Book Overhead

I0024023

A Comprehensive Review of the Federal Budget
By Kevin Connolly
Copyright © 2013 - All Rights Reserved

Paperback ISBN-10: 0984790330
Paperback ISBN-13: 978-0-9847903-3-3
Electronic ISBN-10: 0984790349
Electronic ISBN-13: 978-0-9847903-4-0

Originally published 2/25/2013
http://www.amazon.com/author/kevinconnolly
http://www.kconnolly.net

*Where the people fear the government you have tyranny. Where the
government fears the people you have liberty.*
~ John Basil Barnhill

DEPARTMENTS

Dedication

To Ron Paul, our last true Statesman, our last great hope.

To Bill Whittle, who first interested me in politics.

To my Dad, who taught me to think for myself.

If you have already read my previous book, *Liberty: How America's Increasingly Socialist Agenda Impacts us All*, then you can skip right into the Departments section. I've revised a few things like Tax Reform, but the introductory content remains largely the same. That book was but the introduction to this budget review.

Foreword

There was a dream that was the United States of America, in which people would be free to determine their own path through life, their own needs and wants, and indeed, their own destiny. In this dream, individual liberty would be the basic moral principle of society, and law would be designed only to guarantee the people as much freedom as possible.

Human nature cannot fundamentally change. By instinct, we are greedy, self-righteous creatures who will look out for our own self-interest above all other priorities. Our founders understood that, and designed a government that would use our own nature to the advantage of the people. This government would be constitutionally limited in its power and scope, and its sole purpose would be to secure the rights of its people. This design is the very basis for our prosperity.

This design is based on the concept of Natural Law, which I'll go into further detail on later. The basic idea is that a human is *born free*, and can do whatever they please, until someone comes along and prevents those actions by force. In this case, that someone is Congress, as one of their jobs is to manage law at the Federal level. Being born free, a law can only reduce our otherwise total freedom.

Some laws restrict our activities directly. All laws cost money to enforce, and that money is taken from us. Therefore, every law we pass takes away a little of our freedom. The more laws we have, the less free we are. America has *millions* of laws.

Freedom is the *default* position, and governments are the sole source of restrictions of those freedoms. Governments cannot grant freedoms; they can merely secure or deny them. The Constitution does not grant us freedoms; it merely acknowledges some of the ones that were already there and guarantees that some of them can never be taken away.

As decreed in the 10th amendment to the Constitution, *the powers not delegated to the United States by the Constitution, nor prohibited by the States, are reserved to the States respectively, or to the people*. What that means is that if the Constitution does not explicitly grant a power to the Federal Government, then the Federal Government doesn't have that power and it is then left to the States to decide. If the States do not deny their people such a power, then the people have that power. The genius of the 10th amendment is that if you don't like the laws in your state, you can move to another state. This ingenious design doesn't work when things are done at the federal level. You lose the right to choose; the freedom to decide.

Article I, Sections 8 and 9 of the Constitution are designed explicitly to limit the size and scope of the Federal Government, thus allowing states and the people the maximum possible flexibility and freedom in deciding on the issues for themselves. Unfortunately, it seems the leaders of all three branches have stopped obeying the Constitution. To ignore one part of the Constitution is to invalidate the entire document, and thus the basis of our once great nation.

The Federal Government has ballooned far beyond the size our founders intended, and has metastasized itself so malignantly and deeply into our lives that it may never be possible to treat it without killing the patient.

The Federal Government paid for all this Orwellian control over our lives by enacting the Income Tax in 1913 with the 16th Amendment to the Constitution[1]. Government has multiplied itself 300 times (not inflation adjusted) in size in under a century, and its deficit has increased proportionally. On average, it nearly triples every year.

Gradually, the Income Tax has paid for more and more programs. As people are born and die, a growing number of citizens accept it as "The way things are". A century of people born under the Income Tax has desensitized us to the unchecked growth, violations of our Constitution and freedom, and other evils it delivers.

In order to understand the motivations behind this specific economic solution, you must first understand the Libertarian agenda. To understand Libertarianism, you must first understand Natural Law. Once you understand Natural Law, you will understand what America was designed to be. To that end, I shall explain those concepts before going into the actual budget.

Any time you take money from one group of people and give it to another group of people, that's a form of Socialism known as Redistribution of Wealth. It's evil, it's unnatural, and it's un-American. Somewhere along the line of American history, mostly under FDR, society decided it was everyone's job to take care of people who couldn't or wouldn't take care of themselves. This has been an increasingly prevalent pattern since 1913, and especially since 1936; and it's ruining this country.

---

[1] http://en.wikipedia.org/wiki/Sixteenth_Amendment_to_the_United_States_Constitution

There was a time when accepting help from others was seen as a form of weakness and failure on the part of the provider. As Americans, it is both our tradition and our solemn natural duty to ensure self-sufficiency and provide for ourselves and our families. We must return to that method of thinking if we are ever to recover from our increasingly Socialist way of conducting our society.

There was a dream that was the United States of America.

Natural Law[2]

Introduction

Natural Law is a system by which law is determined by nature. We use it to analyze ourselves and take morals and ethics from the very basis of human nature itself. The United States being founded on this concept, it is imperative that we understand it and its implications. First, I must show that the USA was indeed founded on this concept; then I can demonstrate what this means to us.

The Organic Law of 2007 cites the Declaration of Independence as official law, as there were some who disputed its lawfulness, being enacted prior to the Constitution and thus the Congress as it exist today; and to include it within the United States Code, adopted in 1926.

Declaration of Independence

Analyze the wording of the Declaration of Independence, and the subsequent Constitution. Even the least astute reader will quickly realize the meaning thereof, as the wording was intentionally explicit.

> *We hold these truths to be self-evident, that all men are created equal, that they are endowed by their Creator with certain unalienable Rights, that among these are Life, Liberty and the pursuit of Happiness.*

"We hold these truths"– not these opinions, not this consensus, not this gentlemen's agreement. These are truths that are, by definition, absolutely and irrevocably true. They cannot be disputed, and they cannot be undone.

"To be self-evident"—these truths are so obvious that it seems silly that they even need to be said. Unfortunately, there was a series of tyrant Kings in a faraway land who just didn't seem to get the idea. We didn't create these truths; we don't authorize them; we merely recognize that they are already there. These rights are self-evident because anyone in any society can figure them out for themselves, and because they were here before we were.

"That all men are created equal"—Human rights have come a long way, and we now accept this to mean *all people*. All people are created equal; that is, at the moment of our birth, none of us is any better or any worse than any other. We are equal under the law, and equal under the eyes of our Creator. What we do after that is up to us.

---

[2] http://en.wikipedia.org/wiki/Natural_law

"That they are endowed by their creator"—Call it God, call it Nature, call it whatever you want. Whatever force created us has endowed us; has given to us as our Birthright...

"with certain unalienable Rights"— Not these privileges, not these temporary licenses. *Rights* – Certain actions which we fundamentally must be allowed to do. Certain rights which no mortal power may deny us.

"That among these are life, liberty, and the pursuit of happiness"— Every human has a right to live. Every human has a right to liberty. Every human has a right to pursue happiness.

No mere document, no King, no Constitution; indeed, no human faculty of any kind can grant these rights. They preexist; they are our God-given birthright; they are immortal. They come from a higher authority, and thus they are unalienable.

> *That to secure these rights, Governments are instituted among Men, deriving their just powers from the consent of the governed*

If you believe you have a birthright to something, it makes sense to organize like-minded people; to work together to ensure these rights are never taken away. Fulfilling this guarantee is the **only** purpose of Government.

Government's powers are derived from the people it governs. Not from the States; not from the Corporations; not from God; not from the might of our armies; not even from the Constitution. The people consent to delegate to the government its powers, and the people can take them away by withdrawing our consent.

> *That whenever any Form of Government becomes destructive of these ends, it is the Right of the People to alter or to abolish it*

Humans are imperfect creatures, and thus all our creations are imperfect. Our founders recognized that government in any form can deliver tyranny, and that the people maintain a right to fix that tyranny. We can do so by altering the government in question, or by abolishing it. The Government clearly has no interest in this today, as the destruction of these rights is in the best interest of a tyrant; thus it is the people who must take responsibility.

and to institute new Government, laying its foundation on such principles and organizing its powers in such form, as to them shall seem most likely to effect their Safety and Happiness.

If the people act on their right and go so far as to institute new government, it is further their right to design such government in a way that they think will provide them the best safety and happiness. Clearly, the purpose of such government is to protect the aforementioned unalienable rights from tyrants – Both present and future. It is the position of most Libertarians that the Federal Government has grown unconstitutionally into such a tyrant.

Enumerated Infractions of a Tyrant

Jefferson went on to enumerate the myriad infractions of the King, including:

He has dissolved Representative Houses repeatedly, for opposing with manly firmness his invasions on the rights of the people.

Houses of Representatives, similar to ours today, existed with representatives of the people of the colonies. The King dissolved these houses, tantamount to the Super-Congress we saw recently.

He has refused for a long time, after such dissolutions, to cause others to be elected, whereby the Legislative Powers, incapable of Annihilation, have returned to the People at large for their exercise; the State remaining in the mean time exposed to all the dangers of invasion from without, and convulsions within.

He has prevented the free election of representatives. In this case there were none after such dissolution, but this can be easily compared with the lack of congressional term limits. Much as such lack exposed dangers to the people, today's corrupt congressmen pose such a danger to us; removable only through resignation or impeachment, both of which are nearly impossible to accomplish. As recently as 1995, the Supreme Court ruled that states cannot impose term limits upon their federal Representatives or Senators.

Constitutional amendment proposals have been brought forth to the Congress to impose such term limits upon themselves. As one would expect from any tyrant, they have all failed. I believe such a motion could pass only if the sitting body were exempted thereof, an unfortunate but obvious reflection upon our own history.

He has made Judges dependent on his Will alone for the tenure of their offices, and the amount and payment of their salaries.

Judges could work through the King's permission only, and he directly decided if and what they were paid. Clearly he could impose his will upon our justice system through manipulation thereof. Supreme Court Justices are chosen *only* by the President. Of course, such President chooses such justices as agree with his agenda.

He has erected a multitude of New Offices, and sent hither swarms of Officers to harass our people and eat out their substance.

The King created a great number of new government jobs and offices to oversee and harass us. Today, the DoD alone employs over 3,000,000 people. The Government eats out our substance, not by raiding our kitchens, but by raiding our wallets through taxation, and eating our freedoms by passing such laws as the Patriot Act.

One of the King's greatest infractions against us and humanity in general was the Stamp Act, which allowed British agents to write their own search warrants so they could ensure that every document in your home and on your person bore a taxed and purchased stamp with an image of the King on it. The Patriot Act allows Federal agents to write their own search warrants in exactly this same manner.

> *He has affected to render the Military independent of and superior to the Civil Power.*

The King assumed direct control over the military, and refused to let the people or our representatives decide where and how they were used. Congress hasn't declared a war since World War 2. Since then, Presidents have illegally and unconstitutionally sent our military to fight in Korea, Vietnam, Cuba, Iraq, Afghanistan, Pakistan, and countless other places. Not one of these wars was declared by Congress, as required by the Constitution.

> *He has combined with others to subject us to a jurisdiction foreign to our constitution, and unacknowledged by our laws; giving his Assent to their Acts of pretended Legislation*

The King, in concert with others, imposed his will upon us with utter disregard for the Constitution we had been working under at the time. If we read the 10th amendment to the Constitution, as I outlined earlier, any power not explicitly granted to the government by the Constitution is left to the States and the people. There is not one word about federally controlled education, agriculture, or environmental protection. There is not one word about socialized retirement, healthcare, medicine, food, or housing.

> *For imposing Taxes on us without our Consent*

We're all familiar with the idea of taxation without representation, but I have to wonder how many of us voted for the taxes we have today: Individual income tax, corporate income tax, social security payroll tax, Medicare payroll tax, unemployment insurance, "other retirement receipts", excise taxes, estate and gift taxes, and customs duties. The Federal Reserve, by artificially fiddling with interest rates, has incidentally imposed what we know as the Inflation Tax. That is, if you have a dollar now, and you hold on to it for 50 years, it won't be worth as much. By devaluing your dollar, you have effectively less money.

For depriving us in many cases, of the benefit of Trial by Jury

The President and the CIA occasionally assassinate American Citizens with no trial under the guise of National Security, often citing the unconstitutional Patriot Act as their source of authority. This is a clear and repeated violation of the 5th and 6th amendments to the Constitution.

For taking away our Charters, abolishing our most valuable Laws and altering fundamentally the Forms of our Governments

A colonial charter is a document that gives colonies a legal right to exist. This manipulation and abuse of his power caused the colonial governments to operate in a fundamentally different way. With the Patriot Act, Super Congress, and a Supreme Court that thinks it has the authority to make law, our government has been fundamentally altered in form.

He is at this time transporting large Armies of foreign Mercenaries to compleat the works of death, desolation, and tyranny, already begun with circumstances of Cruelty & Perfidy scarcely paralleled in the most barbarous ages, and totally unworthy the Head of a civilized nation.

Look at the Occupy Wall Street movement. In Oakland, a crowd of legally assembled protestors got a little out of hand and were grossly overreacted to by the government with chemical weapons (tear gas) and large, high velocity projectiles (bean bags). We have seen this same situation unfold time and time again, with the Civil Rights movements for blacks and women, for protests against prohibition and war, and countless other times throughout our history.

People just want to be free.

In nearly every instance, the people persevered and eventually won major victories. The worst factor is that these are battles that should never have been needed in the first place. These people fight for freedom, and freedom is the most basic tenant of what makes America, America.

Constitution of the United States

> *We the People of the United States, in Order to form a more perfect Union, establish Justice, insure domestic Tranquility, provide for the common defence, promote the general Welfare, and secure the Blessings of Liberty to ourselves and our Posterity, do ordain and establish this Constitution for the United States of America.*

Everything you need to know about American Exceptionalism is right there in the Preamble. Here, the framers are introducing the Constitution and explaining its purpose, but it also explains what makes America special.

"We the People of the United States"—The Constitution was ordained and established by **We the People**. Many different Constitutions were tried; this is the one that the states finally (mostly) agreed upon. It was a consensus among the people, which would unite the several states.

"In order to form a more perfect Union"—The Colonies had gone through several different types of government over the course of colonization and expansion. They had tried many times to create a union in one form or another, and none of them lasted.

"Establish Justice"—After many generations of tyranny and oppression, and the suppression of what seemed like the most basic of human rights, the Colonies were ready to run their own system of Justice, free from the King. The colonies believed in a higher form of justice; one that protects our rights and does not succumb to the whim of a tyrant.

"provide for the common defence"—The colonies had basically been a disparate group of largely independent city-states, and recognized that in working together they would be stronger. They also realized that if we decided to tell the King we were going to live our own way and under our own authority, there would be a great need to defend all that we were working so hard to create.

"insure domestic Tranquility"—Since the colonies were defining their own process of law and order, they must have a way to protect and defend them. Peace within the United States.

"promote the general Welfare"— To allow we all the people to benefit from the justice, defense, and tranquility of the more perfect union. It must not be for the specific welfare of a subgroup, and the belief or even fact that

something may benefit the people doesn't mean the government should always do it.

"and secure the Blessings of Liberty to ourselves and our Posterity"—Our forefathers had fought very hard and very recently to obtain and secure their liberty, and they didn't want it whisked away again by a clearly superior military force.

"do ordain and establish this Constitution for the United States of America"—The requisite closing to explain exactly what the document is doing, to name the document, and indeed to reiterate the name of the newly formed nation. To explain the newly united nature of the several states. The use of "ordain" reiterates the idea that our rights are granted by a higher power. The use of "establish" shows that it overrules the failed attempts that came before. The use of "for" shows that the ultimate purpose of the Constitution is to serve the nation, not to rule over it.

Article I, Section 8 enumerates the specific powers of Congress, and ends by granting Congress the authority to make laws "necessary and proper" for executing those specific enumerated powers, or those granted by the Constitution, or "any department or officer" of the Federal Government.

> *To make all Laws which shall be necessary and proper for carrying into Execution the foregoing Powers, and all other Powers vested by this Constitution in the Government of the United States, or in any Department or Officer thereof.*

Clearly the purpose here was to limit the power of Congress to pass only those laws which are needed to let the Government do the job laid out in the Constitution.

Unfortunately to this end, Presidents have created whole departments and many "officers" whose power Congress may then pass law based on the necessity thereof. Article V even allows Congress to invent its own ways to ratify amendments, and the Congress can even create its own officers. Obviously, this was a flawed document, but it's the best we could do with all the disagreement among the States.

During the debates regarding the adoption of the Constitution, its opponents repeatedly exclaimed that the Constitution as drafted would invite tyranny by the Federal Government. With the British violations of our rights so fresh in their minds, they demanded a Bill of Rights to enumerate the immunities of individual citizens.

Bill of Rights

The Bill of Rights was created because several states complained that the rights of the people were explained too implicitly; that without explicitly delineating specific rights, those rights might be "misconstructed or abused".

Examine the wording of the Bill of Rights:

> *"Congress shall make no law..."*
> *"Shall not be infringed"*
> *"Shall not be violated"*
> *"No warrants shall issue"*
> *"No person shall be held to answer"*

I believe the 9th and 10th amendments to be among the most important, and to be the two which most clearly define America's basis in Natural Law:

> 9th: *"The enumeration in the Constitution, of certain rights, shall not be construed to deny or disparage others retained by the people."*
> 10th: *"The powers not delegated to the United States by the Constitution, nor prohibited by it to the States, are reserved to the States respectively, or to the people."*

Conclusion

Clearly, America was founded on Natural Law. Tyranny is the imposition of a leader's will upon the people. The two are mutually exclusive and cannot coexist without the inevitability of violent conflict. Our founders understood this, and thus they designed the Constitution specifically to limit the size and power of the Federal Government.

The 9th amendment clearly and explicitly explains that rights don't have to be enumerated by the Constitution to be rights. The 10th amendment tells us that the states may assume all powers not explicitly delegated to the Federal Government by the Constitution nor denied to them by it, and that any powers not thereby assumed by those states lie with the people.

In short, you are free to do whatever you please until the state legislature or the Congress passes a law making it illegal. **Freedom is the default position;** the very definition of Natural Law.

Now that I have verbosely proven the basis of the United States upon Natural Law, it shall be fairly simple to show its application. Freedom is the default. Laws cannot grant freedoms, because we already have all freedoms until otherwise legislated. Laws can only take freedoms away. By that logic, the more laws we have, the less free we are.

Article I, Section 4 of the Constitution requires that *"the Congress shall assemble at least once in every year"*, implying that it was not intended to be a full-time job. There was a time when we didn't have career politicians. When not in session, Congressmen would go about their regular jobs. There was no retirement package, and there were no benefits packages. You would come in, serve your time, and go back to your trade. As a result, only true statesmen would take on the additional burden of running the nation's business. We would do well to return to such a clean model.

Reading these several documents, it is very evident that our forefathers intended a small, frugal, responsible federal government, just large enough to provide those things which were enumerated in the Constitution. They did not intend a massive, all-controlling *state* with millions of people in its employ and its tentacles in every aspect of our lives.

Libertarianism

There are many conflicting definitions of libertarianism[3]. In this context, I will be discussing the interpretation of Right-Libertarianism[4] and the Libertarian Party, which advocate the Non-Aggression Principle[5], Minarchism[6], Non-Interventionism[7], Constitutionalism, and Classical[8] and Cultural Liberalism. Basically, we want the government to be small and the people to be free.

There is a distinct delineation between Libertarianism and Anarchism. Libertarianism demands small, accountable government in accordance with the Constitution. Anarchism demands no government. It's important to keep that distinction in mind.

To understand the idea of the Federal Government, one must first understand the principles upon which it was created. Libertarianism is a political extension of Natural Law. Libertarians believe that personal liberty is the fundamental moral principle of society. It advocates strict limits to the size and scope of government and its activity, and maximizes individual liberty and freedom. Libertarianism is the very embodiment of what America was supposed to be.

Rightful liberty is unobstructed action according to our will within limits drawn around us by the equal rights of others. I do not add 'within the limits of the law' because law is often but the tyrant's will, and always so when it violates the rights of the individual.

~ Thomas Jefferson

"Unobstructed action according to our will"—is doing whatever we want, with no outside interference.

"Drawn around us by the equal rights of others"—our rightful liberty is limited only by the equal rights of others. In other words, do whatever you want, as long as you don't infringe upon anyone else's rights.

Jefferson goes on to explain that human rights outweigh the law. Clearly, he recognizes that our rights come from a higher authority. Furthermore, he explains that law is always the tyrant's will when it violates the rights of the individual. Clearly, Jefferson believed that law should not infringe upon our

---

[3] http://en.wikipedia.org/wiki/Libertarianism
[4] http://en.wikipedia.org/wiki/Right-libertarianism
[5] http://en.wikipedia.org/wiki/Non-aggression_principle
[6] http://en.wikipedia.org/wiki/Minarchism
[7] http://en.wikipedia.org/wiki/Non-interventionism
[8] http://en.wikipedia.org/wiki/Classical_liberalism

God-given birthrights. To the astute reader, it is clear by his language that Jefferson was exercising these beliefs when he wrote the Declaration of Independence.

Fundamental Concepts

Some of these concepts come from libertarian or classical philosophy. Others are of my own deduction; all are used in the derivation of this proposal.

Non-Aggression Principle – A moral stance which asserts that aggression – The initiation of force - is inherently illegitimate. Nobody has a right to initiate force against anyone else; but only to respond in kind. You can't give to the government a power that you do not yourself possess.

Constitutionalism – If it's not in the Constitution, the federal government has no business meddling in it. It says so right there in Article I, Section 8, and again in the 9th and 10th amendments. The Constitution is our highest law, above all others. To disregard one part of it is to invalidate the entire document, and thus the very fabric of America. Our elected officials swear an oath to uphold it, and doing so hasn't been the pattern in a long time.

Small Government – The smaller government is, the less it costs to run. The less it costs to run, the less it needs to tax. The less it taxes, the more of our money we can keep; the more employees a company can afford to hire. The less government regulates, the easier it is to do *everything*.

Government does not grant rights to people; people delegate some of their power to the government. Adherence to the Constitution that the states ratified is a condition of this delegation of powers. The Constitution lists all of the powers the federal government holds, and it is not allowed to stray beyond those *enumerated powers*.

Low Taxes – Initially, we were able to pay our way with a customs duty. Then we added a land tax, then an excise tax on liquor. As time goes on and the government grows, we add more and more taxes. We didn't even have an income tax until 1913. Since then, we've added taxes on cigarettes, gasoline, and untold numbers of other products.

We need to reduce the government to levels authorized by the Constitution, pay off our debt, and then eliminate and reduce as many taxes as possible. The ideal tax system is none at all.

Individual Liberty – As I've explained in great detail, the rights of the people should trump everything else. Protecting these rights is the main purpose in seceding from Great Britain, and the **only** purpose of having a government. It says so in the Declaration of Independence.

Non-Interventionism – America was not meant to be the world's police force. If it's none of our business, we have no business meddling in it. Unconstitutional new-age ethics aside, we can't afford the warmongering that has pervaded our foreign policy over the past century.

The Constitution defines very clearly when we should go to war and that only the Congress may declare it. War should be declared every time, by the Congress. If the people so choose, we should conduct our war quickly and efficiently.

Antisocialism – Any time you take money from one group and give it to a different group, that's socialism. Any redistribution of wealth is a form of socialism. America is about making it on your own through your own skills and merits. The increasingly prevalent welfare state is ruining this country.

Deregulation – Regulation causes overhead and waste. It forces companies to jump through hoops and hurdles, and reduces the number of people they can employ. Regulation should exist only to protect those freedoms guaranteed to us by our Constitution, such as Life and Liberty. Some estimates put the number of regulations at 81,000 pages, at a cost of $1.75 Trillion per year. If we eliminated these regulations, we could effectively add that number directly to the Gross Domestic Product.

Free Enterprise – The market will correct itself, if only the government would butt out and allow it to do so. One of the reasons for our original secession was that the Crown kept poking its nose into our trading and it interfered with the economy, driving our traders and other businessmen to bankruptcy in many cases.

American Sovereignty - The Constitution decrees that all treaties duly signed are the "supreme law of the land", other provisions of the Constitution notwithstanding. Therefore we must be very careful in our choosing of treaties, and should prefer fewer to more. In the words of Thomas Jefferson:

> *Peace, commerce, and honest friendship with all nations, entangling alliances with none.*

NATO and the United Nations are the two most entangling alliances in American history. I support withdrawing from both, thus obsoleting all security investments therein. Eliminate and save $264 Million in SIP alone.

In every case, services provided by private organizations are better than those provided by governments. Governments can take your money at gunpoint. Businesses have to convince you. If you don't like one company, you can go to a competitor. This option makes every transaction cleaner, more efficient, and cheaper. This is not the case with governments.

The government is not a bank. It is not an investor. It is not a loyal advisor whose advice you can trust. Government intervention makes everything worse for everyone involved. If your business model is not profitable on its own virtue, the economy will show that. Business model viability should not be interfered with; it's dangerous, and on a large scale, it leads to recessions or worse.

Any time the government functions as a bank or an insurance company, it takes profitable business away from a company that could provide such function in the private sector. Taking a rightfully private job function and moving it into the government is a step toward totalitarianism and fascism.

No Foreign Aid – When you provide something to another country for a long period of time, they eventually become dependent on that aid. The longer it continues, the worse the dependency. Iraq will never be strong until we let them rule themselves completely. Israel will never be strong until they learn to supply and defend themselves again. Furthermore, with the sole exception of war cast upon us, the affairs of foreign countries are none of our business.

Finally, we need to fix our own problems before we can even consider fixing those of other countries, assuming we were actually fixing the problems at all. Foreign relations be damned; if a relationship with another country isn't yielding us the same return as what we put into it, then it's not worth it.

No Grants - Giving money in the form of grants doesn't just generate new cash out of thin air; it has to come from somewhere. The government can't give you anything without first taking it away from someone else; and that someone is all of us. Eliminate all federal grants; states can tax their own people for their own programs, if their state legislatures so choose, given the *consent of the governed*.

Private Property – If you own land, then you have sovereign power over that land. You rule your land, more or less, supreme. You can defend it against trespassers, and you can decide who you want to allow onto that land. It then follows that if you offer a product or service on your property, then you should be able to decide who you want to offer those products and services to. The government shouldn't be allowed to force any of these decisions upon you.

Free Trade – Allow products and services to traffic freely and naturally between the US and other countries. Do not embargo them, do not sanction them, do not subsidize them.

Separation of Powers – Cities should tax their own citizens to run their own programs. If the city cannot afford a program, they should not rely on the higher level governments to obtain funding. This would only remove funds from the areas that ran their governments responsibly. Counties and states should run the same way, taxing their citizens as they require to run their own programs, and not to send to lower levels. If your city can tax you to pay for a local police force, there is no need to tax the rest of the state just to pay for your city's needs. It stands to reason that this logic extends to the federal level as well. Taxation and programs should be administered at the lowest possible level.

Overview of the Proposal

I have reviewed the proposed FY2013 Federal Budget in its entirety, and I have identified nearly **$2 Trillion** in spending that can be cut immediately, which in itself would be enough to balance the budget. These aren't the kind of cuts we see from recent administrations, promising a trillion over the course of a decade, which comes out to $100 Billion per year; I do mean $2 Trillion from the **annual** budget. Combined with a reform of the tax system, I have calculated a **$549 Billion surplus** in the first year alone.

This proposal would eliminate all current taxes and replace them with a flat Sales Tax, a flat import tax, and a flat tax on offshore drilling on the Continental Shelf. The benefits of this tax code are that it would greatly simplify the tax code, eliminate the need for the Internal Revenue Service, and motivate companies to bring manufacturing back onto American soil.

This proposal would eliminate all nationalized socialism programs. Unfortunately, a large fraction of Americans have become so utterly dependent on socialized everything that it can't possibly be eliminated all at once. Therefore I have devised a plan to cut them by 10% every year for 10 years, while simultaneously restoring the devastated American manufacturing base. We need to build things again, and we need those people to be building them.

This proposal eliminates seven departments (plus five more after ten years), all ongoing Overseas Contingency Operations, and hundreds of programs within the departments it does not eliminate. My only goal herein is to show that it is possible to fix our economic crisis, and that to do so we need only get serious about it. Cutting a few billion here and there just won't do it. We need to cut in the *trillions*. Not surprisingly, the vast majority of the budget is spent on militarism and wealth redistribution.

After the Ten Year Plan's completion, we would be completely out of debt. At this point, our federal government outlays would measure a paltry few hundred billion dollars and the sales tax could be eliminated. During these 10 years, additional expenditures would certainly be identified and eliminated, further reducing the needed taxes. The goal is to eliminate the need for most taxes altogether, so that people may choose to keep what they earn.

How much money you make and where you work are none of the government's business. In this endgame, the remaining constitutionally authorized programs could be paid for once again with other types of taxes and excises only, like they used to be.

I have reviewed the budgets proposed by President Obama, Paul Ryan, Ron Paul, and Rand Paul. Obama has clearly cut a noticeable amount of fat from the projections of the earlier budgets; but he still puts us hugely in deficit. Paul Ryan's budget puts us in slightly less deficit. The Pauls make a valiant effort, and put us in surplus within a few years, but even their plans have a highly noticeable increase in spending over time. Therefore, while Paul's plan would address our immediate problems, none of these plans goes very far toward eliminating the National Debt.

The only annual increases in outlays should be proportional to the population growth, and even then, only in programs that depend on the size of the population. That basically means the court system, the number of representatives, and possibly new senators as more states are absorbed.

We must eliminate the National Debt in order to realize the full economic potential of America; and to do that, we have to get *really* serious. Unlike Paul, I have the advantage of not requiring the approval of the poor and lazy customers of the National Socialism programs, because I'm not planning to be the President of the United States. Therefore, with all marketing and politics safely out of the way, I could create the wondrous Ten Year Plan.

Once the Ten Year Plan is complete and we have a few trillion in the bank (well, in Fort Knox and various secure, secret, military-controlled locations), we should reduce taxes to just slightly above the allocated spending. Every year, we would take the amount on hand, minus a predetermined stockpile for emergencies, and disperse it **evenly among the citizens** in the form of dividends. Think of it as a nice little stimulus package that actually doesn't cost us any money. It's your money, so here, take back what we didn't need. Divide the stimulus amount by the number of citizens, and send that same amount out to everyone equally. When people get an unexpected check, they spend it; especially so in the lower income brackets.

Let's say one year we have a surplus of $30B. Thirty billion is a drop in the bucket at the federal scale, but divided by 300 million taxpayers, it's a hundred bucks in every pocket. To a lot of Americans, an unexpected $100 is a windfall. Then, obviously, we adjust the tax rate so the surplus isn't so much, since we've long since paid off the debt and accrued what we could call the National Excess. So we give the money back to the people who we took it from in the first place, and it goes right back into the economy; every single year. That's how Stimulus packages **should** work.

For a government that's supposed to be cutting back, reducing the deficit, and balancing its own budgets, I don't see any of that happening. *Let's get extreme.*

Abuse of the Interstate Commerce Clause

Regulation as we know it today makes government bigger and more expensive. Regulation literally means "To keep regular"; Congress has the power to keep commerce regular. In all things, the Interstate Commerce Clause (Article I, Section 8, Clause 3) defines the authority of the Congress to regulate:

> *[The Congress shall have Power] To regulate Commerce with foreign Nations, and among the several States, and with the Indian tribes;*

The Supreme Court decreed in Spectrum Sports, Inc. v. McQuillan, 2003:

> *The purpose of the [Sherman] Act is not to protect businesses from the working of the market; it is to protect the public from the failure of the market. The law directs itself not against conduct which is competitive, even severely so, but against conduct which unfairly tends to destroy competition itself.*

The Supreme Court further decreed in *Gonzales v. Raich, 2005*[9], that the Commerce Clause was originally used to prevent discriminatory state legislation, and that Congress had created its own regulatory authority in the Interstate Commerce Act of 1887 and the Sherman Antitrust Act of 1890. The former was designed to protect farmers from railroad monopolies, and the latter authorized the government to investigate and limit corporate monopolies. The purpose of the Commerce Clause was therefore interpreted to give Congress the authority to prevent corporate monopolies from interfering with competition.

More substantially, between 1778 and 1787, when the colonies were operating under the Articles of Confederation, there was a clause therein reading:

> *Each state retains its sovereignty, freedom, and independence, and every power, jurisdiction, and right, which is not by this Confederation expressly delegated to the United States, in Congress assembled.*

One main problem with the Articles of Confederation was that states tended to create protectionist trade barriers, a clear impediment to free trade. When the Constitution was written in 1787, they wrote the Interstate Commerce Clause to prevent such barriers and create a nationwide free-trade zone. In other words, to keep trade regular between states.

---

[9] http://en.wikipedia.org/wiki/Gonzales_v._Raich

Overview of the Proposal

"The powers delegated by the proposed Constitution to the federal government are few and defined. Those which are to remain in the State governments are numerous and indefinite."[10]

In addition to explicitly limited and enumerated powers, the Federal Government makes everything it touches worse. These are two great reasons to keep Washington as inconsequential in our lives and businesses as possible. The government's job is to "secure these rights" and that's it.

Abuse of the General Welfare Clause

At the beginning of Article I, Section 8, which lists the powers of Congress, the first clause grants Congress the power of taxation:

> *The Congress shall have Power To lay and collect Taxes, Duties, Imposts and Excises, to pay the Debts and provide for the common Defence and general Welfare of the United States; but all Duties, Imposts and Excises shall be uniform throughout the United States;*

The Supreme Court held that the understanding of the General Welfare Clause adheres to the construction defined by Justice Joseph Story in 1833. Specifically he found that *the General Welfare clause is not a grant of general legislative power*, but a qualification on the taxing power. [11]

Second, consider that "general welfare" must apply to the "general" population: Any programs which do not apply equally to everyone are not advancing the general welfare; but rather, to the *specific* welfare of subgroups of people. A government program or law should apply to everyone, or to no one.

Abuse of the Necessary and Proper Clause

At the end of Article I, Section 8, which lists the powers of Congress, there is a clause which provides Congress the power to do all it needs to do to fulfill the powers listed:

> *"The Congress shall have Power [...] **To make all Laws which shall be necessary and proper for carrying into Execution the foregoing Powers,** and all other Powers vested by this Constitution in the Government of the United States, or in any Department or Officer thereof.*

---

[10] James Madison, http://www.constitution.org/fed/federa45.htm
[11] http://en.wikipedia.org/wiki/General_Welfare_clause#United_States

This clause is a blank check to perform all powers listed in the Constitution; it is not a blank check to do anything they want. Even Alexander Hamilton, an infamous statist, argued in the Federalist Papers that this clause only permits the execution of powers already granted by the Constitution.[12]

---

[12] http://en.wikipedia.org/wiki/Necessary_and_Proper_Clause

Jobs Reform

If we want to solve this crisis and restore America to what it was meant to be, we must make Americans self-reliant again. To bring jobs back to America, we must first identify the causes of losing the jobs in the first place.

Contracts – In the bailout programs of the 2000s, the Federal Government unconstitutionally bailed out private corporations and voided legitimate contracts between corporations. This is a dangerous violation of contract law. As the corporations have no way of knowing whether the government will do it again, they are now choosing to hold onto their money for fear of opening new contracts and having them voided by the government. We must repeal the nullification of these contracts and pass a bill that ensures we will *never do this again*.

Regulation – Every regulation we put on an industry makes it more difficult for that industry to produce its goods and services. We must eliminate regulations, and entire regulatory agencies, in order to simplify the process and streamline what little manufacturing and service industries we have left. Maybe we could even start opening new factories and refineries again.

Legislation – Legislation should only be passed when it directly advances an enumerated power in the Constitution. Every single law that has ever been passed by Congress which does not meet this sole criterion must be repealed. We should legalize the use of all drugs, and allow them to be trafficked as any other products on the market. People should have the right to do to their own bodies whatever they choose to do. This will both reduce the size and scope of government, and introduce entirely new industries and taxable revenue into the economy. If you don't like drugs, just don't use them.

Energy Independence – Drill Texas, Montana, North Dakota, and ANWR, and build new refineries in oil-rich areas that don't have any or enough of them. Renew the railroad system by delivering the refined fuel via railways from oil fields that are far from the coasts. We must produce and refine our own oil domestically, while private companies continue to perform their own research and development of newer and cleaner technologies. We won't be switching to electric or hydrogen vehicles overnight, so we must make ourselves as independent as we can while we wait for the industries and the commensurate demand to catch up to the technologies.

Import Tax – One aspect of my proposed tax reform would be a flat import tax on the gross price or value of all goods imported into the United States.

Obviously, any tax increases revenue, but that's not the purpose of this tax. By taxing importation, we incentivize companies to do their manufacturing in the United States. We might exempt raw materials which cannot be found in the United States, and unique cultural items that cannot be made here without losing their cultural significance.

Farm Labor – 53% of all American farm labor is performed by illegal Mexican immigrants. This is a pervasive and well-documented pattern which is costing us **1.325 million jobs**. Each displaced vagrant would introduce one new job for an American citizen to take. It's not great work, but it's work; ideal for teenagers and the grossly unskilled. I would ensure the newly found jobs were advertised nearby. Legalizing drugs would greatly reduce the number of incoming illegals, as well as completely obsolete the underground drug network. We also need to make it a lot easier to immigrate here *legally*.

Eliminate the Minimum Wage – Paying an employee minimum wage is basically saying "I'd pay you less if I could, but it's illegal." There are some jobs which simply aren't *worth* the $7.15 per hour. These jobs can be done by literally anyone, and are completely interchangeable. If the entire McDonald's workforce walked out today, they could be replaced by tomorrow.

For your job to be worth any amount, you must generate more than that amount of profit for the company. If your skills and work are worth more, the companies pay more. This is a natural function of a free market and should be embraced, as many more jobs would be available if each one didn't cost the company so much.

Tax Reform

The current tax code is so convoluted that no tax lawyer, accountant, or auditor could possibly memorize the entire thing. It's famously filled with loopholes and imbalances that employ entire industries that there should be no need for in the first place. With six tax brackets ranging from 10 to 35 percent and a ridiculous number of exceptions, rules, and regulations, it's no wonder companies need to hire entire departments of people to keep track of it all. This overcomplexity forces companies to waste time and money in research and paperwork that could be better spent hiring productive employees and opening new facilities.

This proposal would eliminate the entire federal Tax Code and replace it with three flat taxes: One on all imports, one on all sales, and one on resource mining in areas not claimed by a state (e.g. the continental shelf). No loopholes, exceptions, exemptions, brackets, or IRS. Nobody would need to file taxes; indeed, the government wouldn't even need to know how much money you make or where you work. Everyone could memorize the whole thing in a matter of seconds.

A flat Sales Tax would be enacted on every sale of any product or service, and could therefore be measured directly against the Gross Domestic Product, much as the Import Tax could be measured thusly directly against the Gross Imports. The flat Sales Tax would be excised at the final point of sale. The flat Import Tax would be excised at the port, border, or other point of import.

A flat Sales Tax scales directly in proportion to income. Rich people spend more money than poor people and import more things, and would therefore pay proportionately more taxes. The Sales Tax would be paid by the business providing the goods and services; the consumer need not even think about the tax itself. This tax code would be so simple that combined with reduced regulation and legislation, I believe the decreased cost of manufacturing and providing services could entirely offset this paltry tax.

A flat Sales Tax includes every single person who buys anything, which could potentially add 100 to 150 million new people to the tax base, thereby allowing an overall lower tax rate. The flat Sales Tax imposes taxes on people who currently do not pay taxes, such as drug dealers, illegal immigrants, some of the rich, and some of the poor.

I have looked over the Fair Tax; I would prefer it over the present tax code but would not advocate it as the ideal solution. Its Prebate system is unfair and still requires the government to track your income, it taxes excessively, and it deceptively indicates a lower tax rate than it would actually impose. It is indeed neither flat nor fair.

The 16th amendment to the Constitution does not need to be repealed in order to excise these taxes.

> The Congress shall have power to lay and collect taxes on incomes, from whatever source derived, without apportionment among the several States, and without regard to any census or enumeration.

Nowhere in this amendment does it say the Congress *must* collect these taxes; therefore, we could eliminate the Income Tax without the need to wait for the repeal process. We could certainly do so, but we wouldn't need to. Article I, Section 8, clause 1 already authorized the Congress to collect taxes:

[The Congress shall have Power] to lay and collect Taxes, Duties, Imposts and Excises, to pay the Debts and provide for the common Defence and general Welfare of the United States; but all Duties, Imposts and Excises shall be uniform throughout the United States

Section 8 does not specify from where these taxes may be derived, so long as they are "uniform throughout the United States". Therefore both a flat Income Tax and my proposed Import and Sales flat taxes would be constitutional. The 16th amendment was designed to allow a tax to be excised without it being apportioned among the states (Article I, Section 9, Clause 4) or based on the Census results (Article I, section 2, clause 3). With either my flat tax plan or the Fair Tax, this amendment would become obsolete and could be repealed; however, this would not be required to move forward with either plan.

Import Tax ($616B) – An Excise on all imports, except raw materials and unique cultural items as previously mentioned. Annual imports to the US total $2.239 trillion. At a rate of 30%, subtracting obsolete oil imports, we could expect **$616 Billion** in new annual federal revenue. Perhaps more importantly, American products become relatively cheaper to buy than imported products, thus incentivizing manufacturing, and therefore new jobs.

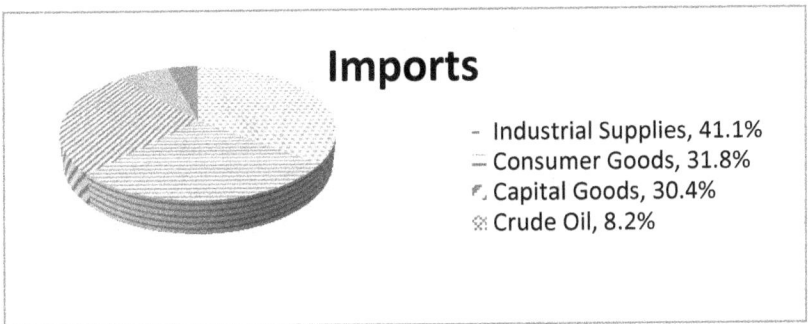

Imports

- Industrial Supplies, 41.1%
- Consumer Goods, 31.8%
- Capital Goods, 30.4%
- Crude Oil, 8.2%

National Sales Tax ($1.8T) – Excise on all purchases at point of sale across the United States and including international transactions not already otherwise taxed. The Gross Domestic Product is $16.6 Trillion. At a tax rate of 11%, we could expect **$1.821 Trillion** in revenue.

Resource Tax ($515B) – Allow private oil companies to set up oil rigs on the continental shelf off the coasts. This is federal territory not claimed by any state, so there's no state to give it back to. Open a contract with such oil companies which would involve the federal government receiving a small stipend; say 10% of the price of each barrel of oil and each 1000 cubic feet of natural gas drilled, which are the standard units of measurement. Require that they leave the water as they found it: Clean up their own spills, and repopulate any species they reduce the population of. Suspend their permit upon any violation thereof. Allow states to handle oil companies within their borders according to their own laws.

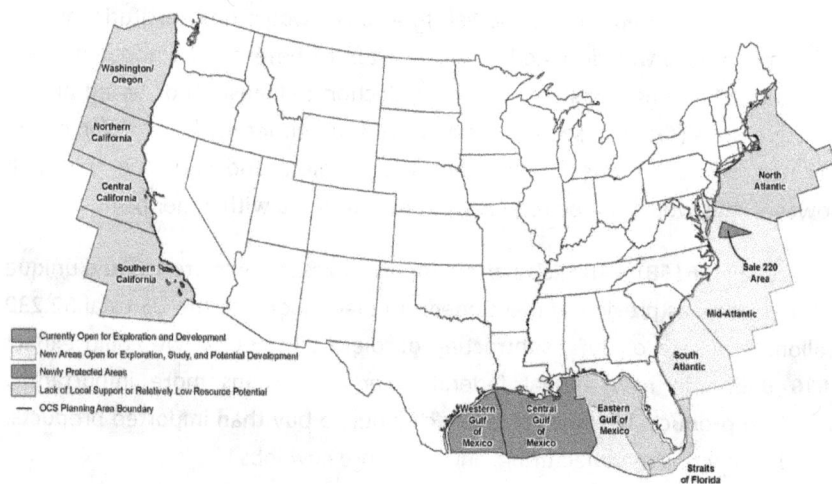

Allow and urge states to allow drilling in their undrilled territory, such as the Arctic National Wildlife Preserve (ANWR), which has nearly zero wildlife. Let the oil companies and states decide on their own pipeline rules; urge them to build new refineries in oil-rich areas. Eliminate all other federal oil-specific legislation, such as subsidies and regulations.

The USA produces roughly 8,000,000 barrels of oil and 68,493,150,684 cubic feet of natural gas[13] per day. Given that the drillable space would roughly double, it stands to reason we would potentially add approximately the same amount of production.

Such a tax, set at 11%, would provide over half a trillion in annual federal revenue, while roughly doubling the supply and number of jobs. Such increased supply would reduce prices, and that's before we even start cutting regulations and taxes. People might start buying new cars and driving for *fun* again!

---

[13] http://en.wikipedia.org/wiki/Natural_gas#United_States

Natural Gas goes for approximately $10-$20 per 1000 cubic feet. A 10% tax on this would add $68-137 Million in revenue. For the purposes of my projections, I am using the lower end of this price range, assuming natural gas is worth $10 / 1000 sq. ft.

Given all these new sources of income, and their plentitude, we can eliminate the entire federal tax code, the Internal Revenue Service, and all other taxes that exist today.

A tax rate of 0% generates zero revenue because it doesn't take any money. A tax rate of 100% generates zero revenue because nobody would bother doing the work if they couldn't keep any of the profit. There is a well-documented phenomenon called the Laffer Curve[14] which shows that there is a point of maximum revenue in between, after which revenue begins to decline again. After some point, high taxes causes business decline. There is a much lower point at which we see maximum growth. The ideal maximum tax rate would have to be somewhere between the two. The point we select between those two points would depend on whether we think economic growth or tax revenue is more important. I favor the former.

The less we tax, the more small and medium businesses have left over to reinvest into their companies. That means hiring more workers, building more facilities, and maybe lowering their prices to increase demand. Therefore we should aim for the lowest taxes possible while still securing the rights of the people.

The combined taxes I have proposed here total $2.952 Trillion in revenue. Eliminating all other taxes, and combined with myriad tax cuts I'll go into in later chapters, this would put us in surplus in the first year.

---

[14] http://www.forbes.com/sites/danielmitchell/2012/04/15/the-laffer-curve-shows-that-tax-increases-are-a-very-bad-idea-even-if-they-generate-more-tax-revenue/

Healthcare Reform

Healthcare is a private industry. You have no right to healthcare; what you have is a right to *pursue* healthcare.

100 years ago, healthcare was cheap and competition was healthy. People could afford their medication, doctors made house calls and worked free one day a week, and hospitals didn't make peoples' conditions *worse*. Today, exactly the opposite is true. As the federal government has nested itself deeper and deeper into the healthcare industry, it has become larger, more expensive, and less responsive to patients' needs.

Throughout the course of this gradual and insidious process, the government began to provide healthcare programs to the people through Medicare and Medicaid. Of course, there were strings attached, such as increased prices, HMOs, giving up your right to choose your own doctor, and the requisite bump in government spending.

Healthcare is a private industry with associated commerce; and the Constitution does not authorize the federal government to interfere in, nor create, industry or commerce. The only authority granted therein is to keep that commerce flowing regularly between the states, the Indian tribes, and other countries.

Therefore, by getting the government out of the healthcare business, it will become cheaper and its quality will improve.

Ten Year Plan

Robin Hood was a dirty thief.

Unfortunately, as I describe several times throughout this book, a huge number of people have become utterly and hopelessly dependent on America's National Socialism programs. Therefore, it would be catastrophic to cut them from the budget altogether and all at once. Due to this, I have designed a Ten Year Plan to eliminate this Socialist pattern over a period of time, while states legislate replacement programs as desired, America recovers from its grossly failed Keynesian dependencies, and its citizens learn to run our own lives again.

If we want to solve this crisis and restore America to what it was meant to be, we must get serious about reducing spending. The welfare state is by far the largest group of expenses in the federal budget. We're talking about orders of magnitude here; no question about it.

If you want to save for retirement, put your own money into your own retirement accounts. Buy CDs, stocks, mutual funds, gold, and silver. If you invest the amount you have been taxed for social security, there would be no difference to your paycheck therefrom, and you would know that the money would be there when you're ready to retire.

If you want healthcare when you can't afford it, save for it while you're healthy. Be responsible and buy health insurance, especially if you're at risk. Your health problems are not my problems, nor are mine yours. Therefore we shouldn't be forced to pay for each other's healthcare. Go to churches, nonprofits, and other charities.

If you can't afford to feed and clothe your children, *don't have children*. Leaving children malnourished or their clothes in a state of disrepair is an encroachment against them.

If you need money to get by and pay your bills while you're between jobs, save your money while you have a job. If you are physically incapable of performing any work of any kind, then seek help from your local churches, charitable organizations, family, friends, and neighbors. Like our ancestors used to do.

If you got Black Lung Disease from working in a coal mine, then you should have made smarter career choices when you were younger.

None of this is the country's fault. Take responsibility for your own life.

At the conclusion of the 10 year program, we would have reduced budgeted expenses by an order of magnitude. The sales tax can be eliminated, and the little that remains could be financed entirely through the Import and Offshore Drilling taxes.

Being in surplus for a decade, the National Debt would be paid in full before the end of the Ten Year Plan. After this decade of rebuilding, we have some serious options. We should slash taxes to a bare minimum, eliminate the Federal Reserve, and shift the country back onto the Gold or Silver Standard. Now, the world's richest and most debt-free nation, with incredibly low taxes and regulations and a strong, sturdy currency, we would unleash the full economic potential of the United States of America. Some of that can be done right now.

Of our $16 Trillion debt, $4.8 Trillion is held by other parts of the government, and $1.7 Trillion is held by the Federal Reserve System. The first part of this can simply be wiped out, as you can't owe yourself money. The second part can be wiped out by eliminating the Federal Reserve. We have $150.73 Billion in foreign reserves, and about $1.2 Trillion that has been taxed, but is not yet obligated to any specific spending.[15] Therefore, if we apply these last two balances directly toward the debt, we really only owe about $8.5 Trillion. This is the amount we must pay off.

---

[15] http://www.whitehouse.gov/sites/default/files/omb/budget/fy2013/assets/balances.pdf

Departments

I have looked through the individual budgets of each Cabinet-level department. I've completely eliminated some, and slashed spending in all that remained. I will here provide a list of cuts and changes, with justifications for each program where feasible.

This budget proposal is based on the FY2013 Federal Budget. In many cases, I have simply eliminated anything that wasn't there several years earlier. In other cases, I eliminated programs based on their unconstitutionality, uselessness, basis in socialism, or a common sense understanding that they should be handled by states, private companies, or citizens.

Descriptions, where possible, have been taken directly from official budgets or organization and program websites. I'm sure there are many possible cuts that I've missed; but the first year budget proposal would only be the first step in a proper economic recovery.

Department of Agriculture (USDA)[16]

Mission Statement

USDA provides leadership on food, agriculture, natural resources, rural development, nutrition, and related issues based on sound public policy, the best available science, and efficient management.

Food and agriculture are private industries and should remain so. Natural resources are the property of whoever owns the land upon which they are located, and it is the landowners' responsibility to ensure they do not deny through their use thereof the use of such resources located on nearby lands. For example, if your property includes a stream, you are responsible for ensuring your downstream neighbors have roughly as steady and clean a water supply as if you were not using it.

Rural development is the responsibility of the landowners and the local governments which oversee such rural areas. Cities, counties, and states have their own governments; separation of powers demands that they run their own areas. If your location can't afford a service you want from the government, then move to a location that has it, or lobby your local government to add the service and increase its taxes accordingly.

Vision Statement

To expand economic opportunity through innovation, helping rural America to thrive; to promote agriculture production sustainability that better nourishes Americans while also helping feed others throughout the world; and to preserve and conserve our Nation's natural resources through restored forests, improved watersheds, and healthy private working lands.

Expansion of economic opportunities is not a government issue. Rural America is the responsibility of the states in which the rural areas are located; and even then, should only be addressed with the consent of the governed. The free market promotes sustainability of agriculture production by buying food, and it does so even without government intervention. Government, however, actually hurts agriculture production with strict regulations on crops, production, farming practices, and by paying some farmers not to grow crops at all.

Nourishment is the responsibility of the citizens purchasing the food. If you buy healthful products, then the market will respond by supplying more. Let your dollar be your vote.

---

[16] http://www.obpa.usda.gov/budsum/FY13budsum.pdf

Helping feed others throughout the world is the responsibility of the countries in which the malnourished are located; feeding people in other countries is not our responsibility. Preserving and conserving our nation's natural resources is the responsibility of the states in which those resources are located. Restoring forests and improving watersheds are the states' responsibility. Healthy private working lands are the option of the private land owners.

None of these visions are authorized by the Constitution, and programs not authorized by the Constitution are not allowed at the federal level. The USDA has $131 Billion in mandatory budget authority and $24 Billion in discretionary budget authority. Eliminate the entire department; **$155 Billion saved** in addition to the value of the sellable assets.

2013 Funding Overview

Between 2010 and 2012, USDA's operating budget was reduced by over 12 percent. Staffing levels have been reduced and USDA has identified a number of areas to reduce costs and streamline operations to increase efficiency while implementing complex programs and increasing performance in a number of areas. The 2013 request for discretionary budget authority to fund programs and operating expenses is about $24 billion, roughly the same level as provided in 2012.

Reducing a department from $176B to $155B (12%) is no way to fix our economy, and no way to reduce government to a constitutional size. Leaving it at the same level as last year is even less effective. We must systematically identify and eliminate everything that's not allowed, and this includes the USDA. Then we can move on to things that are allowed but not necessary.

The discretionary funding request for 2013 reflects the Department's continued efforts to innovate, modernize, and be better stewards of the taxpayers' dollars. For 2013, further administrative efficiencies, reductions in staffing levels and other actions are proposed to reduce costs. In addition, the budget proposes to reduce or terminate selected programs and reallocate resources to fund targeted investments in priority programs and infrastructure to provide a foundation for sustainable economic growth.

If we eliminate the department, then its administration, innovation, modernization, stewardship, and staffing all become irrelevant. Eliminating a program here and there is simply too little, too late.

Funding for mandatory programs is projected to increase in 2013 by almost $8 billion due primarily to a one-time shift in the timing of certain crop insurance costs mandated by the 2008 Farm Bill. In 2013, rising employment and household income are projected to reduce the need for nutrition assistance through the Supplemental Nutrition Assistance Program (SNAP) and lead to fewer program participants, even as SNAP serves a larger share of those eligible. While participation in the program has increased steadily since its last low point in FY 2000, and sharply in the economic downturn, the rate of increase has been declining since around January 2010.

The government is not an insurance company; repeal the 2008 Farm Bill and eliminate all active policies. Feeding the poor is not a federal issue. They should have made better decisions when they had jobs, and should spend this time getting new jobs. If they take jobs on farms, they can replace illegals and probably earn a discount on food at the same time as they begin to eat healthier food. Eliminate SNAP altogether.

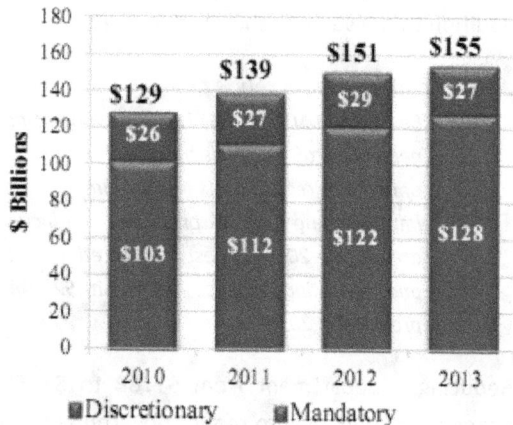

USDA Outlays

Unfortunately, SNAP is relied on by far too many poor people. Move the SNAP program out of the department and put it on the Ten Year Plan while we shift these families into a non-welfare way of life.

USDA's total outlays for 2013 are estimated at $155 billion. Roughly 83 percent of outlays, about $128 billion in 2013, are associated with mandatory programs that provide services as required by law. The majority of these outlays include crop insurance, nutrition assistance programs, and farm commodity programs.

The government is not an insurance company. The government is not your parents. The government is not a farmer. Repeal the 2008 Farm Bill and all associated legislature.

The remaining 17 percent of outlays, estimated at $27 billion in 2013, are associated with discretionary programs such as the Special Supplemental Nutrition Program for Women, Infants and Children (WIC); rural development *loans and grants; research and education; soil and water conservation technical assistance; animal and plant health; management of national forests, wildland fire, and other Forest Service activities; and domestic and international marketing assistance.*

The government is not a job. The government is not a bank. Research should be done by private companies who stand to profit from such innovation. The government is not responsible for education. Farmers who can't figure out how to manage their soil and water without federal involvement should go out of business just like with any other failed business model. The health of livestock and plants is the responsibility of the farmers, not the government. Give all national forests back to the states and let them manage their own land. Managing wildland fire is the responsibility of the landowners, and could understandably be managed by state governments. Eliminate the Forest Service. The government is not a marketing company. Eliminate all international programs.

Farm and Foreign Agricultural Services (FFAS)

The Farm and Foreign Agricultural Services (FFAS) mission area has responsibility for the delivery of programs and services which focus on supporting a sustainable and competitive U.S. agricultural system. According to the Economic Research Service, the U.S. agricultural sector produced $352 billion worth of farm products in 2010 and total production is forecast at $410 billion in 2011, providing a major foundation for prosperity in rural areas as well as a critical element of the Nation's economy.

The free market made our agricultural system sustainable and competitive long before it had a department. Farmers supply food, and everyone demands food. It really is that simple. Managing farm production is not a government issue, and the farms would provide as much production without government interference, if not more.

Agriculture related businesses, accounting for one in 12 jobs in the United States, increased employment between 2008 and 2011, a period when total employment in the United States fell about 3.5 percent. Farm exports in fiscal year 2011 reached a record high of $137.4 billion, exceeding the previous record by $22.5 billion. USDA estimates that every $1 billion worth of agricultural exports supports 8,400 jobs and generates an additional $1.3 billion in economic activity. Exports helped agriculture be one of the bright spots in the economy.

Agriculture is exactly that: A business. Business owners can pay to employ more people if they have less government overhead to deal with, such as regulatory compliance and taxes. All of this can function without the need for government involvement.

> *During 2011, rural families witnessed a record tornado season, a historic drought, record heat, and numerous damaging tropical storms. However, a strong farm safety net helped to mitigate the effects of such disasters, preserving the ability of farmers and ranchers to contribute to American prosperity. Over the past three years, USDA has paid out about $17.6 billion in crop insurance indemnities to more than 325,000 farmers who lost crops due to natural disasters. Further, USDA helped more than 250,000 farmers and ranchers suffering from natural disasters, providing assistance worth more than $3.5 billion since 2008. In response to the tightening financial market, USDA has expanded the availability of farm credit, helping struggling farmers refinance loans. In the past three years, USDA provided 103,000 loans totaling $14.6 billion to family farmers.*

Farm owners should prepare for the disasters they know are inevitable to their location. Lack of preparation on the part of the farmers does not justify taking money from all around the nation. The government is not an insurance company; farmers should seek insurance policies from private insurance companies. If they are refused a policy, there's a good reason for it; such as the risk being too high. The American people should not assume that risk just because a qualified professional decided it would be a bad idea. Natural disasters can be handled by state governments, at the very most, and only with the consent of the governed.

Crop insurance does not magically provide food to the market; it merely compensates farmers who lose their crops. A smart farmer would save some money every season, knowing that the crop is a gamble. A smart farm owner may operate farms in a variety of locations to minimize his losses, such as is the case when diversifying any other investment portfolio. The American people should not have to pay for their lack of foresight and ineligibility for proper insurance.

> *FFAS also plays an important role in the protection and enhancement of the Nation's natural resource base and environment. Thus, the area contributes to multiple USDA Strategic Goals. Specifically, to assist rural communities to create prosperity, the FFAS mission area: (1) Supports a strong farm financial safety net; (2) Promotes the vitality of rural America by improving access to international markets, providing credit guarantees for U.S. farm exports, and supports industry efforts to develop new markets.*

In support of ensuring private working lands are preserved, the FFAS area protects watershed health to ensure clean and abundant water, and enhances soil quality to maintain productive working cropland. Finally, in support of agricultural production, FFAS promotes the international acceptance of new technologies, and promotes sustainable, productive agricultural systems and trade in developing countries to enhance global food security.

Protecting and enhancing the nation's natural resource base is the option of the citizens or companies who own the land upon which the resources are located, and is thus not a federal issue. The government should not provide safety nets; people should plan and prepare for the financial problems which are common in their industries, like they did for thousands of years before the USDA stepped in.

The vitality of rural America is not a federal issue. Access to international markets is already provided by private seaports and trucking companies, and can be augmented with private railways. The government is not a bank; providing credit guarantees is the option of private banks. Diversifying the crops in the markets is not a government issue.

Preserving private working lands is not a government issue, and is the option of the landowners. Watershed health is the responsibility of the people who own the land containing the watershed. Providing clean and abundant water through the irrigation systems is the responsibility of private utility companies. Soil quality is the responsibility of the farm owner who owns the soil.

The government should not step in and interfere in private industries, such as agricultural technologies or agriculture in general. Sustainability of agricultural systems is the responsibility of the owners and operators of the systems. Production of the farms is the responsibility of the farmers. Trade is the options of the farmers and landowners. Developing countries are not a government issue. Food security is the responsibility of whoever owns the food.

Farm Service Agency (FSA)

FSA supports the delivery of farm credit, disaster assistance, and commodity and related programs and also administers some of the USDA conservation programs. FSA provides administrative support for the Commodity Credit Corporation (CCC), which funds most of the commodity, export, and some of the USDA conservation programs. In support of the Department's Blueprint for Stronger Service, in 2012 FSA plans to close 131 Service Center locations in 32 States but still maintain more than 2,100 Service Centers.

If you want credit, go to a bank. If they refuse you credit, it's because you're an unacceptable risk, and the American people shouldn't have to pay for your bad decisions. By the same logic, if you want disaster assistance, go to an insurance company.

Conservation programs should be run by the lowest level of government possible, and are largely unnecessary. Privatize the CCC; the government is not a for-profit company. Eliminate all service centers and sell off the assets. $7.8 Billion saved.

Farm Loan and Grant Programs

The farm loan programs serve as an important safety net for America's farmers by providing a source of credit when they are temporarily unable to obtain credit from commercial sources. In order to meet the growing demand for farm credit, funding for farm loans hit a record of $6 billion in 2010. Despite a strong farm economy, demand for FSA loans remains strong due, in part, to tighter credit standards including higher down-payment requirements.

Farm Loan and Grant Programs
Program Level

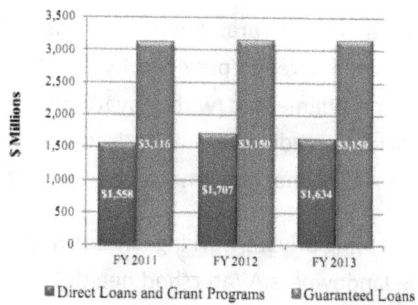

	FY 2011	FY 2012	FY 2013
Direct Loans and Grant Programs	$1,558	$1,707	$1,634
Guaranteed Loans	$3,116	$3,150	$3,150

As covered previously, the government is not a bank. If you are "unable to obtain credit from commercial sources", then you must be an unacceptable risk, and the American people should not have to foot the bill.

The 2013 Budget proposes loan levels that reflect the current demand for credit. The requested program level will support an estimated 29,600 farmers and ranchers to finance operating expenses and provide opportunities to acquire a farm or keep an existing one. The availability of farm operating loans provides farmers with short-term credit to finance the costs of continuing or improving their farming operations, such as purchasing seed, fertilizer, livestock, feed, equipment, and other supplies. For farm operating loans, the 2013 Budget provides about $1.1 billion for direct loans and $1.5 billion for guaranteed loans.

If a farmer is doing so poorly that he can't afford the basic supplies that a farm requires for every crop, then he has bigger problems than securing a loan. The government is not a bank.

Commodity Credit Corporation (CCC)

The Commodity Credit Corporation (CCC) provides funding for commodity programs administered by FSA and many Farm Bill programs such as the conservation programs administered by FSA and the Natural Resources Conservation Service (NRCS) and export programs administered by FAS. CCC borrows funds needed to finance these programs from the U.S. Treasury and repays the borrowings, with interest, from receipts and from appropriations provided by Congress.

Repeal the farm bill; the government is not a bank. Privatize CCC. Let states tax their own people for their own programs and their own lands; give federal land in the states back to the respective states, except where needed for authorized federal programs, like national defense.

If farms didn't have a safety net, farmers would be more incentivized to run their farms responsibly. Given the elimination of all federal regulation, they would have enhanced freedom to run their farm as they desire, thus giving them the freedom to exercise such responsibility in a true American fashion.

Farmers and others in the agricultural community can create their own process for wide distribution through the free market. Failing that, people would end up buying more local, which is a good thing.

Commodity Programs

Commodity loan and income support programs constitute the majority of CCC outlays. These programs provide a major portion of the farm safety net including protection against adverse market fluctuations; hence outlays for many of these programs vary significantly from year to year as market conditions change. The commodity programs are mandated by provisions of the 2008 Farm Bill. The 2008 Farm Bill provided counter-cyclical payments for producers of program crops (feed grains, wheat, upland cotton, rice, soybeans, other oilseeds, and peanuts) when market prices decline below specified target prices.

The government is not a bank. Government interference in markets causes the market to behave in unexpected ways, and causes people to make poor decisions. The buyers and sellers in a given market should have to make their decisions based on the market itself, and not based on government intervention. For example, the government gives milk farmers some revenue when milk demand is low; this deincensivizes the milk farmers from saving money and adjusting their supply for seasonal demand. We must eliminate these "safety nets" to reincentivize the people to make responsible decisions once again. Repeal the 2008 Farm Bill and privatize or eliminate the CCC. The government should not intervene in markets, especially in specific ones.

ACRE is another farm "safety net", whose purpose is to pay off farmers when they produce goods which are not in demand. Having already explained exactly why we should eliminate farm safety nets, I'll eschew the repetition.

Conservation Programs

> The Farm Bill provides authority for conservation programs. The focus of USDA conservation programs administered by FSA and NRCS is to assist producers in using environmentally sound management systems for agricultural production to meet the food and fiber needs of the Nation.

Agricultural production of producers is the producers' business, not the government's. Whether they choose to use environmentally sound management systems therefor is their own decision, as reflected by the market. If the consumers want greener farms, they'll reflect that in their demand and in their purchasing decisions.

Nutritional aspects, such as fiber content, are simply the responsibility of the consumer at the point of purchase. Consumers will buy food with the fiber content of their choosing. This demand will communicate to the producers what they should supply.

CCC Export Credit Guarantee Programs

> The CCC export credit guarantee programs, administered by FAS in conjunction with FSA, provide payment guarantees for the commercial financing of U.S. agricultural exports. These programs facilitate exports to buyers in countries where credit is necessary to maintain or increase U.S. sales. The Budget includes an overall program level of **$5.5 billion** for CCC export credit guarantees in 2013. This estimate reflects the level of sales expected to be registered under the export credit guarantee programs.

The government is not a bank. If overseas export purchasers require credit to buy our exports, they can go to a private bank like anyone else.

Market Development Programs

> FAS administers a number of programs, in partnership with private sector cooperator organizations, that support the development, maintenance, and expansion of commercial export markets for U.S. agricultural commodities and products.

Export markets are not a government issue. The government need only ensure secure trade routes and free trade agreements with other countries.

Quality Samples Program (QSP)

CCC provides funding to assist private entities to furnish samples of U.S. agricultural products to foreign importers in order to overcome trade and marketing obstacles. The program, which is carried out under the authority of the CCC Charter Act, provides foreign importers with a better understanding and appreciation of the characteristics of U.S. agricultural products. The Budget includes $2.5 million of funding for the program in 2013.

If exporters wish to provide samples to foreign importers, they can handle those themselves. Many exporters can even work together to provide a group of samples in a batch, thus overcoming the overhead associated therewith. Repeal the CCC Charter Act.

Market Access Program (MAP)

CCC funds are used to reimburse participating organizations for a portion of the cost of carrying out overseas marketing and promotional activities, such as consumer promotions. MAP participants include nonprofit agricultural trade organizations, State-regional trade groups, cooperatives, and private companies that qualify as small businesses. MAP has a brand promotion component that provides export promotion funding to 600-800 small companies annually and thereby contributes to the National Export Initiative objective of expanding the number of small and medium-sized entities that export. For 2013, the Budget includes a $200 million program level for MAP, the same level provided in 2012.

Your taxes are paying for private enterprises to do their overseas marketing, which is an expense which clearly should be reflected in the prices instead. There is no reason to charge American taxpayers for what is rightfully the expense of foreign purchasers.

Emerging Markets Program (EMP)

EMP Authorizes CCC funding to be made available to carry out technical assistance activities that promote the export of U.S. agricultural products and address technical barriers to trade in emerging markets. Many types of technical assistance activities are eligible for funding, including feasibility studies, market research, industry sector assessments, specialized training, and business workshops.

Overseas distribution expenses are the rightful expense of the exporter, who should reflect these expenses in their prices. A program that isn't funded is a program we can eliminate or privatize.

Biomass Crop Assistance Program (BCAP)

In 2010, a final rule was published implementing all phases of BCAP including financial assistance for the establishment and maintenance of crops for bioenergy production (project areas) as well as the Collection Harvest Storage and Transportation (CHST) payments previously funded through a Notice of Funding Availability (NOFA). On September 15, 2011, an interim rule was published to enable USDA to prioritize the expenditure of program funds in favor of BCAP project areas over CHST. This prioritization was needed to focus BCAP activities on the establishment of the next generation of biomass feed stocks while meeting the Budgetary constraints in 2011.

Bioenergy is a private industry, and government has no business interfering in private industries. Energy production should be handled at the state level or lower, per the 10th amendment. Biomass and biofuel are not government issues.

Salaries and Expenses

The 2013 Budget proposes a level of $1.5 billion, an increase of $24 million above the 2012 enacted level. The increase will provide resources to support continued modernization of FSA's IT infrastructure needed for MIDAS (Modernize and Innovate the Delivery of Agricultural Systems). It will also enable FSA to hire 237 temporary staff to provide critical support for peak workload periods, such as major program signups. Using temporary staff for peak workloads will allow FSA to maintain customer service while keeping FSA's permanent staffing numbers at reduced levels.

If we eliminate the agency, then we can eliminate its staff and expenses. Leave them on for a few months, to give them time to move documents to the filing office, sell off the assets, and transfer other assets elsewhere in the government as needed.

Risk Management Agency (RMA)

Federal Crop Insurance Program (FCIP)

The Federal Crop Insurance Program provides an important safety net that protects producers from a wide range of risks caused by natural disasters, as well as the risk of price fluctuations. In recent years, an increasing proportion of risk protection has been provided by revenue insurance which protects against both a loss of yield and price declines. The Federal Crop Insurance Program is a critical component of the farm safety net.

Great, another safety net; I think we're up to four now. The government is not an insurance company. Protect yourself from price fluctuations by diversifying your crops and saving enough money to get by for a season or two. The market should drive supply with its demand; the government should not step in to affect artificial behaviors into the private farming industry.

Foreign Agricultural Service (FAS)

FAS administers a variety of programs that are designed to facilitate access to international markets and thereby help to support a competitive U.S. agricultural system. FAS also carries out activities that promote productive agricultural systems in developing countries and contribute to increased trade and enhanced global food security. Working bilaterally and with international organizations, FAS encourages the development of transparent and science-based regulatory systems that allow for the safe development and use of agricultural goods derived from new technologies.

Farmers can broker deals through distributors and private exporters, who can then access international markets. The productivity of developing countries is the responsibility of those countries. Artificially increasing trade is not a government issue. Global food security is the responsibility of the owners and distributors of that food. Regulations impede innovation and free trade by adding overhead and expense to the transaction. Safe development of goods is the responsibility of those developing the goods.

Over the past three years, FAS commented on nearly 900 measures proposed by foreign governments that, if implemented, would have significantly affected U.S. exports and/or violated a major World Trade Organization commitment. Through the comment process, USDA not only alerts exporters to expected changes in foreign regulations but also influences their development to minimize the impact on U.S. exports.

Laws and regulations in other countries are not our government's business. Exporters can perform their own research or hire another company to perform research on such foreign regulatory changes. Our government should not influence law and regulation in other countries.

Foreign Market Development Cooperator Program (FMDCP)

FMDCP provides cost-share assistance to nonprofit commodity and agricultural trade associations to support overseas market development activities that are designed to remove long-term impediments to increased U.S. trade. These activities include technical assistance, trade servicing, and market research. Unlike MAP, Cooperator Program activities are carried out on a generic commodity basis and do not include brand-name or consumer promotions.

Your tax dollars should not go toward the bottom line of any private organization, non-profit or otherwise. A program that isn't funded is a program we can eliminate or privatize.

Technical Assistance for Specialty Crops (TASC)

TASC is designed to address unique barriers that prohibit or threaten the export of U.S. specialty crops. Under the program, grants are provided to assist U.S. organizations in activities designed to overcome sanitary, phytosanitary, or related technical barriers to trade. Funding for TASC is not included in the CCC baseline Budget estimates, due to the expiration of the 2008 Farm Bill.

Exporters are responsible for overcoming their own trade barriers. A free market would eschew the products in less demand in favor of those in higher demand. Just because you grow a special orange kiwi blend doesn't mean the government has to go create an artificial market for it. A program that isn't funded is a program we can eliminate or privatize.

Dairy Export Incentive Program (DEIP)

Under the DEIP, CCC funds are used to make bonus payments to exporters of U.S. dairy products to enable them to be price competitive and, thereby, make sales in targeted overseas markets for the purpose of market development or where competitor countries are making subsidized sales.

Your tax dollars are giving farmers cash to lower their prices artificially for overseas buyers, thus discriminating against American buyers. Developing markets is the responsibility of those who stand to profit from those markets.

Foreign Food Assistance

The United States plays a leading role in global efforts to alleviate hunger and malnutrition and enhance world food security through international food aid activities. USDA contributes to these efforts by carrying out a variety of food aid programs which support economic growth and development in recipient countries.

Hunger and malnutrition across the world are the responsibility of those countries, and are not our problem. Eliminate all foreign aid. Countries which rely on our aid will never learn to be self-sufficient; let's kick these dependent little birds out of the nest.

McGovern-Dole International Food for Education and Child Nutrition Program (McDIFE, CNP)

The McGovern-Dole International Food for Education and Child Nutrition Program provides for the donation of U.S. agricultural commodities and associated financial and technical assistance to carry out preschool and school feeding programs in foreign countries. Maternal, infant, and child nutrition programs also are authorized under the program. Its purpose is to reduce the incidence of hunger and malnutrition and improve literacy and primary education. These measures contribute to a healthy, literate workforce that can support a more prosperous, sustainable economy and ensure long-term food security.

Feeding and educating babies, children, and mothers in foreign countries are the responsibility of the foreign countries, and are not our problems. We have starving, illiterate children right here in America, and we need to fix our own problems before we can even consider fixing those of other countries.

Food for Peace Act (P.L. 480)

Assistance provided under the authority of the Food for Peace Act is a primary means by which the United States provides foreign food assistance.

Feeding people in foreign countries is the responsibility of the foreign countries, and is not our problem. We have starving, illiterate children right here in America, and we need to fix our own problems before we can even consider fixing those of other countries.

Food for Progress

The Food for Progress Act of 1985 authorizes U.S. agricultural commodities to be provided to developing countries and emerging democracies that have made commitments to introduce and expand free enterprise in their agricultural economies. Food for Progress agreements can be entered into with foreign governments, private voluntary organizations, nonprofit agricultural organizations, cooperatives, or intergovernmental organizations. Agreements currently provide for the commodities to be supplied on grant terms.

Repeal the Food for Progress Act of 1985. Feeding people in foreign countries is the responsibility of the foreign countries, and is not our problem. The economic systems of developing countries and emerging democracies are none of our government's business. There's no reason why our private industry can't make such deals directly with the governments and organizations in those countries, without the need to involve our own government. We especially shouldn't be incentivizing it, as we would otherwise have greater supply and thus lower prices right here in the states.

Bill Emerson Humanitarian Trust

The Bill Emerson Humanitarian Trust (the Trust) is a commodity and/or monetary reserve designed to ensure that the United States can meet its international food assistance commitments under P.L. 480 Title II. The Trust's assets can be released any time the Administrator of USAID determines that

P.L. 480 Title II funding for emergency needs is inadequate to meet those needs in any fiscal year.

The United States should not make international food assistance commitments. These commitments incentivize other countries to be more dependent on us. Eliminate USAID and repeal P.L. 480. Emergency needs in other countries should be managed by those countries.

Local and Regional Commodity Procurement Pilot Program.

*The 2008 Farm Bill authorized and provided CCC funding for a limited, field-based pilot program of local and regional procurement of food aid commodities for distribution overseas. Under the program, grants are provided to private voluntary organizations, cooperatives, and the World Food Program that undertake the procurement activities. During 2011, FAS issued **$23 million** of grants for procurement projects in Pakistan and six countries in sub-Saharan Africa.*

Procuring food commodities for distribution overseas is the responsibility of private distributors and exporters who desire to do business overseas, and is thus not a government issue. Eliminate all federal grants and foreign aid. We certainly shouldn't be doing business in the same countries that we're simultaneously bombing. Any program that has no funding is a program we can eliminate or privatize.

Trade Adjustment Assistance (TAA) for Farmers

The TAA for Farmers Program was originally authorized by the Trade Act of 2002, extended by the American Recovery and Reinvestment Act of 2009, and more recently by Title II of Public Law 112-40, the Trade Adjustment Assistance Extension Act of 2011. Under the program, USDA is authorized to provide assistance to eligible producers of raw agricultural commodities and fishermen when production in the most recent marketing year yields less than 85 percent of the average national price, production quantity, value of production, or cash receipts for such commodity for the three preceding marketing years, and increases in imports contributed importantly to such declines, as determined by the Secretary.

Repeal the Trade Act of 2002, the ARRA of 2009, P.L. 112-40, and the TAAEA of 2011. Your tax dollars should not subsidize businesses with poor business models and low profit. If your business can't even tread water on its own, then it should fail without government intervention. Not all business models are viable. Some businesses should be seasonal. If you can't get a good price for your goods, the government should not make up the difference just because you happen to sell fish.

Agricultural Reconstruction and Stabilization (ARS)

*The FAS Budget includes **$5.6 million** to support the Department's participation in reconstruction and stabilization activities in Afghanistan, as well as other countries. FAS coordinates closely with the Department of State which sets overall operational and administrative policies for activities in these countries. USDA is supporting implementation of the President's strategy for Afghanistan by providing technical experts who serve as advisors to key government ministries and serve on civilian-military command units, including Provincial Reconstruction Teams, working with farmers and local agricultural officials throughout the countries.*

We spend trillions of dollars destroying a country, and then we spend billions of dollars rebuilding it. Most of Afghanistan is full of peaceful people who wish us no harm; we had no business there in the 80s, and we have no business there today. The reconstruction and stabilization of Afghanistan is the responsibility of the Afghanis, and we should leave them alone so they can prosper or fall under their own merits. If you don't like the way Afghani politics work, don't go to Afghanistan.

Operational and administrative policies in Afghanistan are none of our business, and we certainly shouldn't be setting them. The President should not have a strategy for Afghanistan. Afghani government ministries are Afghani concerns, not ours. Provincial reconstruction is the responsibility of the provinces. Farmers should run their own affairs, or whatever process is set in place by whatever government they have at a given time. Stabilizing strategic areas of Afghanistan and their government capacity are the responsibility of Afghanistan. Eliminate all assistance programs and foreign aid programs. Afghani food security is the responsibility of Afghanistan.

*In addition, the Budget includes an estimated **$169 million** in funding to be made available to FAS through reimbursable agreements. The largest components of this are funding for technical assistance, training, and research activities that FAS carries out overseas on behalf of USAID, foreign governments, and international organizations, and agricultural reconstruction and stabilization activities that are funded by USAID and the Department of State.*

Eliminate USAID and FAS altogether. International organizations, overseas agricultural reconstruction, and stabilization are not US government issues. Most of the Department of State can go, too. Economic development and food security in developing countries are none of our business.

Rural Development (RD)

Rural communities and businesses are implementing innovative technologies and modernizing infrastructure to create jobs, develop new markets, and increase competitiveness, while conserving the Nation's natural resources and providing a safe, sufficient and nutritious food supply for the country and the world. As a leading advocate for rural America, USDA is at the forefront of developing the technology and tools necessary to transform rural America to take advantage of new opportunities.

All of the funding for USDA's Rural Development (RD) programs contributes to the Strategic Goal of assisting rural communities to create prosperity by providing financial and technical assistance to rural residents, businesses, and private and public entities for a broad range of purposes that bring prosperity and better living to Rural America.

Modernizing infrastructure and providing safe food are not federal issues, and should be left to the states. Creating jobs, developing new markets, increasing competitiveness, conserving natural resources, food sufficiency and food nutrition aren't the government's responsibility. Developing technology tools is the responsibility of private companies that stand to profit from newer tools. Transforming Rural America is the responsibility of the states, given the consent of the governed.

Financial assistance does not create prosperity; it creates debt and dependency. People choose to live in rural areas because they are rural; if you don't, then move to a city. We certainly shouldn't be taking away that rural charm by bringing the city to these areas.

The type of assistance offered includes direct loans, loan guarantees, grants, and technical assistance. Some programs provide assistance to intermediaries that make loans or provide technical assistance to the ultimate beneficiaries. Several of the programs require or encourage recipients to contribute their own resources or obtain third-party financing to support the total cost of projects, in which case these programs leverage the Government's support with private sector financing.

The government is not a bank, and shouldn't "provide assistance to" them. Recipients should always use their own resources or obtain their own loans to support their projects, and your taxes shouldn't have to pay for them at all.

Rural Business Cooperative Service (RBS)

Business and Industry Guaranteed Loan Program (B&I)

B&I, with the largest program level of the RBS programs, provides protection against loan losses so that lenders are willing to extend credit to establish, expand, or modernize rural businesses. The 2013 Budget supports a program level of $821 million in B&I loan guarantees, about $10 million above the 2012 level. The 2013 Budget proposes a guarantee fee of three percent on B&I guaranteed loans.

B&I is a safety net for banks. A bank which cannot leverage its own deposits sufficiently to provide loans is a bank which should not be given assistance to exacerbate its flawed business model. This pattern of fractional reserve banking causes banks to be inherently unstable and functions to treat a symptom of a bad design.

Rural Business Enterprise Grant Program (RBEGP)

The Rural Business Enterprise Grant Program provides grants for rural projects that finance and facilitate development of small and emerging rural businesses. The 2013 Budget provides $30 million for grants, an increase of $5.5 million above the 2012 level. The program will also provide support to the Regional Innovation Initiative and help reduce the number of food deserts in rural areas.

Eliminate all federal grants. Rural projects are the responsibility of the states; a taxpayer in Texas should not be forced to pay for a business in California.

Intermediary Relending Program (IRP)

The Intermediary Relending Program provides one percent interest direct loans to entities that relend to rural businesses at a higher interest rate and use their interest earnings to pay for their administrative expenses and develop capital reserves. The 2013 Budget supports a program level of $19 million in direct loans, an increase of $1 million above the 2012 level.

The government is not a bank. A bank that cannot survive on its own business model without government hand-holding is a bank that should fail. Food distribution to rural areas can easily be handled at a state or local level; someone could even set up a business to deliver the food there.

Rural Microentrepreneur Assistance Program (RMAP)

The Rural Microentrepreneur Assistance Program provides one percent direct loans and grants to microenterprise development organizations (MDOs). The loans will be used to establish reserves for relending to microentrepreneurs, and the grants are made to the MDOs which may relend a portion to provide training, operational support, business planning, and market development assistance.

The government is not a bank.

Rural Cooperative Development Grant Program (RCDGP)

*The 2013 Budget includes $12.7 million for this program, a **$1.7 million** increase over the 2012 level. The funding provided will be used to support distribution systems for locally produced products and the development of new cooperatives. The funding level provides modest increases in funding above the 2012 level for rural cooperative centers and grants to assist small socially disadvantaged producers.*

Distribution for locally produced products is the responsibility of private distributors. They can send trucks to the middle of nowhere just as easily as they can send trucks to downtown Los Angeles. Developing new cooperatives is not a rightful government function. Eliminate all federal grants. Producers with a poor business model should not be artificially propped up, as this discriminates against producers in socially advantageous positions. The government should provide a service to everyone equally, or not at all.

Value-Added Producer Grants (VAGP)

*The 2013 Budget provides **$15 million** for the Value-Added Producer Grants Program, an increase of $1 million above the 2012 level. The program provides grants for a wide range of value-added projects, including those that change the physical State of agricultural products or the way such products are marketed. Ten percent of the funding is reserved for mid-tier marketing chains.*

Eliminate all federal grants. The government should not interfere in markets, and should not perform any marketing.

Rural Energy for America Program (Section 9007)

RBS has operated a renewable energy loan and grant program for the purchase of renewable energy systems and energy efficiency improvements since the passage of the 2002 Farm Bill. Section 9007 of the Farm Bill implemented the Rural Energy for America Program (REAP). REAP provides similar assistance as its predecessor program, the Renewable Energy and Energy Efficiency Improvement Program; however, REAP can now offer funding for energy audits and feasibility studies.

The government is not a bank. Repeal the Farm Bills of 2002 and 2008. Providing energy to rural areas can easily be handled at the state level. The government should not be involved in audits and studies of what should be private industries.

Broadband, Distance Learning and Telemedicine (BDLT)

*The Broadband program provides financing to support new or improved broadband access across rural America. The Distance Learning and Telemedicine Grant Program is designed specifically to assist rural communities that would otherwise be without access to learning and medical services over the Internet. The 2013 Budget provides **$9 million** in Budget authority to support $94 million in broadband loans, **$13 million** for Broadband grants and **$25 million** for grants under the Distance Learning and Telemedicine Program. The 2013 Budget does not request funding for grants for analog conversion grants or healthcare services grants.*

Broadband, education, and medicine are commodities and commodities are not a right; therefore it is not the government's responsibility to provide them. This should be handled at the state level. Eliminate all federal grants.

Water and Waste Disposal Program (WWDP)

The Water and Waste Disposal Program provides financing for rural communities to establish, expand or modernize water treatment and waste disposal facilities. These facilities provide safe drinking water and sanitary waste disposal for residential users, and help communities thrive by attracting new business. Projects are designed to improve the energy efficiency of the water and waste facilities and to improve water conservation efforts.

The government is not a bank. Drinking water safety, water treatment, and waste disposal are not federal issues. Modernization of the facilities is the option of the private company providing them. Attracting new business to rural areas is not a government issue.

Rural Housing Service (RHS)

Single Family Direct and Guaranteed Loan Programs

The Single Family Housing programs provide direct and guaranteed loans to low and moderate income families in rural areas. RHS is the only Federal agency that provides direct loans for this purpose. Both direct and guaranteed loans are means-tested. Direct loans are limited to families with incomes less than 80 percent of area median income. The interest rate on these loans is based on the borrower's income and fluctuates from the current prevailing Treasury rate to being subsidized down to one percent interest. Guaranteed loans are limited to borrowers with incomes less than 115 percent of area median income.

A clear duplication of HUD and DHHS programs; If you want a loan, go to a bank. If the bank declines your application, then you must be an unacceptable risk. The government is not a bank. If you can't afford a whole home, look into roommates. This can be handled at the state level.

Multi-Family Housing Programs

The Multi-Family Housing program provides financing for rental housing projects and rental assistance payments for the low-income tenants of those projects. The portfolio currently includes about 16,000 projects that provide housing for about 449,000 low-income tenants, many of whom are elderly. The average annual income of these tenants is about $8,000.

A clear duplication of HUD and DHHS programs; people who make around $8,000 per year are in no place to take on loan payments. If you can't afford a whole home, look into roommates. This can be handled at the state level.

Other Housing Programs

*The 2013 Budget funds additional single family housing activities through **$28 million** for housing repair grants and $10 million for mutual and self-help housing grants. In addition, the 2013 Budget does not fund certain programs in order to focus resources on more efficient and less costly programs. These programs, such as credit sales of acquired property and compensation for construction defects, had been consistently funded at relatively low levels, and will no longer be available.*

A clear duplication of HUD and DHHS programs; Eliminate all federal grants. Eliminate the housing projects and sell off the assets; let the newly privatized landlords deal with their own repairs. If you help someone do something, it's not "self-help".

Community Facilities Loan and Grant Programs

RHS also administers the Community Facilities programs that provide funding for a wide range of essential community facilities. Priority is given to health and public safety facilities and education facilities. The program serves rural communities of up to 20,000 in population.

Health, police, fire, and education are not federal issues. Small rural areas are the responsibility of the small rural towns and their respective states.

Rural Utilities Service (RUS)

Electric and Telecommunications Programs (ETP)

The Electric and Telecommunications programs administered by RUS provide loans to establish, expand, and modernize vital components of the infrastructure of rural America. They are long-standing programs that brought electric and telecommunication services to rural America and ensured universal service for the Nation.

While most borrowers have some access to private credit markets, the programs help to leverage private sector investments as well as fill credit gaps that still exist for some rural areas and borrowers. In addition, the programs facilitate the financing of improvements to facilities that RUS financed in the past and still holds a lien. There are a number of ways USDA's electric program can be used to support energy conservation and efficiency projects.

The 2008 Farm Bill amended the Rural Electrification Act (REA) to make electric program funding available for these purposes. Loans can be made to electric cooperatives that, in turn, offer rebates or provide loans to their customers for energy conservation and efficiency projects. There is also a provision in the REA to provide deferments on certain electric loans for these purposes. The Rural Economic Development Loan and Grant (REDLG) program that is administered by RBS also provides funding for electric cooperatives that may be used to support energy conservation and efficiency projects.

Electricity and telecommunications are private industries which do not require federal involvement. Any rural provisions should be handled at the state level or lower. Privatize the electrical system; the telecommunications infrastructure is already private. The companies that comprise these industries, in turn, are responsible for whatever modernization, establishment, and expansion they so desire based on their own market research. When an electric company saturates its area, it must expand to continue increasing its profit. There's no reason why someone can't start a small power company in a rural area.

The government is not a bank. Privatize all RUS functions and sell all its assets. Energy conservation and efficiency are not government issues.

Repeal the 2008 Farm Bill and the Rural Electrification Act. A taxpayer in Texas should not be forced to pay to give cash to someone in California for installing a solar panel.

Rural Development Salaries and Expenses

*The 2013 Budget maintains funding for salaries and expenses related to carrying out RD programs at the 2012 level of **$654 million**. This level of funding will support a staff level of 5,346 in 2013. An increase in the direct appropriation is requested to specifically fund information technology investments; transfers from the agencies are reduced as a result of lower staff levels in 2013.*

If we eliminate the program, we can eliminate the administrative overhead associated with it, and save nearly a billion additional dollars in the process.

Food, Nutrition, and Consumer Services (FNCS)

The activities and funding of the Food, Nutrition, and Consumer Services, including the Food and Nutrition Service (FNS) and the Center for Nutrition Policy and Promotion (CNPP), support the USDA Strategic Goal to ensure that all of America's children have access to safe, nutritious, and balanced meals. FNS contributes significantly to two activities under this strategic goal, including: (1) increasing access to nutritious food; and (2) promoting healthy diet and physical activity behaviors. FNS is committed to increasing performance, efficiency, and alignment of USDA programs.

Food, nutrition, and consumer services are not government issues; therefore, we can safely eliminate all of these programs. Access to safe, nutritious, and balanced meals is the responsibility of the individual citizens and families. It is not the government's place to tell you what to eat or how to behave.

FNS administers USDA's domestic nutrition assistance programs. The mission of FNS is to increase food security and reduce hunger working in partnership with State agencies and other cooperating organizations to help ensure children and low-income people have access to food, a healthful diet and nutrition education in a manner that supports American agriculture and inspires public confidence. The mission of CNPP is to improve the health of Americans by developing and promoting dietary guidance that links the best evidence-based, scientific research to the nutrition needs of consumers. In addition to providing access to nutritious food, FNS works to empower program participants with the knowledge to eat healthy diets and engage in physical activity.

Domestic nutrition is not a government issue. Food security is the responsibility of the owners of the food. Hunger is not a federal issue. State agencies can do on their own whatever the federal government attempts to coordinate them on. Providing access to food for children is the responsibility of the parents. Providing access to food for low-income people is *nobody's* responsibility; they should look for help in their local communities and from friends and family. More importantly, they should try to increase their income, or learn to live on rice and noodles. Your health is your business and your responsibility. We had access to nutritious food before the FNS existed, and we can continue to purchase from local farms and grocery stores just as easily without it.

Supplemental Nutrition Assistance Program (SNAP)

For 2013, the Budget anticipates participation falling slightly to 46.9 million from 47.1 million in 2012. While the program has increased steadily since its last low point in 2000, and sharply in the economic downturn, the rate of increase has been declining since around January 2010. Continued gradual improvement in the economy is expected to lead to participation declines in 2013, even as the proportion of eligibles who participate is increased. The Recovery Act increased the maximum allotment by 13.6 percent, effective April 2009, a level to remain constant until the statutory SNAP thrifty food plan would increase benefits above the Recovery Act levels, or October 31, 2013, whichever comes first. Consequently, the Department anticipates that the average per person benefit will remain relatively constant through FY 2013.

SNAP is food stamps. As we increase the available welfare for poor people, so increases the demand. It stands to reason, therefore, that a reduction would reduce demand. Feeding poor people is not the government's job. This can be done at the state level; put SNAP on the 10 Year Plan, and immediately stop enrolling new people.

Child Nutrition Programs (CNP)

The 2013 Budget funds the Child Nutrition Programs at a level that will support anticipated participation and food costs, including the changes resulting from the Healthy, Hunger-Free Kids Act of 2010, signed into law in December 2010. USDA is working with State administering agencies, over 100,000 schools participating in the lunch program, hundreds of thousands of school food service workers and suppliers, as well as over 50 million children, their parents and teachers to improve school meals, improve all of the foods sold at school, and help shape child nutritional behaviors to reduce overweight and obesity and help ensure a healthy and productive populace for the future.

Feeding children nutritious food is their parents' job. Repeal HHFKA. States can feed their own kids, though they should elect not to. Parents should pack a lunch for their kids at school, or better yet home school them. Schools may allow private businesses to set up food stands in the schools. Schools should never provide free meals, and should also not exist at the federal level, but I'll get to the schools later. Child obesity, health, and productivity are not government issues.

Women Infants, and Children (WIC)

The WIC Program, USDA's largest discretionary program, helps improve the health and nutritional intake of low-income pregnant, breast-feeding and postpartum women, infants and children up to their fifth birthday. WIC works by providing participants with vouchers redeemable for foods dense in nutrients known to be lacking in the diets of eligible groups and by providing nutrition education and referrals to other important health and social services. In 2010, WIC infant participation was over 53 percent of births in the United States.

If you can't afford to feed yourself while you're pregnant, then you certainly can't afford to have another child! This was your decision, and our tax dollars should not be used to offset your bad decisions. The health and nutritional intake of anyone is not a government issue; nor are nutrition education or general health. Social Services are state issues.

Commodity Assistance Program (CAP)

CAP distributes USDA commodities through several programs. The Emergency Food Assistance Program (TEFAP) provides support to a network of food banks and other programs that assist households in need of immediate, short-term food assistance. TEFAP includes components of both discretionary and mandatory funding. For 2013, State and local program administration would be funded at $49.4 million, any part of which, at State discretion, may be used to purchase additional commodities. Also, under the NAP account, mandatory funding of $269.5 million is available for TEFAP commodities, of which States have the option to convert up to 10 percent for administrative costs.

The government should not distribute commodities. Food banks, similar programs, and poor people are not federal issues and are better left to the states.

CAP includes funding for the Commodity Supplemental Food Program (CSFP) which provides commodities to low-income elderly and pregnant, postpartum and breastfeeding women, infants and children up to age six. The 2013 Budget proposes $186.9 million, an amount sufficient to support current base caseload and participation.

A clear and obviously duplicate function of WIC, it is fair to provide a clear and obviously duplicate explanation. The government should not distribute commodities. Food banks, similar programs, and poor people are not federal issues and are better left to the states.

Nutrition Programs Administration (NPA)

Funding of $143.5 million is requested for NPA to support Federal management and oversight of USDA's investment in nutrition assistance programs, including $2 million for the Congressional Hunger Center. The request includes $2 million to promote MyPlate and the 2010 Dietary Guidelines for Americans. The Budget reflects an increase from the 2012 appropriation to help ensure adequate oversight and program integrity, *simplify and improve the programs, improve nutritional outcomes, encourage healthy and nutritious diets and expand the obesity prevention campaign.*

Nutrition is not a government issue. Eliminate the CHC, MyPlate, and DGA. It's not the government's place to tell you what to eat, or how skinny or fat you should be.

Food Safety (FSIS)

Foodborne illness is recognized as a significant public health problem in the United States. About 48 million people (one in six Americans) get sick, 128,000 are hospitalized, and 3,000 die each year from foodborne diseases, according to estimates from the Centers for Disease Control and Prevention. These diseases can lead to short- and long-term health consequences and, sometimes, can result in death. USDA and other Federal agencies are working in cooperation to ensure that Americans have increased access to safe and healthy food.

Food safety is not a federal issue, and is better left to the states. A private company can perform food inspections and certifications, and people can choose only to buy food with such a certification. Lower quality food could be sold at a lower price, and the poor could buy a lower grade for a fraction of the cost. People should use some basic common sense when selecting and preparing their food.

Organizational Structure

To accomplish its functions, FSIS employees are located at approximately 6,290 slaughtering and processing establishments and import houses, and other Federally-regulated facilities. Headquarters personnel are responsible for overseeing administration of the program and ensuring that scientific and technological developments are incorporated into inspection procedures. The Codex Office coordinates all government and non-government participation in the activities of the Codex Alimentarius Commission.

My copy of the Constitution says nothing about inspecting food. It does, however, state that anything not mentioned in the Constitution is up to the states or the people. There's no reason why the states can't make their own food standards and run their own inspection and enforcement programs.

Inspection, Data Infrastructure, and Outbreak Response

To ensure that FSIS can support its approximately 8,400 Federal in-plant and other frontline personnel, the Federal share of State inspection programs, and continue to improve the data infrastructure supporting the Nation's food safety system, the 2013 Budget proposes a discretionary funding level of $996 million, a net decrease of more than $8 million. The Budget provides the full *amount necessary to meet regulatory responsibilities, which reflects implementation of modernized poultry inspection practices in 2013.*

If we eliminate FSIS, then we no longer have 8,400 personnel to support. Here's a billion dollars we can easily save.

Combating Foodborne Illness

FSIS is instrumental in helping reduce the level of foodborne illness by targeting common and dangerous pathogens for control. In addition to its work ensuring safe and wholesome products are available to the consumer, FSIS also conducts public education campaigns to inform consumers about safe food handling methods to decrease the likelihood of foodborne illness from products that were improperly stored, handled, and/or prepared.

Reducing foodborne illness is not a federal issue, and can be handled at the state level. Ensuring safe and wholesome products are not the role of government at all. Educating the public is not a government issue, as the public is responsible for seeking its own education. If you can't figure out on your own that you should wash your hands after handling raw meat, then perhaps you deserve to catch Salmonella.

User Fees and Trust Funds

*In 2013, FSIS estimates it will collect $162 million through existing user fee and trust fund activities for providing overtime, holiday, and voluntary inspection services. As proposed in the 2012 Budget, FSIS will submit legislative proposals for two user fees in 2013; a user fee collected from plants for additional inspections and related activities made necessary due to the failure in performance by the covered establishment, and a food safety services user fee that would recover a part of the cost of providing FSIS related services at covered establishments and plants, as determined by the Secretary and which would be based on the facility size. Total annual collections from these proposals are estimated at about **$13 million**.*

$162 million is a drop in the bucket compared to the billion allocated for Food Safety. Eliminate all federal user fees and trusts. Food safety is not a federal issue.

Natural Resources and Environment (NRE)

The Natural Resources and Environment (NRE) mission area promotes the conservation and sustainable use of natural resources on the Nation's private lands and sustains production of all the goods and services that the public demands of the national forests. The mission area includes two agencies: the Natural Resources Conservation Service (NRCS) and the Forest Service (FS).

Natural resources are the responsibility of the state in which the resources are located. Give all federal land back to the states, except for military installations and those areas not located in state borders. The sustainability of natural resources is not a federal issue.

The nation's private lands are none of the government's business. Private property is exactly that: Private. You should be allowed to do anything you want on your own land, except infringe on the equal rights of other people without their consent, excepting that others have no right to any resource on or under your land.

Eliminate the NRCS and the FS. Give the states their land back and let them run their own forests. Save $6.2 Billion in the process.

Natural Resources Conservation Service (NCRS)

Conservation Operations (CO)

The 2013 Budget proposes $828 million for CO, which includes $729 million for conservation technical assistance (CTA) as well as $99 million for other CO activities including Soil Survey, Snow Survey, and Plant Materials Centers. The CO Budget is maintained at nearly the 2012 level and will protect the agency's foundation for fulfilling its core mission of delivering conservation to land users.

Let states and land owners conserve their own land, if they so choose at all. The soil, snow, and plants were doing just fine before we showed up, and they'd continue to do just fine without federal involvement.

In 2013 NRCS will continue to focus on the highest priority program areas, such as improving and streamlining technical assistance delivery to farmers, and updating the IT infrastructure, or Common Computing Environment (CCE). NRCS will continue the Conservation Effects Assessment Project (CEAP), which will form the basis for demonstrating the benefits derived from conservation programs and identify opportunities to better target USDA's private lands conservation efforts. CEAP will improve the reliability and accuracy of data sources for national, regional and watershed-scale assessments and allow for more accurate and useful measurement of conservation accomplishments. This data will enhance NRCS's ability to effectively target assistance to areas with the greatest need and practices that can yield the highest benefits.

Farms are not a federal issue. If we eliminate NRCS, then we can eliminate its IT infrastructure. Demonstrating the benefits of its own programs is obsolete, given the plan to eliminate the programs. Give all federally owned land back to the states, except military installations and land not located in a state.

Eliminate federal watershed-scale assessment and conservation measurement programs; let the states manage their own watersheds and conservation measurements. The federal government is not responsible for providing assistance to areas with conservational "needs", and therefore has no responsibility to target such assistance.

Watershed Rehabilitation Program (WRP)

This program provides financial and technical assistance to communities for planning and financing the rehabilitation of Federally-constructed flood prevention dams that have reached the end of their design lives. Although constructed initially with Federal assistance, the continued maintenance of these dams is the responsibility of local and State governments, thus the Budget does not provide funding for this program.

A clear duplication of effort already contained within Conservation Operations, watershed rehabilitation is *still* not a federal issue. Communities should tax their own people to run their own programs. Federally constructed as they may be, flood prevention dams should be given back to the states in which they are located, along with all the other federal land already mentioned. If the responsibility lies with local and state governments, then federal funding is not required. If the budget does not provide such funding, then there is no need to include the program within the NRCS. Stop building federal dams.

Water Bank Program (WBP)

The 2012 Appropriations Act provided $7.5 million for WBP. The program is currently being implemented in the Northern Pothole States of North Dakota, South Dakota, and Minnesota and will focus technical and financial assistance on flooded lands, especially flooded cropland. No funding is requested for this program for 2013.

Minnesota and the Dakotas need to take care of their own flood control problems. If no funding is requested, then the program is clearly unnecessary and can be eliminated.

Emergency Watershed Protection Program (EWP)

The purpose of EWP is to undertake emergency measures, including the purchase of flood plain easements, for runoff retardation and soil erosion prevention to safeguard lives and property from floods, drought, and the products of erosion on any watershed whenever fire, flood or any other natural occurrence is causing or has caused a sudden impairment of the watershed. Funding for EWP is typically provided through emergency supplemental funding rather than annual appropriations. In 2012, $215.9 million was *provided in response to major disasters declared pursuant to the Robert T. Stafford Disaster Relief and Emergency Assistance Act.*

Buying land is not an emergency measure. Handling runoff to prevent floods and manage erosion is the states' option, given the consent of the governed. Responsible landowners should know the dangers of their region and purchase the appropriate insurance. Repeal the RTSDREAA.

Environmental Quality Incentives Program (EQIP)

The purpose of EQIP is to provide assistance to landowners who face serious natural resource challenges that impact soil, water and related natural resources, including grazing lands, wetlands, and wildlife habitat. The 2013 Budget reflects the President's Plan for Economic Growth and Deficit Reduction. The President's Plan reduces the deficit by better targeting conservation funding to high priority areas.

Environmental quality is not a federal issue, and the federal government should not disperse incentives to landowners based on where they happen to live. Soil, water, related natural resources, grazing lands, wetlands, and wildlife habitats are not federal issues. State legislatures should decide on their own environmental laws.

The President's Plan has brought us to the brink of economic disaster, and has shown utter disregard for the Constitution. For a President sworn to uphold the Constitution, and who claims to be a Constitutional scholar, the plan has not worked and needs to be thrown out.

Wetlands Reserve Program (WRP)

WRP is a voluntary program in which landowners are paid to retire cropland from agricultural production if those lands are restored to wetlands and protected, in most cases, with a long-term or permanent conservation easement. Landowners receive fair market value for the land and are provided with cost-share assistance to cover the restoration expenses. The 2008 Farm Bill authorized the program to enroll up to 3,041,200 acres through the end of FY 2012. During 2011, WRP enrolled 200,186 acres and funding for 2012 will allow up to an additional 185,800 acres to be enrolled. The 2013 Budget request includes $224 million, which will allow the servicing of existing contracts. The enrollment of new acres is subject to reauthorization.

The Federal Government is **paying farmers not to farm**. Eliminate the Farm Bill; let states handle their own wetlands.

Conservation Security Program

The Conservation Security Program was established in the 2002 Farm Bill and is a voluntary program that provides financial and technical assistance on Tribal and private agricultural working lands to support ongoing conservation stewardship. The program provides payments to producers who maintain and enhance the condition of natural resources. The program was not reauthorized in the 2008 Farm Bill; the 2013 Budget includes $182 million for the Conservation Security Program to service existing contracts.

This program pays farmers to take care of their own land, which they should do or not do on their own accord. The Constitution gives the Congress the power to regulate commerce with Indian tribes, just as between the states. This literally means the Congress can ensure that commerce between Indian tribes and the states is kept regular. As with the rest of the Commerce Clause, it does not authorize complete power over all things Indian. The government, therefore, does not have authority over tribal or private agriculture.

Conservation Stewardship Program (CSP)

The 2008 Farm Bill replaced the Conservation Security Program with a new Conservation Stewardship Program which is distinguished from the old program in that it encourages participants to undertake new conservation activities in addition to maintaining and managing existing conservation activities. Also, the new program operates under an annual acreage limitation rather than a funding cap. The Budget proposes nearly $1.0 billion, an increase of over $200 million compared to 2012. At this level, CSP will enroll 12 million new acres during 2013 in addition to servicing prior year contracts.

In an unusual move, Congress identified a duplicate function and replaced a program instead of adding a second one. What they failed to consider, however, is that the role of government does not include interfering with private property affairs.

Farm and Ranch Lands Protection Program (FRPP)

FRPP provides matching funds to help purchase development rights to keep productive farm and ranchland in agricultural uses. NRCS partners with State, Tribal, or local governments and non-governmental organizations to acquire conservation easements or other interests in land from landowners. USDA provides up to 50 percent of the fair market easement value of the conservation easement. FRPP is funded at $200 million in 2013, $50 million above the 2012 level. This will enable NRCS to protect a total of 60,000 acres, an increase of 15,000 acres, of prime, unique, or important farmland.

FRPP buys land development rights and delegates the actual development back to the landowners, where it is actually the landowners' job to decide what to do with their land, secure their own funding, and complete the projects. FRPP is redundant to the functions of the landowners and interferes in the market.

Wildlife Habitat Incentives Program (WHIP)

The program provides financial and technical assistance to eligible participants to develop habitats for upland wildlife, wetland wildlife, threatened and endangered species, fish, and other types of wildlife. The purpose of the program is to create needed wildlife habitat that supports wildlife populations with local, State, and national significance. The Budget proposes funding for WHIP at $73 million in 2013, an increase of $23 million over 2012. With this funding, NRCS will increase the number of acres of non-Federal land for fish and wildlife habitat under this program to approximately 1.1 million acres during 2013.

Eliminate all federal grants. The government has no right to give your tax money away to people who plant a few trees or stock a few ponds. Wildlife populations are not a federal issue, and arguably not a government issue at all.

Grassland Reserve Program (GRP)

GRP was authorized in the 2002 Farm Bill as a voluntary program to help landowners and operators restore and protect grassland, including rangeland, pastureland, and certain other lands, while maintaining the lands' suitability for grazing. Participants can enroll acreage in rental agreements with varying lengths or in long-term or permanent easements. The program is jointly administered by NRCS and FSA. FSA has lead responsibility for rental agreement administration and financial activities. NRCS has lead responsibility for technical issues and easement administration. The 2008 Farm Bill reauthorized the program and capped it at 1.2 million additional acres. GRP is funded at $5 million for 2013, which will allow the servicing of existing contracts.

Land suitability for a private industry, restoring and protecting grassland, and feeding cattle on private property are not government issues. End all existing contracts.

Chesapeake Bay Watershed Initiative

The Chesapeake Bay Watershed Initiative provides producers conservation assistance through several USDA programs and is funded at $50 million for 2013, which is the same level authorized for 2012. This program helps agricultural producers improve water quality and quantity, and restore, enhance, and preserve soil, air, and related resources in the Chesapeake Bay watershed through the implementation of conservation practices. The Chesapeake Bay Management Board leads the coordination among agencies from the Department of Agriculture, Environmental Protection Agency,

Department of Defense, State departments of environment, National Oceanic and Atmospheric Administration, the National Association of Conservation Districts, Ducks Unlimited, and others.

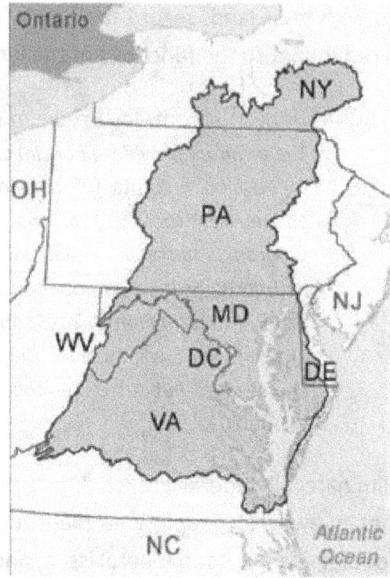

While the Chesapeake Bay Watershed technically includes Washington DC, it extends nearly into Canada. The federal government does not have the authority to manage non-federal lands outside of the District of Colombia, so the states should handle their own parts of the watershed; as it should with any other non-federal parcel of land. Give all federal land back to the states, except where not in a state, military facilities, and Washington DC. As I've stated numerous times, resource conservation is not a federal issue. Agricultural production is a private industry, and the government should not interfere with private industries. Water quality and quantity, soil, air, and related resources are not federal issues.

Voluntary Public Access and Habitat Incentive Program (VPA-HIP)

VPA-HIP was established by the Food Security Act of 1985, as amended by the 2008 Farm Bill. VPA-HIP encourages private landowners to voluntarily open their land to the public for hunting and fishing. It provides environmental, economic and social benefits including, but not limited to, enhanced wildlife habitat, improved wildlife populations, increased revenue for rural communities, and expanded opportunities for re-connecting Americans with the great outdoors. The 2008 Farm Bill provided $50 million for VPA-HIP for fiscal years 2009-2012, and the program was administered by FSA. No funds are available for the program in 2012. The 2013 Budget includes $5 million from the Commodity Credit Corporation for VPA-HIP to be administered NRCS.

Food security is not a federal issue, except for protecting sea trade lanes from piracy. Landowners should decide on their own whether to open their land for hunting and fishing without government interference. The environment and the economy are not federal issues. Rural communities' revenue is the responsibility of those specific rural communities. Re-connecting Americans with the great outdoors is not a government issue; people should be left to decide on their own whether to go outside.

Conservation Reserve Program Technical Assistance

> *NRCS provides technical support including land eligibility determinations, conservation planning and practice implementation for the Conservation Reserve Program (CRP). The 2013 Budget includes $108 million for CRP technical assistance by NRCS. CRP is administered by FSA.*

If we eliminate the NRCS, then we don't need to worry about the eligibility requirements therefor.

Forest Service (FS)

> *The Forest Service (FS), with approximately 33,600 staff years in 2013, is the largest employer in USDA. For 2013, the total request for FS discretionary activities is $4.86 billion, an increase of $15 million from the 2012 enacted level, which includes $240 million in prior year balances directed to be used in the Wildland Fire*

2013 Forest Service Budget Authority
Total = $5.5 Billion

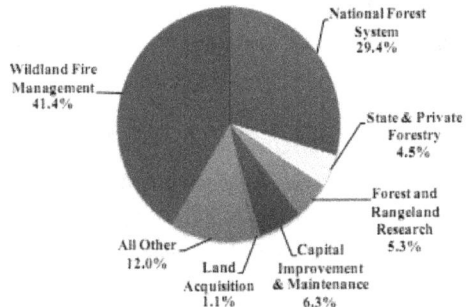

- National Forest System 29.4%
- Wildland Fire Management 41.4%
- State & Private Forestry 4.5%
- Forest and Rangeland Research 5.3%
- Capital Improvement & Maintenance 6.3%
- Land Acquisition 1.1%
- All Other 12.0%

> *Management account. The 2013 Budget will support the America's Great Outdoors (AGO) Initiative, restore large landscapes, improve water quality in priority landscapes, decommission roads, advance the State and Private Redesign effort, fully fund the ten-year average cost of fire suppression, and create green jobs. Through targeted administrative savings, FS will reduce its administrative (specifically cost pool) expenditures by $60 million and reallocate those funds to accomplish more project work.*

Give the forest land back to the states in which the forests reside, let those states manage their own land, and save $4.9 Billion. States should manage their own wildland fires, restore their own landscapes, improve their own water quality, decommission their own roads, and so forth. The states should do so on their own, through their own revenue, and only with the consent of the governed.

Forest and Rangeland Research

> *For 2013, $293 million is proposed for Forest and Rangeland Research, a $2.5 million reduction from 2012, which will be accomplished by focusing research priorities. FS maintains the world's largest forest research organization. While its broad mission is to develop knowledge and technology needed to enhance the economic and environmental values of all of the Nation's forests, the program also supports the specific research needs that arise from managing*

the National Forest System (NFS). The Budget for 2013 will go toward long-term, proactive research, and toward conducting research that responds to currently pressing issues. For example, FS is pioneering new uses for wood through nanotechnology research, but also is developing tools to combat invasive species that have recently been introduced into our Nation's forests.

Enhancing the environmental values of forests is not a government issue. There is no reason for the federal government to own vast stretches of land across the country; give that land back to the states and let them run their own research programs and forest systems. Ideally, they'd sell the land and put caps on how many acres any entity could buy in this fashion. That way, some major corporation can't just come in and buy half of Montana. Nanotechnology research is the responsibility of private companies which stand to profit from nanotechnology products. Combatting invasive species is the responsibility of the landowners, of the federal government should not be one.

State and Private Forestry (S&PF)

*Through S&PF programs, FS addresses forest health concerns on Federal, State, and private lands. For 2013, total funding for S&PF programs is proposed at **$251 million**, a decrease of $2 million below the 2012 level. The Budget proposes **$18 million** to establish a new Landscape Scale Restoration Budget line item that would be used to fund nationally competitive, multi-jurisdictional projects that target issues and landscapes of national importance and require coordination among multiple S&PF programs. The Forest Legacy program—a program that cost-shares the purchase of conservation easements to protect nationally prioritized forest lands from development—will be funded at **$60 million**. Further, **$4 million** is also proposed for the Community Forest & Open Space Conservation program to cost share fee-simple purchases of land. The Budget proposes to shift funding for the Forest Resources Inventory and Analysis program to the Forest Inventory and Analysis Budget line item in the Forest and Rangeland Research account.*

Forest health is not a federal issue. Any concerns on state lands are the responsibility of those states. Any concerns on private lands are the responsibility of the landowner and are not government issues. Restoring the landscape scale is not a government issue. Landscapes of national importance, such as the Grand Canyon and Mount Rushmore, are the responsibility of those states, to which we should give the land back.

Eliminate all federal easements. Private landowners should be allowed to develop their private lands as they so choose. The government should never "cost share" land.

National Forest System

FS manages over 193 million acres of public land in 44 States and Puerto Rico, collectively known as the NFS. These lands are managed for multiple uses on a sustained-use basis. The Agency has placed a focus on restoring forests for the benefit of watersheds, restoring longleaf pine habitat, and re-establishing vibrant local economies.

Managing public land located within state borders is not a federal issue. Give the land back to those states and let them deal with their own projects.

Wildland Fire Activities

*Through the Wildland Fire Activities, FS protects life, property and natural resources on NFS land and an additional 20 million acres on adjacent State and private lands through fee or reciprocal protection agreements. For 2013, total funding for these activities is proposed at **$2.3 billion**, about the same as 2012. The Budget funds the 10-year average cost of fire suppression and focuses on risk-based decision-making when responding to wildfires, as called for in the recently completed, interagency "Cohesive Strategy." This document, prepared by the Department of the Interior and USDA, outlines the Federal government's approach to addressing wildland fire for the next ten years.*

Managing wildland fires is the responsibility of the people who own that land. For very large fires not located in cities, the state governments may choose to step in and provide assistance, if the people so wish. States can work together without federal involvement. Taxes from Oregon should not be used to fight fires in Ohio.

Capital Improvement and Maintenance

*The Capital Improvement and Maintenance account funds construction and maintenance of buildings, recreation sites, facilities, roads, and trails. For 2013, total funding for these programs is proposed at **$346 million**, which reflects a shift of about $50 million to IRR. Within the total, $148 million is provided for road maintenance and reopening. Of the Roads funding, $9 million will be used to construct 4-6 miles of new roads for public access in Alaska. These 4-6 miles of roads are the only new roads FS is proposing to build in 2013 with the exception of possibly building a limited number of roads to support the agency's bark beetle efforts. These roads would be funded under the program that reflects the primary purpose for the project. The Legacy Roads and Trails program would be placed in NFS. The program has set a target of decommissioning 2,028 miles of roads in 2013.*

If we eliminate the Forest Service, then we no longer need to build buildings, recreation sites, facilities, roads, and trails; the states can build their own. Tax dollars from New Hampshire should not pay for new roads in Alaska. Bark beetles are not a federal issue. Roads and trails are not a federal issue. The states should decide for themselves which roads in their own state should be decommissioned.

Land Acquisition

> The Land Acquisition program protects resources, decreases administrative costs, and increases visitor access to the national forests and grasslands by acquiring parcels of land for inclusion in the NFS. The parcels acquired through this program are usually inholdings. For 2013, the Budget proposes **$59 million** in total funding for this program. Up to **$5 million** of this funding will support FS' initiative to target specific parcels that increase the public's access to NFS lands.

If we give all these federal forest lands back to the states, then we no longer need to worry about visitor access, resource, or administrative costs associated therewith.

Marketing and Regulatory Programs (MRP)

> The economic vitality and quality of life in rural America and the U.S. economy at large depends on a competitive, efficient, and productive agricultural system. U.S. agricultural producers are not simply farmers and ranchers; they are often small business owners trying to survive and support their families and rural communities in a challenging global, technologically advanced, and competitive business environment. In an era of market consolidation and intense competition, these producers rely on fair and open access to markets and control over their decisions to thrive. Agricultural producers also need to safeguard animal and plant resources against the introduction of foreign agricultural pests and diseases.

Economic vitality, quality of life, and the economy are not the government issues. Competitive, efficient, and productive agricultural systems are natural byproducts of a free market system, and will exist without government intervention. Small business owners have been able to survive and support their families and rural communities for far longer than this government has even existed, and they do a better job when government is kept out of their work.

Successful business models will rise to new challenges, such as larger and more advanced markets. Poor business models will not. Either should be allowed to succeed or fail by their own merit. This way, at least their success or failure will be their own.

Agricultural producers should indeed safeguard their animals and plants against pests and diseases, as this could impact their profit margins. Having said that, they can do so without government intervention.

> The mission of Marketing and Regulatory Programs (MRP) is to facilitate and expand the domestic and international marketing of U.S. agricultural products, to help protect the agricultural sector from plant and animal health threats, and to ensure humane care and treatment of certain animals. Because these programs provide the basic infrastructure to improve agricultural market competitiveness for the overall benefit of consumers and producers of American agriculture, this mission area contributes to all of USDA's Strategic Goals.

Producers and distributors are responsible for setting up their own international marketing programs, if they so choose. A private organization could easily become a central hub for such marketing programs, making its own profit along the way through a facilitator's or finder's fee. The government does not need to be involved, other than to ensure peace between nations and to protect trade lanes.

Animal and Plant Health Inspection Service (APHIS)

> APHIS works cooperatively with State and local agencies, private groups, and foreign governments to protect the safety of the Nation's agriculture. The APHIS 2013 Budget proposes an appropriation of about **$765 million**, of which approximately **$762 million** is for salaries and expenses and about **$3 million** for buildings and facilities. The total is a net decrease of about $55 million compared to 2012.

> APHIS supports, among others, the Department's strategic goal to ensure children have access to safe, nutritious, and balanced meals by minimizing major diseases and pests that would otherwise hinder agricultural production. This outcome is measured as the value of damage prevented and mitigated annually as a result of APHIS activities.

State and local governments should tax their own people to run their own programs. Private groups are not a government issue. Foreign government involvement need only exist to ensure peaceful relations and eliminate trade barriers between nations.

Ensuring that children have safe, nutritious, and balanced meals is the responsibility of their parents. Minimizing major diseases and pests can be managed at the state level. Preventing reductions in the production of a specific industry is not a government issue.

Safeguarding and Emergency Preparedness/Response

*The 2013 Budget includes discretionary appropriations of **$698 million** for safeguarding and emergency preparedness and response. To combat any sudden, urgent and unforeseen pest and disease outbreaks, the Secretary retains authority to transfer funds from the CCC or other USDA accounts. The Budget provides technical and financial support to help control or eradicate a variety of animal and plant health threats.*

Combatting sudden, urgent, and unforeseen pest and disease outbreaks is not a federal issue. Controlling and eradicating these threats is the responsibility of pest and disease control service companies, which the farm businesses would hire.

Animal Health

*The Budget includes a total of about **$279 million** to protect the health of livestock, poultry, and other animals. The Budget includes an increase of about $5.3 million for Animal Health Technical Services that support the improved animal disease traceability system, which has been developed using stakeholder input. The Budget includes a decrease for Equine and Cervid Health activities of about $1.3 million to eliminate Federal contributions towards addressing chronic wasting disease since States are best positioned to continue managing the disease through voluntary herd certification programs and local surveillance. While USDA will strive to use remaining resources as effectively as possible, States and Tribes may assume greater responsibility for financial support for the program. The Budget includes a decrease of $2.6 million for Sheep and Goat Health activities by discontinuing an ineffective option under the Scrapie Flock Certification Program. Cattle Health activities reflect a $9.0 million reduction, the majority of which is due to amending statistical methods related to cattle health surveillance efforts.*

The Constitution does not authorize the federal government to protect livestock, poultry, and other animals, to certify or survey herds, nor to run sheep, goat, and cattle health activities. The states are best positioned to manage *everything* not listed in Article I, Section 8, and that seems to include the entire Department of Agriculture.

Plant Health

*The Budget includes a total of about **$283 million** to protect plant and forest health. The request includes a decrease of $11.7 million for Tree and Wood Pest activities. APHIS would further reduce its role in addressing the emerald ash borer, scaling back activities to manage an outreach program, provide national coordination and oversight, and continue developing methods development, as there are limited tools currently available. The Budget includes a decrease of $8.9 million stemming from successes in reducing* *acreage infested with cotton pests, although APHIS continues to address the smaller remaining infested areas. APHIS is also requesting a decrease of $2.8 million within Specialty Crop Pests, primarily to pilot an initiative for commercial growers to assume more financial responsibility for pest treatments on their property.*

The health of forests and other plants is the responsibility of the land owners. Tree and wood pests are not government issues, except for those trees and woods located on government property, which should be minimized. Along this same line, emerald ash borer, cotton pests infestation acreage, smaller infested areas, specialty crop pests, and pest treatment are not government responsibilities. Land owners should manage their own land.

Wildlife Services

*About **$84 million** is requested for Wildlife Services. This includes a decrease of about $4.3 million for wildlife damage management as APHIS reduces lower priority program activities, while maintaining focus on critical, higher priority program activities.*

A clear duplication of effort also found in EQIP, WHIP, and VPA-HIP, Wildlife Services can be eliminated for the same reasons: Wildlife is not a federal issue, and managing wildlife is not authorized by the Constitution.

Regulatory Services

*A total of about **$33 million** is requested. APHIS has identified and implemented several process improvements which are expected to yield efficiencies, which allows for a decrease of $1.3 million for biotechnology regulation activities. APHIS will concentrate on further improving the petition process and strengthening NEPA documentation as well as enhancing its compliance program. These activities support the Department's strategic goal of helping promote agricultural production and biotechnology exports by increasing the number of genetically engineered plant lines that are found to be safe by APHIS.*

If we eliminate APHIS, then we don't need to worry about improving its efficiency or processes. Biotechnology is not a government issue, and government should *never* intervene in a specific industry. Promoting agricultural production and any specific type of export are not the proper role of government. The government should neither regulate, nor artificially increase, the number of genetically engineered plant lines, nor any other specific type of products. Managing private industries is not the government's responsibility.

Emergency Management

A total of almost $19 million is requested, representing a $1 million increase. The Budget includes an increase in contingency funds to restore the funding to its previous level and ensure sufficient resources are available to implement emergency, short-term activities.

There is no such thing as a federal agricultural emergency. Land owners should try to manage their own emergencies; for larger issues, they should be handled at the lowest possible level.

Safe Trade and International Assistance

The Budget includes a total of almost $31 million to facilitate a safe U.S. agricultural trade. This includes an increase to implement the Lacey Act amendments included in the 2008 Farm Bill related to preventing importation of products derived from illegally harvested foreign timber. This also includes a decrease in the amount of funding provided to cooperating governments and international organizations. Cooperative efforts against high risk diseases, such as foot-and-mouth disease, will be maintained.

The Agricultural industries will facilitate themselves in a free market; the government's only responsibility is to ensure peaceful relations, free trade, and safe trade lanes. Peaceful relations and free trade can be handled by treaties, without actual programs, and safe trade lanes are the responsibility of the Navy and the Coast Guard.

Animal Welfare

The 2013 Budget proposes $25 million, about $3 million below 2012, for Animal Welfare activities, including $0.5 million for enforcement of the Horse Protection Act. APHIS will achieve the decrease by gaining efficiencies, eliminating unfilled positions and attrition, and prioritizing inspections based on determination of risks, among other efforts.

Protecting horses and ensuring the welfare of other animals are not federal issues. The government should not be in the business of inspecting your animals.

User Fees

In addition to discretionary funding, APHIS collects user fees to cover costs related to agricultural quarantine and inspections that occur at ports of entry. These collections are shared with the Department of Homeland Security's Customs and Border Protection (CBP); APHIS plans to retain $216 million in 2013. Among the many activities conducted by this retained funding, APHIS assesses the risks associated with international trade and develops regulations to protect agricultural health; inspects and quarantines, imported plant *propagative materials; trains agricultural inspectors and detector dog teams; and provides the scientific support necessary to carry out these activities and those carried out by CBP. APHIS will also submit legislative proposals to authorize the collection of about $9 million in user fees for Animal Welfare activities, about $7 million in user fees for Veterinary Biologics activities, and $4 million in user fees for Biotechnology Regulatory Services activities. As recipients of these services are the direct beneficiaries of many of the services provided by the respective division of APHIS, the proposed user fee will place the cost of providing these services on the recipient rather than the U.S. taxpayer.*

The government forces an inspection of your animals upon you, and then it charges you for it on top of the taxes you already pay. Being that there is no authority in the Constitution for the federal government to do any of these things, we can eliminate them. If we eliminate them, then we should also eliminate all fees associated therewith. The 10th Amendment cites that states may still choose to run their own animal inspection "services".

Buildings and Facilities

The Budget maintains funding for general repairs and maintenance of APHIS buildings.

If we eliminate APHIS, then we have no buildings and facilities to repair or maintain. Sell them off at auction.

Agency Management

I could find no description of Agency Management in the budget or the APHIS website, but it stands to reason this is overhead required to manage APHIS. If we eliminate APHIS, we can eliminate its management and save $9 Million.

Agricultural Quarantine Inspection

I could find no description of AQI, but the name implies it is a program designed to inspect agricultural resources and quarantine them as needed. This sounds like a state issue and can be eliminated, thus saving $216 Million.

Agricultural Marketing Service (AMS)

The mission of AMS is to facilitate the competitive and efficient marketing of agricultural products in domestic and international markets, while ensuring fair trading practices.   AMS programs benefit producers, traders, and consumers of U.S. food and fiber products by promoting a strategic marketing perspective that adapts product and marketing decisions to consumer demands, changing domestic and international marketing practices, and new technology.

The Constitution does not authorize the federal government to interfere in private industries. Therefore, it is not authorized to facilitate competition and efficiency in agricultural marketing. Private businesses who wish to compete and improve their efficiency should find their own services to facilitate such desires, or find a way to do it themselves. Therefore, AMS can be eliminated to the tune of $1.3 Billion.

Marketing Services

AMS administers a variety of programs that enhance the marketing and distribution of agricultural products. Activities include the collection, analysis, and dissemination of market information; surveillance of shell egg handling operations; development of commodity grade standards; protection of producers from unfair marketing practices; statistical sampling and analysis of commodities for microbiological contamination and pesticide residues; development and enforcement of organic standards; research and technical assistance aimed at improving efficiency of food marketing and distribution; and monitoring of pesticide recordkeeping.

The Constitution does not authorize the federal government to intervene in the marketing and distribution of any products; only to ensure they are allowed to flow freely between the states, Indian tribes, and foreign nations. This can be accomplished without incentivizing or regulating it; the government need only ensure there are no artificial barriers to such trade.

Collecting, analyzing, and disseminating market information; watching how you handle your eggs, developing grading standards, inspecting marketing practices, looking for germs and chemicals, deciding what to label "Organic", research, hand-holding, and managing the efficiency of marketing and distribution are not authorized by the Constitution. Therefore, states should handle these issues themselves.

Payments to States and Possessions

*Under the Federal-State Marketing Improvement Program (FSMIP), AMS provides matching funds to State Departments of Agriculture for projects aimed at improving marketing efficiency, reducing marketing costs for producers, and lowering food costs for consumers. The 2013 Budget requests a total of **$1.3 million** for the program, an increase of $133,000 to restore grants funding to 2011 levels. The new funding would emphasize value-added projects that spotlight local and regional food marketing initiatives.*

These funds don't just come out of nowhere; the government is redistributing wealth from state to state. States should tax their own people to run their own programs. Yet another in a long line of unconstitutional USDA programs which involve themselves in marketing efficiency and costs, FSMIP can be eliminated to save over a million bucks.

Section 32 Funds

Section 32 of the Act of August 24, 1935, authorizes the appropriation for each fiscal year of an amount equal to 30 percent of the gross receipts from duties collected under customs laws of the United States during the preceding calendar year. These funds are used to encourage domestic consumption of non-price supported perishable commodities and re-establish farmers' purchasing power through a variety of activities, including:

- *Purchases of commodities and removal of surplus commodities from the marketplace for distribution to Federal nutrition assistance programs such as the National School Lunch Program*
- *Diversion programs that bring production in line with demand; and*
- *Disaster assistance for producers.*

Over $1 Billion of your tax dollars are used to tell you what to eat, to buy the extra food the farmers grow and redistribute it to children who should instead be fed by their parents, to tell farmers what to grow, and to give money to farmers who failed to plan properly. A series of disparate and unrelated programs, Section 32 has no authority under the Constitution and does what should rightfully be done by parents, insurance companies, and the free market itself.

User Fee Programs

AMS operates programs funded through license or user fees. The Commodity Grading Services program provides voluntary commodity grading and classing services for dairy products, fresh and processed fruits and vegetables, meat and meat products, poultry, eggs, tobacco, and cotton. AMS also offers certification services to verify contract specifications on quantity and quality, acceptance and condition inspection services for all agriculture commodities upon request, and export certification services for a number of commodities. AMS' audit verification services review production and quality control systems, and verify industry marketing claims. In addition, AMS enforces the Perishable Agricultural Commodities Act which prohibits unfair and fraudulent practices in the marketing of perishable agricultural commodities by regulating shippers, distributors, and retailers. Full and prompt payment for fresh fruits and vegetables is a key objective of the program.

In addition to running a bunch of programs which have no right to exist, the government then charges you for them on top of your tax dollars and your customs duties. The government then steps in and tells the industry how to label its products, what to call them, and tells them they can't sell some of them at all. This is a long list of programs which the government has no constitutional authority to operate, and which therefore belong at the state level, if at all.

Grain Inspection, Packers and Stockyards Administration (GIPSA)

> GIPSA establishes the official U.S. standards and quality assessment methods for grain and related products, regulates handling practices to ensure compliance with the U.S. Grain Standards Act and Agricultural Marketing Act of 1946, and manages a network of Federal, State, and private laboratories that provide impartial, user-fee funded official inspection and weighing services. The agency regulates and monitors the activities of dealers, market agencies, stockyard owners, live poultry dealers, packer buyers, packers, and swine contractors in order to detect prohibited unfair, unjust, discriminatory or deceptive, and anti-competitive practices in the livestock, meat and poultry industries. The agency also reviews the financial records of these entities to promote the financial integrity of the livestock, meat, and poultry industries. As such, its efforts help USDA enhance international competitiveness of American agriculture and the economic viability and sustainability of rural and farm economies.

The assessment methods for grain and related products, regulating handling practices, establishing grain standards, marketing of any kind, managing laboratories, the activities of private businesses and people, financial records, international competitiveness, economic viability, and economic stability of private sectors are not government issues, and none of these programs are authorized by the Constitution. The 10th Amendment tells us that anything that falls into such category is a state issue, and thus we can eliminate GIPSA to save $90 Million.

Research, Education, and Economics (REE)

> Whether measured as crop yield per acre, milk and meat yield per animal, or average output per farm worker, the productivity of U.S. agriculture is among the highest in the world. Economic analysis finds strong and consistent evidence that investment in agricultural research has yielded high returns per dollar spent with net social returns in the United States estimated to be at least 35 percent annually. These returns include benefits not only to the farm sector but also to the food industry and consumers in the form of more abundant commodities at lower prices. In 1929, over 19 percent of a family's income went to paying for food consumed in the home. By 2010, this amount stood at 6.4 percent of the average American's family income. With reduced food costs, families have the resources to spend on other goods and other sectors. Continued investments in research will ensure sustainable agricultural production, economic growth for growers and greater choice for consumers.

The productivity of U.S. agriculture is among the highest in the world *despite*, not because of, federal intervention in the otherwise free market. Loosening restrictions and letting the commerce flow freely could only serve to improve such production, and thus commerce.

The economy being none of the government's business, the analysis thereof is thus moot. Everything the government does is better done by private companies whose profit depends on their competitiveness; therefore, privatizing such research would be in the overall best interest of everyone involved. The government should not involve itself in anything that could be labeled a "social return", and should never interfere with any specific industry or line of business.

Federal interference artificially increases the price of goods by imposing regulation, which causes overhead in time and in financial expense. Any decrease in price due to supply is greatly offset by this increase.

Agricultural Research Service (ARS)

ARS conducts research to develop new scientific knowledge, transfer technology to the private sector to solve technical agricultural problems of broad scope and high national priority, and provide access to scientific information. The agency includes the National Agricultural Library, the Nation's major information resource on food, agriculture and natural resource sciences.

Developing new scientific knowledge is the responsibility of private businesses that stand to profit from the knowledge they're developing. Agriculture is not a federal issue. Access to scientific information is facilitated through the Internet; the farmers can set up a wiki for free. Such a wiki could easily encompass information regarding food, agriculture, and natural resource sciences; saving over $1 Billion in the process.

New Products/Product Quality/Value Added

ARS has active research programs directed toward: (1) improving the efficiency and reducing the cost for the conversion of agricultural products into biobased products and biofuels, (2) developing new and improved products to help establish them in domestic and foreign markets, and (3) providing higher quality, healthy foods that satisfy consumer needs in the United States and abroad.

Bio-based products and biofuels are none of the government's business. Developing new and improved products is the responsibility of private businesses who stand to profit from outperforming their competitors. The quality and health of food produced is the responsibility of the businesses producing the food.

Livestock Production

ARS' livestock production program is directed toward: (1) safeguarding and utilizing animal genetic resources, associated genetic and genomic databases, and bioinformatic tools, (2) developing a basic understanding of the physiology of livestock and poultry, and (3) developing information, tools, and technologies that can be used to improve animal production systems. The research is heavily focused on the development and application of genomics technologies to increase the efficiency and product quality of beef, dairy, swine, poultry, aquaculture, and sheep systems. The 2013 Budget includes a reallocation of $4 million for research to develop integrated, sustainable production systems that will improve food production efficiency and quality and protect the environment. ARS will harness the expanding body of genomic information on ruminants and fish to improve feed and production efficiency thereby reducing feed inputs and waste outputs.

Safeguarding and utilizing animal genetic resources are not government issues. If a company wants to perform genetic research on animals, they can buy their own animals and use their collected data as they wish. Such organizations can create their own database(s) and share their findings across the Internet, if they so choose. Bioinformatic tools, which use computers to facilitate biological research, should be developed and used by the private sector. The physiology of livestock and poultry are not government issues. Improving animal production systems is the responsibility of businesses which produce animal production systems, and such improvement can give them an edge over their competitors.

Genomic technologies should be developed by private businesses and applied by genetic researchers without the need for government involvement. The efficiency and quality of genetically modified meats is not a federal issue. The production of such systems is the responsibility of businesses who stand to profit by selling such systems. The efficiency of feed and production are not government issues.

Livestock Protection

ARS' animal health program is directed at protecting and ensuring the safety of the Nation's agriculture and food supply through improved disease detection, prevention, control, and treatment. Basic and applied research approaches are used to solve animal health problems of high national priority. Emphasis is given to methods and procedures to control animal diseases. The Budget includes a reallocation of $4.1 million for improved animal protection *research which will enhance food production and security. Projects will focus on the detection and elimination of tumor and enteric viruses affecting U.S. poultry production as well as emerging exotic diseases of poultry. Additionally, ARS will expand its research on detection methods and countermeasures to foreign animal diseases thereby reducing the probability of catastrophic losses from these diseases.*

Detecting, preventing, controlling, and treating disease are the responsibilities of the farmers raising the cattle, and of the slaughterhouses while in their care. The health, production, and security of food animals are not federal issues.

The government should not be involved in agriculture. If someone sells you meat from a sick cow, while telling you it was healthy, and you get sick, just sue them and be done with it. The producers should purchase an inspection service from a third party inspection service, who would label it as healthy; just choose on your own not to buy meat that isn't labeled as such.

Crop Production

ARS' crop production program focuses on developing and improving ways to reduce crop losses while protecting and ensuring a safe and affordable food supply. The research program concentrates on effective production strategies that are environmentally friendly, safe to consumers, and compatible with sustainable and profitable crop production systems. Research will focus on improving environmental and resource management strategies, developing superior pest control strategies, and refining production systems. The Budget also reallocates $0.6 million to expand activities to identify, acquire, and secure unprotected genetic resources of plants.

Reducing crop loss is the responsibility of the farmers. Developing and improving new ways to do so can be done by private businesses, who can sell products and services to the farmers. Research should never be done by the government.

Environmental and resource management strategies are not federal issues. Pest control strategies are the business of landowners. Refining production systems is the responsibility of the production system producers, who stand to profit by selling better production systems. Genetic research is not a government issue.

Crop Protection

ARS research on crop protection is directed toward epidemiological investigations to understand pest and disease transmission mechanisms, and to identify and apply new technologies that increase understanding of virulence factors and host defense mechanisms. The 2013 Budget includes a *reallocation of $7.6 million for research to enhance plant health by developing management tools for soil-borne plant pathogenic microbes and nematodes. Specific research will focus on creating and maintaining an environment of soil microbes which will be unfavorable to the establishment or survival of plant pathogens and pathogenic nematodes. By deciphering the complex interactions among microbial populations, ARS will develop consistent and effective biocontrol of soil-borne pathogens in a variety of cropping systems and soils.*

The Budget also proposes to reallocate of $3 million to protect crops from invasive pests. Research will develop molecular and state-of-the-art technologies to control key invasive arthropods of row crops, fruits and vegetables; methods to disrupt insect vectored plant diseases through technologies that reduce arthropod survival; and biologically-based invasive plant control strategies that require minimal inputs and can be used as a component of IPM or a standalone approach.

Understanding virulence factors, pest and disease transmission mechanisms, and controlling the microbial content of every square inch of farmland in the country are not government issues. It is the responsibility of the private businesses which profit more by selling food from healthy crops. Protecting crops from invasive pests, including the government, is the responsibility of the farmers.

Food Safety

Ensuring that the United States has the highest levels of affordable, safe food requires that the food system be protected at each stage from production through processing and consumption from pathogens, toxins, and chemical contaminants that cause diseases in humans. ARS' current food safety research is designed to yield science-based knowledge on the safe production, storage, processing, and handling of plant and animal products, and on the detection and control of toxin producing and/or pathogenic bacteria and fungi, parasites, chemical contaminants, and plant toxins. The 2013 Budget proposes to reallocate $4.1 million for research to develop specific post-harvest pathogen reduction strategies while ensuring that these treatments do not adversely impact product quality.

It is not the government's job to provide food, nor to ensure its food is cheap or safe. A business that sells food that kills people or makes them sick is a business which will quickly go bankrupt as the news spreads. A business that sells its products at a price higher than what people are willing to pay is a business that will go bankrupt as nobody buys its products.

Protecting the food supply from pathogens, toxins, and contaminants is the responsibility of the businesses producing, distributing, storing and transporting the food. A single law at the state level stating "Don't poison people" should be sufficient, but states should be left to come up with their own laws. All research should be done by private businesses, or other interested organizations.

Human Nutrition

Maintenance of health throughout the lifespan along with prevention of obesity and chronic diseases via food-based recommendations are the major emphasis of the ARS human nutrition research program. ARS' research program also actively studies bioactive components of foods that have no known requirement but have health promoting activities. The 2013 Budget proposes to reallocate $2.9 million for research on nutrition and health.

The health of the citizenry, including nutrition, obesity and disease, is not a government issue. The government should never tell you what to eat.

Environmental Stewardship

*ARS research programs in environmental stewardship support scientists at more than 70 locations. Emphasis is given to developing technologies and systems that support profitable production and enhance the Nation's vast renewable natural resource base. The 2013 Budget proposes an increase of **$25 million** to conduct research that will enhance American agriculture's adaptability to environmental challenges and help respond to recommendations in a report (July 2011) released by the President's Council of Advisors on Science and Technology (PCAST), calling for improved accounting of ecosystem services and greater protection of the Nation's environment.*

There is no reason for the government to employ its own scientists and run its own research programs. The profitability and renewability of any given market is not a government issue. The Constitution does not authorize the federal government to monitor the ecosystems of the entire North American continent.

Adapting our agriculture to environmental challenges is the responsibility of those affected by such challenges. If you live in a place with a lot of pests, buy pesticides. If you live in a windy place, build wind breaking fences or grow crops that can survive in the wind. Taking care of you in your own environment is not the government's job.

Being that science and technology are none of the government's business, the President does not require a council of advisors thereon. It is not the government's job to provide ecosystem services, nor to protect the environment at the federal level.

The conditions and trends of the nation's agricultural ecosystems is not a federal issue; thus there is no need for an entire infrastructure to assess them. Developing sciences and technologies is not the role of government; it is the role of private businesses which stand to profit from such development by providing better products or services than their competitors, or at a lower cost, or at higher quality.

Developing crops is not the responsibility of government; thus there is no need to conduct research on such improvements. Enhancing water and nutrient use, minimizing resource losses and environmental impacts, ensuring the availability of water, predicting crop responses, food security in other countries, and enhancing ecosystems services are not federal issues.

National Agricultural Library (NAL)

The NAL is the largest and most accessible agricultural research library in the world. It provides services directly to the staff of USDA and to the public, primarily via the NAL web site: www.nal.usda.gov. The Budget proposes to reallocate $1.5 million for developing and providing unified and accessible sustainability and environmental databases for the scientific community including data sets on carbon sequestration and greenhouse gas emissions, tillage and management studies, and conservation program benefits.

This could be done easily and efficiently with a publically accessible wiki, which could be managed by an interstate cooperative which does not require federal oversight. Such a wiki would provide a centralized, unified, and accessible database for all the sustainability and environmental data anyone could ever want.

Buildings and Facilities

ARS has over 100 research facilities throughout the U.S. and abroad, many collocated with other USDA agencies and university partners. The Budget does not include funding for construction of new laboratories/facilities or their modernization, but requests an increase of $3 million to repair and maintenance of existing facilities.

If we eliminate the ARS, then we can sell off its assets at auction. By doing so, we eliminate the $3 Million in repair in maintenance.

National Institute of Food and Agriculture (NIFA)

NIFA has the primary responsibility for providing linkages between the Federal and State components of a broad-based, national agricultural research, extension, and higher education system. NIFA provides funding for projects conducted in partnership with the State Agricultural Experiment Stations, the State Cooperative Extension System, land grant universities, colleges, and other research and education institutions, as well as individual researchers. Federal funds are distributed to universities and institutions by statutory formula funding, competitive awards, and grants. NIFA is responsible for administering USDA's primary competitive research grants program, the Agriculture and Food Research Initiative, which supports investigator-initiated research with strong potential to contribute to major breakthroughs in agricultural science.

If we eliminate the federal government's involvement in research, education, and the higher education system, then we no longer need to link it to the states. States should tax their own citizens to fund their own programs. The federal government should never give its public money to any private organizations, other than for purchases. Therefore we can eliminate its ties to such universities, colleges, and other institutions and researchers. Eliminate all federal grants. Eliminate NIFA, and save over $1 Billion in the process.

Agriculture and Food Research Initiative (AFRI)

AFRI is the Nation's premier competitive, peer-reviewed research program for fundamental and applied sciences in agriculture. It is broad in scope with programs ranging from fundamental science to farm management and community issues. The 2013 Budget proposes funding of $325 million for AFRI, an increase of

Agriculture and Food Research Initiative

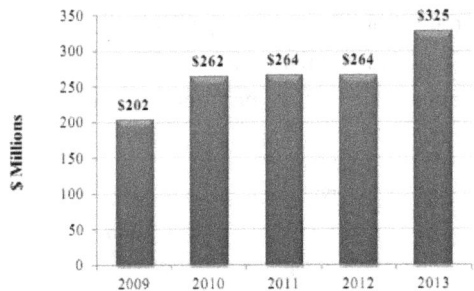

$60.5 million. Major initiatives include an increase of $30 million for the Department's alternative and renewable energy research initiative to develop high-quality, cost-effective feedstocks for biofuel production, conduct targeted research on enhanced value co-products and land-use changes resulting from feedstock production and conversion, and identify the socioeconomic impacts of biofuels in rural communities in order to enhance rural economies; $3.7 million for research to address the adaptation of production systems to climate variables; $7.2 million for international food security to expand research, education and extension efforts on sustainable plant and animal

*production systems as well as plant and animal diseases that threaten public health and agricultural production; **$2.2 million** for an integrated food safety research program which will minimize antibiotic resistance transmission through the food chain and minimize microbial food safety hazards of fresh and fresh-cut fruits and vegetables; **$7.2 million** in nutrition and obesity prevention research; and **$5.2 million** for the NIFA Fellows program which directly supports graduate education in priority research programs through AFRI. Finally, the Budget includes an increase of **$3.2 million** for AFRI's Foundational Research programs. These programs address priority areas needed to continue building a foundation of knowledge in fundamental and applied food and agricultural sciences critical for solving current and future societal challenges.*

Applied sciences in agriculture can be managed by those organizations involved in its research. These organizations can build their own wiki and share their information there. Such a wiki can be built and maintained almost for free, save for web hosting and the time it takes for the people to keep it updated.

Alternative and renewable energy are not government concerns. City governments should allow any energy company to set up, thus encouraging competition. Alternative and renewable energy are more expensive, so such companies would fail, because as it turns out, people care more about their utility bill than they do about where the power comes from.

Changes in land use, feedstock production and conversion, socioeconomic impacts of alternative energy, rural communities and economies, climate adaptation, food security in other countries, production system sustainability, plant and animal diseases, food safety research, graduate education, and applied sciences are not federal issues.

Higher Education Programs

*The 2013 Budget proposes an increase of **$1.8 million** to strengthen training programs in the food and agricultural sciences. Through the Graduate Fellowships Grants Program, Institution Challenge Grants Program, and the Multicultural Scholar Program, NIFA will support the recruitment of highly promising individuals to research and teaching careers, strengthen institutional capacities, and increase the ethnic and cultural diversity of the workforce in the food and agricultural sciences.*

Education is not a federal issue. The government should never intervene in specific industries, nor in their workforces or the training thereof. Eliminate all federal grants. The government should not involve itself in cultures, nor in the diversity of any workforce. Forcing workforce diversity creates artificial discrimination in the workplace, the very facet which it was meant to avoid. Such discrimination exists when highly qualified people are turned away in favor of other qualified people from different backgrounds, for the purpose of claiming the workforce to be "diverse". The hiring people should merely examine the people and hire whoever is most qualified, regardless of their legally protected statuses.

Hispanic-Serving Institutions (HSI)

*The 2008 Farm Bill authorized the establishment of an endowment fund for Hispanic Serving Agricultural Colleges and Universities. The 2013 Budget proposes an increase of **$10 million** to establish the fund that will lead to significant and measurable advancement of Hispanic students in the food and agricultural sciences. Funding will come from the annual interest generated by the Endowment.*

Discriminates against non-Hispanic-serving colleges and universities. Eliminate all such federal discriminatory programs. Eliminate all federal grants, "endowment funds", and similar wealth redistribution programs.

Sustainable Agriculture Research and Education (SARE) Program

*SARE advances agricultural innovations that improve profitability, environmental stewardship and quality of life. The 2013 Budget proposes an increase of **$3.5 million** for the creation of a new Federal-State Matching Grant SARE Program to assist in the establishment and enhancement of State sustainable agriculture research, education and extension programs. The matching requirement will leverage State or private funds and build the capabilities of American agriculture in becoming more productive and sustainable. NIFA estimates that nearly 14,000 farmers and ranchers will gain a benefit from a change in practice learned by participating in a SARE project.*

Profitability, environmental stewardship, and the productivity and sustainability of American agriculture are not government issues. Eliminate all federal grants. States should tax their own people to fund their own programs.

Children, Youth, and Families at Risk (CYFAR) Program

*The 2013 Budget proposes an increase of **$0.8 million** for CYFAR funding to assist Land-Grant universities and Cooperative Extension systems in developing educational community-based programs for at-risk children and their families. Since its inception, CYFAR has supported programs in more than 600 communities in all States and territories and provided access to educational* *resources, and essential technological skills for youth and adults in at-risk environments.*

Eliminate all federal grants and university assistance. Education, technology, children, and families are none of the government's business. Educating at-risk children and their families is completely unrelated to Agriculture.

Grants Management Systems

*With increased funding for AFRI, a significant rise in the number of applications is anticipated requiring increased efficiency of the grant-making processes and systems. Additionally, the breadth and types of grants made will increase requiring the development of new grant management tools. The 2013 Budget proposes an increase of **$3.2 million** to improve and consolidate its grants management systems, which will substantially lower the transaction costs of applying for an AFRI or other NIFA competitive grant, while increasing proposal receipt and acceptance speeds and accuracy.*

Eliminate all federal grants. By doing so, the grant-making processes and systems become obsolete. This is $8 Million just to manage one of the ways in which your money is given away.

Economic Research Service (ERS)

*ERS provides economic and other social science information and analysis on agriculture, food, the environment, and rural development. ERS produces such information and analyses to inform policy and program decisions made across the spectrum of USDA missions, and supplies them in outlets that are also accessible to USDA stakeholders and the general public. The 2013 Budget requests approximately **$77 million** in program funding, which includes the termination of $0.3 million in low-priority programs. ERS' highly trained economists and social scientists will continue to conduct research, analyze food and commodity markets, produce policy studies, and develop economic and statistical indicators which will meet the information needs of USDA, other public policy officials, and the research community.*

Agriculture and food are private industries. They, the environment, and rural development are none of the government's business. Therefore, the economic component and analysis thereof are moot. ERS is used to create new regulations and thus makes government bigger. If we eliminate it, we can save its $77 Million outright in addition to the overhead required to comply with all of the regulations they have caused the creation of. If we eliminate the USDA, then it has no further need for any information. The research community can perform its own research.

County Estimates Program

NASS' programs provide a comprehensive set of unbiased data covering most agricultural commodities as well as economic, environmental, and rural demographic data. This includes county-level statistics for selected commodities that impact billions of dollars of government payments. The Budget proposes to reallocate $3.4 million to improve the data quality of the County Estimates program which is used within the Department to administer crop insurance programs that provide U.S. farmers a safety net ensuring protection against unstable growing conditions, as well as crop revenue support programs, emergency assistance payments, and the Conservation Reserve Program.

Agricultural commodities, industrial data collection, and county commodity statistics are not government issues. At the very most, county commodities should be managed within those counties. The government is not an insurance company; therefore, it should not administer any insurance programs. By eliminating such programs, the Department no longer requires county estimates. Revenue from any industry should not be supported by the government, except in the case of the government purchasing things from those industries; and even then, at fair market rate. Emergency assistance should be handled at the level on which the emergency occurs; very few emergencies occur that justify federal involvement. As the government is not an insurance company, its emergencies do not include agriculture, no matter the scale.

Census of Agriculture

*The 2013 Budget includes **$63 million**, an increase of **$20.9** million, to support the 2012 Census of Agriculture. The Census of Agriculture provides comprehensive data on the agricultural economy with national, State, and county level details. The census data are relied upon to measure trends and new developments in the agricultural sector. This increase supports the normal increase in activity levels due to the cyclical nature of the 5-year Census program. FY 2013 funding for the Census will be the peak year of the 5-year cycle. Funding will be used to secure contract services for significant data collection and processing activities to occur in 2013.*

Agriculture is not a government issue; thus there is no need to obtain information thereon. It is not the government's job to measure trends and developments. Eliminate it and save $63 Million.

Departmental Activities

Office of the Secretary (OSEC)

Assisted by the Deputy Secretary, the Subcabinet, and members of their immediate staffs, directs and coordinates the work of the Department. This involves providing policy direction for all areas of the Department and maintaining liaisons with the Executive Office of the President, members of Congress and the public. The 2013 Budget requests $17.2 million for OSEC to fund on-going policy leadership, Tribal consultation, and cross-cutting trade and biotechnology activities.

If we eliminate the department, then we have no further use for its secretaries, cabinets, staffs, directions, liaisons, consultations, or activities.

Office of the Chief Economist (OCE)

Advises the Secretary and Department officials on the economic implications of Department policies, programs and proposed legislation; and serves as the focal point for the Department's economic intelligence, analysis and review related to domestic and international food and agriculture markets. OCE also provides advice and analysis on bioenergy, new uses of agricultural products, sustainable development, agricultural labor, global climate change, and environmental services markets. The 2013 Budget requests $12 million for OCE to continue its support of USDA policy officials and continue the dissemination of agricultural economic information.

If we eliminate the department, then we have no further use for economic advice, analysis, or review.

National Appeals Division (NAD)

Conducts evidentiary administrative appeal hearings and reviews arising from program operations of the Rural Development mission area, the Farm Service Agency, the Risk Management Agency, and the Natural Resources Conservation Service. The 2013 Budget requests $14.2 million for NAD to continue activities to ensure the fairness of program delivery by the Service Center Agencies.

If we eliminate the department, then Rural Development, the FSA, the RMA, and the NRCS all go away. If they all go away, then we have no need to conduct appeal hearings and reviews arising therefrom.

Office of Communications (OC)

Provides leadership and coordination for the development of communication strategies for the Department and plays a critical role in disseminating information about USDA's programs to the general public. The 2013 Budget requests $9 million for OC to continue to develop effective communications *strategies that make USDA programs and operations more open and transparent to the public.*

If we eliminate the department, then there is no communication to strategize, nor programs to distribute information about.

Office of the General Counsel (OGC)

*Provides legal oversight, counsel, and support to the Department's agencies. OGC's staffing has declined by 32 employees or approximately 10 percent since 2008; however, this decrease has not been accompanied by a commensurate decline in the amount, breadth, and scope of OGC's work, as the office is the primary source of legal support for all USDA programs and activities. The 2013 Budget requests **$45.1 million**, an increase of $5.7 million above the 2012 enacted level for OGC to increase staffing levels, which is critical to achieving the agency's objective of providing effective legal services. This increase also supports information technology improvements, which would increase OGC's efficiency and responsiveness to its clients.*

If we eliminate the department, then it no longer has any use for its squadron of 300 lawyers. Let's give them the commensurate decline in work and eliminate them altogether.

Departmental Management

A major goal for USDA is to transform itself into a high-performing and diverse model organization. Under Cultural Transformation, USDA is focusing on improving several aspects of employee culture, including leadership accountability, employee development, talent management, labor relations forums, customer focus, and diversity of the workforce. By strengthening management operations and engaging employees, USDA will also improve customer services, increase employee satisfaction, and develop and implement strategies to enhance leadership, performance, diversity, and inclusion. These transformations will in turn result in process improvements and increased performance.

Artificial diversity discriminates against non-minorities. DM seems like a series of training classes that only the lawyers and HR people will pay attention to, while everyone just appreciates another day off. Of course, these points are moot, as the department has no constitutional justification and thus needs to go away entirely.

Office of Advocacy and Outreach (OAO)

Established by the 2008 Farm Bill to increase the accessibility of USDA programs to underserved constituents. OAO activities include overseeing the Advisory Committees on Minority Farmers and Beginning Farmers and

Ranchers; administering the Outreach to Socially Disadvantaged Farmers Grant Program (section 2501 Program); overseeing the activities of the Office of Small Farms Coordination and the Farm Worker Coordinator; managing the 1994, 1890, and Hispanic Serving Institutions(HSI) Programs; and coordinating/conducting other outreach functions. The 2013 Budget requests $1.4 million for OAO to carry out these responsibilities and the provisions of the Farm Bill related to outreach to beginning, small, and socially disadvantaged farmers, ranchers, and rural communities.

If we eliminate the department, there will be no programs of which to increase the accessibility. Giving special treatment to minorities and amateurs discriminates against non-minorities and professionals. If we eliminate the services, then there are no minority or novice accessibility concerns to address. Eliminate all federal grants. Coordinating small farms is not a government issue. The government should not offer any services to any group (in this case, minorities) that it does not offer to everyone else. Eliminate all outreach functions.

Office of the Chief Financial Officer (OCFO)

Provides overall direction and leadership in the development of financial management policies and systems and produces the Department's consolidated financial statements and Strategic Plan. OCFO also oversees the provision of administrative accounting, payroll, and related systems for USDA and other agencies through operation of the National Finance Center. The 2013 Budget requests $6.2 million for OCFO to continue its leadership and oversight of the Department's financial management processes, implementation of the Federal Funding Accountability and Transparency Act and the Improper Payments Information Act, and Departmental travel and debarment and suspension policies.

If we eliminate the department, then there are no policies (regulations) to develop, no accounting or management processes to oversee, and no roll to pay.

Office of Budget and Program Analysis (OBPA)

Provides analyses and information to the Secretary and other senior policy officials to support informed decision-making regarding the Department's programs and policies, and Budget, legislative, and regulatory actions. OBPA also serves the key functions of providing information to the Office of Management and Budget and the Appropriations Committees related to the USDA Budget, and coordinating the Department's implementation of the Farm Bill, including providing relevant implementation and mandatory spending information to the Authorizing Committees. The 2013 Budget requests $9 *million for OBPA for the continued delivery of analyses and support to USDA policy officials.*

If we eliminate the department, then there are no secretaries or policy officials to provide information or analyses to; nothing to appropriate, nothing to coordinate, implement, or authorize.

Office of the Chief Information Officer (OCIO)

*Provides policy guidance, leadership and coordination for the Department's information management, technology investment and cyber security activities in support of USDA program delivery. The 2013 Budget requests **$44 million** for OCIO to fund on-going activities, especially the Department's cyber security program.*

If we eliminate the department, then there are no policies (regulations) to guide, no Information Technology to manage, lead, or coordinate; nothing to secure against cyber activities, and no programs to deliver.

Departmental Administration (DA)

*Provides overall direction, leadership and coordination for the Department's management of human resources, ethics, property, procurement, facilities management, small and disadvantaged business utilization programs, and the regulatory hearing and administrative proceedings conducted by the Administrative Law Judges and the Judicial Officer. The 2013 Budget requests **$29.6 million** for DA to maintain critical support activities and oversight for the Department.*

If we eliminate the department, then there is nothing to administer, and no direction or leadership to provide.

Office of Homeland Security and Emergency Coordination (OHSEC)

Provides a central homeland security oversight and assistance capability within USDA. OHSEC is responsible for providing oversight and coordination of the Department's preparation and response to matters of homeland security importance. In addition, OHSEC is responsible for providing the protective services for the Secretary and Deputy Secretary of Agriculture. The 2013 Budget requests $1.5 million for OHSEC to provide leadership and coordination of Departmental security matters and to ensure that USDA is prepared for potential threats or emergency situations.

If we eliminate the department, then there is nothing to coordinate with DHS, no assistance capabilities to oversee, no preparation or response to oversee or coordinate, and no secretaries to protect. The government is not an insurance company.

Agriculture Buildings and Facilities

*Ag B&F and Rental Payments for 2013 is **$244.1 million**. The account provides funding for the rental payments to the General Services Administration (GSA) and security services payments to the Department of Homeland Security (DHS). This account is also responsible for all maintenance, utilities and administration of the more than 2.5 million square feet in the two USDA headquarters buildings. The 2013 Budget includes **$175.7 million** for GSA rental payments, **$54.9 million** for building operations and maintenance, and $13.5 million to DHS for building security.*

If we eliminate the department, then there is nothing to rent, no security to pay for, no buildings to maintain, and no utilities or administration to maintain.

Hazardous Materials Management (HMM)

*Provides for the efficient management and cleanup of hazardous materials on facilities and lands under the jurisdiction, custody, and control of the Department; and the prevention of releases of hazardous substances from USDA facilities. The 2013 Budget requests **$4 million** for the HMM program.*

If we eliminate the department, then there are no hazardous materials to clean up or manage.

Office of Civil Rights (OCR)

*Provides policy guidance, leadership, coordination and training, and complaint prevention and processing for the Department and the agencies. OCR's mission is to facilitate the fair and equitable treatment of USDA customers and employees and ensure the delivery and enforcement of civil rights programs and activities. Through its efforts, OCR strives to: 1) foster a positive civil rights climate at USDA; 2) process Equal Employment Opportunity (EEO) and program complaints in a timely, efficient and cost effective manner; 3) reduce and prevent EEO and program complaints through training and guidance; and 4) offer alternative dispute resolution services. The 2013 budget requests **$22.7 million**, an increase of $1.7 million to meet the Administration's commitment to improving USDA's handling of civil rights matters such as program investigations and compliance reviews.*

If we eliminate the department, then there are no policies to guide, nothing to coordinate, nobody to train, no complaints to prevent, nothing to process, no customers and employees to serve, no civil rights programs and activities to deliver or enforce, no climate to foster, and no disputes to resolve.

*The Budget also requests **$40 million** for costs associated with Equal Credit Opportunity Act (ECOA) claims where the statute of limitations (SOL) for claims settlement has expired. USDA will submit legislation to extend the SOL for* *those ECOA claims filed between July 1, 1997 and October 31, 2009 where claims were not properly resolved or where the SOL has expired. The program will be administered by OCR.*

If we eliminate the department, then there are no claims to generate costs.

Office of Inspector General (OIG)

*OIG Conducts and supervises audits and investigations to prevent and detect fraud, waste, and abuse and to improve the effectiveness of USDA programs and operations. As the law enforcement arm of USDA, OIG also investigates criminal activity involving the Department's programs and personnel. The 2013 Budget requests **$89 million** for OIG for audit and investigation review of the Department's programs. This funding includes an increase of $0.47 million to support the Council of the Inspectors General for Integrity and Efficiency, established under the authority of the Inspector General Reform Act of 2008 to coordinate Federal efforts to improve program delivery. Additional increases include $0.16 million to support mandatory training requirements and $2.5 million to enhance audit and investigations oversight of USDA's programs*

If we eliminate the department, then there is no fraud, waste, or abuse to detect or prevent; no criminal activity to investigate, no programs to investigate, review, or audit, no program delivery efforts to coordinate, no training to require, and no programs to enhance.

Conclusion

I have gone through the entire FY2013 USDA Budget, and I haven't found a single program, agency, office, or other entity which I can find sound constitutional justification for. Instead, I find a variety of organizations whose purposes are to create regulation, to oversee overhead within the department itself, to parent your children *for* you, or to fulfill a function which would be rightfully found the private sector. The government should never function as a parent, a bank, or an insurance company, nor should it ever do the job of any other private business.

I therefore propose we eliminate the entire Department of Agriculture, sell off its assets at auction, repeal all laws which created this mess, and eliminate the regulations created by its authority. By doing so, we can save **$155 Billion** annually, in addition to whatever costs are associated with the overhead it creates, and in further addition to a single massive selloff of assets, facilities, and land.

Department of Commerce (DoC)[17]

Introduction

The mission of the Department of Commerce is to help make American businesses more innovative at home and more competitive abroad. The Department helps American businesses achieve economic growth and job creation by fostering innovation, entrepreneurship, and competitiveness. We accomplish our mission through direct assistance to businesses and communities, targeted investment in world-class research, science, technology, and more. The Secretary of Commerce leads the Department and its 12 bureaus with a budget of about $8.0 billion and nearly 47,000 employees worldwide.

Making American businesses more innovative at home and more competitive abroad is not the government's responsibility; in fact, it's potentially disastrous to interfere in the free market. American businesses should achieve economic growth and job creation on their own merits, or fail naturally on their lack thereof, without government intervention. The government is not a research organization.

In today's challenging budget climate, Commerce is deeply committed to reducing its administrative costs by identifying savings and efficiencies. This helps us act as responsible stewards of taxpayer dollars, but it also ensures that the important programs that support Commerce's primary mission will continue despite current and future budget reductions.

Some people suggest the cuts go too far. I say the "cuts" *don't go too far enough*. The Constitution authorizes the Congress to keep trade regular between the states, meaning to prevent the states from embargoing each other; it does not authorize the government to meddle in the businesses themselves.

The FY 2013 Budget for the Department of Commerce meets the need for fiscal responsibility and the need to promote innovation, entrepreneurship and competitiveness, which will allow us to build it here and sell it everywhere, and put Americans back to work. The FY 2013 President's Budget for the Department of Commerce includes $8.0 billion in discretionary funding, which is a 5% increase from the FY 2012 Enacted level. The Budget also requests $2.3 billion in mandatory funding for new programs. This Budget invests in priorities to create jobs, fuel economic growth, drive innovation and strengthen national security and public safety. It targets efforts to build a 21st

---

[17] http://www.osec.doc.gov/bmi/budget/FY13BIB/fy2013bib_final.pdf

Century infrastructure, promote exports and foreign direct investment, support environmental sustainability, and strengthen science and information.

A "responsible steward of taxpayer dollars" would not request over two billion dollars for new programs; however, this is the mandatory component, so the blame lies with the Congress as usual.

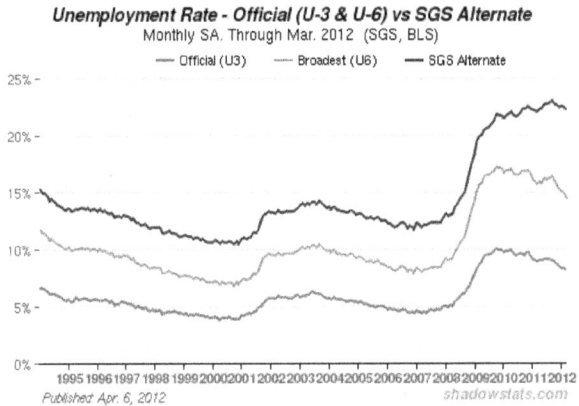

Unemployment Rate - Official (U-3 & U-6) vs SGS Alternate
Monthly SA. Through Mar. 2012 (SGS, BLS)
— Official (U3)   ···· Broadest (U6)   — SGS Alternate

Published Apr. 6, 2012   *shadowstats.com*

The government has proven its utter inability to control the unemployment rate, and thus cannot be trusted to fix it any more than they "fixed" it in 2009.

The government has, however, shown that its interference in the free market has negative economic effects. Therefore, it stands to reason that reversing this interference would reverse the effects, thereby correcting the economy by leaving it alone. If we eliminate such interference, therefore, we can repair the damage done to the economy by the government and promote exports and investment thereby. Environmental sustainability, science, and economic information are not government concerns.

I can find no Constitutional justification for the Department of Commerce, nor for most of the programs it administers. I therefore recommend moving the justified programs out of the department and eliminating the department itself, along with its associated overhead.

International Trade Administration (ITA)

The mission of the International Trade Administration (ITA) is to create prosperity by promoting trade and investment, ensuring fair trade and compliance with trade laws and agreements, and strengthening the competitiveness of U.S. industry.

Prosperity is inherent to the design of any free market, and to that of the United States itself; it requires no creation. It is not the role of government to meddle in trade and investment, other than to ensure peaceful relations between nations and to protect the trade lanes. The government has no right to interfere in our level of competitiveness.

Manufacturing and Services (MAS)

MAS analyzes the domestic and international aspects of U.S. competitiveness by working with U.S. industries to evaluate the needs of the manufacturing and service sectors, conducting economic and regulatory studies aimed at strengthening U.S. industry, obtaining input and advice from U.S. industries for trade policy setting, and participating, as appropriate, with ITA trade policy and negotiation advancement initiatives.

The government should never interfere in private industries, nor should it concern itself with industries' inner workings. A free market will determine its own economic and regulatory needs, and create solutions thereto by the natural course of human greed. If businesses realize it's more profitable to establish standards and comply with them, then they will do so. The government should not interfere with free trade, including via regulatory policies.

Market Access and Compliance (MAC)

MAC concentrates on the development of strategies to overcome market access obstacles faced by U.S. businesses. MAC monitors foreign country compliance with numerous trade-related agreements and identifies compliance problems and other market access obstacles. MAC works with other U.S. Government agencies to rapidly address barriers and ensures that U.S. firms know how to use market opening agreements. It provides information on foreign trade and business practices to U.S. firms and works to find opportunities and to develop current and long-term market strategies in traditional and emerging markets, including information needed to conduct trade negotiations to open markets.

U.S. businesses should be responsible for overcoming their own market access obstacles, other than the government's role of ensuring peaceful relations, free trade, and safe trade lanes. Eliminating regulations would render the compliance thereto moot. As long as the government is fulfilling its responsibilities as I have outlined, addressing barriers is not the their concern; the barriers are not theirs to address.

Businesses can establish their own information on foreign trade and business practices; a wiki could be set up to warehouse such knowledge with little to no overhead. Market strategies are not a government issue; the market should determine its own strategies without external interference.

Import Administration (IA)
> *IA helps ensure fair trade by administering the U.S. antidumping (AD) and countervailing duty (CVD) laws in a manner consistent with U.S. international obligations. IA works extensively with U.S. businesses to educate them about U.S. trade laws related to dumping and foreign government subsidies and how to access U.S. government assistance if they are injured by those practices. IA detects, and where appropriate, confronts unfair competition by monitoring economic data from our global competitors and investigates evidence of unfair subsidization and market distortions.*

The Navy and the Coast Guard should patrol our waters to ensure they are not being dumped into (Authorized under Article I, Section 8, Clauses 14 and 15); dumping in international waters should be permitted on an "at your own risk" basis, as we have no reason to patrol those waters and they are out of our jurisdiction. Businesses and captains should realize on their own merit that deeper, more remote waters are ideal for dumping, as they seem likely to have less impact on the shorelines.

Detecting and confronting unfair competition is not a government issue. If a company is performing unfair practices and you choose to object, do so by withdrawing your business from them. Let your dollar be your vote. If states choose to create their own import laws, those states should administer them. A well-known proponent and source of unfair subsidization and market distortions, the government is in no place to investigate or correct them. The government should never involve itself in any specific industry.

Trade Promotion and the U.S. & Foreign Commercial Service (US&FCS)
> *US&FCS broadens and deepens the base of U.S. exports, particularly small and medium-sized firms (SMEs), by conducting trade promotion programs. US&FCS provides U.S. companies with reliable advice on the range of public and private assistance available and knowledgeably supports all other Federal trade promotion services. Specifically, US&FCS assists exporters by providing information, referral and follow-up services through an integrated global field network. US&FCS includes the Trade Promotion Coordinating Committee (TPCC) secretariat. The TPCC, chaired by the Secretary of Commerce, is composed of 19 Federal agencies that work together to coordinate and streamline trade promotion and financing services.*

There are myriad private services available for small and medium businesses to export their goods and services; there is no need for the government to intervene in the process. Companies can find advice on the Internet and from consultants. Promoting trade is not a government issue and should be done by those doing the trading. Trade project development is not a government issue, other than ensuring free trade agreements and secure trade lanes.

Executive Direction and Administration (ExAd)

> *ExAd directs policy and planning functions to effectively plan and manage ITA. ExAd delivers administrative services to enable ITA's programs to advance their program goals. These administrative services include information technology support systems, strategic planning, performance management services, human capital planning, financial management, and general administrative assistance.*

If we eliminate ITA, then there are no functions left to direct or plan, and no programs to deliver services to.

Economic Development Administration (EDA)

> *The Economic Development Administration (EDA) helps our partners across the Nation (states, regions, and communities) create wealth and minimize poverty by promoting a favorable business environment to attract private capital investments and higher-skill, higher-wage jobs through capacity building, planning, infrastructure investments, research grants, and strategic initiatives. EDA carries out its Economic Development Assistance Program (EDAP) through a network of headquarters and regional personnel that work directly with local organizations and leaders to identify and invest in projects that demonstrate potential for the greatest economic impact in distressed communities.*

Creating wealth and minimizing poverty are natural effects of a free market economy, and the economy is not a government issue. As everything the government touches is worse off as a result thereof, any federal meddling in the economy inevitably leads to a worse economy. For examples, look into the Gold Standard and the New Deal. New wealth is therefore created by removing government interference *from* the economy.

For great examples of the robustness of a free market devoid of government regulation, look into the alcohol black market during prohibition, the drug black market today, or almost any underground economy ever to exist (read: "real" economies). If you want wealth, *go out and create it yourself*. If you are impoverished, *go out and fix it yourself*.

States should tax their own people to run their own programs, and can communicate with each other without the need for federal involvement. The government can best provide a favorable business environment by eliminating regulations and legislation which interferes with those businesses; such as taxes, mandated insurance, registration, standards compliance, and associated overhead. In other words, government best serves you by *leaving you alone*.

Attracting private capital investments is the responsibility of the business owners; investors are better suited by also looking for the businesses. No government facilitation is necessary for the two to find each other. Worker skill levels and wages are a private matter between the workers and the employer, and are thus not government issues.

Capacity building, planning, and infrastructure of any business are the responsibility of that business. Eliminate all federal grants. The government should never invest or interfere in any private enterprise. The economy is not a government issue. Distressed communities are best served by those communities. None of this is authorized by the Constitution.

National Telecommunications and Information Administration (NTIA)

The National Telecommunications and Information Administrations (NTIA) is responsible for: leading the development of domestic and international telecommunications and information policy for the Executive Branch; ensuring the effective and efficient use of Federal radio spectrum; performing state-of-the-art telecommunications research, engineering, and planning; and administering Federal grant programs that promote the use of innovative technology for expanding the use of the Internet, creating jobs and improving public safety.

The Constitution does not authorize the government to develop telecommunications infrastructures, to create legislation pertaining to the electromagnetic spectrum, to do technology research of any kind, to develop the Internet, to create nongovernment jobs, nor to manage most types of public safety. The grants discussed here do not further any enumerated power, and are thus also unauthorized; eliminate all federal grants.

Office of International Affairs (OIA)

NTIA's Office of International Affairs (OIA) formulates and promotes national telecommunications and information policies for presentation in multilateral and international organization settings. OIA also engages in advocacy directly with counterparts in foreign governments and the European Union. OIA draws on its extensive policy and technical expertise to support U.S. negotiators and interagency delegations in strategic international forums.

Telecommunications and information policies in other countries are not government issues. Therefore, no formulation, promotion, advocacy, negotiations, or delegations are necessary.

Office of Policy Analysis and Development (OPAD)

> NTIA's Office of Policy Analysis and Development (OPAD) supports the agency's role as the principal adviser to the President on telecommunications and information policy. OPAD develops, analyzes, and advocates public policies that promote innovation, competition, jobs, and economic growth for the benefit of American businesses and consumers.

If we eliminate the administration, then we can eliminate the policies. If we eliminate the policies, then there is nothing left to advise the President of; nor to develop, analyze, or advocate. Innovation, competition, jobs, and the economy are not government issues.

Office of Spectrum Management (OSM)

> NTIA's Office of Spectrum Management (OSM) is dedicated to protecting the vital Federal government operations that use spectrum while also supporting the growth of commercial wireless broadband and technologies in America. Many federal agencies rely on the use of spectrum, a limited resource, to execute their core missions. There is also increasing demand for spectrum to meet the wireless broadband needs of consumers and businesses, paving the way for continued innovation and economic growth.

Most private communications technologies are forced to use a few very thin slices of the Electromagnetic Spectrum, while the government basically reserves the rest of it. The government may need to reserve a slice for classified military communications, though this could probably be better handled with encryption and packet division technologies. The federal government shouldn't be doing anything within the United States that would require the use of such frequencies, and the rest of the world is far beyond our government's jurisdiction.

The electromagnetic spectrum is a naturally occurring range of naturally occurring frequencies. "Giving" the public access to a few slices is tantamount to giving the public access to a just few water supplies, or just a few miles of coastline. It's not the government's to control.

Commerce and industry are not government issues, and should be left alone to grow or shrink on their own. Given the limited nature of this resource, it's ridiculous to limit the people to only small parts of it. None of the enumerated powers allow the government to use any frequencies within the United States in such a way that would need to be private, given the consent of the governed. That is to say, we delegate the government its power; not the other way around. This proposal is eliminating most federal agencies anyway. They can share the resource just as they share the electrical grid and water supply, which they shouldn't have ultimate control over either.

Office of Telecommunications and Information Applications (OTIA)

NTIA's Office of Telecommunications and Information Applications (OTIA) administers grant programs that further the deployment and use of technology in America, laying the groundwork for sustainable economic growth; improved education, public safety, and health care; and the advancement of other national priorities.

Eliminate all federal grants. The deployment and use of technology, outside of the government, is not a government issue. The economy, education, most types of public safety, and healthcare are not government issues; and none of these programs are encapsulated by the enumerated powers.

Institute for Telecommunication Sciences

The Institute for Telecommunication Sciences (ITS), located in Boulder, Colorado, is the research and engineering arm of NTIA. ITS provides core telecommunications research and engineering services to promote: Enhanced domestic competition and new technology deployment, Advanced telecommunications and information services, Improved foreign trade opportunities for U.S. telecommunication firms, [and] More efficient use of the radio frequency spectrum.

The federal government is not a school, a research foundation, or an engineering company. It is not the government's job to determine or influence economic competition, the rate at which the private sector adopts new technologies, or the ways in which the EM spectrum is utilized. The Constitution does not authorize it to promote any technology or service, nor to meddle in any specific industry, such as telecommunications.

National Technical Information Service (NTIS)

The National Technical Information Service (NTIS) collects and preserves scientific, technical, engineering and other business-related information from Federal and international sources, and disseminates it to the American business and industrial research community. NTIS operates a revolving fund for the payment of all expenses incurred. NTIS reports to the Secretary of Commerce through the National Institute of Standards and Technology.

The Constitution provides no authority to do this, and this function can be fulfilled with a free online wiki.

Bureau of the Census

The Census Bureau's mission is to serve as the leading source of quality data about the Nation's people and economy. We honor privacy, protect confidentiality, share our expertise globally, and conduct our work openly. The Census Bureau performance goals are to provide timely, relevant, and accurate current and benchmark measures of the U.S. population, economy, and governments in order to facilitate this mission.

The wording of the 16th Amendment implies the existence of a census. The wording of Article I, Section 9, Clause 4 expresses such census explicitly. Therefore, a census is authorized. However, this is not enough to justify an entire department. Therefore I propose moving the Census Bureau into a new Department of Internal Affairs, along with all the other internal programs which are authorized but whose departments are not.

Economic and Statistics Administration (ESA)

The Economics and Statistics Administration (ESA) plays three key roles within the Department of Commerce (DOC). ESA provides timely economic analysis, disseminates national economic indicators, and oversees the U.S. Census Bureau (Census) and the Bureau of Economic Analysis (BEA). In this latter role, ESA works closely with the leadership at BEA and Census on high priority management, budget, employment, and risk management issues, integrating the work of these agencies with the priorities and requirements of the Department of Commerce and other government entities.

Analyzing the economy, disseminating economic indicators, and employment are not government issues. The Census bureau can find new oversight in the new Department of Internal Affairs.

National Oceanic and Atmospheric Administration (NOAA)

NOAA generates tremendous value for the Nation—and the world—by advancing our ability to understand and anticipate changes in the Earth's environment, improving society's ability to make scientifically informed decisions, delivering services vital to the economy and public safety, and by conserving and managing ocean and coastal ecosystems and resources. NOAA's mission has three core areas, each individually and separately important, but vital and more effective as a cohesive triad, with each providing the foundation for the others. These missions – Science, Stewardship, Service – are integral to the very design of NOAA as an agency.

No amount of value can supersede the Constitution, which does not provide authority for the government to monitor the entire planet's climate and ecology, nor to interfere in the nation's ecosystems or natural resources (except where needed for overhead and defense purposes).

National Ocean Service

One of NOAA's key goals is to organize our resources and capabilities to promote the environmental and economic sustainability of vibrant coastal communities. The emergence of new industries, such as in renewable energy, and vulnerability to environmental hazards and stresses will change these communities in profound ways. In FY 2013, NOAA will continue to support the economic sustainability of coastal communities We have maintained our commitment to Navigation Services and the stewardship role of the Marine Sanctuary and Coastal Zone Management programs.

The environment and the economy are none of the government's business. Coastal communities should manage themselves. The free market will naturally regulate itself, as seen in every black market ever to exist. The Constitution does not authorize any meddling in private industries such as the electrical grid. Its interference often results in silly regulations like the certification of solar panel installers, and direct corruption like the ethanol subsidies feeding money into Monsanto, which shares many executives with the Presidents' Cabinets and other key federal government positions.

The Constitution says nothing about providing navigation services, marine sanctuaries, or coastal zone management; therefore, the federal government isn't allowed to provide them. By the same token, the government is not an insurance company, and thus can't protect private and state areas from natural disasters. These are programs the states should consider taxing their own people to run.

National Marine Fisheries Service

By continuing efforts to rebuild American fisheries, NMFS will increase the economic output of our fisheries, improve the economic conditions for our fishermen, and create better, more stable and sustainable jobs and opportunities in our coastal communities. In FY 2013, NMFS will continue the trend of putting America's fishing industry on a sustainable and profitable path through targeted investments in fisheries science, observer, and enforcement programs. A small amount of targeted new funding will improve our focus in the following areas: an additional $4.3 million to improve fisheries stock assessments, $5 million to develop integrated ecosystem assessment, used to better understand and manage the complex web that is ocean ecosystems, and $2.3 million to expand our ability to complete fishery-independent survey and monitoring projects, critical to setting appropriate catch limits in valuable fisheries.

Fisheries are not a federal issue; fishing businesses should realize on their own that if they drive fish to extinction, they will go out of business. Therefore it makes economic sense for these businesses to repopulate the waters on their own, or to breed their own fish. The federal government has no authority to interfere in any economy, nor in the job markets; nor to observe and create rules over the fishing industry.

It therefore stands to reason that the federal government has no business in the assessment of fishery stocking, nor that of ecosystem integration; nor the monitoring and surveying thereof, nor to set limits on fish caught.

Office of Oceanic and Atmospheric Research

NOAA's fundamental responsibility is to ensure that complex policy choices are informed by the best available science. As such, data generation and use is the core function of the agency as a whole. Our researchers are examining cutting-edge issues that will guide our approach to resource management for years to come. NOAA's weather data informs millions of people each day, and our resource assessments guide legislative and policy decisions that affect peoples' lives and livelihoods. In addition, NOAA's FY 2013 request continues the necessary investments to improve our climate activities, with a specific focus on the research, which underpins our understanding of climate processes. Continued development and use of state-of-the-art Earth System Models to address urgent climate issues, including sea level rise and Arctic climate change, will be supported by an investment of an additional $8 million[.]

If we eliminate the NOAA, then we have no further policy choices to inform. Any issue that can be described as "cutting edge" is an issue in which the federal government has no business, except perhaps in military defense, and even that should be privatized to the extent feasible. States can tax their own citizens to provide their own weather information, though the private sector does an exemplary job of providing current weather information. There are even grassroots movements involving individuals setting up weather stations at their homes and sharing the information across the country; the federal government does not need to be involved.

Legislation is not a good thing. If you're unclear as to why, refer to my earlier writings on Natural Law. Congress needs fewer sources from which to create new legislation. The federal government has no constitutional authority to have any climate activities; nor to research the climates or *the wind*.

There is no such thing as an "urgent climate issue". The climates have been around for far longer than we have, and they will endure for far longer than we will.

National Weather Service

Concern for public safety drives NOAA to continue to improve the timeliness and accuracy of warnings for all weather-related hazards. In addition, more *and more sectors of the Nation's economy recognize the impacts of weather and water on their activities, and are becoming more sophisticated at using weather and water information to improve commerce. NOAA is committed to enhancing timely and accurate weather and climate forecasts through better observations, improved data assimilation, and collaboration with the research community. The FY 2013 budget requests an additional $7 million to support the critical upgrading and updating of the NWS Telecom Gateway, the backbone of the Weather Service's information delivery system. The request also includes $12.4 million for ground system readiness, ensuring that the NWS will be prepared to ingest data coming from NOAA's investment in new weather satellites. The request also includes an increase of $2.4 million in resources for fundamental climate observations and data management capabilities to maintain and upgrade the TAO array.*

Most forms of public safety are not federal issues. If the government has no authority to create a weather monitoring system, then it has no warnings to issue. The grassroots, private, and state options I mentioned earlier can also provide these alerts. The Constitution does not authorize the government to "improve" commerce, to forecast the weather, or to study the climate.

National Environmental Satellite, Data, and Information Service

One of the greatest challenges facing NOAA today is ensuring continuity of satellite operations to provide unbroken coverage of weather forecasts and climate measurements into the future. The GOES-R satellite acquisition program has been a successful partnership effort between NOAA and NASA to replace and update the existing GOES series of satellites. The first satellite in this program, GOES-R, is expected to launch in 2015. The new satellites in this series will carry improved environmental instrument suites providing more timely and accurate weather forecasts and improved observation of meteorological events that directly affect public safety, protection of property, and ultimately, economic health and development. Thanks to the support of Congress, NOAA's satellite programs received $1,678 million in FY 2012, a substantial increase over FY 2011, which will allow NOAA to make significant progress in the satellite development program. In order to have new satellites ready when needed, the request includes $802 million for the GOES-R program, as well as an investment ($9.4M) for the processing and distribution of NPP data. $916.4 million is requested for the Joint Polar Satellite System. $30 million is also requested to continue progress on Jason-3.

If we eliminate NOAA, then its challenges disappear. If we eliminate the programs that monitor the weather, then there is no further need for the satellites, and they can be sold off to private weather tracking organizations. Most forms of public safety aren't federal issues. Protecting property is the responsibility of the property owners, and is thus not a government issue; only protecting the owners' rights thereto. As previously covered, none of this is authorized by the Constitution.

Program Support / Office of Marine and Aviation Operations

> *The FY 2013 budget continues the recapitalization of the NOAA's fleet, data acquisition platforms critical to meeting fisheries management mandates. NOAA's fleets, both air and sea, are crucial to providing the scientific platforms for key observations and maintenance of our observing systems. This budget requests a modest increase of **$1.9 million** to provide an increase in flight hours. An investment of **$11.7 million** will allow NOAA to perform a Major Repair Period on the Thomas Jefferson, NOAA's primary hydrographic survey vessel. Major Repair Periods are critical to ensuring the ongoing health and well-being of NOAA's fleet; without these periodic refurbishments, ships would be taken out of service. Finally, an additional **$1.5 million** is requested to complete the construction of FSV 6.*

If we eliminate federal fisheries management mandates, then there is no critical need to recapitalize the NOAA fleets. If we eliminate NOAA, then it no longer requires fleets. The government is not responsible to provide scientific platforms. The wording implies NOAA is requesting nearly $2 Million just to let their pilots get more air time; as they otherwise would have cited a more useful purpose than "an increase in flight hours". If we eliminate NOAA and its fleets, it no longer requires repair or refurbishment.

National Institute of Standards and Technology (NIST)

> *The mission of NIST is to promote U.S. innovation and industrial competitiveness by advancing measurement science, standards, and technology in ways that enhance economic security and improve our quality of life. For more than 100 years, NIST has maintained the national standards of measurement, a role that the U.S. Constitution assigns to the Federal Government. Today, the NIST Laboratories address increasingly complex measurement challenges, developing measurements focusing on the very small (e.g. nanotechnology devices) and the very large (e.g. skyscrapers), the physical (e.g. methods for characterizing strands of DNA for forensic testing) and the virtual (e.g. methods for testing electronic health record systems). NIST engages in activities that support trade and global science; provide industry and academia with unique user facilities, and supports development of standards and specifications that define technical and performance requirements for goods and services.*

Article I, Section 8, Clause 5 of the Constitution authorizes the Congress to "fix the Standard of Weights and Measures". Therefore, the Office of Weights and Measures is constitutionally justified. However, this is not enough to justify an entire department. Therefore I propose moving the Office of Weights and Measures into the new Department of Internal Affairs, along with all the other internal programs which are authorized but whose departments are not.

Science, technology, economic security, quality of life, health records, nanotechnology, DNA, forensic testing, industry, academia, specifications, and technical and performance requirements are not government issues; the remainder of the institute is unconstitutional.

Hollings Manufacturing Extension Partnership (MEP)

Through public (Federal-state-local) and private sector partnerships, MEP provides technical and business assistance to small- and medium-sized manufacturers through a network of centers in all 50 states and Puerto Rico. The request includes $128 million for MEP, roughly the same level as in FY 2012.

The government should not provide any assistance to any businesses. States and territories should tax their own people to run their own programs.

Advanced Manufacturing Technology Consortia (AMTech)

The request includes $21.0 million for the new Advanced Manufacturing Technology Consortia (AMTech) program, which will provide grants to leverage existing consortia or establish new industry-led consortia. These consortia will develop road-maps of critical long-term industrial research needs as well as fund research at leading universities and government laboratories directed at meeting these needs. This new program would be based on NIST's experience with the Nanoelectronics Research Initiative (NRI) partnership and would expand and improve on that model.

Eliminate all federal grants. The development of roadmaps, industrial research, education, and electronics on any scale are not government issues, and thus such programs are unauthorized.

Construction of Research Facilities (CRF)

NIST's CRF appropriation supports projects for new buildings and renovation and maintenance of current buildings and laboratories. The CRF account includes an increase of $4.6 Million over the FY2012 enacted appropriations for a total request of $60 Million. Within this total, $48.2 Million is for the Safety, Capacity, Maintenance, and Major Repairs account and $11.8 Million is to fund ongoing work for the Building 1 Renovation project in Boulder, Colorado.

If we eliminate NIST, then NIST no longer requires any buildings or other facilities. Thus there is nothing to build, maintain, repair, or renovate. If the

OWM requires such projects, then finance them as such in its new home under the Department of Internal Affairs.

U.S. Patent and Trademark Office (USPTO)

The United States Patent and Trademark Office (USPTO) is the Federal agency for granting U.S. patents and registering trademarks. In doing this, the USPTO fulfills the mandate of Article I, Section 8, Clause 8, of the Constitution that the Executive branch "promote the progress of science and the useful arts by securing for limited times to inventors the exclusive right to their respective discoveries." The USPTO registers trademarks based on the Commerce Clause of the Constitution (Article I, Section 8, Clause 3). Under this system of protection, American industry has flourished. New products have been invented, new uses for old ones discovered, and employment opportunities created for millions of Americans. The strength and vitality of the U.S. economy depends directly on effective mechanisms that protect new ideas and investments in innovation and creativity. The continued demand for patents and trademarks underscores the ingenuity of American inventors and entrepreneurs. The USPTO is at the cutting edge of the Nation's technological progress and achievement.

Article I, Section 8, Clause 8 of the Constitution authorizes the Congress "to promote the Progress of Science and useful Arts, by securing for limited Times to Authors and Inventors the exclusive Right to their respective Writings and Discoveries". Therefore, the USPTO is constitutionally justified. However, this is not enough to justify an entire department. Therefore I propose moving the Patent and Trademark Office into the new Department of Internal Affairs, along with all the other internal programs which are authorized but whose departments are not.

Minority Business Development Agency (MBDA)

MBDA actively promotes the ability of Minority Business Enterprises (MBEs) to grow and to participate in the global economy through a range of activities that include funding a network of centers that provide MBEs a variety of business assistance services. MBDA provides funding for a network of Minority business centers located throughout the Nation. The Centers provide minority entrepreneurs with one-on-one assistance in writing business plans, marketing, management and technical assistance and financial planning to assure adequate financing for business ventures.

The Constitution does not authorize the government to meddle in the economy, to play favorites with individual market segments, to do entrepreneurs' jobs for them; nor to provide technical assistance, financial planning, or financing of any kind. The government is not a bank. Further, the

General Welfare clause explains that the government is there to promote the general welfare; not the specific welfare of any one individual group. Apply a program to everyone equally, or not at all.

Bureau of Industry and Security (BIS)

*The Bureau of Industry and Security advances U.S. national security, foreign policy, and economic objectives by ensuring an effective export control and treaty compliance system and promoting continued U.S. strategic technology leadership. The President's FY 2013 Budget recognizes the important role of BIS programs to ensuring technologies are not exported to regimes where they may fall into the wrong hands with a request of **$102 million**. Within this request, **$6 million** is provided for the Administration's Export Control Reform initiative that will advance national security and overall economic competitiveness by utilizing the more flexible Commerce dual-use system to control military items of less significance.*

Given complete totalitarian control over all exports, we can probably prevent the export of technologies to regimes where they may fall into the wrong hands. We cannot, however, control these technologies after they leave our jurisdiction. The government has no authority to lead technology, or to drive any economic strategy.

Departmental Management

Within Departmental Management (DM), the Salaries and Expenses (S&E) account provides funding for the Secretary, Deputy Secretary, and support staff. DM develops and implements policy affecting U.S. and international activities as well as internal goals and operations of the Department. DM serves as the primary liaison with the executive branch and Congressional and private sector groups, and acts as the management and administrative control point for the Department. The S&E account contains two activities: Executive Direction, which develops and implements Departmental policies and coordinates Bureau program activities to accomplish the Department's mission; and Departmental Staff Services, which develops and implements the Department's internal policies, procedures, and other administrative guidelines.

If we eliminate the department, then there is nothing left to manage; no secretaries, support staff; no international activities, no policy (regulation), nothing to provide a liaison for, and nothing to administer.

Department of Defense (DoD)[18]

The mission of the Department of Defense is to provide the military forces needed to deter war and to protect the security of our country.

Article I, Section 8, Clause 15 of the Constitution authorizes the Congress to "provide for calling forth the Militia to execute the Laws of the Union, suppress Insurrections and repel Invasions". Article I, Section 8, Clause 12 authorizes the Congress to "raise and support Armies". Therefore, the military itself is constitutionally justified. However, not everything in the department is necessary to fulfill these authorized activities, nor directly advances them.

Defense is a critical issue, and one of the most clearly authorized items in the Constitution. Its organization is gargantuan and its structure is complex. I have attempted to simplify where possible, but I have nevertheless therefore used a very broad interpretation of "necessary and proper" in my interpretations of the programs inclusive therein.

I therefore cut the programs which are clearly unnecessary, and propose a 25% cut across the board among the rest. Bring our troops home. End the wars. Close our overseas bases and give the land back to the countries they rightfully belong to. Let them defend themselves, instead of doing it for them.

I remind you, this is the department of "defense"; not the department of "any military campaign the current President may desire". Station the Army on the borders. Station the Marines at the ports. Station the Navy along our coastlines. Patrol the skies over the cities with the Air Force.

Our military can defend us if they're here. Our military cannot defend us if they're in Iran and Pakistan. Let's secure our own borders instead of Afghanistan's, Japan's, Korea's, and Germany's. Let's make America free and safe again.

Some procurement line items may seem to be duplicated. These items are, in fact, duplicated in the budget and spent multiple times.

---

[18] http://comptroller.defense.gov/defbudget/fy2013/budget_justification/index.html

Defense-Wide Spending

Operation and Maintenance[19]

> *The Operation and Maintenance, Defense-Wide funding request supports critical Department-wide functions and transformational efforts for the Secretary, Military Departments, and warfighters. The funding pays for common information services and system sustainment, contract administration and audits, family support programs, and administrative functions for the Military Departments. This funding supports the activities of the Special Operations Command (SOCOM), numerous Combat Support Agencies, policy and oversight Agencies, and three Intelligence Agencies.*

Civil Military Programs (CMP)

> *The Department of Defense (DoD) Civil Military Programs are managed by the Assistant Secretary of Defense for Reserve Affairs and encompass outreach/service programs identified as: 1) the National Guard ChalleNGe Program authorized under 32 U.S.C. 509; 2) the DoD Innovative Readiness Training Program authorized under 10 U.S.C. 2012; and 3) the DoD STARBASE Program currently authorized under 10 U.S.C. 2193.*

None of the programs within CMP are authorized by the Constitution, and their connection to the Defense of the United States is very tenuous at best. Eliminate CMP; $161 Million saved.

The National Guard Youth ChalleNGe Program

> *ChalleNGe (32 U.S.C. 509) is a youth development program managed by the Assistant Secretary of Defense, Reserve Affairs, and administered by the National Guard Bureau through cooperative agreements with the States. The National Guard Youth ChalleNGe Program provides OSD an opportunity to work with State and local governments to engage our nation's youth and provide graduates an opportunity to join the military. Approximately 20 percent of the 2,000 annual graduates enter military service.*

Developing youths is not the role of government; it is the role of the parents. No special opportunities are required to join the military; people need merely visit a recruiter. State and local governments should tax their own people to run their own programs. Any information and consultation provided by this program can be provided on the DoD's website.

The life skills and employment potential of students and graduates is not a government issue. As I will go into when I get to the Department of Education,

---

[19]http://comptroller.defense.gov/defbudget/fy2013/budget_justification/pdfs/01_Operation_and_Maintenance/O_M_VOL_1_PARTS/Volume_I_Part_I.pdf

education is not a federal issue, and is not authorized by the Constitution. Therefore it is not the responsibility of the federal government, let alone the role of a military department, to assist anyone in attaining a diploma or GED. Leadership development is a part of military training and is already provided upon joining the military. Community service is not a government issue, and there is no need for the military to push it as much as it does.

The life skills, job skills, physical fitness, health, and hygiene of civilians is none of the government's business.

The Innovative Readiness Training Program (IRT)

IRT (10 U.S.C. 2012) is managed by the Assistant Secretary of Defense, Reserve Affairs. IRT contributes directly to military readiness and provides outstanding and realistic combat support and combat service support training in a multi-service environment for National Guard and Reserve members. It also provides a critical link between the military and underserved civilian communities. This pre and post-deployment readiness training (engineering, health care, diving and transportation) provides hands on mission essential training while simultaneously providing renewal of infrastructure improvements and health care to underserved communities throughout the United States and in US territories.

IRT is redundant to the training the armed forces otherwise already have during their military service. As long as they are not being invaded, there is no such thing as a civilian community which is underserved by the military. Providing health care is not the government's job, and providing it to civilians is certainly not the military's job. Providing humanitarian assistance is not a government issue. The government should never interfere in the ecology, such as when creating habitats for fish. South Carolina should tax its own people to run its own fish habitat programs.

The DoD STARBASE Program (10 U.S.C. 2193)

Starbase [...] is designed to raise the interest and improve knowledge and skills of students in kindergarten through twelfth grade in science, technology, engineering and mathematics (STEM). The program targets "at risk" (minority and low socio-economic) students and utilizes instruction modules specifically designed to meet specific STEM objectives.

Getting kids interested in specific areas of study, and mentoring of any kind are not government issues. Education is not a federal issue, but the states reserve the right to involve themselves therein. The government should never target any specific group of people; provide a service to everyone equally, or not at all. The goals of Starbase have nothing to do with national defense, repelling invasions, or protecting our liberty.

Starbase also funds grants, whose nature I could not ascertain; eliminate all federal grants.

Defence Acquisition University (DAU)

> *The Defense Acquisition University (DAU) is a corporate university of the Department of Defense, Office of the Under Secretary of Defense (Acquisition, Technology, and Logistics) (DoD USD (AT&L)). Its mission is to provide a global learning environment to support a mission-ready Defense Acquisition Workforce that develops, delivers, and sustains effective and affordable war fighting capabilities.*

The fact that someone figured we had a large enough Defense Acquisition Workforce to justify an entire university is evidence of the fact that our defense requires too many acquisitions. A workforce of 155,000 FTEs, whose existence is justified solely by acquiring new products and resources, is further evidence thereof. If we eliminate our policy of proactive warmongering, then we can sustain our military with far less wasteful spending. For example, we wouldn't require as many missiles and bombs if we weren't using them continually since at least the 1980s. Establish a large enough stockpile to defend us against all our enemies, plus a small amount for ongoing training, and leave it alone.

An entire university to teach people how to buy stuff for the military is not a "necessary and proper" expenditure for a constitutional government. Eliminate the university, end the wars, bring our troops home, and reduce the acquisition workforce to 10,000. Savings therefrom include $147.2 Million in DAU funding, hundreds of billions in Overseas Contingency Operations, and about $5 Billion in workforce expenditures; not including the actual cost of the acquisitions and procurements. I'll get to that later.

Defense Contract Audit Agency (DCAA)

> *The Defense Contract Audit Agency (DCAA) is responsible for providing audit services and financial advice to all Department of Defense (DoD) acquisition officials to assist them in achieving fair and reasonable contract prices and assuring compliance with contractual terms and conditions. The DCAA responds to specific acquisition official requests for services across the entire spectrum of contract financial and business matters as well as fulfilling recurring audit work required to monitor cost performance and approve contract payments.*

If we eliminate our endless pattern of proactive warmongering and policing the world, none of which was authorized by the Constitution, then our need for acquisition contracts will be greatly diminished. The DoD should enter into no other types of contracts; and even these, only so the private weapons and equipment companies may forecast their manufacturing needs accurately.

By ending our presence in all overseas locations, we obsolete the need for all reconstruction efforts in Iraq and Afghanistan; but I'll get to that later. The United States should never reimburse, finance, initiate, nor intervene in projects in other countries. Eliminate USAID.

I've already covered numerous contracts which can be outright eliminated; that would provide a huge reduction in the audit backlog. The remaining contracts should be few enough in number that auditing can be performed by the DCMA. Therefore, we can eliminate the DCAA and save $574 Million plus $31 Million under the Office of the Inspector General.

Defense Contract Management Agency (DCMA)

The DCMA is a Department of Defense (DoD) Combat Support Agency responsible for ensuring the integrity of the Government contracting process and for providing a broad range of acquisition management services. The DCMA has two primary missions: 1) providing Contract Administration Services (CAS) to their military services worldwide and 2) providing contingency contract support in theater. Their mission is to provide Contract Administration Services to the Department of Defense Acquisition Enterprise and its partners to ensure delivery of quality products and services to the warfighter, on time and on cost.

As discussed previously, the need for defense contracts can be reduced by orders of magnitude. The *"Department of Defense Acquisition Enterprise"* defines itself, almost verbatim, as the "Military-Industrial Complex". Reduce funding by 75%, pending the results of actual contract reduction statistics. Merge all other non-eliminated, contract-related agencies and entities into DCMA. $970 Million saved, plus $70 Million under the OIG.

Defense Finance Accounting Service (DFAS)

The Defense Finance and Accounting Service (DFAS) serves as the Executive Agent, responsible for finance and accounting activities within the Department of Defense (DoD). The DFAS provides finance and accounting management and operational support for appropriated, non-appropriated, revolving and trust funds.

A major simplification of the DoD hierarchy, coupled with massive reductions and eliminations, would greatly reduce the finance and accounting overhead of the department. Eliminate all trust funds; pay contracts up front or COD, and everything else at the point of sale. Combined with the massive reduction in justified contracts, the overhead remaining should be miniscule. Of what remains, the activities, agencies, and subdepartments should be able to administer their own financial and accounting overhead given the oversight already provided therein. Eliminate and save $18 Million.

Defense Human Resources Activity (DHRA)

The Defense Human Resources Activity (DHRA) enhances the operational effectiveness and efficiency of a host of dynamic and diverse programs supporting the Office of the Under Secretary of Defense for Personnel and Readiness (OUSD (P&R)). The Field Activity supports policy development by performing cutting-edge research and expert analysis, supports readiness and departmental reengineering efforts, manages the largest automated personnel data repositories in the world, prepares tomorrow's leaders through robust developmental programs, supports recruiting and retaining the best and brightest, and delivers both benefits and critical services to war-fighters and their families.

Policies do not require ongoing development; the military hierarchy of command has been established for a long time, and it is well known. Obey all lawful orders, disobey and report all unlawful orders. Obey the Uniform Code of Military Justice, all federal laws, and all laws applicable to whatever foreign location you may be located in. No further policy is required.

By eliminating the policy overhead, we obsolete the research, experts, analysis, and departmental reengineering. Good training can provide the benefits of most developmental programs. The remainder of the DHRA can be loosely justified per the previously quoted clauses in Article I, Section 8 of the Constitution. Therefore the DHRA may remain. Reduce by half and save $338 Million.

Defense Information Systems Agency (DISA)

The Defense Information Systems Agency (DISA) is a combat support agency responsible for engineering and providing command and control (C2) capabilities and enterprise infrastructure. The DISA is continuously operating and assuring a global net-centric enterprise in direct support to joint warfighters, National level leaders, and other mission and coalition partners across the full spectrum of operations. The DISA also provides forces to the national command authority that operates the Global Information Grid (GIG).

C2 is the military's acronymic way of saying "Computers". While critical to the way the military works these days, also keep in mind this proposal is reducing its responsibilities significantly. Reduce by 25% and save $337 Million.

Defense Logistics Agency (DLA)

> The Defense Logistics Agency (DLA) continues to execute the plan to improve the oversight of contractor services, acquire those services more effectively, and control costs in the current restricted funding environment. The DLA is primarily a Defense Working Capital Fund (DWCF) activity, so the majority of contractor services will be reflected in the DWCF budget presentation. The DLA Operation and Maintenance (O&M) appropriation is approximately 1% of the overall DLA budget.

"Mobilization Warstoppers" consists of "industrial preparedness" and "the preservation of industrial capability to support the department's readiness". Government should never interfere in private markets. Given the reduction in war mobilization, cut by half; $40 Million saved.

"Other Logistics Services" include finances for homeless blankets and "other logistics programs", including Bosnia/Kosovo support, and the ever-vague Continuing Health. These are not the proper role of government. Eliminate some programs, saving $123 Million. Reduce the rest by 25%, saving $6 Million, for a total of $129 Million.

All hereby justified eliminations total savings of $137.42 Million. Having read through the entire sub-budget for the DLA, I have no qualms cutting the fuding of the remainder by half. Such remainder comes out to a $73.6M savings, for a grand total savings of $241 Million and a total DLA budget of $221 Million.

Defense Standardization Program Office (DSPO)

> DSPO (FY 2013: **$8.420 million** and 12 FTEs) The DSPO was transferred from the OUSD(AT&L) to DLA in FY 1999. The Defense Standardization Program (DSP) is authorized by Sections 2451-2452 of Title 10, United States Code, and the DoDI 4120.24, which implements the DSP in the DoD. The DSPO is the Executive Agent responsible for developing DoD policy and procedures for the DSP, to include the development and use of military specifications and standards; DoD adoption of non-Government standards; Diminishing Manufacturing Sources and Material Shortages; Government-Industry Data Exchange Program; and a variety of related issues.

An office made out of pure overhead, whose sole purpose is to create more rules within the military. Eliminate and save $8.42 Million.

Defense Legal Services Agency (DLSA)

The Defense Legal Services Agency (DLSA) provides legal services to the Office of the Secretary of Defense, Department of Defense (DoD) Field Activities, and the Defense Agencies. The largest component of DLSA, the Defense Office of Hearings and Appeals (DOHA), adjudicates numerous types of cases that arise from all Military Departments and Defense Agencies

Military law should not be tried in civilian courts because civilian judges and lawyers cannot be held accountable to understand military law. Therefore the agency is necessary and proper, and shall receive only the standard 25% cut. $8.8 Million saved.

Defense Media Activity (DMA)

The Defense Media Activity (DMA) is the Department of Defense (DoD) internal news and media production organization. The DMA mission is to support internal communications operations of the Office of the Secretary of Defense (OSD) and each of the Military Departments by gathering information on DoD policies, programs and priorities. The DMA delivers this information to the DoD worldwide military audience – active, reserve, civilian and contractors, including their families, on land and at sea.

DMA directly advances government transparency and disburses information to the entire DoD far more efficiently (albeit less interactively and in less detail) than the chain of command could do. The DMA is thus necessary and proper and shall receive only the standard 25% cut. $56 Million saved.

DoD Dependents Education (DoDDE)

The Department of Defense Dependents Education (DoDDE) programs are the Department of Defense Education Activity (DoDEA), the Family Assistance (FA)/Family Advocacy Program (FAP), and the Relocation Assistance Program (RAP).

Department of Defense Education Activity

DoDEA is the Presidential and National showcase for education excellence. The DoDEA provides a world-class education program that inspires and prepares all students in military communities around the world to be successful and responsible citizens in a dynamic global environment. Courses of study in DoDEA schools are often more rigorous than those found in public schools in the United States.

Education is not a government issue. Having said that, the military way of life actively takes people away from normal education channels, and defense education activities improve personnel training and job effectiveness. Therefore it can be considered necessary and proper, and thus at least parts of it are loosely authorized. However, if we move the people back to areas with normal education channels, then there is no need to provide a special channel for them.

By removing ourselves from all overseas locations, we can move our people back to bases in American lands, near schools. Thus we can eliminate DoDEA and DoDDS. Total savings are approximately $3 Billion.

DoDEA Schools

> *To ensure sustained high levels of student achievement, the DoDEA Community Strategic Plan (CSP) contains goals and benchmarks that drive resources and organizational improvements. The CSP is the catalyst for changing the teaching and learning process; raising the standard of learning to ensure excellence; creating greater local autonomy in devising methods and strategies to meet the standards; creating a common language for communication among all stakeholders; and creating greater accountability for reaching the expected outcomes.*

Civilian education is not a government issue, and has nothing to do with defense. If we eliminate all overseas bases, then all remaining bases will be within the United States. If we further eliminate bases which are not located near a city, then the students can use traditional public or private school systems. Eliminate DoDEA, thus saving $1.3 Billion.

Educational Partnership Program (EPP)

> *EPP responds to Congressional direction in Section 574(d) of P.L. 109-364, as amended (codified at 20 USC 7703b note) to ease the transition of military dependent students to Local Educational Agencies (LEAs). By establishing a Partnership program, DoDEA has the opportunity to enrich and expand partnerships with military connected communities.*

Education is not a government issue. Therefore, transition from one education system to another is not a government issue. If we eliminate civilian education within the military, then there is no transition to perform. The military should not establish partnerships with their communities. Parents should teach their children about the way of life that comes with being a military dependent. Eliminate and save $5 Million.

Family Advocacy (FAP)

> *The FAP funds are sent to each of the Military Services for use in their Family Advocacy Programs to ensure delivery of prevention and clinical intervention programs in the areas of domestic abuse, child abuse, and elder abuse. Funding is distributed to the Military Services for program costs to provide*

services at 300 installations. The FAP staff of over 800 civilians and 650 contractors executes the FAP within the Military Department down to the installation level. The FAP program includes the New Parent Support home visiting program to high risk parents for prevention of child abuse and neglect; and domestic abuse victim advocates[.]

Abuse is a series of criminal law violations, and should be treated as such. Preventing crime is not a government issue; only determining guilt and punishing it. Eliminate and save $793 Million.

Defense Prisoner of War / Missing Personnel Office (DPMO)

The Defense Prisoner of War/Missing Personnel Office (DPMO) provides policy, control, and oversight for the entire Department of Defense (DoD) process of the investigation and recovery related to missing persons in accordance with Sections 1513-13 of Title 10, (including matters related to search, rescue, escape, and evasion). As a Defense field activity, the DPMO leads the national effort to: prepare our personnel for possible isolation while pursuing U.S. national objectives abroad; establish favorable conditions to recover and reintegrate them; and achieve the fullest possible accounting for those lost during our Nation's past conflicts.

DPMO is critical to the troops, in that we should always try to locate and rescue Prisoners of War from our enemies. After all, it was the DoD who put them there. Reducing the active force will not in itself reduce the number of captives abroad. Therefore, leave funding at its current level of $21.964 Million.

Defense Security Cooperation Agency (DSCA)

The Defense Security Cooperation Agency (DSCA) administers funding for the Regional Centers for Security Studies, Warsaw Initiative Fund/Partnership for Peace Program, Combating Terrorism Fellowship Program, Regional International Outreach, Security Cooperation Training and Support (formerly called International Programs Security Requirements Course), Global Train and Equip Program, Minister of Defense Advisors, Defense Institution Reform Initiative, Increasing Partner Capacity Building in Rule of Law Context, Coalition Support Funds, and Lift and Sustain Support. The DSCA also provides program management and program implementation support to the Humanitarian Assistance, Foreign Disaster Relief, and Humanitarian Mine Action programs, which are funded in a separate appropriation. DSCA is continuing to improve the oversight of contractor services and acquire those services more effectively.

DSCA provides security for National Defense University schools in Europe, Hawaii, Washington D.C.. European schools are none of our government's business, American schools should all be in America, Hawaii should tax its own people to run its own programs, and Washington D.C. has no need for the programs. The purpose of these schools is generally to build a community, promote cooperation, and perform outreach and issue research. These are not federal functions and can safely be eliminated.

WIF/PPP is a NATO initiative designed to enhance cooperation and stability in the poor areas of Europe and to democratize the military, thus compromising American sovereignty. Military cooperation with Europe need not extend beyond coexisting peacefully and working together in the event of a mutual war effort. European stability is none of our business, and we should leave them to their own devices.

CTFP is a paramilitary educational program designed to "build partnerships in the struggle against violent extremism". Violent extremism generally manifests itself in the form of criminal acts. Terrorist attacks, such as 9/11, are crimes, and should be treated like crimes. CTFP provides courses on subjects such as international law, intelligence, leadership, coordination, special operations, and homeland defense. In other words, subjects which are already covered in great detail in actual military training. Education by CTFP to anyone outside the military is not a government function. Therefore, CTFP is a combination of obsolete and redundant, and thereby can be eliminated.

Regional International Outreach, now known as GlobalNet, is designed to improve collaboration and outreach efforts among students, graduates, Subject Matter Experts, NDU schools, and communities in general. Its purpose is literally to get people with similar military interests to connect and talk with each other. There are countless public and private systems designed to do this (i.e. Facebook and Google), and thus GlobalNet is completely unnecessary and redundant.

SCTS/IPSRC is a five-day class about international technology transference facilitation, export controls, and foreign disclosure. Within the military, there is already training that covers these areas. Outside of the military is not the DoD's business. SCTS can thus be eliminated.

GTEP supports foreign military and security forces, helps them build their capacity for fighting terrorism, and helps them participate in the United Nations and other coalition military missions. The United States should never interfere in the internal matters of other countries, including training them for free. If other countries want our help, they should pay for it or provide an equivalent value in return. This program's educational component could be provided by a private education facility; the rest is not an American issue; eliminate.

MoDA trains Americans and foreigners on foreign cultures, countries, and languages. This is not a legitimate function of our government, and is redundant to other training already included in the military. Training foreigners is not a government issue. Therefore, MoDA can be eliminated, saving $558 Million.

Defense Security Service (DSS)

The mission of the Defense Security Service (DSS) is to support national security and the war fighter by securing the nation's technological base and overseeing the protection of US and foreign classified information in the hands of industry. The DSS Office of Chief Information Officer (OCIO) supports the Automated Information Systems (AIS) and telecommunications infrastructure and DSS programs that include: National Industrial Security Program (NISP), Counterintelligence (CI), Security Education and Training Awareness (SETA), and support elements.

Critical to certain aspects of military functions as it stands; however, by eliminating our proactive warmongering we will reduce the incentives for terrorist attacks. Further, a reduction in force of 25% across the board reduces the necessity of desktops, network capacity, and support staff. By the combination therein, I propose a standard 25% cut; $127 Million saved.

Defense Threat Reduction Agency (DTRA)

The Defense Threat Reduction Agency (DTRA) is the Department of Defense's (DoD) combat support agency for the WMD mission, executing national missions related to countering WMD threats at their sources, interdict weapons and WMD materials at borders and in transit, as well as mitigate WMD effects. Additionally, the Director, DTRA heads the United States Strategic Command Center for Combating WMD (SCC-WMD) in a dual-hatted role. The SCC-WMD supports the development and advocacy of DoD doctrine, organization, training, material, leadership and education, personnel, and facilities (DOTMLPF) for countering WMD capabilities and synchronizes DoD component countering WMD-related planning efforts.

Weapons programs in other countries are not our problem. Interdicting WMD materials at borders and ports is the job of U.S. Customs. No move in funding is required, however, as this can be accomplished by rotating through the existing military personnel no longer required overseas. Instead, eliminate the civilian component; but I'll get to that later. The military has other, more direct methods for anti-WMD training, doctrine, and other overhead listed herein.

The DTRA is redundant to other functions of the DoD and DHS; eliminate and save $443 Million.

Defense Technology Security Administration (DTSA)

The Defense Technology Security Administration (DTSA) develops and implements, consistent with U.S. policy, national security objectives, and Federal laws and regulations, Department of Defense (DoD)technology security policies on international transfers of dual-use and defense-related goods, services, and technologies to 1) preserve critical U.S. military warfighter technological advantages; 2) support legitimate defense cooperation with foreign friends and allies; 3) assure the health of the U.S. defense industrial base; 4) prevent proliferation and diversion technology that could prove detrimental to U.S. national security interests; and 5) Implement enterprise-wide resources to ensure organizational structures, processes, and procedures to effectively support DTSA's strategic direction.

DTSA is a regulatory body designed to create new rules and push new laws. A free country favors fewer laws, a tyranny favors more laws. There should be no international transfers of defense-related or military goods, except to supply our troops during an overseas war effort; and that can be handled by the Defense Logistics Agency. We should favor a peaceful defense policy, only destroying other countries when they try to attack us. When they do, of course, we should wipe them off the face of the Earth.

Defense cooperation with our allies should be limited to strategic and tactical plans and very limited shared usage of non-critical resources when such cooperation can be obtained without any significant detriment to the capacity or effectiveness thereof. The health of industry, whatever sector, is not a government issue. Preventing the innovation and distribution of new technologies in other countries is not a government issue, except when we're at war with them. If we eliminate the DTSA, then there is no strategic direction to support.

There are myriad duplicate security programs in place. The disclosure of classified military information is handled by the disclosing parties, and anyone who handles such information receives a great deal of training on the handling thereof. This program did not exist prior to 2012, and is clearly therefore unnecessary to the functioning of the DoD. Eliminate all security assistance and armaments cooperation programs. Eliminate the NDPC.

DTSA is comprised of rule makers and obsolete or duplicate functions. Eliminate and save $35 Million.

Missile Defense Agency (MDA)

The MDA maintains a variety of missile systems which provide critical defensive capabilities to the United States, including static and mobile missile and antimissile batteries, Aegis systems, vertical launch systems, other weapons systems, fleet integration, tactical and strategic radar systems, and overhead associated therewith. MDA is critical to the defense of the United States from our enemies, and shall be maintained at 2012 levels, a reduction of $58 Million from the proposed 2013 budget.

National Defense University (NDU)

The National Defense University (NDU) is the premier center for Joint Professional Military Education (JPME) and is under the direction of the Chairman, Joint Chiefs of Staff. The University's main campus is on Fort McNair in Washington, D.C. The Joint Forces Staff College is located in Norfolk, VA. The Commission on Higher Education of the Middle States Association of Colleges and Schools accredits the National Defense University. The NDU conducts world class Joint Professional Military Education (JPME), seminars, symposia and professional development and conferencing for DOD and Congressional representatives.

Necessary and proper for national defense, based on the way the military currently works; NDU is training overhead whose funding needs are correlated to the high-level personnel thereby affected. Eliminate all foreign components, and reduce the remainder by the standard 25%. In sum total, let's call it half; $42 Million saved.

Office of Economic Adjustment (OEA)

The Office of Economic Adjustment (OEA) is the Department of Defense's (DoD) primary source for assisting states and communities that are impacted by Defense changes including the Department's Base Realignment and Closure (BRAC) actions. The OEA's Director testified under oath that technical and financial assistance provided under this program ensures affected communities: 1) can plan and carry out local adjustment strategies; 2) engage the private sector in ventures to plan and/or undertake economic development and base redevelopment; and 3) partner with the Military Departments as they implement Defense actions in support of the DoD mission.

OEA gives money to places after we close a base there, because these cities are apparently unable to function without such bases. The tax and job reforms I have recommended herein may cover the economic adjustment. It would not create the difference in jobs; however, my plan only closes the overseas locations. No economic adjustment is needed; eliminate and save $253 Million.

Special Operations Command (SOCOM)

The United States Special Operations Command's (USSOCOM) mission is to provide fully capable Special Operations Forces (SOF) to defend the United States and its interests, and to plan and synchronize operations against terrorist networks. To achieve this mission, SOF commanders and staff must plan and lead a full range of lethal and non-lethal special operations missions in complex and ambiguous environments. Likewise, SOF personnel serve as key members of Joint, Interagency, and International teams and must be prepared to employ all assigned authorities and apply all available elements of power to accomplish assigned missions. In this capacity, SOF personnel must maintain the highest degree of professionalism, cultural awareness, responsiveness and initiative.

Terrorists are not a sovereign power; they are criminals, and they should be treated that way. Based on my proposed foreign policy reforms, terrorists are projected to lose their incentive and motivation. Further, the elimination of all overseas locations and subsequent relocation of such resources to American soil will significantly improve our national defense and save a large amount of money in the process.

Of course, SOCOM's actual operations are classified, so I have no way of projecting the costs thereof. However, their funding has increased by a quarter from FY2012 to 2013, which tells me they're ramping up for who knows what. I therefore recommend reducing by 25%; $1.3 Billion saved.

United States Court of Appeals for the Armed Forces

This appropriation provides for the salaries of five civilian judges and a staff of 54 other civilian positions. It finances all customary expenses required to operate a government activity, such as salaries, benefits, travel costs, rent, communications services, purchase of equipment, contractual IT support and security services, and the expense of printing opinions and decisions of the Court.

USCAAF is necessary and proper; keep it and reduce by the standard 25%, $3.4 Million saved.

Office of the Inspector General

The Office of Inspector General (OIG) audits, investigates, inspects, and evaluates the programs and operations of the Department of Defense (DoD) and, as a result, recommends policies and process improvements that promote economy, efficiency, and effectiveness in DoD programs and operations.

OIG is necessary and proper. Reduce by the standard 25%; $68 Million saved.

Defense Threat Reduction Agency

The Cooperative Threat Reduction (CTR) Program's overarching mission is to partner with willing countries to reduce the threat from weapons of mass destruction (WMD) and related materials, technologies, and expertise. The CTR Program focuses on eliminating, securing, or consolidating WMD, related materials, and associated delivery systems and infrastructure at their source in partner countries. The CTR Program also focuses on building partner capacity to prevent the proliferation of WMD materials across borders or in transit across international borders.

The internal politics, strategy, tactics, management, delivery systems, and security of other countries and their weapons are not American issues, so long as they remain in those other countries. Thousands of nuclear weapons from the former USSR were lost, and hundreds remain unaccounted for. The United States is more than ready if an attack is made on us, which is far less likely due to my recommended foreign policy reforms. Eliminate; $519 Million saved.

Overseas Humanitarian, Disaster Aid and Civic Assistance Program

The Overseas Humanitarian, Disaster and Civic Aid (OHDACA) appropriation supports the Secretary of Defense and Combatant Commanders' security cooperation strategies to build indigenous capabilities and cooperative relationships with allies, friends, civil society, and potential partners. The appropriation provides low cost, non-obtrusive and highly effective activities that help partners help themselves, improves access to areas not otherwise available to U.S. Forces, and build collaborative relationships with host nation's civil society. The FY 2013 budget estimate requests a total of $108.8 million to finance the humanitarian assistance and mine action programs as well as foreign disaster relief initiatives.

OHDACAP is a series of foreign aid programs, hiding paramilitary training and pro-American propaganda. Disasters, civic issues, internal societies and matters, humanitarian assistance, and mines in other countries are not American issues. Civil society is not a government issue at all. Eliminate; $108 Million saved.

Support for International Sporting Competitions

The Support for International Sporting Competitions (SISC), Defense appropriation is a no-year appropriation that provides for continuing Department of Defense (DoD) support to national and international sporting events that are either certified by the Attorney General or support specific organizations such as the Special Olympics, Paralympics, and the United States Olympic Committee's (USOC) Paralympic Military Program. Funds are still available from the FY 2003 DoD Appropriations Act (P.L. 107-248).

Sports are an industry, and the government should never involve itself in industry or the economy. Despite appropriating no money, SISC still intends to spend money it has already appropriated. Eliminate and move the remaining funds into the Treasury General Fund.

Department of Defense Acquisition Workforce Development Fund

> *The FY 2013 budget supports strengthening of the DoD acquisition workforce to ensure the Department achieves and sustains sufficient workforce capacity and capability. Since 2008, DoD has made significant progress towards bolstering workforce capacity. In addition to completing and maintaining sufficient capacity, DoD will continue efforts to strengthen the quality, readiness and performance results of the workforce. The Defense Acquisition Workforce growth initiative is supported by Title 10 U.S.C. 1705 Defense Acquisition Workforce Development Fund (DAWDF).*

If a department has so many acquisitions that it requires an entire workforce to organize it, and even a fund to develop that force further, then the department has too many acquisitions. This is an overhead program designed to count the people in the military, which can be and previously was accomplished through the chain of command. I'm assuming a misprint in the OM budget and that the 2013 authorization was actually $1.18 Billion, not $1.18 Trillion. Eliminate it and save that amount.

Office of the Secretary of Defense

> *The National Security Act of 1947 unified the United States Armed Forces under a single Secretary of Defense (SECDEF) with cabinet rank. The President exercises his authority as Commander-in-Chief through the SECDEF, who is responsible for setting policy and directing defense programs and planning within the Department of Defense (DoD). The Deputy Secretary of Defense (DEPSECDEF) is delegated full power and authority to act for the SECDEF. The Office of the Secretary of Defense (OSD) supports the SECDEF and DEPSECDEF by performing the duties and responsibilities for policy development, planning, resource management, fiscal, and program evaluation at DoD level.*

Secdef is necessary and proper to raise and maintain armies, navies, and militia. Its two billion in outlays are probably not. Reduce by standard 25%; $524 Million saved.

The Joint Staff

> *The Chairman of the Joint Chiefs of Staff (CJCS) is the principal military adviser to the President, National Security Council, and Secretary of Defense. The Chairman presides over and serves as a member of the Joint Chiefs of Staff. CJCS relies upon the Joint Staff (TJS) to craft and distribute guidance for combatant forces' unified strategic direction, operations under unified*

command, and integration into effective combat forces. On behalf of the Chairman, TJS provides Combatant Commands (COCOMs), the Services, and U.S. war fighters with joint policy, strategy, and doctrine necessary to employ effective joint combat forces in contingencies worldwide.

TJS is necessary and proper to raise and maintain armies, navies, and militia. Its two billion in outlays are probably not. Reduce by standard 25%; $121 Million saved.

Washington Headquarters Service

The Washington Headquarters Services (WHS) was established under DoD Directive 5110.4, on October 1, 1977. WHS is a field activity that provides centralized, consolidated administrative and operational support to the Department of Defense (DoD) activities in the National Capital Region (NCR).

WHS is necessary and proper; thus only cut standard 25%. $130 Million saved.

Overseas Contingency Operations Requests

OCO is the DoD's politically correct way of saying "War" and other "Nation building". The wars we have been fighting constantly over the past century have destroyed our economic base, demoralized our people, and multiplied our enemies. We must return to a peaceful foreign policy, and thus a more liberty-oriented society. Eliminate OCO altogether; save **$7.8 Billion** from Operation and Maintenance of war efforts at the top level of the DoD alone. We haven't even gotten into the actual military yet!

Procurement[20]

Chemical Biological Defense Program

The Installation Force Protection program area provides Chemical, Biological, Radiological, Nuclear (CBRN) and High-Yield Explosive (CBRNE) protection for CONUS/OCONUS DoD installation physical structures as well as military personnel and others within the perimeter of the military reservation. Also, this program supports the acquisition of CBRNE defense equipment requirements for the National Guard Bureau's (NGB) Weapons of Mass Destruction Civil Support Teams (WMD-CST) and the United States Army Reserve (USAR) Reconnaissance and Decontamination Platoons.

Necessary and proper. However, by eliminating all overseas locations and reducing 25% of what's left after that, the need for CBDP is significantly reduced. Cut by half and save $149 Million.

---

[20]http://comptroller.defense.gov/defbudget/fy2013/budget_justification/pdfs/02_Procurement/PB13_FINAL.pdf

Defense Contract Audit Agency

DCAA was eliminated in my general DoD OM proposals; therefore DCAA requires no procurements. Eliminate and save $1.5 Million.

Defense Contract Management Agency

I cut DCMA by 75% in my proposal; thus cut 75% from its procurements; $1.6 Million saved.

Defense Human Resources Activity

I cut DHRA by half in my proposal; thus cut half from its procurements; $5.5 Million saved.

Defense Information Systems Agency

I cut DISA by 25% in my proposal; thus cut 25% from its procurements; $188 Million saved.

Defense Logistics Agency

I cut DLA by 25% in my proposal; thus cut 25% from its procurements; $2.9 Million saved.

Defense Media Activity

I cut DMA by 25% in my proposal; thus cut 25% from its procurements; $3.6 Million saved.

Defense Security Cooperation Agency

I eliminated DSCA in my proposal; thus eliminate its procurements; $971K saved.

Defense Security Service

I cut DSS by 25% in my proposal; thus cut 25% from its procurements; $244K saved.

Defense Threat Reduction Agency

I eliminated DTRA in my proposal; thus eliminate its procurements; $13 Million saved.

Defense Technology Security Administration

I eliminated DTSA in my proposal; thus eliminate its procurements; $447K saved.

Department of Defense Dependent Education Activity

I eliminated DoDDEA; thus eliminate its procurements; $1.5 Billion saved.

Office of the Secretary of Defense
I cut Secdef by 25% in my proposal; thus cut 25% from its procurements; $15.9 Million saved.

The Joint Staff
I cut TJS by 25% in my proposal; thus cut 25% from procurements. $5.5 Million saved.

United States Special Operations Command
I cut SOCOM by 25% in my proposal; thus cut 25% from its procurements. $461.7 Million saved.

Washington Headquarters Service.
I cut WHS by 25% in my proposal; thus cut 25% from its procurements. $6.6 Million saved.

Defense Production Act
Title III of the Defense Production Act (DPA) provides the DoD with a powerful tool to ensure the timely creation and availability of domestic production capabilities for technologies that have the potential for wide-ranging impact on the operational capabilities and technological superiority of U.S. defense systems. Title III is unique in that it is the sole DoD program focused on creating, maintaining, protecting, expanding or restoring domestic production capacity to strengthen domestic industry and to establish the industrial base capacity for essential national defense capabilities.

DPA was not included in the Operations and Maintenance section of the budget, and thus has no correlated cut. DPA interferes in the natural economy of the weapons industry; the production capacity thereof is not a government issue. DPA "incentivizes" manufacturers, though I could not determine through what means. Logic would dictate this is either by procuring stuff we don't need, or by outright handing over cash. Either way is unacceptable. Eliminate; $89 Million saved.

Joint Urgent Operational Needs Fund
Joint Urgent Operational Needs Fund (JUONF): The JUONF, established in FY 2012 by the National Defense Authorization Act, Public Law 111-81, Section 864, provides resources for urgent and compelling requirements that will prevent critical mission failure or casualties. This transfer account will allow immediate action to mitigate emergent capability gaps as identified by Combatant Commanders and validated by the Joint Staff and will enable the Department to provide equipment, supplies, services, and training to quickly respond to Urgent Operational Needs[.]

JUONF was not included in the Operations and Maintenance section of the budget, and thus has no correlated cut. By repealing NDAA, we eliminate JUONF's authority. The DoD has been able to get by through urgent and compelling requirements and critical mission failures or casualties without this brand-new program. Eliminate; $200 Million saved.

Research, Development, Test, and Evaluation (RDT&E)[21]

Defense Advanced Research Projects Agency (DARPA)[22]

DARPA's mission is to maintain the technological superiority of the U.S. military and prevent technological surprise from harming our national security by sponsoring revolutionary, high-payoff research bridging the gap between fundamental discoveries and their military use.

Over the years, DARPA has worked to enhance our national security by funding research and technology development that not only have improved our military capabilities but have changed the way we live. Since the very beginning, DARPA has been the place for people with innovative ideas that lead to groundbreaking discoveries.

It is important that our military be technologically superior to those of our enemies. Having said that, the Constitution does not authorize research at the federal level, and the private sector is better than the government at *everything*. Eliminate and privatize, saving $2.8 Billion.

Missile Defense Agency (MDA)[23]

The Missile Defense Agency (MDA) is a research, development, and acquisition agency within the Department of Defense. Our workforce includes government civilians, military service members, and contractor personnel in multiple locations across the United States. We are focused on retaining and recruiting a dedicated workforce interested in supporting our national security.

Missiles and defense against them are critical to our national defense; thus MDA is necessary and proper. Keep as is.

---

[21]
http://comptroller.defense.gov/defbudget/fy2013/budget_justification/pdfs/03_RDT_and_E/Defense-Wide_PB_2013_1_FINAL_RDTE.pdf
[22]http://comptroller.defense.gov/defbudget/fy2013/budget_justification/pdfs/03_RDT_and_E/Defense_Advanced_Research_Projects_Agency_PB_2013_1%20Final.pdf
[23]http://comptroller.defense.gov/defbudget/fy2013/budget_justification/pdfs/02_Procurement/Missile_Defense_Agency_PB_2013.pdf

Office of the Secretary of Defense (Secdef)[24]

It's important to have one person in charge of each department that we keep around, so secdef is necessary and proper. The majority of programs run by his office, however, are not. For reasons already justified, eliminate US Mission to NATO ($303,000), the Mentor Protégé program ($28.5 Million), and DRIP (which hasn't had funding since 2011). Reduce the remainder by half ($23 Million); $52 Million saved.

Chemical and Biological Defense Programs (CBDP)

> The overarching goal of the CBDP's FY 2013 President's Budget is to develop and field improved chemical, biological, and radiological (CBR) defense capabilities to the Joint Force in support of the 2010 Quadrennial Defense Review (QDR), Defense Planning Guidance (DPG), the CBDP FY 2012-2017 Program Strategy Guidance (PSG), and warfighter priorities. This budget will strengthen and expand programs that prevent, protect, mitigate, respond to, and recover from CBR threats as part of a layered, integrated defense and improve the warfighter's ability to find, track, interdict, and eliminate CBRN weapons or emerging threats.

NBC weapons are becoming more prevalent in modern times, and defending ourselves against them is necessary and proper. However, the private sector is better and more efficient than the government at *everything*. Privatize and eliminate, saving $10.6 Billion. Buy the products that come out of the private sector's research at a much lower price.

Defense Contract Management Agency (DCMA)

> This budget submission sustains Web-basing all new DCMA-unique software applications, and continues supporting Web Services software technology (i.e., machine to machine information exchanges between DCMA, DCMA's customers in the Military Services and Defense agencies, and the Defense industry, based upon the open-standard Extensible Markup Language [XML], Simple Object Access Protocol [SOAP], and so on).

As a C# Developer who has written many SOAP webservices and websites, I know that web-based systems do make more sense than desktop applications from deployment and security perspectives. Having said that, the existing systems are working, and my proposal reduced DCMA by 75%. Such a reduction would make the existing deployment and security about four times easier to manage. I also know that writing a few new webservices and pointing a few

---

[24]http://comptroller.defense.gov/defbudget/fy2013/budget_justification/pdfs/02_Procurement/Office_of_Secretary_Of_Defense_PB_2013.pdf

applications at them shouldn't cost $13 Million, let alone increasing on an ongoing annual basis. Eliminate and save $13 Million.

Defense Human Resources Activity (DHRA)

Distributed Learning Advanced Technology Development

> The Department of Defense Human Resources Activity (DHRA) is a DoD-wide Field Activity chartered to support the Under Secretary of Defense for Personnel and Readiness (USD (P&R)). Advanced Distributed Learning (ADL) Initiative: This program develops the technologies to make learning and performance support available to service members, anytime, anywhere. The ADL concept enables the ability to migrate online learning content to multiple hardware and software applications using the Sharable Content Object Reference Model (SCORM®) standard.

By eliminating our worldwide overseas posture, we no longer require the same degree of distribution across our DoD services. Many parts and types of military training require hands-on experience, testing, and practice, and therefore cannot be done online in any capacity. Public education is not a government issue. Even if it were justifiable, necessary, and proper, it would be better handled as a private contract. Eliminate and save $12 Million.

Homeland Personnel Security Directive Initiative (HSPD-12)

> HSPD-12 requires rapid electronic authentication for all Government employees, uniformed individuals and contractors. The Defense Enrollment and Eligibility System will provide Enterprise capability for the cardholder data repository, common Access interface to multiple types of Access control hardware, common Access software, the ability to control Access to multiple facilities through one authoritative data source, and provide the standards and data to/ form and power efficient gates. Implement Enterprise Access control data for the DoD while providing standards and reducing redundancy. RDT&E funding will be expended to develop the secure interfaces necessary to work with the FBI and first responders for Enterprise authentication.

HSPD-12 is necessary and proper for handling of classified / secured assets and information. Leave it in place, reduce by the standard 25%. $97K saved.

R&D in Support of DOD Enlistment, Testing, and Evaluation

> Joint Service Training & Readiness System Development. Established by the Secretary of Defense to improve the training and readiness of the Active and Reserve Components. This program expedites the prototype development of new training and readiness technologies and Joint Service Training and Readiness systems, which improve training and readiness effectiveness and enhance military forces' performance. It also facilitates the sharing of training

and readiness information, while allowing for the transfer of emerging and innovative technologies among the Services and the private sector.

This project would improve the way enlistment and training are done; but it is not critical to do so. Eliminate; $29 Million saved.

Defense Logistics Agency (DLA)

Agile Transportation for the 21ˢᵗ Century Theater Capability

The Geographic Combatant Commanders (GCCs) lack an automated capability to (1.) manage transportation planning and execution processes for cargo and passenger movement within their respective theaters of operation or (2.) match global movement requirements against available lift assets to produce an optimized transportation schedule that meets delivery requirements. AT21 Increment 3 Theater Capability will provide continuous visibility, collaboration, automated processes, alerts and an exception management capability supporting transportation planning and execution for theater force and sustainment movements.

This can be performed with a wiki, email, or a phone call; each of which is already included in the DISA overhead. Eliminate and save $4 Million.

Logistics Research and Development Technology

The central idea of the Focused Logistics Joint Functional Concept "is to build sufficient capacity into the sustainment pipeline, exercise sufficient control over the pipeline from end to end, and provide a high degree of certainty to the supported joint force commander that sustainment, and support will arrive where needed and on time." The Defense Logistics Agency (DLA) Research and Development (R&D) program helps achieve this vision by pioneering advanced logistics concepts and business processes that provides the leanest possible infrastructure, the use of the best commercial and government sources, and the application of business practices.

This does not appear to address a specific preexisting problem that was not already being addressed otherwise. Eliminate and save $25 Million.

Deployment and Distribution Enterprise Technology

Overseas Contingency Operations (OCO) lessons learned and daily operations indicate that current distribution and logistics processes remain outdated and are rarely capable of providing required warfighter support in an agile, efficient and economical manner. Designation of United States Transportation Command (USTRANSCOM) as the Distribution Process Owner (DPO) and shift within the Department to transform the distribution and logistics processes, demands the examination and improvement of the entire supply chain.

By eliminating all Overseas Contingency Operations, we obsolete the overhead associated therewith. The merely outdated nature of something is not sufficient justification to replace it entirely in a period of economic recession. Eliminate and save $31 Million.

Microelectronics Technology Development and Support
> *The Defense Microelectronics Activity (DMEA) provides a vital service as the joint Department of Defense (DoD) Center for microelectronics acquisition, adaptive operations and support - advancing future microelectronics research, development, technologies and applications to achieve the Department's strategic and national security objectives. An important part of the DMEA mission is to research current and emerging microelectronics issues with a focus on warfighters' needs.*

The government is not the research wing of an electronics company. Eliminate and save $72 Million.

DoD Enterprise Systems Development and Demonstration
> *The mission of the DoD Enterprise Systems is to coordinate and enable business transformation efforts across the Department of Defense. The DLA recognizes that DoD's business enterprise must be closer to its warfighting customers than ever before. Joint military requirements drive the need for greater commonality and integration of business and financial operations.*

This is not an essential function of defense; eliminate and save $133 Million.

Small Business Innovative Research (SBIR)
> *Defense Logistics Agency's (DLA's) ability to deliver Americans the right logistics solution in every transaction requires more than successful management of the Department's wholesale supplies and suppliers. It requires supply chain excellence. Our military's ability to generate and sustain combat readiness indefinitely, anywhere on the globe requires that DLA-managed material flow seamlessly and as needed from the nation's industrial base to where it is ultimately used.*

There are websites where small businesses can view available contracts and compete with each other's bids. No budget for 2013, but eliminate anyway.

Industrial Preparedness Manufacturing Technology
> *The Defense Logistics Agency (DLA) Industrial Preparedness Manufacturing Technology (IP ManTech) Program supports the development of a responsive, world class manufacturing capability to affordably meet the warfighters' needs throughout the defense system life cycle. IP ManTech: Provides the crucial link between invention and product application to speed technology*

transitions. Matures and validates emerging manufacturing technologies to support low-risk implementation in industry and Department of Defense (DoD) facilities, e.g. depots and shipyards.

Manufacturing is the job of private businesses which the government purchases its goods from. Government should not be involved in the innovation, research, manufacturing, or distribution processes, other than telling the businesses where to deliver the products. Eliminate and save $27 Million.

Logistics Support Activities

The Logistics Support Activities (LSA) is under the staff cognizance and oversight of Office of the Secretary of Defense and was transferred to the defense Logistics Agency (DLA) in 1994. In accordance with DoD Directive 5111.1, Defense Continuity & Crisis Management (DCCM) was established to consolidate continuity-related policy and oversight activities within DoD in order to ensure the Secretary of Defense can perform his mission essential functions under all circumstances.

LSA sounds necessary and proper; reduce by half to approximate FY2011 levels. $2.4 Million saved.

Defense Security Cooperation Agency (DSCA)

Regional International Outreach (RIO) – Partnership for Peace Management Systems (PIMS)

Regional International Outreach (RIO) - Partnership for Peace (PfP) Information Management System (PIMS) is an Office of the Secretary of Defense (OSD) initiative to deploy a common information technology platform to improve international partner outreach and collaboration efforts in a federated environment.

The information technology platforms of international partners is not an American issue. Eliminate and save $3 Million.

Overseas Humanitarian Assistance Shared Information Systems

The Overseas Humanitarian Assistance Shared Information System (OHASIS) enables Humanitarian Assistance (HA) offices, including embassy staff, country team members, Combatant Command leads, and DSCA to manage and visualize HA projects on a web-based map display, automate report generation, and perform a variety of analysis.

OHASIS is a quarter million dollars to develop a map with pins on it, which I've done through Microsoft, Google, Yahoo, and Nokia map APIs for free. Eliminate all overseas humanitarian assistance, thereby obsoleting OHASIS. Save $288K.

Defense Security Service (DSS)

Enterprise Security System

The Defense Security Service (DSS) manages the Enterprise Security System (ESS) to provide an effective, real-time, security support capability for the Military Departments, DoD Agencies, the National Industrial Security Program (NISP), and other Federal Agencies. In compliance with the Expanded Electronic Government, President's Management Agenda, and the DoD Enterprise Architecture Framework, ESS is the unified offering of security mission systems which facilitate and automate improved national investigative and adjudicative standards, streamline security processes, and increase DoD community collaboration.

While I was in the Air Force, I once opened a Telnet connection from my snack bar computer to my home network to test an electronic Bulletin Board System I had set up. Within five minutes, I got a phone call from Hawaii and a speech about misuse of government resources. No harm was done, and it showed me how much overhead was associated with the security thereof. Reduce by half and save $4.4 Million.

Defense Technical Information Center (DTIC)

The Defense Technical Information Center (DTIC) is the hub of DoD Scientific and Technical Information interchanges, empowering innovators with greater efficiency, effectiveness, and agility by accelerating the delivery of warfighting technology. Located at Fort Belvoir, Virginia, DTIC leverages DoD's substantial investment in scientific and technical research and development by facilitating the transfer of scientific, technical and program information throughout the national defense community.

The military has no constitutional authorization to partake in its own scientific research, nor to interfere in the innovation of the free market. However, the military does need to maintain a great deal of technical information, which is necessary and proper to fulfill its mission. Compromise and reduce by half, saving $28 Million.

Defense Threat Reduction Agency (DTRA)

DTRA Basic Research Initiative

The Defense Threat Reduction Agency (DTRA) safeguards America and its allies from Weapons of Mass Destruction (chemical, biological, radiological, nuclear, *and high explosives) by providing capabilities to reduce, eliminate, counter the threat, and mitigate its effects. The Basic Research Initiative program provides for the discovery and development of fundamental knowledge and understanding by research performers drawn primarily from academia and world-class research institutions in government and industry. This leverages Department of Defense's $2 billion annual investment in basic research by ensuring a motivation within the scientific community to conduct research benefiting Weapons of Mass Destruction-related defense missions and by improving Agency knowledge of other research efforts of potential benefit to DTRA nonproliferation, counterproliferation and consequence management efforts.*

DTRA BRI is necessary and proper to defend the United States against NBC weapons, so leave it as is. I would reduce it by the standard 25%, but I'll be merging other programs into DTRA BRI, so let's keep funding where it is ($45 Million).

WMD Defeat Technologies

The mission of the Defense Threat Reduction Agency (DTRA) is to safeguard America and its allies from Weapons of Mass Destruction (WMD) by reducing the present threat and preparing for the future threat. This mission directly reflects several national and Department of Defense level guidance/vision documents to include the National Security Strategy, Unified Command Plan, National Strategy to Combat WMD, Counterproliferation Interdiction, National Strategy for Combating Terrorism, National Military Strategy, Global Development of Forces, Global Employment of Forces, National Military Strategy for Combating WMD, [...]

Defeating WMDs is the purpose of DTRA BRI; thus this is a duplicate function. Eliminate and merge into the BRI project, saving $172 Million.

Counterproliferation Initiatives

The Proliferation, Prevention and Defeat program reduces Weapons of Mass Destruction (WMD) proliferation and enhances WMD defeat capabilities through advanced technology development. To accomplish this objective, seven project areas were developed: RA - Systems Engineering and Innovation, RE - Counter- Terrorism Technologies, RF - Detection Technology, RG - Counter WMD Weapons & Capabilities, RI - Nuclear Survivability, RM - WMD Battle Management, and RT - Target Assessment Technologies.

This function seems to be redundant to BRI and WMDDT. Eliminate and merge into BRI, saving $275 Million.

WMD Defeat Capabilities

> *The Weapons of Mass Destruction (WMD) Toolset is the real-time globally accessible net-centric framework which migrates the Defense Threat Reduction Agency (DTRA) chemical, biological, radiological, nuclear, and high explosive (CBRNE) modeling and simulation codes to provide an integrated suite of Combating WMD decision support capabilities.*

WMDDC seems to be redundant to BRI; eliminate and save $6 Million.

Small Business Innovation Research

> *The SBIR program provides the means for stimulating technological innovation in the private sector, strengthens the role of small business in meeting Department of Defense (DoD) research and development needs; fosters and encourages participation of minority and disadvantaged businesses in technological innovation; and increases the commercial application of DoD supported research and development results.*

Technological innovation is not a government issue, let alone a defense issue. The government should never interfere in the natural progression of the private sector. Eliminate and save $8 Million.

The Joint Staff (TJS)

Joint Experimentation

> *JE projects and activities develop and examine potential solutions for combatant command operational needs through targeted Doctrine, Organizational, Training, Material, Leadership and Education, Personnel, Facilities, and Policy (DOTMLPF-P) improvements. JE tackles joint capability issues demanding sophisticated analysis, innovative design and complex experimentation leading to solutions. JE addresses topics that would prove difficult for individual combatant commands and Services to capture in the context of their immediate operational and force generation responsibilities.*

Ongoing force improvement is necessary and proper to the military, to keep up with our enemies. However, it is not necessary to do so at such a rate. Cut by half, and save $11 Million.

Joint Systems Integration

> *The Joint Systems Integration program element provides mission funding for the Joint System Integration Center (JSIC) to conduct interoperability assessments, and develop solutions/recommendations to improve integration of Service, Defense Agency, and coalition systems. JSIC promotes Service/Defense Agency C2 capability integration, and conducts technical, operational, and DOTMLPF assessments of Command and Control (C2) and*

Command, Control, Computer, Communication, Intelligence, Surveillance and Reconnaissance (C4ISR) capabilities.

JSI is redundant to DISA initiatives; eliminate and save $3 Million.

Joint FIRES Integration and Interoperability Team

Employ scientific methods to research, investigate, test, assess, and evaluate current and emergent Joint command and control (C2) information systems and associated procedures. These activities measure capabilities and limitations, identify shortfalls and root cause, recommend and verify solutions, and validate joint capabilities. The resultant empirical outcomes influence Joint Capability development in areas such as Joint Tactics, Techniques and Procedures; integration of capabilities; and digital interoperability.

The government is not the research wing of a military supplier. The mere emergence of new technologies is not a reason to evaluate, assess, or adopt them; if a specific need comes up, then go look for a technology that solves that problem. Interoperability aspects are redundant to DISA initiatives. Eliminate and save $7 Million.

Joint Integrated Air and Missile Defense Organization (JIAMDO)

The Joint Integrated Air and Missile Defense Organization (JIAMDO) is the organization within the Department of Defense (DOD) chartered to plan, coordinate, and oversee Joint Air and Missile Defense (AMD) requirements, joint operational concepts, and operational architectures. As part of the CJCS staff, JIAMDO supports the Chairman in meeting his Title 10 responsibilities as they relate to air and missile defense issues.

Necessary and proper to conduct military operations across the various forces. Keep as is ($56 Million) and make this the *only* central planning and execution platform.

Joint Staff Analytical Support

The Joint Staff Analytical Support (JSAS) family of programs provides defense analytical support capabilities for the CJCS and COCOMs. JSAS encompasses the developmental tools and infrastructure required to conduct analyses and formulate the results to best assist the Chairman in fulfilling his statutory responsibilities. Key deliverables provided by JSAS include wide-ranging force structure assessments, course of action development for the Joint Force environment, analyses and studies to aid in decision-making, and other analysis efforts to implement timely, low-cost initiatives.

JSAS is Red Team and similar activities, which is actually just low-level security exercises, which in turn are rarely effective at identifying security holes due to their policies. Eliminate. No money is saved as no funding is provided in FY2013.

Support to Information Operations Capability

The IO Range provides a secure, flexible, and seamless environment for the Military Services and Joint warfighters to test, train, develop tactics, and exercise selected IO/Cyber capabilities. The basis of the functional structure of the IO Range is the integration of existing ranges, laboratories, information warfare centers, and other Government facilities that currently support IO/Cyber test, training, exercise, and experimentation events. Capabilities at the selected sites are securely connected and integrated into the IO Range.

The military is not responsible for cyber capabilities. Government agencies and private organizations and individuals are responsible for handling their own network security issues. Information Warfare, consisting mostly of duplicate functionality and propaganda, is not a proper use of military funding. Eliminate and save $8 Million.

Joint Integration and Interoperability

The JI&I Program provide resources for a wide range of efforts to define, refine, and deploy integrated joint capabilities. JI&I-funded endeavors aim to improve US and coalition capabilities to conduct coordinated operations. Necessarily, JI&I-funded projects most frequently address Command & Control (C2) and Command, Control, Communications, Computers, Intelligence, Surveillance, and Reconnaissance (C4ISR) - the capstone capabilities for integrating disparate elements of military force for joint and coalition operations.

TJS JI&I is redundant to TJS JSI and DISA initiatives. Eliminate and save $5 Million.

Planning and Decision Aid System (PDAS)

Planning and Decision Aid System (PDAS) is a classified automated information system protected program under Secretary of Defense (SecDef). PDAS supports the planning and execution of Integrated Joint Special Technical Operations.

PDAS is redundant to SIPRNET and JIAMDO. Eliminate and save $4 Million.

Command, Control, Communications, Computers, and Intelligence for the Warrior (C4IFTW)

The Command, Control, Communications, Computers, and Intelligence for the Warrior (C4IFTW) includes all owned and leased communications and computing systems and services, software (including applications), data, security services, and other associated services to support all DOD, National

Security, and related Intelligence Community missions and functions (strategic, operational, tactical and business).

Necessary and proper; reduce by standard 25%. No funding is provided for 2013, so no savings apply.

Management Headquarters

Management Headquarters provides the day-to-day financial resources necessary to support TJS operations. Across the Joint Staff, Management Headquarters supports various efforts including network infrastructure, civilian pay accounts, supplies, travel, training, portfolio management, business process reviews, and transformation initiatives.

This financial overhead is necessary to distribute the money across TJS, but some aspects of it are not. Eliminate transformation initiatives and cut by half, thus saving $2 million.

Special Operations Command (SOCOM)

Special Operations Technology Development

This program element enables USSOCOM to conduct studies and develop laboratory prototypes for applied research and advanced technology development, as well as leverage other organizations' technology projects that may not otherwise be affordable within MFP-11. Applying small incremental amounts of investments to DoD, other government agencies, and commercial organizations allows USSOCOM to influence the direction of technology development or the schedule against which it is being pursued, and to acquire emerging technologies for Special Operations Forces.

The government has no authority to conduct its own scientific research or develop technology; outsource this segment through DCMA and move its financial aspect accordingly. Given our newly homeland-centric defense posture, there will be a reduced need for the Special Forces. However, we must keep them trained and equipped for when that day comes. Reduce by standard 25% and save $7 Million.

Special Operations Advanced Technology Development

This program element conducts rapid prototyping and Advanced Technology Demonstrations (ATDs). ATDs provide a means for demonstrating and evaluating the utility of emerging/advanced technologies in as realistic an operational environment as possible by Special Operations Forces (SOF) users. Evaluation results are included in a transition package, which assists in the initiation of or insertion into an acquisition program. The program element also addresses projects that are a result of unique joint special mission or area-

specific needs for which a few-of-a-kind prototypes must be developed on a rapid response basis, or are of sufficient time sensitivity to accelerate the prototyping effort of a normal acquisition program in any phase.

The government has no authority to conduct its own scientific research or develop technology; outsource this segment through DCMA and move its financial aspect accordingly. Given our newly homeland-centric defense posture, there will be a reduced need for the Special Forces. SOATD is redundant to Special Operations Technology Development; merge its functions and budget into there and reduce by standard 25%, saving $11 Million.

Aviation Engineering Analysis

This program element provides rapid response capability for the investigation, evaluation, and demonstration of technologies for Special Operations Forces (SOF) - unique aviation requirements. Timely application of SOF-unique technology is critical and necessary to meet requirements in such areas as: sensor integration; enhanced situational awareness; near-real-time intelligence to include data fusion, threat detection and avoidance; electronic support measures for threat geo-location and specific emitter identification; navigation; target detection; and future SOF aircraft requirements.

In the military, if you see a deficiency in a product, service, or process, you tell your supervisor and upchannel it through the chain of command. Eventually it gets high enough that someone makes a decision and fixes it. Eliminate and save $861K.

SOF Information and Broadcast Systems Advanced Technology

This Program Element (PE) conducts rapid prototyping, advanced technology demonstrations, and advanced concept technology demonstrations of information and broadcast systems technology. Includes planning, analyzing, evaluating, and production information systems capabilities and distribution/dissemination broadcast systems capabilities. It provides a means for demonstrating and evaluating the utility of emerging/advanced technologies in as realistic an operational environment as possible by Special Operations Forces (SOF) users. This PE integrates efforts with each other and conducts technology demonstrations in conjunction with joint experiments and other assessment events.

The government is not the research wing of a weapons company. Let them do their own research, and just buy through DCMA the products that are best suited to the operations required. Vendors should pay for their own product demonstrations. Eliminate and save $5 Million.

Special Operations for Contingencies

> *This program element develops and deploys special capabilities to perform intelligence, surveillance, and reconnaissance for deployed Special Operations Forces (SOF) using non-traditional means. It provides a mechanism for SOF user combat evaluation of emerging sensor technologies. Special Applications for Contingencies (SAFC) applies focused Research & Development (R&D) for relatively low cost solutions to provide remotely controlled system emplacement and data exfiltration from denied areas.*

Actual Special Forces operations in times of immediate need; necessary and proper. Having said that, our new proposed homeland-centric defense posture, combined with our "Mind our own business" foreign policy, should greatly reduce the need therefor. Per justification previously provided, eliminate the Research and Development aspects hereof. Reduce the remainder by standard 25%; $4.3 Million saved.

Distributed Common Ground/Surface Systems

> *This program element provides for the identification, development, and testing of the Distributed Common Ground/Surface System Special Operations Forces (DCGSSOF). The mission tailored infrastructure interconnects the warfighter and sensor data to find and fix enemy combatants and/or terrorists. The DCGS-SOF program is a network-enabled, interoperable construct allowing continual, unimpeded sharing of intelligence data, information and services within SOF and between the Services, other national intelligence agencies, combatant commands and Multi-National partners in support of a Joint Task Force.*

Necessary and proper; reduce by standard 25% and save $1.8 Million.

MQ-1 Predator A UAV

> *This program element identifies, develops, integrates, and tests Special Operations Forces (SOF) - unique mission kits on the MQ-1 Unmanned Aerial Vehicle (UAV) as a component of the Medium Altitude Long Endurance Tactical Program. USSOCOM is designated as the DoD lead for planning, synchronizing, and as directed, executing Overseas Contingency Operations against terrorist networks.*

This is not to buy an actual Predator drone; this outlay is to continue existing development, testing, and integration between the drones and their battlefield ground control units. The outlay specifies no end date other than "Continuing", which tells me it is a project they do not intend to end. The drones should be developed, tested, and integrated once and be done. Eliminate and save $1.4 Million.

MQ-9 UAV

> *This program element identifies, develops, integrates, and tests Special Operations Forces (SOF) - unique mission kits on the MQ-9 Unmanned Aerial Vehicle as a component of the Medium Altitude Long Endurance Tactical program. USSOCOM is designated as the DoD lead for planning, synchronizing, and as directed, executing Overseas Contingency Operations against terrorist networks. USSOCOM requires the capability to find, fix, finish, exploit, and analyze time-sensitive high-value targets.*

This is not to buy an actual Predator drone; this outlay is to continue existing development, testing, and integration between the drones and their battlefield ground control units. The outlay specifies no end date other than "Continuing", which tells me it is a project they do not intend to end. The drones should be developed, tested, and integrated once and be done. Eliminate and save $3 Million.

RQ-11 UAV

> *This program element identifies, investigates, develops, integrates, and tests Special Operations Forces (SOF) payload requirements and spiral development efforts for SUAS capabilities for standalone employment from world-wide ground locations, from manned/unmanned aircraft, or from maritime craft.*

No funding is provided for 2013, so it looks as if the development, integration, and testing is complete. In combination with the points described in other UAVs above, eliminate.

RQ-7 UAV

> *This program element identifies, develops, integrates, and tests Special Operations Forces (SOF) - Unique Mission Kits for Groups 1 – 3 Unmanned Aircraft Systems (UAS). These mission kits enable SOF to meet continually evolving mission requirements. As the supported combatant command, USSOCOM has been designated as the DoD lead for planning, synchronizing, and as directed, executing Overseas Contingency Operations.*

No funding is provided for 2013, so it looks as if the development, integration, and testing is complete. In combination with the points described in other UAVs above, eliminate.

Small Business Innovative Research

> *This program element consists of a highly competitive three-phase award system that provides qualified small business concerns with the opportunity to propose high quality innovative ideas that meet specific research and development needs of USSOCOM. Small Business Innovative Research (SBIR) is a result of the Small Business Development Act of 1992.*

Technological innovation is not a government issue, let alone a defense issue. The government should never interfere in the natural progression of the private sector. No funding is provided for 2013; eliminate.

Special Operations Aviation Systems Advanced Development
> *This program element provides for the development, demonstration, and integration of current and maturing technologies for Special Operations Forces (SOF)- unique aviation requirements. Timely application of SOF-unique technology is critical and necessary to meet requirements in such areas as: SOF specific avionics; low probability of intercept/low probability of detection, terrain following/terrain avoidance radar; Precision Strike Package for MC-130W Multi-Mission Modification,*

The government is not the research wing of a weapons company. Let them do their own research, and just buy through DCMA the products that are best suited to the operations required. Vendors should pay for their own product demonstrations.

By eliminating our overseas posture, there will be plenty of AC-130s available to conduct the attack and reconnaissance functions of the MC-130W; and plenty of ready AC-130Hs. The rest of these are tools that Special Forces already have. Eliminate and save $97 Million.

Special Forces Tactical Systems Development
> *This program element provides for development, testing, and integration of specialized automation equipment to meet the unique requirements of Special Operations Forces (SOF). Specialized automation equipment will permit small, highly trained forces to conduct required operations across the entire spectrum of conflict. These operations are generally conducted in harsh environments, for unspecified periods and in locations requiring small unit autonomy.*

The government is not the research wing of a weapons company. Let them do their own research, and just buy through DCMA the products that are best suited to the operations required. Vendors should pay for their own product demonstrations. Special Forces have been able to perform these duties with the gear available today; eliminate, save $821K.

Special Operations Intelligence Systems Development
> *This program element provides for the identification, development, and testing of Special Operations Forces (SOF) intelligence equipment to identify and eliminate deficiencies in providing timely intelligence to deployed forces. Sub-projects address the primary areas of intelligence dissemination, sensor systems, integrated threat warning to SOF mission platforms, and tactical exploitation of national system capabilities. USSOCOM has developed an*

overall strategy to ensure that Command, Control, Communications, Computers, and Intelligence (C4I) systems continue to provide SOF with the required capabilities into the 21st century.

The government is not the research wing of a weapons and equipment company. Let them do their own research, and just buy through DCMA the products that are best suited to the operations required. Vendors should pay for their own product demonstrations. Redundant to SOF IBSAT, SOTD, SOATD, and DARPA. Special Forces have been able to perform these duties with the gear available today; eliminate, save $26 Million.

Special Operations CV-22 Development

The CV-22 is a Special Operations Forces (SOF) variant of the V-22 vertical medium lift, multi-mission aircraft. The CV-22 will provide long range, high speed, infiltration, exfiltration, and resupply to Special Forces teams in hostile, denied, and politically sensitive areas. This is a capability not currently provided by existing aircraft.

The government is not the research wing of an aircraft manufacturer. Let them do their own research, and just buy through DCMA the products that are best suited to the operations required. Vendors should pay for their own product demonstrations. Eliminate and save $2 Million.

Mission Training and Preparation Systems (MTPS)

This program element funds the definition, design, development, prototyping, integration, and testing of Mission Training and Preparation Systems (MTPS) to support training, avoid obsolescence, and maintain simulator concurrency with weapon systems' configurations; support mission planning and rehearsal systems enhancements required to meet Special Operations Forces (SOF)-unique mission requirements and correct deficiencies identified in previous testing; and support mission planning and rehearsal capabilities in current MTPS.

The government is not the research wing of a weapons simulator manufacturer. Let them do their own research, and just buy through DCMA the products that are best suited to the operations required. Vendors should pay for their own product demonstrations. Eliminate and save $10 Million.

AC/MC-130J

The AC/MC-130J program element funds core SOF-unique modifications to replace aging MC-130E Combat Talon I, MC-130P Combat Shadow, and AC-130H Spectre airframes. The 8 AC-130H Spectre airframes will be replaced with MC-130J aircraft modified with the Precision Strike Package (PSP) to achieve the AC-130J configuration. These platforms perform clandestine or low visibility, single- or multi-ship low-level missions intruding politically-sensitive or hostile territories; provide air refueling for special operations helicopters and CV-22 aircraft; airdrop of leaflets, small special operations teams, resupply bundles and combat rubber raiding craft; [...]

Maintenance and retrofit of aging aircraft is part of a regularly balanced diet. There will be plenty of parts and other aircraft available with the newly homeland-centric foreign policy. Wait until we can't use them anymore, and then buy a new fleet all at once. Eliminate and save $20 Million.

SOF Communications Equipment and Electronics Systems

This program element provides for communication systems to meet emergent requirements to support Special Operations Forces (SOF). The SOF mission mandates that SOF systems remain technologically superior to any threat to provide a maximum degree of survivability. SOF units require communications equipment that improves their warfighting capability without degrading their mobility. Therefore, SOF Communications Equipment and Electronics is a continuing effort to develop smaller, lighter, more efficient and more robust SOF Command, Control, Communications, and Computer (C4) capabilities.

Merely being "technologically superior" is insufficient justification for more military spending. There's nothing wrong with the equipment they're using now. Eliminate and save $2 Million.

SOF Tactical Radio Systems

This program element is for development of all Special Operations Forces (SOF) tactical radio programs. The SOF mission mandates that SOF systems remain technologically superior to any threat to provide a maximum degree of survivability. SOF units require radio communication equipment that improves their warfighting capability without degrading their mobility. United States Special Operations Command (USSOCOM) has developed an overall strategy to ensure that Tactical Radio Systems continue to provide SOF with the required capabilities throughout the 21st century.

Merely being "technologically superior" is insufficient justification for more military spending. There's nothing wrong with the equipment they're using now. Eliminate and save $3 Million.

SOF Weapons Systems

This program element provides for development, testing, and integration of specialized weapon systems and weapon accessories to meet the unique requirements of Special Operations Forces (SOF). This specialized equipment will permit small, highly trained forces to conduct required operations across the entire spectrum of conflict. These operations are generally conducted in harsh environments, for unspecified periods and in locations requiring small unit autonomy.

The government is not the research wing of a weapons manufacturer. Let them do their own research, and just buy through DCMA the products that are best suited to the operations required. Vendors should pay for their own product demonstrations. Eliminate and save $1.5 Million.

Soldier Protection and Survival Systems

This program element provides for development, testing, and integration of specialized equipment to meet the unique soldier protection and survival requirements of Special Operations Forces (SOF). Specialized equipment will improve survivability and mobility of SOF while conducting varied missions. These missions are generally conducted in harsh environments, for unspecified periods, and in locations requiring small unit autonomy.

The government is not the research wing of an equipment manufacturer. Let them do their own research, and just buy through DCMA the products that are best suited to the operations required. Vendors should pay for their own product demonstrations. Eliminate and save $1.5 Million. Repeal the NDAA.

SOF Visual Augmentation, Lasers, and Sensor Systems

This program element provides for development, testing, and integration of specialized visual augmentation, laser and sensor systems equipment to meet the unique requirements of Special Operations Forces (SOF). Specialized equipment will permit small, highly trained forces to conduct required operations across the entire spectrum of conflict.

The government is not the research wing of an equipment manufacturer. Let them do their own research, and just buy through DCMA the products that are best suited to the operations required. Vendors should pay for their own product demonstrations. Eliminate and save $4.5 Million.

SOF Tactical Vehicles

This program element provides for the development and testing of a variety of spiral upgrades to Special Operations Vehicles and ancillary equipment. The current SOF tactical vehicles include: All Terrain Vehicles and Lightweight Tactical All Terrain Vehicles (Individual), Light Mobility Vehicles (Light), Ground Mobility Vehicles (Medium), Non-Standard Commercial Vehicles (Commercial) for use in tactical missions, and Mine Resistant Ambush Protected Vehicles (Heavy).

Vehicles are not a subscription service; if you stop buying them, then you still have the ones you had. The government is not the research wing of an equipment manufacturer. Let them do their own research, and just buy through DCMA the products that are best suited to the operations required. Eliminate and save $11 Million.

SOF Munitions

This program element provides for the advanced engineering operational system development and qualification efforts related to Special Operations Forces peculiar munitions and equipment. Funding supports development of IM technology and evaluation, in accordance with statutory requirement set forth in U.S. Code, Title 10, Chapter 141, Section 2389 (December 2001).

The government is not the research wing of a weapons manufacturer. Let them do their own research, and just buy through DCMA the products that are best suited to the operations required. Eliminate and save $1.5 Million.

SOF Rotary Wing Aviation

This program element develops SOF-unique modifications and upgrades to SOF rotary wing aircraft that operate in increasingly hostile environments. Rotary wing aircraft supported by this project include: MH-60L/M, MH-47G, and A/MH-6M. These aircraft provide aviation support to Special Operations Forces (SOF) in worldwide contingency operations and low-intensity conflicts. They must be capable of rapid deployment; undetected penetration of hostile areas; and operating at extended ranges under adverse weather conditions to infiltrate, provide logistics for, reinforce, and extract SOF.

With the new homeland-centric defense posture, there will be plenty of helicopters available for SOF's needs. Eliminate and save $24 Million.

SOF Underwater Systems

This program element provides for engineering and manufacturing development and operational systems development of small combat underwater submersibles and underwater support systems and equipment. This program element also provides for pre-acquisition activities (material solutions analysis, advanced component development and prototypes) to respond to emergent requirements. These submersibles, systems, and equipment are used by Special Operations Forces (SOF) in the conduct of infiltration/extraction, hydrographic/inland reconnaissance, beach obstacle clearance, underwater ship attack, and other missions.

SOF already has underwater systems. The government is not the research wing of an equipment manufacturer. Let them do their own research, and just buy through DCMA the products that are best suited to the operations required. Eliminate and save $26.4 Million.

SOF Surface Craft

> *This program element provides for engineering & manufacturing development and operational systems development of light, medium, and heavy surface combatant craft and selected items of specialized equipment to meet the unique requirements of Special Operations Forces (SOF). This program element also provides for pre-acquisition activities (material solutions analysis, advanced component development & prototypes) to quickly respond to new requirements for surface craft and equipment, such as the light and heavy combatant crafts that are currently being studied in the Joint Capabilities Integration and Development System process.*

SOF already has light, medium, and heavy surface combatant craft and specialized equipment. The government is not the research wing of an equipment manufacturer. Let them do their own research, and just buy through DCMA the products that are best suited to the operations required. Eliminate and save $9 Million.

Military Information Support Operations

> *Beginning in FY2012, Program Element 1160488BB was renamed Military Information Support Operations (MISO). Former name was SOF PSYOP. The Military Information Support Operations (MISO) program element provides for the development, test and integration of MISO equipment. MISO are planned operations to convey selected information and indicators to foreign audiences to influence their emotions, motives, objective reasoning, and ultimately, the behavior of foreign governments, organizations, groups, and individuals.*

SOF already has MISO equipment. The government is not the research wing of an equipment manufacturer. Let them do their own research, and just buy through DCMA the products that are best suited to the operations required. Eliminate and save $3 Million.

Washington Headquarters Service (WHS)

IT Software Development Initiatives

> *The Washington Headquarters Services (WHS) Information Technology (IT) program provides ongoing research, test, development, and enhancement initiatives for the Office of the Secretary of Defense (OSD), OSD Principal Staff Assistants, and WHS Directorates. Ongoing initiatives include enterprise storage testing, enterprise performance and productivity analysis, enterprise/business applications development and enhancements, operational support enhancements, and information assurance testing and development.*

In the interest of government transparency, I give this one some leeway and say this is vaguely necessary and proper to support other authorized functions within the DoD, as it's only enough to support one or two employees. Keep as is ($104K)

Operational Test and Evaluation

DOT&E was created by Congress in 1983. The Director is responsible under Title 10 for policy and procedures for all aspects of Operational Test and Evaluation (OT&E) within the Department of Defense (DoD). Particular focus is given to OT&E that supports major weapon system production decisions for acquisition programs included on the Office of Secretary of Defense Test and Evaluation Oversight List that is prepared and approved annually.

There needs to be exactly one department-wide plan to test and evaluate new weapons and equipment. For the moment, I'm willing to let the military branches have their own, but there don't need to be so many at the top level. One should do the trick. Merge into TJS Joint Experimentation and eliminate; $72.5 Billion saved (not including the following sub-bullet-points).

Live Fire Test and Evaluation

This Program Element consists of three programs: Live Fire Test and Evaluation, Joint Aircraft Survivability Program (JASP) and Joint Technical Coordinating Group for Munitions Effectiveness (JTCG/ME). Starting in FY 2013 the JASP and JTCG/ME programs are realigned from the Operational Test Activities and Analyses program (0605814OTE) to the Live Fire Test and Evaluation program element (0605131OTE).

There needs to be exactly one department-wide plan to test and evaluate new weapons and equipment. For the moment, I'm willing to let the military branches have their own, but there don't need to be so many at the top level. One should do the trick. Merge into TJS Joint Experimentation and eliminate; $49.2 Billion saved.

Operational Test Activities and Analyses

The Test and Evaluation programs are continuing efforts that provide management and oversight of test and evaluation functions and expertise to the Department of Defense (DoD). The T&E programs consist of five activities: Joint Test and Evaluation (JT&E); Threat Systems (TS); Center for Countermeasures (CCM); Joint Technical Coordinating Group for Munitions Effectiveness (JTCG/ME); and Joint Aircraft Survivability Program (JASP). Starting in FY 2013 the JTCG/ME and JASP programs are realigned from the Operational Test Activities and Analyses program element (0605814OTE) to the Live Fire Test and Evaluation program element (0605131OTE). Since the JTCG/ME and JASP programs focus on the survivability of currently fielded systems the two programs are more appropriately funded within the Live Fire Test and Evaluation program element.

Given the magnitude of purchases of the DoD, the vendors would almost certainly provide free demonstrations out of their own self-interest. Have the deciding generals present at the demonstrations, give them the relevant fact sheets and documentation, and let them make the call as to whether to make the purchase. If the relevant generals and admirals can't be mustered to attend all such demonstrations, then the number of potential programs is too high. Eliminate and save $63.6 Billion.

Defense Information Systems Agency (DISA)

Advanced IT Services Joint Program Office (AITS-JPO)

> The Advanced IT Services Joint Program Office (AITS-JPO) identifies and integrates new, mature commercial Information Technology (IT) and advanced operational concepts into net-centric battlespace capabilities to: access and exchange critical information; exploit opportunities to enhance current force capabilities; and project future force IT requirements.

AITS-JPO performs functions which have already been done within the DOD. Thus, this program adds redundancy at unnecessary expense. Eliminate; $26 Million saved.

Global Combat Support System

> The Global Combat Support System-Joint (GCSS-J) is an information technology (IT) application that continues to transition to a service oriented architecture to deliver asset visibility to the joint logistician (i.e., essential capabilities, functions, activities, and tasks necessary to sustain all elements of operating forces in theater at all levels), and facilitates information interoperability across and between Combat Support and Command and Control functions. In conjunction with other Global Information Grid elements including Global Command and Control System-Joint (GCCS-J), Computing Services, and Combatant Commands/Services/Agencies information architectures, GCSS-J will provide the IT capabilities required to move and sustain joint forces throughout the spectrum of military operations.

$20 Million per year to rewrite a computer program that was already working just fine. Eliminate; $20 Million saved.

C4I Interoperability

> JITC is the sole interoperability certifier for all Information Technology/National Security Systems (IT/NSS) for DoD. Additional core missions include testing of DoD terrestrial, space, and tactical communications capabilities, supporting warfighters on technical IT/NSS issues, and assisting Combatant Command to Coalition partner interoperability. JITC, as the only Joint Operational Test Agency (OTA), plans and conducts operational tests and

evaluations (OT&E) for DISA, the National Security Agency (NSA), Defense Intelligence Agency (DIA), military services, and other DoD agencies.

This sounds vaguely important, so I'll give them the benefit of the doubt on the Necessary and Proper issue. Reduce by the standard 25%; save $18 Million.

Joint/Allied Coalition Information Sharing

Through the Combined Enterprise Regional Information Exchange System (CENTRIXS) and Pegasus (formally GRIFFIN), the Multinational Information Sharing (MNIS) Program enables secure sharing of operational and intelligence information and enhances collaboration amongst United States forces, their most trusted allies and additional multinational partners in the ongoing war. This effort also increases overall combat effectiveness by leveraging capabilities and information from all partners and reducing the possibility of fratricide.

Necessary and proper; reduce by standard 25%, save $1.6 Million.

National Military Command System-Wide Support

The National Military Command System (NMCS), operated by the Chairman of the Joint Chiefs of Staff, provides the President, Secretary of Defense, and other national senior leaders the ability to maintain situational and operational awareness and command and control of military forces in all crisis and/or national emergency contingencies.

Necessary and proper. Leave it as is ($499K).

Defense Information Infrastructure Engineering and Integration

The Global Information Grid (GIG) Enterprise Wide Systems Engineering (EWSE) project resolves near term (1 to 3 years) high-priority technical issues defined by Department of Defense Chief Information Officer (DOD CIO) and DISA, that impact operational capabilities affecting GIG end-to-end (E2E) interoperability and performance.

By eliminating our overseas posture, we reduce the need for our information grid to be global. Reduce by 75%; save $11 Million.

Long-Haul Communications – DCS

The Defense Information Systems Network (DISN) is the Department of Defense (DoD) consolidated worldwide telecommunications capability that provides secure, end-to-end information transport for DoD operations. It also provides the warfighter and the Combatant Commands (COCOMs) with robust Command, Control, Communications, Computing, and Intelligence (C4I) infrastructure to support DoD netcentric missions and business requirements. The Defense Red Switch Network (DRSN) is a DoD Secure Voice, Command and

Control Network that is controlled and directed by the Joint Staff and the
Office of the Secretary of Defense.

The DOD only requires one worldwide telecommunications network; I don't care which one. I will eliminate this one for budgetary purposes, assuming the selected one would be approximately the same cost. Let's take the NMCS and GIG budgets as left, described earlier; and eliminate DCS. Save $26 Million.

Minimum Essential Emergency Communications Network

Minimum Essential Emergency Communications Network (MEECN) provides the Nuclear Command, Control, and Communications (NC3) engineer with plans and procedures; systems analysis; operational assessments; systems engineering; and development of concepts of operation and architectures. The NC3 System provides connectivity from the President and the Secretary of Defense through the National Military Command System (NMCS) to nuclear execution forces integral to fighting a "homeland-to-homeland," as well as theater nuclear war. MEECN includes the Emergency Action Message (EAM) dissemination systems and those systems used for integrated Tactical Warning/Attack Assessment (TW/AA), presidential decision-making conferencing, force report back, re-targeting, force management, and requests for permission to use nuclear weapons.

Necessary and proper; keep as is, but reduce by half. Most of these functions can be merged into the redundant NMCS, GIG, and DCS. Save $6.5 Million.

Information Systems Security Program

The Community Data Center (CDC) provides research, designs, builds, tests, demonstrates, and evaluates an innovative system to analyze a significant portion of the DoD's and associated network traffic for anomalous network behavior using unique techniques and processes. This unique capability, that addresses the massive data overload associated with analyzing network traffic and raw data, significantly improves the ability of the DoD to operate, defend, and protect its networks.

The DOD does not need a brand-new system redundant to preexisting functionality. Eliminate and save $4.5 Million.

Global Command and Control System

Based on the termination of the Net Enabled Command Capability (NECC) Program and the renewed focus on the existing Global Command and Control System – Joint (GCCS-J), this submission reflects the shift in the GCCS-J program from funding only the GCCS-J Program Management Office (PMO) activities to sustaining a portfolio of Joint command and control (C2) activities within DISA in support of the overall Department. These Joint C2 activities include GCCS-J,

Joint Planning and Execution Services (JPES), and the support to the development and sustainment of the Joint C2 architecture.

GCCS performs mission-essential combat coordination, and I haven't found any systems which this is redundant with. Necessary and proper; keep but reduce by standard 25%. Save $9 Million.

Defense Spectrum Organization

Electromagnetic Spectrum Management enables information dominance through effective spectrum operations. In direct support of Combatant Commanders, Assistant Secretary of Defense for Networks and Information Integration (ASD/NII), Military Services, and Defense Agencies, the Defense Spectrum Organization (DSO), a component of DISA, provides a full array of electromagnetic spectrum services and capabilities, ranging from short notice on-the-ground operational support at the forward edge, to long range planning in pursuit of national strategic objectives.

The electromagnetic spectrum is not the government's to control. Eliminate; save $24.3 Million.

Net-Centric Enterprise Services

The Program Executive Office (PEO) for Global Information Grid (GIG) Enterprise Services (GES) provides a portfolio of enterprise level services that enable communities of interest and mission applications to make their data and services visible, accessible, and understandable to other anticipated and unanticipated users. The PEO GES portfolio supports 100 percent of the active duty military and Government civilians; 258 thousand embedded contract personnel; 75 percent of the active Guard and Reserve; and 25 percent of the Guard and Reserve users. This meets the Department's requirement to support 2.5 million users on the Non-Classified Internet Protocol Router Network (NIPRNet) and 300 thousand users on the Secret Internet Protocol Router Network (SIPRNet).

I don't know about proper, but GIG is certainly necessary, based on the descriptions of other DISA projects. Leave as is ($3 Million).

Teleport Program

The Department of Defense (DoD) Teleport system is a Satellite Communications (SATCOM) gateway that links the deployed warfighter to the sustaining base. It provides high-throughput, multi-band, and multi-media telecommunications services for deployed forces. The system provides centralized integration capabilities, contingency capacity, and the necessary interfaces to access the Defense Information System Network (DISN) in a seamless, interoperable, and economical manner.

Necessary and proper; however, given our eliminated overseas posture and the end of proactive warmongering, less so. **Increase** from $6.05 Million to $10 Million, and make this the ONLY communications system for deployed personnel.

Cybersecurity Initiative

The budget lists the details of CI as classified. However, I was able to obtain a description from the White House website:

> The activities under way to implement the recommendations of the Cyberspace Policy Review build on the Comprehensive National Cybersecurity Initiative (CNCI) launched by President George W. Bush in National Security Presidential Directive 54/Homeland Security Presidential Directive 23 (NSPD-54/ HSPD-23) in January 2008. President Obama determined that the CNCI and its associated activities should evolve to become key elements of a broader, updated national U.S. cybersecurity strategy.

The government's departments and the private sector should implement their own security systems. While security breaches of various kinds can be considered attacks, they are not a military issue. Eliminate and save $4.2 Million.

Distributed Common Ground/Surface Systems

> DCGS Programs of Record (PoRs) and Coalition partners use the DDTE network to integrate architecture, standards, and capabilities for implementation of the DCGS Integration Backbone (DIB) and supports the migration to net-centricity [...] Net-enabled enterprise testing is designed to more closely simulate the complexities of an actual combat environment. JITC engineered the DDTE network to support the assessment of the DCGS Enterprise under the DCGS Governance.

This is integration overhead associated with other systems. The DOD has already created another program for the purpose of integrating these systems together: The Internet. Eliminate, and save $3.2 Million.

Family Housing[25]

> The FY 2013 Family Housing Operation and Maintenance, Defense-Wide request is $6,083,000 (excludes leasing costs, which will be addressed separately). The Operation and Maintenance includes maintenance and repair of government-owned housing units and associated real property; utility

---

[25]http://comptroller.defense.gov/defbudget/fy2013/budget_justification/pdfs/04_Family_Housing /PB13_Family_Housing_DW.pdf

services; repair, replacement, transportation and handling of furniture and furnishings; refuse collection and disposal services; management services; and other miscellaneous support. Furnishings support for members of the Defense Attaché System are also included.

Giving our military personnel a place to stay is necessary and proper for the operation of the military. While I would prefer they live off base when possible, their pay is increased to make up the difference, so it makes negligible difference from a budgetary perspective.

By eliminating our overseas posture and bringing our troops back home, we will probably fill our U.S. bases to capacity. Unfortunately, due to the grossly increased size of the military over the past decade, we will likely still need to construct new facilities to house them. Further, existing and authorized facilities do require maintenance and operation. Therefore I'm calling this necessary and proper for the first year.

Unfortunately, we have hundreds of thousands of troops afloat, deployed, or stationed overseas to contend with; all of which I propose bringing back home. Based on numbers from 2010, the U.S. has around 1,429,367 military personnel (plus a roughly equivalent number of contractors and other civilians), 1,137,716 of whom are in the United States and its territories. A standard reduction of 25% (357,341) would be 1,072,026 people. Add our deployed people to the larger number (202,880) and we really have around 494,531 people overseas.

Bases have enough room for the people they have deployed, as they're technically stationed at their home base. Therefore, we need enough space for (1,429,367 * .75 = 1,072,026) total personnel. Since we have enough space for all domestic personnel plus the deployed numbers, real capacity is at least 1,137,716, assuming all bases are filled to capacity.

Therefore, the number of personnel who would be stationed at our U.S. bases (1,072,026) is less than the capacity thereof (1,137,716), and no new housing construction is necessary. I therefore recommend subtracting the new construction, improvements, and planning and design parts from the Housing budget.

The military component of the FY2013 Housing Budget has no outlays for these items ($0). Therefore, a standard 25% cut across the board saves us $14 Billion.

I was surprised to find that we are providing such housing for members of the NSA, DIA, and DLA; but "across the board" is "across the board".

DoD Base Realignment and Closure (BRAC)[26]

Closing a base should not be a complicated process. Decide where to send the people, equipment, documents, files, etc; and send them there. Once the base is devoid of these items, hand it over to the state or other country, and wash our hands of it.

The realignment half is more involved, as it involves logistics, deciding what functions to put on what bases, and balancing personnel more precisely. Therefore I propose BRAC is necessary and proper and should remain, but only for a period of one year. We should identify how we want our bases configured, configure them that way, and end the project once and for all.

Prior-Round BRAC

> The Defense Secretary's Commission on Base Realignment and Closures was chartered on May 3, 1988 to recommend military installations within the United States, its commonwealths, territories, and possessions for realignment and closure. The Congress and the President subsequently endorsed this approach through legislation that removed some of the previous impediments to successful base closure actions. The Defense Authorization Amendments and Base Closure and Realignment Act, Public Law 100-526, as enacted October 24, 1988, provides the basis for implementing the recommendations of the 1988 Commission.

Restoring and taking care of the environment is not a federal issue, let alone an ongoing one 25 years later. Give the land back to the states and be done with it. Eliminate and save $349.4 Million.

BRAC Parts I-IV Continuing Environmental and Caretaker Costs

This program level is for ongoing projects; bases which haven't been closed yet. These are necessary and proper, so they can continue for the time being.

Army

Eliminate Environmental component, save $4.4 Million.

Navy

Eliminate Environmental component, save $130 Million.

Air Force

Eliminate Environmental component, save $113 Million.

---

[26]http://comptroller.defense.gov/defbudget/fy2013/budget_justification/pdfs/05_BRAC/BRAC_Exe c_Sum_Book_FY13.pdf

Eliminate Environmental component, save $318 Million.

BRAC 2005

> *The FY 2013 budget request includes $126.7 million of new budget authority for environmental restoration and caretaker costs for facilities closed under the recommendations from the BRAC 2005 Commission. The Department has prepared separate budget justification books to address BRAC 2005 funding requirements.*

Having previously justified the elimination of preexisting BRAC projects, eliminate and save $126.7 Million. It does not take seven years to move people and equipment from one place to another.

Base construction costs are listed in the linked BRAC budget. Such projects include $6.8 Million for a new Child Development Center, $9 Million for a Recruiting Operations Building, $13.5 Million for a dental clinic, aircraft parking aprons (read: a slab of concrete with some canvas over it) ranging from six to seven million dollars, and other ridiculously large, expensive projects.

There's even a museum ($12.2 Million); the DoD should not be building museums on your dollar. These things do not cost this much to build in the real world. Additional construction projects are provisioned for programs I have proposed the elimination of; therefore it makes sense that they require no new buildings. I therefore propose a further reduction of 25% of the construction project funding (which does not appear to be budgeted), saving $6.2 Billion. However, as the construction projects are not in the BRAC budget, I will take the $6.2 Billion out of the general DoD Military Construction budget forecast, which is where that money appears to come from.

Defense Working Capital Fund[27][28][29]

Revolving Fund Budget

Washington Headquarters Service

> *The FY 1991 Defense Authorization Act established the Pentagon Reservation Maintenance Revolving Fund (PRMRF) and 10 USC 2674 codified it. The fund is responsible for the maintenance, sustainment, protection, repair and*

---

[27] http://comptroller.defense.gov/defbudget/fy2013/budget_justification/pdfs/06_Defense_Working_Capital_Fund/DW_Narrative_FY2013_PB.pdf
[28] http://comptroller.defense.gov/defbudget/fy2013/budget_justification/pdfs/06_Defense_Working_Capital_Fund/PB_13_DWWCF_Capital_Budget.pdf
[29] http://comptroller.defense.gov/defbudget/fy2013/budget_justification/pdfs/06_Defense_Working_Capital_Fund/PB_13_DWWCF_Operating_Budget.pdf

renovation of the Pentagon Reservation. As established, the "Pentagon Reservation" refers to approximately 280 acres located in Arlington, Virginia, on which stand the Pentagon Building, Federal Office Building #2 {(FOB #2) (Also known as the Navy Annex)}, the Pentagon Heating and Sewage Treatment Plants, and all Reservation grounds and parking areas.

It bothers me that the Pentagon has so many people that it requires its own sewage treatment plant and police force (PFPA), and that its renovation had to be broken into its own budget instead of included in the general defense-wide Operations and Maintenance budget. Of course, providing a central military planning location and a bug-out location for the top brass are necessary and proper. Reduce by standard 25%, saving $142.4 Million.

Defense Logistics Agency

The Defense Logistics Agency (DLA) Strategic Materials (formerly known as the National Defense Stockpile) operates under the authority of the Strategic and Critical Materials Stock Piling Act (50 U.S.C. §98, et seq.). The Stock Piling Act provides that strategic and critical materials are stockpiled in the interest of national defense to preclude a dangerous and costly dependence upon foreign sources of supply in times of national emergency. The DLA Strategic Materials administers the acquisition, storage, management, and disposal of the stockpile.

The National Defense Stockpile is imperative to our national defense, and is thus very necessary and proper. We should never sell our weapons, so eliminate its excess weapons sales component, costing $153 Million in lost revenue. Leave the rest as is, for a new cost of $534.5 Million.

Capital Budget

Consists of infrastructure costs such as phone systems, computer networks, security, and replacing old or broken equipment. Reduce by standard 25% and save $8.7 Million.

Operating Budget

The DWWCF consists of six activity groups. The Defense Logistics Agency (DLA) operates three of these activity groups, the Defense Information Systems Agency (DISA) operates two activity groups, and Defense Finance and Accounting Service (DFAS) operates one activity group.

This is additional overhead for DISA, DFAS, and DLA to operate. Why their operating budgets are separate from their regular budgets is beyond me. Includes a number of programs related to overseas operations. Reduce by standard 25% and save $306 Million.

Military Construction

Eliminate all overseas construction, as we're closing those bases by this proposal anyway. Eliminate all pollution abatement, energy conservation, floodplain management, wetlands protection, and environmental protection projects, as they are not the federal government's business. Eliminate non-defense-related projects such as a laboratory to study the physiological effects of living in moderately high altitudes. Reduce the remainder by the standard 25% and save a total of around $2 Billion.

Defense Health Program

> The medical mission of the Department of Defense (DoD) is to enhance DoD and our Nation's security by providing health support for the full range of military operations and sustaining the health of all those entrusted to our care. The Defense Health Program (DHP) appropriation funding provides for worldwide medical and dental services to active forces and other eligible beneficiaries, veterinary services, medical command headquarters, specialized services for the training of medical personnel, and occupational and industrial health care.

Necessary and proper; less necessary due to reduced force size and newly defense-oriented military position. Standard 25% cut, save $10.6 Billion.

NATO Security Investment Program

> NATO Security Investment Program projects meet Alliance military requirements for a wide range of facilities and capabilities. Projects include effective surveillance and intelligence capabilities, flexible command and control systems (including secure and reliable communications), mobility within and between regions, adequate logistics and transportation support, and the infrastructure to support both forward deployed and reinforcing forces.

The Constitution decrees that all treaties duly signed are the "supreme law of the land", other provisions of the Constitution notwithstanding. Therefore we must be very careful in our choosing of treaties, and should prefer fewer to more. In the words of Thomas Jefferson:

> Peace, commerce, and honest friendship with all nations, entangling alliances with none.

NATO and the United Nations are the two most entangling alliances in American history. I support withdrawing from both, thus obsoleting all security investments therein. Eliminate and save $264 Million in SIP alone.

Department of the Army[30]

After a decade of war, the United States Army remains the best led, best trained, and best equipped ground force in the world. In the uncertain security environment our country faces, the Army–which in the future will be smaller and leaner, agile, flexible, ready, and technologically advanced–remains central to our Nation's defense as part of the Joint Force. In 2011, the Army successfully completed the drawdown of all forces from Iraq.

Article I, Section 8, Clause 15 of the Constitution authorizes the Congress to "provide for calling forth the Militia to execute the Laws of the Union, suppress Insurrections and repel Invasions". Article I, Section 8, Clause 12 authorizes the Congress to "raise and support Armies". Therefore, the Army is constitutionally justified. However, not everything in the Army is necessary to fulfill these authorized activities, nor directly advances them.

Military Personnel

The Military Personnel, Army (MPA) appropriation provides pay and benefits for both Active Component Soldiers and Reserve Component Soldiers activated for current contingencies. The appropriation plays a critical role in National Military Strategy by enabling the Army to meet its manning objectives (having the right number of high quality Soldiers in the appropriate grades and skills to satisfy force structure requirements) while maintaining the All-Volunteer Force. In addition to manning force structure requirements, the appropriation provides for Soldiers in a variety of individual accounts including Cadets and TTHS (trainees, transients, holdees, and students).

An army without soldiers is no army; so the personnel are necessary and proper to the purpose of raising armies per the Constitution. Keep military personnel at the standard 25% reduction, and save $10.3 Billion. Keep reserve personnel at the standard 25% reduction, and save $1.24 Billion. Keep the National Guard personnel at the standard 25% reduction, and save $2.2 Billion.

Operation and Maintenance

The Operation and Maintenance, Army (OMA) appropriation provides the resources to organize, equip, and train forces for the conduct of prompt and sustained combat operations on land and in support of Combatant Commanders. This appropriation provides funds for recruiting and training the Army's All-Volunteer Force, sustains Families, and funds the Army's day-to-day operating costs at 74 installations world-wide.

---

[30] http://www.asafm.army.mil/offices/BU/BudgetMat.aspx?OfficeCode=1200

This appropriation sustains Army training with Ground Operating Tempo (OPTEMPO), flying hours, fuel, supplies, and the maintenance of weapons systems and airframes. It funds quality of life and vital programs and services for Soldiers, Civilians, and their Families at installations where they live and work. It also funds educational and developmental programs for Soldiers and Civilians.

Given my proposed changes in foreign policy, we can eliminate all regular costs of doing business overseas. The operations and maintenance of the Army is critical to the army itself, and is thus necessary and proper. This is a $36.6 Billion program level.

Operating Forces

The Operating Forces budget activity provides funding for day-to-day operations of the Army's Soldiers, combat units, installations, and those facilities required for the training and readiness of our combat elements. This budget activity consists of three activities: Land Forces, Land Forces Readiness, and Land Forces Readiness Support.

Necessary and proper; even after bringing our troops home, they should continue to train as if we were at war. That way, when war comes, we're always ready for it. I identified $10.4 Billion in total outright eliminations under Operating Forces. Cut the remainder by the standard 25%, saving a total of $13.4 Billion.

Maneuver Units

Executes the training and operations required to maintain readiness in the active Army's Brigade Combat Teams (BCTs) and all organic forces associated with those BCTs in a phased, expeditionary Army Force Generation (ARFORGEN) cycle. Funds training for units available to train at home station in FY 2013. The Army has taken a deployment offset equivalent to 12 BCTs (10 Active Component and two Army National Guard) programmed for deployment for current and planned contingency operations.

Necessary and proper; no funding change at this level, as funding was reduced at the Operating Forces level.

Modular Support Brigades

Executes the training and operation of modular, multi-functional support brigades in a phased, expeditionary Army Force Generation (ARFORGEN) cycle. Included are Fires Brigades, Battlefield Surveillance Brigades, Sustainment Brigades, and Maneuver Enhancement Brigades.

Necessary and proper; no funding change at this level, as funding was reduced at the Operating Forces level.

Echelons Above Brigade

Executes the training and day-to-day operations of echelons above brigade operational units whose mission is to provide critical, actionable intelligence, force protection, and area logistics support to Brigade Combat Teams (BCTs) in a phased, expeditionary Army Force Generation (ARFORGEN) cycle. It includes critical tactical and national assets such as Patriot Air Defense Battalions and Chemical, Biological, Radiological/Nuclear, and Explosive (CBRNE) units/operations required to protect both deployed units and the homeland.

Necessary and proper; no funding change at this level, as funding was reduced at the Operating Forces level.

Theater Level Assets

Includes military units that directly support worldwide operations, the deployable elements of the Army Service Component Command's (ASCC) headquarters in a phased, expeditionary Army Force Generation (ARFORGEN) cycle.

Given that my proposal eliminates worldwide operations, we can eliminate TLA and save $707 Million.

Land Forces Operational Support

Executes force related maneuver training at the four Combat Training Centers (CTCs) which include the maneuver CTCs at National Training Center, the Joint Readiness Training Center, the Joint Multinational Readiness Center, and U.S. Army Combined Arms Center (Mission Command Training Program). Funds support joint training integration during CTC exercises. This funds ground OPTEMPO for the Opposing Force (OPFOR) units at each of the CTCs, the deployment costs for the units training at the CTCs, and contracts for the operation and maintenance of training devices used at the CTCs.

Necessary and proper; no funding change at this level, as funding was reduced at the Operating Forces level.

Aviation Assets

Executes training and operations required to maintain readiness in the Army's aviation units and all organic forces associated with those units in a phased, expeditionary Army Force Generation (ARFORGEN) cycle. This includes Combat Aviation Brigades (CAB); Echelons Above Brigade (EAB) aviation units; and theater aviation assets including the headquarters, aviation support, aviation maintenance support, and aviation operations support.

Necessary and proper; no funding change at this level, as funding was reduced at the Operating Forces level.

Force Readiness Support

Provides support of key activities essential to the readiness for the Land Forces. Includes operation of training ranges and associated facilities, incremental expenses of Joint Chiefs of Staff (JCS) exercises, active component support to the reserve components, including Title XI; centralized procurement and issue of Operations and Maintenance, Army (OMA) funded clothing and equipment, and operation of key communication and tactical intelligence and related activities (TIARA) intelligence systems. Finances manpower authorizations, equipment, necessary facilities, and the associated cost specifically identified and measurable to the units.

Necessary and proper; no funding change at this level, as funding was reduced at the Operating Forces level.

Land Forces Systems Readiness

Finances maintenance below the depot level, plus support of land forces equipment performed or managed at the national level. It includes national maintenance contracts performed by in-house or Contractor Logistics Support (CLS) personnel for the Army's watercraft and below depot Test Measurement and Diagnostic Equipment (TMDE) support

Necessary and proper; no funding change at this level, as funding was reduced at the Operating Forces level.

Land Forces Depot Maintenance

This program funds depot level maintenance for equipment and digital technology associated with Army weapon systems. Depot maintenance is the national maintenance standard that restores equipment condition and service life - it includes overhaul (restores equipment, or components, to a completely serviceable condition with a measurable [expected] life), rebuild (this is a near zero/zero mile maintenance process requiring end item total tear down involving the replacement of all expendable components, all aged components, reconditioning of structural components, in addition to the procedures identified for overhaul) and recapitalization (which includes rebuild, restoring items to a standard configuration, installing modification work orders / engineering change proposals, and technology insertion).

Necessary and proper; no funding change at this level, as funding was reduced at the Operating Forces level.

Base Operations Support (BOS)

Finances the Active Army's installation services worldwide, ensuring an environment in which Soldiers and Families can thrive, and provides a structure that supports an expeditionary Army. BOS is vital in all aspects of mission readiness and training, and provides for operating and maintaining installations worldwide that serve as our Nation's power projection platforms, and provides essential services and programs that promote quality of life for our Soldiers, Families, and civilian workforce. Installation support is provided through the following programs and services.

Given the elimination of our overseas deployments, locations, and other installations, we can make some big changes here. Eliminate Overseas Security Guards ($200 Million) and OCO Funding ($1.2 Billion). Reduce the remainder by one third (my standard for programs including overseas base overhead), and save $3.4 Billion.

Sustainment, Restoration, and Modernization, and Energy

Finances worldwide operations, activities, and initiatives necessary to maintain and sustain the Army's facilities; restores facilities to industry standards; and modernizes facilities to meet the full range of tasks necessary to provide relevant and ready land power for the Nation. These facilities are our community based installations and training sites. The Army leverages geographical locations of installations as power projection and support platforms and utilizes information infrastructure in support of reach-back capabilities. This program also supports the reduction of excess and obsolete inventory. The Army's Energy Program enables Soldiers and Leaders to maximize available resources by providing the capability to manage energy status, and resources.

Given that my proposal eliminates worldwide operations, and that land power is the responsibility of the states and the energy companies, we can eliminate this and save $3 Billion.

Management and Operational Headquarters

Finances the day-to-day operation of Army Management Headquarters Activities (AMHA). Funds civilian pay and other support costs (travel, contracts, supplies, and services) for civilian and military personnel. The Army Management Headquarters develop policy and guidance, performs long-range planning, programming and budgeting, manages and distributes resources, and conducts program performance reviews and evaluations.

Necessary and proper; no funding change at this level, as funding was reduced at the Operating Forces level. Having said that, I think our military has a bit too much "policy and guidance".

Combatant Commands Core Operations
> *Supports day-to-day operations of the unified commands' headquarters (HQ) and HQ support. The Army as the Combatant Command Support Agent (CCSA) for U.S. Africa Command (USAFRICOM), U.S. European Command (USEUCOM), and U.S. Southern Command (USSOUTHCOM) is responsible for funding their Headquarter requirements and activities. The Unified Command Plan establishes the missions and geographic responsibilities among the combatant commanders . Additionally, the Army provides funding to the United States Forces Korea (USFK) under this program.*

Given that my proposal eliminates worldwide operations, we can eliminate this and save $178 Million.

Additional Activities
> *Beginning in FY 2010, all base funding in SAG 135 has been transferred to other SAGs in order to realign funds to more appropriate areas. Only Overseas Contingency Operations (OCO) funding will be executed in this SAG.*

No funding since 2011, except OCO; eliminate and save $24.5 Billion.

Combatant Commands Direct Mission Support
> *Supports Combatant Commands mission activities that promote regional stability and shape the international security environment in ways that favor U.S. National Security. The Army is the Combatant Command Support Agent (CCSA) for U.S. Africa Command , U.S. European Command, and U.S. Southern Command . The Army is responsible for funding the Combatant Commands mission areas such as conducting Theater Security Cooperation to build positive relationships, developing partner nation security capabilities, promoting the exchange of information, and affording U.S. forces with peacetime and contingency access to support training and military operations.*

Given that we no longer have overseas missions under my proposal, we can eliminate this and save $461 Million.

Mobilization
> *The Mobilization budget activity supports the National Military Strategy and the Strategic Planning Guidance by providing an immediate response capability to deploying forces. It affords the ability to maintain a viable deterrence and an adequate defense of the nation's vital interests with less reliance on forward deployed forces. The prepositioning of equipment required for wartime operations is a major component of the Army's response capability. Mobilization consists of three activity groups: Strategic Mobility, Army Prepositioned Stocks (APS), and Industrial Preparedness. Mobilization is the act of assembling and preparing troops and supplies for war. This includes the Army Power Projection efforts, material amassed in peacetime to meet an*

increase of military requirements at the outbreak of war, and analysis of the industrial base toward mitigating shortfalls in industrial capacity.

The great thing about our military being in our own territory is that we don't need to deploy anyone. If we need to go to war, Congress should appropriate money for such war after having declared it. Therefore, we can eliminate this from the budget and save $607 Million.

Strategic Mobility

This program directly supports the National Military Strategy, the Strategic Planning Guidance (SPG), the Army Vision deployment objectives, and the Geographic Combatant Commanders' Operational Plans, in an effort to link current capabilities with future force projection requirements. The three major efforts for Strategic Mobility are: prepositioning of combat material (both afloat and ashore), power projection out-loading, and readiness training.

Given that future deployments will be significantly limited, there is therefore no future force projection to require. Eliminate and save $405 Million.

Army Prepositioned Stocks

APS supports the current National Military Strategy and the Strategic Planning Guidance (SPG) by providing a rapid response capability to deploying forces. APS are a key component of a relevant and ready land force as the Army enhances its strategic mobility capabilities to execute Overseas Contingency Operations (OCO) and transformation to meet the emerging strategic realities of the 21st century. APS supports the Army's capability to project combat-ready forces from CONUS, Europe, Southwest Asia, South Korea, Japan, and Hawaii to conduct operations anywhere in the world.

We have no right to deploy our weapons throughout the world when we're not at war, and we have no right to be at war without the support of the people through a declaration by Congress. We haven't declared a war since the 40s, so it's time to bring our stuff home. Eliminate and save $195 Million.

Industrial Preparedness

Executes industrial analysis tools to help the Army obtain end-item and repair parts support (excluding ammunition). Additionally, it provides for a planning base with private industry and government owned industrial plants. Such planning includes program administration, project management, and industrial base management. Industrial analysis is performed on industrial sectors, which support weapon system acquisition, readiness, and sustainment. An integral element of this program is the evaluation of industrial base capability and development of recommendations to mitigate the risk of sector deficiencies and shortfalls in capability.

Sell all government owned industrial plants; let the private sector produce what we need, and just buy the products. They can forecast their manufacturing needs with a phone call, email, or contract. Eliminate and save $6.4 Million.

Training and Recruiting

I identified $456.82 Million in programs we can eliminate entirely. Reduce the remainder by 25% and save a total of $1.2 Billion.

Officer Acquisition

Funds three mission-essential institutions: U.S. Military Academy (USMA), U.S. Military Academy Preparatory School (USMAPS), and Officer Candidate School (OCS). These institutions provide the Army with qualified officers. In addition, it finances the costs for Class III (fuel and oils) and Class IX (repair parts) to operate and maintain equipment sets at all their locations.

Necessary and proper; no funding change at this level, as funding was reduced at the Training level.

Recruit Training

This program funds civilian pay and benefits, trainee processing at reception stations, trainee support, resident instruction, local replication of training aids and training literature, procurement of supplies and equipment, and contractual services. It also includes temporary duty (travel and per diem) for staff and faculty, organizational clothing, and equipment issued for use during the training period. This program also funds costs for Class III (fuel and oils) and Class IX (repair parts) to operate and maintain equipment sets.

Necessary and proper; no funding change at this level, as funding was reduced at the Training level.

One Station Unit Training

This program funds trainee support, resident instruction, local preparation of training aids and training literature, procurement of supplies and equipment, and contractual services. It also includes temporary duty (travel and per diem) for staff and faculty, civilian pay and benefits, and organizational clothing and equipment issued for use during the training period. Also finances costs for Class III (fuel and oils) and Class IX (repair parts) and to operate and maintain equipment sets.

Necessary and proper; no funding change at this level, as funding was reduced at the Training level.

Senior Reserve Officer Training Corps (SROTC)
> This program funds the SROTC program, which produces over 70 percent of all U.S. Army officers and remains the broadest avenue of entry for men and women seeking to serve as officers in the Army. Provides for campus detachment operations and training, scholarships for students, summer camp operations, operation of SROTC Brigade Headquarters, and the Cadet Command Headquarters. Campus detachment support includes funds for civilian pay and benefits; temporary duty (travel and per diem); contractual support; transportation; and the purchase of organizational clothing, equipment, textbooks, reference publications, and supplies. Scholarship funds provide for tuition costs, academic textbooks, laboratory fees, and other academic expenses for the students who are awarded or continue on scholarships each school year.

Necessary and proper; no funding change at this level, as funding was reduced at the Training level.

Junior Reserve Officer Training Corps (JROTC)
> Funds programs located in all 50 states, the 4 territories, and on 7 U.S. bases in foreign countries as mandated by the U.S. Congress, 10 USC 2031. JROTC, a public service program available to high school students, provides a citizenship program that motivates young people to be strong leaders and better citizens. Funding supports retired military instructor salaries, costs of unit supplies, equipment, summer camps for 10 percent of enrolled cadets, and travel and per diem costs for instructors.

Necessary and proper; no funding change at this level, as funding was reduced at the Training level.

Specialized Skill Training
> Funds Military Occupational Specialty (MOS) and mid-level promotion qualifying courses for all Soldiers. Cost includes student support, resident instruction, local preparation and replication of training aids and training literature, procurement of supplies and equipment, civilian pay and benefits, and contractual services. Funds temporary duty (travel and per diem) for staff and faculty trips, organizational clothing, and equipment issued for use during the training period.

Necessary and proper; no funding change at this level, as funding was reduced at the Training level.

Flight Training
> Funds Initial Military Training for Initial Entry Rotary Wing undergraduate flight students and graduate flight training. This subactivity group also funds the support costs of training flight students including equipment maintenance,

POL (Petroleum, Oil, and Lubricants), repair parts, depot level reparable parts, and the operation of the aviation school airfields and airfield equipment. The purpose of undergraduate flight training is to generate qualified aviators for the Army. The purpose of graduate flight training is threefold. First, it training trains aviators as maintenance test pilots. Second, it provides training of instructor test pilots. Finally, it qualifies aviators in the use of advanced aircraft.

Necessary and proper; no funding change at this level, as funding was reduced at the Training level.

Professional Development Education

Funds the operation and support of the Army War College, Command and General Staff College, and the Army Sergeants Major Academy. Funds the tuition and fees for the Advanced Civil Schooling Program and tuition, fees, and temporary duty (travel and per diem) for Army officers attending foreign military schools (schools of other nations).

Necessary and proper; no funding change at this level, as funding was reduced at the Training level.

Training Support

Funds Army-wide support of the training establishment and its development of training programs and materials. Additionally, it funds the following programs: Tactical Equipment Maintenance for institutional training equipment - reparable and major end items used to operate and maintain equipment sets. Automation training support efforts throughout the various Army and Joint schools.

Necessary and proper; no funding change at this level, as funding was reduced at the Training level.

Recruiting and Advertising

Funds a key component of the Army's mission to maintain the highest quality force possible. Program provides funding to recruit sufficient manpower to sustain the Active Army. Innovative marketing methods are required to attract recruits with the particular qualifications needed to operate the Army's modern, technologically advanced weaponry, telecommunications systems, and equipment.

Necessary and proper; no funding change at this level, as funding was reduced at the Training level.

Examining

> *Funds the U.S. Military Entrance Processing Command (USMEPCOM). Army is the Executive Agent for the USMEPCOM. Also funds the U.S. Army Accessions Support Brigade, the U.S. Army Marksmanship Unit (USAMU), and the U.S. Army Parachute Team. These organizations provide support to the Recruiting and Cadet Command forces.*

Necessary and proper; no funding change at this level, as funding was reduced at the Training level.

Off Duty and Voluntary Education

> *Finances three Army programs: First, the Army Continuing Education System (ACES). ACES is an integrated system of self-development education providing programs and services that support Army readiness, recruitment, and retention. It provides the Soldier with academic and vocational counseling services to aid in establishing professional and educational goals.*

This isn't really an important part of defending the country. Eliminate and save $244 Million.

Civilian Education and Training

> *Funds Army civilian training to achieve optimum performance through five major programs: Senior Executive Onboarding, Financial Management Certification Program, Army Intern Program, Army Civilian Training Program, and the Acquisition Corps Training Program. Training is performed at military installations, training centers, colleges, universities, and civilian contract facilities.*

This isn't really an important part of defending the country. Eliminate and save $212 Million.

Administration and Servicewide Activities

> *The Administration and Servicewide Support budget activity provides funding for administration, logistics, communications, and other servicewide support functions required to support Army forces worldwide. This budget activity consists of four activities: Security Programs, Logistics Operations, Servicewide Support and Support of Other Nations.*

I identified $2 Billion in programs which can be eliminated altogether. Cut the remainder by my standard 25% and save a total of $3.7 Billion.

Security Programs

> *Includes the Consolidated Cryptologic Program (CCP), General Defense Intelligence Program (GDIP), the Foreign Counterintelligence Program (FCIP), National Geospatial-Intelligence Program (NGIP), Military Intelligence Program*

(MIP), Security and Related Activities, and Arms Control Treaties implementation and compliance.

Necessary and proper; no funding change at this level, as funding was reduced at the Administration level.

Servicewide Transportation

Finances worldwide movement of material for Army force modernization, sustainment, and restructuring. Servicewide transportation operations include the movement of material between the Army depots and Army customers, movement of goods and mail to support service members worldwide, management of ground transportation, and port operations.

Given the elimination of our worldwide posture, there is no worldwide movement to execute. Having said that, stuff still needs to move around within the U.S. and we'll need to move a lot of weapons and equipment out of our overseas bases. Reduce by half after the first year and save $301 Million.

Central Supply Activities

Finances end-item procurement, management, and sustainment of material and equipment to equip, deploy, and sustain the Army and other U.S. military services worldwide.

Given the elimination of our worldwide stance, and the fact that we shouldn't equip, deploy, or sustain anyone's military services but our own, this can be significantly reduced. Cut by 75% and save $556 Million.

Logistics Support Activities

Finances a variety of logistics support functions, which equip, deploy, and sustain the Army and other Services worldwide. LSA contains the worldwide Logistics Management Systems for Class VII end-item fielding and redistribution; Class IX unit-level and wholesale requisitioning and distribution; and readiness and asset visibility reporting.

Given the elimination of our worldwide posture, there is no worldwide movement to execute. Having said that, stuff still needs to move around within the U.S. and we'll need to move a lot of weapons and equipment out of our overseas bases. Reduce by half after the first year and save $305 Million.

Ammunition Management

Finances the Army in its role as the Department of Defense (DoD) Single Manager for Conventional Ammunition (SMCA). It resources the acquisition planning and logistical support for conventional ammunition assigned to the

SMCA. Conventional ammunition includes all explosive and kinetic energy munitions but excludes nuclear and biological devices.

Necessary and proper; no funding change at this level, as funding was reduced at the Administration level.

Administration

Finances the operation (civilian pay, training, supplies, equipment, and contracts) of the Headquarters, Department of the Army, Field Operating Agencies, Information Management, Army Enterprise Architecture, Soldier Modernization, and Public Affairs.

Necessary and proper; no funding change at this level, as funding was reduced at the higher Administration level.

Servicewide Communications

Finances communications to key organizations: Headquarters Department of the Army, the Network Enterprise Technology Command (NETCOM), the U.S. Army Material Command, the Army Space and Missile Defense Command (SMDC), and the U.S. Army Acquisition Command. The functional categories resourced are Information Services, Communication Systems Support, Information Security, Computer Security, Defense Satellite Communications System, Connect the Logistician, and Integrated Personnel and Pay System (IPPS-A).

Necessary and proper; no funding change at this level, as funding was reduced at the Administration level.

Manpower Management

Finances the administration and professional personnel management of the Army's active and reserve service members as well as its civilian employees. Supports the U.S. Army Human Resources Command workforce infrastructure and automated personnel management systems which integrate and coordinate military personnel systems to develop and optimize the use of the Army's human resources. Manpower Management also finances the Civilian Human Resources Agency operations which recruit, access, and retain Army's civilian personnel through continued modernization, restructure of programs, and by streamlining processes and procedures.

Necessary and proper; no funding change at this level, as funding was reduced at the Administration level.

Other Personnel Support
> *Finances a system of personnel management programs in support of Army's active service members and civilian employees during all phases of their careers to include recruitment, training, assignments, and career progression.*

Necessary and proper, except as listed below; no funding change at this level, as funding was reduced at the Administration level.

Strong Bonds - A chaplain-led program for commanders which builds relationship resiliency. The Strong Bonds mission is to increase Soldier and Family readiness through relationship education and skills training.

The family life of our soldiers is none of the government's business; eliminate and save $79 Million.

Army Career Alumni Program - *Provides separating and retiring Soldiers, family members, and civilians with skills they require to obtain appropriate post-Army employment and to maximize the use of benefits earned through their Army service.*

It is not the Army's job to train people to be civilians again. Eliminate and save $90 Million.

Other Service Support
> *Finances a wide array of worldwide support functions that are vital to overall Army readiness which enable the Army to comply with public laws and Department of Defense (DoD) directives. Other Service Support addresses centralized functions, which benefit DoD, Defense Finance and Accounting Service (DFAS), Army Audit Agency (AAA), Inspector General (IG), Judge Advocate General activities, and the Army as a whole, which yield efficiencies through consolidation.*

Given the elimination of our worldwide operations, we no longer require as much support therefor. Necessary and proper; no funding change at this level, as funding was reduced at the Administration level.

Army Claims
> *Funds administrative, personnel and logistical support for Army centralized legal functions executed by Judge Advocate General Corps Organizations: United States Army Legal Services Agency (USALSA), United States Army Claims Service (USARCS), and Office of the Judge Advocate General (OTJAG), Information Technology Division, Center for Law and Military Operations, and Army Claims Fund.*

Necessary and proper; no funding change at this level, as funding was reduced at the Administration level.

Other Construction Support and Real Estate Management
> Resources U.S. Army Corps of Engineers (USACE) Headquarters and its Subordinate Commands. Resources policy formulation, program management, national and regional coordination, and quality assurance of the construction support and real estate management worldwide. Resources the supervision and direction of USACE activities engaged in developing and publishing guidance.

Necessary and proper; no funding change at this level, as funding was reduced at the Administration level.

Financial Improvement and Audit Readiness
> Complies with the Department of Defense's strategy to commit to having fully auditable statement of budgetary resources by 30 September 2014 in accordance with the National Defense Authorization Act of 2012. Financial improvement activities are managed through the FAIR plan, which provides the strategy, methodology and means for monitoring progress to achieve Congress' audit readiness requirement.

Having looked through the federal budget, I can tell you the government is grossly unqualified to manage its own finances. Eliminate and save $222 Million.

International Military Headquarters
> Supports the North Atlantic Treaty Organization (NATO) and U.S. Forces Korea.

For reasons already justified, withdraw from NATO. Korea is none of our business as long as they don't attack us. Eliminate and save $460 Million.

Miscellaneous Support of Other Nations
> Supports Office of the Secretary of Defense (OSD) directed missions to other nations to promote regional stability and shape the international security environment in ways that favor U.S. National Security. It provides support to Army programs designed to promote and facilitate multinational force compatibility; to enhance the Army's ability to fight as a member of an alliance or coalition; and supports data and technology exchange programs including Senior National Representatives, Engineer/Scientist Exchange Program, Data Exchange Agreements, Subject Matter Expert Exchanges, and NATO's Council of National Armaments Directors.

For reasons already justified, withdraw from NATO. Other nations are not our concern, our own defense notwithstanding. Eliminate and save $26 Million.

Army Reserve[31]

Operation and Maintenance

> *The FY 2013 Operation and Maintenance, Army Reserve (OMAR) appropriation supports operations, logistics, engineering, administration and management support capabilities for the Army Reserve. Additionally, the OMAR appropriation supports installation management, maintenance of real property, records management; and personnel support to retirees, veterans and their families. Costs incurred in providing support include civilian pay, information systems, networks, telecommunications, supplies, fuel, equipment and base operations support. Funding is provided in two budget activities. Budget Activity One (Operating Forces) consists of the following SubActivity Groups: Land Forces, Land Forces Readiness, and Land Forces Readiness Support. Budget Activity Four (Administrative and Service-wide Activities) consists of the following Sub-Activity Groups: Logistics Operations and Service-Wide Support.*

Reserve O&M has a structure similar to that of Army Proper. Necessary and proper; standard 25% cut, saving $790 Million.

Army National Guard[32]

Operations and Maintenance

> *The Operation and Maintenance, National Guard (OMNG) appropriation supports operating and maintaining Army National Guard units in the 50 States, 3 Territories, and the District of Columbia. Funding supports two Budget Activities and eighteen Subactivity Groups. Programs funded in this appropriation include: training and operations support; air and ground OPTEMPO; Chemical, Biological, Radiologicial, Nuclear, and High-yield Explosive (CBRNE) Enterprise, to include Civil Support Teams; pay and benefits for Military Technicians and Department of the Army Civilians; automation and information systems; base operations; education programs; medical readiness; mission support; [...]*

NG O&M has a structure similar to that of Army Proper. Necessary and proper; standard 25% cut, saving $1.8 Billion.

---

[31]http://asafm.army.mil/Documents/OfficeDocuments/Budget/BudgetMaterials/FY13/opmaint//omar-v1.pdf
[32]http://asafm.army.mil/Documents/OfficeDocuments/Budget/BudgetMaterials/FY13/opmaint//omng-v1.pdf

Procurement

Aircraft Procurement[33]

Utility Fixed Wing Aircraft

The budget line covers the acquisition of Army fixed wing aircraft to include the procurement of utility fixed wing aircraft to support Operational Support Airlift (OSA) requirements, Special Electronic Mission Aircraft (SEMA), Special Mission Aircraft (Utility), and training. This budget line also provides for the acquisition of new commercial-off-the shelf, non-developmental fixed wing aircraft systems. In accordance with section 1815 of the FY 2008 National Defense Authorization Act P.L. 110-181), this item is necessary for use by the active and reserve components of the Armed Forces for homeland defense missions, domestic emergency responses and providing military support to civil authorities.

I'll let the military get away with replacing combat losses as being necessary and proper, but expanding our military to larger scales is unjustifiable. Repeal NDAA. If we bring our people and equipment back from overseas, we'll have plenty of utility aircraft to cover the four this purchases for homeland defense. Domestic emergencies which do not involve insurrection are not a federal concern. Military support to civil authorities should be provided by the National Guard, which will have plenty of aircraft available. Eliminate and save $18.6 Million.

C-12 Cargo Airplane

The C-12 fixed wing aircraft platform hosts a number of Army Intelligence, Surveillance and Reconnaissance/Reconnaissance Surveillance and Target Acquisition (ISR/RSTA) sensor systems that support irregular warfare in Overseas Contingency Operations (OCO). Included in those systems are Red Ridge, Guardrail Common Sensor (GRCS), Aerial Reconnaissance Multi Sensor (ARMS) (Iraq), the Medium Altitude Reconnaissance and Surveillance Systems (MARSS) (Iraq and Afghanistan), and Constant Hawk (Afghanistan). The ARMS system is composed of B-200 (C-12) aircraft equipped with imagery sensors, specialized communications intelligence (COMINT) sensors, and an array of line of sight and beyond line of sight communications equipment. The aircraft were fielded to Operation Iraqi Freedom (OIF) in FY06 and have been providing daily support to the Task Force Observe, Detect Identify, Neutralize (TF ODIN) commander. Constant Hawk (CH) in Afghanistan is hosted on a King Air 350 (C-12) aircraft. CH is a persistent surveillance wide field of view airborne intelligence, surveillance and reconnaissance (AISR) system conducting Counter Improvised Explosive Device (IED) surveillance and forensic force protection

---

[33]http://asafm.army.mil/Documents/OfficeDocuments/Budget/BudgetMaterials/FY13/pforms//aircraft.pdf

mission. CH uses high resolution Electro Optic (EO) cameras mounted on manned aircraft to provide persistent surveillance of a designated Named Area of Interest (NAI). The MARSS aircraft are primarily King Air 300's (C-12 variant) equipped with numerous sensors to include imagery and COMINT payloads. They also include several line-of-sight and beyond line of sigint communications systems and on board (manned) processing of the imagery and COMINT. The Enhanced MARSS (EMARSS) program provides additional MARSS systems based on a King Air 350 Extended Range (ER) aircraft. Laser Detection and Ranging (LIDAR) is a persistent surveillance AISR system.

My proposal eliminates all OCO, thus obsoleting the purchases therefor. No purchases are requested in 2013, so just eliminate. Why items *not* being purchased are in the budget is beyond me; these were bought and delivered in 2011.

MQ-1 UAV

The production MQ-1C Gray Eagle Unmanned Aircraft System (UAS) has changed based on new Army guidance from a Company sized unit equipped with (12) Unmanned Aircraft (UA) and associated support equipment to balanced Platoons, each capable of operating independently with (4) aircraft.

We already have plenty of UAVs; we certainly don't need 29 more during peacetime. Eliminate and save $27 Million.

RQ-11 Raven UAV

The Small Unmanned Aircraft System (SUAS) provides the battalion and below ground maneuver elements critical situational awareness and enhances force protection. The system provides the small unit commander an organic and responsive tactical Reconnaissance, Surveillance, and Target Acquisition (RSTA) capability through the ability to view real-time Full Motion Video (FMV) and sensor data via the system ground control station. Other compatible receivers, such as the One Station Remote Video Terminal (OSRVT) and appropriately equipped manned platforms may also receive the SUAS products.

This one is nifty because it can be launched by hand, like the toy R/C planes we grew up with, except each one costs as much as a middle class house. We already have plenty of UAVs; we certainly don't need 234 more during peacetime. Eliminate and save $26 Million.

BCT UAV Incr 1

Brigade Combat Team Unmanned Aerial Vehicle (UAVS) Increment 1. The program has no FY13 funding requirements. Based upon the ADM, dated February 3rd 2011, the Army cancelled this program. Based upon this ADM, the Army withheld this entire budget for the ATR Raven Program.

Programs not funded and procurements not procured do not belong on the budget; eliminate.

UH-72A LAKOTA Light Utility helicopter

> The Light Utility Helicopter, UH-72A LAKOTA will provide general aviation support for Continental United States (CONUS) based Table of Distribution and Allowance (TDA) and Table of Organization and Equipment (TOE) aviation units in the active and reserve components. The UH-72A platform will provide the flexibility to respond to Homeland Security (HLS) requirements, conduct civil search and rescue operations, support damage assessment, support test and training centers, perform generating force missions, augment the HH-60 Medical Evacuation (MEDEVAC) aircraft, and provide support to CONUS counterdrug operations.

The only homeland security requirement that we require is "Defend us if we're attacked". Therefore, since we're not under attack, there should be no such requirements. Civil search and rescue operations should be conducted by the states. Though states should be able to ask for help from the military when needed, we shouldn't plan around it. Try to have fewer emergencies. By legalizing drugs, we eliminate all counterdrug operations. Hospitals have their own medevac helicopters. Eliminate and save $272 Million.

AH-64 Apache

> Apache Block IIIA (AB3A) REMAN is an aircraft remanufacture program that refurbishes aging Longbow Apaches to extend their service life and upgrades the aircraft with updated technologies and performance enhancements to keep the Apache viable throughout its lifecycle.

Extending the service life of existing aircraft, thus preventing the purchase of new ones, is a good use of military funding. That component thereof is thus necessary and proper; however, there is an advance acquisition component of this acquisition which is not. Keep the recapitalization project ($19 Million) and eliminate the new acquisitions ($541 Million) and the overhead (i.e. "other costs" and initial spares) associated with the bulk deal ($210 Million).

AH-64 Apache Advance Procurement

> Apache Block IIIA (AB3A) REMAN is an aircraft remanufacture program that refurbishes aging Longbow Apaches to extend their service life and upgrades the aircraft with updated technologies and performance enhancements to keep the Apache viable throughout its lifecycle. AB3A addresses obsolescence and reliability challenges as well as adds significant combat capability to the aircraft.

This is the ongoing future version of the same AH-64 project. Eliminate and save $108 Million.

AH-64 Apache New Build

> *Apache Block IIIB (AB3B) New Build is based on the AB3A REMAN program which is an aircraft remanufacture program that refurbishes aging Longbow Apaches to extend their service life and upgrades the aircraft with updated technologies and performance enhancements to keep the Apache viable throughout its lifecycle. While AB3A remanufactures aircraft in production, AB3B assembles all new components resulting in completely NEW aircraft at the end of the production process. New aircraft fill shortages in the Apache fleet due to combat losses.*

This is an ongoing project, building new helicopters out of old parts. Eliminate and save $33 Million.

AH-64 Apache New Build Advance Procurement

> *Apache Block IIIB (AB3B) New Build is based on the AB3A REMAN program which is an aircraft remanufacture program that refurbishes aging Longbow Apaches to extend their service life and upgrades the aircraft with updated technologies and performance enhancements to keep the Apache viable throughout its lifecycle. While AB3A remanufactures aircraft in production, AB3B assembles all new components resulting in completely NEW aircraft at the end of the production process. New aircraft fill shortages in the Apache fleet due to combat losses.*

This is putting away future funding for the same New Build project. Eliminate and save $146 Million.

AH-64 WRA

> *The AH-64D Longbow Apache aircraft incorporates the Longbow weapon system and provides the US Army with a significant improvement in target acquisition and firepower effectiveness, increasing the survivability, lethality, and adverse weather fighting capabilities of the Apache. Principal aircraft components include the Target Acquisition Designation Sight (TADS) housed in a turret on the nose of the AH-64 and consisting of a TV, Forward Looking Infrared (FLIR), Direct View Optics, Laser Designator/Rangefinder and Spot Tracker. The Pilot Night Vision Sensor (PNVS) is a FLIR which allows Nap-of-Earth operations at night by the pilot independent of the co-pilot/gunner's FLIR.*

This is to replace a combat loss in Operation New Dawn / Operation Enduring Freedom; however, it was funded in 2011. No further funding is requested; irrelevant.

Kiowa Warrior WRA

> *To replace aircraft lost during Overseas Contingency Operations (OCO) and to return the fleet to the Army Authorized Objective (AAO) of 368 the Army will build Wartime Replacement Aircraft (WRA). These new Kiowa Warriors will be delivered in the OH-58D(R) configuration, including upgrades that are being installed on the fielded fleet.*

This is to replace nine combat losses; keep it ($11.5 Million).

UH-60 Black Hawk M

> *In accordance with section 1815 of the FY 2008 National Defense Authorization Act P.L. 110-181), this item is necessary for use by the active and reserve components of the Armed Forces for homeland defense missions, domestic emergency responses and providing military support to civil authorities.*

Repeal NDAA. There will be plenty of Black Hawks available when we leave the Middle East; eliminate and save $22 Million.

UH-60 Black Hawk M Advance Procurement

> *FY 2013 procures long lead and Economic Order Quantities (EOQ) items such as T700-GE-701D engines and avionics components for the FY12-FY16 multiyear contract.*

Withdraw from the contract, eliminate and save $115 Million.

CH-47 Helicopter

> *FY13 Base procurement dollars in the amount of $1159.4 million will procure 19 new build (12 CH-47Fs and 7 MH-47Gs) aircraft and 19 renew aircraft. FY13 OCO procurement dollars in the amount of $231.3 million will procure 6 war replacement new build CH-47F aircraft. Note: The 7 MH-47Gs are not part of the planned FY13-17 Multiyear Procurement.*

No new purchases except combat losses; withdraw from the contract, eliminate and save $32 Million.

CH-47 SLEP

> *The ReNew program will provide a more reliable, less costly to operate aircraft compatible with Joint digital connectivity requirements in the Future Force. The ReNew Program produces an identical aircraft as the CH-47F New Build program with the exception of dynamic components including engine, transmission and drive train. During production, the aircraft receives a new airframe, cockpit, wiring and plumbing.*

No new purchases except combat losses; withdraw from the contract, eliminate and save $634 Million.

CH-47 Advance Procurement

FY 13 Base procurement dollars in the amount of $83.3 million will procure avionics and airframe advance procurement.

No new purchases except combat losses; withdraw from the contract, eliminate and save $83 Million.

MQ-1 Payload UAV

FY 2013 base procurement dollars in the amount of $231.508 million supports procurement of 32 STARLite ER, 32 CSP HD and 12 TSP payloads. This will be the first year CSP HD payloads (CSP baseline capability enhancement) will be procured with a retrofit plan starting FY 2014 to retrofit all of the previously procured CSP Baselines. CSP HD and STARLite payloads support the Gray Eagle UAS fielding schedule for the 8-15th Units Equipped (UE). Along with the CSP HD, STARLite ER and TSP procurement, the funding also procures spares, contractor support, initial fielding support, and Depot Facilitization. There are no FY 2013 OCO Procurement dollars.

Indeed there are no OCO dollars; they're all under the 2013 Base column. Eliminate new programs and non-combat-loss purchases. Save $232 Million.

Guardrail Mods (MIP)

The GR Modernization program includes three main efforts: cockpit modernization, external aircraft modifications, and payload upgrades. Initial planning established an overall schedule to integrate all of these efforts, while minimizing impacts to current GR operations in support of Operation New Dawn (OND) & Operation Enduring Freedom (OEF). The GR/CS modernization effort provides A-Kits for the fleet of 14 mission aircraft (designated RC-12X) with capabilities that allow GR/CS to keep pace with a flexible enemy. Communications High Accuracy Location Subsystem-Compact (CHALS-C) provides precision geo-location and supports Theater for Net-Centric Geo-location (TNG) Architecture Cooperative Operations.

This is an improvement to existing platforms to provide better battlefield intelligence. However, we already have the best signal intelligence in the world, and the general idea is not to have a battlefield. Eliminate and save $16 Million.

Multi Sensor ABN Recon (MIP)

FY13 Base procurement dollars in the amount of $4.294 million supports the procurement of interoperability data links and installation, procurement of workstation architecture software for the ARL Modernization Program. This modernization and standardization effort represents critical technology insertions to improve system capability, target relevance, and improves the *system long term sustainability. The upgrades provide critical capability, target relevance, and improves the ARL's long term sustainability.*

This is an improvement to existing platforms to provide better battlefield intelligence. However, we already have great target relevance determination in the field, and we shouldn't be buying equipment that doesn't work right in the first place. Eliminate and save $4 Million.

For some reason, this jumps to $116 Million in 2015. I'm a little worried about that.

AH-65 Mods

The AH-64 MODS program provides for modernization of the fielded AH-64D Longbow Apache (LBA) fleet. Modifications accomplished by this funding line are not included in the Block III Program. FY13 Base funding in the amount of $178.805 Million supports modification efforts for the Airframe, Armament, Mission Command, Sensors, Survivability, Support Elements, and Training Systems.

This improves existing aircraft, though I have to wonder why such improvements are necessary. The Longbow is a reliable and effective weapons platform. Eliminate and save $179 Million.

CH-47 Cargo Helicopter Mods

The CH-47 Chinook is a twin-turbine, tandem-rotor, heavy lift transport helicopter with a useful load of up to 25,000 pounds. As the Army's only heavy lift helicopter, the mission of the CH-47 is to transport troops (including air assault), supplies, weapons, and other cargo in general support operations. The CH-47 is vital to the Overseas Contingency Operations and Homeland Security needs of our nation. Secondary missions include medical evacuation, aircraft recovery, parachute drops, disaster relief, and search and rescue. These aircraft are fielded to heavy helicopter companies and Special Operations Aviation.

While the budget goes into detail on the types of modifications, this program provides no justification, so let's take the AH-65 mods as a basis for comparison. It also doesn't look important, as the aircraft is already able to perform its missions. Eliminate and save $39 Million. For some reason, this skyrockets to $487 Million in 2017; I wonder what they're planning.

Utility/Cargo Airplane Mods

FY13 Base procurement dollars in the amount of $24.842 million supports communications, navigation, and surveillance equipment that meets current and future air traffic management requirements. In addition, equipment *included in the modifications will enhance the safety of passengers and crew. The upgrades will also permit the Army fixed wing aircraft to operate in compliance with other existing and emerging regulations.*

Air traffic management is not a justification to spend millions of dollars upgrading aircraft. The aircraft can already communicate, navigate, and survey. My proposal eliminates most existing regulations and would generally not allow for more to emerge. A lot of the requirements specified are "international requirements", and no other country should be allowed to tell us how to manage our aircraft. Eliminate and save $30 Million.

Utility Helicopter Mods

Utility Helicopter Mods include modifications to the UH-60 BLACKHAWK helicopter and the UH72A LAKOTA helicopter. The UH-60 BLACKHAWK helicopter is the Army's utility helicopter in the future force. The UH-72A LAKOTA helicopter provides general aviation support for aviation units in the active and reserve components.

The Blackhawk is already a highly reliable and fully mission-capable aircraft. Both of these aircraft have proven their ability to perform their missions, and thus require no mods. Eliminate and save $74 Million.

Kiowa Warrior

FY 2013 Base Funding in the amount of $192.484 Million will procure Cockpit and Sensor Upgrade Program (CASUP) (OH-58F) long-lead and Recap components ($122.693 Million), and continue Weight Reduction and Fielded Fleet Upgrade programs for the fielded fleet of OH-58D(R) aircraft ($69.791 Million). CASUP modifications will allow the Kiowa Warrior to safely serve as the Army's, armed reconnaissance, aviation platform until replaced/retired.

These aircraft have proven their ability to perform their missions, and thus require no mods. Eliminate and save $192 Million.

Network and Mission Plan

The Network and Mission Plan budget line includes the Aviation Mission Planning System (AMPS), the Improved Data Modem (IDM), the Aviation Data Exploitation Capability (ADEC), the Aircraft Notebook (ACN), Apache Interoperability, the Helicopter Terrain Avoidance and Warning System (HTAWS), and the Aviation Logistics Enterprise-Platform (ALE-P).

These aircraft have proven their ability to perform their missions, and thus require no mods. Eliminate and save $101 Million. This skyrockets to over a billion dollars in 2016.

Comms, Nav Surveillance

The Global Positioning System (GPS) provides Army Aviation with extremely accurate and secure navigation and timing, assists in situational awareness, and aids in prevention of fratricide. GPS is installed in two configurations based upon mission profile, operational requirements, and avionics architecture of the aircraft.

This program supports engineering projects, kit incorporation, and new radios on certain aircraft. These aircraft have proven their ability to perform their missions, and thus require no mods. Eliminate and save $133 Million.

GATM Rollup

This budget line supports procurement of Global Air Traffic Management equipment for both Fixed Wing (FW) and Rotary Wing (RW) aircraft.

It seems to me that our military air traffic is being managed well enough, and we shouldn't be thinking about globalizing any more than we already have. Eliminate and save $87 Million.

RQ-7 UAV Mods

FY2013 Base funding of $104.339 million supports acquisition of 7 Shadow TCDL retrofit kits (and associated spares), 7 launchers, 44 enhanced mission computers, 8 Universal Mission Simulators, 400 OSRVT modification kits, and Program Management, Engineering and Logistics support.

The aircraft we have are serving us just fine, and we have more than enough heavily armed UAVs to defend ourselves with. Eliminate and save $104 Million.

Aircraft Survivability Equipment

The Aircraft Survivability Equipment (ASE) budget line includes ASE Laser Countermeasures (AZ3508), ASE Trainers (AZ3506), and ASE Radio Frequency Countermeasures (AZ3511).

No justification is provided, but it's pretty obvious this is new kinds of countermeasures. The chaffs and flares we were using before worked very well, and we don't need to be at war anymore, so no new types are required. Eliminate and save $34 Million.

CMWS

The US Army operational requirements concept for infrared (IR) countermeasure systems is known as the Suite of Integrated Infrared Countermeasures (SIIRCM). SIIRCM is an integrated warning and countermeasure system to enhance aircraft survivability against IR guided threat missile systems. The core element of the SIIRCM concept is the

Advanced Threat Infrared Countermeasure/Common Missile Warning System (ATIRCM/CMWS) Program. The ATIRCM/CMWS is an integrated ultraviolet (UV) missile warning system, an IR Laser Jamming and Improved Countermeasure Dispenser (ICMD) serving as a subsystem to the host aircraft.

The chaffs and flares we were using before worked very well, and we don't need to be at war anymore, so no new types are required. Eliminate and save $128 Million.

Avionics Support Equipment

Consists of a family of avionics support equipment. Current program consists of the Aviators' Night Vision Imaging System (ANVIS). FY13 Base procurement dollars, in the amount of $4.886 million, support the procurement of 415 AN/AVS-6(V)3 systems for fielding to Active Units. The increased capability of the AN/AVS-6(V)3 yields enhanced mission performance and improved safety of flight, compared to what is now possible using previous AN/AVS-6 systems. The AN/AVS-6(V)3 enhances the survivability, lethality, and tactical mobility for aviators.

These aircraft have been working fine, have proven they can fulfill their mission, and thus do not require upgrades. Eliminate and save $12 Million.

Common Ground Equipment

FY 2013 Base procurement dollars in the amount of $82.511 million supports and provides various types of ground support equipment. In accordance with section 1815 of the FY 2008 National Defense Authorization Act P.L. 110-181), this item is necessary for use by the active and reserve components of the Armed Forces for homeland defense missions, domestic emergency responses and providing military support to civil authorities.

The Second Amendment and a military to defend against invasions are all the Homeland Defense we require. Eliminate and save $83 Million.

Aircrew Integrated Systems

FY2013 Base procurement dollars in the amount of $77.381 million supports production and fielding of the following Air Warrior products for deploying units: Electronic Data Manager (EDM); Encrypted Aircraft Wireless Intercom System (EAWIS), including A Kit and B Kit production and installations; Survival Kit, Ready Access, Modular (SKRAM); Communication Enhancement/Protection System (CEPS); and Microclimate Cooling for Apache Block 3. These funds also will procure Personnel Recovery Support System (PRSS) platform interoperability hardware and software improvements.

These aircraft have been working fine, have proven they can fulfill their mission, and thus do not require upgrades. Eliminate and save $77 Million.

Air Traffic Control

> FY 2013 Base procurement dollars in the amount of $47.235 million supports tactical and fixed base ATC systems and P3I modifications to these systems. Funds for tactical ATC systems provide for upgrades, modifications, to TAIS, ATNAVICS, TTCS, and MOTS. ATNAVICS upgrades will address joint interoperability and networking capabilities, as well as Information Assurance requirements, improved radio communications, and integrating the TPX-57 to interrogate Mode 5/S equipped aircraft. These modifications will allow the ATNAVICS to transmit critical air picture information to TAIS.

Our military air traffic control, communications, networking, and computers is working just fine, so no upgrades are required. Eliminate and save $47 Million.

Industrial Facilities

> At RTC, FY 2013 procures upgraded telemetry equipment used to capture and process real-time data transmitted at high data rates and frequencies during open air developmental flight tests. At YPG, FY 2013 procures replacement aircraft instrumentation for the time-stamping and on-board recording and telemetering of data from standard 1553 multiples bus, analog video from sensors, intercom (voice), and analog sensors; and on-board recorders and telemetry equipment that can meet the environment and data speeds needed for production base aviation programs.

This is a program to send data from planes to a base station during flight tests. We have had great success in flight testing in recent decades, and require no further upgrades. Furthermore, aircraft manufacturers should test their own products. Eliminate and save $1.6 Million.

2.75 Rocket Launcher

> FY 2013 procurement dollars in the amount of $.516 million supports the M260 7-tube analog launcher for OH-58D Kiowa Warrior and AH-6J helicopters and the M261 19-tube analog launcher for the AH-64 Apache, MH-60L Blackhawk, and AH-6J helicopters. Procurement replaces disposable launchers as a result of annual rocket firing for training and replenishes the limited issuable stockage that has been depleted below levels acceptable to support training and war reserve requirements of Active Army, Special Operations Forces and Reserve Components usage.

Necessary and proper; keep as is ($516K)

Missile Procurement[34]

PATRIOT System

> Patriot is an advanced Surface-to-Air guided missile system with a high probability of kill capable of operation in the presence of Electronic Countermeasures (ECM) and able to conduct multiple simultaneous engagements against high performance air breathing targets and ballistic missiles likely to be encountered by U.S. Forces. The system utilizes a multifunction Phased Array Radar, a digital computer controlling system function, a guidance system combining command and homing (track-via-missile) features, and provides the operator the ability to control operations.

PATRIOT missiles shoot down nukes. This is necessary and proper; keep as is ($7.7 Billion). No further procurements are forecasted, so this would not be an ongoing purchase.

MSE Missile

> The Missile Segment Enhancement (MSE) missile evolves from the PAC-3 (Patriot Advanced Capability 3) missile. The MSE upgrade takes the PAC-3 Cost Reduction Initiative (CRI) missile design and improves on it with a higher performance, dual pulse, eleven-inch diameter Solid Rocket Motor (SRM) design, improved Lethality Enhancer, thermally hardened front end for longer fly out, upgraded batteries, enlarged fixed fins, more responsive control surfaces, and upgraded guidance software. These improvements provide a more agile, lethal interceptor missile, which results in a substantial missile performance improvement while enhancing Insensitive Munitions (IM) compliance.

We don't need two types of missiles that do the same thing; one or the other should go away. Since the MSE system is still under development, eliminate this one until it is ready to replace all PATRIOT procurements. Even then, replace them gradually as they are used. Eliminate and save $12.8 Billion.

Hellfire System

> The Laser HELLFIRE II system family of air-to-ground missiles (all variants) provides attack helicopters and Unmanned Aircraft Systems (UAS) with point-target precision strike capability to defeat heavy, advanced armor, individual hard point and non-traditional targets. HELLFIRE II Missiles use a semi-active laser terminal guidance and are the primary armament of the AH-64 Apache, OH-58 Kiowa Warrior, Army UAS and Special Operations aircraft.

---

[34] http://asafm.army.mil/Documents/OfficeDocuments/Budget/BudgetMaterials/FY13/pforms//missiles.pdf

There is no justified need to replace the four existing Hellfire configurations, so we should merely choose the new system when replenishing the expended munitions. In the meantime, there will be plenty coming in from overseas, so we don't need to buy new ones for the time being. Eliminate and save $189 Million.

Javelin System

> Javelin provides the US Army and USMC a man-portable, fire-and-forget, medium-range missile with enhanced situational awareness and precision direct-fire effects to defeat armored vehicles, fortifications, and soft targets in range of military operations. Javelin has a high kill rate against a variety of targets at extended ranges under day/night, battlefield obscurants, adverse weather and multiple counter-measure conditions.

Our guys on the ground need a way to take down armored targets from the ground, but our newly homeland-centric stance places less demand therefor. Since we don't need to use them normally other than for training, and we have the ones currently located overseas, we can eliminate this for a while and save $203 Million.

TOW 2 System

> TOW missiles (BGM-71 Series) are combat proven missiles that provide heavy anti-armor/assault capability to the Army's Infantry Brigade Combat Teams (IBCT), the Stryker Brigade Combat Teams (SBCT) and the Bradley equipped Heavy Brigade Combat Team (HBCT). TOW continues to be used consistently in Operation Enduring Freedom (OEF) as the weapon of choice in precision combat engagements. TOW missiles are the primary heavy anti-armor / assault missile for the U.S. Marine Corps (USMC) and 43 allied nations.

Our guys on the ground need a way to take down armored targets from the ground, but our newly homeland-centric stance places less demand therefor. Since we don't need to use them normally other than for training, and we have the ones currently located overseas, we can eliminate this for a while and save $80 Million.

Guided MLRS Rocket

> Guided Multiple Launch Rocket System (GMLRS) munitions are the Army's primary organic Joint Expeditionary, all-weather, 24/7, tactical precision guided rockets employed by modular Fires Brigades supporting Brigade Combat Teams, Divisions, Joint Special Operations Force, and Joint Force combatant commanders and is also a key component of the Marine Corps Future Fighting Effort. GMLRS are the primary munitions for units fielded with

the High Mobility Artillery Rocket System (HIMARS) and Multiple Launch Rocket System (MLRS) M270A1 rocket and missile launcher platforms.

Since we don't need to use them normally other than for training, and we have the ones currently located overseas, we can eliminate this for a while and save $239 Million.

MLRS Reduced Range Practice Rockets (RRPR)

The Multiple Launch Rocket System (MLRS) Low Cost Reduced Range Practice Rocket (LCRRPR) is the only live training rocket or missile for the U.S. Army Field Artillery rocket and missile units/crews.

This is necessary and proper to train the military, and much cheaper than using live rockets. Keep ($7M)

High Mobility Artillery Rocket System (HIMARS)

The M142 High Mobility Artillery Rocket System (HIMARS) is a full spectrum, combat proven, all weather, 24/7 lethal and responsive, precision strike weapon system that fully supports more deployable, affordable and lethal, Brigade Combat Teams, Fires Brigade, Modular Forces, and Joint Expeditionary Forces.

By ending all OCO, we can bring our existing munitions home and store them for when they're needed, rather than blowing them up and buying replacements. Eliminate and save $12 Million.

Modification of Missiles

Patriot Mods

The Patriot weapon system modernization program implements modifications to the weapon system and maintains Integrated Logistics Support. Required modifications are identified through various means, including the following: material changes identified in the Patriot Product Improvement Program (PIP); corrections identified in the field; obsolescence issues; emerging technologies; software improvements; crew interface and communication upgrades.

The Patriot systems and missiles we have are working just fine. If they weren't, then we never should have bought them in the first place. Eliminate and save $7 Million.

MLRS Mods

FY 2013 Base procurement dollars in the amount of $2.466 million procures Enhanced Command and Control (C2), M993A1 Carrier Upgrades, Obsolescence Mitigation/Engineering Change Proposal Integration to include measures for other hardware and software required in support of launcher *upgrades. The MLRS product improvement program provides funding for integration efforts to the MLRS necessary for obsolescence mitigation, reliability improvements, incorporation of system hardware and software technologies.*

The MLRS systems and missiles we have are working just fine. If they weren't, then we never should have bought them in the first place. Eliminate and save $2.5 Million.

HIMARS Mods

FY 2013 Base procurement dollars in the amount of $6.068 million supports the installation fielding of the ICP Cab, Enhanced Command and Control (C2), and the continuation of the hardware/software obsolescence mitigation and reliability enhancement programs.

The HIMARS systems and missiles we have are working just fine. If they weren't, then we never should have bought them in the first place. Eliminate and save $6 Million.

Spares and Repair Parts

Provides for the procurement of spares to support initial fielding of new or modified end items.

Necessary and proper; keep ($7.8M)

Support Equipment and Facilities

Air Defense Targets

The Air Defense Artillery (ADA) Targets program provides target hardware and associated scoring, payload, and ground support equipment that enables Air Defense Artillery Soldiers and units to conduct required training. This training consists of Department of the Army Pamphlet (DA PAM) 350-38 (Standards in Training Commission) required gunnery tables and aerial target tracking, training and scoring.

Necessary and proper; keep ($3.8M)

Items less than $5 Million

Provides for the procurement of various tools and shop sets to perform missile maintenance repair tasks on the Army's missile systems worldwide. FY13 Base procurement dollars in the amount of $1.540 million supports the procurement of tools and shop sets for support of Patriot, Tube-launched, Optically-tracked, Wire-guided (TOW 2A) missile, TOW/ Improved Target Acquisition System (TOW 2B Aero/ITAS) missile, Multiple Launch Rocket System (MLRS), High Mobility Artillery Rocket System (HIMARS), Javelin, and Avenger.

I'm generally against items as vague as "less than $5 Million", but this assorted hardware does seem important. Necessary and proper, keep ($1.5 Million)

Production Base Support

> *This program provides Production Support and Equipment Replacement (PSR) of Government-owned equipment used in production and production testing of missile systems or missile components. FY 2013 Base procurement dollars in the amount of $5.200 million support the establishment, modernization, expansion, or replacement of Army-owned industrial facilities. These funds are essential to sustain the Army's missile warhead production capability to eliminate safety hazards by replacing worn equipment, and to refurbish facilities.*

Necessary and proper; keep ($5.2M)

Weapons and Tracked Combat Vehicles Procurement[35]

Stryker Vehicle

> *A dynamic asymmetric threat and operational environment demands full spectrum, strategically responsive, agile and dominant land forces. Immediate response by a lethal, versatile, tactically agile joint force capable of operational maneuver is essential to fulfilling the Army's Warfighting needs. The Stryker-equipped Brigade Combat Team (BCT) is this force. The use of a common platform/common chassis design reduces requirements for repair parts and logistics support in the area of operations.*

The Army doesn't need to fight wars, they need to defend America. We have plenty of Strykers out across the world; bring them home and we can forego the procurements for a while. Eliminate and save $4.9 Billion.

Stryker Mods

> *Modifications to the Stryker Family of Vehicles (FOV) are required to resolve various obsolescence issues, safety and operational related issues such as Targeting Under Armor, and system specific training devices to support the requirement for a new 91S Stryker Vehicle Maintainer Training Course.*

The Stryker seems to be a highly reliable and versatile vehicle which is working just fine. Eliminate and save $61 Million.

Bradley Mods

> *Bradley Program (MOD) procures Operation Desert Storm (ODS) vehicle upgrades to improve its Situational Awareness (SA).*

---

[35] http://asafm.army.mil/Documents/OfficeDocuments/Budget/BudgetMaterials/FY13/pforms//wtcv.pdf

The Bradley is working just fine. Eliminate and save $148 Million.

Howitzer, Med Sp Ft 155MM M109A6 Mods

> The funding profile supports all aspects of the M109A6 & M992A2 Life Cycle, to include Program Acquisition, Logistics, Engineering and in-house contractor support to the field. Additionally, it enables control of the physical and functional characteristics of items installed on both platforms.

Necessary and proper; keep ($10M)

Paladin PIM Mods

> Paladin Integrated management (PIM) is an ACAT ID, Engineering and Manufacturing Development (EMD) Phased Acquisition Program, in Government Developmental Testing that is intended to replace the current fleet of M109 Family of Vehicles.

The M109 vehicles are working just fine and require no replacement. Eliminate and save $12 Billion.

Improved Recovery Vehicle (M88A2 Hercules)

> The M88A2 Heavy Equipment Recovery Combat Utility Lift and Evacuation System (HERCULES) is a 70 ton armored, full tracked, diesel powered recovery vehicle based on the M88A1 chassis. The hull is armored for protection against small arms fire, artillery fragments, and anti-personnel mines.

We have plenty overseas to bring home; eliminate and save $3.5 Billion.

Assault Breacher Vehicle

> The Assault Breacher Vehicle (ABV) is a combined program with the United States Marine Corps (USMC) that is the Lead Service. It is a tracked combat engineer vehicle for the Marine Air Ground Task Force and the Army Heavy Brigade Combat Team (HBCT).

We have plenty overseas to bring home; eliminate and save $5 Billion. Not that we have many minefields here that need breaching.

M88 FOV Mods

> The M88 Fleet Modification Program applies Material Developer and Combat Developer approved modifications to the fielded M88 family of vehicles (FOV). These improvements include the Blue Force Tracking and the M88 FOV modifications to maintain operational readiness rates, improve vehicle safety and operation, and minimize the effects of component obsolescence. Operational Modification Kits will be procured for the M88 FOV. Specific modifications include an automatic fire extinguishing system, upgraded electrical circuit panel, improved operational and task lighting, a driver's vision

enhancer for optimal night operation, enhanced vehicle diagnostics tied to the vehicle's interactive electronic technical manuals, and an improved metal cutting tool to reduce recovery time in combat situations.

The M88s we have are working fine; eliminate and save $30 Million.

M1 Abrams Tank Mod

The Abrams Tank Fleet Modification Program applies Material Developer and Combat Developer approved modifications to the fielded Abrams family of vehicles.

The M1s we have are working fine; eliminate and save $129 Million.

Abrams Upgrade Program (more M1 mods)

This program upgrades M1/M1A1 tanks to the M1A2 System Enhancement Package (SEP) configuration. Therefore, for each M1A2 SEP produced, there was a corresponding decrease in the Army's M1/ M1A1 inventory.

The M1s we have are working fine; eliminate and save $74 Million.

Production Base Support

This program provides for the Provision of Industrial Facilities (PIF). Funds are used to establish, modernize, expand or replace facilities owned by the Army. It provides Production Support Equipment Replacement and Modernization to Government-owned equipment and real property used in the production of Weapons and Tracked Combat Vehicles.

Necessary and proper; keep ($1M)

Integrated Air Burst Weapons Systems Facility

The Maneuver Center of Excellence (MCoE), Ft Benning, GA (User Representative) identifies the XM25 Individual Semi-Automatic Airburst System (ISAAS) as their number one material solution to mitigate a critical capability gap Counter Defilade Target Engagement (CDTE) for our Soldiers in combat (defeating defilade targets from 15-500m).

IAB explodes rounds in the air above a concealed enemy 50 to 1500 feet away. A grenade launcher can burst in the air and hit a concealed enemy at 50 to 1500 feet, and is already part of the standard combat unit loadout; use those. Eliminate and save $500K.

Lightweight .50 Caliber Machine Gun

The Lightweight .50 Caliber (Cal) Machine Gun (MG) system (to include the XM205 Tripod) meets the U.S. Army requirement for a Lightweight Enhanced .50 Caliber MG. This weapon enables the Soldier to effectively suppress and

> incapacitate exposed personnel targets out to 2,000 meters and provide the
> capability to defeat lightly armored vehicles out to 1,500 meters.

This new program did not exist prior to 2013, and the procurement continues indefinitely; eliminate and save $25 Million. This is unfortunate, as it sounds like a good weapon.

Mortar Systems

> Mortar Systems includes the production of M224/A1, 60mm; M252/A1, 81mm;
> and M120/M121, 120mm Mortar Weapon Systems and includes production of
> associated equipment to include procurement of the M326 Mortar Stowage Kit
> and M1101 trailer that are used with the M120 120mm towed mortar system.

Repeal the NDAA. The military has plenty of mortar systems, and we can remove the ones from overseas. Eliminate and save $8 Million.

XM320 Grenade Launcher Module

> The M320 Grenade Launcher Module (GLM) is a 40mm low-velocity grenade
> launching weapon that attaches underneath the barrel of both the M4 carbine
> series and M16 rifle series. The weapon replaces the M203 low-velocity
> grenade launcher.

Withdraw from NATO. The M203 and the M320s we already have are plentiful and working fine, in addition to the many being removed from overseas. Eliminate and save $6 Million.

Carbine

> This funding is used to procure carbine weapons for the Army. The carbine is
> more compact than the M16 rifle series since it uses a shorter barrel and
> collapsible stock. Currently the Army uses the M4 andM4A1 Carbines. These
> carbines are 5.56mm, gas operated, air-cooled, selective-rate, shoulder fired
> small arms weapons.

This new program did not exist prior to 2013; eliminate and save $2 Million.

M4 Carbine Mods

> The M4 Carbine Modification Program provides combat optics, a Close
> Quarters Battle Kit (CQBK), an improved buttstock, a modular weapon system
> and a product improvement kit. The Modular Weapon System includes an
> adapter rail system, back-up iron sight, and M203 Grenade Launcher Kit.

The M4s we have are working just fine; eliminate and save $27 Million.

Shotgun, Modular Accessory System

> *The M26 Modular Accessory Shotgun System (MASS) is a 12 gauge shotgun that attaches underneath the barrel of the M4 and M4A1 Carbine. The MASS can also be fired in a standalone mode. The MASS provides the capability to fire lethal, non-lethal, and door breaching 12 gauge rounds. The MASS enables Soldiers to transition between their primary lethal weapons to a less-than-lethal capability without carrying a separate shotgun. Features include a recoil-absorbing buttstock, box magazine, flip-up sights and an extendable standoff device for door breaching. The weapon system can be zeroed to the sighting system of the host weapon for improved accuracy.*

This procurement ends in 2013, so we can eliminate it and save $3 Million.

Common Remotely Operated Weapon Station (CROWS)

> *The M153 Common Remotely Operated Weapon Station (CROWS) is an integrated system that provides the capability to remotely operate all standard U.S. Army machine guns (i.e., M2 Heavy Barrel Machine Guns, MK-19 Grenade Machine Guns, M240B/L Medium Machine Guns and M249 Squad Automatic Weapons) on a variety of vehicles from an Up-Armored High Mobility Multi-Purpose Wheeled Vehicle (HMMWV) to a M1A2 Main Battle Tank.*

This sounds like a great way to protect tank gunners from incoming fire. Necessary and proper; keep ($57M)

LW155 Howitzer 155m

> *The Lightweight 155mm Howitzer (LW155), also known as the M777A2, provides direct, reinforcing, and general support fires to maneuver forces. It replaces all howitzers in all missions in the USMC and replaces the M198 howitzer as the general support artillery for light forces in the Army.*

The howitzers we had before were just fine, and this program ends in 2013. Eliminate and save $14 Million.

LW155 Howitzer Mods

> *The LW155 (also known as the M777A2 howitzer) provides direct, reinforcing, and general support fires to maneuver forces as well as direct support artillery. It is an excellent example of a successful joint service program with the Marine Corps and Army working together to develop, produce, and field the howitzer. The LW155 was first fielded by the Marine Corps in April 2005 and since then the 10th, 11th, 12th, and 14th Marines and the schoolhouses have been fielded.*

This new program didn't exist before 2013; eliminate and save $27 Million.

M2 50 Cal Machine Gun Mods

The M2A1 Quick Change Barrel (QCB) Kit provides enhancements for the .50 Caliber M2 Heavy Barrel Machine Gun to provide the Soldier with the ability to quickly change the barrel without the need to reset the headspace and timing and reduce the visible muzzle flash.

The M2s we have are working just fine. Eliminate and save $40 Million.

M249 SAW Machine Gun Mods

The M249 Squad Automatic Weapon (SAW) is a 5.56mm, lightweight machine gun that can be utilized in either the automatic rifle role or light machine gun role. Various system enhancements have been identified that improve the use of this weapon system. These include the addition of a feedtray cover rail and forward rail assemblies.

The M249s are working just fine; eliminate and save $5 Million.

M240 Medium Machine Gun Mods

The M240B/L Medium Machine Gun is an infantry version of the M240 Armored Machine Gun used to replace the M60 Series Machine Gun in Light Infantry, Mechanized Infantry, Armor, Rangers, Special Forces, and select Combat Engineer units. Since the initial fielding of the M240B, various system enhancements have been identified that further improves the use of this weapon system by increasing functionality and performance capabilities, while improving training capability

The M240s are working just fine; eliminate and save $7 Million.

Sniper Rifle Mods

Program to procure modification or conversions of sniper weapons, advanced sniper accessory kits (ASAK), and M151 Spotting Scope Tactical Tripod Kit (TTK) components, combat optics, sophisticated laser range finders and fire control systems. Initial buys of items to support or meet operational needs and lighten sniper load.

The sniper rifles we have are working just fine; eliminate and save $15 Million.

M119 Mods

The M119A2 Towed Howitzer provides direct fire support for the Infantry Brigade Combat Teams. Funding in the M119 Modifications budget supports the application of modernization system enhancements and includes the integration of digital fire control components previously type classified on other weapons.

The M119s are working just fine; eliminate and save $21 Million.

M16 Mods

> *The M16 Rifle Modifications Program provides combat optics, Close Quarters Battle (CQB) Kit, collapsible buttstock, and a Modular Weapon System (MWS) suite for the M16A2 and the M16A4 Rifles. The MWS includes a rail system, a flashlight mount, a quick attach bracket kit for the M203 Grenade Launcher, and back-up iron sight for the M16A4 Rifle.*

The M16s we have are working just fine; eliminate and save $19 Million.

Modifications Less than $5 Million

> *This program procures modifications of small arms with a cost less than $5.000 million to include the procurement of accessory components of optics, mounting systems, bipods, and tripods. Optic sights allow the Soldier to identify and engage targets at longer ranges more effectively than standard iron sights.*

Some of these items have been obsoleted earlier in this section, and others are unnecessary. Eliminate and save $3 Million.

Items Less Than $5 Million

> *Program provides for the procurement of small arms and auxiliary components such as combat optics, fire controls, suppressors, weapon mounts/platforms, and adaptors to meet urgent needs or initial buys.*

Some of these items have been obsoleted earlier in this section, and others are unnecessary. Some are necessary, like magazines and cleaning kits. Cut by 75% and save $1.5 Million.

Production Base Support

> *This program provides funding to establish, modernize, expand or replace Army-owned industrial facilities and equipment used in production and production testing of Weapons and Tracked Combat Vehicles and their components.*

Necessary and proper; keep ($10M)

Industrial Preparedness

> *This program provides for Maintenance of Laid-away Industrial Facilities (MLIF), the maintenance of laid away portions of active weapons production plants, and the storage, protection, and maintenance of laid away Government-owned equipment being stored on-site at Government-owned plants.*

Necessary and proper; keep ($442K)

Small Arms Equipment

This Soldier Enhancement Program (SEP) provides ancillary small arms equipment to the Soldier. The purpose of SEP is to identify and evaluate commercially available individual weapons, munitions, Soldier equipment and accessories, etc., which can be adopted and provided to Soldiers in three years or less. The nature of the items determines the acquisition strategy, market survey, candidate evaluation and down select method, scope of testing, adoption decision and fielding process.

Necessary and proper; keep ($2M)

Spares and Repair Parts

Necessary and proper; keep ($31M)

Ammunition[36]

Ammo is necessary and proper for the Army to function. Keep ($2M)

Tactical and Support Vehicles Procurement[37]

Semitrailers, Flatbed

FY 2013 Base procurement dollars in the amount of $7.097 million procures 27 M870A4 Semitrailers to transport engineering equipment, including pavers, compactors, the Hydraulic Excavator (HYEX), and dozers. IAW Section 1815 of the FY08 NDAA this item is necessary for use by the active components and reserve components of the Armed Forces for homeland defense missions, domestic emergency responses and providing military support to civil authorities.

Repeal and rewrite the NDAA; it bothers me that many items on the budget are using it for justification. The Army can continue using whatever else it had before. This program ends in 2014; eliminate and save $263 Million.

Medium Tactical Vehicles

FY 2013 Base Procurement dollars in the amount of $346.115 million supports a quantity of 1,149 various armor capable trucks and 99 various trailers to fill 2-1/2-ton and 5-ton truck and trailer requirements, fulfill Army modularity requirements and modernize the medium fleet, reduce operating and support costs, resolve potential operational deficiencies and operate throughout the theater as a multi-purpose transportation vehicle used by combat, combat support, and combat service support units.

---

[36]http://asafm.army.mil/Documents/OfficeDocuments/Budget/BudgetMaterials/FY13/pforms//ammo.pdf
[37]http://asafm.army.mil/Documents/OfficeDocuments/Budget/BudgetMaterials/FY13/pforms//opa1.pdf

The medium fleet seems to be doing just fine as it is; eliminate and save $374 Million.

Firetrucks and associated firefighting equipment

This line is a roll-up of various Fire Trucks. These vehicles are used for fighting fires, and as a safety precaution at airfields and ammunition storage areas. In addition, these vehicles respond to forest fires, train and automobile accidents, and hazardous material incidents.

Take the trucks and equipment we have overseas, and use them here in the U.S. Eliminate and save $19 Million.

Heavy Tactical Vehicles

FY13 Base procurement dollars in the amount of $52.933 million supports 103 M983A4 Light Equipment Transporters (LETs), 7 HEMTT Load Handling System (LHS), and 327 E-CHUs to transport ammunition, petroleum, oils and lubricants, and support unit resupply and other tactical missions. Funds support Stryker and Modular Brigade Combat Teams (BCT) activations, Patriot Units, Combat Engineers, Army Pre-positioned Stocks (APS), 82nd Airborne Division, Korea.

We have plenty of these overseas which can be retasked to support domestic missions. Eliminate and save $55 Million.

Palletized Load System

The Palletized Load System Extended Service Program (PLS ESP) is a Department of the Army (DA) supported RECAP program critical to increasing the 16.5 ton payload, 10 wheel drive PLS fleet armor ready capability to include trucks and trailers.

We have plenty of these overseas which can be retasked to support domestic missions. Eliminate and save $1 Billion.

Truck Tractor, Line Haul, M915/M916

This family of vehicles consists of the M915A5 Truck and Tractor, and the M916A3 Light Equipment Transporter (LET). The M915A5 Line Haul Tractor tows the M871 and M872 flatbed semitrailers, the M967 and M969 series 5000 gallon tankers, and the M1062 7500 gallon tanker. The M915A5 is more expeditionary-ready through increased safety, range and fuel efficiency, reliability, on-board diagnostics, service intervals and Manpower and Personnel Integration (MANPRINT) considerations.

We have plenty of these overseas which can be retasked to support domestic missions. Eliminate. No procurement was requested for FY2013, but budgets resume in 2014.

Heavy Expanded Mobile Tactical Truck

The Heavy Expanded Mobility Tactical Truck Extended Service Program (HEMTT-ESP) is a Vice Chief of Staff of the Army approved RECAP program critical to increasing the 11.5 ton load, 8 wheel drive HEMTT fleet armor ready capability.

We have plenty of these overseas which can be retasked to support domestic missions. Eliminate and save $448 Million.

High Mobility Multipurpose Wheeled Vehicle (HMMWV / Humvee)

The High Mobility Multipurpose Wheeled Vehicle (HMMWV) Recapitalization (RECAP) program will support the recapitalization of Up-Armored HMMWVs (UAH) returning from theater. The recapitalization of UAHs will support the incorporation of the latest HMMWV technical insertions common to the fleet and upgrading vehicle components (frame rails, air conditioning, on-board vehicle power, etc).

We have plenty of these overseas which can be retasked to support domestic missions. Eliminate and save $127 Million.

Tactical Wheeled Vehicle Protection Kits

The Heavy Tactical Vehicle Protection Kits program provides an Armor Survivability Suite protection which includes B-Kits, Fire Suppression, Fuel Tank Fire Suppression Blanket (FTFS), Fuel Tank Self Sealant (FTSS) and Tank Armor Module (TAM) to enhance survivability. The Armor Survivability Suite components are mounted to an A-kit Heavy Tactical Vehicle (HEMTT, HETs, PLS, Line Haul, Tanker Trailer) configuration to address numerous threats that the DoD has identified.

The DoD's vendors really should integrate these items into the vehicles when they sell them in the first place. We have plenty of these overseas which can be retasked to support domestic missions. Eliminate and save $73 Million.

Modification of In Service Equipment

This line funds the Army's plan to recapitalize Mine Resistant Ambush Protected (MRAP) RG33L+ variant vehicles originally bought to fulfill Operational Needs Statement (ONS) or Joint Operational Needs Statement (JUONS) into a Program of Record (PoR) Medium Mine Protected Vehicle (MMPV) for Engineer Route Clearance and Explosive Ordnance Disposal (EOD). In addition, starting in FY13, this line implements the plan to upgrade a mix of

ONS/JUONS vehicles (Husky, Panther MMPV, RG-31, and Buffalo) in coordination with a concurrent reset program to field PoR vehicles to Engineer; EOD; Chemical, Biological, Radiological and Nuclear Units; and Area Clearance Platoons.

These vehicles are just fine as they are. Eliminate and save $92 Million.

Mine Resistant Ambush Protected (MRAP) Mods

This budget line implement's the Army's plan to upgrade the Mine Resistant, Ambush Protected (MRAP) fleet returning from theater for Army enduring requirements in accordance with the Army's Tactical Wheeled Vehicle (TWV) strategy.

These vehicles are just fine as they are. Eliminate and save $464 Million.

Passenger Carrying Vehicles

This line is a roll-up of Sedans, Ambulances and Buses. Passenger Carrying Vehicles Vehicles are of commercial design intended to provide transportation for Army personnel and family members.

We have plenty of these overseas which can be retasked to support domestic missions. Eliminate and save $3 Million.

Other Non-Tactical Vehicles

This line is a roll-up of Special Purpose Vehicles, General Purpose Vehicles, and the Personnel Carrying Semi-Trailer Vans. Special and General Purpose vehicles are used in the direct support of facility engineering, maintenance activities, and for general administrative use in transporting personnel and cargo.

We have plenty of these overseas which can be retasked to support domestic missions. Eliminate and save $17 Million.

Communications and Electronics Procurement[38]

Joint Combat Identification Marking System

Joint Combat Identification Marking System (JCIMS) is comprised of three separate devices used to enhance friendly object identification capabilities by providing the ability to display controlled, discrete, visible cues that can be identified at extended ranges and under conditions of limited visibility by sensor-equipped ground and air observers, and individuals equipped with the proper equipment. JCIMS devices emit or reflect either near infrared or far infrared (IR) radiation.

---

[38]http://asafm.army.mil/Documents/OfficeDocuments/Budget/BudgetMaterials/FY13/pforms//opa2.pdf

This seems a bit much, we've been buying them for several years, and procurement ends after 2013. Eliminate and save $1.4 Million.

Warfighter Information network Tactical (WINT) – Ground Forces Tactical Network

> Warfighter Information Network-Tactical (WIN-T) is the Army's strategy to achieve a world-class Joint expeditionary network enabled by information technologies that support the goals of the Army Campaign Plan and other Army/Joint mandates.

Redundant to DISA functions; eliminate and save $412 Million. There should be *one* DoD-wide information network; the rest are redundant.

Signal Modernization Program

> The Signal Modernization program will increase the number of communication nodes (generally one node per command post) an Expeditionary Signal Battalion (ESB) can support from 30 to approximately 69 nodes. The additional nodes will be modular, scalable and fully interoperable with WIN-T Increments 1 and 2.

There's nothing wrong with the communication nodes we have; eliminate and save $46 Million.

JCSE Equipment

> The Joint Communications Support Element (JCSE) mission is to provide, on short notice, those critical communications required to support Joint Task Force support (JTF) and Joint Special Operations Task Force (JSOTF) headquarters.

No reason they can't use existing radio technologies, which have been around for decades. Eliminate and save $5M.

Defense Enterprise Wideband Satcom Systems

> The Defense Enterprise Wideband SATCOM Systems (DEWSS) provides super high frequency (SHF) wideband and anti-jam (AJ) satellite communications supporting critical national strategic and tactical Command, Control, Communications and Intelligence (C3I) requirements.

No reason they can't use existing radio technologies, which have been around for decades. Eliminate and save $152M.

Transportable Tactical Command Communications

> Transportable Tactical Command Communications (T2C2) provides small teams and company-sized early entry units robust voice and data communications capabilities in the early phases of joint operations. T2C2 will

also provide transportable communication systems to enable these units to be integrated into a higher capacity network. T2C2 transitions Global Rapid Response Information Package (AN/PSC-15 GRRIP systems), [...]

No reason they can't use existing radio technologies, which have been around for decades. Eliminate and save $7M.

SHF Terminal

Super High Frequency (SHF) terminal, also referred to as the Phoenix satisfies tactical, highly mobile, command and control, intelligence, fire support, air defense and logistics wideband communications requirements in support of Army and multi-service users. Phoenix provides the Army operational flexibility by operating over four bands (C, X, Ka, and Ku) on military and commercial satellites resulting in less dependency on costly and high demand commercial satellites.

No reason they can't use existing radio technologies, which have been around for decades. Eliminate and save $9M

NAVSTAR GPS

The Navstar Global Positioning System (GPS) is a passive, space-based, radio positioning and navigation system providing precise, three-dimensional position, navigation, velocity and timing information to warfighters. The Navstar GPS program is designated as a DoD Space Program and the United States Air Force (USAF) is the executive service. The Joint Program Office develops GPS User Equipment (PE 35164F) with direct Army management and participation.

As my proposal eliminates all ground vehicle procurements, and the Army has already procured tens of thousands of these devices, we don't need any more. Eliminate and save $8 Million.

SMART-T

Secure Mobile Anti-Jam Reliable Tactical Terminal (SMART-T) is a multi-channel satellite terminal that provides beyond line of sight support for the current and future tactical communications network. The SMART-T provides a robust, protected satellite capability to permit uninterrupted communications, as our advancing forces move beyond the line-of-sight of terrestrial systems.

The Army doesn't need yet another way to talk with its units. Pick one, and go with it. Eliminate; save $3.3 Billion.

Global Broadcast Service

Global Broadcast Service (GBS) program provides high speed broadcast of large volume data and multimedia products including Unmanned Arial

Vehicles (UAV) video, imagery, intelligence, weather, and biometric data, access to national level repositories of intelligence products and other critical mission planning tools to deployed Soldiers and garrisoned forces world-wide. The Air Force (USAF) is designated as the executive service and leads the Joint Program Office (JPO) with Army supporting JPO for the development and procurement of the Transportable Ground Receive Suites (TGRS) and the Theater Injection Point (TIP) and is the ACAT III manager for these items.

We have the Internet now, and broadcasting can be done for free; this technology is obsolete. Eliminate and save $363 Million.

TAC SAT Mods

Mod of In-Svc Equipment (TACSAT) funds the upgrades to Army tactical satellite communications equipment. This Mod of In-Svc funding procures and fields Tactical Computer Digital Mission Planner (TCDMP) AN/PYQ-19. T-CDMP replaces the current Communications Planning System (CPS)(AN/PSQ-17). The T-CDMP is an integrated tool on which Milstar, and future AEHF planning will be performed. The T-CDMP supports real-time mission planning and network management to efficiently use limited satellite resources.

The tac sat system is working just fine. Eliminate and save $597 Million.

Army Global Command and Control System

Global Command and Control System-Army (GCCS-A) provides critical automated Command and Control (C2) tools for Combatant Commanders (COCOMs) and Army Component Commanders (ACCs) to enhance warfighter capabilities throughout the spectrum of conflict during Joint and combined operations in support of National Security.

Redundant to DISA functions. There should be *one* DoD-wide information network; the rest are redundant. The Army doesn't need yet another way to talk with its units. Pick one, and go with it. Eliminate; save $11 Million.

Army Data Distribution System

The Army Data Distribution System (ADDS) is a Command, Control, Communication and Intelligence (C3I) program which currently consists of the Enhanced Position Location Reporting System (EPLRS). EPLRS is a critical mobile wireless data communications backbone for the Army's Tactical Internet.

Redundant to DISA functions. There should be *one* DoD-wide information network; the rest are redundant. The Army doesn't need yet another way to talk with its units. Pick one, and go with it. Eliminate; save $1 Million.

Joint Tactical Radio System

JTRS is the Department of Defense (DoD) family of common software-defined programmable radios that will form the foundation of information radio frequency transmission for Joint Vision 2020. JTRS will provide transformational communication capabilities for the warfighter.

The Army doesn't need yet another way to talk with its units. The Army has been buying radios for decades and should require no further radios. Eliminate; save $50 Million.

Mid-Tier Networking Vehicular Radio

Joint Tactical Radio System (JTRS) is the Department of Defense (DoD) family of common radios that will form the foundation of information radio frequency transmission for Joint Vision 2020. The Mid-Tier Networking Vehicular Radio (MNVR) Program complements the JTRS family of interoperable, modular software-defined radios which operate as nodes in a network to ensure secure wireless communication and networking services for mobile and fixed forces.

The Army doesn't need yet another way to talk with its units. The Army has been buying radios for decades and should require no further radios. Eliminate; save $387 Million.

Radio Terminal Set, MIDS LVT

The Multifunctional Information Distribution System Low Volume Terminal (MIDS LVT) is a communications device that provides situational awareness information exchange between aircraft, airborne command and control, Ground Air Defense and shipboard platforms in the Tactical Data Link-16 Network.

Redundant to DISA functions. The Army doesn't need yet another way to talk with its units. The Army has been buying radios for decades and should require no further radios. Eliminate; save $8 Million.

Sincgars Family

The Single Channel Ground and Airborne Radio System (SINCGARS) Very High Frequency-Frequency Modulated (VHF-FM) Radio Communications System provides the primary means of command and control for combat/combat support/combat service support units.

Redundant to DISA functions. The Army doesn't need yet another way to talk with its units. The Army has been buying radios for decades and should require no further radios. Eliminate; save $9 Million.

AMC Critical Items

The AMC Critical Items Program oversees the process by which Class II and VII end items that are out of production and, consequently, now under AMC management, are re-procured to fill shortages. The program supports major end-item (weapon system) inventory management through item managers. The program requirements represent actual and projected equipment deficiencies and do not include obsolete items or items replaced by modernized successors managed by G8.

The Army should not have to keep track of which of its procurements will no longer be produced. Rather, weapons and equipment manufacturers should present information and demonstrations to the Army in hopes of making major sales. The Army, in turn, should choose from the available options, like any other consumer. Eliminate and save $24 Million.

Tractor Desk

The details for this program are reported in accordance with Title 10, United States Code, Section 119(a)(1)."

This is not a good way to justify a federal budget procurement. Very well. Let us examine 10 USC 119(a)(1) [39]...

Not later than March 1 of each year, the Secretary of Defense shall submit to the defense committees a report on special access programs. (2) Each such report shall set forth the total amount requested for special access programs of the Department of Defense in the President's budget for the next fiscal year submitted under section 1105 of title 31 [...]

This tells me nothing pertaining to a "tractor desk". The program provides no justification, I could find no committee report on it, and it sounds silly. Tractors do not need desks, and desks do not need tractors. Eliminate and save $8 Million.

Spider APLA Remote Control Unit

The Spider is a hand emplaced, remotely controlled, anti-personnel munition system that was designed to replace the capability of the persistent anti-personnel landmines banned from use after December 2010 per US Landmine policy. Spider, as a Man-in-the-Loop system, offers numerous capabilities for asymmetric warfare focusing on the control of insurgents and small unit force protection. The system is made up of 4 subsystems: Man-in-the-Loop (the human operator), Remote Control Station (the system command and control

---

[39] http://www.law.cornell.edu/uscode/text/10/119

station), Repeater (a communication link to the munitions that provides extended range), and Munition Control Units (delivers anti-personnel effects).

Eliminate the persistent anti-personnel landmines ban and go back to them, though this does not necessitate the elimination of the RC units we've already bought. Eliminate and save $155 Million.

Soldier Enhancement Program Communications and Electronics

The Soldier Enhancement Program (SEP) identifies and evaluates commercially available individual weapons, munitions, optics, combat clothing, individual equipment, water supply, shelters, communication and navigational aids which can be adopted and provided to Soldiers in three years or less. The nature of the item determines the acquisition strategy, market survey, candidate evaluation and down select method, scope of testing, adoption decision and fielding process.

Weapons and equipment manufacturers should present information and demonstrations to the Army in hopes of making major sales. The Army, in turn, should choose from the available options, like any other consumer. Eliminate and save $2 Million.

Tactical Communications and Protective System

The Tactical Communications and Protective System (TCAPS) enhances survivability through improved threat detection in operational environments and supports situational awareness by enabling clear and understandable communications over radios in combat situations where hearing can be temporarily impaired from gunfire and explosions. By reducing noise-induced hearing damage, TCAPS contributes to the reduction of post-service disability compensation.

A more effective way to reduce hearing damage and disability compensation needs is to stop invading countries and telling them how to live. Eliminate and save $2 Million.

Gunshot Detection System

The Gunshot Detection System (GDS) was identified by the Vice Chief of Staff of the Army for insertion into the Capabilities Development for Rapid Transition (CDRT) process. A Capabilities Production Document (CPD) was approved on 13 Feb 2009. On 3 May 2010 an Army Acquisition Objective (AAO) was approved for 13,424 systems. The system uses passive acoustic and / or another sensor modality for detection, computer-based signal processing, and both aural and visual indications to help troops locate a hostile shooter, by reporting relative shooter azimuth, range, and elevation from incoming small *arms fire. The visual data is displayed on a single ruggedized display and the verbal/voice over a speaker.*

Any soldier who's passed basic training knows how to identify a gunshot and can probably tell where it came from. The need to identify the few remainders can easily be eliminated by not being in a gunfight-prone area in the first place. Bring our troops home and eliminate GDS, saving $51 Million.

Radio, Improved HF (COTS) Family

Radio Improved High-Frequency (HF) Commercial Off the Shelf (COTS) Family consists of the AN/PRC-148/152 Tactical Handheld Radio (HHR), the AN/PRC-150 HF Radio, and the AN/PSC-5D & AN/ PRC-117 COTS Tactical Satellite (TACSAT) Radios.

The Army doesn't need yet another way to communicate with its mobile units. It needs, in fact, exactly one and only one way to do so. Eliminate and save $1 million.

Medical Comm for CBT Casualty Care

The Medical Communications for Combat Casualty Care (MC4) System provides multipliers to the medical force structure through the acquisition of information technology solutions for the deployable medical forces. The MC4 System will fulfill the requirements highlighted in United States Code: Title 10, Subtitle A, Part II, Chapter 55, Section 1074f, mandating the proper documentation of deployed service members' medical treatment to include pre- and post-deployment screening and its associated medical surveillance, enabling each soldier to have a comprehensive, life-long medical record of all illnesses and injuries.

The Army doesn't need yet another way to transfer records from one place to another. This could be accomplished with an email. Eliminate and save $9 Million.

CI Automation Architecture

This program provides the Army, as a member of the DoD counterintelligence (CI) community, with an advanced CI operational equipment to enhance Army's ability to counter the global threat through significant improvements in information sharing, common situational awareness, and knowledge management in a joint operational environment.

If we eliminate the worldwide posture of our Army operations, this becomes less important. If we then consider the size, scope, and pervasiveness of our intelligence community, this becomes unnecessary. Eliminate and save $1.6 Million.

Reserve CA/MISO GPF Equipment

This program is vital in conventional operations and irregular warfare. Combined, Civil Affairs (CA) and Military Information Support Operations (MISO) are comprised of 17 systems. These systems are critical to the war fighter's capabilities in all overseas contingency operations, theater security cooperation, and stability, transition and reconstruction operations

In our day to day operations, combatant commanders shouldn't need to engage with foreign audiences, and we should have no need for joint interagency or multinational operations. In fact, our troops should be here, defending our borders, instead of Afghanistan's. Eliminate and save $24 Million.

TSEC - Army Key Management System (AKMS)

Army Key Management System (AKMS) is the Army's system to automate the functions of Communications Security (COMSEC) key management control and distribution, Electronic Counter-Countermeasures(ECCM) generation and distribution and Signal Operation Instructions (SOI) management. AKMS electronically generates and distributes Army key and key-related material, thereby limiting adversarial access to, and reducing the vulnerability of, Army Command, Control, Communications, Computers, Intelligence (C4I) systems. It provides key management to communications and network planning.

Necessary and proper; keep ($23M).

Information System Security Program – ISSP

This program procures and fields Communications Security (COMSEC) solutions to secure the National Network Enterprise. New and emerging architectures are driving the need to replace current inventory of stove pipe systems with technologically advanced (network centric/GIG compliant) devices that incorporate Chairman of the Joint Chiefs of Staff and Joint Requirements Oversight Council directed cryptographic modernization, advanced key management and network centric performance capabilities.

The availability of something newer does not obsolete the older equivalent. Eliminate and save $18 Million.

Terrestrial Transmission

The Army Special Access Program Enterprise Portal (ASEP) is the Army's only Top Secret compartmented enterprise wide area network providing a secure communications capability (email, video, teleconferencing, document storage/sharing, instant messaging, etc) for the transmission of highly classified Special Access Required (SAR) information between the Army Operations Center (AOC), the Army staff, Major Army Commands, Army

Special Access Programs (SAPs) and Army Sensitive Activities (SAs). ASEP was directed by the Army G3 in May 2005 to address immediate operational needs.

Redundant to SIPRNET and DISA functionality. The DoD needs one and only one global enterprise-wide information network, and SIPRNET is even compartmentalized. Eliminate and save $3 Million.

Base Support Communications

This program funds Army-wide requirements for garrison Land Mobile Radio (LMR) systems. Army non-tactical garrison LMR systems and radios are commercial solutions that provide mobile and portable radio support to garrison safety, force protection, homeland defense, and facilities maintenance operations. Garrison LMR systems and radios are used by installation military police, fire departments, medical personnel, and other emergency response activities to both synchronize emergency response efforts and for critical communications support during mobilization, deployment, and split-based operations.

The Army needs a way to communicate with its mobile units, but it only needs one radio communications network. Keep this one, and make it the single communications network across the entire Army ($14M).

Worldwide Technical Control Improvement Program (WWTCIP)

The World Wide Technical Control Improvement Program (WWTCIP) is a continuing program to initiate, improve, expand and automate the Army's Technical Control Facilities (TCF) in support of the Global Defense Network (GDN). The TCFs enable technical control personnel to gain full use of communication resources in support of the Soldier and gain information dominance.

The Army's technical control facilities and the GDN are working fine and require no new initiation, improvement, or automation; let alone expansion. Eliminate and save $10 Million.

Information Systems

This program provides for improvement/modernization of Army base level voice, data and video networks worldwide. It encompasses nontactical telecommunications services in support of Army base operations, Army Knowledge Management (AKM) Goal 3, Army Campaign Plan and Information Systems for Command and Control (C2) requirements and also acquires common user information systems in support of Military Construction, Army (MCA) projects.

The Army's voice, data, and video networks are working fine, and require no new improvements nor modernizations. The Army's networks in general are redundant to DISA functions. Eliminate and save $142 Million.

Installation Information Infrastructure Modernization Program (I3MP)

> *The Installation Information Infrastructure Modernization Program (I3MP) encompasses the modernization and upgrade of the Telecommunications/Information Infrastructure on Army installations in the Continental United States (CONUS), Europe and Pacific theaters, as well as Army Enterprise Systems.*

The Army's base infrastructures are working fine and require no modernization or upgrades. However, upgrades may become necessary to support the additional capacity of the hundreds of thousands of troops I want to bring home. Eliminate for now and bring back in if it is determined that the additional capacity is needed. Save $58 Million.

Pentagon Information Management and Telecom

> *The U.S. Army Program Executive Office Enterprise Information Systems (PEO EIS) is responsible for providing continued modernized integrated information technology and telecommunication capabilities to Defense and Army activities within the Pentagon and worldwide. PEO EIS supports a cadre of optimized network operations, enterprise level services, and applications to the Defense and Army acquisition, technology, logistics, and business system community. This includes net-centric secure access to data, voice, communication, knowledge, collaboration, and identity management infrastructures for classified and unclassified domains that ensures interoperability and preserves the Warfighters global infrastructure, connectivity, and worldwide presence.*

Modernization of I.T. and telecommunications capabilities is not necessary for a functioning army, or our army wouldn't have had one for centuries. However, the computer and phone networks themselves are necessary. Keep and reduce by 25%, saving $1.25 Million.

JTT/CIBS-M

> *The Joint Program Office (JPO) supports all Services and Special Operations Command (SOCOM). The Integrated Broadcast Service (IBS) is the worldwide Department of Defense (DoD) standard network for transmitting time-sensitive tactical and strategic intelligence and targeting data to all echelons of Joint Service operational users. The JPO's role is to consolidate and replace existing IBS terminal functionality and capability, and to expedite execution of the IBS Technical Transition Plan (TTP).*

Redundant to DISA, DoD SOCOM, and other Army procurements. The Army doesn't need yet another way to communicate with its field units. Eliminate and save $2 Million.

Prophet Ground

> Prophet Enhanced (PE) is the tactical commander's sole organic ground-based Signals Intelligence (SIGINT)/Electronic Warfare system for the Brigade Combat Team (BCT), Stryker Brigade Combat Team (SBCT), and Battlefield Surveillance Brigade (BfSB). Its primary mission is to provide 24-hour Situation Development and Information Superiority to the supported maneuver brigade to enable the most effective engagement of enemy forces.

This seems redundant to DISA and other Army procurements. The Army doesn't need yet another way to communicate with its field units. Eliminate and save $49 Million.

Distributed Common Ground System - Army (DCGS-A (MIP))

> Distributed Common Ground System - Army (DCGS-A) is the Intelligence, Surveillance and Reconnaissance (ISR) System of Systems (SoS) for Joint, Interagency, Allied, Coalition, and National data analysis, sharing and collaboration. The core functions of DCGS-A are: the vertical and horizontal synchronization of ISR Processing, Exploitation and Dissemination (PED); operating in a networked environment at multiple security levels; [...]

This seems redundant to DISA, DoD SOCOM, NSA, NIA, and other Army procurements and projects. Eliminate and save $274 Million.

Joint Tactical Ground Station (JTAGS)

> The Joint Tactical Ground Station (JTAGS) system provides the only means for directly downlinking raw data from the Defense Support Program satellites, processing that data into ballistic missile early warning, alerting, cueing and disseminating that information reliably to theater combatant commanders. JTAGS currently has five systems and is deployed in three theaters (PACOM, EUCOM, and CENTCOM).

This seems redundant to DISA and other Army procurements and projects. Eliminate and save $3 Million.

TROJAN (MIP)

> TROJAN, as an Army Intelligence system, has been providing a direct support and an operational readiness capability to soldiers since 1983. TROJAN exists to provide value added to the tactical commander with remote access to signal environments, in order to maintain a high state of operational readiness and enhance the training and sustainment of highly perishable intelligence skills.

Additionally, the TROJAN architecture provides the infrastructure enabling split-based and force protection operations in direct support of the warfighter.

This seems redundant to DISA and other Army procurements and projects. Eliminate and save $21 Million.

Mod of In-Service Equipment (Intel SPT / MIP)
Special Purpose Systems (BZ9751): Upgrades/enhancements will be made to the ground-based Signals Intelligence (SIGINT) system with additional Technical Insertion (TI) Capabilities. Prophet Enhanced (PE) is the tactical commander's sole organic ground-based SIGINT/Electronic Warfare system for the Brigade Combat Team (BCT), Stryker Brigade Combat Team (SBCT), and Battlefield Surveillance Brigade (BfSB).

The ground-based sigint systems we have now are working just fine. Eliminate and save $2 Million.

CI Humint auto reporting and collection (CHARCS)
The Counterintelligence (CI) and Human Intelligence (HUMINT) Automated Reporting and Collection System (CHARCS) is the Army's CI and HUMINT tactical collection and reporting system. CHARCS provides automation support for information collection, reporting, investigations, source & interrogation operations and document exploitation. The CHARCS automation architecture extends from the individual HUMINT team soldier or CI agent to the Division and Corps Analysis and Control Element (ACE).

This big, fancy, expensive system could be replaced with a free wiki. Eliminate and save $14 Million.

Lightweight Counter Mortar Radar
The AN/TPQ-50 (formerly known as AN/TPQ-48(V)3) Lightweight Counter Mortar Radar (LCMR) is a digitally connected, day/night mortar, cannon, and rocket locating system. It is used to detect, locate, track, and report enemy indirect firing systems and also provides observed fires from friendly units. The AN/TPQ-50 is capable of being deployed in two configurations, standalone or vehicle mounted. It can be set up and operational in 20 minutes and disassembled in 10 minutes.

This sounds like a very useful piece of equipment, but entirely unnecessary when we're not at war and expecting incoming mortars. Given that my proposal eliminates all ongoing wars, this would not be the case. We have already procured hundreds of these devices; eliminate and save $100 Million.

Counter Radio Controlled Improvised Explosive Devices Electronics Warfare (RCIED/CREW)

> *The Counter Radio Controlled Improvised Explosive Devices (RCIED) Electronics Warfare (CREW) family of Electronic Counter Measure (ECM) systems is used to provide essential force protection for fixed sites, vehicle platforms and soldiers.*

The most effective way to protect against IEDs is to remove our troops from the areas prone to the IEDs. Eliminate and save $15 Million.

Family of Persistent Surveillance Capabilities

> *Persistent Threat Detection System (PTDS) and Persistent Ground Surveillance System (PGSS) comprise the tethered component of Persistent Surveillance Systems (PSS-T). PTDS is under Program Executive Office for Intelligence, Electronic Warfare and Sensors (PEO IEW&S), and PGSS is under NAVAIR. PSS-T is a critical Quick Reaction Capability (QRC) program[.]*

Procurement for this item ends after 2013; the Army has plenty of ways to survey targets. Eliminate and save $52 Million.

Counterintelligence / Security Countermeasures

> *Program description information identified in Volume II of the Military Intelligence Program Congressional Justification Book.*

Fair enough, I'll assume it's classified since I can't find this MIPCJ book. Eliminate the OCO component and save $205 Million.

Counterintelligence Modernization

> *The Counterintelligence (CI) Modernization effort provides resources for the sustainment of the CI IT infrastructure used by the CI components of the Army. This architecture and infrastructure includes shared databases, workstations, global communications, and adequate connectivity for CI agents and specialists.*

This can be done with a free wiki. Eliminate and save $1 Million.

Forward Area Air Defense Command and Control (FAAD) GBS

> *The Improved Sentinel system is used with the Forward Area Air Defense Command and Control [FAAD C2] element, and is a supporting program to the Integrated Air and Missile Defense architecture via the Integrated Air and Missile Defense Battle Command System [IBCS] to provide critical air surveillance of the forward areas.*

This procurement ends after 2013, and our systems are plenty modern. Eliminate and save $8 Million.

Sentinel Mods

> The Improved Sentinel system is used with the Forward Area Air Defense Command and Control [FAAD C2] element, and it is a supporting program to the Integrated Air and Missile Defense architecture via the Integrated Air and Missile Defense Battle Command System [IBCS] to provide critical air surveillance of the forward areas.

Our forward area air defense systems are plenty modern. Eliminate and save $33 Million.

Sense Through the Wall (STTW)

> Sense Through The Wall (STTW) (AN/PPS-26) is a lightweight, handheld sensor that provides dismounted Soldiers with the capability to detect and locate targets through walls from a standoff distance up to 20 meters. The AN/PPS-26 provides near real time detection and location of moving and stationary targets behind obstructions.

A fancy way of referring to infrared or similar cameras, this program is unnecessary. Eliminate and save $6 Million.

Night Vision Devices

> FY2013 Base funding in the amount of $166.516 mllion will support the procurement of 6,906 Enhanced Night Vision Goggles, 587 Laser Target Location Modules and 44 TS-3895A Test Sets. Also, it will support fielding and management of AN/PVS-14 Night Vision Goggles and Clip-On Sniper Night Sight systems.

When we bring our troops home, we'll have plenty of these left over in addition to the others we've procured over the years. Eliminate and save $167 Million.

Night Vision, Thermal Weapon Sight

> The AN/PAS-13 Thermal Weapon Sight (TWS) allows the Soldier to acquire and engage targets in all weather conditions. The TWS program supports the Army's objectives by increasing the individual Soldier's situational awareness, lethality, mobility and survivability during periods of significantly reduced visibility.

When we bring our troops home, we'll have plenty of these left over in addition to the others we've procured over the years. Eliminate and save $19 Million.

Small Tactical Optical Rifle Mounted MLRF

> *The AN/PSQ-23 Small Tactical Optical Rifle Mounted (STORM) Micro-Laser Range Finder (MLRF) is a weapon-mounted multi-function laser system. It provides an eye safe laser range finder, digital compass, Infrared (IR) and visible aiming lights, and an IR illuminator for far target location with continuous range, accuracy, weight and power performance enhanced capabilities. It also has an embedded training system, Multiple Integrated Laser Engagement System (MILES).*

When we bring our troops home, we'll have plenty of these left over in addition to the others we've procured over the years. Eliminate and save $15 Million.

Green Laser Interdiction System (GLIS)

> *The Green Laser Interdiction System (GLIS) is a rifle-mounted (M4/Modular Weapon System (MWS) carbine or M16A4) laser system that allows the Soldier to interdict non-combatants through non-lethal effects up to 300 meters. It is also designed to divert, disrupt, or delay potential enemies before they can engage friendly forces.*

This program ends after 2014. When we bring our troops home, we'll have plenty of these left over in addition to the others we've procured over the years. Eliminate and save $1 Million.

Indirect Fire Protection Family of Systems

> *Indirect Fire Protection Capability (IFPC) Increment 1, will be the Army's acquisition program to provide the existing C-RAM Warn capability to all Maneuver Brigade Combat Teams (BCT). IFPC Increment 1 is a horizontal technology insertion, using current   C-RAM Warning equipment, to provide early, localized warning.*

Our troops were clearly able to handle themselves in the field before this brand-new procurement was added in 2013. Eliminate and save $1.8 Billion.

Profiler

> *The AN/TMQ-52 Meteorological Measuring Set-Profiler (MMS-P) uses a ground tactical meteorological (TACMET) sensor and Meteorological (MET) data from communication satellites along with an advanced weather model to provide highly accurate MET data covering an operational area of 500 kilometers with a tested range of 60 kilometers.*

When we bring our troops home, we'll have plenty of these left over in addition to the others we've procured over the years. Eliminate and save $92 Million.

Modification of In-Service Equipment
> *funds the modifications to the Firefinder Radars, the AN/TPQ-36 Mortar Locating Radar and the AN/TPQ-37 Artillery Locating Radar. The Firefinder Radars were designed to meet the Army's critical need to quickly and accurately locate the large number and variety of hostile indirect fire weapons.*

When we bring our troops home, we'll have plenty of these left over in addition to the others we've procured over the years. Eliminate and save $18 Million.

Join Battle Command Platform (JBC-P)
> *Joint Battle Command - Platform (JBC-P) provides true Joint Force Command and Control (C2) and Situational Awareness (SA) capability at the platform level and enables mission accomplishment across the entire spectrum of Joint military operations.*

This can be done with a wiki or a SharePoint site. Eliminate and save $137 Million.

Modification of In-Service Equipment
> *MOD OF IN-SERVICE EQUIPMENT (LLDR) funds the retrofit of the Lightweight Laser Designator Rangefinder (LLDR, AN/PED-1) to incorporate Target Acquisition improvements. The LLDR is a modular system designed for crew-served, man-portable day/night all-weather use for determining the precise location of threat targets, and for designating threat targets for engagement by Global Position System (GPS) precision and laser guided munitions for a variety of Army and Joint weapons systems.*

There's nothing wrong with our rangefinders. If there were, then we shouldn't have bought them in the first place. Eliminate and save $191 Million.

Mortar Fire Control System
> *The Mortar Fire Control System (MFCS) accurately determines weapon position and orientation, navigates, calculates ballistics, and communicates digitally on the fire support net. The MFCS consists of the M95/M96 version that is used on mounted 120mm mortars in Heavy and Stryker Brigade Combat Teams, and the M150/M151 version that is used on the M120A1 120mm Towed Mortar[.]*

When we bring our troops home, we'll have plenty of these left over in addition to the others we've procured over the years. Eliminate and save $246 Million.

Enhanced Sensor and Monitoring System

> This program addresses requirements validated by the Office of the Under Secretary of Defense, Acquisition, Technology & Logistics (OUSD AT&L) as related to Weapons of Mass Destruction (WMD) arms control and disarmament. The Department of Defense (DoD) has responsibility to manage the implementation, compliance, monitoring and inspection for existing and emerging nuclear arms control activities.

Necessary and proper; keep ($2M).

Tactical Operations Centers

> Product Manager for Command Post Systems and Integration (CPS&I)(formerly Tactical Operation Centers: TOCs) manages the Standardized Integrated Command Post System (SICPS) Program. SICPS provides standardized Command Post infrastructure allowing Commanders and their staffs to digitally train, plan, prepare and execute Mission Command in support of Unified Land Operations.

Necessary and proper; keep and cut by standard 25%, saving $57 Million.

Fire Support C2 Facility

> Fire Support Command and Control (FSC2) systems automate the planning and execution of fire support so that a suitable weapon or group of weapons adequately covers targets.

This seems to be the job of any well-trained field commander. Eliminate and save $34 Million.

Battle Command Sustainment Support System (BCS3)

> The Battle Command Sustainment Support System (BCS3) is the logistics Command and Control (C2) Logistics (LOG)C2 solution for U.S. land forces.

Redundant to DISA, DoD, and other Army procurements. Eliminate and save $24 Million.

FAAD C2

> FY 13 Base procurement dollars in the amount of $5.031 million provides Software Maintenance Support and Common Hardware Support (CHS) upgrades. IAW Section 1815 of the FY08 NDAA this item is necessary for use by the active components and reserve components of the Armed Forces for homeland defense missions, domestic emergency responses, and providing the military support to civil authorities.

Necessary and proper; keep and reduce by standard 25%, saving $1.3 Million.

Air and Missile Defense Planning and Control Systems

The Air and Missile Defense Planning and Control System (AMDPCS) is an Army Objective Force System that provides integration of Air and Missile Defense (AMD) operations at all echelons. AMDPCS systems are deployed with Air Defense Artillery (ADA) brigades (Bdes), Army Air Missile Defense Commands (AAMDCs), and Air Defense and Airspace Management (ADAM) Cells at the Brigade Combat Teams (BCTs), Multi-Functional Support Brigades, Corps and Divisions. AMDPCS systems also provide air defense capabilities to Homeland Defense systems. The fielding of ADAM Cells is essential in fulfilling the Army's Campaign Plan requirement. ADAM Cells provide the Commander at BCTs, Bdes and Divisions with air defense situational awareness and airspace management capabilities. They also provide the interoperability link with Joint, multinational and coalition forces.

Necessary and proper; keep and reduce by standard 25%, saving $1.3 Billion.

Knight Family

The M1200 Armored Knight provides precision strike capability by accurately locating and designating targets for ground, precision guided, air-delivered, and laser-guided ordnance and conventional munitions. It replaces the M707 Knight High Mobility Multi-Purpose Wheeled Vehicle (HMMWV base) and M981 Fire Support Team Vehicle (M113 base) used by Combat Observation Lasing Teams (COLT) in both Heavy and Infantry Brigade Combat Teams. Also, the M1200 Armored Knight is used in Fire Support Teams (FIST) in the Reconnaissance Surveillance and Target Acquisition (RSTA) Squadron in the IBCTs and Battlefield Surveillance Brigades (BFSB). It operates as an integral part of the brigade reconnaissance element, providing COLT and fire support mission planning and execution. The Armored Knight Approved Acquisition Objective is 465.

This procurement ends after 2013. When we bring our troops home, we'll have plenty of these left over in addition to the others we've procured over the years. Eliminate and save $12 Million.

Lifecycle Software Support

Life Cycle Software Engineering (LCSE) support, by the Software Engineering Center (SEC), provides the essential equipment needed to maintain Communications-Electronics Life Cycle Management Command (C-E LCMC) managed fielded Battlefield Automated Systems (BAS) and Information Systems (IS) in a state of operational readiness. Approximately 100 BASs in Post Production Software Support (PPSS) directly depend on LCSE support to maintain a posture of mission critical readiness.

Necessary and proper; cut by standard 25% and save $463K.

Automatic Identification Technology

Radio Frequency-Intransit Visibility (RF-ITV) utilizes cutting edge RF technologies in concert with automatic identification technology to provide near real-time logistics visibility to on-site commanders, Combatant Commanders (COCOMs), NATO allies and Coalition partners. This is accomplished through the use of various applications of Radio Frequency Identification (RFID) tags. Shipments are tracked and monitored by land, air and sea as cargo transits throughout the global Defense Transportation System through a collection of tag read sites strategically located world-wide transmitting to satellite uplinks, downloaded to a collection tactically located servers and accessed by PC using a CAC card or user ID/Password.

This line item ends after 2013. AIT is redundant to DISA and other Army procurements; eliminate and save $14 Million.

Network Management Initialization and Services

The Network Management Initialization and Services (NMIS) program supports the Army's objectives of an integrated Network Operations capability. There are three components to the program: Tactical Service Management (TSM), Network Management System (NMS), and Data Products. TSM provides the S-6/G-6 the capability for real time management of servers, applications, and clients used in the Tactical Operations Centers.

The Army's networks are doing just fine, and many are redundant to DISA projects and even each other. Eliminate and save $60 Million. Also eliminate most of those other networks.

Maneuver Control System (MCS)

Tactical Mission Command (TMC) is a suite of products that provide Army and joint community commanders and their staff a human-centered collaborative capability with integrated Voice over Internet Protocol (VoIP), a user-defined common operational picture (COP) and real-time situational awareness. TMC supports Mission Command Connvergence/ Common Operating Environment (COE), Army Battle Command System (ABCS) interoperability, as well as coalition interoperability to support Battle Staff functions.

This is the fancy video game helmets we issue the soldiers. When we bring our troops home, we'll have plenty of these left over in addition to the others we've procured over the years. Eliminate and save $80 Million.

Single Army Logistics Enterprise (SALE)

The Single Army Logistics Enterprise is the overarching concept for achieving Army-wide integration of Combat Service Support (CSS) (supply, maintenance, ammunition supply, and personnel management) data. SALE has the funding subcomponents of Standard Army Management Information Systems (STAMIS) Tactical Computers (STACOMP), Army Enterprise System Integration Program (AESIP), Standard Army Maintenance System (SAMS), Standard Army Retail Supply System (SARSS), Unit Level Logistics Systems (ULLS), Property Book User System Enhanced (PBUSE), Standard Army Ammunition System (SAAS) and Installation Fixed Base (IFB). The SALE program acquires hardware and fielding resources for the current operations of CSS units across the Army, and for the support of emerging CSS applications such as the Global Combat Support System Army (GCSS-Army), and the Personnel Transformation-Army enterprise Human Resource (Army eHR) System.

This is a very expensive way to integrate the logistics and HR systems together. The Army was working just fine before we made up this new system, and can continue to do so. Eliminate and save $28 Million. This goes into the hundreds of millions within two years.

Reconnaissance and Surveying Instrument Set (ENFIRE)

The Instrument Set, Reconnaissance and Surveying (commonly known as ENFIRE) is a tactical engineering tool set designed to modernize the collection and dissemination of engineer related information while minimizing exposure to enemy observation. ENFIRE incorporates the ability to automatically populate field data on digital forms used for road, bridge, hasty minefield, and Improvised Explosive Device (IED) reconnaissance/reporting with relevant information from peripheral devices included in the ENFIRE set.

When we bring our troops home, we'll have plenty of these left over in addition to the others we've procured over the years. Eliminate and save $99 Million.

Army Training Modernization (ATM)

Army Training Modernization (ATM) includes three related efforts to acquire Digital Training Facilities (DTF). DTFs allow rapid delivery of high quality instruction to Army personnel. Infrastructure acquired is based on industry standards and complies with the Joint Technical Architecture (JTA) and Defense Information Infrastructure Common Operating Environment (DII COE), where applicable.

The Army's training has always been among the best in the world and requires no modernization, let alone on an ongoing, neverending basis. Eliminate and save $9 Million.

Automated Data Processing Equipment

This program supports the Army's sustaining base automation systems. The Army's primary sustaining base Information Management (IM) goal is to provide information services for the sustainment and readiness of the forces at minimum cost.

The budget implies this project saves more money than it costs, so I'll allow it to get by with "necessary and proper". Cut by standard 25% and save $32 Million.

General Fund Enterprise Business Systems Family

The General Fund Enterprise Business System (GFEBS) is a Major Automated Information System (MAIS)(ACAT-1AM) project that replaces 30+-year-old financial systems including the Standard Finance Systems (STANFINS), Standard Operations and Maintenance, Army R&D System (SOMARDS), and Database Commitment Accounting System. GFEBS will become the Dept of the Army's new core financial and asset management system for administering its general fund, improving performance, standardizing processes and ensuring future needs are met. GFEBS is a commercial off-the-shelf (COTS) Enterprise Resource Planning (ERP) System certified by the Chief Financial Officers Council (CFOC).

This sounds very similar to Automated Data Processing Equipment to me. Eliminate and merge the two together; save $9 Million.

CSS Communications

This Combat Service Support (CSS) Communications program supports the Army's full spectrum logistics communication requirements under two programs: Combat Service Support Automated Information System Interface (CAISI) and Combat Service Support Satellite Communications (CSS SATCOM).

Redundant to DISA and other Army programs. Eliminate and save $21 Million.

Reserve Component Automation System

The Reserve Component Automation System (RCAS) is an automated information system (AIS) that provides the capability to administer, manage, and mobilize the Army's Reserve Component(RC) forces more effectively. Specifically, RCAS supports the mobilization planning and unit administration functions of the Army National Guard (ARNG) and Army Reserve (USAR) by integrating commercial off-theshelf (COTS) hardware and office automation (OA) software, Government off-the-shelf (GOTS) software, and developed functional software applications into a common operating environment (COE), personal computer (PC)-based architecture.

Redundant to Automated Data Processing Equipment and other DISA and Army programs. The military needs ONE program for each need, regardless of duty status or even branch. Eliminate and save $36 Million.

Items less than $5 Million

Multimedia Visual Information Systems Program (M/VISP)

> The M/VISP supports central management of Multimedia/Visual Information (M/VI) requirements. The M/VISP restructures and consolidates assets to a network-centric workspace, which allows centralization and streamlining to reduce overall operating expenses while expanding services

There's no reason the government can't use free services like Skype or Google for their videoconferencing needs. Eliminate and save $8.5 Million, which is not less than $5 Million.

Automated Integrated Survey Instrument (AISI)

> This budget line supports the procurement and upgrade of the Automated Integrated Survey Instrument (AISI) (both Long and Short versions), Digital Levels and Global Positioning System - Survey (GPSS). This equipment supports the survey mission of both the Topographic and Construction Engineer.

The Army shouldn't be building anything overseas, and can hire contractors to build most stuff here. Most types of construction do not require any GPS capability. Placement of weapons platforms can be guided by a map, available for free on the Internet. Aircraft should not require registration, engineering surveys can use a map, and software only needs to be bought once. Eliminate and save $5.4 Million.

Production Base Support

> This program provides funding to the Army Test and Evaluation Command (ATEC), Developmental Test Command (DTC) to establish, modernize, expand or replace test facilities used in production testing of Communications and Electronic material. It sustains Army production test capabilities through upgrade and replacement of instrumentation and equipment that is technologically and/or economically obsolete. Modernization of test instrumentation and equipment provides increased automation and efficiencies, improved data quality and quantity and cost avoidances to Army Program Managers. Programmed funding will be used to upgrade or replace production test instrumentation and equipment at the Electronic Proving Ground (EPG), Fort Huachuca, AZ.

The Army should not need to do extensive testing on communications and electronic material. Rather, it should be tested before being sold to the Army, and the Army's testing needs should be minimal. If a company sells them a bad product, just don't buy anything from them again. Eliminate and save $586K.

Other Support Equipment and Spares Procurement[40]

Family of Non-Lethal Equipment

> *This line contains Non-Lethal Equipment, All Types. It currently contains the Launched Electrode Stun Device (LESD) and the Acoustic Hailing Device (AHD).*

Necessary and proper; however, tasers and high frequency loudspeakers don't run out of ammo. Keep and cut by half, saving $16 Million.

Base Defense Systems

> *Base Defense Systems (BDS) includes Non-Intrusive Inspection Systems (NIIS) (M90108), Battlefield Anti-Intrusion System (BAIS) (M90202) and Lighting Kit Motion Detection (LKMD) (M90204). NIIS is a family of systems that inspect for the presence of explosives, weapons and other contraband in vehicles, cargo containers and personnel from a distance providing stand-off ballistic and blast protection. The current family of systems includes the Z-backscatter Van (ZBV), Military Mobile Vehicle and Cargo Inspection System (MMVACIS) and personnel scanners such as the Secure-1000. All systems are either mobile or fully relocatable.*

Base defense systems are necessary and proper. Keep ($79.5 Million).

CBRN Soldier Protection

> *Funds support acquisition of critically required Chemical Biological equipment needed to support Army mission requirements. Collective protection platforms include hard and soft wall shelters, vehicles, and structures. The Decontamination program consists of the Joint Service Transportable Decontamination System, Small Scale (JSTDS-SS). The Contamination Avoidance program includes systems that provide detection, identification, collection and reporting of CBRN hazards. The Individual Protection program provides Protective Masks and test equipment.*

Necessary and proper; keep ($52 Million).

Tactical Bridging

> *The Dry Support Bridge (DSB) is a mobile, rapidly erected, modular military bridging system used by the Multi-Role Bridge Company (MRBC). The DSB can span a 40-meter gap or two 20-meter gaps up to Military Load Class (MLC) 100 Wheeled/MLC 80 Tracked. The DSB has a road width of 4.3 meters and an emplacement time of 90 minutes or less, with little or no site preparation. The DSB will support the Joint Force Commander's ability to employ and sustain forces throughout the global battlespace.*

---

[40] http://asafm.army.mil/Documents/OfficeDocuments/Budget/BudgetMaterials/FY13/pforms//opa34.pdf

These are the machines that provide temporary bridges where none exist, allowing troops and equipment to cross gaps that would be otherwise very difficult. Necessary and proper, but we'll have plenty available when we bring them back from overseas, in addition to others we've procured over the years. Eliminate and save $41 Million.

Tactical Bridge, Float-Ribbon (TBFR)

The Tactical Float Ribbon Bridge line supports the Multi-Role Bridge Company (MRBC). One Tactical Float Ribbon Bridge System consists of the Improved Ribbon Bridge (IRB) bays (30 Interior and 12 Ramp); 14 Propulsion Bridge Erection Boats (BEB) and 56 Common Bridge Transporters (CBT).

Necessary and proper, but we'll have plenty available when we bring them back from overseas, in addition to others we've procured over the years. Eliminate and save $33 Million.

Robotic Combat Support System (RCSS)

This Robotic Combat Support System (RCSS) Budget line procures both the M160 and the Man Transportable Robot System (MTRS). The M160 is a 6.1-ton tracked, combat engineer vehicle designed for teleoperation by soldiers from either mounted or dismounted positions to perform area clearance of antipersonnel mine sown areas. The Army Acquisition Objective (AAO) is 65.

We'll have plenty available when we bring them back from overseas, in addition to others we've procured over the years. Eliminate and save $30 Million.

Explosive Ordnance Disposal Equipment

The Explosive Ordnance Disposal (EOD) equipment is used by EOD soldiers to defuse unexploded ordnance and improvised explosive devices throughout the world. The equipment provides the capability to examine, identify, and defuse ordnance effectively and safely. This program covers various types EOD equipment for Force Protection and Homeland Defense.

We'll have plenty available when we bring them back from overseas, in addition to others we've procured over the years. Eliminate and save $29 Million.

Remote Demolition Systems

This line includes Remote Demolition Systems, All Types. It includes Radio Frequency - Remote Activated Munition System (RF RAMS) and Magneto Induction - Remote Activated Munition System (MI RAMS) and other system components.

We'll have plenty available when we bring them back from overseas, in addition to others we've procured over the years. Additionally, blowing stuff up remotely doesn't seem like a proper peacetime SOP. Eliminate and save $8 Million.

Countermine Equipment

> *This line covers procurement of countermine equipment with a total cost of less than five million dollars. This line includes detectors, neutralizing devices, training aids and devices to support New Equipment Training (NET), initial entry training, and institutional training, as well as any related tasks. It also funds initial fielding and deployment of equipment to support Military Working Dogs.*

We'll have plenty available when we bring them back from overseas, in addition to others we've procured over the years. Eliminate and save $4 Million.

Heaters and Environmental Control Units

> *The 60,000 British Thermal Units per hour (BTU/H) Improved Environmental Control Unit (IECU) program is a joint Army and Air Force effort to replace the heavy and inefficient field Environmental Control Units that utilize ozone depleting refrigerants. The 60,000 BTU/HR IECU will be a replacement for the existing Army 54,000-BTU/HR Environmental Control Unit (ECU) and Air Force developed 66,000-BTU/HR Field Deployable Environmental Control Unit. The 60,000 BTU/H IECU will be lighter in weight than the existing military ECUs.*

We'll have plenty available when we bring them back from overseas, in addition to others we've procured over the years. Eliminate and save $21 Million.

Soldier Enhancement

> *The emphasis of this Soldier Enhancement Program (SEP) is on Soldier modernization and enhancements. It procures items that improve Soldier lethality, survivability, mobility and command and control. Items procured include the M25 Stabilized Binocular, Sniper Tripod, M1950 Weapons Case, and the Advanced Emergency Bailout Parachute.*

We'll have plenty available when we bring them back from overseas, in addition to others we've procured over the years. Eliminate and save $7 Million.

Personnel Recovery Support System (PRSS)

> *The Personnel Recovery Support System (PRSS) consists of items including personal locator beacons and personnel recovery equipment to report and locate Isolated, Missing, Detained, and Captured Soldiers.*

We'll have plenty available when we bring them back from overseas, in addition to others we've procured over the years. Eliminate and save $13 Million.

Ground Soldier System

> *The Nett Warrior (NW) program leverages commercial smart devices and secure Army tactical radios to provide an integrated dismounted leader Mission Command (MC) and Situational Awareness (SA) system for use during combat operations. The system provides unparalleled situational awareness and understanding to the dismounted leader allowing for faster and more accurate decisions in the tactical fight.*

We'll have plenty available when we bring them back from overseas, in addition to others we've procured over the years. Eliminate and save $120 Million.

Force Provider

> *Force Provider is a fully integrated system providing critical basic life support for soldiers deployed in remote areas. A Force Provider module provides billeting, field feeding, and hygiene capabilities that include all the integrated utilities to include climate control, power generation, water and waste water systems, and fuel storage. A single Force Provider module is capable of sustaining 600 personnel. Force Provider is fully containerized for rapid deployment and is transportable by rail, sea, land, and air using C-130, C-141, C-17 or C-5A aircraft. With the addition of Cold Weather Kits (CWKs), the module is deployable in temperatures as low as -15 degrees Fahrenheit.*

Soldiers should not regularly be deployed in remote areas. We'll have plenty available when we bring them back from overseas, in addition to others we've procured over the years. Eliminate and save $40 Million.

Field Feeding Equipment

> *The Field Feeding and Refrigeration program provides equipment to conduct tactical food service operations. Field Feeding is a combat multiplier which improves morale and enhances the warfighters physical and cognitive capabilities. Associated with food service operations are storage, preparation, serving and cleanup. Equipment items include: field kitchens, food sanitation centers, and refrigerated containers. In conjunction with food service personnel and field rations, this equipment comprises the Army Field Feeding*

System (AFFS) which supports the Army standard of one hot cook-prepared meal per day in the field. This program provides a critical capability that supports Army transformation and the modularity concept and maintains readiness through fielding and integrating new equipment. It enhances the field Soldier's well being and reduces sustainment requirements, related Combat Support/Combat Service Support (CS/CSS) lift demands, combat zone footprint, and logistical support costs.

The fact that this exists is a symptom. We shouldn't fight wars, let alone in such a way that these are necessary. Eliminate and save $147 Million.

Joint Improvised Explosive Device Defeat Fund[41]

The improvised explosive device (IED) persists as the most serious threat to U.S. and Coalition forces. Recognizing the IED as an enduring battlefield condition, JIEDDO's mission is to lead all Department of Defense (DoD) actions and support Combatant Command efforts to eliminate the IED as the predominant strategic weapon against our Nation and its partners. This mission is executed across three concurrent and complementary lines of operation: attacking the networks that employ IEDs, devising ways to defeat the device, and training our forces to counter the threat. This FY 2013 Budget Estimate and Overseas Contingency Operations (OCO) Request is formulated to continue JIEDDO's counter-IED (C-IED) efforts to defeat the global, asymmetric threat posed by IEDs.

It's interesting to note that we never hear news of IEDs being detonated within the United States; only overseas, where we don't belong. By ending all OCO, we thus eliminate the majority of IED threats.

As the "Artillery of the 21st Century", the IED requires a dedicated, multi-faceted approach to mitigate and defeat the networks and devices used against American interests. When discussing future threats, it is important that both the networks that employ IEDs as well as the device itself are considered. The IED is the weapon of choice for the overlapping consortium of networks operating along the entire threat continuum.

It's amusing that the Army makes such a big deal out of how cheap and simple IEDs are, yet requests hundreds of billions of dollars to deal with this simple, cheap threat. IEDs account for many of the thousands of American deaths we've suffered in the past decades in the Middle East, and every single one of those soldiers and civilians would have been spared if we simply understood proper foreign policy.

---

[41]http://asafm.army.mil/Documents/OfficeDocuments/Budget/BudgetMaterials/FY13/pforms//jieddf.pdf

Given the combination of the ridiculous expense of combating IEDs, fact that we brought the threat upon ourselves, and the rampant duplication of effort across the military, the elimination of our proactive warmongering foreign policy yields us the ability to eliminate this program in its entirety. If nobody is planting IEDs to blow up our people and our vehicles, then we need not fight them. $227 Million saved.

Research, Development, Test, and Evaluation

Budget Activity 1[42]

Budget Activity 1 consists of doing research that businesses should be doing, or contracting this research out to universities. The whole thing can be eliminated, saving $9 Billion.

In-House Laboratory Independent Research

> *This program element (PE) supports basic research at the Army laboratories through the In-House Laboratory Independent Research (ILIR) program. Basic research lays the foundation for future developmental efforts by identifying fundamental principles governing various phenomena and appropriate pathways to exploit this knowledge.*

The military should not conduct its own weapons and equipment research. Weapons and equipment companies should pay for their own Research and Development based on cues through which the military indicates what kind of purchases it's interested in making. From there, the weapons companies should produce and demonstrate a prototype. If the military decides to buy it, they should place a purchase order and receive the finished products. This is not a complicated process. In short, the Army is not the R&D department of a weapons company. Eliminate and save $21 Million.

Defense Research Sciences

> *This program element (PE) builds fundamental scientific knowledge contributing to the sustainment of US Army scientific and technological superiority in land warfighting capability and to solving military problems related to long-term national security needs, investigates new concepts and technologies for the Army's future force, and provides the means to exploit scientific breakthroughs and avoid technological surprises.*

The Army is not the R&D department of a weapons company. This effort duplicates other efforts within TJS and elsewhere in this budget. Eliminate and save $219 Million.

---

[42] http://asafm.army.mil/Documents/OfficeDocuments/Budget/BudgetMaterials/FY13/rforms//vol1.pdf

University Research Initiatives

> *This program element (PE) supports Army basic research efforts in the Multidisciplinary University Research Initiative (MURI) program, the Defense University Research Instrumentation Program (DURIP) and the Presidential Early Career Awards for Scientists and Engineers (PECASE) program by funding basic research in a wide range of scientific and engineering disciplines pertinent to maintaining the U.S. land combat technology superiority.*

The Army, universities, and other educational facilities are not the R&D department of a weapons company. This effort duplicates other efforts within TJS and elsewhere in this budget. The government should never provide money to schools, especially at the federal level, let alone selectively. Eliminate and save $81 Million.

University and Industry Research Centers

> *This program element (PE) fosters university and industry based research to provide a scientific foundation for enabling technologies for future force capabilities. Broadly, the work in this project falls into three categories: Collaborative Technology Alliances (CTAs), University Centers of Excellence (COE), and University Affiliated Research Centers (UARCs).*

The Army, universities, and other educational facilities are not the R&D department of a weapons company. This effort duplicates other efforts within TJS and elsewhere in this budget. The government should never provide money to schools, especially at the federal level, let alone selectively. Eliminate and save $123 Million.

Budget Activity 2[43]

Budget Activity 2 consists of doing research that businesses should be doing, or contracting this research out to universities.

Materials Technology

> *This program element (PE) evaluates materials for lighter weight and more survivable armor and for more lethal armaments. Project H7G researches and explores nanostructure materials properties and exploits the strength and durability of these materials to enable lighter weight, increased performance in Soldier weapons and protection applications. Project H84, researches a variety of materials and designs, fabricates and evaluates performance of components for lighter weight Soldier and vehicle armors, armaments, and electronics.*

---

[43]http://asafm.army.mil/Documents/OfficeDocuments/Budget/BudgetMaterials/FY13/rforms//vol2.pdf

The Army is not the Research and Development department of a Materials or Textiles company. Eliminate, buy the resulting products from the private sector, and save $24 Million.

Sensors and Electronic Survivability

> *This program element (PE) investigates designs and evaluates sensors and electronic components and software that enhance situational awareness, survivability, lethality, and autonomous mobility for tactical ground forces.*

The Army is not the Research and Development department of an Electronics company. Eliminate, buy the resulting products from the private sector, and save $13 Million.

Tractor Hip

> *The details of this program are reported in accordance with Title 10, United States Code, Section 119(a)(1).*

The Army is not the Research and Development department of a... wait, what exactly is a tractor hip? Tractors don't have hips, and hips don't have tractors. 10 USC 119.a.1 just explains that it shall be reported to a committee, whose reports I could not find; and in the FY2010 Army Performance Budget Justification Book, which I could not find. Eliminate and save $22 Million.

Aviation Technology

> *This program element (PE) conducts rotary wing vehicle component design, fabrication and evaluation to enable Army aviation transformation. Emphasis is on developing rotary wing platform technologies to enhance manned and unmanned rotary wing vehicle combat and combat support operations for attack, reconnaissance, air assault, survivability, logistics and command and control missions.*

The Army is not the Research and Development department of an aircraft manufacturer. Eliminate, buy the resulting products from the private sector, and save $52 Million.

Electronic Warfare Technology

> *This program element (PE) designs and validates electronic warfare (EW) components that deny, disrupt, or degrade the enemy's use of the electromagnetic spectrum for offensive or defensive operations.*

The Army is not the Research and Development department of a weapons manufacturer. Eliminate, buy the resulting products from the private sector, and save $15 Million.

Missile Technology

This program element (PE) designs, fabricates and evaluates advanced component technologies for tactical missiles, rockets, guided munitions, and their launch systems in order to increase lethality, precision, and effectiveness under adverse battlefield conditions while reducing system cost, size and weight. Major goals in Project 214 include enhancing the survivability of the munition, launch and fire control systems; and increasing kill probabilities against diverse targets.

The Army is not the Research and Development department of a weapons manufacturer. Eliminate, buy the resulting products from the private sector, and save $49 Million.

Advanced Weapons Technology

This program element (PE) investigates enabling technologies for High Energy Laser (HEL) weapons. Project 042 develops component technologies such as efficient, high energy, solid state lasers, advanced beam control components, and lethality / effectiveness measurements that enable better models and simulations for future HEL weapon designs.

The Army is not the Research and Development department of a weapons manufacturer. Eliminate, buy the resulting products from the private sector, and save $26 Million.

Advanced Concepts and Simulation

This program element (PE) investigates and designs enabling technologies to create effective training capabilities for the Warfighter and supports the underpinning technologies and understanding to establish architecture standards and interfaces necessary for realizing the Army vision of creating a realistic synthetic "electronic battlefield" environment for use across the spectrum of doctrine, organization, training, leader development, material, personnel, and facilities (DOTLM-PF).

The Army is not the Research and Development department of a weapons manufacturer. Eliminate, buy the resulting products from the private sector, and save $24 Million.

Combat Vehicle and Automotive Technology

This program element (PE) researches, designs, and evaluates combat and tactical vehicle automotive technologies that enable the Army to have a lighter, more survivable, more mobile and more deployable force. Project C05 investigates, researches, and evaluates advanced ground vehicle design and occupant protection technologies in such areas as armor concepts, ballistic defeat mechanisms, blast mitigation, survivability modeling and simulation

(M&S), hit avoidance, kill avoidance, safety, sensors, instrumentation and survivability packaging concepts to achieve superior survivability/protection for soldiers and military ground vehicles.

The Army is not the Research and Development department of a weapons or automobile manufacturer. Eliminate, buy the resulting products from the private sector, and save $69 Million.

Ballistics Technology

This program element (PE) investigates and evaluates materials and ballistic technologies required for armaments and armor that will enable enhanced lethality and survivability.

The Army is not the Research and Development department of a weapons manufacturer. Eliminate, buy the resulting products from the private sector, and save $61 Million.

Chemical, Smoke, and Equipment Defeating Technology

This program element (PE) investigates and evaluates obscurant technologies to increase personnel and platform survivability and develop and validate forensic analysis methods for military and homemade explosive devices, including their precursors and residue. Project 552 pursues research in materials science as well as dissemination methodologies, mechanisms, technologies, and techniques to enable forensic analysis of explosive signatures.

The Army is not the Research and Development department of a weapons manufacturer. Eliminate, buy the resulting products from the private sector, and save $5 Million.

Joint Service Small Arms Program

This program element (PE) investigates designs and evaluates individual and crew-served weapon technologies that enhance the fighting capabilities and survivability of the dismounted Warfighter in support of all the Services. All work is done under the Joint Service Small Arms Program (JSSAP) (Project H21) and are based upon the Joint Service Small Arms Master Plan (JSSAMP) and the Joint Capabilities Integration Development System's Small Arms Analyses.

The Army is not the Research and Development department of a weapons manufacturer. Eliminate, buy the resulting products from the private sector, and save $7 Million. Be worried any time you hear about a government "Master Plan".

Weapons and Munitions Technology

> *This program element (PE) investigates, designs and evaluates enabling technology to develop lethal and nonlethal weapons and munitions with increased performance and the potential for lower weight, reduced size, and improved affordability.*

The Army is not the Research and Development department of a weapons manufacturer. Eliminate, buy the resulting products from the private sector, and save $35 Million.

Electronics and Electronic Devices

> *This program element (PE) designs and evaluates, power components, frequency control and timing devices, high power microwave devices, display technologies; and electronic components.*

The Army is not the Research and Development department of a weapons manufacturer. Eliminate, buy the resulting products from the private sector, and save $60 Million.

Night Vision Technology

> *This program element (PE) conducts applied research and investigates core night vision and electronic sensor components and software to improve the Army's capability to operate in all battlefield conditions.*

The Army is not the Research and Development department of an electronics manufacturer. Eliminate, buy the resulting products from the private sector, and save $53 Million.

Countermine Systems

> *This program element (PE) investigates, designs, and evaluates technologies to improve countermine, signature management and counter-sensors capabilities. The focus is on sensor components, sub-components and software algorithms to improve detection of mines, explosive threats and directed energy; ballistic methods to defeat mines and explosive threats; and signature management technologies to reduce reconnaissance capabilities of the enemies.*

I've seen this title in at least one other place in the DoD budgets. The Army is not the Research and Development department of a weapons manufacturer. Eliminate, buy the resulting products from the private sector, and save $19 Million.

Human Factors Engineering Technology

> This program element (PE) is to conduct applied research on aspects of human factors engineering that impact the capabilities of individual and teams of Soldiers operating in complex, dynamic environments. The results of the research will enable maximizing the effectiveness of Soldiers and their equipment for mission success. The aspects of human factors that will be studied include sensing, perceptual and cognitive processes, ergonomics, biomechanics and the tools and methodologies required to manage interaction within these areas and within the Soldiers' combat environment.

The Army is not the Research and Development department of a weapons manufacturer. Eliminate, buy the resulting products from the private sector, and save $20 Million.

Environmental Quality Technology

> This program element (PE) investigates and evaluates enabling tools and methodologies that support the long-term sustainment of Army training and testing activities. Project 048 improves the Army's ability to comply with requirements mandated by federal, state and local environmental/health laws and reducing the cost of this compliance.

The Army is responsible for the defense of the United States, not the environment. Repeal all federal environment laws. Eliminate and save $20 Million.

Command, Control, Communications Technology

> This program element (PE) researches and investigates communications, command and control (C2), and electronics components, sub-components, software and protocols that provide the Army with enhanced capabilities for secure, mobile, networked communications, assured information delivery, and presentation of information that enables decision-making.

The Army is neither a phone company nor the Research and Development department of an electronics manufacturer. Eliminate, buy the resulting products from the private sector, and save $29 Million.

Computer and Software Technology

> This program element (PE) develops and evaluates hardware and software algorithms enabling enhanced understanding and accelerating the decision cycle time for commanders and leaders operating in a mobile, dispersed, highly networked environment. Project Y10 supports research on information and communications technology.

The Army is not a software company. Eliminate and save $10 Million.

Military Engineering Technology

This program element (PE) investigates, evaluates, and advances technologies, techniques and tools for depiction and representation of the physical and human environment for use in military operations; for characterizing geospatial, atmospheric and weather conditions and impacts on systems and military missions; for conducting mobility, counter-mobility, survivability and force protection; and for enabling secure, sustainable, energy efficient facilities.

The Army is not the Research and Development department of an equipment manufacturer. Eliminate, buy the resulting products from the private sector, and save $71 Million.

Manpower / Personnel / Training Technology

This program element (PE)conducts applied behavioral and social science research that provides non-material solutions to ensure that Soldiers can adapt and excel and improve the Army's capability to fully leverage advances in networks, systems, and technologies as they evolve. This research provides the scientific basis to recruit, select, assign, promote, educate, train, and retain Soldiers and leaders that comprise a ready and relevant Landpower capability.

The Army is not a psychologist or a sociologist. Eliminate and save $18 Million.

Warfighter Technology

This program element (PE) investigates and develops technologies which improve Soldier and Small Combat Unit survivability, sustainability, mobility, combat effectiveness, and field quality of life.

The Army is not the Research and Development department of a weapons or equipment manufacturer. Eliminate, buy the resulting products from the private sector, and save $28 Million.

Medical Technology

This program element (PE) supports application of knowledge gained through basic research to refine drugs, vaccines, medical devices, diagnostics, medical practices/ procedures, and other preventive measures essential to the protection and sustainment of Warfighter health.

The Army is not a pharmaceutical or other medical company. Eliminate, buy the resulting products from the private sector, and save $108 Million.

Budget Activity 3[44]

Warfighter Advanced Technology

> This program element (PE) provides Soldiers and Small Combat Units with the most effective personal clothing, equipment, and combat rations, and shelters and logistical support items at the least weight and sustainment burden. This PE supports the maturation and demonstration of technologies associated with air delivery of personnel and cargo (Project 242), rapid ammunition/munitions deployability and resupply (Project 543), combat rations and combat feeding equipment (Project C07), combat clothing and personal equipment (including protective equipment such as personal armor, helmets, and eye wear) (Project J50) and expeditionary base camps (Project VT5).

The Army is not a clothier, a food supplier, a construction company, or an equipment manufacturer. Eliminate, buy the resulting products from the private sector, and save $39 Million.

Medical Advanced Technology

> This program element (PE) matures and demonstrates advanced medical technologies including drugs, vaccines, medical devices, and diagnostics and developing medical practices and procedures to effectively protect and improve the survivability of US Forces across the entire spectrum of military operations.

The Army is not a pharmaceutical company or a medical device manufacturer. Eliminate, buy the resulting products from the private sector, and save $70 Million.

Aviation Advanced Technology

> This program element (PE) matures and demonstrates manned and unmanned rotary wing vehicle (RWV) technologies to enable Army aviation modernization. Within this PE, aviation technologies are advanced and integrated into realistic and robust demonstrations. Project 313 matures and demonstrates enabling component, subsystems and systems in the following areas: rotors, drive trains, structures and survivability.

The Army is not the Research and Development department of an aircraft manufacturer. Eliminate, buy the resulting products from the private sector, and save $64 Million.

---

[44]http://asafm.army.mil/Documents/OfficeDocuments/Budget/BudgetMaterials/FY13/rforms//vol3.pdf

Weapons and Munitions Advanced Technology

> This program element (PE) matures weapons and munitions components/subsystems and demonstrates lethal and non-lethal weapons and munitions with potential to increase force application and force protection capabilities across the spectrum of operations. The weapons and munitions include artillery, mortars, medium caliber, tank fired, and shoulder fired.

The Army is not the Research and Development department of a weapons manufacturer. Eliminate, buy the resulting products from the private sector, and save $68 Million.

Combat Vehicle and Automotive Advanced Technology

> This program element (PE) matures, integrates and demonstrates combat and tactical vehicle automotive technologies that enable a lighter, more mobile and more survivable force.

The Army is not the Research and Development department of a weapons or automotive manufacturer. Eliminate, buy the resulting products from the private sector, and save $104 Million.

Command, Control, Communications Advanced Technology

> This program element (PE) matures and demonstrates advanced space technologies that support the Army's ability to control and exploit space assets that contribute to current and future military operations as defined in the national, DoD, and Army space policies.

The Army is not the Research and Development department of an electronics manufacturer. Eliminate, buy the resulting products from the private sector, and save $4 Million.

Manpower, Personnel, and Training Advanced Technology

> This project element (PE) matures and demonstrates advanced behavioral and social science technologies that enhance performance to ensure that the Warfighter keeps pace with the transformations in systems, weapons, equipment, and mission requirements to meet the goals of the future force.

The Army is not a psychologist or a sociologist. Eliminate, buy the resulting products from the private sector, and save $10 Million.

Electronic Warfare Advanced Technology

> This program element (PE) matures and demonstrates technologies to address the seamless integrated tactical communications challenge with distributed, secure, mobile, wireless, and self-organizing communications networks that will operate reliably in diverse and complex terrains, in all environments.

The Army is not the Research and Development department of a weapons or equipment manufacturer. Eliminate, buy the resulting products from the private sector, and save $51 Million.

Next Generation Training and Simulation Systems

This program element (PE) matures and demonstrates tools to enable effective training capability for the Warfighter. Project S28 matures and demonstrates simulation technologies developed by the Institute for Creative Technology.

The Army is not the Research and Development department of a weapons or equipment manufacturer. Eliminate, buy the resulting products from the private sector, and save $17 Million.

Military HIV Research

This program element (PE) matures and demonstrates advanced technology of candidate human immunodeficiency virus (HIV) vaccines, prepares and conducts human clinical studies to assess safety and efficacy of candidate HIV vaccines, conducts research to control HIV infection in military environments, protects the military blood supply from HIV, and protects military personnel from risks associated with the HIV infection.

The Army is not the Research and Development department of a pharmaceutical company, and an HIV vaccine has already been developed. The biggest thing in the way is FDA trials and government approval. Eliminate, buy the resulting products from the private sector, and save $7 Million.

Combatting Terrorism – Technology Development

This program element (PE) demonstrates technologies with high payoff potential to address current technology shortfalls or future force capability gaps. Work in this PE complements and is fully coordinated with PE 0602105A (Materials Technology), PE 0602303A (Missile Technology), PE 0602601A (Combat Vehicle and Automotive Technology), PE 0602618A (Ballistics Technology), PE 0602705A (Electronics and Electronic Devices), PE 0602784A (Military Engineering Technology), PE 0603005A (Combat Vehicle and Automotive Advanced Technology, PE 0603734A (Military Engineering Advanced Technology), and PE 0603710A (Night Vision Advanced Technology).

The Army is not the Research and Development department of a weapons or equipment manufacturer, and the best defense against terrorism is to stop pissing of the extremists in the first place. Eliminate, buy the resulting products from the private sector, and save $10 Million.

Tractor Nail

> The details of this program are reported in accordance with Title 10, United States Code, Section 119(a)(1).

More classified Black Budget projects. Eliminate and save $3 Million.

Tractor Eggs

> The details of this program are reported in accordance with Title 10, United States Code, Section 119(a)(1).

More classified Black Budget projects. Eliminate and save $2 Million.

Tractor Rose

> The details of this program are reported in accordance with Title 10, United States Code, Section 119(a)(1).

More classified Black Budget projects. Eliminate and save $10 Million.

Tractor Hike

> The details of this program are reported in accordance with Title 10, United States Code, Section 119(a)(1).

More classified Black Budget projects. Eliminate and save $9 Million.

Tractor Gage

> The details of this program are reported in accordance with Title 10, United States Code, Section 119(a)(1).

More classified Black Budget projects. Eliminate and save $11 Million.

Electronics Warfare Technology

> This program element (PE) matures and demonstrates electronic warfare (EW) sensors and software intended to deny, disrupt, locate or destroy the enemy's command, control, and communications (C3) systems and intelligence, surveillance and reconnaissance assets. This PE matures both countermeasures (CM) and counter-countermeasures (CCM) to deny the enemy the use of their systems while protecting US assets from enemy deception and jamming.

The Army is not the Research and Development department of a weapons or equipment manufacturer. Eliminate, buy the resulting products from the private sector, and save $22 Million.

Missile and Rocket Advanced Technology

> This program element (PE) matures, fabricates, and demonstrates advanced rocket, missile, interceptor, and guided munition

technologies to enhance weapon system lethality, survivability, agility, deployability, and affordability.

The Army is not the Research and Development department of a weapons manufacturer. Eliminate, buy the resulting products from the private sector, and save $71 Million.

High Performance Computing Modernization Program

This program element (PE) demonstrates and provides high performance computing hardware, parallel software, wide area networking services, and expertise that enable the Department of Defense (DoD) Research, Development, Test, and Evaluation (RDT&E) community to investigate and understand physical phenomena and behavior of systems through large scale computational simulation.

The Army is not the Research and Development department of a computer manufacturer. Eliminate, buy the resulting products from the private sector, and save $181 Million.

Landmine Warfare and Barrier Advanced Technology

This program element (PE) matures components, subsystems and demonstrates sensor and neutralization technologies that can be used by dismounted forces and on ground and/or air platforms to detect, identify and then mitigate the effects of landmines, minefields, other explosive hazards and obstacles.

The Army is not the Research and Development department of a weapons manufacturer. We only encounter minefields overseas; not when we're at home, minding our own business. Eliminate, buy the resulting products from the private sector, and save $27 Million.

Joint Service Small Arms Program

This program element (PE) matures and demonstrates advanced technologies that integrate into individual and crew served weapons for all Services. All work is done under the Joint Service Small Arms Program (JSSAP) (Project 627) and are based upon the Joint Service Small Arms Master Plan (JSSAMP) and the Joint Capabilities Integration Development System's Small Arms Analyses.

The Army is not the Research and Development department of a weapons manufacturer. A small follow-up Army testing period may be acceptable prior to making a purchase. Eliminate, buy the resulting products from the private sector, and save $6 Billion.

Night Vision Advanced Technology

Project K70 pursues technologies that improve the Soldier's ability to see at night, provide rapid wide area search, multispectral aided target detection (AiTD), and enable passive long range target identification (ID beyond threat detection) in both an air and ground test-beds. Project K86 matures and evaluates sensors and algorithms designed to detect targets (vehicles and personnel) in camouflage, concealment and deception from airborne platforms, and provides pilotage and situational awareness imagery to multiple pilots/crew members independently for enhanced crew/aircraft operations in day/night/adverse weather conditions.

The Army is not the Research and Development department of a weapons manufacturer. Privatize and buy the resulting products from the weapons industry; but not until existing systems are really obsolete. Eliminate and save $15 Million.

Environmental Quality Technology Demonstrations

This program element (PE) matures and demonstrates technologies that assist Army installations in becoming environmentally compatible without compromising readiness or training critical to the success of the future force.

Protecting the environment is not a military function, and has nothing to do with national defense. Evaluate products coming out of the private sector, prefer those which are better for the environment if all other factors are of sufficient quality, and eliminate; $8 Million saved.

Military Engineering Advanced Technology

This program element (PE) matures and demonstrates data and information architectures and software applications, as well as sensing systems, that can be used to provide Warfighters with timely, accurate, easily interpretable data and information for the operational and tactical mission environments [...]

The Army is not an electronics or computer company. Eliminate, buy the products that come out of the private sector, and save $29 Million.

Advanced Tactical Computer Science and Sensor Technology

This program element (PE) matures and demonstrates technologies that allow the Warfighter to effectively collect, analyze, transfer and display situational awareness information in a network-centric battlefield environment. It matures and demonstrates architectures, hardware, software and techniques that enable synchronized Command and Control (C2) during rapid, mobile, dispersed and Joint operations.

The Army is not a weapons, electronics or computer company. Eliminate, buy the products that come out of the private sector, and save $14 Million.

Budget Activity 4[45]

Army Space Systems Integration
> *The program element funds space systems integration efforts performed by the US Army Space and Missile Defense Command/ Army Forces Strategic Command (USASMDC/ARSTRAT) and the Program Executive Office for Intelligence, Electronic Warfare, and Sensors (PEO IEW&S).*

This project provides commanders with battlefield intelligence, so they know what's going on at the battlefield without even needing to be near it. We already have drones, satellites, radios, and realtime maps with integrated digital readouts. They do not need more tools to provide the same information. Eliminate and save $10 Million.

Landmine Warfare and Barrier Advanced Development
> *This program element provides for advanced development of all landmine and counter landmine technologies. It also covers other close combat systems to include demolitions, grenades and pyrotechnics. Currently only one project line is funded: Project 606 - Countermine/Barrier Advanced Development. It provides for component development of new countermine systems for neutralizing, clearing, and detection concepts that will enhance the effectiveness of the Route Clearance Family of Systems Capabilities Development Document.*

The Army already has advanced landmine and counter landmine technologies, and the development thereof is the responsibility of the research and development departments of weapons companies. Eliminate and save $5 Million.

Smoke, Obscurant, and Target Defeating Systems Advanced Development
> *Project supports Screening Obscuration Module (SOM) in the development and improvement of an array of obscurant agents, and devices to improve survivability of the combined armed forces, support extended range capability, complement combined weapon systems, and enhance force effectiveness and combat power.*

The Army is not a weapons company. Eliminate, buy the products that come out of the private sector, and save $3 Million.

---

[45]http://asafm.army.mil/Documents/OfficeDocuments/Budget/BudgetMaterials/FY13/rforms//vol4.pdf

Tank and Medium Caliber Ammunition

The Direct Fire Advanced Technology (DFAT) Program Element (PE) encompasses a comprehensive program to develop, rapidly transition to production, and field advanced tank, medium and small caliber munitions.

The Army is not a weapons company. Eliminate, buy the products that come out of the private sector, and save $31 Million.

Advanced Tank Armament Systems

This Program Element (PE) supports the development of the Stryker Family of vehicles (FOV) in three separate projects.

The Army is not a weapons company. Eliminate, buy the products that come out of the private sector, and save $14 Million.

Soldier Support and Survivability

This program element supports component development and prototyping for organizational equipment, improved individual clothing and equipment that enhance Soldier battlefield effectiveness, survivability, and sustainment. This program element also supports the component development and prototyping of joint service food and combat feeding equipment designed to reduce logistics burden.

The Army is not a weapons company. Eliminate, buy the products that come out of the private sector, and save $26 Million.

Tactical Electronic Surveillance System Advanced Development

The Tactical Exploitation of National Capabilities (TENCAP) program serves as the Army's centralized lead to perform National Intelligence cross-agency engineering to evaluate, enhance, prototype, and transition Intelligence, Surveillance, and Reconnaissance (ISR) technologies/capabilities developed by Science and Technology (S&T) and other activities across the National Intelligence Community into Army systems and architectures.

The Army is not a weapons 7company. Eliminate, buy the products that come out of the private sector, and save $9 Million.

Night Vision Systems Advanced Development

This program element focuses on efforts to evaluate and integrate technologies and representative prototype systems that facilitate the development of Soldier-borne sensor devices transitioning from the laboratory to operational use. Efforts focus on proving out commonality across as broad a spectrum of users as possible to provide enhanced Soldier products, giving them superiority on the battlefield.

Duplication of effort from a BA3 activity. The Army is not a weapons company. Eliminate, buy the products that come out of the private sector, and save $11 Million.

Environmental Quality Technology Demonstration

> *There is a broad application potential for environmental quality technology (EQT) to be applied to multiple Army weapon systems and installations. However, technology must be demonstrated and validated (total ownership cost and performance data identified) before potential users will consider exploiting it. Therefore, this program element includes projects focused on validating the general military utility or cost reduction potential of technology when applied to different types of infrastructure, military equipment or techniques.*

Environmental quality is not a military function. In the few instances where the use of military force is required, the environment would not be much of a priority. Eliminate and save $5 Million.

Warfighter Tactical Information Network

> *The Defense Acquisition Executive (DAE), through the Nunn-McCurdy certification process, certified a restructured WIN-T program on June 5, 2007. The certification Acquisition Decision Memorandum (ADM) stated that the Army will restructure the WIN-T Major Defense Acquisition Program (MDAP) to absorb the former Joint Network Node (JNN) Network program.*

Duplication of efforts in DoD and TJS R&D projects and of those which have already made it to production. Eliminate and save **$275 Million**.

NATO Research and Development

> *This program implements the provisions of Title 10 U.S. Code, Section 2350a, Cooperative Research and Development (R&D) Projects: Allied Countries. The objective is to improve, through the application of emerging technologies, the conventional defense capabilities of the United States and our cooperative partners, including the North Atlantic Treaty Organization (NATO), U.S. major non-NATO allies and Friendly Foreign countries.*

The United States has greater conventional defense capabilities of the next 20 countries combined. Every other developed nation in the world would have to attack us at the same time for our current defenses to falter; and most of those are our allies. Our partners' defense is our partners' business, though I personally am against exporting weapons and military technology. Eliminate and save $5 Million. Withdraw from NATO, as Article VI of the Constitution allows our sovereignty to be ceded thereto.

Aviation Advanced Development

This PE provides advanced development aviation support of tactical programs associated with air mobility, advanced maintenance concepts and equipment, and Aircrew Integrated Systems (ACIS).

The Army is not an aircraft or electronics manufacturer. Eliminate and save $9 Million.

Logistics and Engineer Equipment Advanced Development

This program element supports advanced component development and prototypes of new and improved technologies for combat support and combat service support equipment essential to sustaining combat operations.

The Army is not a weapons, boat, utility, or logistics company. Outsource and eliminate, saving $15 Million.

Combat Service Support Control System Evaluation and Analysis

The Battle Command Sustainment Support System (BCS3) is the logistics Command and Control (C2) solution for U.S. land forces. BCS3 provides commanders the capability to execute end-to-end distribution and deployment management and brings better situational awareness resulting in better decision-making capability to warfighters.

The existing solutions seem to be working just fine, and there will be reduced demand in peacetime. Eliminate and save $5 Million.

Medical Systems Advanced Development

This program element (PE) funds development of medical material at the start of an official program of record, within the early system integration portion of the System Development and Demonstration phase of the acquisition life cycle using 6.4 funding.

The Army is not a medical company. Outsource and eliminate, saving $24 Million.

Soldier Systems Advanced Development

This Program Element (PE) for Advanced Component Development and Prototypes manages the Soldier as a system in order to increase combat effectiveness, test and deliver tangible products that save Soldier's lives, and improve Soldier's quality of life. It evaluates, develops, and tests emerging technologies and critical Soldier support systems to reduce technology risk.

The only systems the soldier needs to be a part of is the chain of command and the unit. They use methods proven over hundreds of years, and work just fine. Eliminate and save $32 Million.

Integrated Broadcast Service

> *The Joint Program Office (JPO) for IBS Terminals supports all Services and Special Operations Command (SOCOM). The Integrated Broadcast Service (IBS) is the worldwide Department of Defense (DoD) standard network for transmitting time-sensitive tactical and strategic intelligence and targeting data to all echelons of Joint Service operational users.*

The Army already has plenty of secure radios, walkie talkies, telephones, and satellite phones. They don't need a new kind. Eliminate and save $96K, and we shouldn't still be "researching and testing" a "DoD standard".

Technology Maturation Initiatives

> *This Program Element (PE) develops and demonstrates selected technology enabled capabilities to support advanced ground and aviation systems, precision weapons, and soldier equipment. Funding facilitates demonstration of relatively mature technologies and systems in relevant environments and tactical / operational scenarios, taking technologies through and beyond Technology Readiness Level (TRL) 6.*

The Army is not a weapons, electronics, or aircraft manufacturer. Eliminate and save $25 Million.

Tractor Jute

> *The details of this program are is reported in accordance with Title 10, United States Code, Section 119(a)(1).*

10 USC 119.a.1 just explains that it shall be reported to a committee, whose reports I could not find; and in the FY2010 Army Performance Budget Justification Book, which I could not find. Eliminate and save $59K.

Indirect Fire Protection Capability Increment 2

> *This program supports the overall Air and Missile Defense (AMD) architecture and provides a robust intercept capability against rocket, artillery, and mortar (RAM) and residual Unmanned Aerial System (UAS) threats for deployed forces supporting stability and counterinsurgency operations. Indirect Fire Protection Capability Increment 2 (IFPC2) will integrate with current Counter-Rocket, Artillery, and Mortar (C-RAM), and RAM Warn Capability.*

The stability of, and insurgencies in, other countries, are none of our business. If we eliminate the missions, then we eliminate the threats brought up by those missions. Perhaps we should instead focus on why these weapons are being fired on our soldiers in the first place. Further, we should buy our weapons from weapons companies instead of developing them ourselves. Eliminate and save $76 Million.

Integrated Base Defense (IBD)

> *Provides integration of software and analytical capability to support the integration of systems in the field. IBD employs an enterprise approach to enable Integrated Base Defense capabilities across the operational spectrum by leveraging interoperability efforts in support of the Integrated Unit, Base, and Installation Protection (IUBIP) framework.*

No American military base has been attacked since Pearl Harbor; our base defenses have been upgraded plenty since then. We can start by eliminating the private security guards at our bases and protecting them with our actual military instead of protecting foreign cities with them. Eliminate and save $4 Million.

Long Endurance Multi-Intelligence Vehicle (LEMV)

> *This program element (PE) evaluates unmanned aerial vehicle (UAV) prototype systems that provide increased flight and/or mission duration for Intelligence, Surveillance, and Reconnaissance (ISR) and communications capabilities. These systems include the aerial platform integrated with existing and/or developmental payloads.*

We already have solar-powered UAVs that can stay airborne indefinitely. We can put fancy cameras and sensors on existing UAVs. Eliminate and save $26 Million.

Budget Activity 5A[46]

Aircraft Avionics

> *The FY 2013 budget request funds the development of Aircraft Avionics systems required to horizontally and vertically integrate the battlefield and the integration of those systems into Army aircraft. Tasks in this PE support research, development, and test efforts in the Engineering and Manufacturing Development (EMD) phases of these systems. Beginning in FY 2013, funding on this Program Element was split into Projects C97 Aircraft Avionics and VU3 Networking and Mission Planning.*

The Army is not an aircraft manufacturer. Eliminate and save $79 Million.

Armed, Deployable Helos

> *The Kiowa Warrior (KW) funding line (Project 538) develops, integrates and tests modifications which will allow the OH-58D to continue to safely serve as the Army's armed reconnaissance aviation capability until replaced/retired. An ACAT II program, KW Cockpit and Sensor Upgrade Program (CASUP), was*

---

[46] http://asafm.army.mil/Documents/OfficeDocuments/Budget/BudgetMaterials/FY13/rforms//vol5a.pdf

established to address capability shortfalls, obsolescence, and safety issues with the current fielded fleet. KW CASUP is not the alternative solution to meet the Armed Scout Helicopter capability.

The helicopters the Army uses seem to be working fine so far, and would be less important in peacetime. Eliminate and save $90 Million.

Electronic Warfare Development

FY 2012 budget request funds Electronic Warfare Development. This program element (PE) encompasses engineering and manufacturing development for tactical electronic warfare (EW), signals warfare (SW), aircraft survivability equipment (ASE), battlefield deception, rapid software reprogramming and protection of personnel and equipment from hostile artillery.

The Army is not a weapons company. Eliminate and save $181 Million.

Mid-Tier Networking Vehicular Radio (MNVR)

MNVR encourages an industry solution for a multi-channel vehicular radio which will host JTRS networking waveforms. The MNVR will be a Non-Development Item (NDI) procurement. The MNVR represents a subset of functionality which was demonstrated in the JTRS Ground Mobile Radios (GMR) development program.

The Army's existing radios seem to be working just fine. Eliminate this brand-new program and save $13 Million.

All Source Analysis System (ASAS)

The All Source Analysis System (ASAS) provided US Army commanders at all echelons from battalion to Army Service Component Command (ASCC) with automated support to the management and planning, processing and analysis, and dissemination of intelligence, counterintelligence, and electronic warfare. ASAS provided the means to enhance the commander's timely and comprehensive understanding of enemy deployments, capabilities, and potential courses of action.

The Army has done a pretty good job of planning, processing, and analyzing intelligence and warfare so far. Eliminate and save $6 Million.

Tractor Cage

The details of this program are is reported in accordance with Title 10, United States Code, Section 119(a)(1).

10 USC 119.a.1 just explains that it shall be reported to a committee, whose reports I could not find; and in the FY2010 Army Performance Budget Justification Book, which I could not find. Eliminate and save $32 Million.

Infantry Support Weapons

FY 2012 budget request funds Infantry Support Weapons. This program element (PE) Engineering and Manufacturing Development (EMD) manages the Soldier as a system, with the goal of increasing Soldiers' combat effectiveness, increasing survivability, and improving the Soldiers' quality of life. It develops and tests prototypes of weapons, clothing, equipment, and other items useful to support the Soldier.

The Army has plenty of weapons, and they've done a pretty good job so far. They do not need new ones, and I've already debunked the SaaS system. Eliminate and save $96 Million.

Medium Tactical Vehicles

This Program Element (PE) supports continued modernization of the Army's medium truck and trailer fleet and the Armored Security Vehicle (ASV). In the medium fleet, the Family of Medium Tactical Vehicles (FMTV) replaces aging M35 2 1/2-ton trucks, and M809 and M900 Series 5-ton trucks that are beyond their economic useful life of 15-20 years.

The Army already has medium tactical vehicles, which are working just fine, and which are already leaps and bounds ahead of the old Jeeps, Humvees, and other trucks. Eliminate and save $3 Million.

Javelin

FY13 RDTE funding will support qualification testing of the multi-purpose warhead (MPWH), software modifications and upgrades, and Javelin Block I missile range verification testing.

The Army's existing Javelin systems are working just fine; they don't need upgrades. Eliminate and save $5 Million.

Family of Heavy Tactical Vehicles

This program element aligns system development and demonstration of Heavy Tactical Vehicles with Future Modular Force requirements to support combat and combat support missions. These missions include the following: line haul, local haul, and unit resupply.

The Army already has heavy tactical vehicles, which are working just fine, and which are already leaps and bounds ahead of the old ones. Eliminate and save $3 Million.

Air Traffic Control

This program element funds continuous efforts in the development of modernized tactical and fixed base Air Traffic Control (ATC) systems that will enable safety of aircraft landings in both the tactical and strategic ATC domains.

The Army's ATC efforts seem to be doing just fine. Aircraft are able to land safely today, and require no new technology to continue doing so. Eliminate and save $10 Million.

Tactical Unmanned Ground Vehicle

One program is covered by the Tactical Unmanned Ground Vehicle Program Element 0604641A: The Small Unmanned Ground Vehicle (SUGV) platform. The Small Unmanned Ground Vehicle (SUGV), designated as the XM-1216, is a lightweight (32 lbs), man-portable, DC powered UGV capable of conducting Military Operations in Urban Terrain (MOUT) to include tunnels, sewers, and caves.

EOD already has bomb diffusing robots; they don't need robots to do the actual soldering, too. If we eliminate our wartime stance, there will be reduced need for silly robots to do our shooting for us. Eliminate and save $13 Million.

Night Vision Systems Engineering Development

This program element provides night vision/reconnaissance, surveillance and target acquisition technologies required for U. S. defense forces to engage enemy forces twenty-four hours a day under conditions of degraded visibility due to darkness, adverse weather, battlefield obscurants, foliage and man-made structures.

This is at least the fourth night vision research project I've found so far, just within the Army's budget. This should be done by the companies that are making the night vision equipment, and they have great night vision technology already. Eliminate and save $33 Million.

Combat Feeding, Clothing, and Equipment

This project supports the development and demonstration and Non-Developmental Item (NDI) Commercial Off The Shelf (COTS) evaluation of combat feeding equipment to enhance soldier efficiency and survivability, and to reduce food service logistics requirements for all four services. The project supports multi-fuel, rapidly deployable field food service equipment initiatives and engineering and manufacturing development to improve equipment, enhance safety in food service, and decrease fuel and water requirements.

The military already has MREs, which are tasty, nutritious, and convenient. They do not need a new meal form factor. Eliminate and save $2 Million.

Non-System Training Devices Engineering Development
> Program Element funds development of Non-System Training Devices to support force-on-force training at the Combat Training Centers (CTC), general military training, and training on more than one item/system, as compared with system devices which are developed in support of a specific item/weapon system.

The Army does not need to spend $45 Million to research how to train in a realistic battlefield scenario. They already have realistic battlefield simulations on and off their bases. Eliminate and save $45 Million.

Terrain Information Engineering Development
> Distributed Common Ground System - Army (DCGS-A) is the Intelligence, Surveillance and Reconnaissance (ISR) System of Systems (SoS) for Joint, Interagency, Allied, Coalition, and National data analysis, sharing and collaboration.

The Army already has systems that perform these functions. Eliminate and save a million bucks.

Air Defense Command, Control, and Intelligence Engineering Development
> The Forward Area Air Defense Command and Control (FAAD C2) system collects, digitally processes, and disseminates real-time target cuing and tracking information; the common tactical 3-dimentional air picture; and command, control, and intelligence information to all Maneuver Air and Missile Defense (MAMD) weapon systems (Avenger and Man-Portable Air Defense System (MANPADS)), and joint and combined arms systems.

We already have systems that do this; we don't need a new one. Eliminate and save $73 Million.

Constructive Simulation Systems Development
> This program element funds the development of constructive and wargame simulations used to realistically train commanders and their battle staffs on today's complex battlefield conditions.

The Army already has wargame simulations and realistic training. Eliminate and save $29 Million.

Automatic Test Equipment Development
> This program element (PE) provides for development and testing of general-purpose test equipment and of state-of-the-art diagnostics and prognostics technology, software and systems to support the increasingly complex electronic components of the Army's new and upgraded weapon systems. It focuses on implementation of commercial test and diagnostic technologies

across multiple weapon platforms to minimize the cost of troubleshooting and maintenance of Army equipment in the field.

If we stop making the Army's equipment and weapons more complex, then we can stop compensating for that complexity. Eliminate and save $11 Million.

Distributive Interactive Simulations Engineering Development

Applies to the Army's Advanced Simulation Program, which enables operational readiness and the development of concepts and systems for the Future Force through the application of new simulation technology and techniques.

The Army's existing concepts are working pretty well so far. Eliminate and save $14 Million.

Combined Arms Tactical Trainer (CATT) Core

CATTs represent a family of combined arms simulation systems designed to support the Army's simulation-based Combined Arms Training Strategy. CATT enables units, from crew to the battalion task force level, to conduct a wide variety of combat tasks on a realistic, interactive, synthetic battlefield.

The Army's existing training strategies are working just fine. Eliminate and save $18 Million.

Brigade Analysis, Integration, and Evaluation

Provides funding for the Industry and government programs that meet or exceed known technological gaps and funds their platform and network integration into the Army's Network Integration Evaluation (NIE) Events.

The Army has no business meddling in industry and government, and should base its technology on what the private sector has to offer. Eliminate and save **$214 Million.**

Budget Activity 5B[47]

Weapons and Munitions Engineering Development

This program element funds engineering development of precision guidance systems applicable to Indirect Fire artillery weapon systems. The Precision Guidance Kit (PGK) is a Global Positioning Guidance Kit with fuzing functions.

The Army is not a weapons company. Eliminate and buy from the private sector; save $15 Million.

---

[47]http://asafm.army.mil/Documents/OfficeDocuments/Budget/BudgetMaterials/FY13/rforms//vol5b.pdf

Logistics and Engineer Equipment Engineering Development

> *This Program Element (PE) provides system development and demonstration for various projects. This PE includes the development of military tactical bridging, material handling equipment, construction equipment, engineer support equipment, soldier support equipment (to include shelter systems, environmental control, field service equipment, camouflage systems and aerial delivery equipment), water purification equipment, petroleum distribution equipment, mobile electric power and water craft.*

The Army's job is to defend our borders, not to demonstrate projects or research new technology. Eliminate and privatize; save $44 Million.

Command, Control, Communications Systems Engineering Development

> *This Program Element (PE) supports efforts to develop interoperability of Army programs and products, horizontally and vertically for the digitized battlefield. Project D485 supports Information Standards Interoperability Engineering and Joint Interoperability Certification. It provides the critical elements of the Army/Joint Technical Architecture, the mandated standards and communication protocols for Army/Joint ground and air operations, and crucial certification test tools to evaluate systems' interoperability for the Warfighter in support of the Vice Chief of Staff of the Army (VCSA) and Army Acquisition Executive (AAE).*

The Army's communications systems are just fine as they are, and require no additional research. Eliminate and save $21 Million.

Medical Material / Medical Biological Defense Equipment Engineering Development

> *This program element (PE) funds advanced development of medical material within the System Demonstration and Low Rate Initial Production portions of the acquisition life cycle using 6.5 funding. It supports products successfully developed in the Systems Integration portion of the Systems Development and Demonstration phases through completion of the Milestone C Decision Review.*

The military really doesn't need its own fancy hospitals; they could just train medics and use private hospitals, but I'll let that slide. Having said that, they really don't need special materials that aren't available in the private sector. For example, this line item funds HIV research, which has nothing to do with the military. If a soldier gets HIV, they should have to go through the same process as anyone else who made an equally bad decision. Eliminate and save $43 Million.

Landmine Warfare/Barrier Engineering Development

> This program element (PE) provides for System Development and Demonstration of networked munitions and countermine systems. This PE implements the National Landmine Policy to develop alternatives to the non-self-destructing anti-vehicle and anti-personnel landmine systems.

The Army already has effective countermine systems. Eliminate and save $105 Million.

Artillery Munitions

> Excalibur provides improved fire support through a Precision Guided Extended Range family of munitions with greatly increased accuracy and significantly reduces collateral damage in most urban environments. The Excalibur is interoperable with the M777A2 Lightweight 155mm howitzer (LW155), the M109A6 (Paladin) howitzer, and Sweden's Archer howitzer.

Our existing precision long-range munitions are doing a fine job already. Compatibility with other countries' platforms is irrelevant. Eliminate and privatize, saving $4 Million.

Army Tactical Command & Control Hardware & Software

> The umbrella program to exploit automation technology for the conduct of combat operations is the Army Tactical Command and Control System (ATCCS) program which is a component of the Army Battle Command System (ABCS). The ATCCS program provides automation in the five battlefield functional areas (BFAs)

The Army already has effective C&C systems. Eliminate and save $77 Million.

Radar Development

> This system is a supporting program of the overall Air and Missile Defense (AMD) architecture and will provide for an incrementally fielded Integrated Air and Missile Defense Fire Control System/capability for the composite Army Air and Missile Defense Brigades.

The Army is not a radar manufacturer, and our existing radar systems work just fine. Eliminate and save $3 Million.

General Fund Enterprise Business System

> The General Fund Business Enterprise System (GFEBS) is a Major Automated Information System (MAIS) program and completing the developmental phase. It will follow the DoD Business Enterprise Architecture which is aligned to the mandated Federal Enterprise Architecture.

Eliminate federal enterprise architecture mandates. Improve federal finances by not spending ten million bucks on a new computer system. This is the last year of funding, so it won't be needed in FY2014; but it probably should either have been done a long time ago or not at all. We can restructure this after we restructure the government. Eliminate and save $10 Million.

Firefinder

This Program funds design, development and test of primary target acquisition and counterfire radars to automatically detect, locate and classify hostile indirect fire weapons (mortars, artillery, and rockets). This PE directly supports the prioritization, tracking, and locating of targets, and dissemination of that information for simultaneous attack of multiple threats.

This is microphones set up at stationary points that can detect gunfire. If we eliminate our overseas posture, we need only detect gunfire in the U.S., and those will generally be crime as opposed to war. Gunshots can be detected just as easily with a call to 9-1-1. This would, however, be useful for base defense. For that, we can use the $32 Million the program has already been funded. Eliminate and save $21 Million.

Soldier Systems – Warrior Demonstration

This program element contains three projects: Project S56 for Mounted Soldier System (MSS), Project S65 for Soldier Power and Project S75 for Nett Warrior (NW)[.] MSS provides an integrated suite of enhancements to the combat vehicle crew member and commander to address identifiable capability gaps in their ability to fight, communicate, and maneuver across the full spectrum of operations.

Our soldiers and commanders have shown they can fight, communicate, and maneuver quite effectively without Nett. Eliminate and save $52 Million.

Artillery Systems – EMD

This program element supports the Joint Light Weight 155mm Howitzer (LW155) and the Paladin/FAASV Improvement programs. Beginning in FY11, only the Paladin/FAASV Improvement program has RDTE funding in this program element.

The Army is not a weapons manufacturer. Eliminate and save $168 Million.

Patriot / MEADS Combined Aggregate Program (CAP)

Medium Extended Air Defense System (MEADS) provides joint and coalition forces critical asset and defended area protection against multiple and simultaneous attacks by short-to-medium range ballistic missiles, cruise missiles, manned and unmanned aerial systems, and tactical air-to-surface missiles. This system leverages current technology for an Integrated Air and Missile Defense Fire Control System/capability.

We already have Patriot and MEADS systems in place. CAP ends this year, and is a NATO initiative. Withdraw from NATO. Eliminate and save **$401 Million**.

Nuclear Arms Control Monitoring Sensor Network

This project provides Research, Development, Testing & Evaluation (RDTE) to meet technology requirements in support of implementation, compliance, monitoring and inspection for existing and emerging nuclear arms control activities and dual use technology for missile defense integration activities. The project addresses requirements validated by the Office of the Under Secretary of Defense, Acquisition, Technology & Logistics (OUSD AT&L).

The Army already has systems to implement, monitor, and inspect our nukes. Eliminate and save $8 Million.

Information Technology Development

Supports efforts to plan, design, develop, and test information technology solutions to fulfill the Army's Warfighter Support Mission and accommodate changing Army requirements while fulfilling future Army needs. Provides for development and acquisition of Combat Service Support (CSS) and business information technology solutions to help arm, sustain, fix, move, train and man the force.

The Army is not a computer company. Eliminate and save $51 Million.

Army Integrated Military Human Resources System

The funds increased due to the Army's commitment to fully funding the program for completion of Increment I development and integration, as well as initial system Design, Development, and Integration efforts associated with critical activities for Increment II, Release 2.0. The Increment II Releases require ramp-up efforts of the System Integrator in order to meet our current schedule of fielding capabilities every 12 months. Release 2.0 is twice the size of Increment I in terms of efforts required for development and integration.

Use an existing commercial product like every other major employer. Eliminate and save **$159 Million**.

Joint Air-to-Ground Missile (JAGM)

The Joint Air-to-Ground Missile (JAGM) is an air-launched missile system that provides the Joint warfighter advanced targeting capabilities beyond currently fielded legacy missile variants. The funding allows continuation of the Technology Development phase to focus on affordability and risk reduction prior to additional investment in the Engineering and Manufacturing Development phase.

The Army is not a weapons company. Eliminate and save $10 Million.

PAC-3/MSE Missile

This system is an integral part of the overall Air and Missile Defense (AMD) architecture and will provide for an incrementally fielded Integrated Air and Missile Defense Fire Control System/capability for the composite Army Air and Missile Defense Battalions.

Our existing missile defense systems have been tested extensively and are doing just fine. The Army is not a weapons manufacturer. Eliminate and save $69 Million.

Army Integrated Air and Missile Defense (AIAMD)

This system is an integral part of the overall Air and Missile Defense (AMD) architecture and will provide for an incrementally fielded Integrated Air and Missile Defense Fire Control System/capability for the Army Air and Missile Defense Battalions. Funding in this program element provides for the overarching Army Integrated Air and Missile Defense (AIAMD) Architecture and Army IAMD Battle Command System (IBCS) components necessary to produce an AIAMD capability.

Our existing missile defense systems have been tested extensively and are doing just fine. The Army is not a weapons manufacturer. Eliminate and save $277 Million.

Manned Ground Vehicle

The Ground Combat Vehicle (GCV) program is based on an Initial Capabilities Document (ICD) that was approved 10 December 2009 and a draft Capabilities Development Document (CDD) developed by the U.S. Army Training and Doctrine Command (TRADOC). The accomplishments and funding reflected in this justification are based on these documents and on program milestone decision memoranda. A Milestone A Defense Acquisition Board was conducted on 21 July 2011. An Acquisition Decision Memorandum (ADM) was signed 17 August 2011.

This program doubles in 2014 and triples by 2015. It replaces existing APCs with a new acronym, IFVs, which do the same thing. Eliminate and save **$640 Million**.

Aerial Common Sensor

The Enhanced Medium Altitude Reconnaissance and Surveillance System (EMARSS) is the Army's next generation C-12 based, direct support, manned airborne intelligence collection, processing, and targeting support system. EMARSS provides a persistent capability to detect, locate, classify/identify, and track surface targets with a high degree of timeliness and accuracy.

The Army already has UAVs and satellites that can collect intelligence, look at stuff, and identify targets. Eliminate and save $47 Million.

Joint Light Tactical Vehicle

Joint Light Tactical Vehicles (JLTV): Funding supports the development and testing of the JLTV Family of Vehicles (FoV), which is being developed as a joint system between the Army and Marine Corps. International participation will be offered during this phase. The JLTV goal is a FoV with companion trailers capable of performing multiple mission roles that will be designed to provide protected, sustained, networked mobility for personnel and payloads across the full Range of Military Operations (RoMO).

How many different product families of light tactical vehicles do we really need? One. What's wrong with the ones we already have? Nothing. Why is the Army doing its own product research? Eliminate and save $72 Million.

TROJAN RH12 MIP

This project is a Military Intelligence Program (MIP). Trojan research and development supports Trojan Classic XXI (TCXXI) and next generation (NexGEN) future capabilities to fulfill the Army's need for a worldwide, deployable, remotable, intelligence, surveillance and reconnaissance support that can dynamically execute operations from sanctuary-based to deployed assets in theater.

The Army already has worldwide, deployable, remotable recon systems. We call them satellites and UAVs. Elimiante and save $4 Million.

Electronic Warfare Development

FY 2011 budget request funds Electronic Warfare Development. This program element (PE) encompasses engineering and manufacturing development for tactical electronic warfare (EW). EW encompasses the development of tactical EW equipment and systems mounted in both ground and air vehicles.

The Army is not a weapons, aircraft, or electronics manufacturer. Eliminate and privatize; save $14 Million.

Budget Activity 6[48]

Threat Simulator Development

> This program supports the design, development, acquisition, integration and fielding of realistic mobile threat simulators and realistic threat simulation products utilized in Army training and developmental and operational tests. While this project originally funded simulators representing Soviet equipment, the changing world order has expanded the scope of this program to address other world threats.

The Army already has systems and exercises to simulate threats. The Army is not a threat simulation product manufacturer. Eliminate and save $18 Million.

Target Systems Development

> This program funds aerial and ground target hardware and software development, maintenance, and upgrades. The overall objective is to ensure validation of weapon system accuracy and reliability by developing aerial and ground targets essential for test and evaluation (T&E). These targets are economical and expendable, remotely controlled or stationary, and often destroyed in use.

The Army does not need to spend millions of dollars developing remote-controlled toys that can be picked up at any local electronics store. Eliminate and save $14 Million.

Major Testing and Evaluation Investment

> This program funds the development and acquisition of major developmental test instrumentation for the U.S. ATEC test activities: White Sands Test Center, Yuma Test Center, Aberdeen Test Center, Electronic Proving Ground , Redstone Test Center, AL; and for the Reagan Test Site (RTS) at the U.S. Army Kwajalein Atoll (USAKA), which is managed by the Space and Missile Defense Command. The program also funds development and acquisition of Operational Test Command's (OTC) major field instrumentation.

The Army is not a weapons or electronics manufacturer. We probably don't need so many testing centers, either. Eliminate and save $37 Million.

Rand Arroyo Center

> This program funds the RAND Arroyo Center, the Department of the Army's Federally Funded Research and Development Center (FFRDC) for studies and analysis. The Arroyo Center draws its researchers from RAND's staff of nearly 700 professionals trained in a broad range of disciplines. Most staff members

---

[48]http://asafm.army.mil/Documents/OfficeDocuments/Budget/BudgetMaterials/FY13/rforms//vol6.pdf

work in RAND's principal locations-Santa Monica, California; Arlington, Virginia; and Pittsburgh, Pennsylvania. The RAND Arroyo Center provides for continuing analytical research across a broad spectrum of issues and concerns, grouped in four major research areas: Strategy, Doctrine, and Resources; Military Logistics; Manpower and Training; and Force Development and Technology.

The Army should not do much of its own research; rather, buy the products that private companies create based on their own research. Eliminate and save $21 Million.

Army Kwajalein Atoll

The U.S. Army Kwajalein Atoll/Ronald Reagan Ballistic Missile Defense Test Site (USAKA/RTS), located in the Republic of the Marshall Islands, is a remote, secure activity of the Major Range and Test Facility Base (MRTFB). Its function is to support test and evaluation of major Army and DoD acquisition programs and to provide space operations (surveillance and object identification) in support of U.S. Strategic Command (USSTRATCOM) and National Aeronautics and Space Administration (NASA) scientific and space programs.

There is a series of Army airfields on this remote island chain, which should thereby be funded through the regular Operations budget. Space surveillance can be done on literally any military installation or testing area, and we do have our own series of remote oceanic islands. Eliminate and save **$177 Million**.

Concepts Experimentation Program

The Army Experimentation mission enables integrated examinations with US Joint Forces Command (USJFCOM), Army Test and Evaluation Command (ATEC), Research, Development, and Experimentation Command (RDECOM), Army battle laboratories, operational units, research labs, material developers, industry and academia to collaborate in the development, refinement, and assessment of future force concepts.

The Army should not be doing its own experimentation. This should be done by the companies that make whatever we're testing; we should merely test them a few times and buy them. Eliminate and save $28 Million.

Army Test Ranges and Facilities

This project provides the institutional funding required to operate the developmental test activities, in accordance with Section 232 of the FY2003 National Defense Authorization Act (NDAA), required by Department of Defense (DOD) Program Executive Officers, Program and Product Managers, and Research, Development, and Engineering Centers.

The Army should not be doing its own experimentation. This should be done by the companies that make whatever we're testing; we should merely test them a few times and buy them. Most of these operations can probably be concentrated DoD-wide into one remote island or desert region; especially since we're supposedly not doing nuclear testing anymore. Reduce funding by 90% and save **$333 Million**.

Army Technical Test Instrumentation and Targets
> *This Program Element provides critical front-end investments for development of new test methodologies; test standards; advanced test technology concepts for long range requirements; future test capabilities; advanced development of M&S and instrumentation prototypes; and the full development of systems for [list of bases].*

Vendors should use their sales profits to fund research and development efforts. Eliminate and save $69 Million.

Survivability/Lethality Analysis
> *This project funds analytical products necessary for inherently-governmental Army Test & Evaluation Command/Army Evaluation Center's (ATEC/AEC) mission. Products result from investigating, analyzing, assessing, and reporting on the survivability of Soldiers, and on the survivability, lethality and vulnerability (SLV) of the highest priority Army systems whether those systems are employed during stability, support, defensive, or offensive missions.*

Parts of this are the responsibility of the product vendors, and other parts are the responsibility of the mission commanders. In peacetime, there wouldn't be much data to analyze anyway; eliminate and save $45 Million.

Aircraft Certification
> *The Airworthiness Certification program ensures flight safety and safe operation of Army aircraft and aviation systems by means of technical design approval and qualification of systems to appropriate airworthiness standards. It provides independent airworthiness qualification of all assigned developmental and in-production Army aircraft, both manned and unmanned, as required by AR 70-62, and is essential for ensuring the safe operation of Army aircraft.*

I understand that the Army needs aircraft, but do they need so many new lines of them that the need justifies a whole certification program? How often do we really need an entirely new line of aircraft; especially in peacetime? Why not just put a qualified pilot in the plane and tell him to run it through the gauntlet? Eliminate, privatize, and/or integrate into Army Test Ranges and Facilities and save $6 Million.

Meteorological Support to RDT&E Facilities

All functions and resources in this Program Element (PE) are managed by the U.S. Army Test and Evaluation Command (ATEC). Meteorological support to research, development, test, and evaluation (RDT&E) activities provides standard and specialized weather forecasts and data for test reports to satisfy Army/ Department of Defense RDT&E test requirements for modern weaponry

There are already plenty of different weather forecasts and data for test reports; this is redundant. Eliminate and save $7 Million.

Material Systems Analysis

This program element funds Department of the Army (DA) civilians at the Army Material Systems Analysis Activity (AMSAA) to conduct responsive and effective material systems analysis in support of senior Army decision making for equipping the U.S. Army. AMSAA conducts systems and engineering analyses to support Army decisions in technology; material acquisitions; and the design, development, fielding, and sustaining of Army weapon/material systems. As part of this mission, AMSAA develops and certifies systems performance data used in Army studies, and develops systems performance methodology and Models and Simulations (M&S).

Testing processes have become overcomplicated. Just give the equipment to a team who knows the subject area and get their sign-off. Eliminate and save $20 Million.

Exploitation of Foreign Items

Maximize[s] the efficiency of research and development for force and material development by reducing the uncertainties concerning these threats. The program also answers general scientific and technical intelligence requirements, aids in the development of countermeasures to threat material and threat technology, and provides material for realistic testing and training. Operations in Afghanistan have increased the number of items of captured threat material that require immediate exploitation to develop countermeasures and force protection measures for deployed forces. Acquisitions and exploitations are executed according to an Army Foreign Material Program Plan and with the approval of the Army, Director of Intelligence (G2).

Looking at an IED and determining whether it contains radiological material, etc. doesn't seem like it should cost seven digits. Have a lab technician run some swabs, have an engineer look at its design, and have a battlefield commander examine it for threats. Eliminate and save $6 Million.

Support of Operational Testing

> *This Program Element provides the resources to operate the Army's operational test directorates[.] Also funds the Test and Evaluation Coordination Offices (TECOs)[...]; as well as recurring support costs of Headquarters, Army Test and Evaluation Command (HQ ATEC), joint testing, operational test and evaluations without an Army Program Executive Officer/Project Manager and follow-on test and evaluations, all of which are managed by HQ, ATEC.*

By eliminating most testing, we can eliminate most needed support. Reduce by 90% and save $61 Million.

Army Evaluation Center

> *The Army Evaluation Center (AEC) provides independent and integrated technical and operational evaluations, and life-cycle Continuous Evaluation (CE) of assigned Major Defense Acquisition Programs (MDAP), Major Automated Information Systems, and In-Process Review (IPR) programs for major milestone decisions, material changes, and material releases in support of the Army Acquisition Executive, other Service Acquisition Executives, Joint Program Executive Officers, other governmental agencies, and force development. AEC is The Army's independent evaluator.*

First off, the military really doesn't need to evaluate and buy so many products. Many are duplicated or never looked feasible in the first place, and some are just pointless. Given a massive reduction in purchasing and evaluation, we can eliminate some of this overhead associated therewith. Save $63 Million.

Army Modeling and Simulation Cross-Command Collaboration and Integration

> *M&SC3I promotes the Army's goal to achieve affordable, interoperable and networked Modeling and Simulation (M&S) capabilities. In support of Army operations, Generating-Force functions and institutional processes, M&S Cross-Command Collaboration and Integration addresses analytical efforts underlying decision making, capability development, and life-cycle costs by capitalizing on M&S technologies (accomplished through collaborative efforts of the training/operations and acquisition communities).*

This is overhead that appears necessary due to the sheer volume of testing. By reducing testing, this becomes obsolete. Eliminate and save $2 Million.

Programwide Activities

This program funds the continued operation of non-Army Management Headquarters Activities (AMHA) management and administrative functions at U.S. Army Research, Development and Standardization Groups overseas, Army Research, Development, Test, and Evaluation (RDTE) commands, centers and activities required to accomplish overall assigned general research and development missions and international research and development not directly related to specific research and development projects.

This is more overhead associated with the large scale testing. Eliminate and save $83 Million.

Technical Information Activities

This program element (PE) supports upgrading the accuracy, timeliness, availability, and accessibility of scientific, technical, and management information at all levels of the Army Research and Development (R&D) community. Management of this information is critical to achieve the goals established by the Army's Senior Leadership.

This is more overhead associated with the large scale testing. Eliminate and save $51 Million.

Munitions Standardization, Effectiveness, and Safety

This Program Element supports continuing technology investigations. It provides a coordinated tri-service mechanism for the collection and free exchange of technical data on the performance and effectiveness of all non-nuclear conventional munitions and weapons systems in a realistic operational environment.

This program tests for interchangeability and compatibility between similar rounds per NATO and similar standards. Our ammo really doesn't need to be interchangeable with anyone else's; rather, manufacturers should agree on what constitutes a 9mm round, etc. Eliminate and save $47 Million.

Environmental Quality Technology Management Support

This program resources environmental quality technology (EQT) related management support functions including support of RDT&E required for EQT technical integration efforts at demonstration/validation test sites, technical information and activities, test facilities and general test instrumentation, and EQT requirement assessments.

Eliminate military environment requirements; eliminate EQTMS, save $5 Million.

R&D Management Headquarters

>This project provides for the salaries and related personnel benefits for the management headquarters authorized civilian personnel who support the U.S. Army Test and Evaluation Command (ATEC) mission.

Overhead associated with research programs. Given the reduction in RDT&E scale, this can probably be moved down a few command levels and no longer requires a headquarters. Eliminate and save $19 Million.

Budget Activity 7[49]

MLRS Product Improvement Program

>The M142 High Mobility Artillery Rocket System (HIMARS) is a full spectrum, combat proven, all weather, 24/7 lethal and responsive, precision strike weapon system that fully supports more deployable, affordable and lethal, Brigade Combat Teams, Fires Brigades, Modular Forces, and Joint Expeditionary Forces. The HIMARS launcher is a C-130 transportable, wheeled, indirect fire, rocket/missile launcher capable of firing all rockets and missiles in the current and future Multiple Launch Rocket System (MLRS) Family of Munitions (MFOM) and Army Tactical Missile System (ATACMS) Family of Munitions (AFOM) engaging targets with precision out to ranges of 300 kilometers.

The Army is not a weapons manufacturer. Eliminate and privatize; save **$143 Million**.

Patriot Product Improvement

>Patriot is an advanced Surface-to-Air guided missile system with a high probability of kill capable of operation in the presence of Electronic Countermeasures (ECM) and able to conduct multiple simultaneous engagements against high performance air breathing targets and ballistic missiles likely to be encountered by US Forces.

This duplicates efforts within the Army's procurement budget, and the Patriot missile systems are already working fine. Eliminate and save $110 Million.

Aerostat Joint Project Office

>Joint Land Attack Cruise Missile Defense Elevated Netted Sensor System (JLENS) is a supporting program of the Army and Joint Integrated Air and Missile Defense, providing a persistent surveillance and tracking capability for Unmanned Aerial Vehicle and Cruise Missile defense to the current and projected defense forces. JLENS will provide fire control quality data to Surface

---

[49]http://asafm.army.mil/Documents/OfficeDocuments/Budget/BudgetMaterials/FY13/rforms//vol7.pdf

to Air missile systems such as Army Patriot and Navy Aegis; increasing the weapons' capabilities by allowing these systems to engage targets normally below, outside or beyond surface based weapons' field of view.

We already have systems like this and likely require no further research. If we do, then we should buy products that have already been researched by the private sector companies who stand to profit from it. Eliminate and save **$190 Million**.

Advanced Field Artillery Tactical Data System

The Advanced Field Artillery Tactical Data System (AFATDS) automates fire support planning and coordination for the Army, Navy, and Marine Corps. AFATDS automates the planning, coordinating and controlling of all fire support assets in the Joint battlespace (field artillery, mortars, close air support, naval gunfire, attack helicopters, and offensive electronic warfare) from Echelons Above Corps to Battery or Platoon in support of all levels of conflict. As a result of Operation Iraqi Freedom (OIF)/Operation Enduring Freedom (OEF), AFATDS has implemented precision fires capabilities in new/improved munitions such as Multiple Launch Rocket System (MLRS) Unitary Vertical Attack, Excalibur, Smart and 155 Bonus.

The Army has shown that it is capable of aiming and firing artillery (etc.) effectively; it need not be automated. If it must be, then buy a solution from a weapons company. Eliminate and save $33 Million.

Combat Vehicle Improvement Program

This Program Element (PE) corrects vehicle deficiencies identified in Army operations; continues technical system upgrades to include the integration of applicable technologies on ground systems; addresses needed evolutionary enhancements to tracked combat vehicles; and develops technology improvements which have application to or insertion opportunities across multiple Ground Combat Systems vehicles. This PE provides combat effectiveness and Operating and Support (O&S) cost reduction enhancements for the Abrams tanks and Bradley Fighting Vehicles through a series of product improvements.

If the Army is buying defective products, then the manufacturer should be held accountable through a warranty program of some kind. For what remains, the Army has legions of vehicle maintainers and does not require special research projects. The people using the vehicles can simply report deficiencies as they are detected in normal use. Eliminate and save **$254 Million**.

Maneuver Control System

> *Tactical Mission Command (TMC) is a suite of products and services that provide commanders and staffs executive decision making capability in a collaborative environment, planning tools, and Common Operational Picture (COP) management and other maneuver functional tools. TMC satisfies requirements and capabilities identified in the Maneuver Control System (MCS) Good Enough Operational Requirements Document (ORD) and MCS 6.4 Capability Production Document (CPD) which includes Army migration to Department of Defense (DoD) net-centric environment.*

The Army has plenty of existing collaboration tools, and many more are available online for next to nothing. Pick up a phone or a radio. Eliminate and save $68 Million.

Aircraft Modifications / Product Improvement Program

> *FY 2011 budget request funds aviation development of modifications and improvements for the Guardrail Common Sensor/Aerial Common Sensor, the Improved Cargo Helicopter (ICH), the UH-60A/L Black Hawk Recapitalization/ Modernization.*

The description is clearly outdated, but it is funded for the foreseeable future. The Army's equipment is working just fine and needs to be replaced only when it is destroyed or otherwise stops working. Further, other Army budget areas already request funds for aircraft recapitalization and that is duplicated here. Eliminate and save **$280 Million**.

Aircraft Engine Component Improvement Program

> *Aircraft Engine Component Improvement Program (CIP) develops, tests, and qualifies improvements to aircraft engine components to correct service-revealed deficiencies, improve flight safety, enhance readiness and reduce operating and support (O&S) costs.*

Identifying engine improvements is the responsibility of the engine manufacturers and Army mechanics while on duty. Eliminate and save $898K.

Digitization

> *Horizontal Battlefield Digitization is a strategy that allows warfighters, from the individual soldier and platform to echelons above corps, to share critical situation awareness (SA) and command and control (C2) information. It conducts analysis and evaluation of new information technologies, concepts, and applications of integrated management activities to meet the dynamic Army acquisition technology requirements.*

Soldiers already have HUD readouts on some helmets, and battlefield commanders already have digital maps delivered through satellite surveillance and point to point systems. Eliminate, let the private sector do it, and save $35 Million. Maybe we'll even start seeing this stuff show up in the private sector sooner that way.

Missile / Air Defense Product Improvement Program
Project 036: Patriot is an advanced Surface-to-Air guided missile system with a high probability of kill capable of operation in the presence of Electronic Countermeasures (ECM) and able to conduct multiple simultaneous engagements against high performance air breathing targets and ballistic missiles likely to be encountered by US Forces.

Yet another duplication of effort; this is the third Patriot improvement project I've seen so far. Eliminate and save $21 Million.

Tractor Card
The details of this program are reported in accordance with Title 10, United States Code, Section 119(a)(1).

The Army is not the Research and Development department of a... wait, what exactly is a tractor card? 10 USC 119.a.1 just explains that it shall be reported to a committee, whose reports I could not find; and in the FY2010 Army Performance Budget Justification Book, which I could not find. Eliminate and save $63 Million.

Joint Tactical Ground System (JTAGS)
This system is an integral part of the overall Air and Missile Defense (AMD) architecture and will provide for an incrementally fielded Integrated Air and Missile Defense Fire Control System/capability for the composite Army Air and Missile Defense Brigades. This program element supports development of critical improvements and insertion of technology upgrades to the Joint Tactical Ground Station (JTAGS) and the research and development of the JTAGS Pre-Planned Product Improvement (P3I).

This system is already in use and research should be done by the manufacturers. Eliminate and save $32 Million.

Joint High Speed Vessel
The Joint High Speed Vessel (JHSV) program is a merger of the Army's Theater Support Vessel (TSV) program and the Marine Corps/Navy High Speed intra-theater surface Connector (HSC) program into a joint (multi-service) High Speed Vessel program.

If they need the same boats, then they should just buy the same boats. Eliminate and save $35K.

Special Army Program

This is a classified program.

No funding is outlined in the budget, so no funding shall be provided.

Security and Intelligence Activities

INSCOM's RDTE program provides the Army with low-density, high-demand, extremely advanced offensive cyberspace technologies designed to degrade, deny, disrupt, or destroy adversary C4I and shape the operational warfighting environment in order to create conditions favorable to the application of other elements of national power.

This program is already being used and requires no further development. Eliminate and save $8 Million.

Information Systems Security Program

The Cryptographic Modernization (CM) program supports the implementation of the National Security Agency (NSA) developed Communications Security (COMSEC) technologies into the Army by providing COMSEC system capabilities through encryption, trusted software or standard operating procedures, and integrating these mechanisms into specific systems in support of securing the National Network Enterprise.

The Army's communications are already encrypted and this duplicates TJS and DoD efforts. Eliminate and save $16 Million.

Global Combat Support System

The Global Combat Support System-Army (GCSS-Army) program has two components: a functional component titled GCSS-Army and a technology enabler component titled Army Enterprise Systems Integration Program (AESIP) (formerly Product Lifecycle Management Plus (PLM+)). GCSS-Army coupled with AESIP are information and communications technology investments that will provide key enabling support to the transformation of the Army into a network-centric, knowledge-based future force.

This is a duplication of several Army and DoD projects, and provides nothing the Army doesn't already have. Elimiante and save $121 Million.

SATCOM Ground Environment

Military Satellite Communication (MILSATCOM) systems are joint program/project efforts to satisfy ground mobile requirements for each Service, the Joint Chiefs of Staff (JCS), the National Command Authority, the combatant commanders, the Office of the Secretary of Defense, and other governmental, non-DoD users.

Yet another duplicate effort to coordinate ground activity and present them on screens and each other's visors. How many different ways do people need to see the same information? Eliminate and save $16 Million.

WWMCCS / Global Command and Control System

Global Command and Control System-Army (GCCS-A): This project is the Army component system that directly supports the implementation of the Global Command and Control System Family of Systems. GCCS-A provides automated command and control tools for Army Strategic and Operational Theater Commanders to enhance warfighter capabilities throughout the spectrum of conflict during joint and combined operations in support of the National Security.

Yet another duplicate effort to coordinate ground activity and present them on screens and each other's visors. How many different ways do people need to see the same information? Eliminate and save $14 Million.

Tactical Unmanned Aerial Vehicles

Project 114: Tactical Unmanned Aerial Vehicle (TUAV) Shadow 200 provides the Army Brigade Commander with dedicated Reconnaissance, Surveillance and Target Acquisition (RSTA), Intelligence, Battle Damage Assessment (BDA) and Force Protection. The Shadow provides the Brigade Commander with critical battlefield intelligence and targeting information in the rapid cycle time required for success at the tactical level.

The Army is not an aircraft manufacturer. Eliminate, privatize, and save $331 Million.

Distributed Common Ground/Surface Systems

Distributed Common Ground System - Army (DCGS-A) is the Intelligence, Surveillance and Reconnaissance (ISR) System of Systems (SoS) for Joint, Interagency, Allied, Coalition, and National data analysis, sharing and collaboration.

A duplicate effort to coordinate ground activity and collaborate between people, both of which have already been addressed. Eliminate and save $41 Million.

MQ-1 Gray Eagle UAV

The production MQ-1C Gray Eagle Unmanned Aircraft System (UAS) has changed based on new Army Guidance from a company sized unit equipped

> with twelve (12) Unmanned Aircraft (UA) and associated support equipment to balanced Platoons, each capable of operating independently with four (4) Aircraft.

The Army is not an aircraft manufacturer. Eliminate and save $75 Million.

RQ-11 Raven UAV

> The Small Unmanned Aircraft System (SUAS) provides the battalion and below ground maneuver elements critical situational awareness and enhances force protection.

The Army is not an aircraft manufacturer. Eliminate and save $4 Million.

RQ-7 Shadow UAV

> Tactical Unmanned Aerial Vehicle (TUAV) Shadow 200 provides the Army Brigade Commander with dedicated Reconnaissance, Surveillance and Target Acquisition (RSTA), Intelligence, Battle Damage Assessment (BDA) and Force Protection.

The Army is not an aircraft manufacturer. Eliminate and save $31 Million.

UAV/UAS Modifications / Product Improvement Program

> The Army has a requirement to provide Intelligence, Surveillance, and Reconnaissance (ISR) platforms capable of operating in and near unfriendly territories/areas of conflict. The system shall be a rotary wing unmanned vertical takeoff and landing (VTOL) aircraft system not conducive to standard airfields but forward deployable to support extended operations in austere environment.

The Army is not an aircraft manufacturer. Eliminate and save $2 Million.

Biometrics Enabled Intelligence

> Joint Personnel Identification Version 2 (JPIv2) will provide an Army tactical biometric collection capability to capture an adversary or neutral person's biometric data and enroll them into the Department of Defense (DoD) enterprise authoritative biometric database to positively identify and verify the identity of actual or potential adversaries.

This is at least the third biometrics research project I've found so far. We only need one biometrics solution at the most. Eliminate and save $15 Million.

End Item Industrial Preparedness Activities

> This program element (PE) develops and demonstrates manufacturing processes that enable improvements in producibility and affordability of emerging and enabling components and subsystems of Army air, ground,

Soldier, and command/control/communications systems. Initiatives within the PE result in cost savings and reduced risk of transitioning military-unique manufacturing processes into production. Project E25 fosters the transfer of new/improved manufacturing technologies to the industrial base, including manufacturing efforts that have potential for high payoff across the spectrum of Army systems.

The Army is not a manufacturer. Eliminate and save $60 Million.

Military Construction[50]

Inside the United States
My plan does not significantly reduce domestic military forces, and in fact notably increases them. Keep this section as is.

Alaska	$18.3M	California	$8.9M
Colorado	$18M	District of Columbia	$7.2M
Georgia	$88.95M	Hawaii	$210M
Kansas	$12.2M	Kentucky	$81.8M
Missouri	$123M	New Jersey	$57.2M
New York	$287M	North Carolina	$98M
Oklahoma	$4.9M	South Carolina	$24M
Texas	$116.6M	Virginia	$259M
Washington	$169.1M		

Total $1,590,150,000

Outside the United States
My plan eliminates all overseas bases; therefore, no construction is required. All following funding is eliminated:

Italy	$68M	Japan	$96M
Korea	**$45M**		

Total $209,000,000

Worldwide
My plan eliminates all overseas bases; therefore, no construction is required. All following funding is eliminated:

Host Nation Support	$34M	Planning and Design	$65M
Minor Construction	**$25M**		

Total $124M

---

[50]http://asafm.army.mil/Documents/OfficeDocuments/Budget/BudgetMaterials/FY13/milcon//mca.pdf

Chemical Agents and Munitions Destruction and Defense[51]

Operation and Maintenance

If our enemies have chemical weapons, it behooves us to be able to respond in kind, under the understanding that we shall not use them proactively. Eliminate and save $1.1 Billion; some of these disposal facilities can probably be closed as well.

Research, Development, Test, and Evaluation

This budget activity provides resources for the development and testing of technologies for the destruction of chemical munitions that are alternatives to the baseline incineration program, and the design, acquisition and testing of prototype equipment for the recovery and treatment of the non-stockpile chemical material.

The Army is not a research organization. Eliminate; save $647 Million.

Procurement

This budget activity provides for the procurement of all process and support equipment used in the incineration disposal facilities for destroying the unitary chemical stockpile, equipment to support the closure of the incineration facilities, Chemical Stockpile Emergency Preparedness Project equipment, and Non-Stockpile Chemical Material Project equipment.

The Army is not a research organization. Eliminate; save $19 Million.

Having found nothing in this budget that is "Defense"-oriented, I move we eliminate the entire thing; $1.3 Billion saved.

Chemical Demilitarization Construction, Defense[52]

For expenses, not otherwise provided for, necessary for the construction of facilities and infrastructure upgrades to support destruction of the United States stockpile of lethal chemical agents and munitions in accordance with the provisions of Section 1412 of the National Defense Authorization Act, 1986 (50 U.S.C. 1521), $151,000,000 to become available on October 1, 2012 and to remain available until September 30, 2017.

Having found nothing in the CDCD budget that is "Defense"-oriented, I move we eliminate the entire thing; $151 Million saved.

---

[51]http://asafm.army.mil/Documents/OfficeDocuments/Budget/BudgetMaterials/FY13//camdd.pdf
[52]http://asafm.army.mil/Documents/OfficeDocuments/Budget/BudgetMaterials/FY13//cdcd.pdf

Army Working Capital Fund[53]

> *Working capital funds were established by Congress to more effectively control and account for the cost of programs and work performed in the Department of Defense. Under the provisions of Title 10 United States Code § 2208, the Secretary of Defense may establish working capital funds to finance inventories of supplies and industrial-type activities that provide common services such as repair, manufacturing, or remanufacturing.*

With our new peacetime stance, there would be a significantly reduced need for supply throughput, repair, manufacturing, and remanufacturing. What remains really should be part of the Operations and Maintenance budget. With these two sources of standard maintenance and overhauls, combined with similar programs in the various Procurements budgets, it's no wonder how large sums of money go missing from time to time. The work is simply being duplicated and accountability may be lost in the process.

The AWCF's mission is to break even, requiring no extra money to be funneled into any programs, despite employing over 26,000 people. If they have no funding, then they have no choice. I therefore recommend we move the AWCF into the Operations and Maintenance budget and eliminate all funding, saving **$14 Billion.** Whatever remains can come out of the O&M budget. Try to think of it as an incentive.

Army National Cemeteries Program[54]

> *Army is almost quadrupling the resources in FY 2013 that will be obligated for Arlington National Cemetery (ANC) operations and improvements to address the issues identified in the recent Army Gravesite Accountability Report, Army Inspector General Reports, Government Accountability Office, Army Audit Agency and other reviews*

There are no war heroes in peacetime. Eliminate all new construction and save $103 Million. What's left can be transferred or merged into the VA.

Operation Enduring Freedom Military Personnel[55]

> *In response to the terrorist attacks on the United States on September 11, 2001, the President invoked his authority (10 U.S.C 12302) to order to active duty Ready Reserve members and delegated his authority to the Secretary of Defense in Proclamation 7463 of September 14, 2001.*

---

[53] http://asafm.army.mil/Documents/OfficeDocuments/Budget/BudgetMaterials/FY13//awcf.pdf
[54] http://asafm.army.mil/Documents/OfficeDocuments/Budget/BudgetMaterials/FY13//usa-ncp.pdf
[55] http://asafm.army.mil/Documents/OfficeDocuments/Budget/BudgetMaterials/FY13/OCO//milpers.pdf

The only national emergency we're facing is the economic collapse that inevitably follows any spiraling government spending and rampant devaluation of the national currency. End all Overseas Contingency Operations, including Operation Enduring Freedom. Bring home all our personnel, equipment, documents, etc; save $10.1 Billion.

Overseas Contingency Operations Operation and Maintenance[56]

> *Operation Enduring Freedom encompasses all actions to restore stability and provide security in Afghanistan, the Horn of Africa, and the Philippines. The Operation and Maintenance, Army (OMA) appropriation supports day-to-day operations in these theaters*

Stability and security in other countries is the business of those countries. Therefore, America does not need the Army to perform any day-to-day operations, to train any foreigners, to police anyone anywhere, to maintain bases overseas, nor to deploy units.

> *Operation New Dawn (OND) encompasses all actions to return national security responsibility to the nation of Iraq.*

We're done with Iraq. If they want democracy, let them build and hold it themselves. If not, whatever.

Eliminate and save **$28.6 Billion.**

Overseas Contingency Operations Army Reserve Operation and Maintenance[57]

> *Operation New Dawn (OND): Historically, the Army Reserve supported Operation New Dawn with soldiers performing various combat support and combat service support missions in Iraq to include nation building throughout the CENTCOM area of operation. Of the total FY 2013 request, 0% supports OND.*

My proposal is eliminating all overseas operations. Eliminate and save $155 Million.

Overseas Contingency Operations Army National Guard Operation & Maintenance[58]

> *The Army National Guard supports Overseas Contingency Operations (OCO) with Soldiers performing various combat, combat support, and combat service support missions such as physical security, nation building, and Counter-*

---

[56] http://asafm.army.mil/Documents/OfficeDocuments/Budget/BudgetMaterials/FY13/OCO//oma.pdf
[57] http://asafm.army.mil/Documents/OfficeDocuments/Budget/BudgetMaterials/FY13/OCO//omar.pdf
[58] http://asafm.army.mil/Documents/OfficeDocuments/Budget/BudgetMaterials/FY13/OCO//omng.pdf

> *insurgency (COIN) Operations. The Army National Guard utilizes OCO funding to provide these formations with pre-mobilization training and support as well as post-redeployment and re-integration activities upon completion of the deployment.*

If we eliminate all OCO, then we eliminate the need to support it with the National Guard. Eliminate and save $382 Million.

Afghanistan Security Forces Fund[59]

> *Recent Afghanistan Security Forces Fund (ASFF) Budgets have provided the resource foundation needed to Train and Equip a 352,000 Afghan National Security Force (ANSF) and 30,000 Afghan Local Police (ALP). The Fiscal Year (FY) 2013 Budget request marks a shift as emphasis moves from building, equipping, and training to professionalizing and sustaining the force.*

Afghanistan is none of our business. It wasn't in 1979, it wasn't in 2001, and it isn't today. We should never equip (especially with weapons) foreign military, paramilitary, or civilian forces for any reason. It makes no sense whatsoever to invade a country and then build them an army; one might think they had been the victors. Eliminate and save $5.7 Billion.

Conclusion

By eliminating our wartime stance, eliminating all unconstitutional spending, and returning to a peacetime stance, we can reduce the Army's budget by more than half without any impact to our national *defense*. The Army's official budget claims $184.6 Billion in outlays, but I counted $224.226 Billion. The new spending totals $92 Billion, a **reduction of $131.8 Billion.**

---

[59] http://asafm.army.mil/Documents/OfficeDocuments/Budget/BudgetMaterials/FY13/OCO//asff.pdf

Department of the Navy[60]

Article I, Section 8, Clause 13 of the Constitution authorizes the Congress to "To provide and maintain a Navy". Therefore, the Navy is constitutionally justified. However, not everything in the Navy is necessary to serve the Navy's purpose.

Military Personnel, Navy[61]

The Navy would be useless without personnel, so the personnel are necessary and proper to the purpose of providing and maintaining a navy per the Constitution. Keep military personnel at the standard 25% reduction, and save $7 Billion.

Military Personnel, Marine Corps[62]

I think the Marines can get away with calling themselves constitutionally authorized by calling themselves an army or a navy; their job is really a hybrid thereof. Reduce by the standard 25% and save $3.6 Billion.

Operation and Maintenance, Navy[63]

> For expenses, not otherwise provided for, necessary for the operation and maintenance of the Navy and the Marine Corps, as authorized by law; to be expended on the approval or authority of the Secretary of the Navy, and payments may be made on his certificate of necessity for confidential military purposes, $41,606,943,000.

Given my proposed changes in foreign policy, we can eliminate all regular costs of doing business overseas. The operations and maintenance of the Navy is critical to the navy itself, and is thus necessary and proper. This is a $41.6 Billion program level.

> The Operation and Maintenance, Navy (O&M,N) appropriation finances the day-to-day costs of operating naval forces, including fuel, supplies, and maintenance of ships, Navy and Marine Corps aircraft, related weapon systems, and the support establishment ashore. The primary focus of the Department's FY 2013 budget is to continue to ensure the readiness of deployed forces.

Peacetime means fewer operations, which in turn means less maintenance.

This budget starts with the FY 2013 Base, and completely ignores the FY 2013 OCO funding. OCO spending is spending that shall not happen under my plan.

---

[60] http://www.finance.hq.navy.mil/fmb/13pres/books.htm
[61] http://www.finance.hq.navy.mil/fmb/13pres/MPN_Book.pdf
[62] http://www.finance.hq.navy.mil/fmb/13pres/OMMC_Book.pdf
[63] http://www.finance.hq.navy.mil/fmb/13pres/OMN_Vol1_book.pdf

Operating Forces

Air Operations

Mission and Other Flight Operations include all Navy and Marine Corps Tactical Air (TACAIR) and Anti-Submarine Warfare (ASW) forces, shore-based Fleet Air Support, and irregular warfare. Funding provides flying hours to maintain required levels of readiness enabling Navy and Marine Corps aviation forces to perform their primary missions as required in support of national objectives. In addition, the Flying Hour Support program provides funding for transportation and travel of equipment and squadron staff & personnel, aircrew training systems, commercial air services, and various information technology systems.

Eliminate all flying hours requirements and the Flying Hour Support program; people shouldn't have to fly solely for the purpose of having done so. Flying hours should be accomplished through regular training. Eliminate all warfare except when we are attacked, but not the preparation therefor.

DoD adopted "operations tempo" as a measure of the pace of an operation or operations in terms of equipment usage -- aircraft "flying hours," ship "steaming days" or "tank [driving] miles." In the military way, the term became jargon: optempo.

Optempo exists solely for the purpose of keeping people busy. Manpower wasted on busy work is manpower that's going to waste. Eliminating the Flying Hours system will save **$4.3 Billion**, more than twice the entire Navy training budget. The cost is $7,041 per flying hour.

Fleet Air Training

Fleet Air Training provides funding for two critical components of the Department of the Navy's Flying Hour Program, the Fleet Replacement Squadrons (FRS) and Chief of Naval Air Training (CNATRA). The FRS train replacement aircrews for each Navy and Marine Corps type/model/series in weapons tactics, weapons delivery qualifications, carrier landing qualifications, and provide fleet squadrons the ability to develop and maintain required air-to-air combat skills.

Obviously, pilots need to train in order to be effective. Reduce by standard 25%; save $472 Million.

Aviation Technical Data and Engineering Services

The Engineering Technical Services (ETS) program provides formal and on-the-job technical information, instruction and training to aviation maintenance personnel at the organizational and intermediate levels of maintenance for a network of 30 detachments dispersed worldwide. This training is performed by Navy Engineering Technical Service and Contractor Engineering Technical Service (NETS/CETS) personnel.

OJT, instruction, and training are critical aspects of a proper military. Keep as is ($44M).

Air Operations and Safety Support

Air Traffic Control (ATC)

Provides logistics, engineering, and maintenance support for identification and landing systems for facilities ashore and afloat.

Air Traffic has to be controlled near airports due to the tendency of airplanes to fly into each other. When you think about it, it's really not all that important on clear days with low air traffic. Reduce by standard 25% and save $11.4 Million.

Marine Air Traffic Control and Landing Systems (MATCALS)

Provides depot maintenance and engineering support for tactical shore-based landing aids and Marine Air Traffic Control systems. Systems include Airport Surveillance Radars, Precision Approach Radars, control and communications systems, air navigation aids, towers, and the ancillary equipment associated with the systems. MATCALS provides life-cycle support of electronic and other systems used by the Marine Air Traffic Control Detachments (MATCD) in support of Marine expeditionary forces.

Airports need radars and communications. However, with our new peacetime stance, they will go through less wear and tear, so we can save on maintenance. Reduce by standard 25% and save $3.3 Million.

Aircraft Launch and Recovery Equipment (ALRE)

Provides life-cycle management including launchers, recovery, visual landing aids, information systems, fleet technical support, and policy management.

Carriers need catapults; most of this is necessary and proper. We could probably do without some of the policies being managed. Reduce by standard 25% and save $4.5 Million.

Expeditionary Airfields (EAF)

Supports airfield matting refurbishment, in-service engineering, life-cycle management, logistical and technical efforts, and fleet direct and technical support for expeditionary airfields.

Airfields need to be maintained; but our reduced activity would require less thereof. For example, we really wouldn't need to move people and equipment around so much in peacetime. Reduce by standard 25% and save $2.5 Million.

Aviation Life Support Systems

> *Supports in-service basic design engineering and logistics management support for over 785 Aircrew Systems products for the total life cycle. Examples of Aircrew Systems products that are essential to aircrew safety and survival include clothing and equipment that Navy and Marine Corps aircrew and passengers need to function within all flight envelopes (helmets, oxygen masks, flight suits, gloves, in-flight personal communications), escape safely from disabled aircraft (ejection seats, parachutes,*

In peacetime, there would be less flying and thus less need to move people and equipment around. The existing suits and survival packs will do fine and would rarely need to be replaced. Reduce by standard 25% and save $1.4 Million.

Aviation Facilities and Landing Aids

> *Supports improvements in shore-based landing aids, installation of the Naval Air Systems Command (NAVAIR) provided equipment, development/revision of aviation facilities planning and design criteria, and NAVAIR facilities management functions.*

In peacetime, there would be less shore landing, less equipment to install, fewer and new facilities to build. Reduce by standard 25% and save $717K.

Aviation Mobile Facilities

> *Supports aviation mobile facility configurations for the Navy and Marine Corps.*

For the same reasons as other Air Operations programs, reduce by standard 25%; save $774 Million.

> *[AOSS] Also includes funding for pollution prevention, environmental protection, and other miscellaneous operations and services.*

Eliminate pollution prevention and environmental protection; save $1.1 Million.

Air Systems Support

> *Air Systems Support provides funding for engineering and logistics analysis necessary to sustain aircraft systems and equipment. This includes support to sustain aircraft platforms across Navy and Marine Corps Training and Test and Evaluation Commands.*

Obviously, aircraft systems and equipment need to be engineered; though this should be done by the aircraft systems and equipment manufacturers, and the Navy should just buy the resulting products and sometimes support contacts. Some support can be done within the Navy, when it's cheaper or more efficient to do so. Reduce by standard 25% and save $93 Million.

Aircraft Depot Maintenance

> The Aircraft Depot Maintenance program funds repairs, overhauls, and inspections within available capacity to ensure sufficient aircraft quantities are available for operational units. The readiness based model distributes funding to achieve the best readiness mix for airframe and engine maintenance based on the squadron inventory authorization necessary to execute assigned missions.

Depot is a regularly scheduled maintenance done periodically or upon the need for emergency repairs on aircraft. This is an important maintenance event which happens regardless of flying hours. Keep as is ($961 Million).

Aircraft Depot Operations Support

> Sustains and enhances fleet readiness by providing unscheduled services and expeditious solutions for the correction of unplanned maintenance problems incurred during fleet operations.

This is required by ADM; keep as is ($37.5 Million).

Aviation Logistics

> The Aviation Logistics program provides Navy and Marine Corps aviation programs a budget line item for Contractor Logistics Support (CLS) and Performance Based Logistics (PBL). CLS is the performance of maintenance and/or material management functions for a DoD system by a commercial activity. PBL is the purchase of support as an integrated, affordable, performance package designed to optimize system readiness and meet performance goals for a weapon system through long-term support arrangements with clear lines of authority and responsibility.

Peacetime means fewer operations, which means we don't need to move people and equipment around so much. Reduce by standard 25% and save $82 Million.

Mission and Other Ship Operations

> This sub-activity group provides resources for all aspects of ship operations required to continuously deploy combat ready warships and supporting forces in support of national objectives. Programs supported include operating tempo (OPTEMPO), fleet and unit training, operational support such as

command and control, pier side support and port services, organizational maintenance, and associated administrative & other support.

A warship works like a self-contained military base, but they won't be doing war anymore. War is expensive. Reduce by standard 25% and save $1.2 Billion.

Ship Operations

Ship Operational Support and Training

Ship Operational Support and Training provides for the detailed pre-planning, engineering, training and range operations necessary to ensure that all operating force ships and nuclear attack submarines and their crews are operating at high levels of readiness. Specific programs funded include submarine support, surface ship support, and Receipt, Segregation, Storage, and Issue (RSSI).

Ships need not operate at high levels of readiness during peacetime. Operating at high levels of readiness increases wear and tear. Reduce by standard 25% and save $192 Million.

Ship Maintenance

Financing within this program supports maintenance ranging from Overhauls (OH) to Restricted Technical Availabilities (RA/TA) performed at Naval Shipyards (public) or private shipyards. Ship overhauls restore the ship, including all operating systems that affect safety or combat capability, to established performance standards.

Peacetime means reduced operations; thus reduced maintenance needs. Reduce by standard 25%; save $1.3 Billion.

Ship Depot Operations Support

A variety of depot maintenance programs are funded within this sub-activity group. The planning and technical support function supports management for availabilities, life cycle maintenance, and class maintenance impacts due to alterations, repair material management, and special projects for ship logistics managers.

Peacetime means reduced operations; thus reduced maintenance needs. Reduce by standard 25%; save $329 Million.

Combat Operations / Support

Combat Communications

The Naval Network and Space Operations Command operates and maintains space systems including spacecraft and ground-based components to fulfill

Naval and national requirements. Also performs daily satellite health (Telemetry, Tracking, and Commanding (TT&C)) monitoring, long-term system performance analysis, and communications resource management.

Peacetime means fewer naval and national requirements and a reduced need for satellites. Reduce by standard 25% and save $155 Million.

Electronic Warfare

Funding provides for ship operations electronic warfare support including Quick Reaction Capability Support and various electronic warfare decoys and deception devices, and a wide spectrum of electronic warfare support including radar and anti-ship missile warning and defense systems maintenance and software support.

This all sounds fairly important if we're actually at war, but under my plan we are not. Reduce by standard 25% and save $23 Million.

Space Systems and Surveillance

This subactivity group includes funding for Naval Network and Space Operations Command (NNSOC); space systems management; tracking, telemetry and control; and undersea surveillance. The NNSOC supports naval space policy and strategy by providing direct support to fleet units world-wide through integrated control of naval space programs. The command coordinates Navy-wide operational space resources and personnel required to fulfill Fleet missions.

This all sounds fairly important if we're actually at war, but under my plan we are not. Reduce by standard 25% and save $44 Million.

Warfare Tactics

Funding in this subactivity group supports a variety of warfare tactics, development and execution efforts designed to improve and enhance naval warfighting capabilities. These efforts include: Enhanced Naval Warfare Gaming System (ENWGS); naval warfare management; warfare tactics development/documentation; exercise support and analysis; fleet training administration and range operations; Navy Air and Missile Defense Center of Excellence (NAMDC COE); Ballistic Missile Defense (BMD) training; and unified commands

A tactic is merely a strategy on a smaller scale, and requires no special funding in and of itself. It's not a product you buy, it's a thing you do. Our Navy has shown itself to be very capable of warfighting, except against Somali pirates. Reduce by standard 25% and save $110 Million.

Op Meteorology and Oceanography

> *Funding within this subactivity group supports the performance of Naval meteorological and oceanographic mission functions worldwide and provides a wide array of essential operational meteorological and oceanographic products and services to operating forces afloat and ashore. These services include collecting and processing environmental data using resources such as oceanographic ships, aircraft, and computing systems.*

This all sounds fairly important if we're actually at war, but under my plan we are not. Reduce by standard 25% and save $83 Million.

Combat Support Forces

> *Funding in Combat Support Forces sustains a vast array of programs that support and maintain combat ready forces necessary to respond to national objectives in Joint, Naval, and combined operations. Funding supports the operations of the Navy Expeditionary Combat Command (NECC), Amphibious Craft Units, Special Combat Support Forces, other Mission support programs, and Fleet management headquarters and staffs.*

This all sounds fairly important if we're actually at war, but under my plan we are not. Reduce by standard 25% and save $227 Million.

Equipment Maintenance

> *This funding provides maintenance and engineering technical support for Hull, Mechanical and Electrical (HM&E) equipment including marine gas turbines, command and control equipment, equipment calibration, ground support equipment, aerial targets and cameras and mine countermeasures equipment.*

Gotta maintain equipment, even if the planes aren't flying as much. Keep as is ($167M).

Depot Operations Support

> *This program provides depot operations support services for test and monitoring systems, and General Purpose Electronic Test Equipment (GPETE). Efforts include In-Service Engineering (ISE) to develop, review and verify changes, maintain equipment data, plan equipment modifications, manage equipment and ship system configuration changes, develop and review technical manuals, and distribute and verify computer programs.*

Gotta maintain that technical data. Keep as is ($4M).

Combatant Commander Core Operations

> *Funding in this sub-activity group supports operation and administration of the Combatant Commanders Core Operations headquarters staff, including civilian personnel, travel, supplies, and training.*

By reducing the number of bases and overall scope of the military, we reduce the need for what is clearly overhead. Reduce by standard 25% and save $24 Million.

Combatant Commander Direct Missions Support

Funding in this sub-activity group supports the Combatant Commanders Direct Mission Funding. Beginning in FY 2012, USJFCOM was disestablished and retained only those critical functions necessary to maintain essential joint capability. These functions were transferred to the Chairman of the Joint Chiefs of Staff.

By reducing the scope of the military's jurisdiction and operations, we reduce the need for what is clearly overhead. Remove war-related appropriations component ($14 Million), and reduce the remainder by standard 25%; save $62 Million.

Weapons Support

Cruise Missile

Funding provides for overall operations and maintenance support of the Tomahawk Weapons System including All-Up-Round (AUR) missile, Weapons Control System on ships and submarines, and Mission Planning Systems ashore and afloat.

In peacetime, there is no need for cruise missile operations, other than occasional test firing to make sure they still work. Eliminate and save $112 Million.

Fleet Ballistic Missile

Funding for this program provides for the operational readiness and reliability of the Navy's Strategic Weapons Systems aboard fleet ballistic missile submarines (SSBNs). SSBN forces currently supported are the TRIDENT I (C-4) (system retirement and disposal) and TRIDENT II (D-5) SSBNs deployed in the Pacific and Atlantic.

In peacetime, the need for this will be significantly reduced. Reduce by half and save $591 Million.

In-Service Weapons Systems Support

Funding for this program provides maintenance engineering support services for aviation, undersea and surface weapons systems. Weapons systems supported include: Major gun weapons and gun fire control systems, surface/undersea/aviation anti-submarine warfare (ASW) systems, mine warfare systems and data processors.

In peacetime, guns and other weapons will fire less often and thus require less maintenance. Reduce by standard 25% and save $21 Million.

Weapon Maintenance

Funding for this program provides depot level maintenance and overhaul for missile systems, rockets, gun systems and surface/undersea/aviation and anti-submarine warfare (ASW) systems. Ammunition and ordnance rework and certification are also performed in this program. Funding is also provided for maintenance of electronic components, data processors and guidance systems that are integral with weapons systems operations.

In peacetime, weapons will fire less often and thus require less maintenance. Reduce by standard 25% and save $130 Million.

Other Weapon Systems Support

Funding is required for operational planning support to integrate products and responses into Combatant Commanders (COCOM) operational planning; support to peacetime exercises; and COCOM support teams to forward deploy to a COCOM/Joint Force Commander's headquarters in support of contingency planning with associated deployable gear. In FY 2013, Joint Warfare Activity Center (JWAC) is transferred to the Department of Air Force. Funding is also included in this Sub-Activity Group in support of Navy Systems Management Activity (NSMA) Classified Programs. Accordingly, the details specific to these programs are held at a higher classification.

Most of this sounds fairly important. Reduce by standard 25% and save $75 Million.

Base Support

Enterprise Information Technology

Enterprise Information Technology includes Information Technology resources for various Department-wide initiatives, including Navy Marine Corps Intranet (NMCI). NMCI was the Navy's information technology (IT) initiative and procurement strategy that provided secure, seamless, global end-to-end connectivity for Naval war fighting and business functions. NMCI contract and funding ended on 30 Sep 10 and was replaced with the Continuity of Services Contract (CoSC), which will act as a transition to the follow on Next Generation Enterprise Network (NGEN).

Most of this sounds fairly important. Reduce by standard 25% and save $269 Million.

Group Sustainment, Restoration, and Modernization

Facility Sustainment, Restoration and Modernization (FSRM), and Demolition includes funding for shore activities that support ship, aviation, combat operations and weapons support operating forces. FSRM funding provides maintenance and repair for all building, structures, ground and utility systems to permit assigned forces and tenants to perform their mission.

Military branches procure their needed funds in their Procurements budgets and don't need a duplicate effort here. There is no need to demolish anything; if you're done with the land, sell it as is. If not, get it out of the construction budget. Repair is also requisitioned in the Procurement budgets. Reduce by half and save $1 Billion.

Base Operating Support

Base Operating Support includes funding for shore activities that enable sea, air, and land operations by the Navy's fleet forces. Base Support includes port and airfield operations, operation of utility systems, public works services, base administration, supply operations, and base services such as transportation, environmental and hazardous waste management, security, personnel support functions, bachelor quarters operations, morale, welfare and recreation operations, and disability compensation.

Most of this sounds fairly important. Eliminate war-related appropriations ($395 Million), payments to GSA ($32 Million), and Child and Youth Development Programs ($202 Million). Reduce the remainder by standard 25% and save $1.7 Billion.

Mobilization

Ship Prepositioning and Surge

The Navy's Sealift Program provides the worldwide capability to deploy combat forces and/or supporting material that may be required to meet national contingency objectives. The program is divided into two functional areas: (1) Prepositioned assets and (2) Surge assets.

In peacetime, we have no such need. Our assets will be prepositioned along our borders and ports, and there will be no surges. Eliminate and save $335 Million.

Aircraft activations/inactivations

The aircraft activations/inactivations program removes aircraft from active service, and then prepares and maintains these aircraft for either later potential mobilization or disposal through scrapping and sales. This program also funds special tooling storage and demilitarization of aircraft.

This all sounds fairly important if we're actually at war, but under my plan we are not. Reduce by standard 25% and save $1.6 Million.

Ship Activations/Inactivations

> *Inactivation of surface ships includes depot level and hull maintenance to ensure that retention assets are maintained in the highest practical state of material readiness, and that stricken ships are maintained in a safe stow condition that ensures security of the ship and protection of the environment. The program also includes environmental abatement of hazardous materials onboard stricken inactive ships, and ship dismantling and recycling.*

If we can trust civilians to recycle our ships, then we can just sell them off. Eliminate and save $1 Billion.

Expeditionary Health Service Systems

> *Expeditionary Health Services Systems (EHSS) provides comprehensive medical support to U.S. and allied forces in the event of combat or contingency operations. Traditional fleet hospitals have and continue to be transformed into Expeditionary Medical Facilities (EMFs). EMFs are easily adaptable, capabilities-based modules/packages that can be tailored to meet a myriad of mission requirements.*

In peacetime, there are no combat or contingency operations. Eliminate and save $84 Million.

Industrial Readiness

> *The Industrial Readiness program is managed in two functional areas. Industrial Readiness program provides technical and administrative support for the lease administration and inspection of Government/Contractor Owned, Contractor Operated (GO/CO) facilities, including inventory control, plant cost appraisal, storage, preservation and shipment of Special Tooling and Special Test Equipment.*

This all sounds like pure overhead. Eliminate and save $3 Million.

Coast Guard Support

> *The Coast Guard Support program funds the maintenance, overhaul, and calibration of Navy-Type Navy-Owned (NTNO) equipment installed on Coast Guard ships and aircraft. This process complies with an agreement between the Department of Homeland Security and the Department of the Navy, which ensures necessary interoperability between Coast Guard and Navy forces both in peacetime and in the event of Coast Guard wartime service.*

My plan will merge the Coast Guard into the Navy and eliminate DHS, thus obsoleting this program. Eliminate and save $24 Million.

Training and Recruiting

Officer Acquisition

Officer Acquisition programs provide orientation and indoctrination for officer candidates, preparatory training for selection for an officer accession program, and academic study at higher education institutions for baccalaureate degrees

Officers should be selected out of the pool of applicants and of qualified enlisted members. Orientation is unnecessary; just give them a few classes on leadership, management, military tradition, and the like. Indoctrination is reprehensible, as it brainwashes people; and unnecessary, as the bad apples shall be weeded out during training. Cut by half and save $74 Million.

Recruit Training

Recruit Training indoctrinates every new enlisted accession (recruit) by providing basic military principles, basic naval skills, and practical experience of fleet environment and shipboard life. Operations are conducted at the Navy Recruit Training Command (RTC) located at Naval Training Center, Great Lakes, IL. .

Obviously, recruits need to be trained. However, peacetime will reduce turnover attributable to suicide and combat. Further, a 25% reduction in manpower and elimination of military growth reduces the need to train new recruits. Reduce by standard 25% and save $3 Million.

Reserve Officer Training Corps

The Naval Reserve Officer Training Corps (NROTC) program produces unrestricted line Navy and Marine Corps officers. Training is conducted at civilian colleges and universities providing instruction to highly qualified baccalaureate degree students who, upon graduation, receive a commission in the Navy or Marine Corps.

ROTC sends your tax money to private universities and colleges, while funding scholarships and indoctrinating people who aren't even military yet. Eliminate and save $139 Million.

Specialized Skill Training

Specialized Skill Training resources are used to maintain a trained force of personnel able to man and support surface, sub-surface, and aviation operating forces and their installed complex weapons systems. Enlisted personnel receive broad career-field and Naval Enlisted Classification (NEC) ratings upon completion of initial and advanced training programs in areas such as general skill, intelligence, cryptologic/signals and nuclear power operation.

Tech school is an important part of training military people for their job. Reduce by standard 25% and save $146 Million.

Flight Training

> *Flight Training provides for the operation of the Naval Aviation Schools Command (NASC) whose mission is to provide an educational foundation in technical and leadership professionalism to support pipeline training and fleet requirements. NASC vision projects global preeminence in military indoctrination, leadership and our focus is the development and conduct of safe, quality aviation training. Curriculum of academics and physical training produces the highest quality of officers and enlisted of the United States Uniformed Services and selected International Military students.*

Pilot training is an important part of having pilots. Eliminate all international programs and reduce the remainder by standard 25%, saving $2 Million.

Professional Development Education

> *Professional Development Education prepares career officers for more demanding assignments, particularly command and staff positions. It is concerned with broad professional goals in subjects such as military science, engineering and management. Students attend either a Service school or a civilian institution.*

Training military for higher ranks and responsibility is a critical part of having a rank structure in the first place. Reduce by standard 25% and save $43 Million.

Training Support

> *Training Support encompasses various programs which provide Navy-wide support to training headquarters, activities and equipment. Headquarters support includes personnel and associated costs for the Naval Education and Training Command (NETC). Contractors and in-house personnel maintain simulators and other training equipment. This includes depot, intermediate and organizational maintenance, maintainability, reliability and safety modifications, technical publication updates, logistical support, modification kits, and software support.*

This overhead is, unfortunately, necessary to do the job. Reduce by standard 25% and save $38 million.

Recruiting and Advertising

> *Recruiting and Advertising activities provide for the operation and maintenance costs necessary to recruit men and women for enlisted, officer candidate, and officer status in the Active and Reserve components of the Navy. The Navy's advertising for recruiting is built around a national advertising plan which is complemented by local advertising and an active*

public service campaign. Included in the overall Advertising Program is a media campaign targeted at diversity segments with the objective of increasing the number of quality diversity accessions.

A recruiting process of some kind is essential to obtaining new recruits. Eliminate the advertising component ($194 Million), reduce the remainder by the standard 25%, and save $206 Million.

Off-Duty and Voluntary Education

Off-Duty and Voluntary Education programs include Tuition Assistance (TA), Navy College Offices (NCO), Navy College Program for Afloat College Education (NCPACE), Navy College Center (NCC) and Defense Activity for Non-Traditional Education Support (DANTES).

Unfortunately, some college education is necessary to do some military tasks. However, my plan would greatly reduce the cost of education, and we wouldn't have as many people getting this free ride. Reduce by half and save $54 Million.

Civilian Education and Training

The Civilian Education programs are designed to develop and upgrade the professional knowledge and skills of Department of the Navy (DON) civilian employees through training, education and career management at various points in the employees' careers. The Naval Acquisition Intern Program (NAIP) consists of the Acquisition Intern Program (AIP), the Acquisition Workforce Tuition Assistance Program (AWTAP) and the Continuous Learning Program.

Hire only already-qualified civilians, giving strong preference to Navy veterans. For jobs where there are no qualified civilians, use military. Eliminate and save $106 Million.

Junior ROTC

The Naval Junior Reserve Officers Training Corps (NJROTC) Program is a congressionally sponsored youth citizenship program mandated by Public Law 88-647. NJROTC is a highly visible program in the local community receiving high level political interest. The program enhances the image of the military in the eyes of the community by providing a chance for success to the nation's youth. NJROTC is intended to instill in students in American High Schools the value of citizenship, service to the United States, personal responsibility and a sense of accomplishment.

If you want to enhance the image of the military, just point out that we haven't been attacked since 1941. The government is not responsible for its own image; only for obeying the Constitution. Eliminate all youth programs; the government is neither a babysitter nor an educator. Save $52 Million.

Administration and Service-Wide Activities

Administration

> *The Secretary of the Navy staff serves as the principal policy advisors and assistants in the administration of the affairs of the Department of the Navy. The Chief of Naval Operations (OPNAV) staff advises and assists the Chief of Naval Operations in the discharge of his responsibilities as the principal naval advisor and naval executive to the Secretary of the Navy on the conduct of the activities of the Department of the Navy, and as the Navy member of the Joint Chiefs of Staff. The OPNAV Support Activity performs functions of an operational nature that support the Chief of Naval Operations Staff Offices.*

This has overhead written all over it. Reduce by standard 25% and save $199 Million.

External Relations and Public Affairs

> *External Relations and Public Affairs is a function that covers all responsibility for contacts with the public and the effect of these contacts on the Navy, evaluation and consideration of public opinion and its role in formulating and administering public policy, and dissemination of information about the Navy in the United States and overseas. External Relations programs provide for communications, contracts, printing, and supplies. Public Affairs staffs are responsible for enhancing the awareness and support for the mission and operations of the Department of the Navy among the general public, the media and members of Congress and other personnel support programs.*

This is a duplication of effort of the DCMA and somewhat of the GAO. Units should publish their nonclassified activities on a website, available for free; possibly on a Facebook page as many do now. Administration, DoD, and GAO should cover the dissemination of budgets, procurements, etc. No further information dissemination is required; and none whatsoever is required overseas. Eliminate all public relations programs. Eliminate and save $13 Million.

Civilian Manpower and Personnel Management

> *This activity group supports Department of the Navy (DON) civilian personnel and equal employment opportunity (EEO) policy and programs, regionalized operational human resources servicing for DON civilians, and DON Human Resources (HR) Information Technology (IT) systems. Funds provided are for the Office of Civilian Human Resources (OCHR), Defense Civilian Personnel Data System-Navy (DCPDS-Navy), and Human Resources Service Center (HRSCs). The OCHR strategic goal is to integrate and strengthen civilian HR policy development, program management, and operations across the entire DON HR community.*

Reduce this overhead by standard 25% and save $30 Million.

Other Personnel Support

> *The Legal Services Support Group provides the Navy's senior-level officials with advice and counsel on issues such as environmental law, real estate, base closure, and handles all suspension and debarment actions against government contractors for the General Counsel. The Navy Litigation Office supports the joint Justice Department/Navy Department contract analysis and review effort concerning the pending A-12 contract termination case.*

A significant reduction in the regulations and laws in this country will reduce everyone's need for legal representation. Eliminate all federal-level environmental laws. Base closures should consist of removing all personnel, media, and equipment, and giving or selling the facility and land back to the state or other government to which the land belongs. Debarment can be dealt with by simply eliminating bar requirements in the first place. Reduce by half and save $132 Million.

Servicewide Communications

> *The Servicewide Communications program provides funding for communication systems, which support both fleet and shore establishments of the Navy. These systems include Electronic Command and Control systems, which provide command, control, readiness and intelligence information. Funding also provides for information security, which is required to prevent access to classified material, the engineering and logistics support required to maintain these systems, and Fleet Ballistic Missile (FBM) Strategic Communications High/Very Low/Low Frequency broadcast subsystems.*

Eliminate the DoD DSN system. Use encrypted radios or DoD systems for classified communications and regular phone systems for all other communications. The remainder of this is a duplication of DoD-level programs. Eliminate and save $363 Million.

Medical Activities

> *The Navy supports a comprehensive drug demand reduction program to eliminate/reduce illegal drug use in the Department of the Navy through testing, prevention, education, and outreach programs. The Navy's Demand Reduction Program supports the National Drug Control Strategy. The Drug Reduction Program funds are realigned from the Central Transfer Account during the year of execution.*

Legalize drugs and eliminate all drug programs and drug strategies; just court martial anyone whose drug use interferes with their jobs. Eliminate this program, which requests no funding.

Servicewide Transportation

> The Servicewide Transportation (SWT) program provides funding for the majority of the Navy's worldwide cargo shipments. This includes First Destination Transportation (FDT), Second Destination Transportation (SDT), and continental United States terminal services in conjunction with cargo movements. FDT costs are associated with the movement of material, after purchase, on a Free-On Board basis, from the contractor's facilities to the first point of use or storage. The SWT program also provides financing for worldwide Second Destination shipment of regular and emergency readiness material including ammunition, chemicals, medicine, subsistence, mail repair parts, and high value repairable items.

By eliminating our worldwide posture, we can significantly reduce the logistics overhead associated therewith. Just put the stuff and the people on a truck, a plane, or *gasp* a ship! Reduce the frequency with which people and equipment are shifted around, which seems to have no particular purpose other than to keep them rotated. Eliminate and save $182 Million.

Environmental Programs

> The Department of the Navy's Environmental Restoration requirements are budgeted in the ER,N appropriation. The Environmental Restoration Account (ER,N) is a centrally managed transfer account that funds analysis and cleanup of past contamination from toxic and hazardous substances, low-level radioactive materials and petroleum, oil and lubricants at DOD installations.

Eliminate this and all other environmental programs. No funding is requested.

Planning, Engineering, and Design

> This sub-activity group provides funding for the acquisition, planning, engineering, and design of engineering programs. This includes the sustainment and development of physical security equipment and mishap prevention and hazard abatement programs.

This is pure overhead designed to make the Navy bigger and fund research that should be done by the vendors from which the products are purchased in the first place. The DoD and Army already fund CBRNE research and can simply share that with everyone else. Eliminate and save $282 Million.

Acquisition and Program Management

> This sub-activity group provides funding for salaries and administrative expenses for personnel involved in program management and logistics support for both air and ship systems. Funding also provides non-salary program management for several other Department of Navy programs.

This is a duplication of effort by DMCA. Eliminate and save $1 Billion.

Hull, Mechanical, and Electrical Support

This program provides funding for total ship engineering, logistics, and technical support of shipboard environmental protection that is structured to both protect the environment and comply with existing legislation. Funding also supports ship design methodology, studies to reduce ship maintenance, energy conservation, and marine gas turbine engine programs.

This is critical to the sustainability of our warships. Eliminate ship design programs and let the ship manufacturers do that. Eliminate studies and let the ship captains do that. Eliminate all environment programs. Reduce the remainder by standard 25% and save $13 Million.

Combat/Weapon Systems

This program provides funding to manage and administer tests in compliance with Radiation, Detection, Indication, and Computation (RADIAC) regulations. Additionally, funding is used to manage nuclear material permits, prepares for responses to nuclear accidents, and provides for low level radioactive waste disposal in the Radiation Control and Health program.

Put up radiation sensors near the nukes and test fire the conventional weapons from time to time. Eliminate all permit requirements. Reduce by half and save $13 Million.

Space and Electronics Warfare Systems

The Space and Electronic Warfare Systems sub-activity group provides technical and life-cycle support for ocean surveillance and several other electronic programs. Engineering and technical support is provided for electronic test and repair, maintenance engineering, technical publications, cover and deception, electronic warfare, naval information programs, portable electronic support measures, tactical electromagnetic programs, electromagnetic compatibility programs, and other engineering services.

None of this seems particularly important in peacetime. Eliminate and save $64 Million.

Naval Investigative Service

The Naval Criminal Investigative Service (NCIS) has reorganized to make force protection it highest priority. The NCIS force protection mission is designed to identify, mitigate, and neutralize threats from criminal, terrorists, and spies, which would prevent naval forces from meeting their operational commitments. In its traditional role, the Naval Criminal Investigative Service

(NCIS) conducts investigation of felony violations of the U.S. Code of Military Justice (UCMJ) as they occur throughout the Navy and Marine Corps.

We can reduce the need for NIS by reducing the number of laws, by reducing terrorism through a hands-off approach, and by having less to spy on in the first place. Reduce by half and save $290 Million.

Security Programs

Funding provides for classified programs in areas of signal intelligence, electronic warfare support measures, operation of special security communications, direction finding and exploitation of hostile command/control signals, detection/classification/tracking of platforms beyond radar range in support of weapons targeting and signal intelligence surveillance.

Eliminate most classified programs, and reduce the scope of most others. The special security people can use the same encrypted radios as all the other field people. Reduce by half and save $26 Million.

Funding provides for classified programs including statistics on foreign military forces, weapons, target and personnel; analysis of worldwide developments that affect U.S. security interests and personnel/equipment; assessments of military capabilities and actions and projections of developments in forces, weapons, plans, and intentions.

Eliminate most classified programs, and reduce the scope of most others. Reduce by half and save $169 Million. This is actually a different program from the one right above it; they both have the same name.

This classified program provides funding for protecting installations, material, operations information and personnel from espionage, sabotage, terrorism, and other clandestine intelligence activities.

Eliminate most classified programs, and reduce the scope of most others. Reduce by half and save $58 Million. This is actually a different program from the one right above it; they both have the same name.

This sub-activity group provides funding to support Security Programs.

This one doesn't say it's classified and doesn't provide what kind of security programs or what kind of support. Eliminate and save $8 Million.

International Headquarters and Agencies

This program provides support to other nations, including the Latin American Cooperation Program; emergency medical travel for Navy personnel and their families at Military Assistance Advisory Groups (MAAGS), Missions and Defense Attache Offices worldwide; International Cooperative Administrative Support Services (ICASS) Program; the Technology Transfer Program; and payment of the administrative fee waiver on Foreign Military Sales (FMS) Training Cases. Resources support review and evaluation of munition cases, strategic trade cases, technical exchange agreements, science and technology agreements, reciprocal Memoranda of Understanding, and other similar agreements.

By eliminating all overseas locations and agencies, we can eliminate this overhead. Save $5 Million.

Operation and Maintenance, Marine Corps[64]

This budget starts with the FY 2013 Base, and completely ignores the FY 2013 OCO funding. OCO spending is spending that shall not happen under my plan.

Operating Forces

Operational Forces

The Operating Forces are considered the core element of the Marine Corps. Operational Forces constitute the forward presence, crisis response and fighting power available to the Combatant Commanders. This sub-activity group provides for the operating forces that constitute the Marine Air-Ground Team and Marine Security Forces at naval installations and aboard Naval vessels. The funds finance training and routine operations; maintenance and repair of organic ground equipment; routine supplies, travel, per diem and emergency leave; information technology and internet support; and replenishment and replacement of both unit and individual equipment.

Under my plan, there is no forward presence. There are no crises to respond to, and no one to fight. There will be less turnover, so less need for training. Reduce by half and save $394 Million.

Field Logistics

The Field Logistics sub-activity group provides resources necessary for overall weapons system management and logistics support required to meet the operational needs of the Marine Corps.

Under my plan, there is a reduced tendency to move people and equipment around all the time. Reduce by half and save $381 Million.

---

[64] http://www.finance.hq.navy.mil/fmb/13pres/OMMC_Book.pdf

Depot Maintenance

> *This sub-activity group finances the depot maintenance (major repair/rebuild) of active Marine Corps ground equipment. Depot Maintenance programs fund the overhaul, repair, and maintenance of combat vehicles, automotive equipment, constructive equipment, electronics/communications systems, missiles, and ordnance/weapons/munitions performed at both public (DoD) and private (contractor) facilities.*

USMC equipment must be maintained, but will undergo less wear and tear in peacetime. Reduce by standard 25% and save $42 Million.

Maritime Prepositioning

> *The Marine Corps' Maritime Prepositioning Force (MPF) provides operational capabilities in support of our nation's interests throughout the world and across the globe. MPF provides essential elements needed to execute crisis response, global reach, and forward presence. Prepositioning key warfighting equipment and supplies, MPF has significantly reduced reliance on strategic lift while providing powerful and integrated warfighting capabilities to combatant commanders.*

Under my plan, there is a reduced tendency to move people and equipment around all the time. There are literally no activities "throughout the world and across the globe". There are no crises to respond to, we need not reach globally under most circumstances, and we will have zero forward presence. The warfighting equipment and supplies will be recalled to domestic bases and other stockpiles. Eliminate and save $100 Million.

Sustainment, Restoration, and Modernization

> *This sub-activity group funds all Marine Corps Facilities Sustainment, Restoration, and Modernization (FSRM). Sustainment provides resources for maintenance and repair activities necessary to keep an inventory of facilities in good working order. It includes regularly scheduled adjustments and inspections, preventive maintenance tasks, and emergency response and service calls for minor repairs. Sustainment also includes major repairs or replacement of facility components (usually accomplished by contract) that occur periodically throughout the life cycle of facilities. This work includes regular roof replacement, refinishing of wall surfaces, repairing and replacement of heating and cooling systems, replacement of tile and carpeting, and similar work.*

Military branches procure their needed funds in their Procurements budgets and don't need a duplicate effort here. There is no need to demolish anything; if you're done with the land, sell it as is. If not, get it out of the construction budget. Repair is also requisitioned in the Procurement budgets. Reduce by half and save $413 Million.

Base Operating Support

> Base Operating Support (BOS) enables activities associated with supporting Marine Corps' most valuable assets—the individual Marine and family members.

Most of this sounds fairly important. Reduce by standard 25% and save $547 Million.

Training and Recruiting

Recruit Training

> The Recruit Training Program finances 89 basic skill training days to prepare new enlistees for assignment into the Active and Reserve Marine Forces. This training is designed to produce Marines who can assimilate well into units. During recruit training, Drill Instructors train new recruits in basic military skills, help recruits build confidence within themselves and their units. Marines graduating from recruit training are assigned to formal schools for specialized training in a military occupational specialty (MOS).

Obviously, recruits need to be trained. However, peacetime will reduce turnover attributable to suicide and combat. Further, a 25% reduction in manpower and elimination of military growth reduces the need to train new recruits. Reduce by standard 25% and save $5 Million.

Officer Acquisition

> The Officer Acquisition Program finances Officer Candidate School (OCS) and Naval Reserve Officers' Training Course (NROTC) training requirements. Before appointment into the Marine Corps Active and Reserve Forces as commissioned officers, candidates must undergo and complete a complex screening process concentrated in leadership, basic military subjects, Marine Corps history and tradition, and physical conditioning.

Officers should be selected out of the pool of applicants and of qualified enlisted members. Orientation is unnecessary; just give them a few classes on leadership, management, military tradition, and the like. Indoctrination is reprehensible, as it brainwashes people; and unnecessary, as the bad apples shall be weeded out during training. Cut by half and save $435K.

Specialized Skills Training

> Upon completion of Officer Acquisition Training or Recruit Training, Marines are assigned to courses of instruction to acquire the requisite skills to meet the

minimum requirements of a Military Occupational Specialty (MOS). Officer Training involves completion of The Basic School at Marine Corps Combat Development Command (MCCDC), Quantico, Virginia, and follow-on MOS qualifying courses such as the Infantry Officer's Course or Command and Control Systems School.

Recruits have to be trained. Reduce by standard 25% and save $20 Million.

Professional Development Education

This sub-activity group allows career Marines to enhance their overall professional development and to qualify them for increased command and staff responsibilities. Funded in this sub-activity group are programs for officers and Staff Non-Commissioned Officers (SNCOs) within the Marine Corps, at other Services schools, and at civilian institutions. Training and Education Command, Marine Corps University (MCU) as the subordinate command, has the primary responsibility of professional development education[.]

Training military for higher ranks and responsibility is a critical part of having a rank structure in the first place. Reduce by standard 25% and save $11 Million.

Training Support

The Training Support Program finances training ranges, training support equipment, computer-assisted training programs, formal school training, training battalions, warfare training groups, cultural language training, security cooperation and education training, the Marine Air Ground Task Force Training Staff Training Support Program (MSTP) and other core training functions.

This overhead is, unfortunately, necessary to do the job. Reduce by standard 25% and save $73 million.

Recruiting and Advertising

Recruiting: Operations financed in this sub-activity include expenses incurred in developing a proficient military recruiting force, civilian labor associated with recruiting, administrative supplies, communications, travel, per diem, leasing of recruiting vehicles, recruiter out-of-pocket expenses (ROPE), applicant processing costs, and equipment.

Advertising: Marine Corps advertising supports all recruiting missions, including enlisted and officer, active duty and reserve. Advertising programs and strategies are grouped into three primary and complementary categories: Awareness (broadcast TV, PSA, online, print, outdoor, etc.); Lead Generation (direct mail, database, call centers, prospect websites, etc.); and Recruiter Support (collateral materials, incentive items, online applications, etc).

A recruiting process of some kind is essential to obtaining new recruits. Eliminate the advertising component ($194 Million), reduce the remainder by the standard 25%, and save $100 Million.

Off-Duty and Voluntary Education

> This sub-activity finances off duty and voluntary education for Marines. The Marine Corps Off-Duty Education program provides Marines an opportunity to enhance their career through education programs. This program includes the Military Academic Skills Program (MASP), formerly the Basic Skills Education Program (BSEP), and an on-duty program which is designed to remedy deficiencies in reading, mathematics, and communications skills.

Unfortunately, some college education is necessary to do some military tasks. However, my plan would greatly reduce the cost of education, and we wouldn't have as many people getting this free ride. Reduce by half and save $28 Million.

Junior ROTC

> Marine Junior Reserve Officers Training Corps (MJROTC) Program is a congressionally sponsored youth citizenship program mandated by Public Law 88-647. MJROTC is intended to instill the value of citizenship, service to the United States, personal responsibility, and a sense of accomplishment in high school students.

Instilling a basic sense of human decency, integrity, and responsibility is the job of the parents. Eliminate all youth programs; the government is neither a babysitter nor an educator. Save $20 Million.

Administration and Service-Wide Activities

Servicewide Transportation

> This sub-activity group funds transportation of Marine Corps owned equipment, material and supplies by the most economical mode that will meet Department of Defense Uniform Material Movement and Issue Priority System in-transit time standards.

Given the elimination of our worldwide posture, there is no worldwide movement to execute. Having said that, stuff still needs to move around within the U.S. and we'll need to move a lot of weapons and equipment out of our overseas bases. Eliminate and save $40 Million.

Administration

> Headquarters, U.S. Marine Corps (HQMC) consists of the Commandant of the Marine Corps and those staff agencies that assist and support him in the discharge of his lawfully prescribed Title X responsibilities. The Commandant is

the principal Marine Corps advisor to the Secretary of the Navy on the total performance of Marine Corps; including administration, discipline, internal organization, training, resource requirements, efficiency, operations, and the overall readiness of the force. Since the Commandant is a member of the Joint Chiefs of Staff, HQMC also aids and supports him in his interaction with the Joint Staff.

This has overhead written all over it. Reduce by standard 25% and save $87 Million.

Acquisition and Program Management

Acquisition and Program Management provides leadership, management policies and resources necessary to operate Marine Corps Systems Command. This sub-activity group provides funding for salaries and administrative expenses for personnel involved in acquisition, program management, and logistics support associated with Marine Corps weapons, supply, and Information Technology systems. Over 60 percent of budgeted resource pay salaries and benefits for personnel who oversee and manage our acquisition programs.

This sounds like overhead necessary to run the USMC, but also somewhat duplicates DCMA and other DoD and Navy programs. Reduce by standard 25% and save $21 Million.

Operation and Maintenance, Navy Reserve[65]

Given my proposed changes in foreign policy, we can eliminate all regular costs of doing business overseas. The operations and maintenance of the Navy is critical to the navy itself, and is thus necessary and proper. This is a $1.3 Billion program level.

The Operation and Maintenance, Navy Reserve (O&M,NR) appropriation provides for the cost of operating Navy Reserve forces and maintaining their assigned equipment at a state of readiness that will permit rapid employment in the event of full or partial mobilization and meet fleet operational support requirements. The Navy Reserve's mission is to provide strategic depth and deliver operational capabilities to our Navy and Marine Corps team and Joint forces from peace to war. In FY 2013, the Navy Reserve will continue to contribute significantly to the effectiveness of the Navy's Total Force.

Peacetime means fewer operations, which in turn means less maintenance.

---

[65] http://www.finance.hq.navy.mil/fmb/13pres/OMNR_Book.pdf

This budget starts with the FY 2013 Base, and completely ignores the FY 2013 OCO funding. OCO spending is spending that shall not happen under my plan.

Mission and Other Flight Operations

The Commander, Naval Air Force Reserve Flying Hour Program funds Navy Reserve and Marine Corps Reserve air operations including flying hours, specialized training, maintenance, and [...] associated support programs[.]

Eliminate war-related and disaster supplemental appropriations ($38M) and reduce the remainder by 25%; save $183 Million.

Intermediate Maintenance

This sub-activity group provides funding for all aspects of Navy Reserve Fleet Readiness Centers (FRC) and Marine Corps Reserve Mobile Maintenance Facilities (MMFs). These activities perform intermediate level maintenance that enhances and sustains the combat readiness and mission capability of supported activities by providing quality and timely material support at the nearest location with the lowest practical resource expenditure.

Aircraft and equipment need to be maintained, of course. However, our reduced Optempo and new peacetime stance will reduce the wear and tear; thus the need for maintenance. Reduce by standard 25% and save $4 Million.

Aircraft Depot Maintenance

The Aircraft Depot Maintenance program funds repairs, overhauls and inspections within available capacity to ensure sufficient aircraft quantities are available for operational units. The readiness-based model determines airframe and engine maintenance requirements based on the squadron inventory authorization necessary to execute assigned missions.

Aircraft and equipment need to be maintained, of course. However, our reduced Optempo and new peacetime stance will reduce the wear and tear; thus the need for maintenance. Reduce by standard 25% and save $27 Million.

Aircraft Depot Operations Support

Aircraft and equipment need to be maintained, of course. However, our reduced Optempo and new peacetime stance will reduce the wear and tear; thus the need for maintenance. Reduce by standard 25% and save $89 Million.

Mission and Other Ship Operations

This subactivity group provides resources for all aspects of ship operations required to continuously deploy combat ready warships and supporting forces in support of national objectives. Programs supported include operating tempo (OPTEMPO), fleet and unit training, operational support such as

command and control, pier side support and port services, organizational
maintenance, and associated administrative & other support.

A warship works like a self-contained military base, but they won't be doing war anymore. War is expensive. Reduce by standard 25% and save $21 Million.

Ship Operational Support and Training

This subactivity group provides funding for the Naval Tactical Command Support System (NTCSS) which incorporates the functionality of the Maintenance Resource Management System (MRMS) for ship intermediate maintenance management to Navy Reserve Force (NRF) ships.

Ships need not operate at high levels of readiness during peacetime. Operating at high levels of readiness increases wear and tear. Reduce by standard 25% and save $148K.

Ship Maintenance

This subactivity group provides funding for Depot and Intermediate repairs for both scheduled and emergent availability of Navy Reserve Force (NRF) ships. This program is designed to ensure the safe and reliable operation of Reserve ships in fulfilling their assigned combat and combat-support related missions. Depot repairs include Selected Restricted Availabilities (SRAs), Emergent Repairs (EM), Continuous Maintenance (CM), and miscellaneous Restricted Availability/Technical Availability (RA/TA) programs.

Peacetime means reduced operations; thus reduced maintenance needs. Reduce by standard 25%; save $12 Million.

Combat Communications

This subactivity group provides communications support for the Navy Reserve Intelligence Program. Resources for this program fund supplies, travel, and civilian personnel associated with operations of the national headquarters in Fort Worth, Texas and regional offices nationwide.

Peacetime means a reduced need for supplies, travel, and personnel. Reduce by standard 25% and save $4 Million.

Combat Support Forces

Funding is provided for the readiness and peacetime support of combat support forces of Navy Expeditionary Combat Command (NECC) as well as the operations of the Navy Reserve Force Headquarters and its subordinate commands.

This all sounds fairly important if we're actually at war, but under my plan we are not. Reduce by standard 25% and save $31 Million.

Weapons Maintenance

FFG 7 TECHNICAL SUPPORT: The Navy Tactical Data System (NTDS) provides Reserve Component FFG 7 class ships with the core combat direction system element required to implement self-defense to detect, control and engage tracks of interest, and to maintain multi-unit Interoperability with Model 4 Link 11 capability.

Peacetime means less weapons firing and therefore less maintenance. Reduce by standard 25% and save $495K.

Enterprise Information Technology

Enterprise Information Technology (IT) includes resources for IT requirements and the replacement of Navy Marine Corps Intranet (NMCI) with the Continuity of Services Contract (CoSC) which will act as a transition to the follow on Next Generation Enterprise Network (NGEN). Next Generation Enterprise Network (NGEN) is intended to integrate the existing Department of Navy (DON) networks into a seamless, reliable, interoperable, and highly secure net-centric enterprise network environment.

This is pretty important, but in peacetime and in eliminating all overseas locations, the need thereof is reduced. Reduce by standard 25% and save $11 Million.

Sustainment, Restoration, and Modernization

Facility Sustainment, Restoration and Modernization (FSRM) includes funding for shore activities that support ship, aviation, combat operations and weapons support of operating forces. FSRM funding provides maintenance, repair, and minor construction for all building, structures, ground and utility systems to permit assigned forces and tenants to perform their mission.

This is pretty important, but in peacetime and in eliminating all overseas locations, the need hereof is reduced. Reduce by standard 25% and save $15 Million.

Base Operating Support

Base Operating Support includes funding for shore activities that sustain sea, air, and land operations in support of Navy's fleet forces. Base Support includes port and airfield operations, operation of utility systems, public works services, base administration, supply operations, and base services such as transportation, environmental and hazardous waste management, security, personnel support functions, bachelor quarters operations, morale, welfare and recreation operations, and disability compensation.

This is pretty important, but in peacetime and in eliminating all overseas locations, the need hereof is reduced. Reduce by standard 25% and save $26 Million.

Administration

This subactivity Group provides resources for the operation of the Office of the Chief of Navy Reserve. The Chief of Navy Reserve provides policy, control, administration, and management direction, including the management of all resources (manpower, hardware, and facilities) assigned to facilitate an optimum training posture and mobilization readiness.

This clear overhead is, unfortunately, necessary for the Navy Reserve to function. Reduce by standard 25% and save $779K.

Military Manpower and Personnel Management

The Navy Reserve Order Writing System (NROWS) is the single, enterprise-wide application for putting a Reservist on Annual Training (AT), Active Duty (ADT) and Inactive Duty Training Travel (IDTT) orders. This system produces 150,000 sets of training orders annually, and is used by all Navy Reservists to support every major claimant.

It seems pretty obvious to me that this belongs under Administration. This clear overhead is, unfortunately, necessary for the Navy Reserve to function. Reduce by standard 25% and save $4 Million.

Servicewide Communications

Funding for this subactivity is for base communications service and support to Navy and non-Navy activities worldwide. Funding is used to operate, maintain, and manage the communications infrastructure supporting the transport of voice, video, and data including pier side connectivity.

Eliminate the DoD DSN system. Use encrypted radios or DoD systems for classified communications and regular phone systems for all other communications. The remainder of this is a duplication of DoD-level programs. Eliminate and save $2 Million.

Acquisition and Program Management

This subactivity group funds logistics operations and program management at Naval Supply Systems Command (NAVSUP) Reserve Component field activities and Headquarters in the areas of supply operations, contracting, resale, fuel, card management, security assistance, conventional ordnance, food service and other quality of life programs.

This is a duplication of effort by DMCA. Eliminate and save $3 Million.

Operation and Maintenance, Marine Corps Reserve[66]

Given my proposed changes in foreign policy, we can eliminate all regular costs of doing business overseas. The operations and maintenance of the Navy is critical to the navy itself, and is thus necessary and proper. This is a $41.6 Billion program level.

Peacetime means fewer operations, which in turn means less maintenance. This budget starts with the FY 2013 Base, and completely ignores the FY 2013 OCO funding. OCO spending is spending that shall not happen under my plan.

Operating Forces

This subactivity group provides funds for the day-to-day cost to train and support to the Marine Forces Reserve. This program includes funding for material readiness, purchase and replacement of expense type items authorized by unit training allowances, local repair of equipment, training centers, and mount out materials for training and preparation for mobilization.

Peacetime means a reduced need for forces to operate; they need only train and be prepared to be called up. There will be fewer repairs to perform, and less mobilization to actualize. Reduce by standard 25% and save $22 Million.

Depot Maintenance

Maintenance of major end items of equipment is accomplished on a scheduled basis by Marine Corps Logistics Command. Depot level repair and rebuild has proven to be an effective program whereby major end items of equipment can be sustained and operated for their maximum useful life. Funding ensures that major end items are available to meet unit training and mobilization requirements. Items programmed for repair have been screened to ensure that valid requirements exist and the repair and rebuild is the most effective and economical means of satisfying requirements.

Peacetime means there will be reduced operations, and thus less wear and tear on weapons and other equipment. Reduce by standard 25% and save $4 Million.

Sustainment, Restoration, and Modernization

This subactivity group funds Facilities Sustainment, Restoration, and Modernization (FSRM) for the Marine Forces Reserve (MARFORRES).

Peacetime and eliminating our overseas positions means there will be less to sustain, restore, and modernize. Reduce by standard 25% and save $9 Million.

---

[66] http://www.finance.hq.navy.mil/fmb/13pres/OMMCR_Book.pdf

Base Operating Support

> *Base Operations Support funding finances Marine Forces Reserve base support, administrative services, and civilian labor. Additionally, funding is provided for Reserve civilian personnel assigned to HQMC. Base support funding provides for utilities, janitorial services, public affairs, Morale, Welfare and Recreation (MWR) support, postage, base communications, and environmental compliance.*

Peacetime and eliminating our overseas locations means fewer bases to operate, fewer operations to support, an d less civilian labor. Eliminate all environmental compliance programs. Reduce by half and save $52 Million.

Servicewide Transportation

> *This subactivity group finances the transportation of Marine Corps Reserve owned material and supplies by the most economical mode that meets Department of Defense Uniform Material Movement and Issue Priority Systems in-transit time standard. All resources within this program finance commercial transportation carrier services.*

Peacetime and eliminating our overseas locations means a reduced need to move people and equipment around so much. Reduce by standard 25% and save $218K.

Administration

> *This subactivity group provides funding for Marine Forces Reserve Headquarters, New Orleans, LA, it accomplish the mission of providing administrative and logistical support for Reserve Component mobilization.*

Unfortunately, this overhead is necessary for the Marine Reserves to operate. Reduce by standard 25% and save $4 Million.

Recruiting and Advertising

> *Recruiting: Operations financed in this subactivity include expenses incurred in developing a proficient military recruiting force, civilian labor associated with recruiting, administrative supplies, communications, travel, per diem, leasing of recruiting vehicles, recruiter out-of-pocket expenses (ROPE), applicant processing costs, and equipment. Advertising: Marine Corps advertising supports all recruiting missions, including enlisted and officer, active duty and reserve.*

Eliminate the advertising component; reduce the remainder by standard 25% and save $5 Million.

Aircraft Procurement, Navy[67] [68] [69] [70]

Any procurement budget that is so large that it requires seven volumes to describe itself is clearly too large. I do not support the continued expansion of the military and the spiraling Military-Industrial Complex. We could easily reduce our military funding by half and still have more power and funding than every other developed nation on Earth, combined. I will therefore support only combat losses and upgrades that are absolutely necessary for the Navy to continue functioning. Let's dive in, shall we?

Combat Aircraft

EA-18G

> *The EA-18G is replacing the EA-6B aircraft. The EA-18G's electronic attack upgrades meet or exceed EA-6B (with ALQ-218, ALQ-99, USQ-113) Airborne Electronic Attack (AEA) capability to detect, identify, locate and suppress hostile emitters; provide enhanced connectivity to National, Theater and strike assets; and provide organic precision emitter targeting for employment of onboard suppression weapons(HARM) to fulfill operational requirements.*

The budget does not indicate that there is anything wrong with the existing EA-6B line, other than something newer is available. The quantity is justified by saying there is a minimum per year if produced at all. Eliminate and save **$1 Billion ($9 Billion** total).

FA-18E/F

> *The F/A-18E/F Naval Strike Fighter is a twin-engine, mid-wing, multi-mission tactical aircraft. F/A-18E/F can be missionized through selected use of external equipment to accomplish specific fighter or attack missions. This capability allows the Operational Commander more flexibility in employing his tactical aircraft in a dynamic scenario.*

The budget does not indicate any specific need for more F-18s, other than force projections for the year 2030. The quantity is justified by saying there is a minimum per year if produced at all. Eliminate and save **$2 Billion ($44 Billion** total).

FA-18E/F Advanced Procurement

If we eliminate the buy contract, we thereby eliminate the need to pre-fund FY2014's buys as well. Eliminate and save $30 Million.

---

[67] http://www.finance.hq.navy.mil/fmb/13pres/APN_BA1-4_BOOK.pdf
[68] http://www.finance.hq.navy.mil/fmb/13pres/APN_BA5_BOOK.pdf
[69] http://www.finance.hq.navy.mil/fmb/13pres/APN_BA6_BOOK.pdf
[70] http://www.finance.hq.navy.mil/fmb/13pres/APN_BA7_BOOK.pdf

Joint Strike Fighter CV

> *Joint Strike Fighter (JSF) program will develop and field a family of aircraft that meets needs of USN with Carrier Variant (CV), USAF with Conventional Take Off and Landing (CTOL) variant, and USMC with Short Take-Off and Vertical Landing (STOVL) variant, and allies, with optimum commonality among the three variants to minimize life cycle costs.*

I don't see why the Navy needs to buy both traditional carrier-bound fighters and non-carrier-bound fighters designed to replace them at the same time. This program procures 4 to 14 per year until 321 total aircraft are procured. The budget does not provide any real justification for this program; eliminate and save **$1.1 Billion ($55 Billion** total).

Joint Strike Fighter CV Advanced Procurement

If we eliminate the buy contract, we thereby eliminate the need to pre-fund FY2014's buys as well. Eliminate and save $65 Million (**$5 Billion** total).

JSF STOVL

> *Joint Strike Fighter (JSF) program will develop and field a family of aircraft that meets needs of USN with Carrier Variant (CV), USAF with Conventional Take Off and Landing (CTOL) variant, and USMCwith Short Take-Off and Vertical Landing (STOVL) variant, and allies, with optimum commonality among the three variants to minimize life cycle costs.*

More F-35s, the entire fleet of which has been grounded multiple times, this variant for the short takeoff variant, still with no real justification. Eliminate and save **$1.5 Billion ($50.1 Billion** total).

JSF STOVL Advanced Procurement

If we eliminate the buy contract, we thereby eliminate the need to pre-fund FY2014's buys as well. Eliminate and save $106 Million (**$5.6 Billion** total).

V-22 Medium Lift

> *The V-22 is a tilt-rotor vertical takeoff and landing aircraft currently being produced for joint service application. The program provides an aircraft to meet the amphibious/vertical assault needs of the Marine Corps, the strike rescue needs of the Navy, and supplements USSOCOM special mission aircraft.*

Once again, the justification provided is to procure 17 MV-22s and to save money with a longer term contract than a single year contract. The budget doesn't actually explain why we need them in the first place. If Special Forces requires 50 Ospreys, then we're probably doing way too many special operations. Eliminate and save **$1.5 Billion ($35.6 Billion** total).

V-22 Medium Lift Advanced Procurement

If we eliminate the buy contract, we thereby eliminate the need to pre-fund FY2014's buys as well. Eliminate and save $154 Million (**$1.9 Billion** total).

UH-1Y/AH-1Z

> *The mission of the AH-1Z attack helicopter is to provide rotary wing close air support, anti-armor, armed escort, armed/visual reconnaissance, anti-helicopter and point air defense and fire support coordination during day/night conditions.*

The Justification section in the budget for this procurement is literally blank. They provide absolutely no reason to buy these. Eliminate and save $820 Million (**$10.8 Billion** total).

UH-1Y/AH-1Z Advanced Procurement

If we eliminate the buy contract, we thereby eliminate the need to pre-fund FY2014's buys as well. Eliminate and save $70 Million ($623 Million total).

MH-60S (MYP)

> *The Helicopter Combat Support (HC) mission of the MH-60S is to maintain forward fleet supportability through rapid airborne delivery of materials and personnel and to support amphibious operations through search and rescue coverage.*

Again we see no real justification. Eliminate and save $454 Million (**$7 Billion** total).

MH-60S (MYP) Advanced Procurement

If we eliminate the buy contract, we thereby eliminate the need to pre-fund FY2014's buys as well. Eliminate and save $69 Million (**$1.2 Billion** total).

MH-60R

> *The MH-60R Multi-Mission helicopter provides battle group protection and adds significant capability in coastal littorals and regional conflicts. The MH-60R Multi-Mission Helicopter represents a significant avionics improvement to the H-60 series helicopters by enhancing primary mission areas of Undersea Warfare (USW) and Surface Warfare (SUW).*

Again we see no real justification. Eliminate and save $873 Million (**$12.3 Billion** total).

MH-60R Advanced Procurement

If we eliminate the buy contract, we thereby eliminate the need to pre-fund FY2014's buys as well. Eliminate and save $186 Million (**$1.8 Billion** total).

P-8A Poseidon

The P-8A Multi-mission Maritime Aircraft (MMA) system is a commercial derivative aircraft based on Boeing's 737-800 ERX. The P-8A is the replacement system for the P-3C. The P-8A will sustain and improve the armed maritime and littoral Intelligence, Surveillance, and Reconnaissance capabilities for U.S. Naval Forces in traditional, joint and combined roles to counter changing and emerging threats.

Again we see no real justification. Eliminate and save **$2.7 Billion ($25.2 Billion total).**

P-8A Poseidon Advanced Procurement

If we eliminate the buy contract, we thereby eliminate the need to pre-fund FY2014's buys as well. Eliminate and save $326 Million (**$2.3 Billion** total).

E-2D AHE

The E-2D Advanced Hawkeye (AHE) is an all-weather, twin engine, carrier-based, Airborne Command, Control and Surveillance aircraft designed to extend task force defense perimeters. The AHE mission is to provide advance warning of approaching enemy surface units and aircraft, to vector interceptors or strike aircraft to attack, and to provide area surveillance, intercept, search and rescue, communications relay, and strike/air traffic control.

Again we see no real justification. Eliminate and save $985 Million (**$19.7 Billion** total).

E-2D AHE Advanced Procurement

If we eliminate the buy contract, we thereby eliminate the need to pre-fund FY2014's buys as well. Eliminate and save $123 Million (**$2.5 Billion** total).

Trainer Aircraft

JT Primary Aircraft Trainer System (JPATS)

Joint Primary Aircraft Training System (JPATS) is a joint USAF/USN Acquisition Category 1C program. JPATS includes the T-6 Texan II (a single turboprop engine, stepped tandem seat, commercially derived aircraft), ground based training system (aircrew training devices, development courses, conversion courses, and operational support), and contractor logistics support.

Finally, a justification for a line item; but it doesn't indicate that there's anything wrong with the existing T34s and T37s other than being old. Eliminate and save $279 Million (**$2.1 Billion** total).

Other Aircraft

KC-130J

> The KC-130J aircraft is an all metal, high-wing, long-range, land-based monoplane. It is designed for cargo, tanker and troop carrier operations. For tanker operations, the aircrew will consist of a pilot, co-pilot, augmented crew member and two air refueling observers. Features include wing mounted refueling pods, an internal cargo ramp and door, crew and cargo compartment pressurization, ground and in-flight refueling, thermal deicing systems and a Heads-Up Display (HUD).

The justification area for this procurement is literally blank; the Navy provides no reason for buying them. Eliminate and save $36 Million ($10.5 Billion total).

KC-130J Advanced Procurement

If we eliminate the buy contract, we thereby eliminate the need to pre-fund FY2014's buys as well. Eliminate and save $23 Million ($947 Million total).

RQ-4 UAV Advanced Procurement

> The Broad Area Maritime Surveillance (BAMS) Unmanned Aircraft System (UAS), which is an adjunct to the P-8A Multi-Mission Maritime Aircraft (MMA)/P-3, is integral in recapitalizing the Navy's Maritime Patrol and Reconnaissance Force. The BAMS UAS capability will be based upon the Block 20 variant of the Global Hawk with specific capabilities developed for the maritime persistent Intelligence, Surveillance and Reconnaissance (ISR) mission.

This is a brand-new program which the Navy has clearly done just fine without. Eliminate and save $51 Million (**$1.3 Billion** total).

MQ-8 UAV

> The MQ-8 Vertical Take-Off and Landing Tactical Unmanned Aerial Vehicle (VTUAV, popular name "Fire Scout") provides real-time and non-real-time Intelligence, Surveillance and Reconnaissance (ISR) data to tactical users without the use of manned aircraft or reliance on limited joint theater or national assets. The baseline MQ-8 can accomplish missions including over-the-horizon tactical reconnaissance, classification, targeting and laser designation and battle management (including voice relay).

Again we see no real justification. This program procures about six per year to a total of 168 units, and has 41 so far; so they intend it to go on for roughly another 20 years. Eliminate and save $125 Million (**$2.3 Billion** total).

STUASLO

> The Small Tactical Unmanned Aircraft System (STUAS) is a combined Navy and Marine Corps program that provides Persistent Intelligence, Surveillance, and Reconnaissance/Target Acquisition (ISR/TA) support for tactical level maneuver decisions and unit level force defense/force protection for Naval amphibious assault ships (multi-ship classes) and Navy and Marine land forces. This system will fill the ISR capability shortfalls currently filled by the ISR services contracts.

This new program was just introduced in FY2011 and is intended to run through FY2015. The Navy already had systems that did these jobs before the program was created, and no real justification is provided. Eliminate and save $9.6 Million ($57 Million total).

Modification of Aircraft

EA-6 Series

> This line item funds modifications to the EA-6B aircraft. The EA-6B Prowler is a four-seat, twin-engine, mid-wing, tactical, electronic attack aircraft. The EA-6B is employed in both Navy and Marine Corps squadrons to provide DoD tactical electronic attack capability.

There's nothing wrong with the ones we have now, and there is no justification whatsoever. Eliminate and save $30 Million (**$3.4 Billion** total).

AEA Systems

> This line item funds modifications to Airborne Electronic Attack (AEA) products used on multiple platforms.   Modifications budgeted and programmed include: procurement of Low Band Transmitter Antenna Group (LBT AG) inventory, AN/ALQ-99 Tactical Jamming System upgrades and related sustainability, capability, and viability modifications, Airborne Electronic Attack Expendable (AEAE) upgrades and integration, and Area Chaff Dispenser (ALE-43) upgrades and integration.

There's nothing wrong with the ones we have now, and there is no justification whatsoever. Eliminate and save $50 Million.

AV-8 Series

> This line item funds modifications to T/AV-8B aircraft. The AV-8B is a single engine, single crew member aircraft capable of vertical/short take-off and landing operations (V/STOL). The AV-8B meets the Marine Corps requirements for a light attack aircraft to provide responsive offensive air power that can operate from ships and austere forward bases in direct support of ground forces.

There's nothing wrong with the ones we have now, and there is no justification whatsoever. Eliminate and save $81 Million ($1.5 Billion total).

Adversary

> This line item funds modifications to convert a total of 10 F-16A Aircraft, regenerated from the Aircraft Maintenance and Regeneration facility into a Navy approved configuration. It allows the U.S. Navy to maintain as close a standardized configuration with the Air Force as possible based on need. It also allows the Navy to initiate unique structural, avionics, and other safety related modifications.

If you want to have aircraft similar to the Air Force's, just buy the same planes in the first place. There's nothing wrong with the ones we have now, and there is no justification whatsoever. Eliminate and save $4 Million.

F-18 Series

> The overall goal of the modifications budgeted in FY 2013 is to implement commonality/capability and structural safety and reliability improvements.

The Navy's existing F-18s seem to be working fine, and the aircraft manufacturers should be held responsible for correcting their own defects. Eliminate and save $689 Million (**$15.3 Billion** total).

H-46 Series

> This line item funds modifications to the H-46 aircraft. The H-46 is a twin-turbine powered dual-piloted tandem-rotor helicopter. The cabin contains provisions for accommodating 25 troops and crew members. The cabin also contains an integral cargo and rescue system. The overall goal of the modification budget in FY 2013 is to keep the H-46 a viable platform until a replacement aircraft can be fielded. H-46 helicopters are used by the Marine Corps for troop transport and search and rescue missions.

These aircraft have been around for longer than they were intended, and I'm eliminating most other procurements. Keep as is for now ($2.3 Million).

AH-1W Series

> This line item funds modifications to the AH-1W aircraft. Modifications prior to FY 1997 were funded in the H-1 Series P-1 line item. In FY13 we project 126 AH-1Ws. The AH-1W is a tandem-seat, two-place attack helicopter. The mission of the AH-1W attack helicopter is to provide rotary wing close air support, anti-armor, armed escort, armed/visual reconnaissance, survivability enhancements, and fire support under day/night and adverse weather conditions and special operations support; supporting arms coordination and aeromedical evacuation.

The ones we have seem to be doing just fine; eliminate and save $9 Million ($800 Million total).

H-53 Series

> *This line item funds modifications to the CH-53D/CH-53E/MH-53E aircraft. The aircraft inventories to be modified vary by OSIP, dependent on kit modification production lead-time. The CH-53E is a seven blade main rotor and a four-blade canted tail rotor helicopter powered by three T64-GE-416/416A/419 turbo shaft engines while the CH-53D has six main rotor blades and two T64- GE-413/416 engines. The CH-53D/E aircraft are capable of both land and ship based transport of heavy equipment, supplies, and personnel.*

The ones we have seem to be doing just fine; eliminate and save $61 Million (**$2 Billion** total).

SH-60 Series

> *This line item funds modifications to H-60 series aircraft. The H-60 series program of record for modification is comprised of: 30 HH-60H, 138 SH-60B, 65 SH-60F, 173 MH-60S, 84 MH-60R [...] The overall goal of the modifications budgeted is for the Integrated Mechanical Diagnostic System (IMDS), Safety Related Systems Upgrade, AMCM/Armed Helo (Correction of Deficiencies) for the MH-60S, Armed Block I Upgrade for the MH-60R, H-60 Helicopter Visit, Board, Search, and Seizure (HVBSS), H-60 Overland Missions, SH-60B KG-45A, MH-60S Warfighting Capability, SH-60B Datalink (KuBand), MH-60R/S Crew Workload - Operator System Interface (OSI), Automatic Radar Periscope Detection Discrimination (ARPDD), and H-60 Aircraft Sustainment.*

The ones we have seem to be doing just fine; eliminate and save $84 Million (**$1.8 Billion** total).

H-1 Series

> *The overall goal of the modifications budgeted in FY 2013 is to eliminate safety hazards, improve survivability, fulfill operational requirements, remedy obsolescence, and maintain significant mission capability and Joint interoperable data link circuit capable of transmitting, receiving, and display digital information and video which includes Full Motion video. Additionally, the H-1 will continue to upgrade the applicable aircraft sensor and avionics systems and subsystems as well as weapons rocket delivery system which includes the Advance Precision Kill Weapon System (APKWS). In addition, air vehicle improvements needing critical reliability enhancements will be incorporated.*

The ones we have seem to be doing just fine; eliminate and save $7 Million ($520 Million total).

EP-3 Series

> *This line item funds modifications to the EP-3E aircraft. The EP-3E is a land based, long range aircraft with electronic intercept devices for detection and tracking of enemy RADARs and communications.*

The ones we have seem to be doing just fine; eliminate and save $79 Million (**$1.3 Billion** total).

P-3 Series

> *This line item funds modifications to P-3 aircraft. The P-3 Orion is a four turbo-prop engine, long-range maritime surveillance aircraft which performs Under Sea Warfare (USW), Surface Warfare (SUW) and Intelligence, Surveillance and Reconnaissance (ISR) in support of battle group and littoral operations in direct support of Sea Shield and Forcenet pillars of Seapower 21.*

The ones we have seem to be doing just fine; eliminate and save $148 Million (**$5 Billion** total).

E-2 Series

> *This line item funds modifications to the E-2 aircraft. The E-2 is an all weather, carrier based, airborne early warning and command and control aircraft that extends task force defense perimeters by providing early warning of approaching enemy units and by vectoring interceptors into attack position.*

The availability of something newer does not justify spending billions of dollars on it. The ones we have seem to be doing just fine; eliminate and save $16 Million (**$1.6 Billion** total).

Trainer Aircraft Series

> *This line item funds modifications to a group of trainer aircraft which includes T-44A/C, and TH-57. [...] The overall goal of the modification is to maintain safe and reliable operation of the trainer aircraft through the timely installation of necessary changes. Total numbers for T-44 and TH-57 aircraft are 54 and 126, respectively.*

Aircraft do not need to be modified to maintain preexisting levels of safety or reliability. Parts often need to be replaced, but that is part of regular maintenance. They need not be upgraded. Eliminate and save $34 Million ($337 Million total).

C-2A

> *The C-2A(R) Greyhound is a high wing monoplane, twin engine turbo-prop aircraft capable of operating from both a shore base and all operational United States Navy aircraft carrier classes. [...] The design service life of the C-*

2A(R) is 10,000 flight hours with 15,000 landings. Service Life Extension Program (SLEP) modifications increase the service life to 15,000 flight hours and 36,000 landings, remove and replace all aircraft wiring and install various upgrades to allow C-2A(R) to meet requirements into the next decade.

As my proposal largely eliminates new spending, it is important to extend the service life of existing aircraft. Keep as is for now ($4.7 Million).

C-130 Series

This item funds modifications to C/KC-130 aircraft. The Lockheed C/KC-130 aircraft is a four engine, high-wing, all metal, long range, land based monoplane capable of all weather transport of cargo or personnel and in-flight refueling. There are currently 90 aircraft in the Navy and Marine Corps inventory (42 active and 48 reserve).

It occurs to me that since every branch has C-130s, the aircraft need not be assigned to one specific branch. A reorganization may be in order so that when one branch isn't using them, another can be. The budget does not specify the reason for this outlay, so eliminate it and save $17 Million ($933 Million total).

Fleet Electronic Warfare Support Group

This line item funds modifications to avionics equipment used for Fleet Operational Forces and Adversary Air Electronic Warfare (EW) training exercises. The overall goal is to accurately simulate the known and postulated electronic warfare characteristics and tactics of various radar and jammer threats for fleet training[...]

The Navy seems to be able to train just fine without this special equipment, and we've already bought plenty. Eliminate and save $670K ($108 Million total).

Cargo/Transport Aircraft Series

This line item funds modifications to the following cargo and transport aircraft: C-9B, C-40A, C-20A/D/G, C-37A/B, UC-35C/D, RC-12F/M, UC-12B/F/M/W, NC-12B and C/EC/RC-26D.

The budget doesn't actually explain the reason for these modifications; eliminate and save $26 Million ($426 Million total).

E-6 Series

This line item funds modifications to E-6 "Take Charge and Move Out", TACAMO aircraft. All sixteen (16) aircraft in the TACAMO fleet will receive each modification. The E-6 TACAMO is a manned airborne communications relay platform designed to provide a survivable, reliable, endurable airborne

> *Command and Control Communications link between the President, Secretary of Defense and U.S. strategic and non-strategic forces.*

The budget doesn't actually explain the reason for these modifications; eliminate and save $158 Million (**$1.9 Billion** total).

Executive Helicopters Series

> *This line item funds modifications to the (11) VH-3D, (8) VH-60N, (1) TH-3D, and (1) TH-60N. These aircraft are assigned to Marine Helicopter Squadron One to support the President of the United States. The VH-60N Cockpit Upgrade consists of an upgrade to all-glass instrumentation.*

That seems like an excessive number of aircraft to support the President. The budget doesn't actually explain the reason for these modifications; eliminate and save $58 Million (**$1 Billion** total).

Special Project Aircraft

> *The Special Projects program modifies and/or replaces obsolete special mission equipment and integrates Quick Reaction Capability as required in six P-3 aircraft. Procurements vary in each fiscal year and include common Navy systems for increased capability, reduced operator workload and common logistics, as well as procurement of special mission equipment as directed by the Chief of Naval Operations. Active PAA inventory is 4 with additional 2 BAA aircraft in the Special Mission inventory.*

The availability of something newer doesn't automatically obsolete existing equipment. Eliminate and save $15 Million ($558 Million total).

T-45 Series

> *This line item funds modifications to T-45A/C aircraft [...] The overall goal of the modifications budgeted in FY 2013 is to correct discrepancies and deficiencies discovered after delivery of the aircraft and to commence upgrades to the aircraft cockpit and navigation systems.*

They seem to be working well enough, and manufacturers should be held responsible to correct their own deficiencies. Eliminate and save $64 Million (**$1.7 Billion** total).

Power Plant Changes

> *This line item funds modifications to all in-service aircraft engines. Power Plant Changes (PPC) are required throughout the service life of each aircraft to correct flight deficiencies and improve operational readiness while reducing engine operating costs. This program finances the procurement and installation of retrofit kits for all Navy and Marine Corp aircraft engines and related propulsion hardware such as propellers, starters and transmissions.*

Manufacturers should be held responsible to correct their own deficiencies; it's called a warranty. Eliminate and save $22 Million ($667 Million total).

JT Primary Aircraft Trainer System (JPATS)

> *This line item funds modifications to the Joint Primary Aircraft Training System (JPATS) [...] The overall goal of the modifications budgeted in fiscal year 2013 is to correct discrepancies and deficiencies discovered after delivery of the aircraft; and to maintain, where appropriate, joint configuration with Air Force aircraft. The T-6B derivative incorporates major upgrades to the aircraft cockpit, navigation system, and aircrew life support system. 131 Aircraft will receive modifications in FY13.*

Manufacturers should be held responsible to correct their own deficiencies; it's called a warranty. Eliminate and save $2 Million ($56 Million total).

Aviation Life Support Mods

> *This line item funds the installation of the new aircraft endurance modifications in legacy non-ejection seat equipped aircraft due to extended range missions. Installation of the Joint Helmet Mounted Cueing System (JHMCS) night mission Electronic Control Unit (ECU) into tactical aircraft. The ECU works with the JHMCS night vision system to provide the ability to cue and display weapons and sensors at night using Night Vision Devices (NVD) that integrate JHMCS cueing, display symbology, and scene viewed through NVD. Also funds the installation of the crashworthy troop and gunner seats for fielded MH-60S aircraft.*

Stop sending aircraft on missions they weren't designed for; there are plenty of other aircraft available to choose from. Eliminate and save $2 Million ($46 Million total).

Common ECM Equipment

> *This line item funds common Electronic Countermeasures (ECM) equipment (B kits) for multiple aircraft. The overall goal of the modification budget is to provide a reprogrammable radar and missile warning system, provide attacking missile declaration and sector direction finding, laser detection, and self protection capability devices to applicable user aircraft.*

The aircraft already seem to be able to countermeasure or evade incoming missiles effectively, and my plan would pretty much eliminate incoming missiles for the foreseeable future. Eliminate and save $115 Million (**$3.4 Billion** total).

Common Avionics Changes

> This line item funds common avionics equipment for multiple aircraft. With the exception of OSIPs 43-94 (Flight Data Recorders), 14-97 (KC-130T GPWS), 17-98 (Helo GPWS), and 24-99 (CAS), the individual aircraft platforms fund the "A" kits and installation in the appropriate aircraft line. The overall goal of the modifications budgeted in FY 2013 is to procure the common equipment required for the individual aircraft platforms.

Procuring equipment is not a reason in itself to procure equipment; the aircraft seem to be working just fine without these upgrades. Eliminate and save $97 Million (**$3.8 Billion** total).

ID System

> MK XIIA Mode 5 provides improved secure cooperative combat identification via Identification Friend or Foe (IFF). MODE 5 is a product improvement which is designed to be installed through engineering changes to digital MK XII interrogators and transponders including, but not limited to the APX-118/123, UPX-37/41C, APX-111, and APX-119. Mode 5 is designed to be installed in all Navy T/M/S aircraft which are currently Mode 4 IFF capable. Mode 5 is developed in cooperation with NATO and is governed by STANAG 4193.

Existing IFF systems are working fine, and under my plan there would be few to no foes to identify in the fist place. Withdraw from NATO. Eliminate and save $40 Million ($427 Million total).

P-8 Series

> This line item funds correction of deficiencies, modernization to the P-8 aircraft and the retrofit of future P-8A mission system/avionics as developed under P-8A sequential increment programs. Increment 2 includes upgrades to the Automatic Identification System, Multi-Static Active Coherent, and Acoustic Processor Tech Refresh. Increment 3 includes upgrades to Integrated Broadcast System, Net-Ready, Net-Enabled Weapon and Rapid Capability Insertion Upgrade. This is an FY 2013 new start.

The ones we have now seem to be working fine. Eliminate this brand-new program and save $5 Million (**$2.2 Billion** total).

MAGTF EW for Aviation

> This line item funds modification efforts for the System of Systems (SOS) that support the Marine Air Ground Task Force Electronic Warfare (MAGTF EW) mission. These SOS are designed to support improved capabilities to close gaps in MAGTF EW sufficiency and integration in the EW arena, they are designed for carriage on a variety of organic air and ground MAGTF assests and include: Software Reprogrammable Payload (SRP), Collaborative EW/EW

Battle Management, EW Services Architecture (formerly Collaborative On-Line Reconnaissance Provider of Operational Responsive Attack Link (CORPORAL)), and Intrepid Tiger series. MAGTF EW will support procurement of new technologies and equipment as needed to combat emerging electronic warfare (EW) technologies and systems.

This seems to duplicate DoD-level troop coordination efforts, and the existing systems are working fine. Eliminate and save $34 Million ($103 Million total).

RQ-7 Series

This line funds modifications to the RQ-7 UAV and associated support systems. The RQ-7B Shadow UAV system provides dedicated Reconnaissance, Surveillance and Target Acquisition, Intelligence, Battle Damage Assessment and Force Protection to the Marine Air-Ground Task Force. The RQ-7B Shadow UAV system provides the Marine Expeditionary Force with critical battlefield intelligence and targeting information in the rapid cycle time required for success at the tactical level.

The ones we have now seem to be working fine. Eliminate this brand-new program and save $49 Million ($87 Million total).

V-22 Osprey

The overall goal of the modifications budgeted in FY 2013 is to maintain commonality, implement structural safety and reliability improvements, and improve capability. These modifications will also improve readiness, increase aircraft availability, and decrease operating costs. FY 2013 focus will be on reducing flight hour costs, and improving Time On Wing, as reflected in the Readiness OSIP.

The ones we have now seem to be working fine. Eliminate this brand-new program and save $96 Million (**$1.7 Billion** total).

Aircraft Spares and Repair Parts

The initial spares requirement funds all repairables and consumables allowances to support the quantity and type/model/series of aircraft in new procurement, during Interim Contractor Support and to support. The initial spares category includes interim spares for recently introduced equipment without adequate demand history using prescribed weapons utilization rates, as well as all aircraft engines and module spares. All spares requirements are developed using accredited sparing models. Funding requirements for major avionics are calculated on an item-by-item basis where possible.

Maintenance requires spare parts. Keep as is ($1.2 Billion). This program ends in FY2017.

Aircraft Support Equipment and Facilities

Common Ground Equipment

The Common Ground Equipment line funds procurement of Automatic Test Equipment (ATE), various aircraft systems trainers and training aids, the Consolidated Automated Support System (CASS), support equipment for the Rapid Deployment Force, mobile maintenance facilities for Marine expeditionary forces, and other aircraft ground support equipment that is either peculiar to out-of-production aircraft or common in applicability to more than one aircraft.

This is necessary for proper maintenance; Eliminate OCO component, reduce the remainder by standard 25% and save $97 Million.

Aircraft Industrial Facilities

Calibration Equipment funds are used to procure Calibration Standards (CALSTDs) and ancillary equipment for Aviation Fleet Intermediate Calibration Activities, Fleet Training Activities, Aviation Navy Calibration Laboratories (NCLs), and the Navy Primary Standards Laboratory (NPSL). CALSTDs procured for Fleet Intermediate ('I') level use are to replace obsolete and/or irreparable equipment, expand technical measurement capabilities to decrease Depot support costs, reduce out-of-service turn around times, provide enhanced forward deployed geographic support and reduce/control the Naval Air Systems Command (NAVAIR) cost of ownership associated with Calibration.

Training falls under the Operations budget. The remainder reduces maintenance and extends equipment and aircraft service lifetime; reduce by standard 25%.

NAVAIR owns one active, contractor operated aircraft manufacturing plants and several hundred acres of environmentally contaminated land at two former plants. NAVAIR is the environmental permitee at one site, legally responsible for environmental compliance including cleanup of offsite private property contaminated by activity originating on NAVAIR property.

It is wrong to require a company to meet certain environmental standards and then to pay them to do so. This falls under NAVAIR's own internal costs and is not a proper taxpayer expense. Stop contaminating private property. Eliminate all federal environmental laws and let the states deal with them, thus exempting the ongoing bill. Eliminate and save $23 Million plus indefinite ongoing costs.

War Consumables

> The WAR CONSUMABLES P-1 line item has two subcategories: Common Aircraft Ancillary Equipment (AAE) and Aerial Refueling Stores (ARS). The Common AAE program procures, modifies and upgrades common bomb racks, peculiar bomb racks, missile launchers and related support for USN/USMC platforms. In FY11, External Fuel Tank (EFT) funds were realigned from PE 0204164N to PE 0204161N. The ARS portion procures, modifies, and upgrades aerial refueling stores, External Fuel Tanks (EFT) and related support.

By eliminating war, we eliminate the consumption thereof. Eliminate and save $43 Million.

Other Production Charges

> The Other Production Charges line provides funds for miscellaneous production support and testing services, aircraft pods, and instrumentation packages supporting tactical aircrew combat training and mobile sea range systems.

This sounds like it could be potentially important. Keep for now and reevaluate in more detail as the budget settles down ($3 Million).

Special Support Equipment

> Details of this P-1 item are classified.

We'll just see about that. This program runs from 2011 through 2017; reduce by half for now and save $16 Million.

First Destination Transport

> This line finances the movement of newly procured equipment and material from the contractor's plant to the initial point of receipt by the Government.

My plan has greatly reduced procurements, and thus the need to move them around. Reduce by 90% and save $1.6 Million.

Weapons Procurement, Navy[71]

Since my plan involves being in peacetime, we can reduce the ongoing expenditure of weapons and ammunition by a great deal. They need only be used in training, criminal investigations, and defense as needed.

Ballistic Missiles

Trident II Mods

> The TRIDENT II (D5) missiles carried on OHIO CLASS Fleet Ballistic Missile Submarines through 2042. The D5 Life Extension (D5LE) program will ensure

---

[71] http://www.finance.hq.navy.mil/fmb/13pres/WPN_BOOK.PDF

that the United States continues to maintain a highly survivable strategic deterrent well into the 21st century. The TRIDENT II missile (1) enhances Fleet Ballistic Missile Submarine survivability as it increases the Sea Launched Ballistic Missile range at full payload to exploit the total patrol area available to the TRIDENT submarine, (2) minimizes total weapon system costs as it has increased the Sea Launched Ballistic Missile payload to the level permitted by the size of the TRIDENT submarine launch tube, thereby allowing mission capability to be achieved with fewer submarines, and (3) and it has added an efficient hard target kill capability to the Sea Launched Ballistic Missile.

Peacetime means a reduced need for missiles. Eliminate the START I and SORT requirements which reduced the payload from 12 to only five sub-warheads. We've been buying these things for a long time; we have plenty of them now. Eliminate and save **$1.2 Billion ($21 Billion** total).

Missile Industrial Facilities

Funding for Missile Industrial Facilities provides for capital maintenance projects at Navy-owned Naval Industrial Reserve Ordnance Plants (NIROPS) at Sunnyvale and Santa Cruz, California, and Bacchus, Utah, in support of the Fleet Ballistic Missile program. The Bacchus, Utah, ATK facility alone consists of 583 acres, 130 buildings and 13 miles of road.

This sounds fairly important; reduce by standard 25% and save $1.4 Million.

Other Missiles

Tomahawk

Tomahawk provides an attack capability against fixed and mobile/moving targets, and can be launched from both surface ships (RGM) and submarines (UGM).

We have thousands of these things now, and we won't require an ongoing supply as long as we stay at peace. Eliminate and save $309 Million (**$14.9 Billion** total).

AMRAAM

The Defense Acquisition Board approved AMRAAM Full Rate Production (Milestone IIIB) in April 1992. The next version, AIM-120D, completed Engineering and Manufacturing Development (EMD) Sep 09. Procurement of limited quantities to support Air Force and Navy operational test and Initial Operational Capability (IOC) requirements began in FY06.

We have tons of these things now, and won't be expending them in peacetime. I don't see any reason to continue procurement through 2024; eliminate and save $102 Million (**$5 Billion** total).

Sidewinder

> The AIM-9X Sidewinder short-range air-to-air missile is a long term evolution of the AIM-9 series of fielded missiles. The AIM-9X missile program provides a launch and leave, air combat munition that uses passive infrared (IR) energy for acquisition and tracking of enemy aircraft and complements the Advanced Medium Range Air-to-Air missile (AMRAAM). Air superiority in the short-range air-to-air missile arena is essential and includes first shot, first kill opportunity against an enemy employing IR countermeasures.

We have tons of these things now, and won't be expending them in peacetime. Eliminate and save $80 Million (**$2.2 Billion** total).

Joint Standoff Weapon (JSOW)

> Joint Standoff Weapon (JSOW) is a joint USN/USAF program with the USN as the lead service. The JSOW program provides an air-to-ground glide weapon (AGM-154) capable of attacking a variety of targets during day, night, and adverse weather conditions for use against fixed area targets. The JSOW enhances aircraft survivability as compared to current interdiction weapon systems by providing the capability for launch aircraft to standoff outside the range of most target area surface-to-air threat systems.

We've procured thousands of these things and won't be expending them in peacetime. Eliminate and save $128 Million (**$3.9 Billion** total).

Standard Missile

> The STANDARD Missile SM-2 Medium Range (MR) and Extended Range (ER) missiles are solid-propellant, tail-controlled surface-to-air missiles which are the main air defense battery for AEGIS guided missile cruisers and destroyers. The SM-2 Block IIIB, SM-2 Block IV and earlier variants are currently deployed.

AEGIS Missile Cruisers have been around for decades, long before we had Standard missiles. Eliminate and save $399 Million (**$13.7 Billion** total).

Rolling Airframe Missile (RAM)

> Rolling Airframe Missile (RAM) is a high fire-power, low cost, lightweight ship self-defense system to engage anti-ship missiles. Block 1 adds the capability of Infrared all-the-way guidance while maintaining the original dual-mode passive Radio Frequency/Infrared (RF/IR) guidance (Block 0). The RAM missile is fired from a RAM Guided Missile Launching System (GMLS)(MK-49), which holds 21 RAM rounds.

This new program sounds pretty useful for defending our fleets. Keep but reduce by standard 25% and save $17 Million.

Hellfire

> *AGM-114 Hellfire is a family of laser guided missiles employed against point and moving targets by both rotary and fixed wing aircraft. The family of Hellfire missiles includes, but is not limited to, AGM-114B/ K/K2/K2A/M/N/N-5/P/P+/R variants. These variants include shaped charge warheads (B/K/K2/K2A) for use against armored targets and blast fragmentation warheads (M/N) for use against urban structures. The AGM-114N is a Thermobaric blast fragmentation warhead that maintains the capability provided by the AGM-114M while adding a unique capability against confined compartmented spaces, a typical target type observed in current combat operations.*

We have procured around 13,000 Hellfire missiles over the years, with a significant bump in the FY2013 budget. One has to wonder what that bump is for. We won't expend many of these in peacetime, so we don't need to replenish them. Eliminate and save $92 Million.

Stand Off Precision Guided Munitions (SOPGM)

> *SOPGM weapons, Viper Strike and Griffin, are threshold weapons for the KC-130J Intelligence, Surveillance and Reconnaissance (ISR) Weapon Mission Kit USMC requirement. Both weapons are portions of the required roll-on/roll-off capability inherent in the ISR Weapon Mission Kit. The Viper Strike is a glide weapon with Global Positioning System/Inertial Navigation System (GPS/INS) navigation to the target vicinity and a semi-active laser (SAL) seeker used for terminal guidance to target impact.*

This new program began in FY2012; the Navy and USMC seemed fine without them in 2011. After 2013, the program continues to budget outlays but does not procure any quantity. Eliminate and save $7 Million.

Aerial Targets

> *The Aerial Targets Program provides powered targets, towed targets and necessary Target Auxiliary and Augmentation Systems (TA/AS) equipment for fleet training and weapons systems test and evaluation. This program is composed of a series of continuing target production programs.*

The Navy still needs to train in peacetime, and it's better than paying for expensive wars to do their practice. Keep as is ($62 Million).

Other Missile Support

The MK-41 Vertical Launching System (VLS) is a surface combatant missile launching system, designed to store, select and launch various STANDARD Missile configurations, TOMAHAWK, Tactical TOMAHAWK, EVOLVED SEASPARROW (ESSM) and Vertical Launch ASROC (VLA) missiles. The MK-41 VLS significantly improves missile capacity, flexibility, multi-mission capability, reaction time and rate of fire and is designed to be adaptable to present and future weapon systems.

If we stop buying Standard missiles, then we don't need any more of their launchers. Eliminate and save $4 Million.

Evolved Sea Sparrow Missile (ESSM)

The Evolved SEASPARROW Missile (ESSM) Program is an international cooperative effort to design, develop, test, produce and provide in-service support to a new and improved version of the SPARROW missile (RIM-7P) with the kinematic performance to defeat current and projected threats that possess low altitude, high velocity and maneuver characteristics beyond the engagement capabilities of the RIM-7P.

International cooperation in missile-building is not a very good reason to build missiles. The availability of something newer and shinier does not obsolete the preexisting ones. No quantities are procured for the foreseeable future. Eliminate and save $58 Million.

HARM Mods

AARGM is an ACAT-1C acquisition program to upgrade the Legacy AGM-88 High Speed Anti-Radiation Missile (HARM) with multimode guidance and enhanced targeting capability. AARGM program will integrate multi-mode guidance (passive Anti-Radiation Homing (ARH)/active Millimeter Wave (MMW) Radar/Global Positioning system(GPS)/Inertial Navigation System) on the HARM AGM-88 missile.

The availability of something newer and shinier does not obsolete the preexisting ones. Eliminate and save $87 Million.

Weapons Industrial Facilities

Close, deactivate, prepare, and convey the Government-Owned Contractor Operated (GOCO), Naval Weapons Industrial Reserve Plant (NWIRP) in Bedford, MA under the cognizance of NAVSEA supported by WPN funds. Support for Capital Type Rehabilitation projects at the GOCO plant, Naval Industrial Reserve Ordnance Plant (NIROP) Allegany Ballistics Laboratory (ABL) in Rocket Center, WV. NIROP ABL supports weapons systems such as AARGM, RAM, Sparrow, ESSM, ERGM, AIM-9X, AGS, Tomahawk GG and Trident GG.

> *Federal Acquisition Regulation Part 52.245-7 specifies that Facilities Use contracts require that the Government fund capital type rehabilitation projects to support and maintain these facilities.*

The government should not fund weapons research or support thereof; merely buy the resulting products from the private sector. Having said that, some of this sounds fairly important. Keep and reduce by half, saving $1 Million. Eliminate environmental and energy conservation components.

Fleet Satellite Communications Follow-On

> *This Budget Line funds the Mobile User Objective System (MUOS) satellites and launch vehicles. MUOS will provide a worldwide, multi-service population of mobile and fixed-site terminal users with narrowband beyond line of sight satellite communications (SATCOM) services. Capabilities will include a considerable increase to current narrowband SATCOM capacity as well as a significant improvement in availability for small terminals.*

This at least somewhat duplicates DoD/TJS projects, and the Navy seems to be doing just fine without it. Eliminate and save $21 Million (**$2.9 Billion** total).

Ordnance Support Equipment

> *Additional details with respect to this line item are held at a higher classification. This line item is reported in accordance with Title 10, United States Code, Section 119(a)(1) in the Special Access Program Annual Report to Congress.*

We'll just see about that. Reduce by half in the meantime.

Torpedoes and Related Equipment

Surface Ship Torpedo

> *The Surface Ship Torpedo Defense (SSTD) WPN account procures surface ship Acoustic Device Countermeasures (ADCs) and the Countermesure Anti-Torpedo (CAT). The ADC is a 3-inch expendable torpedo countermeasure (CM) that provides an over-the-side soft-kill defense against threat torpedoes. The CAT is an autonomous seek-and-destroy Anti-Torpedo torpedo. ADC funding replaces expiring units and raises inventory to Navy requirements.*

Ships definitely need countermeasures, but peacetime would result in almost none being expended. Buy enough for all our ships and a bit extra, then eliminate; save $3 Million.

ASW Targets

> *MK39 quantity total is 10,074 which is a combination of MK39 Mod 1 and MK39 Mod 2 Expendable Mobile ASW Training Target (EMATT) Targets. The*

MK39 Mod 2 EMATT is a small self-propelled underwater vehicle launched from fixed wing and rotary wing Anti-Submarine Warfare (ASW) aircraft and ASW surface ships for the purpose of providing basic, open ocean sonar training and torpedo placement exercises.

The Navy still needs to train in peacetime, and it's better than paying for expensive wars to do their practice. Keep as is ($10 Million).

MK-54 Torpedo Mods

This line item procures MK54 Mod 0 Torpedo Kits, MK 54 Mod 1 Torpedo Kits, MK54/Vertical Launch Anti-submarine Rocket (VLA) Conversion Kits, VLA Components and High Altitude ASW Weapon Capability (HAAWC) kits for lightweight torpedoes.

There's nothing wrong with the MK54 torpedoes we already had, and this program has no end date. Eliminate, buy the right torpedoes in the first place, and save $74 Million (**$1.4 Billion** total).

MK-48 Torpedo ADCAP Mods

This line item procures MK48 Mod 7 Common Broadband Advanced Sonar System (CBASS) kits for Heavyweight Torpedo Upgrades. The MK-48 ADCAP MODs kit incorporates a new Guidance and Control (G&C) modification. The G&C Modification provides a common G&C with the Mod 7 CBASS replacing obsolete electronic components with Commercial Off-The-Shelf (COTS) Processors and increased processing capacity.

There's nothing wrong with the MK48 torpedoes we already had, and this program has no end date. Eliminate, buy the right torpedoes in the first place, and save $54 Million (**$1.5 Billion** total).

Quickstrike Mine

The QUICKSTRIKE (QS) family of air delivered mines has 3 variants based on size - the MK 62, MK 63, and MK 65. The MK 62 and MK 63 (500 lb. and 1000 lb.) QS are created by adding mine hardware to the MK 82 and MK 83 general purpose bomb (respectively) to form a mine. The MK 65 (2000 lb.) QS consists entirely of hardware designed for use as a mine.

This sounds pretty useful, but we won't need to expend many mines in peacetime. Reduce by half and save $3 Million.

Torpedo Support Equipment

The Torpedo Support equipment account procures various 4T and associated torpedo components required to ready weapons for Surface Ships, Submarines, Fixed Wing and Rotary Wing to achieve and maintain a reeadiness posture sufficient to provide Anti-Submarine Warfare (ASW) and Anti-Surface Warfare

> *(ASUW) readiness. The objective of this line is to provide the Fleet with ready exercise weapon for conducting training maneuvers which involve actually firing the torpedoes and to maintain warshot inventories in an operational ready-for-issue (RFI) status in support of combat ready deployment by ASW forces. After a torpedo is fired during a training exercise it is recovered and all expendable components such as batteries, cables, igniters (as well as various accessories required for air-launched torpedoes), must be replaced.*

Peacetime means reduced torpedo usage, which means less need for support thereof. Reduce by standard 25% and save $12 Million.

ASW Range Support

> *The AntiSubmarine Warfare (ASW) Range support program provides training range equipment and Fleet support equipment for use on the Navy's underwater ranges. This equipment is used to instrument*

> *Fleet exercises and torpedo firings and ASW readiness assessment testing. The Weapon Fleet training ranges supported are Southern California Offshore Range (SCORE), Barking Sands Tactical Underwater Range/Barking Sands Underwater Range Extension (BARSTUR/BSURE) and Atlantic Underwater Test and Evaluation Center (AUTEC).*

The Navy still needs to train in peacetime, and it's better than paying for expensive wars to do their practice. Keep as is ($12 Million).

First Destination Transportation

> *First Destination Transportation (FDT) provides for the movement of newly procured equipment and material from the contractor's plant to the initial point of receipt for subsequent shipment to its destination.*

By eliminating our worldwide posture, we can significantly reduce the logistics overhead associated therewith. Just put the stuff and the people on a truck, a plane, or *gasp* a ship! Reduce the frequency with which people and equipment are shifted around, which seems to have no particular purpose other than to keep them rotated. Reduce procurements significantly. Reduce by 90% and save $3 Million.

Other Weapons

Small Arms and Weapons

> *Quantities of weapons procured with the above funding are to meet small arms allowances and inventory objectives. This line item provides for initial issue procurement, modernization, standardization and stock replenishment procurement of a wide variety of small arms and weapons (caliber .50 and below), including required gun mounts and associated support components.*

This line also provides for procurement of sufficient types and quantities of weapons to support training, security afloat and shore missions of approximately 1,300 ship/ashore activities Navy-wide.

I can't imagine that the Navy expends a whole lot of 9mm rounds compared to the Army, but I'll give them the benefit of the doubt. People on ships have to be armed in case someone tries to take the ship or in case of mutiny. Reduce by standard 25% and save $3 Million.

Close-In Weapons Systems (CIWS) Mods

Phalanx Close-In Weapon System (CIWS) is a high fire rate weapon system that automatically acquires, tracks and destroys Anti-Ship Missiles that have penetrated all other ship's defenses.

The Phalanx systems we have now seem to be working fine, and the program goes on for the foreseeable future. Why not just buy a better gun in the first place or hold manufacturers accountable for defects? Eliminate and save $59 Million.

Coast Guard Weapons

The Coast Guard Equipment line funds the Coast Guard Combat System Suite for USCG cutters under the Coast Guard Surface Asset Acquisition Program. Under inter-service agreement (delineated in OPNAVINST 4000.79B), DON plans, programs, and budgets for specific Navy military equipment, systems and logistic support requirements for Coast Guard units to ensure the Coast Guard is prepared to execute naval warfare tasks in consonance with US Navy units. Ship construction and installation costs are funded under the Department of Homeland Security appropriation.

USCG needs weapons, too. Reduce by standard 25% and save $5 Million.

Gun Mount Mods

Gun Mount Mods supports various types of Gun Weapon System and sub-system modifications and upgrade requirements.

In peacetime, there would be less wear and tear on the guns and their mounts. They seem to be working fine so far; eliminate and save $55 Million.

Cruiser Modernization Weapons

Modernized CG47 Class ships will operate independently, or as units of Carrier Strike Groups and Surface Action Groups, in support of Underway Replenishment Groups and the Marine Amphibious Task Forces in multithreat environments that include air, surface and subsurface threats. These ships will respond to Low Intensity Conflict/Coastal and Littoral Offshore Warfare

(LIC/CALOW) scenarios, Joint Missions, as well as open ocean conflicts, providing and augmenting power projection and forward presence. In addition, these ships will conduct Air Dominance, Land Attack and Force Protection missions.

With the Aegis system, we already have very modern cruisers and weapons. In peacetime, they would have very few or no threats to respond to. Eliminate and save $1.6 Million.

Airborne Mine Neutralization Systems

Airborne Mine Countermeasures (AMCM) Equipment is currently used by MH-53E helicopters to counter the threat of sea mines. The MH-60S helicopter will be adapted for the AMCM mission in support of the development of an Organic Fleet AMCM program.

The Navy already has a variety of mine detection and neutralization systems, and in peacetime there would be no mines to neutralize. Eliminate and save $21 Million.

Spares and Repair Parts

This budget activity provides all WPN Spares funding formerly separately identified in the other WPN budget activities. The procurement of spares and repair parts and assemblies for WPN equipment requiring support by the acquisition activities prior to the Navy Supply System Material Support Date is outlined below for Initial and Vendor Direct spares.

Spares and parts are parts of regular maintenance. Keep as is ($60 Million).

Shipbuilding and Conversion, Navy[72]

Other Warships

Battle Force Tactical Training System: The Navy still needs to train in peacetime, and it's better than paying for expensive wars to do their practice. Keep as is ($8 Million).

CANES: The Navy doesn't need yet another tactical display system. Eliminate and save $29 Million.

---

[72] http://www.finance.hq.navy.mil/fmb/13pres/SCN_BOOK.pdf

AN/USG-2 Cooperative Engagement Capability: Networks ships' sensors together to display the battlefield as one picture. This looks pretty useful; keep but reduce by 25%; save $3 Million.

Digital Modular Radio (DMR) Satcom: Duplicates TJS/DoD/Army efforts; the Navy doesn't need yet another form of encrypted radios. Eliminate and save $14 Million.

AN/UPX-29(V) Interrogator Friend or Foe (IFF): The Navy needs to identify friends and foes in battle. Keep but reduce by standard 25%, saving $5 Million.

Automatic Carrier Landing System: Exactly what it implies, this is important for bad weather. Keep but reduce by standard 25%, saving $4 Million.

Ship Self Defense System: Exactly what it implies, this is important in case of close battle. Keep as is ($91 Million).

Carrier Air Traffic Control Center: Exactly what it implies, this is somewhat important to prevent planes from flying into each other. Keep but reduce by standard 25%; save $2 Million.

Navy Multiband Terminal: Part of the MILSTAR communications system; keep as is ($8M).

Electronic Surveillance Suite Sewip Block 2: Mitigates EMI and combat system interference. Reduce by half and save $11M.

Ships Signal Exploitation Equipment: Acquires encrypted signals from enemy ships and identifies enemy locations. The Navy seemed to be fine without this; eliminate and save $13 Million.

Electronic Consolidated Automated Support System (eCASS): This brand-new procurement tests weapon systems and related circuitboards. The Navy seemed to work without it; eliminate and save $39 Million.

Electronic Surveillance Suite Sewip Block 3: Improves electronic attack capabilities. The availability of something newer doesn't justify replacing the existing systems. Eliminate and save $37 Million.

High Frequency Radio Group (HFRG): The Navy doesn't need yet another encrypted radio system. All of the DoD should really use one system. Eliminate and save $7 Million.

Sea-Based Joint Precision Approach & Landing System (JPALS): An ALS system that plugs into GPS navigation. The availability of something newer doesn't justify replacing the existing systems. Eliminate and save $10 Million.

Electromagnetic Aircraft Launching System (EMALS): This is the carrier catapult system; the Navy wants to upgrade it to support future aircraft. Since we aren't procuring future aircraft for the time being, eliminate and save $847 Million.

Dual Band Radar: The availability of something newer doesn't justify replacing the existing systems. Eliminate and save $243 Million.

Advanced Arresting Gear: Replaces the arresting hook system on some carriers despite the existing ones working just fine. Eliminate and save $212 Million.

Phalanx Block 1B Mk 15 Close-In Weapons Systems: Improves ship self-defense, which is working just fine. Eliminate and save $27 Million.

Carrier Tactical Support Center: A new sensor data processing system the Navy doesn't need. Eliminate and save $8 Million.

Guided Missile Launching System: Provides exactly two ships with an upgraded launch system to replace the existing ones which are working fine. Eliminate and save $16 Million.

Aviation Data Management and Control System: A new interface for existing systems. Eliminate and save $9 Million.

Integrated Launch and Recovery Television Systems: This is just a CCTV system. 18 cameras and monitors cost a few grand, tops. But of course it all has to be secure, because our enemies would totally win a war if they could see the planes landing. Eliminate and save $5 Million.

Rolling Airframe Missile: This was already authorized under Weapons Procurement and requires no additional funding. Eliminate and save $18 Million.

Improved Fresnel Lens Optical Landing System (IFLOLS): How many landing systems does the Navy need? Have our pilots forgotten how to land without computers? Eliminate and save $10 Million.

Ready Room Transformational Technologies Upgrade: Rearranges the CNC area of carriers. Eliminate and save $3 Million.

Amphibious Ships

Combat Sonar Control and Architecture: A new electronics suite for the Navy's newest line of attack submarines. Are our newest subs seriously already obsolete? Were the existing electronics that bad? Are the submarine manufacturers doing that bad a job? Eliminate and save $201 Million.

Electronic Support Measures Subsystem: Part of CSCA; an internal ship communications system. What was wrong with the old one? Eliminate and save $55 Million.

Photonics Mast: Two infrared cameras and monitors do not cost this much. Eliminate and save $37 Million.

Universal Modular Mast: Eight telescopic pieces of metal do not cost this much. Eliminate and save $21 Million.

Exterior Communications System Recurring: A stealthy, encrypted antenna array should not have recurring costs associated with it. Buy it once and be done with it. Eliminate and save $50 Million.

Propulsor: A new alloy for propeller blades. The old ones seem to be working fine, and the cost per ship is going up by seven digits every year; eliminate and save $70 Million per ship.

Auxiliaries, Craft, and Prior-Year Program Costs

Completion of Prior Year Shipbuilding Program: Completes ships already started. Keep as is ($1.2 Billion, non-recurring).

Other Procurement, Navy [73] [74] [75] [76] [77]

Ships Support Equipment

LM-2500 Gas Turbine

> The LM2500 Marine Gas Turbine and its associated Engineering Control Systems provide main propulsion for the Navy's surface combatants including the FFG 7 OLIVER HAZARD PERRY Class, CG 47 TICONDEROGA Class, DDG 51 ARLEIGH BURKE Class, and LCS Class. The LM2500 is composed of two major sub-assemblies: the gas generator and power turbine sections. It is coupled to

---

[73] http://www.finance.hq.navy.mil/fmb/13pres/OPN_BA1_BOOK.pdf
[74] http://www.finance.hq.navy.mil/fmb/13pres/OPN_BA2_BOOK.pdf
[75] http://www.finance.hq.navy.mil/fmb/13pres/OPN_BA3_BOOK.pdf
[76] http://www.finance.hq.navy.mil/fmb/13pres/OPN_BA4_BOOK.pdf
[77] http://www.finance.hq.navy.mil/fmb/13pres/OPN_BA_5-8_Book.pdf

> *the ship drive-train by a high speed coupling shaft. The control system provides for both local and remote engine operations.*

This program repairs and replaces ship engines to keep them running over time, which is much cheaper than buying new ships. Reduce by standard 25% and save $2.7 Million.

Allison 501K Gas Turbine

> *This program provides the life-cycle support for the following Marine Gas Turbine systems: The Rolls Royce (Allison) 501-K Series Gas Turbines are used to drive electrical generators in Ship Service Gas Turbine Generators (SSGTG). The 501-K17 is used on the CG-47 Class ships. The 501-K34 is an upgraded version used on the DDG-51 Class ships and is not interchangeable with the 501-K17. The Rolls Royce MT-30 are used on LCS-1 variant for main propulsion and DDG 1000 for electrical generation. Rolls Royce 250-KS4 is used as a starter gas turbine for the 501-K34 on DDG 79 and above.*

This program repairs and replaces ship engines to keep them running over time, which is much cheaper than buying new ships. Reduce by standard 25% and save $2.1 Million.

Other Navigation Equipment

> *This program provides procurement and improvements of navigation equipment to include Inertial Navigation equipment for Ballistic Missile Defense such as gyrocompasses, speed sensors, radars, Electronic Chart Display and Information System - Navy (ECDIS-N) and major components for other navigation systems. ECDIS-N provides Fleet-wide electronic charting capability, increases navigation and situational awareness, improves safety at sea, and eliminates reliance on paper charts. These systems provide mission critical navigation data to Ballistic Missile Defense, shipboard, combat, and gun and missile systems.*

The Navy's navigation equipment seems to be working just fine. Eliminate and save $24 Million.

Sub Periscope and Imaging Equipment

> *The Submarine Periscopes and Imaging Equipment Program procures the Type 18 and Type 8 periscope upgrades, Photonics Mast (PM), improved imaging capabilities incorporated in the Integrated Submarine Imaging System (ISIS), and VIRGINIA Class imaging upgrades and Photonics land based spares. Commander Naval Submarine Force (CNSF), Operations Review Group (ORG) selected the Periscope Acquisition, [...]*

The periscopes and imaging systems on our subs today seem to be working fine. Eliminate and save $54 Million.

DDG Mod

The DDG Modernization Program is required to upgrade the 28 in-service Flight I and II DDG-51 Class ships in order to keep them relevant and affordable components of the Navy's Sea Power 21 Plan. The DDG Modernization Program is composed of a series of improvements in both the HM&E and Combat Systems (CS) areas installed in two respective phases beginning with the oldest ships first. The modernization installations are planned for each ship at approximately the midlife point for each hull.

The Aegis systems seem to be working fine as is; eliminate and save $452 Million.

Firefighting Equipment

The Navy decided that a number of survivability improvements needed to be incorporated into mission-essential ship and combat systems during their acquisition and modernization. Shipboard fires have emphasized the urgent need to upgrade features and design standards that contribute to survivability.

Fires tend to cause more damage costs than prevention costs; reduce by standard 25% and save $4 Million.

Command and Control Switchboard

The switchboard program provides mission critical switching capability required to link shipboard combat equipment including weapons, launchers, sensors, computers and navigation equipment. In essence, switchboards serve as the central connection point for most elements of combat and weapon systems, interior communications, data transfer, and command and control systems. They are designed to accommodate either analog, digital interfaces, or a combination of both. In total, this budget item supports approximately 200 ships and 1,000 pieces of equipment throughout the acquisition life cycle.

The Navy's existing C&C systems seem to be working fine; eliminate and save $2 Million.

Pollution Control Equipment

This item provides funds for the procurement of pollution control systems and equipment that are required by Navy ships in order for them to comply with international regulations, federal laws, DOD Directives and Navy environmental protection regulations. These regulations, laws and directives restrict the discharge of oily waste, sewage, solid waste, plastic waste, medical waste and hazardous waste.

Protecting the environment isn't the government's responsibility. If that's really a big deal, then tell the manufacturers to produce cleaner equipment in the first place. Eliminate and save $21 Million.

Submarine Support Equipment

The Submarine Support Equipment budget provides funding for equipment technical refresh and upgrades that consists of hardware, software, system engineering, integrated logistics support, system test and evaluation, training, data, installation assistance teams and program management. This funding also procures equipment and material required to implement the military high priority Submarine Silencing Program for operating nuclear submarines. These equipment technical refreshes and upgrades are not supported by other NAVSEA program offices and support SSN/SSBN/SSGN Class Submarines and land based laboratories/facilities.

The subs seem to be working fine as is. Eliminate and save $12 Million.

Virginia Class Support Equipment

This provides a wide range of material required to operate, test, support and maintain the viability of VIRGINIA SSN774 Class ships. The "Major Shore Spares" component includes rotatable pool and insurance spares. Rotatable pool assets support planned maintenance during scheduled availabilities by decreasing equipment turn-around time/availability duration. Rotatable pool program equipment includes the high pressure air compressor, various pump/motor assemblies, radar mast, ventilation fans and Thin Line Towed Array components and other components.

Ships need to operate viably, but a lot of these upgrades are unnecessary. Reduce by half and save $40 Million.

LCS Class Support Equipment

This budget provides for the procurement of long-lead major end items required for Littoral Combat Ship (LCS) construction and repairs, for both variants of ships, while production lines are still active. Spares procurement mitigates major long-lead replacement times due to unplanned system failures and increases operability of vital fleet assets.

Ships need to operate, but a lot of these upgrades (and a few lines of ships, but I digress) are unnecessary. Reduce by half and save $10 Million.

Submarine Batteries

Procurement of Valve Regulated Lead Acid (VRLA) batteries and Shipalt installation to modify submarines from use of legacy flooded battery (no longer in production at former sole source manufacturer) to new design VRLA battery. Initial installations of VRLA battery also requires the installation of an

Automatic Battery Monitoring system (ABMS). The budget procures and installs initial VRLA batteries for 31 SSN688 Class, 3 SSN21 Class, 4 SSGN Class, 10 SSBN Class and 6 SSN774 Class Submarines.

Submarines need batteries, and the old ones can't be bought anymore. Keep as is ($42 Million).

LPD Class Support Equipment

This budget provides funding for the in service LPD 17 class program support equipment. Previous funding for LPD 17 class support equipment (FY 12 and earlier) was provided line item OPN 0981, Items Less Than $5 Million. Funding is required to upgrade mission critical electronic and HM&E systems including the Engineering Control Systems (ECS), Ship Control Systems (SCS), Degaussing Systems, Shipboard Wide-Area Network (SWAN), commercial software products for ECS, SCS, C4ISR and Administrative Communications

Ships need to operate, but a lot of these upgrades are unnecessary. Reduce by half and save $15 Million.

Strategic Platform Support Equipment

Funding in this P-1 line provides for the procurement of tactical Hull, Mechanical and Electrical (HM&E) equipment that will be installed aboard ships and in the facilities at the TRIDENT Refit Facility (TRIREFFAC), Navy Intermediate Maintenance Facility (NAVIMFAC) and TRIDENT Training Facility (TRITRAFAC). The TRIDENT Refit Facility and Navy Intermediate Maintenance Facility (NAVIMFAC) are dedicated shore support facilities providing a full range of industrial support. The TRITRAFAC provides the crews for the SSBN 726 Class Submarines with realistic training experience in operating and maintaining shipboard equipment.

Upgrades to existing drydock and related facilities. Reduce by standard 25%, saving $4 Million.

Deep Submergence Systems Project Equipment

The Advanced Undersea Systems (AUS) Program, formerly Deep Submergence Systems Program (DSSP), is responsible for the procurement, life cycle support, and improvement and modernization of assigned platforms and programs. The AUS Program provides for the procurement of equipment to support the establishment and maintenance of fleet capability for a number of programs which perform submarine search and rescue, inspection, and object location and retrieval from the ocean environment. AUS procurements replace obsolete, non-supportable equipment and subsystems through phased improvement and modernization projects.

Replaces existing equipment that can no longer be replaced, but with newer versions thereof. Keep as is ($4 Million).

CG Modernization

> Modernized CG47 Class ships will operate independently or as units of Carrier Battle Groups and Surface Action Groups, in support of the Marine Amphibious Task Forces in multi-threat environments that include air, surface and subsurface threats. These ships will respond to Low Intensity Conflict/Coastal and Littoral Offshore Warfare and joint mission scenarios as well as open ocean conflict, providing and augmenting power projection and forward presence. These ships will conduct Air Dominance, Land Attack, and Force Protection missions.

I have trouble believing that we have significant air, surface, and subsurface threats that we can't deal with already. Other than that, these already-new Aegis cruisers seem to be working fine. Eliminate and save $101 Million.

Landing Craft Air Cushion

> The LCAC (Landing Craft Air Cushion) mission is to transport weapons systems, equipment, cargo, and personnel of the assault elements for the Marine Air/Ground Task Force from ship-to-shore and across the beach. The LCAC weighs 150 tons, is 88ft long with a beam of 47ft, rides on a cushion of air contained in a flexible skirt and is propelled by two aft-mounted, reversible, variable pitch propellers. It is capable of speeds in excess of 40 knots. The LCAC sustainment funding is programmed for equipment procurement using OPN to replace selected engines, personnel transport modules and propeller shrouds that the fleet urgently requires to maintain acceptable levels of readiness.

The landing craft we have now are working fine, and are still pretty new to the Navy. Eliminate these upgrades and save $17 Million.

Underwater EOD Programs

> Underwater Explosive Ordnance Disposal (EOD): This program supports EOD Groups, Units and Detachments worldwide. This program supplies EOD forces with the necessary diving and diving related equipment to fulfill assigned missions that includes Underwater Mine Countermeasures (UMCM). All equipment must have inherently low acoustic and magnetic signatures. This program also includes the Marine Mammal Systems (MMS).

It seems pretty smart to have a way to blow up underwater explosives, but in peacetime we'll have far fewer of them to deal with. Reduce by half and save $18 Million.

Items less than $5 Million

> This budget provides for "S" cognizance (Shipboard, Hull, Mechanical & Electrical (HM&E) equipment for submarines, surface ships, and aircraft carriers) which are not in any specific category. This equipment accomplishes Program alterations for installation during CNO and Fleet availabilities, fills Fleet requisitions from casualties and attrition, provide tech refresh upgrades, and replaces obsolete equipment.

This area supports the installation of systems I've eliminated, additional parts to programs I've eliminated, and various other items which I haven't covered. Reduce by half and save $33 Million.

Chemical Warfare Detectors

> Public Law 103-160, Section 1703 created a Joint Service Chemical and Biological Defense Program (CBDP) to address ever growing threats from the aggressive proliferation of chemical and biological weapons. Joint CBDP funds the development and procurement of Chemical and Biological Defense (CBD) Equipment to enhance the warfighter's ability to survive and complete their mission in a chemical biological contaminated environment.

This program duplicates Army and TJS projects; how many different NBC research projects do we really need? Eliminate and save $4 Million.

Submarine Life Support System

> The review and approval of any production contract technical documentation, or the separate development of this documentation to include, technical manuals, Preventive Maintenance Schedule (PMS), Level III production drawings, provisioning technical documentation (PTD), Program Support Data (PSD) and Allowance Parts Lists (APL); Engineering & support for final design reviews. This work can be accomplished by NSWC PHILA as the in-service engineering agent, other Naval activities or contractors as appropriate.

Submarine life support systems seem to be working fine; we haven't heard of anyone suffocating on a submarine lately. Eliminate and save $10 Million.

Reactor Power Units

> The details of this program are classified CONFIDENTIAL and are submitted to Congress annually in the classified budget justification books.

We'll just see about that. In the meantime, reduce by half and save $143 Million.

Reactor Components

> The details of this program are classified CONFIDENTIAL and are submitted to Congress annually in the classified budget justification books.

We'll just see about that. In the meantime, reduce by half and save $139 Million.

Diving and Salvage Equipment

> This request provides funding for procurement of modern equipment to replace the Navy's archaic diving systems. The demand for divers' services for salvage, ship husbandry, repair and sanitizing work is rapidly increasing. The requested funding buys diving hardware which increases the efficiency and safety of the working diver. Program objectives are to: (1) provide increased safety for diver decompression and better recompression chamber patient monitoring capability, (2) increase underwater ship maintenance capabilities, (3) improve quick response capability, and (4) standardize the configuration of diving systems in the Fleet.

This program is almost over, so keep as is ($9 Million) for now. This funding ends in 2017.

Standard boats

> Naval Sea Systems Command (NAVSEA) -- Boats are procured to fill allowances established by CNO and NAVSEA and to replace boats now in service which are beyond economical repair at shore activities and aboard ships. Total inventory objectives change based on Fleet requirements. Strategic Systems Programs (SSP) -- Nuclear Weapon Security Manual (DoD S-5210.41M) requires armed escort of TRIDENT submarines (SSBNs) transiting on the surface near homeport. The procurement of a variety of vessels armed with specialized weapons is required to meet this DoD armed escort requirement.

We're buying boats just to buy boats? I have mixed feelings about this; cut by half and save $15 Million.

Other Ships Training Equipment

> The equipment procured under the Other Ships Training Equipment line supports Hull, Mechanical, and Electrical (HM&E) training requirements.

The Navy still has to train in peacetime. Keep as is ($30 Million).

Operating Forces IPE

> These funds are used to procure industrial plant equipment for afloat (surface combatant) activities which provide maintenance capabilities for Sailors to maintain Ship's mission essential, operational readiness while deployed. The upgraded IPE increases deployed maintenance capability and enhances strike group's ability to remain on station through Casualty Report (CASREP) avoidance. The program provides new industrial plant equipment to replace equipment beyond economical repair and to upgrade capabilities for ship maintenance and repair.

In peacetime, there will be no deployments. However, we must still be ready for them. Cut by half and save $32 Million.

Nuclear Alterations

The details of this program are classified CONFIDENTIAL and are submitted to Congress annually in the classified budget justification books.

We'll just see about that. In the meantime, cut by half ($77 Million).

LCS Common Mission Modules Equipment

Littoral Combat Ship (LCS) focused mission packages provide the operational commander with capabilities to perform littoral mine countermeasures (MCM) operations, a detect-to-engage capability to counter small boat threats, and a detect-to-engage capability to counter enemy submarines. A mission package is a combination of warfare mission modules with specialized crew, support equipment, and vehicles, including embarked manned helicopters and unmanned maritime systems.

The Navy already has mine countermeasure systems, and won't be losing any in peacetime. Eliminate and save $31 Million.

LCS MCM Mission Modules

The LCS Mine Countermeasures (MCM) mission package will counter bottom, deep, shallow, surface, near surface, and tethered mines in the littoral without putting Sailors in the minefield. When the MCM mission package is embarked, LCS is capable of conducting detect-to-engage operations (hunting, sweeping, and neutralization) against shallow and deep-water sea mine threats. The MCM mission package provides these capabilities through the use of sensors and weapons deployed from an embarked MH-60S multi-mission helicopter and unmanned off-board vehicles.

The Navy already has littoral countermine systems, and we won't be losing any in peacetime. Eliminate and save $38 Million.

LCS SUW Mission Modules

The Surface Warfare (SUW) mission package increases firepower and offensive/defensive capabilities against large numbers of highly maneuverable, fast, small craft threats, giving LCS the ability to protect the sea lanes and move a force quickly through a choke point or other strategic waterway. With the SUW mission package embarked, LCS has enhanced detection and engagement capability against enemy small craft and similar littoral surface threats.

In peacetime, there are no highly maneuverable threats. Eliminate this brand-new program and save $33 Million ($476 Million total).

LSD Midlife

This budget provides funding for the LSD Mid-life Program. The LSD Mid-life Program replaces obsolete/unsupported HM&E systems and implements Total Operating Cost (TOC) savings upgrades to maintain amphibious warfare capabilities through DECOM (2038). Primary objectives are to maintain or improve readiness, safety, reliability, lower maintenance costs, improve sailor quality of life, and/or sustain the LSD ship class through their notional service life or beyond. The budget purchases equipment including generators, Low Pressure Air Compressors (LPAC), Canned Lube Oil Pumps, A/C Plants and deck crane control systems.

We don't have to replace equipment just because it's out of warranty; the Navy has plenty of its own mechanics and technicians, and nothing is in danger of becoming unusable. Eliminate and save $50 Million.

Communications and Electronics Equipment

SPQ-9B Radar

This program provides for procurement of AN/SPQ-9B Radars whose primary mission is to detect and track low flying Anti-Ship Missile targets in heavy clutter. The mission of the AN/SPQ-9B is currently being expanded to include the capability to detect and classify periscopes with the completion and incorporation of a Periscope Detection and Discrimination (PDD) capability designed to operate concurrently with the Anti-Ship Missile Defense (ASMD) capability.

Ships won't have low-altitude missiles flying at them in peacetime, and when's the last time you heard of a missile blowing up one of our subs anyway? Eliminate and save $20 Million.

AN/SQQ-89 Surface Anti-Submarine Warfare Combat System

The 'Vision for Anti-Submarine Warfare (ASW) Superiority' provides a foundation on which to base the operational principles and force attributes needed to prevail against future adversary submarines. Fully aligned with 'A Cooperative Strategy for 21st Century Seapower', it is intended to establish a consistent sense of urgency, and guide the development of a comprehensive long-term strategy and attendant execution plans to achieve and sustain a strategic and operational advantage, and maximize the potential for tactical advantage in future operationally-relevant environments. Our nation and maritime forces face an evolving submarine threat of increasing lethality.

Having a vision of future high-tech military and cooperating with other countries are not implicitly justifications to spend more money on the military.

The AN/SQQ-89(V) Surface Ship ASW Combat System provides integrated Undersea Warfare (USW) combat management, fire control, command and control, and on-board training to enable surface combatants to engage USW targets in both open ocean and littoral environments. The AN/SQQ-89(V) is a system comprised of many subsystems, which integrate the helo and its sensors, the ship's own organic sensors, weapons, torpedo detection, and a high fidelity Surface ASW Synthetic Trainer (SAST). The AN/SQQ-89(V) was established as an Acquisition Category (ACAT) I acquisition program in 1983 and re-designated an ACAT IC program in 1990. In 1998, the AN/SQQ-89(V) program was deemed to be 90% complete and removed from the Major Defense Acquisition Program (MDAP) list.

Several of our enemies have fallen since 1983, and we have no remaining enemy superpowers. This program has upgraded some combat systems since then, but we're on top now. Eliminate and save $89 Million.

SSN Acoustics

This program procures submarine systems and equipment for installation on all classes of submarines to maintain clear acoustical, tactical, and operational superiority over submarine and surface combatants in all scenarios through detection, classification, localization, and contact following. All future acoustic upgrades of Acoustic Rapid COTS Insertion (A-RCI) equipment are incorporated into this budget item. Future procurements, detailed below, are focused on supporting Littoral Warfare, Regional Sea Denial, Strike Group Support, Diesel Submarine Detection, Surveillance, and Peacetime Engagement.

Ships don't need to be upgraded to maintain superiority; only to obtain it. We've long been militarily superior to the entire rest of the world; in fact we are stronger than every other developed nation combined. We no longer need to work at becoming the best. Eliminate and save $191 Million.

Undersea Warfare Support Equipment

Acoustic Communications provides two-way and one-way acoustic communications equipment for submarines and surface ships. The equipment consists of: (1) AN/WQC-2/2A, a stand alone, single side band, general purpose, voice, continuous wave, multiple tone communication for surface ships, submarines, and shore activities; (2) AN/WQC-6, which provides long range coded signaling from surface ASW ships to attack submarines when interfaced with the AN/SQS-53 and AN/BQQ-5; (3) AN/BQC-1, a stand-alone emergency voice and signal beacon for submarines; and (4) technical improvements (Engineering Changes (ECs)) to acoustic communication equipment.

I've generally been against duplicate communications systems, but this one has the unique property of being designed to communicate underwater. It's pretty useful for subs not to have to surface to send and receive messages; but I can't understand the justification for an ongoing program. I would expect this to be a series of products we'd by once and be done with. Reduce by half and save $9 Million.

Sonar Switches and Transducers

> *This program procures hydrophones, transducers, cables, associated Out-Board Electronics bottles (OBE), and acoustic windows for In-Service Undersea Warfare Sonars on all classes of submarines. The components are required to support units in the fleet on a replacement basis, at regularly scheduled ship overhauls, and at interim availabilities when units are defective, and for upgrades.*

The sonar systems we have now seem to be working fine, and my proposed peacetime stance will reduce our areas of responsibility. Unfortunately, this seems to be an ongoing requirement, albeit not an ongoing procurement – the program ends in 2017. Ultimately, we do need to protect our own coasts. Keep as is for now ($13 Million).

Electronic Warfare MILDEC

> *Integrated Communications and Data Systems (ICADS) is a Chief of Naval Operations (CNO) directed mission critical system which provides limited back-up, mobile communications capability for large deck naval platforms. The system provides reliable, limited solution for re-establishing command and control for high value unit, subordinate units, and controlling fleet entities. ICADS is a Rapid Deployment Capability (RDC) and is a system of systems. Specific program details held at a higher classification.*

Yet another radio system, a clear duplication of several TJS, DoD, and Army systems. The military doesn't need this many different radio systems, though this item is not procured in 2013. Procurement occurred in 2012 and resume in 2014; just keep it off the budget. Save $16K in spares for 2013 despite not being actively procured.

Submarine Acoustic Warfare System

> *The Submarine Acoustic Warfare System (SAWS) provides submarines with an enhanced capability against torpedoes and the means to reduce the acoustic and non-acoustic effectiveness of enemy sensors. This program provides ongoing production of countermeasure devices needed to sustain fleet inventories, production of preplanned improvements to enhance the readiness*

and effectiveness of countermeasure devices acoustic intercept receivers and processors, and associated countermeasure launcher systems.

This program has been going on for several years, meaning several subs have already been upgraded with it. We can just try to keep the others away from enemy subs, and it will all be moot if we avoid warfare altogether. Unfortunately, countermeasures are a standard component of any warship and needed for a fully functioning fleet. Reduce by half and save $11 Million.

Surface Ship Torpedo Defense

The Surface Ship Torpedo Defense (SSTD) program is comprised of three major projects, the AN/SLQ-55 (NIXIE) system, Torpedo Warning System (TWS), and the Countermeasure Anti-Torpedo (CAT). The CAT program does not have OPN funding. TWS does not require funding until FY2014.

Yet another torpedo defense system, SSTD has been going on for a long time and will continue for the foreseeable future. Nixie is a countermeasure system a ship actually has to tow, which just screams "battlefield liability" to me. However, the system is designed specifically to detect torpedoes, so it seems pretty useful. We have a bunch of these already procured, and don't need them all the time; we can probably leave them somewhere in peacetime. Eliminate new procurement and save $11 Million.

Fixed Surveillance System

Additional details with respect to this line item are held at a higher classification. This line item is reported in accordance with Title 10, United States Code, Section 119(a)(1) in the Special Access Program Annual Report to Congress.

FSS is designed to survey undersea areas for enemy ships and the like. It appears to be a sea-deployable system designed to watch a static area, which seems useful for protecting our shores. Keep as is ($99 Million).

Surveillance Towed Array Sensor System (SURTASS)

[SURTASS] is the mobile, tactical and strategic arm of the Navy's undersea surveillance capability that provides deep ocean and littoral acoustic detection and cueing for tactical weapon platforms against diesel and nuclear submarines as well as surface vessels in any given Area of Operations worldwide. Dedicated ASW T-AGOS ships tow long acoustic arrays that collect acoustic data and relay that data to shore facilities via SHF satellites for processing and fusion of the resulting contact data with other sensors. Currently, there are five T-AGOS ships operating in the Pacific area.

Patrolling our shores is a critical part of national defense; keep as is ($3 Million).

Maritime Patrol and Reconnaissance Force

> Maritime Patrol & Reconnaissance Force (MPRF) Mission Support Systems: MPRF Mission Support Systems provide the MPRF commanders with the capability to plan, direct, control and evaluate the tactical operations of MPRF and other assigned units within their respective area of responsibility. These operations include littoral, open ocean, and over land all sensor (e.g., Electro Optical (EO), Infrared (IR), Inverse Synthetic-Aperture Radar (ISAR)) surveillance, anti-surface warfare, over-the-horizon targeting, counter-drug operations, power projection, antisubmarine warfare, mining, search and rescue, homeland defense, and special operations.

We already had a force to patrol and recon these areas; we call it the Coast Guard. Their job is, quite literally, to guard the coast. In peacetime, this would be supplemented by whatever Navy ships aren't in drydock; Navy ships already have these capabilities. Eliminate and save $18 Million.

AN/SLQ-32

> The AN/SLQ-32(V) provides a family of modular shipborne electronic warfare equipment which is installed on all surface combatants, aircraft carriers, amphibious ships and auxiliaries in the surface Navy. The system consists of eight configurations and provides early detection, analysis, threat warning and protection from anti-ship missiles.

This is a set of improvements to already-proven systems, which are working fine. Eliminate and save $92 Million.

Shipboard IW Exploit

> CDLS provides network interface capability, wideband encryption, and command link upgrades to the Common High Bandwidth Data Link-Shipboard Terminal (CHBDL-ST) baseline system. CDLS provides a wideband data link between Navy/Joint airborne sensor systems and the shipboard processors of national and tactical reconnaissance programs. It is designed to communicate with the Signals Intelligence Mission and the Distributed Common Ground Station.

That's darned expensive for just being a link between two systems. Also includes funding for other programs I have reduced or eliminated in this proposal. Reduce by half and save $53 Million.

Automatic Identificaton System (AIS)

> Automatic Identification System (AIS) is an international maritime Very High Frequency (VHF) communication system that allows ships to exchange information (machine to machine) on navigation (position, course, speed, etc), ship information (ship name, call sign, length/beam), cargo information (draft, type, destination, route, estimated time of arrival), and messaging (safety, text).

We used to be able to handle all this with radios; I don't understand why we spend so much money on completely unnecessary things. Eliminate and save $91 Million.

Submarine Support Equipment Program (SSEP)

> [SSEP] was established to develop and support systems which provide the capability to exploit signal intercepts for tactical support and early warning of threat sensors. The Electronic Warfare Support (ES) Operational Requirements Document (ORD) Serial. No. 570-77-00 dated 20 Dec. 2000, established funding to procure AN/BLQ-10(V) Electronic Warfare Support and Improved Communication Acquisition/Direction Finding (ICADF) systems to provide a modern ES capability to LOS ANGELES, SEAWOLF, and SSGN Class submarines.

Cooperative Engagement Capability

> Cooperative Engagement Capability (CEC) significantly improves Battle Force Anti-Air Warfare (AAW) capability by coordinating all Battle Force AAW sensors into a single, real-time, composite track picture capable of fire control quality. CEC distributes sensor data from each ship and aircraft, or cooperating unit (CU), to all other CUs in the battle force through a realtime, line of sight, high data rate sensor and engagement data distribution network.

Seems to me our anti-air warfare is very effective as is; as if we had any enemies with an air force. In peacetime, this will be even less important; eliminate and save $28 Million.

Trusted Information System

> Trusted Information System (TIS) Radiant Mercury (RM) system provides the core on-line, automated guarding, sanitization, and transliteration services that provides the United State Navy (USN)'s primary command and control systems with the capability to move data between multiple security domains. RM is a critical component in the Navy's Automated Identification System Global Command Control Systems-Maritime (GCCS-M), and Maritime Operation Center (MOC) and Distributed Common Ground System-Navy (DCGS-N) architectures providing the capability to move data between security domains in order to maintain Maritime Domain Awareness.

Things don't need to be expensive to be secure. Secure networks can be interconnected via VPN for four digits, and if you're already inside such a secure network, you can just copy the files or data across with the built-in operating system. Eliminate and save $448K.

Naval Tactical Command Support System

The Naval Tactical Command Support System (NTCSS) is a multi-function program designed to provide standard tactical support information systems to various afloat and associated shore-based fleet activities. The mission is to provide the full range of responsive tactical support Automated Data Processing (ADP) hardware and software in support of the management of information, personnel, material and funds required to maintain and operate ships, submarines, and aircraft. management requirements for force sustainment.

We shouldn't buy computer programs that have ongoing eight-digit costs every year; if support is really that involved, then we should build it ourselves (DoD-internal). Providing tactical information over an already existing network couldn't possibly cost as much as we've put into this thing. Eliminate and save $36 Million ($772 Million total).

Advanced Tactical Data Link System (ATDLS)

funds the Time Division Multiple Access family of Link 16 terminals including the Multifunctional Information Distribution System - Low Volume Terminal, Joint Tactical Information Distribution System (JTIDS) and the Tactical Digital Information Link - Joint (TADIL-J) message standard databases resident in the Command & Control Processor (C2P)/ Common Data Link Management System (CDLMS).

This program ran for several years, and continues indefinitely; but oddly, it skips FY 2013 altogether. It runs what is basically a 2G cell phone network. The Navy seems to be doing fine as is, and if we don't have to spend anything on it in 2013, I don't see why that can't continue. Eliminate and save recurring costs.

Navy Command and Control System

Funding includes Global Command and Control System- Maritime (GCCS-M), the Navy fielded portions of GCCS-Joint, and Theater Battle Management Core System (TBMCS). GCCS-M is further delineated by Afloat and Ashore.

Upgrades and modifications to systems that are already in place and working. Eliminate and save $10 Million.

Minesweeping System Replacement

> *Provide systems, subsystems, and engineering change kits for minehunting, navigation, and tactical display operations by the surface Mine Countermeasure (MCM) force. Engineering change kits improve reliability and maintainability and correct deficiencies to allow equipment to perform in accordance with operational requirements.*

I can't find any instances of a ship hitting a mine since 1988 in the Persian Gulf; which never would have happened if we had minded our own business and stayed in our hemisphere. Rather, we should be deploying mines at our own perimeters (trade lanes excepted). Therefore, our existing minesweeping systems seem to be working fine. Eliminate and save $60 Million.

Shallow Water Mine CM Ship

> *This program provides a combination of US Navy projects planned to counter the threat to amphibious landing forces from known and projected foreign land/sea mines, obstacles in the beach zone and surf zone approaches to amphibious assault areas.*

I can't find any instances of a ship hitting a mine since 1988 in the Persian Gulf, so our existing minesweeping systems seem to be working fine. Eliminate and save $7 Million.

NAVSTAR GPS Receivers

> *NAVSTAR Global Positioning System (NAVSTAR GPS) provides assured and protected navigation solutions to war fighters through supported, affordable, and integrated systems, and is the primary source of positioning, navigation and timing information for the DoD.*

For a procurement that equips ships, I would expect this program to end when all required ships are equipped. This program, however, continues indefinitely. A GPS is a one-time purchase, and a system to monitor all those GPS devices goes for a few grand a month, tops. Eliminate and save $9 Million.

Armed Forces Radio and TV Service

> *American Forces Radio and Television Service (AFRTS) Program - AFRTS shipboard systems provide Command Information to deployed Sailors and Marines, and allow for the distribution of AFRTS programming in order to provide situational awareness for forward deployed commanders with real-time news and information. The systems also provide programming to Sailors and Marines at sea worldwide as a Navy Quality of Life (QOL) initiative, staying in compliance with the Chief of Naval (CNO) Shipboard Habitability Program.*

AFN is an important aspect of transparency; but in order to say so, we should open the network up to the whole country. Maybe that way, the news channels can even subsidize it instead of the other way around. Keep as is ($8 Million).

Strategic Platform Support Equipment

> The OBSOLETE EQUIPMENT REPLACEMENT (OER) Program is the replacement of existing hardware/software that, though functional, has become operationally obsolete, is no longer in production or supportable with spare parts, or has a high failure rate making them no longer cost effective to maintain. OER hardware/software changes are expected to provide significant cost savings via reduced maintenance costs and use Commercial-Off-The-Shelf (COTS) technology wherever possible as long as all technical requirements are met.

This program specifically replaces equipment that's working just fine. Eliminate and save $4 Million.

Other Training Equipment

> Other Training Equipment line supports various types of Communication and Electronic training requirements

Training is of paramount importance, even in peacetime. Keep as is ($43 Million).

METCALS

> Marine Air Traffic Control and Landing Systems (MATCALS) is a fully automated all-weather expeditionary terminal Air Traffic Control (ATC) System that provides arrival/departure and enroute surveillance control, automated precision approach and landing control or Ground Controlled Approach, Tactical Air Navigation (TACAN), and other ATC services.

This duplicates other Navy ATC systems, and there's no reason why the Marines shouldn't use the same systems as the Navy. Eliminate and save $6 Million.

Shipboard Air Traffic Control

> Shipboard Air Traffic Control (SATC) systems are responsible for safe and expeditious control of air traffic within 50 Nautical Miles of a ship. SATC systems include the air traffic surveillance radar, AN/SPN-43, and the air traffic central tracking and control system, AN/TPX-42, which has two major configurations: Carrier Air Traffic Control Center-Direct Altitude and Identity Readout (CATCC-DAIR) and Amphibious Air Traffic Control Center-Direct Altitude and Identity Readout (AATCC-DAIR).

Controlling air traffic near a ship can be a pretty big deal, but I can't imagine why it would have ongoing recurring costs. Reduce by standard 25% and save $2 Million.

Automatic Carrier Landing System (ACLS)

> *Provides the primary precision electronic guidance for landing aircraft under all weather conditions on CVNs, LHAs, LHDs and selected Naval Air Stations. Many of the components in the system have been in service for more than twenty years. This program funds maintainability, reliability and supportability improvements to existing equipment components that can no longer be maintained and supported, as well as items providing upgraded operational capability*

Being able to land on a carrier is a pretty big deal, but when did our pilots forget how to do so without all the computers? Reduce by standard 25% and save $4 Million.

National Air Space System

> *The Joint Department of Defense (DOD)/Federal Aviation Administration (FAA) National Airspace System (NAS) Modernization (MOD) program upgrades the DOD Air Traffic Control (ATC) systems at Approach Control Facilities in concert with the FAA's upgrade of the National ATC System. Since existing DOD ATC facilities interface with the FAA's facilities, the military must maintain interoperability and retain vital special-use airspace for combat readiness training. These funds will procure ATC systems for the Navy/Marine ATC facilities.*

The DoD has *yet another* ATC system? No, we shouldn't modernize any of them until we're ready to replace them with a single, defense-wide system. Eliminate and save $17 Million. Eliminate the FAA and just call the airports up on the radio. I'm sure they'll want to come up with a system of their own, given the risk of not coordinating air traffic.

Fleet Air Traffic Control Systems

> *The Chief of Naval Operations (CNO) tasked the Naval Air Systems Command (NAVAIR) with the requirement to provide shore based Air Traffic Control (ATC) terminal facilities and equipment that are required in joint efforts to efficiently and safely monitor and direct military and commercial air traffic in national and international air space.*

How many different ATC systems could the DoD possibly need? Eliminate and save $7 Million.

Landing Systems

> The Chief of Naval Operations (CNO) tasked Naval Air Systems Command (NAVAIR) with the requirement to provide shore based Air Traffic Control (ATC) terminal facilities and equipment that are required to efficiently and safely monitor and direct military and commercial air traffic in national and international air space. Many of these systems are required to interface through automated means with the Federal Avaiation Administration (FAA).

How many different ATC systems could the DoD possibly need? Eliminate and save $8 Million.

ID Systems

> The Identification Systems program funds procurements, installations, and certifications for the following systems: AN/UPX-37 Digital Interrogator (DI), AN/APX-118 Common Digital Transponder (CXP), AN/ UPX-29(V) Interrogator System, Mark XIIA Mode 5 and Identification Friend Foe (IFF) support equipment.

> The Air Traffic Control (ATC) Radio Beacon System, IFF, Mark XII System (AIMS) is a DOD directed tri-service program designed to provide a universal air traffic control radar beacon system compatible with the National Airspace System Program. It provides a secure identification system for military use on all combatant ships, selected auxiliaries, patrol craft, and selected Coast Guard ships by allowing all friendly forces to identify each other and neutral forces.

Instead of developing just a universal beacon system, we should have a universal Air Traffic Control system. All that really means is radars and a commonly agreed upon set of radio frequencies; it couldn't be that complicated. The Navy already has systems that fulfill these functions; this line item merely replaces some of the older ones.

IFF is really not that complicated. When the IFF antennae are turned on, just send a public key encrypted signal and use private keys to decrypt them like many currently-available and completely free systems do over the Internet.

None of this is critical. Eliminate and save $35 Million.

Naval Mission Planning Systems

> This line item provides funding to procure Joint Mission Planning System (JMPS) workstations, Software/Production Engineering Support and Integrated Logistics Support (ILS). JMPS is the Chief of Naval Operation's (CNO) designated automated mission planning system for the Navy. JMPS enables weapon system employment by providing the information and decision aids needed to rapidly plan aircraft, weapon or sensor missions, load mission data

into aircraft and weapons, and conduct post mission analysis. JMPS consists of two types of workstations - Maritime (JMPS-M) and Expeditionary (JMPS-E). JMPS-M is the primary product within the Naval Mission Planning System (NavMPS). failure rates, emerging technology and increased memory requirements.

Mission planning can be done in a joint fashion with a videoconference and a shared online whiteboard, which can be had at prices that most individuals can afford. Even the equipment is cheap; all you really need is a computer made within the past 5-10 years. Logistics support can be added in via a wiki, which is completely free; or just send an email. Even a custom-written piece of software that does all these things could be developed for five or six digits. Eliminate and save $10 Million.

Deployable Joint Command and Control (DJC2)

Deployable Joint Command and Control (DJC2) is a Secretary of Defense (SECDEF) and Chairman, Joint Chiefs of Staff (CJCS) priority Department of Defense transformation initiative that is providing a standardized, integrated, rapidly deployable, modular, scalable, and reconfigurable joint command and control (C2) capability to designated Geographic Combatant Commands (GCCs). DJC2 is the material solution to Defense Planning Guidance that called for the development of Standing Joint Task Forces (JTFs) with a deployable C2 capability. DJC2 will ensure that Joint Force Commanders (JFC) are equipped, as well as trained and organized, to carry out their C2 responsibilities.

That can be accomplished with a computer and a satellite modem, or even just a mobile radio. Eliminate and save $9 Million.

Maritime Integrated Broadcast System

Project charter is to deliver Integrated Broadcast Service (IBS) data to operational and tactical decision makers aboard United States Navy surface ships, shore headquarters, and other joint platforms. It disseminates organic and non-organic derived data from Navy platforms to other theater tactical, operational, and strategic users.

We have the Internet now, which is specifically designed – by the DoD no less – to deliver information to anywhere in the world. Eliminate and save $16 Million.

Tactical / Mobile C4I Systems

The TacMobile program provides evolutionary C4I capabilities and ancillary equipment upgrades to support the unified, fleet, and Navy component commanders, the maritime patrol and reconnaissance, theater, and the naval liaison element commanders (ashore) with the capability to plan, direct and control the tactical operations of joint and naval expeditionary forces and other assigned units within their respective area of responsibility.

The command, control, communications, computers, and intelligence systems the Navy has today seem to be doing a pretty good job. Eliminate and save $15 Million.

Distributed Common Ground System – Navy

The Distributed Common Ground System - Navy (DCGS-N) is the Navy's portion of the Under Secretary of Defense, Intelligence (USD (I)) DCGS-N Family of Systems (FoS). The Department of Defense (DoD) has defined a DCGS architecture that will be verifiably compatible and interoperable across all of the Services' Intelligence, Surveillance and Reconnaissance (ISR) systems and operations.

This can be done with a wiki for free. Eliminate and save $12 Million.

CANES

Consolidated Afloat Networks & Enterprise Services (CANES) is a Department of Navy (DoN) Efficiency Initiative and is the Navy's only Program of Record to replace existing afloat networks and provide the necessary infrastructure for applications, systems, and services to operate in the tactical domain. CANES is the technical and infrastructure consolidation of existing, separately managed afloat networks currently under PE 0204163N (LI 3050) Ship Communications Automation[.]

This is one of the most expensive money savers I've ever seen. All of these parts can be accomplished either for free or dirt cheap using preexisting technologies; eliminate and save $342 Million.

RADIAC

The Radiation Detection, Indication and Computation (RADIAC) Program is responsible for providing radiation monitoring instruments that detect and measure ionizing radiation. These instruments are used on all Navy, Coast Guard and Military Sealift Command vessels, and at every Navy shore installation, in order to ensure the safety of personnel, continuity of operations in radiological or nuclear contingencies, and protection of the environment.

This sounds important, especially on nuclear ships, but how expensive could it possibly be to install a Geiger counter and wire up the speaker circuit to an indicator light at CNC? Find a cheaper option and reduce by standard 25%, saving $2 Million.

CANES Install

CANES is the technical and infrastructure consolidation of existing, separately managed afloat networks currently under PE 0204163N (LI 3050) Ship Communications Automation, including Integrated Shipboard Network Systems (ISNS), Combined Enterprise Regional Information Exchange System - Maritime, Sensitive Compartmented Information (SCI) Networks, and Submarine Local Area Network.

If we eliminate the CANES program, then we can eliminate the installation segment; save $79 Million.

General Purpose Electronic Test Equipment

This program provides for the initial procurement and distribution of General Purpose Electronic Test Equipment (GPETE). This equipment is essential to the operational readiness of the Navy for repair, installation, and maintenance (preventive and routine) of electronic systems and equipments, both afloat and ashore.

Multimeters and the like are an important part of keeping the electronics working; but my peacetime proposal would reduce wear and tear, thus reducing needed maintenance. Reduce by standard 25% and save $2 Million.

Integrated Combat System Test Facility

This program supports various Navy Integrated Combat System Test Facility (ICSTF) sites as required to support the conduct of integration and interoperability testing. Sites include, but are not limited to: Naval Surface Warfare Center (NSWC) Dahlgren, Surface Combat System Center (SCSC) Wallops Island, and NSWC Dam Neck.

Given that I'm eliminating most newfangled combat systems, there is a reduced need to test them. Reduce by half and save $2 Million.

EMI Control Instrumentation

The EMI Control Instrumentation Program provides Cradle to Grave Systems Engineering for Mission Assurance by implementing Electromagnetic Compatibility (EMC) hardware solutions and Spectrum Management (SM) software solutions. This ensures equipment, systems, and ships meet their Operational Mission Requirements and goals within their intended operational EM environment. This Program provides EMI (Hardware and Software) fixes to correct mission degrading EMI problems on deploying ships and submarines, thereby restoring combat capability and Fleet Readiness.

This sounds like it's treating a symptom; the root problem is buying electromagnetically incompatible systems. Eliminate and save $5 Million.

Items less than $5 Million

A bunch of "cheap" items. Given the rate at which I've been proposing cuts, we could probably cut 75% from here, but just to be safe, let's call it half. $41 Million saved.

Shipboard Tactical Communications

> *Digital Modular Radio (DMR) - DN105: The DMR is a 2 MHz to 2 GHz software defined radio that provides Satellite Communications, Line of Sight (LOS) and High Frequency (HF) communication capability to surface, submarine, and shore facilities.*

What's wrong with the radios the Navy has now? This new line item started in FY2012, requests no funding in FY2013, but continues on indefinitely resuming next year. Eliminate and save ongoing costs.

Ship Communications Automation

> *With the evolution of afloat networks programs migrating into the Consolidated Afloat Networks and Enterprise Services (CANES) program, the Ship Communications Automation budget line will provide even more comprehensive capabilities across the fleet. While the networks capabilities of the Integrated Shipboard Network Systems (ISNS), Combined Enterprise Regional Information Exchange System - Maritime (CENTRIXS-M), Submarine Local Area Network (SubLAN), Automated Digital Network System (ADNS), and their associated personal computer hardware and software continue to be supported, CANES will reduce the infrastructure footprint and collapse a significant amount of afloat networks through the use of mature cross domain technologies.*

Given that I eliminated the CANES program, we can eliminate the peripheral programs that come with it; $57 Million saved.

Maritime Domain Awareness (MDA)

> *The CENTRIXS program provides US Navy ships with secure, reliable, high-speed Local Area Network with access to the Coalition Wide Area Network (WAN) to include CENTRIXS Four-Eyes, Global Counter Terrorism Task Force, NATO Information Data Transfer System, Multinational Coalition Force - Iraq, bilateral networks such as Combined Enterprise Regional Information Exchange System - US/Japan and Combined Enterprise Regional Information Exchange System - US/ Korea, and Communities Of Interest virtual networks such as Coalition Naval Forces - CENTCOM and Cooperative Maritime Forces - Pacific.*

This is all either already done or available for cheap or free. This program ends this year anyway, so eliminate and save a million bucks.

Communications Items Under $5 Million

A bunch of "cheap" items. Given the rate at which I've been proposing cuts, we could probably cut 75% from here, but just to be safe, let's call it half. $14 Million saved.

Submarine Broadcast System

> The Submarine Broadcast Support program was established to improve the reliability, availability, maintainability, efficiency and performance of the Very Low Frequency (VLF) and Low Frequency (LF) submarine broadcast systems. These transmission mediums, VLF/LF, comprise the primary line of Fleet Ballistic Missile Nuclear Command, Control and Communications (NC3). Shore based transmitter sites are Emergency Action Message relay points providing primary connectivity between the Senior Leadership and Ship Submersible Ballistic Nuclear Submarines (SSBN). Upgrades to shore infrastructure include integrating Internet Protocol capability in Broadcast Control Authorities.

The submarine communications we have now seem to be doing the job. Eliminate and save $4 Million.

Submarine Communication Equipment

> The Submarine Communications Program mission is to create a common, automated, open system architecture radio room for all submarine classes. The program provides for the procurement and installation of systems incorporating the technical advances of network centric warfare to allow the submarine force to communicate as part of the Battle Group. The program addresses the unique demands of submarine communications, obsolescence issues and higher data rate requirements.

We shouldn't be developing a universal communications system just for the submarines; we should be developing one for the entire DoD. Eliminate and save $69 Million.

Satellite Communications Systems

> The Satellite Communications (SATCOM) Systems P-1 line provides funds for procurement of shipboard terminal equipment for ship-to-ship, ship-to-shore and ship-to-aircraft tactical communications via earth orbiting relay satellites in the Ultra High Frequency (UHF), Super High Frequency (SHF), and Extremely High Frequency (EHF) bands.

As if we didn't already have satellite radio systems. Eliminate and save $49 Million.

Navy Multiband Terminal (NMT)

Procurement of ship, submarine, and shore protected and wideband Military Satellite Communications (MILSATCOM) terminals via earth orbiting relay satellites in the SHF, Ka, and EHF bands. NMT provides warfighters with the assured, jam resistant, secure SATCOM for message traffic, data transfer and secure voice communications. These procurements are scheduled to meet the satellite communications requirements established by the Chief of Naval Operations in the Fleet Communications Planning and Programming documents.

As if we didn't already have secure satellite radio systems. Eliminate and save $185 Million.

JCS Communications Equipment

This line funds the Department of the Navy's portion of the Joint Communications Support Element Program. This program is jointly funded by Army, Navy, Marine Corps and Air Force in support of Joint Tactical Force and Joint Special Operations Task Force Headquarters.

Satellite radio systems, line of sight transmission systems, and computers to control it all. We already have systems that do all this; eliminate and save $2 Million.

Electrical Power Systems

Procure, install, replace generators and UPS systems. The Electrical Power Program is designed to provide highly reliable, continuous, high quality power subsystems to support Navy Cyber Forces. Basic deficiencies in current power sources, coupled with recent telecommunication system trends toward sophisticated, highly reliable, high speed, continuous accurate systems (e.g., various High Frequency, Low Frequency, Very Low Frequency Facilities), necessitate a continuing program to upgrade power systems.

This is important to keep shipboard and base electrical systems operational during a blackout, which would be fairly likely if we were attacked. Keep as is ($1 Million).

Information Systems Security Program (ISSP)

Information Systems Security Program (ISSP) ensures the protection of Navy and joint cyberspace systems from exploitation and attack. Cyberspace systems include wired and wireless telecommunications systems, information technology (IT) systems, and the content processed, stored, or transmitted therein. ISSP includes protection of the Navy's National Security Systems (NSS).

Quality computer spyware and virus protection is available for free. What they can't do can be done by a qualified IT / network technician or electronic warfare officer. Eliminate and save $144 Million.

Cryptologic Communications Equipment

> Cryptologic Carry-On Equipment: The Cryptologic Carry-On Program (CCOP) procures state-of-the-art, commercial off-the-shelf signal acquisition equipment (hardware and software) in response to combatant commander requirements for a quick-reaction surface, subsurface, and airborne cryptologic carry-on capability. The equipment is procured according to the overall requirements detailed in the Shipboard Information Warfare/Cryptologic System Operational Requirements Document (Serial Number: 537-06-99) of 9 Dec 99 and specific execution year fleet requirements as defined by the Signals Of Interest (SOI) Integrated Product Team (IPT).

While this is important, the Navy has been using encrypted communications for decades. I have difficulty believing this is anything new, let alone has any ongoing costs. Eliminate and save $13 Million.

Coast Guard Equipment

> The Coast Guard Equipment line funds the Coast Guard Combat System Suite for USCG cutters under the Coast Guard Surface Asset Acquisition Program. Under inter-service agreement(delineated in OPNAVINST 4000.79B), DON plans, programs, and budgets for specific Navy military equipment, systems and logistic support requirements for Coast Guard units to ensure the Coast Guard is prepared to execute naval warfare tasks in consonance with US Navy units. Ship construction and installation costs are funded under the Department of Homeland Security appropriation.

Coastal defense and patrol is more important than ever (in recent history, anyway). Keep as is ($7 Million).

Civil Engineering Support Equipment

It's eerie how many of these programs started in 2011.

Passenger Carrying Vehicles

> This P-1 line is for passenger-carrying vehicles consisting of buses, automobiles, ambulances, and various utility and carryall trucks up to 9200 lbs. Gross Vehicle Weight Rating (GVWR). These vehicles are utilized by Naval operating forces and shore activities for essential transportation of personnel in the execution of official Navy business. Beginning in FY 2010 funding in this line supports the Joint POW/MIA Accounting Command (JPAC).

I have serious difficulty believing that the Navy couldn't sufficiently carry their passengers around prior to this program's inception in 2011. Eliminate and save $11 Million.

General Purpose Trucks

This P-1 line item is for various sizes of utility and cargo trucks of commercial design. Cargo pickup trucks are used to transport personnel and equipment in support of fleet operations where such mobility is necessary to support the mission.

I have serious difficulty believing that the Navy couldn't sufficiently move their cargo around prior to this program's inception in 2011. Eliminate and save $4 Million.

Construction and Maintenance Equipment

This P-1 line is for equipment used for a variety of construction, maintenance, and repair operations. This equipment is used by the Naval Expeditionary Combat Command, Naval Beach Group, Maritime Prepositioning Force, and other Special Operating Units, in support of advance bases and camp sites.

I have serious difficulty believing that the Navy couldn't sufficiently construct and maintain things prior to this program's inception in 2011. Eliminate and save $11 Million.

Firefighting Equipment

This P-1 line is for aircraft fire/rescue trucks and structural/brush fire trucks. The aircraft fire/rescue trucks are used at Naval Air Stations for combating aircraft fires and rescue of aircraft crews. The trucks range in size from a small 11,000 pound Gross Vehicle Weight Rating (GVWR) pickup with utility body and twin engine fire fighting unit to the 68,000 pound GVWR crash truck which carries 3,000 gallons of water and 200 gallons of AFFF (foam). The structural/brush fire trucks are used at Naval activities in the same manner as municipal fire trucks in fighting structural and grass fires.

I have serious difficulty believing that the Navy couldn't sufficiently fight fires prior to this program's inception in 2011. Eliminating a procurement doesn't eliminate the equipment the Navy already has. Eliminate and save $18 Million.

Tactical Vehicles

This P-1 line is for light and medium duty tactical equipment used primarily by the Naval Expeditionary Combat Command (NECC), Maritime Prepositioning Force (MPF), Naval Beach Group (NBG), and other special operating units. This line also includes Force Protection requirements for Tactical Vehicles.

The Navy's preexisting tactical vehicles seem to be working just fine; eliminate and save $29 Million.

Amphibious Equipment

> *This P-1 line provides equipment which significantly enhances the Navy's capability to support Marine Corps amphibious and Logistics Over the Shore (LOTS) operations through ship-to-shore transfer of both dry and liquid cargo. This program is a key part of the Strategic Sealift Program.*

I have serious difficulty believing that the Navy couldn't sufficiently take stuff off boats prior to this program's inception in 2011. Eliminate and save $11 Million.

Pollution Control Equipment

> *This P-1 line supports the Navy Ashore Pollution Control Equipment program. Funding requirements for the Navy's oil spill program include procurements of oil spill containment boom and related deployment equipment.*

The Navy is responsible for protecting our shores, and to a lesser extent, trade lanes; they are not responsible for protecting the environment. If the media are doing their job, oil companies will clean up their own messes to prevent the inevitable PR disaster. Eliminate and save $7 Million.

Items under $5 Million

> *This program includes special purpose vehicles and trailers of commercial design which support the Naval Expeditionary Combat Command (NECC), shore activities, and other special operating units. Included are tank trucks used to transport fuel to construction equipment at remote locations, waste disposal trucks used to transport waste oil/water, overhead maintenance trucks with insulated buckets and pole and line trucks used for repair/replacement of power systems, wreckers used in vehicle recovery/towing, field servicing vehicles used for on-site preventive maintenance of construction equipment in the field, and ammunition handling trucks used in loading/unloading and transporting munitions. Truck tractors and trailers required by the active operating forces in the logistics support of the fleet are also included in this program. Representative types and uses include van and stake bed semi-trailers to support loading/unloading of ships and aircraft and movement of materials and equipment for fleet operations, lowbed semitrailers for transport of construction equipment, tank trailers for transport and dispensing of water, fuel, and hazardous liquids, and semi-trailers transport of materials.*

Given the drastic cuts I've made to the budget, it stands to reason similar cuts can be made at the more minute levels. Reduced shore activities and operations, the complete elimination of war, and a much leaner Navy mean less overhead associated therewith. Cut by half and save $8 Million.

Physical Security Vehicles

The Physical Security Vehicle line includes armored sedans and armored cargo/utility trucks assigned to Antiterrorism (AT), Counterintelligence (CI), and Counternarcotics (CN) missions in high threat OCONUS locations. Sedans and cargo/utility trucks are armored to various levels of protection and are on platforms of varying sizes and gross vehicle weights, dependent upon the level of threat and the operating environment. These vehicles are generically referred to as either Commercial Heavy Armored Vehicles (CHAVs) or Commercial Light Armored Vehicles (CLAVs).

The Navy can continue using last year's sedans and trucks, in addition to all of the overseas locations being closed whose vehicles would be moved. Eliminate and save $1 Million.

Supply Support Equipment

Materials Handling Equipment

The MHE program funds the procurement of Material Handling Equipment to satisfy operational requirements and replaces overaged non-repairable equipment used in material handling operations at worldwide Navy activities. Major using activities include ships, naval magazines, air stations, weapon stations, and overseas support activities such as Sigonella and Sasebo.

Equipment must be kept in working order, but there would be less need for it. Reduce by standard 25% and save $4 Million.

Other Supply Support Equipment

NAVY CASH PROGRAM - This program funds the procurement of the Navy CashTM system. Navy CashTM is a teaming effort between the Naval Supply Systems Command (NAVSUP), U.S. Department of the Treasury (Treas, FMS), Industry, and the Fleet to replace the existing ATMs-at-Sea Program. The program is essential to the Navy's Direct Deposit System. Navy Cash improves the Quality of Life for Sailors and Marines on board ship by providing improved access to their financial accounts ashore and better service shipboard. Navy Cash improves shipboard business practices by reducing the collecting, counting, recounting, sorting, moving, and monitoring of paper currency and coins for retail location, disbursing office, and other functions that collect funds. By providing a form of electronic banking, Navy Cash provides fundamental support for other key initiatives in the Disbursing Office, Ship's Store, and Post Office and addresses optimal manning issues for retail and

> *services operations on future ship classes. This program is a direct improvement of fleet support.*

Funny how a system designed to save money costs seven figures. Under my peacetime plan, there would be fewer ships at sea; thus fewer sailors at sea at any given time. Reduce by standard 25% and save $2 Million.

First Destination Transportation

> *This program funds the procurement of First Destination Transportation services providing for the movement of newly procured equipment from the contractor's plant to the initial point of receipt by the government. Major using activities include ships, systems commands, and overseas support activities.*

By eliminating our worldwide posture, we can significantly reduce the logistics overhead associated therewith. Just put the stuff and the people on a truck, a plane, or *gasp* a ship! Reduce the frequency with which people and equipment are shifted around, which seems to have no particular purpose other than to keep them rotated. Reduce procurements significantly. Reduce by 90% and save $6 Million.

Special Purpose Supply Systems

> *Funding reported in this line item is classified and is reported in accordance with Title 10, United States Code, Section 119(a)(1) in the Special Access Program Annual Report to Congress.*

We'll just see about that. Reduce by half in the meantime and save $17 Million.

Personnel and Command Support Equipment

Training Support Equipment

A series of 16 programs which have their own descriptions, all under one funding umbrella with no overall description in the budget. Given our peacetime stance, the entire Navy will be either on patrol or training at any given time, so training is more important than ever. Keep as is ($23 Million).

Command Support Equipment

> *Enterprise Networks Command and Control, Communications, and Computer (C4) Systems Directorate (J6) implements and manages global communications and computer networks for USJFCOM and its components; ensures reliability of Command, and Control, Communications, Computer (C4) Systems and protects and defends these systems.*

The Navy's computer networks are fine the way they are today; they don't need yet another duplicate attempt to plug things into each other in ways they were probably never meant to. Ongoing maintenance doesn't require new procurements, other than a three or four digit item here or there. Such items can be accounted for and presented in the next budget request; let's be realistic here. **One new server for Human Resources does not cost $900,000;** a brand-new top of the line server is about a hundred times cheaper. Eliminate and save $43 Million.

Education Support Equipment

> The U. S. Naval Academy's mission is to ensure the best educated and most qualified junior officers enter the naval service. The Academy must maintain the highest standards in academic disciplines and supporting infrastructure. Planned upgrades and replacements are vital in ensuring graduates are technologically prepared to serve in tomorrow's Fleet and Fleet Marine Force while supporting institutional accreditation and competitiveness with peer institutions.

Training is important, as I have more than established here already. However, I'm eliminating a lot of the "tomorrow's fleet" ideas, so reduce by standard 25% and save $563K.

Medical Support Equipment

> This line item provides funding for the Medical Support Equipment program in support of new medical capability and new technology on naval operating ships. Requirements are determined through Commander, U.S. Fleet Forces Command and Commander, U.S. Pacific Fleet, and procurement is managed by Naval Medical Logistics Command (NMLC). Funding is used to procure changes or additions to the ships' allowance items that are identified within the Authorized Medical Allowance List (AMAL) and Authorized Dental Allowance List (ADAL). AMALs and ADALs are unique to specific classes or types of ship or Command to fulfill its intended health care mission. AMAL and ADAL allowances are approved by the respective Fleet Type Commander (TYCOM) Force Surgeon with concurrence by the Commander, Fleet Forces Command Surgeon. Medical Support Equipment configuration management, spares, technical manuals and installations are also funded through this line item.

Sailors need to be medically taken care of, but there will be fewer healthcare-required situations in peacetime. Cut by standard 25% and save $1 Million.

Naval MIP Support Equipment

> This effort is to procure, install and configure critical Maritime Intelligence applications to include servers and remaining storage systems at the Eastern Disaster Recovery Center (DRC)

I can find no record of any existing DRC, so I guess I'll let this one fly. Given the gross overspending I found under Command Support Equipment, I anticipate the same pattern here. Therefore reduce by 90% and save $3 Million.

Intelligence Support Equipment
  Classified programs

We'll just see about that. In the meantime, reduce by half and save $7 Million.

Operating Forces Support Equipment
  Mobile Aircraft Fire Training Device: Trailer mounted fully-contained device that allows firefighters to conduct live firefighting techniques to meet Naval Air Systems Command (NAVAIR) requirements. The device has interior and exterior fire scenario props to fully prepare the firefighters for aircraft firefighting and rescue missions.

A trailer that simulates a burning building. If you're training for buildings, train in old buildings. If you're training for planes, train on old planes. I'm sure there are decommissioned carriers and other ships that could be used for this purpose as well.

  Aircraft Fire Mobile Training Devices: Procurement of mobile live fire training devices designed for aircraft and structural operations for required firefighter training to ensure certification and proficiency of First Responders, DoD, and Foreign National firefighters. Training devices allows responders to conduct realistic CBRN response exercises to properly prepare for Overseas Contingency Operations missions. The training devices are very flexible and allow set up for different training evolutions related to terrorist events or emergency incidents.

A trailer that simulates a burning airplane. Why not just burn a decommissioned airplane? We have huge aircraft graveyards filled with these things.

The list of sub-programs continues in this manner. It also includes some special buoys that have lights in them, which I'm sure could be picked up off the shelf; cranes, which the Navy has plenty of; mobile buildings specifically designed to be deployed in Djibouti, and maintenance enhancements to facilities I want to get rid of anyway. Eliminate and save $16 Million.

C4ISR Equipment
  Consists of Mobile Inshore Undersea Warfare (MIUW) units and Harbor Defense Command (HDC) units operating Mobile Ashore Support Terminal IIIs (MAST IIIs). NCW also includes Inshore Boat Units (IBUs) and Maritime Security Force (MSF), which are separately funded.

Upgrades to networks and other communications systems. They seem to be working fine right now; eliminate and save $7 Million.

Environmental Support Equipment
26 programs that upgrade systems which measure things, locate things, look at things, or listen to things. The Navy was able to do all of this before this program started in FY2011, so they can do without them. Eliminate and save $19 Million.

Physical Security Equipment
New surveillance systems, access controls, materials that help with taking over other ships at sea, remote-controlled and auto-tracking machine guns (ROSAM), and more special radios. Six digits for a motorized tripod? None of this will be very important in peacetime, and the Navy has done just fine without these things. Eliminate and save $186 Million.

Enterprise Information Technology
> NGEN is an enterprise network which will provide secure, net-centric data and services to Navy and Marine personnel and represents the continuous evolution of information technology at the Department of Navy (DoN). NGEN forms the foundation for the DoN's future Naval Network Environment that will be interoperable with and leverage other Department of Defense-provided Net-Centric Enterprise Services. Prior year funds procured Early Transition Activities (ETAs) software tool suites that were required to replace current vendor owned proprietary tools. A license to access vendor owned Intellectual Property (IP) was procured to facilitate government control and oversight of the NMCI network.

The Navy's existing networks seem to be working fine. Eliminate and save $184 Million.

Spares and Repair Parts
> The Spares budget provides for the initial spares, outfitting spares, and vendor direct spares for equipment financed in OPN BAs 1-7.

I cut most of OPN BAs 1-7, so appropriately most of the spares and parts for those items can be cut. However, just to be on the safe side, I'll only cut 75% of this one. Use it to buy extras of the parts for things I kept; extend service life and such. Save $188 Million.

Aviation Support Equipment

Sonobuoys

The AN/SSQ-36, Bathythermograph (BT) is a bathythermograph sonobuoy used to provide a vertical temperature profile of the ocean with respect to depth. The data is transmitted to aircraft to assist in the selection of hydrophone depths and tactics for localizing and tracking submarines and long-range forecasts of acoustic conditions in the ocean.

Localizing and tracking submarines are pretty important to defending our coastlines. Keep as is ($105 Million).

Weapons Range Support Equipment

This budget line item provides the resources to implement the Navy Fleet Training Range (FTR) Instrumentation Program Plan. These FTRs provide the primary means of fleet combat readiness training.

The fleet must train for combat readiness, even more so in peacetime. Keep as is ($71 Million).

Expeditionary Airfields

This program provides for procurement of aircraft recovery equipment, landing mat and accessories, airfield lighting, and Visual Landing Aids for Naval Aviation EAF. EAF recovery equipment consists of the M31 arresting gear and its accessories. This equipment is used to stop aircraft in less than 1000 ft. EAF landing mats and accessories are used to construct airfields of varying configurations such as, 5000+ ft conventional airport runways and taxiways, Forward Arming and Refueling Points (FARPs), Forward Operating Bases (FOBs), Landing Zones (LZs) and Helo Pads. EAF Lighting equipment augments the many types of EAFs with lighting of the runways, taxiways, LZs, FARPs, FOBs and Helo pads.

In peacetime, there will be reduced or no need to create new airfields dotting the world. Eliminate OCO funding and reduce the remainder by standard 25%, saving $60 Million.

Aircraft Rearming Equipment

This program funds the procurement of common Armament Support Equipment (ASE), and Weapons Support Equipment (WSE) under the procurement and inventory control of the Naval Inventory Control Point and the Naval Air Systems Command.

The Navy must be able to rearm their aircraft, but they've been doing that since they had planes. Eliminate and save $11 Million.

Aircraft Launch and Recovery Equipment

> *This program provides for procurement of major aircraft Launch, Recovery, and Visual Landing Aids (VLA) equipment as well as ancillary items required for installation aboard aircraft carriers, air capable combatant vessels, amphibious assault ships and shore stations.*

This is generally needed due to unforeseen wartime activities or expanding operations. Since my plan would eliminate these two points altogether, there would be a reduced need for this. However, equipment breaks and has to be repaired and replaced, so let's just reduce it by half and save $41 Million.

Meteorological Equipment

> *This item provides new and replacement meteorological equipment for all Navy and Marine Corps Air Stations, all Navy ships, USMC Operational Forces units and other activities required to provide weather observations and safety of flight capabilities.*

In peacetime, the Navy will not have any increased need to monitor the weather. However, equipment breaks from time to time. Keep but reduce by half and save $9 Million.

DCRS/DPL

> *Digital Camera Receiving Station/Digital Photo Lab (DCRS/DPL) The Naval Air Systems Command (NAVAIR) is tasked to support digital imagery shipboard photographic requirements. In FY13, the DPL will transition to the Naval Sea Systems Command (NAVSEA).*

No digital camera receiving and processing requires that much funding; the cameras should be designed in such a way that they can just download them easily like *every other digital camera ever made*. Eliminate and save $1 Million.

Aviation Life Support

> *This account provides for the acquisition, upgrade, and production support of aviation life support systems required for the personal safety and protection of aircrew against the hazards encountered in the aircraft operating environment and for safe recovery of downed aircrew.*

The Navy won't need a lot of new oxygen bottles and such, but stuff breaks sometimes. Reduce by half and save $20 Million.

Airborne Mine Countermeasures

> *Airborne Mine Countermeasures (AMCM) Equipment is currently used by MH-53E helicopters to counter the threat of sea mines. The MH-60S helicopter will be adapted for the AMCM mission in support of the development of an*

Organic Fleet AMCM program. The equipment is divided into three categories -- minesweeping, minehunting and mine neutralization. (1) Minesweeping is performed by mechanical or influence sweeps.

I don't expect to encounter a whole lot of enemy mines around our own shores, but we do need to be able to fight them off just in case. Reduce by half and save $31 Million.

LAMPS Mk 3 Shipboard Equipment

This program provides for non-recurring engineering, procurement and installation of AN/SRQ-4(Ku) field install kits. This system encompasses hardware and software to transmit sensor data from the Light Airborne Multi-Purpose System (LAMPS) MK III aircraft to the host ship classes (cruisers, destroyers, and frigates). The minimum sustaining production rate is 6 kits per Fiscal Year.

For a non-recurring program, this program sure does continue indefinitely. Their minimum is six and they procure eight, so reduce by 25% and save $5 Million.

Portable Electronic Maintenance Aids

Aviation Support Equipment end items used by fleet technicians to assist in performing maintenance and diagnostics of aircraft. Funding is required to procure the necessary hardware, software applications, initial stand up, and production support. PEMAs are a portable display device used in the Automated Maintenance Environment (AME) to read digital maintenance publications and Integrated Electronic Technical Manuals (IETMs).

If a broken plane has to land in an unprepared location, it makes sense to have some portable tools to bring with us when we go fix it; but in peacetime, the planes will break less often. Cut by half and save $4 Million.

Other Aviation Support Equipment

Procures upgrades and enhancements to Test Equipment supporting the Sonobuoy Quality Assurance Program at San Clemente Island and ongoing sonobuoy engineering reviews at Naval Air Warfare Center Patuxent River.

Gotta test those sonobuoys and protect our shores from enemy submarines. Keep as is ($10 Million).

Autonomic Logistics Information System

ALIS controls all aspects of aircraft mission planning, maintenance, logistics, and supply functions. ALIS Ship Integration efforts will ensure the ship modification and classified/unclassified network integration, as well as installing related equipment, conducting security accreditation, and verifying system operations.

I've already covered how to reduce the expenses of mission planning, maintenance, logistics, and supply. Eliminate this **brand-new program** and save $4 Million.

Ordnance Support Equipment

Naval Fires Control System

The Naval Fires Control System (NFCS) is an automated mission planning and coordination system for the Naval Surface Fire Support (NSFS) System. It automates shipboard land attack battle management duties to be interoperable and consistent with joint C4ISR systems.

I've already covered how to reduce the expenses of mission planning, maintenance, logistics, and supply. Eliminate and save $3 Million.

Gun Fire Control Equipment

This program provides for the procurement of equipment, materials and Ordnance Alterations (ORDALTs) to improve combat effectiveness and maintain logistic supportability of Gun Fire Control Systems (GFCS) and Optical Sight Systems (OSS) and procures night vision devices.

The Navy is already highly combat effective and its logistics are already supportable. Eliminate and save $5 Million.

NATO Seasparrow

A shipboard Self-Defense Missile System designed to protect the ship and crew from Anti-Ship Cruise Missiles (ASCM), Fast Attack Craft/ Fast Inshore Attack Craft (FAC/FIAC), Low Velocity Air Threats (LVAT) and a wide range of asymmetrical threats (Unmanned Aerial and Surface vehicles, small Rigid Hull Inflatable Boats (RHIBS), etc.) as well as the standard mission of Anti-Air and Anti-Surface Defense (AAW, ASUW).

When was the last time you heard of someone launching a cruise missile at one of our ships? They already have self-defense systems; this is just a new one. Eliminate and save $9 Million.

RAM GMLS

Rolling Airframe Missile (RAM) - MK-49 Guided Missile Launching System (GMLS): RAM is a cooperative project with the Federal Republic of Germany, produced under a series of production MOUs/MOAs executed between the U.S. and the Federal Republic of Germany.

I reduced RAM by 25%, so let's reduce the support equipment by 25% and save $300K. Why we need to work with Germany to make a new missile is beyond me.

Ship Self Defense System

> Provides ship self-defense capabilities against Anti-Ship Cruise Missiles (ASCM) for LSD 41/49 class ships. It integrates several existing stand-alone sensor and Anti-Air Warfare weapons systems to provide an automated detect-to-engage capability against low flying, high speed ASCMs with low radar cross sections in the littoral environment. System design emphasizes physically distributed non-developmental items, commercial standards and computer program reuse in an open system architecture computer network. It includes a command table that uses components of the Navy's AN/UYQ-70 standard display for human-system interface, commercially available local area network access units and circuit cards, and commercially available fiber optic cabling. SSDS MK 1 requires a COTS obsolescence technology refresh and transitioned to an SSDS MK2 Open Architecture Computing Environment (OACE) beginning with FY10 procurement.

Defends dock-landing ships against cruise missiles, a worthwhile endeavor. Cut by standard 25% and save $14 Million.

AEGIS Support Equipment

> This program provides equipment for shore facilities and for shipboard upgrades to support the battle readiness of AEGIS Cruisers and Destroyers[.]

AEGIS is a very useful and worthy weapons system which will still be useful in defending our waters and trade lanes. Keep as is ($82 Million).

Tomahawk Support Equipment

> Surface and Submarine Tactical Tomahawk Weapon Control System (TTWCS) (5C220, 5C700, 5C800, 5C830, 5C890) is a post milestone III program in sustainment and fielding periodic refreshes to hardware and software to mantain capability. TTWCS functions include: Tasking validation (missile mission matching), planning of over the water routes, initialization, preparation and launch of BLK III/IV missiles.

We need our Tomahawk missiles to function correctly, so just reduce by standard 25% and save $19 Million.

Vertical Launch Systems

> The MK-41 Vertical Launching System (VLS) is a surface combatant missile launching system, designed to store, select and launch various STANDARD Missile configurations, TOMAHAWK, Tactical TOMAHAWK, EVOLVED

SEASPARROW (ESSM) and Vertical Launch ASROC (VLA) missiles. The MK-41 VLS significantly improves missile capacity, flexibility, multi-mission capability, reaction time and rate of fire and is designed to be adaptable to present and future weapon systems.

Some missiles launch vertically, and those systems have to be maintained. Keep as is ($754K).

Maritime Integrated Planning System (MIPS)

Maritime Integrated Air and Missile Defense (IAMD) Planning System (MIPS) is an automated air and missile defense planning tool that supports Joint Force Maritime Component Commander operational level of war air defense planning by automatically and optimally allocating ship stationing options in support of Ballistic Missile Defense (BMD) or Anti-Air Warfare (AAW).

I've already covered how to plan missiles and missions; eliminate and save $5 Million.

Strategic Missile Systems Equipment

The SSP funding in this P-1 line provides for the procurement of Strategic Weapons System (SWS) equipment for deployed SSBNs and shore support sites to support the TRIDENT II (D5) program. Included are shipboard subsystem equipment modernization and technical refresh efforts associated with the TRIDENT II (D-5) life extension program. TRIDENT II SSBN hull life has been extended, therefore extending system life to FY 2042.

Gotta support those submarines. Reduce by standard 25%, saving $45 Million.

SSN Combat Control Systems

A variety of upgrades to our submarines. The systems being upgraded are working fine, but some of these upgrades do look pretty useful (i.e. being able to launch missiles more quickly). Reduce by half and save $35 Million.

Submarine ASW Support Equipment

This line item procures modifications and improvements to Attack and Ballistic Missile Submarine fire control interface systems, torpedo tube system components and torpedo tube test equipment. These requirements arise as a result of the introduction of new or modified weapons and sensors and their subsequent evaluation test and operational use. Also procured are reliability, maintainability, functional and safety modifications and tactical improvements resulting from operational use experience.

Upgrades to systems that are working just fine; but it's a relatively cheap line item and the changes have been requested by the people who are actually using the systems. Further, protecting against enemy subs is a big deal, even in peacetime. Keep as is ($4 Million).

Surface ASW Support Equipment

This line item provides funding to procure Reliability, Maintainability and Availability (RM&A) and safety modifications through the Ordnance Alteration (ORDALT) process to Anti-Submarine Warfare (ASW) Fire Control, Surface Vessel Torpedo Tubes (SVTT), and related ASW Fire Control/SVTT support and test equipment to maintain the current envelope.

Upgrades to systems that are working just fine; but it's a relatively cheap line item and the changes have been requested by the people who are actually using the systems. Further, protecting against enemy subs is a big deal, even in peacetime. Keep as is ($6 Million).

ASW Range Support Equipemnt

Funding provides for the procurement of training range and shore support equipment, Test and Evaluation (T&E), acoustic trial range equipment, and weapon system and test support equipment. Equipment procured includes instrumentation for Fleet Operational Readiness Accuracy Check Sites (FORACS), support equipment required to conduct fleet exercises at Navy ASW Training ranges, Submarine Combat System Certification and Assessment Program (SCS CAP), Surface Ship Combat Ship Qualification Trial (CSSQT), and Surface Ship Radiated Noise Measurement (SSRNM).

Protecting against enemy subs is a big deal, even in peacetime. Keep as is ($48 Million).

Explosive Ordnance Disposal Equipment

All procurement of EOD tools and equipment, both initial outfitting and replenishment, for all military services is made by the Navy. The Navy provides all procurement services. There is an annual average of 300 procurement actions for this material. Each military service funds its own hardware.

That's a strange way to organize a procurement, but we do need to be able to dispose of IEDs, mines, etc. Keep as is ($3.6 Million).

Items less than $5 Million

Given the drastic cuts I've made to the budget, it stands to reason similar cuts can be made at the more minute levels. Reduced shore activities and operations, the complete elimination of war, and a much leaner Navy mean less overhead associated therewith. Cut by half and save $2 Million.

Anti-Ship Missile Decoy System

> The Anti-Ship Missile Decoy Program covers a family of decoys and the equipment to deploy them. It is an essential element of the Anti-Ship Missile Defense tactics to counter the threat of enemy homing missiles. NULKA is a joint program with Australia, and is currently in service with the Australian, Canadian, and United States Navies.

Assuming they're effective, decoys are a great way to protect the fleet against our enemies. Keep as is ($32 Million).

Surface Training Device Mods

> This line provides funds to procure, modify and modernize Aegis Ashore, LCS, DDG 1000 and surface shore-based navigation, combat systems, engineering, damage control and amphibious warfare individual and team Technical Training Equipment, Training Devices, Training Unique Equipment and Training systems.

We'll still need to train in peacetime; keep as is ($34 Million).

Submarine Training Device Mods

> This line provides funds to modify/upgrade training devices to keep them compatible with equivalent changes made to Fleet operational equipment and to implement Training Enhancement Changes (TECs) to the trainer systems capabilities.

We'll still need to train in peacetime; keep as is ($23 Million).

Procurement, Marine Corps[78]

Weapons and Combat Vehicles

AAV7A1 PIP [mod]

> The AAV Modifcation Kit Program provides life-cycle support to ensure cost-effective combat readiness for the AAV Family of Vehicles (FOV). This is accomplished through continuous review of sub-systems to maintain system supportability, safety, reduce total ownership costs, and improve fleet readiness.

It's important to keep Assault Amphibious Vehicles working, as amphibious assault is a huge part of what the USMC actually does. The upgrades are less important, and there will be a reduced need for them in peacetime, so we have more time to get them done. Reduce by standard 25% and save $4 Million.

---

[78] http://www.finance.hq.navy.mil/fmb/13pres/PMC_Book.pdf

LAV PIP

> *The LAV-C2 Upgrade Program is designed to meet and maintain the command and control requirements of the Operational Requirements Document (ORD). LAV-C2 upgrade provides a hardware and software module for the LAV-C2 to support complex radio configurations.*

Light Armored Vehicles are a big part of the Marine Corps, so we should do what we can to keep them working. The upgrades are less important, and there will be a reduced need for them in peacetime, so we have more time to get them done. Reduce by standard 25% and save $50 Million.

Expeditionary Fire Support System

> *EFSS is an all-weather, ground based indirect fire system designed to support the vertical assault element of a Ship-To-Objective Maneuver (STOM) force. EFSS is defined as a Launcher, Mobility Platform (prime mover), Ammunition, Ammunition Supply Vehicle, and Technical Fire Direction and Control equipment necessary for orienting weapons to an azimuth of fire.*

STOM is a big part of how the USMC operates in concert with Naval operations in general, so we should make sure they can fulfill their mission. Keep as is ($3 Million).

155mm Lightweight Towed Howitzer

> *LW155 (also known as the M777A2 howitzer) provides direct, reinforcing, and general support fires to maneuver forces as well as direct support artillery. It is a successful joint service program between the Marine Corps and Army working together to develop, produce, and field the howitzer.*

Ground troops need howitzers, but they require no ongoing support and the program is almost over anyway. Eliminate and save $18 Million. The Marines will still have the howitzers they already have.

High Mobility Artillery Rocket System (HIMARS)

> *A C-130 transportable, wheeled, indirect fire, rocket/missile system capable of firing all rockets and missiles in the current and future Multiple Launch Rocket System Family of Munitions (MFOM). The system includes a launcher, two Re-Supply Systems (RSS) and the MFOM. An RSS consists of a Re-Supply Vehicle (Medium Tactical Vehicle Replacement (MTVR) based truck with Material Handling Equipment) and a Re-Supply Trailer.*

By ending all OCO, we can bring our existing munitions home and store them for when they're needed, rather than blowing them up and buying replacements. Eliminate and save $157 Million.

Weapons and Combat Vehicles under $5 Million

This is a roll-up line that contains multiple Weapons and Tracked Combat Vehicle items. The funds are used to enhance the existing kits within the USMC inventory with improved, state-of-the-art electronics and tools for units that have been added or changed due to Table of Organizational (TOO) changes and Table of Equipment (TOE) changes. Funds also support the ongoing changes to the various stock lists prescribing those components of sets of test equipment and tools.

Spares and repair parts, extra ammo and guns, and related equipment. While we need those things, we won't be expending them in nearly the quantity we do now and can thus reduce by half, saving $9 Million.

Modification Kits

Mods for existing tanks, bridge vehicles, and mobile cranes. We do have to keep them working, but they're already doing just fine. Cut by half and save $24 Million.

Weapons Enhancement Program

The Weapons Enhancement Program provides funding for various force protection items and weapons upgrades. Additionally, the program funds commercially available equipment, non-developmental items (NDI) that can be rapidly fielded to support Infantry Marine Units.

Some potentially useful combat items here, so let's keep it around. Cut by standard 25% and save $1 Million.

Guided Missiles and Equipment

Ground Based Air Defense (GBAD)

Ground Based Air Defense Transformation (GBAD-T) supports the Low Altitude Air Defense (LAAD) Battalion's mission of Short Range Air Defense (SHORAD) and Force Protection Missions. The Advanced Man-Portable Air Defense System (A-MANPADS) Fire Unit is a mobile, Stinger missile-based low altitude surface-to-air weapons system designed to provide close-in short range air defense. A-MANPADS assets are organic to the low altitude air-defense (LAAD) battalion of the Marine Air Control Group (MACG).

Ground-to-air weapons are an important part of defending any ground force. Reduce by standard 25% and save $3 Million.

JAVELIN

Javelin provides the US Army and USMC a man-portable, fire-and-forget, medium-range missile with enhanced situational awareness and precision direct-fire effects to defeat armored vehicles, fortifications, and soft targets in full spectrum operations. Javelin has a high kill rate against a variety of targets at extended ranges under day/night, battlefield obscurants, adverse weather and multiple counter-measure conditions.

I don't understand why they need more than one type of ground-to-air missile, and this program ends this year anyway. Further, there will be nothing to defend ground troops against in peacetime, and they'll still have the missiles they already bought. Eliminate and save $29 Million.

Follow on To Smaw

The solution to the Follow on to Shoulder-Launched Multipurpose Assault Weapon (SMAW) (FOTS) capability requirement has been defined as the SMAW II system. Marine Expeditionary Forces will employ the SMAW II across the spectrum of conflict, under all environmental conditions, to destroy a variety of ground targets. As defined in the FOTS Capability Development Document (CDD), the program will consist of two distinct blocks which will be fielded using an evolutionary (incremental) acquisition strategy.

This is an important system for destroying tanks and similar targets, but there won't be any tanks to destroy in peacetime and they already have plenty of them. This program element replaces the launchers and rockets with new ones. Eliminate and save $20 Million.

Anti Armor Weapons Systems – Heavy (AAWS-H)

The Improved Target Acquisition System (ITAS) is a combat proven system that provides long-range, lethal anti-armor and precision assault fires capability for USMC Infantry, Tank and Light Armored Recognizance Battalions across the spectrum of contemporary operational environments.

The USMC has already procured plenty of these, and I'm assuming the writer here actually meant "reconnaissance". Eliminate and save $21 Million.

Modification Kits

The Tube-Launched Optically-Tracked, Wire-Guided (TOW) missiles (BGM-71 Series) are combat proven missiles that provide heavy anti-armor/assault capability to the USMC Infantry, Tank, and Light Armored Vehicle Battalions. TOW continues to be used consistently in Operation Enduring Freedom (OEF) as the weapon of choice in precision combat engagements. Marines employ TOW missiles against buildings and field fortifications taking advantage of the missile's inherent precision assault capability against such targets. The TOW missiles are launched from a variety of combat systems to include HMMWV, MRAP's, and LAV's, as well as having the capability for ground mounted operations. The TOW missile provides the warfighter with a highly lethal, cost effective, interoperable, multi-purpose weapon.

My plan puts OEF to an abrupt and permanent end, so there would be no precision engagements to fight. They have plenty of these left from previous procurements; eliminate and save $42 Million.

Unit Operations Center

Combat Operations Center (COC) - AN/TSQ-239 (V)2/3/4 is a deployable, self-contained, modular, scalable and centralized facility which provides digital, shared Command and Control/Situational Awareness functionalities to enhance the Common Operational Picture.

An expensive radio and digital map system. An equivalent could be produced using Google or OpenStreetMap for pretty much free, and the DoD has way too many different radio systems. Eliminate and save $1 Million.

Repair and Test Equipment

This budget line item provides funding for repair and test equipment consisting of 250+ different items of equipment (seperate TAMCNs) required to support the operation and maintenance of USMC ground based weapon systems or major end items. Repair and test equipment includes tool kits, shop sets, manual and automatic test equipment, as well as metrology and calibration equipment.

They seem to be getting by with the repair and test equipment they already have, and peacetime will mean fewer repairs and tests. However, stuff breaks even in training, so we'll have to keep it. Reduce by half and save $19 Million.

Other Support (Tel)

Global Combat Support System

Global Combat Support System-Marine Corps (GCSS-MC) is the physical implementation of the enterprise Information Technology (IT) architecture designed to support both improved and enhanced Marine Air Ground Task Force (MAGTF) Combat Support Services (CSS) functions and MAGTF Commander and Combatant Commanders/ Joint Task Force (CC/JTF) combat support information requirements.

If we mind our own business and keep our military where it belongs, then we need not worry about the globe as a whole. However, we do need to be ready in case of war, and a lot of this stuff is in place here at home. Reduce by standard 25% and save $7 Million.

Modification Kits

Printers, laptop computers and Client Suites and Servers to support the Biometric Automated Toolset System (BATS), as well as refresh both Badge Printers and Client Suites for the MAGTF Integrated Systems Training Center (MISTC).

End all OCO programs, and thus all OCO spending. Cut the remainder by standard 25% and save $4 Million in total.

Command and Control System (Non-Tel)

Items under $5 Million (Communications and Electrics)

A series of line items too small to justify their own individual outlays; reduce by standard 25% and save $1 Million.

Air Operations C2 Systems

Will address four of the 26 capability gaps identified in the validated Combat ID – Friendly Force Tracker (CID-FFT) Joint Capabilities Document (JCD). A Jun 2010 JFCOM-led AoA concluded, and the USMC concurred, that pursuit of a new material solution and introduction of a new system would not be cost effective.

I couldn't find this document, so I don't know what those gaps are. Obviously they aren't preventing us from waging war effectively, so it seems we can live without them. Looks like a ground IFF system so our troops will stop shooting each other by accident, among other things. Let's keep it for now but cut by half, saving $13 Million.

Radar and Equipment (Non-Tel)

Radar Systems

A series of different radar systems. Radars are important, of course; but we can just use the ones we currently have overseas and will end up bringing back home. Eliminate and save $136 Million.

RQ-21 UAS

The Small Tactical Unmanned Aircraft System (STUAS) program is a combined Navy and Marine Corps program that will provide persistent maritime and land-based tactical Reconnaissance, Surveillance and Target Acquisition (RSTA) data collection and dissemination capabilities to the warfighter. For the United States Marine Corps, STUAS will provide the Marine Expeditionary Force and subordinate commands (divisions and regiments) a dedicated Intelligence, Surveillance, and Reconnaissance system capable of delivering intelligence products directly to the tactical commander in real time.

This **brand-new** UAV is to be used for recon. We already have tons of UAVs, other aircraft, and satellites capable of doing exactly this, and we'll be recalling our UAVs from overseas. Further, this duplicates the preexisting RQ-11 UAV program. Eliminate and save $28 million.

Intelligence / Communications Equipment (Non-Tel)

Fire Support System

> MIMM: Provides the ability to derive highly accurate meteorological data through the use of Numerical Weather Prediction (i.e. meteorological models).

We already have plenty of these and don't need to buy any more for peacetime.

> **Fire Support Mods (Sustainment):** Funding will provide improvements and upgrades to the Ground Counter Fire Sensor (GCFS), Marine Artillery Survey Set (MASS), Improved Position Azimuth Determining System (IPADS), Long Range Thermal Imager (LRTI), Thermal Laser Spot Imager (TLSI), Joint Terminal Attack Controller Laser Target Designator (JTAC LTD), the Portable Lightweight Designator Rangefinder (PLDR), and the Meteorological Support Group (MSG).

These systems seem to be working fine as they are now.

> **Common Laser Range Finder (CLRF):** CLRF will equip operating forces with the technological capability to reduce the target location error, increasing target location accuracy. CLRF is a comprehensive program fulfilling requirements for eye-safe laser rangefinders.

The Marines already have plenty of rangefinders, and they're very good at hitting targets, so they seem to be working.

Eliminate and save $7 Million. This program ends soon anyway.

Intelligence Support Equipment

> A semi-automated, man/team portable system providing intercept, collection, direction-finding, reporting and collection management to Marine Air-Ground Task Force (MAGTF) commanders. It provides special signals intercept, and Direction Finding (DF) capability for each system and is modular, lightweight and team transportable.

Special Intelligence

> Additional details with respect to this line item are held at a higher classification.

We'll just see about that. In the meantime, cut in half and save $1 Million.

RQ-11 UAV

> *Procures a capability for unmanned aircraft systems (UAS) to provide the company/detachment level with airborne reconnaissance to aid in detecting, identifying, and engaging or avoiding enemy units. The UAS air vehicle autonomously gathers and transmits imagery of the tactical situation in near-real time at a range of up to ten kilometers.*

How many different UAVs do we really need? We've been procuring this one for years, and this ends soon anyway. Eliminate, bring our existing UAVs home, and save $2 Million.

Distributed Common Ground System (DCGS-MC)

> *a Service-level effort to migrate select USMC Intelligence, Surveillance and Reconnaissance (ISR) processing and exploitation capabilities into a single, integrated net-centric baseline consisting of functional capability sets that support Marine intelligence analysts across the Marine Air-Ground Task Force (MAGTF) by making organic ISR data more visible, accessible, and understandable.*

We shouldn't be consolidating systems within the Marine Corps; we should be consolidating them DoD-wide. Eliminate and save $18 Million.

Night Vision Equipment

> *Night Vision Equipment (NVE) consists of multiple optical, Electro-Optical (EO) and laser systems which allow the dismounted Marine the ability to acquire, locate, identify, and engage targets during daylight and limited visibility conditions, and perform navigation and manual tasks during limited visibility conditions utilizing ambient or covert illumination.*

We've already procured thousands of these things; how could we not have enough already? Eliminate; use the ones we bring back from overseas, and save $49 Million (**$1.5 Billion** total).

Other Support

Common Computer Resources

> *Workstations (desktop/laptop), servers and other information technology (IT) hardware to support the Operating Forces and other non-Navy Marine Corps Intranet (NMCI) Marine Corps customers. MCHS provides support for two principal groups: 1) approximately 50 United States Marine Corps (USMC) Tactical and Functional Programs of Record that use COTS IT hardware as part of their fielded systems; and 2) tactical and other Marine Corps customers not supported by NMCI such as Marine Corps Forces, Europe/Marine Corps Forces, Korea and stand-alone Marine Corps units and schoolhouses. MCHS is also responsible for ADHOC emerging priority requirements approved by C4.*

Some Marines need computers, just like anyone else, to get their job done. Having said that, we don't need to plan on having any overseas anymore. Eliminate all OCO spending and cut the remainder by the standard 25%, saving $71 Million.

Command Post Systems

Will provide Beyond Line of Sight (BLOS)/Line of Sight (LOS) transmission capability to the operating forces for network connectivity while on the move to enable access to Command and Control (C2) applications, streaming video and collaboration tools. NOTM will also provide remote and dynamic network management to eliminate the burden on end-users and incidental operators to perform technical functions.

In peacetime, we won't need any mobile command posts; but we do need to be ready for war. Reduce by standard 25% and save $9 Million.

Radio Systems

The BFT System is a commercial L-Band satellite-based Tracking and Communication System. USMC was directed to converge to the BFT Family of Systems (FoS) based on OIF/OEF lessons learned. The BFT FoS is comprised of the BFT, Mounted Refresh Computer (MRC) and Tactical Operations Center (TOC) Kit.

My plan puts OEF to an abrupt and permanent end. We shouldn't be merging a few communications systems together across just the USMC; we should be merging them together across the entire DoD, if not the entire federal government itself. Eliminate and save $126 Million.

Comm Switching and Control Systems

A transit case solution that will provide reach back capability to the Global Information Grid (GIG) to access the Defense Switch Network (DSN), Defense Information System Network (DISN) Secret Internet Protocol Router Network (SIPRNET), Non-secure Internet Protocol Router Network (NIPRNET), and DISN Video Services (DVS), enabling a small advance force/liaison team to communicate with a Marine Air-Ground Task Force (MAGTF), Joint Task Force (JTF) or other Joint Force Commander, and to maintain situational awareness.

This new program didn't exist prior to FY2011, so we can live without it. Eliminate and save $64 Million.

Communications and Electronic Infrastructure Support

Supports organizational messaging for all classification levels from General Service (GENSER) unclassified through Top Secret/Sensitive Compartmented Information (TS/SCI) for the United States Marine Corps (USMC). DMS organizational messages are used to direct and commit resources, provide user authentication, non-repudiation, confidentiality, and integrity. It also maintains an archive and retrospective search capability to the warfighter and requires security at the Class 4 level.

Under my plan, there would be a whole lot less deemed worthy of being classified, but people need a way to communicate about classified stuff in a secure way. Of course, that could be done much cheaper, given the encryption technologies available to everyone these days. This program ends in 2017 anyway. Reduce by half and save $21 Million.

Commercial Passenger Vehicles

Funds in this line are used for the replacement of centrally managed non-tactical sedans, station wagons, and buses at Marine Corps bases and stations. Commercial Passenger Vehicles are acquired through commercial contracting procedures. This program provides commercial design various size buses for overseas bases and stations supporting the deployment and resetting of operating forces.

There's nothing wrong with the ones they already have, and we'd bring all those vehicles back from overseas. Under my plan, there are no overseas bases. Eliminate and save $3 Million.

Commercial Cargo Vehicles

Funds in this line are used for the replacement of centrally managed non-tactical general purpose heavy duty and light trucks and special purpose trucks; refuse collection trucks; and all types of trailers and low speed electric motor scooters at bases and stations throughout the Marine Corps to transport material and supplies to support the deployment and resetting of Operating Forces.

There's nothing wrong with the ones they already have, and we'd bring all those vehicles back from overseas. Under my plan, there are no overseas bases. Eliminate and save $14 Million.

5/4T Truck HMMWV (MYP)

High Mobility Multipurpose Wheeled Vehicle Expanded Capacity Vehicle (HMMWV ECV) is the 4th generation design of the HMMWV. The HMMWV ECV serves as the primary light tactical ground transport platform for command and control, troop transport, light cargo transport, shelter carrier, towed weapons prime mover, and weapons platform throughout all areas of the battlefield or mission area.

This **brand-new program** upgrades our Humvees, which they do not require. Eliminate and save $8 Million.

Motor Transport Modifications

> *The modifications program funds numerous extremely important modifications and initiatives that are required to address operational priorities, engineering change proposals, safety concerns, support equipment inefficiencies, tool malfunctions, product quality deficiencies, beneficial suggestions and other issues that affect vehicle reliability, availability and readiness.*

Well, if the modifications are that important to keep the equipment running, I guess we have to do it. Keep as is ($50 Million).

Medium Tactical Vehicle Replacement

> *The MTVR (Medium Tactical Vehicle Replacement) fleet of vehicles replaced the medium tactical motor transport fleet of M809/M939 series trucks with cost-effective, state-of-the-art technologically improved trucks. The MTVR has 22 years of economic useful life and markedly improved performance plus Reliability, Availability, Maintainability and Durability (RAM-D).*

What's wrong with the vehicles we have now? The availability of something shiny and new does not automatically obsolete the existing equipment. Eliminate and save $10 Million; this program ends this year anyway.

Logistics Vehicle System Replacement

> *The Logistics Vehicle System Replacement (LVSR) is replacing the LVS legacy fleet as the Marine Corps' heavy tactical logistics vehicle. The fleet is composed of three variants to replace the 5 LVS variants. Cargo, tractor, and wrecker variants are currently being procured.*

What's wrong with the vehicles we have now? The availability of something shiny and new does not automatically obsolete the existing equipment. Eliminate and save $37 Million; this program ends this year anyway.

Family of Tactical Trailers

> *Family of Tactical Trailers provides for procurement of new tactical trailers in the light, medium and heavy trailer fleet in support of the Marine Corps tactical vehicle fleet mobility capability. This program includes multiple initiatives.*

What was wrong with the ones we had before? There's nothing tactical about these trailers. Eliminate and save $56 Million.

> **Motor Transport Modifications -** *Funds Marine Corps unique improvements to fielded ground transportation systems, to include any required government or contractor configuration management for technology improvement insertions*

> **Marine Security Guard (Vehicles) -** *Provides various types of vehicles for the Marine Security Guard depending on the requirement of the command / country.*

Some of this is probably useful in some way, but a lot of it can be worked around by the items returning from overseas and a new peacetime way of life. Cut by half and save $3 Million.

Environmental Control Equipment Assorted

> *The Marine Corps Systems Command supports and fields a number of tactical Environmental Control Units (ECUs) in various sizes that provide heating, ventilation, air conditioning, and dehumidification for soft wall (tents) and rigid wall shelters, as well as Small and Large Field Refrigeration Systems and a unique Cooling and Refrigeration Tool Kit.*

Heat and cooling can be important in some deployed environments, but they already have plenty of these, in addition to whatever they replaced. EPA compliance will be far less important when I eliminate the EPA. Eliminate and save $14 Million.

Bulk Liquid Equipment

> *Family of Expeditionary Water Systems: Funding for Bulk Liquid Equipment and Family of Water Supply Support Equipment was combined beginning in FY12.*

Sanitizing water in the field, etc. can be important during a war; but we won't be at war. Eliminate OCO funding and cut the remainder by standard 25%, saving $23 Million.

Tactical Fuel Systems

> *Family of Expeditionary Fuel Systems - Funding for Tactical Fuel Systems and Expeditionary Fuel Systems was combined beginning in FY12.*

Fuel is important in war, but we won't be at war. Eliminate OCO funding and cut the remainder by standard 25%, saving $56 Million.

Power Equipment Assorted

> *This joint DoD program includes mobile electric power equipment used throughout the Fleet Marine Forces and Reserves. These are centrally managed items. Sizes and types of Generators and Mobile Electric Power*

Distribution Systems range from 2 kW to 100 kW in both 60HZ and 400HZ. All generators are selected from the standard family of DoD Mobile Electric Power (MEP) sources. Current generators are from the Tactical Quiet Generator (TQG) family.

Marines need power in the field to maintain equipment and run the war; but we won't be at war. Eliminate OCO funding, cut the remainder by standard 25% and save $34 Million.

Engineer and Other Equipment

Amphibious Support Equipment

Amphibious Support Equipment supports multiple capabilities, enhancements, life cycle replacements and personnel equipment shortfalls existing in reconnaissance units throughout operating forces for airborne/parachuting programs, specialized reconnaissance programs and underwater reconnaissance capability programs.

Gotta support that amphibious stuff. Cut by standard 25%, save $3 Million.

EOD Systems

A rollup of explosive ordnance disposal equipment. There will be a great reduction in the amount of explosive ordnance needing to be disposed of in peacetime and with all our guys back home where they belong. Eliminate all OCO funding, cut the remainder by standard 25% and save $363 Million.

Physical Security Equipment

Physical security systems are used at base flight lines and Arms, Ammunition and Explosive (AA&E) sites, in expeditionary environments, Other Critical Assets (OCA), Mission Essential Vulnerable Areas, support the Marine Corps Critical Infrastructure Protection (CIP) Program and include capital plant equipment specifically designed for physical security/electronic security systems (ESS) in military construction (MILCON) projects. [...etc.]

Physical security is a critical part of securing our bases, borders, shores, and ports. Eliminate all OCO funding and **double** the remainder, since physical security is pretty much all the Marines will be doing in peacetime. $5 Million saved.

Garrison Mobile Engineering Equipment

Command Support Equipment - Funds in this line provide for the procurement/replacement of Class 3 (non-industrial) and Class 4 (Industrial) equipment to support the operation and mission of United States Marine Corps ground bases, air stations and districts.

The operation of Marine bases is pretty important; keep as is ($11 Million).

Material Handling Equipment
> *A roll-up line that funds the replacement and service life extension of Material Handling Equipment which includes forklifts, cranes, and container handlers. The replacement/service life extension program has been developed on an 'as required' basis. T*

Improving existing equipment is cheaper than buying new ones; Eliminate all OCO funding, saving $19 Million.

First Destination Transportation
> *This funding supports timely shipments for end items procured with PMC funds from manufacturers/suppliers to Marine Corps users or facilities in accordance with fleet requirements.*

By eliminating our worldwide posture, we can significantly reduce the logistics overhead associated therewith. Just put the stuff and the people on a truck, a plane, or a ship. Reduce the frequency with which people and equipment are shifted around, which seems to have no particular purpose other than to keep them rotated. Reduce procurements significantly. Reduce by 90% and save $100K.

Field Medical Equipment
There will be a significantly reduced need for medical equipment in peacetime, as nobody will be getting shot at or blown up. Eliminate all OCO funding and cut the remainder by standard 25%, saving $24 Million.

Training Devices
Training is as important as ever, if not more so. Eliminate all OCO funding and keep the rest as is, saving $4 Million.

Container Family
> *The Container Family provides the Fleet Marine Force with a fully intermodal transport capability emphasizing dimensional standardization and International Organization for Standardization compatibility. Two types of containers are procured, Pallet and Quadruple. The containers are end items and assets owned by the unit, expeditionary in nature. Components for the containers such as racks, horizontal connectors and inserts are not end items and do not have Acquisition Objectives.*

If we don't buy as much stuff, and try not to move existing stuff around so much, then we don't need as many containers. Also consider that we've been procuring containers for many years and they can be reused. Eliminate and save $6 Million.

Family of Construction Equipment

> *The Family of Construction Equipment (FCE) line is a roll-up line that provides for the replacement and service life extension program (SLEP) of Marine Corps construction equipment.*

Eliminate all OCO funding, but keep the rest as is. After all, we may need to build up our defenses and bases here at home. $16 Million saved.

Rapidly Deployable Kitchen

> *Consists of those items used to store, prepare, transport, & serve combat rations in a non-garrison environment while maintaining force protection through distributed operations and sanitation capabilities.*

Troops have to eat on the move, too; but I don't understand why they can't just eat MREs or field rations. If they're deployed for so long that this becomes a real problem, then they've been deployed too long. In peacetime, they should pretty much always be fairly close to a base or other source of food. Eliminate and save $8 Million.

Items Less than $5 Million

> *A series of line items too small to justify their own individual outlays; reduce by standard 25% and save $2 Million.*

Spares and Repair Parts

> *Funds are required to reimburse the Navy Working Capital Fund for both repairable and consumable components at the time the initial spare parts package is released with the principal end item (PEI) to the Fleet Marine Force. This concept complies with the Navy Working Capital Fund funding of Initial Spares with reimbursement from the Procurement Account.*

Spares and parts are an important part of any maintenance; keep as is ($3 Million).

Procurement of Ammunition [79] [80]

Ammo is important, but we won't need nearly as much of it if we just stop shooting at people and things. Eliminate all OCO spending and reduce the remainder by standard 25%; save $480 Million saved.

---

[79] http://www.finance.hq.navy.mil/fmb/13pres/PANMC_1_BOOK.pdf
[80] http://www.finance.hq.navy.mil/fmb/13pres/PANMC_2_BOOK.pdf

National Defense Sealift Fund[81]

NDSF exists to fund construction, including that of vessels; operation and maintenance of charter vessels, installation of defense features on privately owned and operated vessels; research and development; etc.

Research and Development should be funded by the companies manufacturing the equipment we buy; we should not do their job for them. Eliminate R&D and save $48 Million. Reduce the remainder by standard 25% and save a total of $18 Million.

Base Closure and Realignment[82]

Eliminate environmental component (studies, compliance, and restoration) and save $130 Million (this may reduce the resale value). The remainder is actually very cheap due to selling off existing assets, and we have thus reduced the total cost from $147 million to $20 million.

Military Construction and Family Housing Programs[83]

Eliminate the "Outside the United States" component and save $287 Million. Keep the rest as is due to the influx of military from current overseas locations. The "Inside the United States" component may need to be expanded.

Military Construction, Navy and Marine Corps Reserve Programs[84]

Keep as is ($50 Million) due to the influx of military from current overseas locations. The "Inside the United States" component may need to be expanded.

Research and Development (Navy) [85] [86] [87] [88][89]

The Navy should not be funding **$17 Billion** for research that should be done in the private sector. Therefore, most of these programs will be eliminated.

Basic Research

University Research Initiatives

This program includes support for multidisciplinary basic research in a wide range of scientific and engineering disciplines that enable the U.S. Navy to

---

[81] http://www.finance.hq.navy.mil/fmb/13pres/NDSF_book.pdf
[82] http://www.finance.hq.navy.mil/fmb/13pres/BRAC_Book.pdf
[83] http://www.finance.hq.navy.mil/fmb/13pres/MCON_Book.pdf
[84] http://www.finance.hq.navy.mil/fmb/13pres/MCNR_book.pdf
[85] http://www.finance.hq.navy.mil/fmb/13pres/RDTEN_BA1-3_BOOK.pdf
[86] http://www.finance.hq.navy.mil/fmb/13pres/RDTEN_BA4_book.pdf
[87] http://www.finance.hq.navy.mil/fmb/13pres/RDTEN_BA5_book.pdf
[88] http://www.finance.hq.navy.mil/fmb/13pres/RDTEN_BA6_book.pdf
[89] http://www.finance.hq.navy.mil/fmb/13pres/RDTEN_BA7_book.pdf

> *maintain technological superiority, and for university research infrastructure to acquire research instrumentation needed to maintain and improve the quality of university research important to the Navy.*

Technological superiority, university infrastructures, and research are not the federal government's job. We should simply let the free market come up with what it may, and buy the products that come therefrom. Eliminate and save $114 Million.

In-House Lab Independent Research

> *This program element (PE) sustains U.S. Naval Science and Technology (S&T) superiority by providing new technological concepts for the maintenance of naval power and national security and by helping to avoid scientific surprise while exploiting scientific breakthroughs and providing options for new Future Naval Capabilities (FNCs).*

Technological research is not the federal government's job. We should simply let the free market come up with what it may, and buy the products that come therefrom. Eliminate and save $19 Million.

Defense Research Sciences

> *This program element (PE) sustains U.S. Naval Science and Technology (S&T) superiority, provides new technological concepts for the maintenance of naval power and national security, and helps avoid scientific surprise. It is based on investment directions as defined in the Naval Science & Technology Strategy approved by the S&T Corporate Board (Sep 2011).*

Technological research is not the federal government's job. We should simply let the free market come up with what it may, and buy the products that come therefrom. Eliminate and save $473 Million.

Applied Research

Power Projection Applied Research

> *This strategy provides the vision and key objectives for the essential science and technology efforts that will enable the continued supremacy of U.S. Naval forces in the 21st century.*

The Navy already knows how to project power anywhere in the world. The Navy's supremacy is in no danger whatsoever. Research is not the federal government's job. We should simply let the free market come up with what it may, and buy the products that come therefrom. Eliminate and save $89 Million.

Force Projection Applied Research

This strategy provides the vision and key objectives for the essential science and technology efforts that will enable the continued supremacy of U.S. Naval forces in the 21st century.

The Navy already knows how to project force anywhere in the world. We should simply let the free market come up with what it may, and buy the products that come therefrom. Eliminate and save $143 Million.

Marine Corps Landing Force Tech

This strategy provides the vision and key objectives for the essential science and technology efforts that will enable the continued supremacy of U.S. Naval forces in the 21st century.

The Marines have been around for a long time; I think they've figured out how to land on a beachhead by now. Eliminate and save $47 Million.

Common Picture Applied Research

The Strategy focuses and aligns Naval S&T with Naval missions and future capability needs that address the complex challenges presented by both rising peer competitors and irregular/asymmetric warfare.

The Navy should have only two objectives: Protect our shores, and protect our trade lanes. My plan merges the Coast Guard into the Navy, which would add a third objective: Protect major inland waterways and ports. By ending the wars, we eliminate the need to fight them. Eliminate and save $42 Million.

Warfighter Sustainment Applied Research

The Strategy focuses and aligns Naval S&T with Naval missions and future capability needs that address the complex challenges presented by both rising peer competitors and irregular/asymmetric warfare.

We certainly shouldn't be looking for ways to sustain wars for longer timeframes. Eliminate and save $44 Million.

Electromagnetic Systems Applied Research

[This] strategy focuses and aligns Naval S&T with Naval missions and future capability needs that address the complex challenges presented by both rising peer competitors and irregular/asymmetric warfare.

Railguns should be produced as a natural product of the private sector, equally available to the Navy or the citizens. The Navy shouldn't be doing its own research; eliminate and save $78 Million.

Ocean Warfighting Environment Applied Research

> *This PE provides the unique, fundamental programmatic instrument by which basic research on the natural environment is transformed into technological developments that provide new or enhanced warfare capabilities for the Battlespace Environment (BSE).*

I think the Navy understands how to protect an ocean environment by now. Eliminate and save $50 Million.

JT Non-Lethal Weapons Applied Research

> *The efforts described in this Program Element (PE) reflect science and technology (S&T) investment decisions provided by the Joint Non-Lethal Weapons (NLW) Integrated Product Team, a multi-service flag level corporate board that executes the JNLWP for the Commandant of the Marine Corps.*

Non-lethal weapons should just come out of the free market like any other product. If the Navy really needs to shoot at someone, then lethality is probably OK. Eliminate and save $6 Million.

Undersea Warfare Applied Research

> *This PE funds applied research efforts in undersea target detection, classification, localization, tracking, and neutralization. Technologies being developed within this PE are aimed at enabling Sea Shield, one of the core operational concepts detailed in the Naval Transformational Roadmap.*

These are all aspects of warfare that should be researched by the weapons and equipment manufacturers; private companies that develop technology are supposed to have R&D departments. Eliminate and save $97 Million.

Future Naval Capabilities Applied Research

> *The FNC Program represents the requirements-driven, delivery-oriented portion of the Navy Science and Technology (S&T) portfolio. FNC investments respond to Naval S&T Gaps that are generated by the Navy and Marine Corps after receiving input from Naval Research Enterprise (NRE) stakeholders.*

These are all aspects of warfare that should be researched by the weapons and equipment manufacturers; private companies that develop technology are supposed to have R&D departments. Eliminate and save $162 Million.

Mine and Expeditionary Warfare Applied Research

> *This PE provides technologies for Naval Mine Countermeasures (MCM), Expeditionary Warfare, U.S. Naval sea mining, Naval Special Warfare (NSW), and Joint Tri-Service Explosive Ordnance Disposal (EOD). This program is strongly aligned with the Joint Chiefs of Staff Joint Warfighting Capability*

Objectives through the development of technologies to achieve military objectives with minimal casualties and collateral damage.

These are all aspects of warfare that should be researched by the weapons and equipment manufacturers; private companies that develop technology are supposed to have R&D departments. Eliminate and save $32 Million.

Advanced Technology Development

Power Projection Advanced Technology

The efforts described in this Program Element (PE) are based on investment directions as defined in the Naval S&T Strategic Plan approved by the S&T Corporate Board (Sep 2011).

These are all aspects of warfare that should be researched by the weapons and equipment manufacturers; private companies that develop technology are supposed to have R&D departments. Eliminate and save $57 Million.

Force Protection Advanced Technology

This PE addresses advanced technology development associated with providing the capability of Platform and Force Protection for the U.S. Navy. This program supports the development of technologies associated with all naval platforms (surface, subsurface, terrestrial and air) and the protection of those platforms.

The less war you have, the less protection your forces need. My proposal involves having zero.

These are all aspects of warfare that should be researched by the weapons and equipment manufacturers; private companies that develop technology are supposed to have R&D departments. Eliminate and save $19 Million.

Electromagnetic Systems Advanced Technology

Activities and efforts in this Program Element (PE) address technologies critical to enabling the transformation of discrete functions to network centric warfare capabilities which simultaneously perform Radar, Electronic Warfare (EW), and Communications and Network functions across platforms through multiple, simultaneous and continuous communications/data links.

These are all aspects of warfare that should be researched by the weapons and equipment manufacturers; private companies that develop technology are supposed to have R&D departments. Eliminate and save $57 Million.

MC Advanced Technology Demo

> *Continued development of enhanced warfighting capabilities through field experiments with Marine operating forces; rapid response to low-, mid-, and high-intensity conflicts in the Overseas Contingency Operation (OCO); methods for countering irregular threats; and expansion of seabasing and naval force packaging capabilities.*

Development of weapons should be done by weapons manufacturers, and the same holds true for electronics, avionics, etc. Eliminate all OCO and commensurate funding thereof. Eliminate and save $43 Million.

JT Non-Lethal Tech Development

> *This program funds Advanced Technology Development of next-generation Non-Lethal Weapons (NLWs) and includes performing analysis, technical development efforts, and modeling and simulation necessary to ensure optimum weaponization and use of these NLWs.*

Development of weapons should be done by weapons manufacturers. Eliminate and save $12 Million.

Future Naval Capabilities Advanced Tech Development

> *This project supports the naval pillars of Capable Manpower, Enterprise and Platform Enablers, Expeditionary Maneuver Warfare, Force Health Protection, Forcenet, Power and Energy, Sea Basing, Sea Shield and Sea Strike.*

You don't need to spend a quarter billion dollars per year to understand how to staff your bases and ships properly. The rest of these components are the responsibility of whoever we're buying the technology from. Eliminate and save **$256 Million.**

Warfighter Protection Advanced Technology

> *This program supports the development and demonstration of field medical equipment, diagnostic capabilities and treatments; technologies to improve warfighter safety and to enhance personnel performance under adverse conditions; and systems to prevent occupational injury and disease in hazardous, deployment environments.*

Field medical equipment should be developed by field medical equipment manufacturers. Diagnostic capabilities should be developed by diagnostic equipment manufacturers and doctors. Treatments should be developed by doctors and researchers in the private sector, with input from medics on the battlefield. Battle in adverse conditions and most other warfighter safety issues can be avoided by establishing peacetime, which need only that we stop attacking other countries so much. Eliminate and save $4 Million.

Navy Warfighting Experimentation & Demo

This Program Element (PE) addresses the development of recent technology breakthroughs to meet current operational needs from a subscale proof-of-principle into a full-scale prototype for warfighter experimentation during laboratory and operational demonstrations, Fleet Battle Experiments (FBE), Limited Objective Experiments (LOEs) and Sea Trial Exercises.

Evaluating technologies for their application in the battlefield is an important part of keeping the fleet up to date, though we must ensure these technologies come from the private sector. Keep as is ($52 Million).

Advanced Component Development and Prototypes (ACD&P)

Air/Ocean Tactical Applications

New state-of-the art government and commercial technologies are identified, transitioned, demonstrated and then integrated into Combat Systems and programs of record and Tactical Decision Aids that determine in real-time and near-real-time the operational effects of the physical environment on the performance of combat forces and their new and emerging platforms, sensors, systems and munitions.

Evaluating technologies for their application is an important part of keeping the fleet up to date, though we must ensure these technologies come from the private sector. Keep as is ($34 Million).

Aviation Survivability

Aviation Survivability addresses the issues of aircrew and platform survivability, focusing on enhancing overall opportunity for aircrew and platform protection and enhanced performance.

In peacetime, there would be fewer or no situations requiring a pilot egress or other potentially deadly situations, and aircraft ejection systems are pretty reliable. Eliminate and save $9 Million. Make sure future aircraft procured are thoroughly tested.

Deployable JT Command and Control

Providing a standardized, integrated, rapidly deployable, modular, scaleable, and reconfigurable joint command and control (C2) capability to designated Geographic Combatant Commands (GCCs).

The Navy does not need yet another shiny new C&C system, not to mention all the other RDT&E projects that this duplicates. They need exactly **one** C&C system. Eliminate and save $4 Million.

Aircraft Systems

> This program element supports the study, evaluation, optimization and enhancements of fielded aircraft systems not supported by a system specific RDTEN program element. The supported efforts will provide a basis to recommend options for improved efficiency, minimization of life cycle cost, and other affordable options.

It's important to keep aircraft working reliably, so I'd keep this one in. However, it ends in 2014, so I'm excluding it from my budget proposal as it would not be part of an ongoing requirement.

ASW Systems Development

> Includes RDT&E funds for advanced development and developmental testing of airborne anti-submarine warfare (ASW) systems, including aircraft, equipment, and devices for use against all types of submarine targets; and advanced, high-performance, underwater, mobile target for use in fleet ASW training exercises and for the operational evaluation of the MK-30 torpedo and the MK-48 torpedo weapons system improvement program.

Evaluating technologies for their application in the battlefield is an important part of keeping the fleet up to date, though we must ensure these technologies come from the private sector. Keep as is ($8 Million).

Tactical Airborne Reconnaissance

> This program element funds efforts to develop Concept of Operations in support of the Navy's overall Unmanned Aircraft System (UAS) strategy integrating UASs into the Chief of Naval Operations Navy Vision of Sea Power 21 (Sea Shield, Sea Strike, Sea Basing, and FORCEnet).

The Navy doesn't need a special R&D budget to sit and think of new strategies, but the money will get spent either way. Keep as is for now ($5 Million) and see what it develops.

Advanced Combat Systems Tech

> The Advanced Combat System Technology line is to evolve the technical and business practices for programs to change to an open architecture construct. The program was constructed to mature both technical and business model integration for C5I systems programs of record in an open architecture environment.

Spending seven digits to move to an open architecture is like putting a dollar in the "Give a penny take a penny" tray so you don't feel guilty about taking a penny next time. Eliminate and save $1.5 Million.

Surface and Shallow Water MCM

> *The program provides for developments to combat the threat of known and projected foreign mines against U.S. Naval and merchant shipping in harbors, channels, choke points, sea lines of communications and amphibious and other fleet operating areas.*

The Navy already has vessels which are specifically designed to combat threats in shallow littoral waters and on surfaces, to hunt and combat mines, to land craft on beachheads, and to operate amphibiously. Eliminate and save $191 Million.

Surface Ship Torpedo Defense

> *The Surface Ship Torpedo Defense (SSTD) program provides a detect-to-engage hardkill torpedo defense capability through two development programs*

This is a weapons system, which should be developed by weapons manufacturers. Eliminate and save $93 Million.

Carrier Systems Development

> *(2208) - Development of ship hull, mechanical, propulsion, electrical, aviation, and combat support systems, subsystems and components to significantly improve aircraft carrier affordability, manpower requirements, survivability, and operational capabilities, and to meet the requirements of existing and pending regulations and statutes critical to the operation of existing and future aircraft carriers.*

Development of ship structure and parts is the responsibility of the shipbuilders.

> *(3216) - Development of block upgrades to the MH-60R sensor suite into the AN/SQQ-34 Aircraft Carrier Tactical Support Center (CV-TSC).*

Development of sensor upgrades is the responsibility of the sensor manufacturers. If it's that big a deal, they'll upgrade or build new ones for the right price.

> *(4004) - Development of an advanced technology aircraft launch system in support of the CVN 78 Class design and construction schedule.*

Catapult development is the responsibility of catapult manufacturers.

> *(4005) - The In-Service Carrier Systems Development Demonstration and Validation program exploits available technologies to deliver an*

affordable, robust, operator-friendly automation control environment for Navy Aircraft Carrier shipboard equipment.

Equipment automation is the responsibility of equipment manufacturers, or equipment automation engineer types who can be hired or who can sell products and services.

Eliminate and save $109 Million.

Pilot Fish

This program is reported in accordance with Title 10, United States Code, Section 119(a)(1) in the Special Access Program Annual Report to Congress.

We'll just see about that. In the meantime, cut by half and save $50 Million.

Retract Larch

This program is reported in accordance with Title 10, United States Code, Section 119(a)(1) in the Special Access Program Annual Report to Congress

We'll just see about that. In the meantime, cut by half and save $37 Million.

Retract Juniper

This program is reported in accordance with Title 10, United States Code, Section 119(a)(1) in the Special Access Program Annual Report to Congress

We'll just see about that. In the meantime, cut by half and save $45 Million.

Radiological Control

The Radiation Detection, Indication and Computation (RADIAC) Program is responsible for providing radiation monitoring instruments that detect and measure ionizing radiation.

A Geiger counter hooked up to a speaker or monitor does not require ongoing funding once installed, and we shouldn't be building more ships as long as they aren't getting disabled. Eliminate and save $800K.

Surface ASW

The Anti-Submarine Warfare (ASW) Advanced Development project provides advanced development demonstration and validation of technology for potential surface sonar and combat system applications. Program Element (PE) 0603553N has been designated to support emerging multi-static technologies, and the Chief of Naval Operations' (CNO) ASW Initiative.

We don't seem to have any problem with enemy submarines, except the ones that are used to smuggle drugs which the government has utterly failed to take care of. Eliminate and save $7 Million.

Advanced Submarine System Development

> *Project Unit 0223: The Advanced Submarine Combat Systems Development non-acquisition (NON-ACAT) Project supports Navy Submarine Acoustic Superiority and Technology Insertion Initiatives through the application of advanced development and testing of sonar and tactical control systems improvements.*

Submarines are weapons, and weapons development should be done by weapons companies.

> *Project Unit 2033: The Advanced Submarine Systems Development (ASSD) Program is a non-acquisition program that develops and matures technologies for successful integration into future and modernized submarine classes, thus lowering acquisition and life cycle program costs while improving mission capability.*

Submarines are weapons, and weapons development should be done by weapons companies.

> *Project Unit 3197: The Undersea Superiority Project supports offboard Anti-Submarine Warfare (ASW) technologies selected by the Chief of Naval Operations (CNO) ASW Cross Functional Team for technologies that hold the potential for deployment and/or use by submarine platforms. Efforts associated with these technologies include design, development, integration and testing of future Undersea Superiority systems.*

Weapons development should be done by weapons companies.

Eliminate and save **$555 Million.** Note this doubles in size by 2017 and continues indefinitely.

Submarine Tactical Warfare System

> *The objective is to improve submarine operational effectiveness through the development and implementation of advanced Research and Development (R&D).*

Submarines are weapons, and weapons development should be done by weapons companies. Eliminate and save $9 Million.

Ship Concept Advanced Design

The objective is a more affordable, mission capable surface ship force including increased ship production capability; ships with reduce manning, reduced operating and support costs, and greater utilization of the latest technology.

Ships are weapons, and weapons development should be done by weapons companies. Eliminate and save $25 Million.

Ship Prel Design and Feasibility Studies

Advanced ship concepts and research. Ships are weapons, and weapons development should be done by weapons companies. Eliminate and save $14 Million.

Advanced Nuclear Power Systems

The details of this program element are classified CONFIDENTIAL and are submitted annually to Congress in the classified budget justification books.

Research and development for nuclear propulsion and related power subsystems. Ships are weapons, and weapons development should be done by weapons companies. Eliminate and save $250 Million.

Advanced Surface Machinery System

In October 2009, SECNAV outlined a set of specific objectives supporting U.S. Navy energy reform including several aimed at significantly reducing Fleet fuel consumption and improving our energy security posture.

Another great way to reduce fleet fuel consumption is by not sending the fleet all over the world. Eliminate and save $30 Million.

Chalk Eagle

This program is reported in accordance with Title 10, United States Code, Section 119(a)(1) in the Special Access Program Annual Report to Congress.

We'll just see about that. In the meantime, cut by half and save $255 Million.

Littoral Combat Ship

This Program Element (PE) provides funds for detailed design, development, construction, integration, and testing of the Littoral Combat Ship (LCS). LCS is a fast, agile, and networked surface combatant with capabilities optimized to defeat asymmetric threats, and assure naval and joint force access into contested littoral regions.

Design and development of ships is the responsibility of shipbuilders. Tell them what you want, maybe front some cash for expenses, and they will build it.

Eliminate and save $435 Million plus $1.8 Billion in LCS procurements elsewhere.

Combat System Integration

> Chief of Naval Operations (CNO) created the Navy's Strike Force Interoperability (SFI) Program in 1998 in response to critical shortfalls in the introduction of integrated and interoperable system of systems to deploying Strike Forces.

The success of our Navy in times of war indicates that these shortfalls must not be so critical after all. Eliminate and save $57 Million.

Conventional Munitions

> Insensitive Munitions Advanced Development (IMAD) (Project 0363) - Most Navy munitions react violently when exposed to unplanned stimuli such as fire, shock and bullet or fragment impact, thus presenting a great hazard to ships, aircraft and personnel. This program will provide, validate and transition technology to all new weapon developments and priority weapon systems and enable production of munitions insensitive to these stimuli with no reduction in combat performance.

Another great way to prevent violent munitions' reactions is by preventing exposure to fire, shock, and impacts. Eliminate and save $7 Million.

Marine Corps Assault Vehicles

> This Program Element (PE) includes funds for the Expeditionary Fighting Vehicle (EFV) and the Amphibious Combat Vehicle (ACV) Programs.

The Marines have been a very effective fighting force and require no more newfangled trucks. Eliminate and privatize; save $95 Million.

Marine Corps Ground Combat/Support System

> This PE supports the demonstration and validation of Marine Corps Ground/Supporting Arms Systems for utilization in Marine Air-Ground Expeditionary Force amphibious operations. This program is funded under DEMONSTRATION & VALIDATION because it develops and integrates hardware for experimental test related to specific ground weapon system.

Demonstration and validation of privately developed technologies is a valid use of military spending, as it is necessary and proper for keeping the Marines well-equipped. Keep as is ($10 Million, ongoing at $1.4 million).

JT Service Explosive Ordnance Disposal

> This program provides for the development of EOD tools and equipment for use by all military services. Responsibility is assigned to the Navy[.]

> *Proliferation of sophisticated types of foreign and domestic ordnance and IEDs necessitate a continuing development program to provide Explosive Ordnance Disposal personnel of all military services with the special equipment and tools required to support this mission.*

Or we could just send the data we recover on the IEDs, or even the exploded IEDs themselves, to equipment manufacturers and tell them we'll pay for any effective countermeasure they come up with. Eliminate and save $57 Million.

Cooperative Engagement

> *Cooperative Engagement Capability (CEC) significantly improves Battle Force Anti-Air Warfare (AAW) capability by coordinating all Battle Force AAW sensors into a single, real-time, composite track picture capable of fire control quality. CEC distributes sensor data from each ship and aircraft, or cooperating unit (CU), to all other CUs in the battle force through a real-time, line of sight, high data rate sensor and engagement data distribution network.*

That's exactly what we need: One single system to give our commanders a picture of the battlefield. Ideally it would completely replace whatever duplicated systems are in use. Too bad it's not a proper government function; but we should definitely buy it when the private sector comes up with it. Eliminate and save $57 Million.

Ocean Engineering Technology Development

> *Developments in this program will enable the U.S. Navy to overcome deficiencies that constrain underwater operations in the areas of search, location, rescue, recovery, salvage, construction, and protection of offshore assets. This program develops medical technology, diver life support equipment, and the vehicles, systems, tools, and procedures to permit manned underwater operations.*

In peacetime, there will be a reduced need for search, location, rescue, recovery, and salvage. Construction and most salvage should be privatized, and protection can be accomplished with Naval patrols and sonar buoys. Eliminate and save $7 Million.

Environmental Protection

> *Many environmental laws, regulations, and policies impose restrictions on Navy vessels, aircraft, and facilities that interfere with operations and/or increase the cost of operations. The Navy must be able to conduct its national security mission in compliance with applicable environmental requirements in the U.S. and abroad without compromising performance, safety, or health, while simultaneously minimizing the cost of compliance.*

Repeal all federal environmental laws, regulations, and policies. States and overseas governments can grant the Navy waivers for their local environmental laws if they want Navy protection. The Navy, of course, should only be used to protect our shores and critical trade lanes. Eliminate and save $21 Million.

Navy Energy Program

This program supports projects to evaluate, adapt, and demonstrate energy related technologies for Navy aircraft and ship operations[.]

Evaluation and demonstration of potential product purchases is an important step in making such big-dollar decisions. Eliminate all except the weapons effectiveness components (i.e. range and time on station); save $47 Million.

Facilities Improvement

This program provides for capabilities to: a) overcome performance limitations and reduce the life cycle cost of shore facilities and, b) provide protection against terrorist attacks for shore installations and their operations.

That sounds pretty important. Reduce by standard 25% and save $1 Million.

Chalk Coral

This program is reported in accordance with Title 10, United States Code, Section 119(a)(1) in the Special Access Program Annual Report to Congress.

We'll just see about that. In the meantime, cut by half and save $23 Million.

Navy Logistic Productivity

Includes development and evaluation of incentive systems for improving the productivity of civilian and military personnel. Identifies barriers to increased productivity and evaluates the effect of removing them.

The military already has incentive programs for FWA prevention: Identify a way to save money, and they give you cash. Maybe they just need to make this program better known or increase the payouts. Eliminate and save $4 Million.

Retract Maple

This program is reported in accordance with Title 10, United States Code, Section 119(a)(1) in the Special Access Program Annual Report to Congress

We'll just see about that. In the meantime, cut by half and save $171 Million.

Link Plumeria

This program is reported in accordance with Title 10, United States Code, Section 119(a)(1) in the Special Access Program Annual Report to Congress

We'll just see about that. In the meantime, cut by half and save $91 Million.

Retract Elm

This program is reported in accordance with Title 10, United States Code, Section 119(a)(1) in the Special Access Program Annual Report to Congress

We'll just see about that. In the meantime, cut by half and save $87 Million.

Link Evergreen

This program is reported in accordance with Title 10, United States Code, Section 119(a)(1) in the Special Access Program Annual Report to Congress.

We'll just see about that. In the meantime, cut by half and save $34 Million.

Special Processes

This program is reported in accordance with Title 10, United States Code, Section 119(a)(1) in the Special Access Program Annual Report to Congress.

We'll just see about that. In the meantime, cut by half and save $22 Million.

NATO Research and Development

Provides funding for research and development (R&D) programs with approved allies under international agreements. [...] This program historically does not meet established execution benchmarks.

Withdraw from NATO and eliminate all overseas spending and all foreign aid, including joint research projects. Eliminate this admittedly failing program and save $9 Million.

Land Attack Technology

The Advanced Minor Caliber Gun project will support non-recurring engineering, component integration, testing and qualification efforts required for the Task Force Defense (TFD) capability upgrade to the MK38 Mod 2, a minor caliber gun weapon system. TFD creates a near term improvement to address ship based, close range solutions for FIFTH Fleet Counter- Swarm.

Gun development should be done by gun manufacturers, and we should buy some of the products they come out with. Eliminate and save $16 Million.

Joint Non-Lethal Weapons Testing

The efforts in this Program Element (PE) reflect Joint Service research and development (R&D) investment decisions provided by the Joint Non Lethal Weapons Integrated Product Team, a multi-service flag level corporate board that executes the JNLWP for the Executive Agent. Research conducted is based on the needs and capabilities of the Services, the Special Operations Command

and the Coast Guard, as identified in the DoD's Non-Lethal Weapons Joint Capabilities Document.

Testing new weapons is an important part of keeping our military well-equipped, but I can't understand how test firing a few types of weapons could possibly cost this much. Reduce by 75% and save $33 Million.

JT Precision Approach and Landing System

Provides for the development, integration, and testing of the Joint Precision Approach and Landing System (JPALS), which will be applicable to Department of Defense (DoD) Ground systems, DoD aircraft, and Navy and Coast Guard air capable surface ships.

The government shouldn't be doing research and development projects, but rather should just buy them from the private sector. Navy planes don't seem to have a problem landing on carriers now; eliminate and save $137 Million.

Tactical Aircraft Directed Infrared Countermeasures

This element includes development of electronic warfare systems for the United States Navy and United States Marine Corps assault and strike aircraft.

The government shouldn't be doing research and development projects, but rather should just buy them from the private sector. Our planes don't seem to have a problem deflecting missiles now; eliminate and save $74 Million.

Self Protection Optimization

This element includes development of Aircraft Survivability equipment and Electronic Warfare/Countermeasures solutions for the United States Navy, United States Marine Corps and Coalition Aircraft to include studies and evaluations of current and future aircraft threats, Modeling and Simulation for improved countermeasure capabilities, and development and testing to address new and emerging threats.

The government shouldn't be doing research and development projects, but rather should just buy them from the private sector. Eliminate and save $1 Million.

Joint Cntr Radio Control IED Elec Warfare

Provides for the research and development of EW systems, equipment, procedures, and tactical aids for all military services against the threat posed by Radio Controlled Improvised Explosive Devices (RCIEDs) and to prevent initiation of RCIEDs across the spectrum of Joint military operations.

The government shouldn't be doing research and development projects, but rather should just buy them from the private sector, and this program ends in 2014. Eliminate and save $71 Million.

Precision Strike Weapons Development Program
> *The Precision Strike Weapons Development program provides for initial and continuing development of strike weapons consisting of armament, munitions, and weapon subsystems to allow for the horizontal integration among current and future weapon system capabilities to include Anti-Surface Warfare and the weaponization of Unmanned Aerial Systems.*

The government shouldn't be doing research and development projects, but rather should just buy them from the private sector, and this program ends in 2014. Eliminate and save $6 Million.

SEW Architecture / Engineering Support
> *Maritime Battle Center (MBC), Fleet Experimentation, Allied/ Coalition Interoperability and Information Dominance (ACIID), and Space and Electronic Warfare (SEW) Engineering.*

Experimentation is pretty important for keeping an up-to-date military, so we can keep this one. Reduce by standard 25% and save $8 Million.

Offensive Anti-Surface Warfare Weapon Development
> *The Offensive Anti-Surface Warfare (OASuW) Weapon Dev program was previously funded under Program Element 0605853N, Project Unit 2221 and assigned to Budget Activity (BA) 06: RDT&E Management Support. In May of 2011, PE 0604786N PU 3337 was established as the principal budget line for the OASuW program assigned as BA 04: Advanced Component Development and Prototypes. The transition from PE 0605853N to PE 0604786N continues the transfer of program with the alignment of funding associated with the OASuW program.*

The government shouldn't be doing research and development projects, but rather should just buy them from the private sector. Eliminate and save $87 Million.

Joint Light Tactical Vehicle
> *This Program Element (PE) funds the Joint Light Tactical Vehicle (JLTV) Family of Vehicles. Funding supports the development and testing of the JLTV Family of Vehicles (FoV), which is being developed as a joint system between the Army and the Marine Corps. International participation will be offered during the Engineering, Manufacturing and Development (EMD) phase.*

The government shouldn't be doing research and development projects, but rather should just buy them from the private sector. Eliminate and save $45 Million.

ASW Systems Development – MIP

The mission of Airborne Acoustic Intelligence (AAI) (CNO Project K-0416) is to provide Sound Pressure Level quality recordings of targets of interest and an associated new technology, rapid prototyping mechanism for the application of state-of-the-art collection sensors.

The government shouldn't be doing research and development projects, but rather should just buy them from the private sector. Eliminate and save $13 Million.

Electronic Warfare Development – MIP

This project supports systems development and collection of Specific Emitter Identification (SEI) information from National Technical Means (NTM) to track commercial ships over 200 gross registered tons world-wide. Research and development will cover improvements and enhancements to Electronic Intelligence technology.

The government shouldn't be doing research and development projects, but rather should just buy them from the private sector. Eliminate and save $1 Million.

Development and Demonstration

Other Helicopter Development

This Program Element includes funding for the development support for improvements to current systems for CH/MH-53, MH-60 development, and VH-3/VH-60. The H-53 is the premier heavy lift helicopter for the Marine Corps and only operational airborne mine sweeping platform for the Navy. H-53 RDT&E efforts focus on trade studies and risk reduction measures to identify candidate survivability, safety, avionics, cargo handling, cockpit and other airframe specific improvements to extend the service life.

The government shouldn't be doing research and development projects, but rather should just buy them from the private sector. Eliminate and save $34 Million.

AV-8B Aircraft Engine Development

The program provides for AV-8B Design, Development, Integration and Test of various platform improvements such as: Engine Life Management Program (ELMP), Escape Systems, Joint Mission Planning System (JMPS), and Block

> *upgrades to various mission systems, communications systems, navigation equipment, weapons carriage and countermeasures, and the Aircraft Handling/Readiness Management Plan (RMP).*

The government shouldn't be doing research and development projects, but rather should just buy them from the private sector. Eliminate and save $33 Million.

Standards Development

> *This project provides for the identification, study, design, development, demonstration, test, evaluation, and qualification of standard avionics capabilities for Navy use, and wherever practicable, use across all Services and Foreign Military Sales.*

The military seems to be doing just fine without such standards so far. Eliminate and save $85 Million.

Multi-Mission Helicopter Upgrade Developement

> *This Program Element includes funding for the development support for the improvements to current systems for the MH-60R. The MH-60R Multi-Mission Helicopter provides battle group protection and adds significant capability in coastal littorals and regional conflicts.*

The government shouldn't be doing research and development projects, but rather should just buy them from the private sector. Eliminate and save $7 Million.

Air / Ocean Equipment Engineering

> *The Air/Ocean Equipment Engineering (AOEE) Program Element provides future mission capabilities to support naval combat forces. This program engineers and developmentally tests organic and remote sensors, communication interfaces, and processing and display devices.*

The government shouldn't be doing research and development projects, but rather should just buy them from the private sector. Eliminate and save $4 Million.

P-3 Modernization Program

> *This program provides for P-3C aircraft systems development and test in subsurface and surface surveillance, search, detection, localization, classification, attack and communications in support of Sea Shield/Sea Power 21. The P-3C Sensor Integration project integrates advanced and future Anti-Submarine Warfare (ASW) and Anti-Surface Warfare (ASuW) sensors, weapons*

systems, and supporting technology into legacy P-3C systems and phased capabilities upgrades.

The government shouldn't be doing research and development projects, but rather should just buy them from the private sector. Eliminate and save $3 Million.

Warfare Support System

The Naval Coastal Warfare (NCW) community consists of 22 Mobile Inshore Undersea Warfare (MIUW) units and 8 Harbor Defense Command (HDC) units operating Mobile Ashore Support Terminal IIIs (MAST IIIs). NCW also includes 14 Inshore Boat Units (IBU) comprised of 6 small craft (boats) each on which are installed C4I systems.

The government shouldn't be doing research and development projects, but rather should just buy them from the private sector. Eliminate and save $13 Million.

Tactical Command System

Project 0709 Global Command & Control System Maritime (GCCS-M) Applications: *In FY 2012, the Navy Command Control Air Planning Capability effort was realigned from Global Command and Control System Maritime (GCCS-M) Maritime Applications (x0709) to the Navy Air Operations Command and Control (NAOC2) program (Project Unit x3324).*

Project 2351 Maritime Domain Awareness (MDA): *MDA RDTEN funding was realigned to Distributed Common Ground System-Navy (DCGS-N) PE 0305208N in FY 2012 and out.*

Project 3320 Trident Warrior (TW): *Funding transferred from Project 9123 FORCEnet into Project 3320 beginning in FY 2012.*

Project 3323 Maritime Tactical Command & Control (MTC2): *Beginning in FY 2013, the development of maritime tactical command and control capabilities will be realigned from Global Command and Control System Maritime (GCCS-M) Maritime Applications (Project Unit x0709) to the MTC2 program (Project Unit x3323).*

The government shouldn't be doing research and development projects, but rather should just buy them from the private sector. Eliminate and save $72 Million.

Advanced Hawkeye

The E-2D Advanced Hawkeye (AHE) program develops, demonstrates, tests, and procures the replacement of the AN/APS-145 radar system and other aircraft system components including Cooperative Engagement Capability Pre-Planned Product Improvement and Dual Transmit Satellite Communications that modernize the E-2 weapon system to maintain open ocean mission capability while providing the United States Navy with an effective littoral surveillance, battle management, and Theater Air and Missile Defense (TAMD) capability.

Existing radar systems and components are working fine. Eliminate.

Operational Systems Development

E-2 Squadrons

E-2 Improvements (0463) provides for incorporation of technologies for the evolution of E-2 Battle Management and Command and Control capabilities in support of naval warfare command and control requirements. It funds developments for the modification or replacement of Weapon Replaceable Assemblies of currently installed subsystems, as well as providing for experimentation with narrowband and wideband internet protocol (IP) concepts[...]

The Navy should not be funding development efforts. Internet Protocol concepts should be fleshed out by the companies that build networking equipment and organizations like the Internet Engineering Task Force (IETF) and the Internet Society (ISOC). Eliminate and save $9 Million.

Fleet Tactical Development

The Communications Automation Program - This project is a continuing program that provides for automation and communications upgrades for fleet tactical users. It includes Battle Force Tactical Networks (BFTN) (formerly High Frequency Internet Protocol/Sub Network Relay), Maritime Aerial Layer Network (MALN) and Automated Digital Network System (ADNS).

The Navy should not be building its automation systems, but rather should buy the ones that come out of the private sector. Recurring outlays need not apply. Eliminate and save $16 Million.

Surface Support

The Surface Support RDT&E funding will be used for the research, design, development, integration testing, and documentation of a new AN/WSN-7 Inertial Measuring Unit (IMU) to support the Ballistic Missile Defense (BMD) mission.

The Navy shouldn't be performing research, design, or development of any kind. That's the economy's job. Eliminate and save $4 Million.

Tomahawk Mission Planning Center

Includes RDT&E funds for development of the Tomahawk encompassing Tomahawk Land-Attack Missile (TLAM) upgrades, Tactical Tomahawk Weapons Controls System, Tomahawk Command and Control System upgrades and other missile system improvements. The Tomahawk Weapons System provides a Tomahawk cruise missile attack capability against fixed and mobile targets.

In peacetime, there would be no Tomahawk missions to plan, other than maybe an occasional test fire to make sure they still work. We already have Tomahawk control systems. Eliminate and save $11 Million.

Integrated Surveillance System

Project 0766 provides for Integrated Undersea Surveillance Systems (IUSS) Research and Development Projects under the Maritime Surveillance Systems (MSS) Program Office (PEO SUB PMS 485). IUSS provides the Navy with its primary means of submarine detection both nuclear and diesel.

If these systems are working, then they require no more Research, Development, Test, and Evaluation. Eliminate and save $46 Million.

Amphibious Tactical Support Units

Provides for research efforts on Landing Craft Air Cushioned (LCAC) Future Naval Capabilities to transfer technologies to functional uses on current LCACs.

Existing LCAC capabilities are plenty amphibious for the Navy's and Marines' needs. If the manufacturer releases a newer model, we can buy those. Eliminate and save $8 Million.

Ground/Air Task Oriented Radar (G/ATOR)

Ground/Air Task Oriented Radar (G/ATOR) (formerly known as the Multi-Role Radar System (MRRS)) is an expeditionary, 3-dimensional, high-mobility, multi-purpose wheeled vehicle, short/medium range multi-role radar designed to detect cruise missiles, air breathing targets, rockets, mortars, and artillery.

"Air breathing targets" sounds an awful lot like "mostly innocent people" to me. If the Gator is working, then it requires no additional RDT&E. Eliminate and save $75 Million.

Consolidating Training Systems Development

The Training Range and Instrumentation Development Systems (TRIDS) program provides development of range systems including Large Area Tracking Range (LATR), Test & Training Enabling Architecture (TENA)

> *interoperability and Tactical Training Ranges (TTR) infrastructure improvements.*

The Navy has plenty of training systems. If they're working, then they require no additional RDT&E. Elimiante and save $20 Million.

Cryptologic Direct Support

> *The Advanced Cryptologic Systems Engineering - Cryptologic Carry On Program develops state-of-the-art signal acquisition software in response to Combatant Command requirements for a quick-reaction surface, subsurface, and airborne cryptologic carry-on capability.*

Sounds to me like combatant commanders are too whiny; the military was still effective before we had this. Eliminate and save $2 Million.

Elect Warfare Readiness Support

> *Research, assess, and develop information warfare capabilities*

That's about as vague a description as you can hope for from the military-industrial complex. Research and development should be done by the private sector, and assessment is procured elsewhere. Eliminate and save $20 Million.

Harm Improvement

> *Research, Development, Test and Evaluation funding for the Joint Service Pre-Planned Product Improvement program which will include near and far term performance improvements, cost reduction, and studies that establish future development requirements.*

The Navy's missiles are already quite effective, and research on them should be done by missile manufacturers. Eliminate and save $11 Million.

Tactical Data Links

> *This Program Element develops and improves the Navy's Tactical Data Link (TDL) systems. It includes the Advanced Tactical Data Link Systems (ATDLS) Integration Programs, specifically Link 16 Network, Command and Control Processor (C2P) and Link Monitoring and Management Tool (LMMT) (formerly Air Defense System Integrator (ADSI))*

The Navy shouldn't be doing its own development; eliminate and save **$119 Million**.

Surface ASW Combat Systems Integration

> *The objective of this Program Element (PE) is to significantly improve existing Surface Ship Undersea Warfare (USW) sonar system capabilities through quick and affordable development/integration of emergent, transformational*

technologies in support of Littoral ASW, Theater ASW, Mine Reconnaissance, and overall Sea Shield efforts required to pace the threat. Detection and classification play uniquely vital roles in the success of any ASW campaign.

Existing surface ship undersea warfare sonar systems are plenty effective right now, and R&D should be done by the manufacturers of said equipment. Eliminate and save $27 Million.

Aviation Improvements

Common Ground Equipment is a Naval Aviation Project to apply new technology to common support equipment necessary to support multiple aircraft.

Yes, but existing ground equipment is doing the job just fine.

Consolidated Automated Support System is a standardized Automated Test Equipment with computer assisted, multi-function capabilities to support the maintenance of aircraft subsystems and missiles.

There's nothing wrong with the way tests were done before.

Aircraft Equipment Reliability/Maintainability Improvement Program is the only Navy program that provides engineering support for in-service out-of-production aircraft equipment, and provides increased readiness at reduced operational and support cost.

So hire some contractors or buy an extended service plan.

Aircraft Engine Component Improvement Program develops reliability and maintainability and safety enhancements for in-service Navy aircraft engines, transmissions, propellers, starters, auxiliary power units, electrical generating systems, fuel systems, fuels, and lubricants.

Aircraft engine components should be improved by aircraft engine manufacturers.

The description continues in this manner. Eliminate and save $89 million.

Navy Science Assistance Program

The Naval Science Advisor Program ensures the Fleet/Force (F/F) helps shape the Department of the Navy (DoN) investment in Science and Technology (S&T), develops teaming relationships to rapidly demonstrate and transition technology, supports development of technology-based capability options for naval forces, and enables warfighting innovations based on technical and conceptual possibilities.

If we eliminate the Navy's investments, then we can eliminate this overhead and save $3 Million.

Operational Nuclear Power Systems

> The details of this program element are classified CONFIDENTIAL and are submitted annually to Congress in the classified budget justification books.

We'll just see about that. We can infer from the title that is has to do with the nuclear propulsion systems of Navy ships. Which seem to be working fine. Eliminate and save $86 Million.

Marine Corps Comm Systems

> This program element provides funding to develop the command and control (C2) support and information infrastructures for the Fleet Marine Force and supporting establishment.

Now, in the 21st century, we shouldn't still be developing individual communications systems. We should be developing one single communication system that spans the entire DoD. By "we", of course, I mean the private sector. Eliminate and save $219 Million.

MC Ground Combat Support Arms System

> This PE provides modification to Marine Corps Expeditionary Ground Force Weapon Systems to increase lethality, range, survivability and operational effectiveness.

The Marines are plenty lethal as they are now. They can be anywhere in the world in under a day, they operate effectively, and their occupational safety record is pretty good if you disregard the number who get shot or blown up in foreign countries. Eliminate and save $182 Million.

Marine Corps Combat Services Support

> This program element (PE) provides funding for Marine Air-Ground Task Force requirements for Combat Service Support equipment improvement. It will enhance combat breaching capabilities of the ground combat elements, logistics, maintenance and transportation.

Marines are already highly effective against ground forces, being that they are in fact ground forces. If we eliminate war, then they won't need improvements to their ground equipment. Eliminate and save $65 Million.

USMC Intelligence / Electronic Warfare Systems

> This Program Element (PE) includes funds for Intelligence Command and Control (C2) which supports the employment of reconnaissance, surveillance,

and target acquisition resources and the timely planning and processing of all-source intelligence. It ensures that all-source tactical intelligence is tailored to meet specific mission requirements.

Once again, the development of these systems is the job of the private sector. Hand the economy back to them and let it fix itself. Eliminate and save $23 Million.

Tactical Aim Missiles

This program supports the integration of the Advanced Medium Range Air-to-Air Missile (AMRAAM) into Navy aircraft with analysis of Navy unique applications, aircraft missile integration tasks, product improvement efforts including missile software upgrade development and procurement of hardware to support Navy test and evaluation tasks.

Missile development is the job of missile manufacturers. Eliminate and save $21 Million. Submit the budget again with only the evaluation component, and we can talk.

AMRAAM

This program supports the integration of the Advanced Medium Range Air-to-Air Missile (AMRAAM) into Navy aircraft with analysis of Navy unique applications, aircraft missile integration tasks, product improvement efforts including missile software upgrade development and procurement of hardware to support Navy test and evaluation tasks.

Missile development is the job of missile manufacturers. Eliminate and save $3 Million. Submit the budget again with only the evaluation component, and we can talk.

Joint High Speed Vessel

Future joint forces will be responsive, deployable, agile, versatile, lethal, survivable and sustainable. The nation will need lift assets that can provide for assured access, decrease predictability and dwell time, and have the capacity to quickly deliver troops and equipment together in a manner that provides for unit integrity.

This program ends in 2014, so it needn't be considered as part of any ongoing budget. Having said that, the Navy seems to be doing just fine with whatever they have now, so eliminate and save $2 Million.

Satellite Communications (Space)

The Navy Multiband Terminal (NMT) Program is the required Navy component to the Advanced Extremely High Frequency (AEHF) Program for enhancing protected and survivable satellite communications to Naval forces. The NMT system provides an increase in single service capability from 1.5 Megabits per second (Mbps) to 8 Mbps, increases the number of coverage areas and retains Anti-Jam/Low Probability of Intercept (AJ/LPI) protection characteristics.

The private sector is routing much more traffic than this over satellites today. Eliminate this program, which provides communications slower than a household DSL connection, and buy one of those products. $188 Million saved.

Consolidated Afloat Network Enterprise Services (CANES)

CANES is a DoN Efficiency Initiative and is the Navy's only Program of Record (POR) to replace existing afloat networks and provide the necessary infrastructure for applications, systems, and services to operate in the tactical domain.

Existing afloat networks seem to be working just fine. Eliminate and save $17 Million.

Information Systems Security Program

Information Systems Security Program (ISSP) ensures the protection of Navy and joint cyberspace systems from exploitation and attack. Cyberspace systems include wired and wireless telecommunications systems, Information Technology (IT) systems, and the content processed, stored, or transmitted therein. ISSP includes protection of the Navy's National Security Systems and Information (NSSI).

There are plenty of security programs available in the private sector for much less. Many of them are even free. Eliminate and save $26 Million.

WWMCCS / Global Command and Control System

PE 0303150M reflects a portion of the Global Force Management-Data Initiative (GFM-DI) advocated by the VCJCS. Funding enhancements support GFM-DI implementation of the Force Management and Adaptive Planning Processes by FY13 and Financial, Health Records, and Information Assurance by FY16.

Systems that do these things are available today, and they cost a lot less. Eliminate and save $500K.

Cobra Judy

Cobra Judy Replacement funds will replace the current U.S. Naval Ship (USNS) Observation Island which has become unsustainable and due to leave service in 2014. This program funds the development of a single ship-based radar suite for ballistic missile treaty verification.

Ship-based radar suite development should be done by ship-based radar suite manufacturers. Additionally, we need to eliminate and rethink most of our treaties. Eliminate and save $17 Million.

Navy Meteorological and Ocean Sensors – Space (METOC)

> *This program element supports the Navy's requirements in meteorological and oceanographic (METOC) space-based remote sensors. These requirements include commitments to satellite, sensor, and operational demonstration/development activities as well as the transition to fleet applications associated with three satellite programs[.]*

A private company can perform this task and provide the data to the Navy, but I suppose it could be described as necessary and proper. On the other hand, we already have a system that this development project is replacing; so eliminate and save $810K.

JT Military Intel Programs

> *The details of this program element are classified CONFIDENTIAL and are submitted annually to Congress in the classified budget justification books.*

We'll just see about that. In the meantime, but by half and save $4 Million.

Tactical Unmanned Aerial Vehicles

> *This Program Element (PE) includes non-lethal joint tactical Unmanned Aerial Vehicle system support for DoD to provide the warfighters with the capability for day/ night aerial Reconnaissance, Surveillance and Target Acquisition, intelligence, communications/data relay, and minefield detection in limited adverse weather.*

The UAV is a worthy project, but its applications have already stretched far beyond military authority. Privatize and eliminate, saving $9 Million.

Manned Reconnaissance System

> *This program is reported in accordance with Title 10, United States Code, Section 119(a)(1) in the Special Access Program Annual Report to Congress.*

We'll just see about that. In the meantime, cut by half and save $15 Million.

Distributed Common Ground / Surface Systems

> *DCGS-MC, in compliance with the Department of Defense DCGS Family of Systems (FOS) concept, is a service-level effort to migrate select USMC Intelligence, Surveillance and Reconnaissance (ISR) processing and exploitation capabilities into a single, integrated, net-centric baseline that will be interoperable with other services and agencies. Multiple functional capability sets will be configured to support Marine intelligence analysts across the*

> *MAGTF. The goal of DCGS-MC is to make external and internal ISR data more visible, accessible, and understandable.*

We shouldn't be migrating select USMC capabilities into a single integrated system; we should be migrating the entire Department of Defense. Now we have all these different disparate systems being migrated into slightly fewer disparate systems which barely talk to each other and thereby justify R&D projects for decades to come. Eliminate and save $26 Million.

Distributed Common Ground System

> *The Department of Defense (DoD) has defined a DCGS architecture that will be verifiably compatible and interoperable across all of the Services' Intelligence, Surveillance and Reconnaissance (ISR) systems and operations. DCGS accesses and ingests data from space borne, airborne, subsurface, and surface ISR collection assets, intelligence databases and intelligence producers.*

A fair integration effort, but it doesn't go far enough. Go big or go home. Eliminate and save $15 Million.

FY 2013 Overseas Contingency Operations Request [90]

> *The FY 2013 Overseas Contingency Operations (OCO) requests funding so that the United States may continue security stabilization efforts in Afghanistan and continue the global fight against terror. These efforts are in addition to ongoing daily military operations around the globe. Without additional funds in FY 2013, the Navy would have to use funds from readiness and investment accounts to finance the continuing costs of military operations. Absorbing costs of this magnitude will seriously degrade combat operations and weaken the nation's ability to react to future threats.*

We drove the Al Qaeda out of Afghanistan, so they just fled to Pakistan. We drove them out of there and they went to Libya. Clearly, the trillions we have spent are not getting the job done. Further, every single terrorist attack against us that was connected to the Al Qaeda or other Muslim extremist groups has been attributed by the attackers as because of our foreign policy. We must change the policy or we will destroy ourselves in the process.

As outlined myriad times already, we must eliminate all OCO funding and bring our military home. All of them. Right now. We need to worry about our own borders, security, and economy; let them deal with their own problems. **$914 Million** saved.

---

[90] http://www.finance.hq.navy.mil/fmb/13pres/FY13_OCO_Book.pdf

Department of the Air Force [91]
Article I, Section 8, Clause 12 authorizes the Congress to "raise and support Armies". Given that there were no airplanes when this was written, it's easy to see the parallel between the Air Force and a traditional ground army. Therefore, the Air Force is constitutionally justified. However, not everything in the Air Force is necessary to fulfill these authorized activities, nor directly advances them.

Military Family Housing [92]
The Air Force would be useless without personnel, and people need a place to live, so the housing is (generally) necessary and proper to the purpose of providing and maintaining an Air Force (read: "armies") per the Constitution. Keep military housing at the standard 25% reduction, and save $150 Million.

Military Construction [93]

Construction outside the United States
Since my plan eliminates all overseas locations, we can safely eliminate all overseas military construction and save $69 Million.

New Mission
New mission projects all support new and additional programs or initiatives that do not revitalize the existing physical plant. These projects support the deployment and bed-down of new weapons systems: new or additional aircraft, missile and space projects; new equipment, e.g. radar, communication, computer satellite tracking and electronic security.

All New Mission requirements shall be put on hold while we reevaluate our place in the world. Eliminate and save $113 Million.

Operations, Utilities, and Maintenance
Cut by standard 25% to estimate the reduction caused by closing all overseas locations; save $30 Million.

Utilities
Cut by standard 25% to estimate the reduction caused by closing all overseas locations; save $190 Million.

---

[91] http://www.saffm.hq.af.mil/budget/
[92] http://www.saffm.hq.af.mil/shared/media/document/AFD-120207-056.pdf
[93] http://www.saffm.hq.af.mil/shared/media/document/AFD-120209-048.pdf

Maintenance
Cut by standard 25% to estimate the reduction caused by closing all overseas locations; save $50 Million.

Privatization
Cut by standard 25% to estimate the reduction caused by closing all overseas locations; save $10 Million.

Leasing
Cut by standard 25% to estimate the reduction caused by closing all overseas locations; save $20 Million.

Keep all other Military Construction as planned; total saved $477 Million.

Reserve Military Construction[94]
Pollution Abatement requests no funding, but is nonetheless part of the budget and adding overhead. Eliminate. All Reserve construction is within the United States; keep as is for now ($10M).

Air National Guard Construction[95]
All ANG construction is within the United States; keep as is for now ($42M).

Military Personnel[96]
Since my plan eliminates social security, Medicaid, and the like, we can eliminate all funding that goes into those programs, thus saving over $**2 Billion**.

Since my plan eliminates all overseas stations, we can eliminate Overseas Extension Pay, saving $206K; Station Allowance Overseas, saving $544 Million.

Since my plan eliminates being positioned anywhere that involves being fired at by hostiles, we can eliminate all Hostile Fire Pay and save $31 Million.

We should eliminate the practice of discharging people who fail to earn promotions, saving $2.2 Million in Severance Pay, Non-Promotion.

The practice of moving people around from base to base should be minimized, so people can build houses and have some stability in their lives. Let's cut PCS Travel by our standard 25% and save $323 Million.

---

[94] http://www.saffm.hq.af.mil/shared/media/document/AFD-120202-054.pdf
[95] http://www.saffm.hq.af.mil/shared/media/document/AFD-120127-064.pdf
[96] http://www.saffm.hq.af.mil/shared/media/document/AFD-120206-029.pdf

Unemployment Insurance is a form of Redistribution of Wealth. Eliminate it and instead disburse its $72 Million back into the primary Military Pay fund. That is, just give them their money up front instead of withholding it; and teach them to save that money "just in case".

The government should never subsidize adoption, nor involve itself therein to any extent. Eliminate the Adoption Reimbursement pay and save $519K.

My plan eliminates the Federal Reserve and the ongoing process of printing more and more money, so inflation should be eliminated. Therefore, eliminate all increases that result to offset inflation, saving $611 Million.

The number being brought back from overseas will offset a reduction of 25% of our active force, so we can reduce the remainder by 25%, thus saving an additional **$7.4 Billion**.

These cuts save a total of **$10.24 Billion**.

Air Force Reserve Personnel[97]
Since my plan eliminates FICA, cut that and save $530K. Our military probably shouldn't have to pay taxes anyway.

I didn't see most of what I cut anywhere in the Reserve budget, so let's go ahead and cut the remainder by the standard 25%, which is well below the 33% I cut from Active. $473 Million saved.

Air National Guard Military Personnel[98]
Since my plan eliminates Medicare, let's cut that and save $227 Million.

I didn't see most of what I cut anywhere in the ANG budget, so let's go ahead and cut the remainder by the standard 25%, which is well below the 33% I cut from Active. **$1.2 Billion** saved.

Operations and Maintenance [99] [100]

Summary - All Inclusive O&M Cuts
Foreign National Direct Hire: Eliminate based on the name alone; $70 Million and $169 Million saved.

---

[97] http://www.saffm.hq.af.mil/shared/media/document/AFD-120207-057.pdf
[98] http://www.saffm.hq.af.mil/shared/media/document/AFD-120202-052.pdf
[99] http://www.saffm.hq.af.mil/shared/media/document/AFD-120206-061.pdf
[100] http://www.saffm.hq.af.mil/shared/media/document/AFD-120206-062.pdf

Voluntary Separation Incentive Pay: We shouldn't bribe people to leave the military; $33 Million saved.

Unemployment Compensation: Take this $15 Million and instead put it right back into the base pay.

Counter-Drug Activities: Let the people do what they want; take appropriate action when it is found to affect their duties. $35K saved.

Grants: Eliminate all federal grants; $33 Million saved.

Overseas Contingency Operations Funding: Eliminate per new foreign policy; save **$10.4 Billion**.

Environmental Restoration: Eliminate and save **$4.5 Billion**.

Operating Forces

Air Operations

Primary Combat Forces

> *Primary Combat Forces are comprised of three major subcategories: Fixed wing combat aircraft to include its front-line fighters, bombers, and strike assets; Nuclear assets to include Intercontinental Ballistic Missiles (ICBMs), the helicopters that support them and the bomber force's air launched missiles; and Conventional weapons that provide a strong capability to counter a wide range of threats to the U.S. and its allies, as well as assure a viable deterrent posture.*

The primary combat forces are, of course, a critical part of the military. Keep as is ($3 Billion).

Combat Enhancement Forces

> *Combat Enhancement Forces include Electronic Warfare (EW) and manned destructive suppression assets employed to enhance the effectiveness of other operational weapons systems, civil and combat rescue and recovery, Air Force Special Operations, and combat communications. Electronic Warfare programs include EC-130H (Compass Call) aircraft, mission planning systems, electronic combat support, shore-based electronic warfare squadrons, combat identification, information warfare flights, intelligence support to information operations and joint information operations support.*

Knowing what's going on around the battlefield is an important part of conducting the battle. Keep as is ($1.6 Billion).

Air Operations Training

Air Operations Training consists of fighter lead-in training, combat mission and advanced tactical training for aircrew, and missile launch training for ballistic missile crews. Funding supports the operation and maintenance of training and aggressor squadron aircraft; training range activities, facilities and equipment; combat simulation training; dissimilar air combat training; ground training munitions and training deployments and exercises.

People have to train, even in peacetime, so that we're ready for war if it comes upon us. Keep as is ($1.5 Billion).

Depot Maintenance

The Air Force enhances the management and programming for Total Force sustainment requirements by reviewing sustainment requirements at the enterprise level. This concept, Weapon System Sustainment (WSS), includes Depot Purchased Equipment Maintenance (DPEM), Contractor Logistics Support (CLS), Sustaining Engineering (SE) and Technical Orders (TO) commodities.

A new peacetime foreign policy means the aircraft will not be pushed as far nor flown as much, so let's reduce this by 25% and save **$1.4 Billion**.

Facilities Sustainment

Facilities Sustainment and Restoration/Modernization (FSRM) functions include facility and infrastructure sustainment, restoration, modernization and demolition activities. This Subactivity Group predominantly supports and maintains Air Combat Command (ACC), Pacific Air Forces (PACAF), United States Air Forces in Europe (USAFE), Air Force Space Command (AFSPC), Air Force Special Operations Command (AFSOC) and Air Force Global Strike Command (AFGSC) operating installations.

We're eliminating all overseas locations, which easily covers a quarter of our bases, so let's cut this by 25% and save $339 Million.

Base Support

This program provides funding for installation support functions, engineering and environmental programs[.] The program sustains mission capability, quality of life, workforce productivity and infrastructure support.

These are important aspects of being ready for war, and thus protecting the homeland. Eliminate the environmental components and reduce the remainder by the standard 25%, saving $649 Million.

Combat Related Operations

Global C3I and Early Warning

> *Global Command, Control, Communication, Intelligence (C3I) & Early Warning includes resources that provide Strategic Offensive C3I, Strategic Defensive C3I and Air Force-wide communications. Strategic Offensive C3I and Computer (C4I) assets comprise the media through which interconnected airborne and ground-based command centers execute commands for offensive strikes against opposing threats.*

We need to be ready in case we do get attacked; keep as is ($958M).

Other Combat Operations Support Programs

> *Resources provide manpower, support equipment, necessary facilities and other items in support of combat evaluation groups and strategic missile evaluation squadrons; defensive training; civil engineer heavy repair squadrons (Red Horse); Defense System Evaluation Squadrons and Radar Evaluation Squadrons.*

These are mostly necessary aspects of defending the homeland. Eliminate all Major Commands, and move everything into what is currently NORTHCOM, but removing that layer of overhead in between. Essentially everything below MAJCOM needs to move into the United States and move up one level in the hierarchy. Obviously, this is a DoD-level change. Keep as is for the time being ($916M).

Tactical Intelligence and Special Activities

> *The description of operations financed under Tactical Intelligence & Special Activities is classified. Details will be provided under a separate cover upon request.*

If everything is on the up-and-up, and we're in peacetime, then there really isn't a need for most classified programs. Let's cut this by half until we figure out what it is ($352 Million).

Space Operations

Launch Operations

> *Launch operations are composed of Spacelift Ranges and the Launch Vehicles program. Spacelift ranges provide tracking, telemetry, communications, range safety, weather and other support for Department of Defense (DoD), civil and commercial space launches, intercontinental and sea-launched ballistic missile Test and Evaluations (T&E), missile defense developmental T&E and aeronautical T&E. The spacelift ranges are responsible for infrastructure*

> *maintenance functions, to include heating and air conditioning, fire protection/detection and corrosion control.*

Satellites don't just launch themselves. Let's cut by the standard 25% and save $79 Million.

Space Control Systems

> *Space Operations is composed of Space Control Systems, Satellite Systems, and Other Space Operations. Space Control Systems include the Air Force Satellite Control Network (AFSCN) and the Space and Missile Test Evaluation Center. AFSCN deploys and provides assured access to operational Department of Defense (DoD) and classified satellites and provides the global network of control centers, remote tracking stations and communications links required to operate national security satellites for both operations and research and development.*

Satellites don't just control themselves. Let's cut by the standard 25% and save $122 Million.

COCOM

Combatant Commands Direct Mission Support

> *Funding in this Subactivity Group supports the combatant commands (COCOM) and their mission to provide for the functional combatant capability and geographic worldwide mobility of U.S. forces. This funding is critical to defending the homeland and deterring foreign adversaries by executing the National Security Strategy and National Military Strategy of the United States.*

By eliminating our geographic worldwide posture, we thusly obsolete the entire Expeditionary Force system. Eliminate and save $863 Million.

Combatant Commands Core Operations

> *Funding supports the operation and administration of the combatant command (COCOM) headquarters staff, including civilian pay, travel, supplies, and training.*

By eliminating our geographic worldwide posture, we thusly obsolete the entire Expeditionary Force system. Eliminate and save $222 Million.

For those of you who haven't been counting, this means we can eliminate COCOM altogether. Its very existence is a symptom of a warmongering way of life, which is not what America was supposed to be about.

Mobilization

Airlift Operations

Airlift operations support day-to-day mission activity for C-17 and C-5 strategic airlift, C-130 tactical airlift, KC-10 and KC-135 strategic air refueling, and Operational Support Airlift (OSA) and Very Important Person Special Airlift Missions (VIPSAM) for movement of personnel, cargo, and fuel with time, place, or mission-sensitive requirements.

In a peacetime environment, the only day-to-day mission activity for these cargo planes and cargo plane derivatives would be training. Cut by half and save $893 Million.

Mobilization Preparedness

Mobilization preparedness supports mobility operations with the capability to sustain contingency operations and wartime requirements through the provision and prepositioning of war readiness materials, theater nuclear weapon storage and security systems, industrial preparedness, inactive aircraft storage, deployable contingency hospitals and clinics, and installation Medical Counter-Chemical, Biological, Radiological, Nuclear (C-CBRN) Installation Response Program.

We do need to be prepared for war, even though we don't want to be at war. Keep as is ($154M).

Depot Maintenance

The Air Force enhances the management and programming for Total Force sustainment requirements by reviewing sustainment requirements at the enterprise level.

In peacetime, there will be less wear and less use on aircraft and equipment. Cut by standard 25% and save $369 Million.

Facilities Sustainment

Facilities Sustainment and Restoration/Modernization (FSRM) functions include demolition, sustainment, restoration and modernization projects. This Subactivity Group supports Air Force District of Washington (AFDW) and maintains Air Mobility Command's (AMC) main operating bases.

There is no indication of how much of this funding goes toward overseas facilities, so let's cut by the standard 25% and save $77 Million.

Base Support

This program provides funding for installation support functions, engineering and environmental programs in support of Air Mobility Command (AMC) and

Air Force District Washington (AFDW). The program sustains mission capability, quality of life, workforce productivity and infrastructure support.

Installations need support and, to a lesser extent, engineering. The rest is unnecessary. The budget doesn't indicate how much of this money goes toward the environmental component, so let's cut it by the standard 25% and save $177 Million.

Training and Recruiting

Officer Acquisition

Operations support three of the four officer accession training programs within the Air Force. The majority of the funding supports the United States Air Force Academy (USAFA) to include direct mission support for cadets, preparatory school students, and faculty.

The military needs officers, though I would argue that the government shouldn't be subsidizing prep schools. Keep as is ($115 Million).

Recruit Training

Program supports recruiting and basic military training that transforms civilian recruits into disciplined, dedicated, physically fit Airmen ready to serve in the United States Air Force. Operations financed include support for the 737th Training Group located at Lackland AFB, TX.

The military needs recruits; keep as is ($18 Million).

Reserve Officer Training Corps (ROTC)

Air Force Reserve Officer Training Corps (AFROTC) is the largest source of new officer accessions for the Air Force and the primary source of commissioning for technical Air Force Specialty Codes.

Necessary and proper; but cut by 25% and save $23 Million.

Facilities Sustainment

Facilities Sustainment and Restoration/Modernization (FSRM) functions include demolition, sustainment, restoration and modernization projects. This Subactivity Group supports and maintains base infrastructure and personnel support functions at the United States Air Force Academy (USAFA) and Air Education and Training Command (AETC).

There is no indication of how much of this funding goes toward overseas facilities, so let's cut by the standard 25% and save $84 Million.

Accession Training

Base Support

> This program provides funding for installation support functions, engineering and environmental programs in support of the United States Air Force Academy (USAFA) and Air Education and Training Command (AETC). The program sustains mission capability, quality of life, workforce productivity and infrastructure support.

Installation support functions need funding, but we're supporting fewer installations. Reduce by standard 25% and save $211 Million.

Specialized Skill Training

> Operations provide Air Force and other service members the initial skills training (Air Force Specialty Code awarding) and education essential to managing complex weapon systems and performing other mission-related tasks. Additionally, this training provides the enhanced technical skills needed throughout a member's career to accomplish the Air Force mission.

Air Force trainees wouldn't be very good airmen without tech school. Cut by standard 25% and save $121 Million.

Flight Training

> Flying training programs include Academy Glider and Powered Flight Programs, Joint Specialized Undergraduate Pilot Training (JSUPT), Joint Specialized Undergraduate Pilot Training-Helicopter (JSUPT-H), Combat System Officer (CSO) Training, EURO-NATO Joint Jet Pilot Training (ENJJPT), Introduction to Fighter Fundamentals (IFF), and Pilot Instructor Training (PIT).

We didn't build the greatest Air Force on the planet by skimping on pilot training. Keep as is ($751 Million).

Professional Development Education

> Professional Military Education (PME) programs located at Air University (AU) enhance and develop critical leadership skills of commissioned officers, civilians, and Noncommissioned officers and prepare them for progressively more responsible positions.

The promotion training system seems to be working well, so let's keep this as is for now ($235M).

Training Support

> Activities support essential training functions encompassing Management Headquarters Training, Advanced Distance Learning, and Training Support to units. Headquarters Air Education and Training Command (AETC) provides

> positive command, control, and guidance to the Air Force Training
> Establishment. Field Training Detachments conduct on-site training at Active,
> Guard and Reserve installations on weapon systems identified to specific
> commands.

The promotion training system seems to be working well, so let's keep this as is for now ($101M).

Depot Maintenance

> The Air Force enhances management and programming for Total Force
> sustainment requirements by reviewing sustainment requirements at the
> enterprise level. This concept, Weapon System Sustainment (WSS), includes
> Depot Purchased Equipment Maintenance (DPEM), Contractor Logistics
> Support (CLS), Sustaining Engineering (SE) and Technical Orders (TO)
> commodities.

I don't understand why Depot Maintenance shows up in so many different places. The reduced wear and use of equipment means reduced need for maintenance; cut by 25% and save $58 Million.

Judgement Fund

> Judgment Fund provides funding for monetary judgments under the Contract
> Disputes Act of 1978 which are awarded by the Armed Services Board of
> Contract Appeals or the Court of Federal Claims. These are paid by the
> Department of the Treasury from Judgment appropriation, Claims for Contract
> Disputes.

The fact that we have a fund set up to pay the revolving and ongoing costs of contract disputes is a symptom of a grossly flawed contract management process. Eliminate; there is no funding.

Recruiting and Advertising

> Recruiting operations provide officer and enlisted personnel the required
> quantity, quality, and skills, both non-prior and prior service, to fulfill Air Force
> manpower requirements. Advertising supports the following programs:
> Enlisted Accessions, Air Force Academy, Reserve Officer Training Corps, Officer
> Training, Physician, Nurse, Dentist, Bioenvironmental Sciences Corps,
> Attorneys, Chaplains, and Specialized Recruiting needs.

Eliminate the advertising component and save $9 Million.

Examining

> Examining Activities optimize selection and classification of accessions to
> provide the best match of skills and aptitudes for Total Force mission capability
> to include emerging requirements (e.g. Remotely Piloted Aircraft Operator

Selection, Cyber, Competencies) and the legal requirements for testing & Department of Defense requirements for joint-service testing.

I suppose it's OK to examine recruits before letting them into the military. Keep as is ($3M).

Logistics Operations

Logistics operations funds readiness requirements for Air Force Material Command's (AFMC) air logistics centers, product centers, headquarters, Air Force acquisition program executive offices and several field operating agencies. Funds civilian workforce and associated travel and transportation costs. Also, logistics operations funds key information technology enablers for Air Force logistics transformation efforts.

By eliminating all overseas locations, we can cut this pure overhead by 25%, saving $260 Million.

Technical Support Activities

Technical support activities fund Acquisition and Command Support for Headquarters, Air Force; the Air Force Material Command product centers; and the Air Force Operational Test and Evaluation Center.

By eliminating all overseas locations, we can cut this pure overhead by 25%, saving $228 Million.

Depot Maintenance

The Air Force enhances the management and programming for Total Force sustainment requirements by reviewing sustainment requirements at the enterprise level. This concept, Weapon System Sustainment (WSS), includes Depot Purchased Equipment Maintenance (DPEM), Contractor Logistics Support (CLS), Sustaining Engineering (SE) and Technical Orders (TO) commodities.

Peacetime means less use and less wear; cut by 25% and save $7 Million.

Facilities Sustainment

Facilities Sustainment and Restoration/Modernization (FSRM) functions include demolition, sustainment, restoration and modernization projects. This Subactivity Group supports Air Force Material Command's (AFMC) main operating bases and FSRM activities ensure installation facilities, utility systems and infrastructure are capable of fully supporting mission requirements throughout their economic lives.

By eliminating all overseas locations, we can cut this pure overhead by 25%, saving $76 Million.

Base Support

> *This program provides funding for installation support functions, engineering and environmental programs in support of Air Force Material Command (AFMC), Air Force District Washington (AFDW) and Headquarters Air Force (HAF). The program sustains mission capability, quality of life, workforce productivity and infrastructure support.*

By eliminating all overseas locations, we can cut this pure overhead by 25%, saving $317 Million.

Servicewide Activities

Administration

> *Administrative programs include funding for the Air Force Combat Operations Center which provides senior leadership real-time global information concerning Air Force operations. It also supports the Air Force crisis action team, Air Force official representation funds, and miscellaneous current expenses funds designated to maintain the standing and prestige of the United States by extending official courtesies to United States and foreign dignitaries.*

By eliminating all overseas locations, we can cut this pure overhead by 25%, saving $147 Million.

Servicewide Communications

> *Air Force Servicewide Communications programs play a major role in providing reliable and secure communications to our combat forces around the globe. These services range from robust fiber networks at our main bases to global high-frequency radio broadcast stations providing worldwide connectivity for a variety of aircraft, primarily airlifters.*

By eliminating all overseas locations, we can cut this pure overhead by 25%, saving $274 Million.

Civil Air Patrol Corporation

> *The Civil Air Patrol (CAP) is a federally chartered non-profit organization. Established and purposed under USC Title 36, the CAP is a federal grant recipient. As a grant recipient, the CAP uses federally provided resources via a cooperative agreement to provide public purpose missions and support mandated by law. As executive agent, the United States Air Force is required to provide fiscal oversight of funding provided via the cooperative agreement and maintain operational substantial involvement processes.*

Eliminate all federal grants. The federal government should not own or control corporations. Eliminate and save $24 Million.

Security Programs

Security Programs include the Air Force Office of Special Investigations (AFOSI), the Department of Defense Cyber Crime Center (DC3), and counterintelligence (CI) which support the Comprehensive National Cybersecurity Initiative (CNCI).

Some of this is necessary to maintain an Air Force, but is not broken down by program. Cut by standard 25% and save $302 Million.

International Support

Operations support the North Atlantic Treaty Organization (NATO), Supreme Headquarters Allied Powers Europe (SHAPE), North Atlantic Treaty Organization Airborne Early Warning and Control (NATO AEW&C) program, Cooperative Defense Initiative program, and other international headquarters. The Technology Transfer Program, which controls the transfer of critical Air Force technologies to foreign governments, is also included in this Subactivity Group.

Needless to say, eliminate and save $81 Million.

Air Force Reserve Operations and Maintenance[101] [102]

Reserve forces are authorized under Article I Section 8 as "militia". The AFR O&M budget consists of largely the same programs and hierarchy as the active O&M budget, so let's cut this by the standard 25% and save $792 Million.

Air National Guard Operations and Maintenance [103] [104]

National Guard forces are authorized under Article I Section 8 as "militia". The NG O&M budget consists of largely the same programs and hierarchy as the active O&M budget, so let's cut this by the standard 25% and save **$1.5 Billion**.

Aircraft Procurement [105] [106]

F-35

The JSF program will develop and field a family of aircraft that meets the needs of the United States and its international partners. Specifically, the Joint Strike Fighter (JSF) will meet USAF Conventional Take Off and Landing (CTOL) requirements with the F-35A variant, the USMC with the Short Take-Off and Vertical Landing (STOVL) requirements with the F-35B variant, and USN Carrier Variant (CV) requirements with the F-35C variant.

---

[101] http://www.saffm.hq.af.mil/shared/media/document/AFD-120210-064.pdf
[102] http://www.saffm.hq.af.mil/shared/media/document/AFD-120210-071.pdf
[103] http://www.saffm.hq.af.mil/shared/media/document/AFD-120208-058.pdf
[104] http://www.saffm.hq.af.mil/shared/media/document/AFD-120208-059.pdf
[105] http://www.saffm.hq.af.mil/shared/media/document/AFD-120210-115.pdf
[106] http://www.saffm.hq.af.mil/shared/media/document/AFD-120210-116.pdf

As I have explained several times already, aircraft development is the responsibility of the Research and Development department of the aircraft manufacturers. They should use their profits to fund their own research, and the Air Force should simply buy the ones which best suit the AF's needs.

The DoD has bought 68 of the 2,443 F-35s it intends to buy. In the meantime, our fleets of F-18s, F-16s, A-10s, and Harriers which the F-35 replaces have been getting the job done for 40 years. It seems to me that modernization can be worth the expense, if the extra expense of maintaining the older aircraft is getting near the cost of replacing them. I have been unable to locate the actuarial tables thereof.

It also occurs to me that to recover some of the cost of these programs, we should strip down and sell the older models they're replacing instead of converting them into target practice drones. The Air Force has 1,018 F-16s[107], each of which cost $14.6 Million[108] when new. From there we calculate that we have bought $14.9 Billion in F-16s.

The DoD also owns 343 A-10s and 948 F-18s. I couldn't find a number of AV-8Bs owned by the DoD, but they bought about half of the other models, so we can estimate they bought about 160 Harriers.

So sell off the old aircraft being replaced, one per F-35 purchased, at five million bucks each. F-18s and Harriers cost a lot more, so we'll sell those off for ten million, still a fraction of the original price. I'm sure there are some rich people out there who would jump at the chance to buy and fly an F-16 instead of their slower Learjet, and used combat aircraft have always been good enough for the poorer among our allied countries.

The procurement request of about $3.4 Billion per 19 F-35s comes out to $180 Million per F-35, well over ten times what the F-16 cost. Given that 2,443 F-35s are replacing 2,469 other aircraft, the old fleet would need to be sold off at about a one-to-one rate.

Based on the price structure I have come up with out of thin air, our sales would generate $17.885 Billion in profit. While a paltry sum compared to the $212 Billion total F-35 program cost, it would certainly help reduce the pain.

[107] http://www.af.mil/information/factsheets/factsheet.asp?id=103
[108] http://en.wikipedia.org/wiki/General_Dynamics_F-16_Fighting_Falcon

If all our military are here at home, they won't have nearly as much airspace to defend. Therefore we can apply my standard 25% cut to this procurement and save $1.7 Billion on the annual budget. Further, this would bring down the total program cost to $159.3 Billion. If we subtract the sales profit, the price is then $141.4 Billion.

Now we multiply this number by the ratio of the 2013 procurement to the total program procurement, and the final price for 2013 is about $2.3 Billion. Excluding the reduced maintenance costs, this saves us **$1.2 Billion** for FY2013.

F-35 Advance Procurement

The manufacturers can build the products on the profit they took from us last year. Eliminate and save $293 Million.

C-130J

The FY13 budget does not procure a C-130J aircraft. The budget provides for logistics support for the USAF C-130J fleet, logistics support for aircrew and maintenance training devices, and program management support.

During peacetime, the only regular operations I can predict being performed by airlifters would be ongoing training. During the first year, of course, they would be used a great deal, to move our people and equipment back to U.S. territory; so I'll keep this as is for now ($68 Million).

H-130 Recapitalization

HC-130 recapitalization will replace and augment the aging USAF fleet of combat rescue HC-130P/N aircraft which are experiencing airworthiness, maintainability and operational limitations.

Overhauling our existing cargo planes is certainly cheaper than buying new ones; but they'll see far less use in peacetime. Reduce by standard 25% and save $41 Million.

MC-130 Recapitalization

MC-130 recapitalization will replace and augment the aging USAF fleets of special operations MC-130E/H/P/W aircraft which are experiencing airworthiness, maintainability and operational limitations.

Overhauling our existing cargo planes is certainly cheaper than buying new ones; but they'll see far less use in peacetime. Reduce by standard 25% and save $104 Million.

AC-130 Recapitalization

The AC-130 Recapitalization will replace and augment the aging USAF fleet of AC-130H Gunship aircraft which are experiencing airworthiness, maintainability, and operational limitations.

Overhauling our existing gunships is certainly cheaper than buying new ones; but they'll see far less use in peacetime. Reduce by standard 25% and save $46 Million.

HH-60 Loss Replacement and Recapitalization

This line item supports the acquisition of HH-60 Operational Loss Replacement (OLR) helicopters to replace HH-60Gs lost through attrition. The HH-60G currently supports the Air Force's core function of Personnel Recovery.

In peacetime, there will be a significantly reduced need to recover personnel. Reduce by standard 25% and save $15 Million.

CV-22 Osprey

The CV-22 is a Special Operations Forces (SOF) variant of the 1st Generation V-22 tiltrotor, multi-mission aircraft. The CV-22 will provide long range, high speed, critical capability to insert, extract, and resupply special operations forces into politically or militarily denied areas, not currently provided by existing aircraft. The Navy is the lead service for the joint V-22 program and is responsible for managing all V-22 medium-lift variants, including the CV-22.

By the same math as was used to deduce the F-35 deduction, we know we can cut this program by about a third. Further, peacetime means significantly reduced Special Operations, which have generally been getting a 25% cut in this proposal. Cut by half and save $157 Million.

CV-22 Osprey Advance Procurement

The manufacturers can build the products on the profit they took from us last year. Eliminate and save $15 Million.

Civil Air Patrol

The Civil Air Patrol (CAP) is a Congressionally chartered non-profit corporation that serves as the Auxiliary of the Air Force. CAP uses federally provided resources to provide assistance requested by the DoD, federal, state or local government authorities and non-governmental organizations (NGO's) to perform emergency or non-emergency public purpose missions and activities.

As far as the DoD is concerned, here are two kinds of emergencies and non-emergency missions: The kind the military needs to handle internally, and the kind that are not military issues at all. Eliminate and save $2 Million.

Target Drones

Full-scale and subscale targets assure warfighters weapon systems will perform effectively against real-world enemy fighters and cruise missiles. Aerial Targets provide adherence to Public Law Title 10, Section 2366 "Live Fire/Lethality" developmental/operational test requirements. Target drones are used to validate operational missile/weapon system effectiveness and fighter Operational Flight Program (OFP) updates.

Pilots have to train, shooting at real things improves training, and they won't have any enemies to train against in peacetime. Having said that, this program is fairly new and recently jumped in price, so let's cut this back by two thirds and save $87 Million. We shouldn't be firing a whole lot of live missiles in training anyway.

RQ-4 UAV

The Global Hawk Unmanned Aircraft System (UAS) provides high altitude, deep look, long endurance intelligence, surveillance, reconnaissance (ISR), and Battle Management Command & Control (BMC2) enabler capability that complements space and other airborne collectors during peacetime, crisis, and war-fighting scenarios.

This program ends in 2014, and no more items are being procured, so let's go ahead and cut this one off. $147 Million saved.

MQ-9 UAV

This program has associated Research Development Test and Evaluation AF funding in PEs 0305219F MQ-1 Predator UAV, 0305206F Airborne Reconnaissance Systems, 0304260F Airborne SIGINT Enterprise, and associated APAF funding in 0305206F Airborne Reconnaissance Systems.

With the success of the MQ-1 in combat, General Atomics anticipated the Air Force's desire for an upgraded aircraft and, using its own funds, set about redesigning Predator.[109] This is the model by which all military procurement research and development should be done.

24 MQ-9s are requested. An unknown number confirmedly belong to the CIA and the Department of Homeland Security, so let's move those over to the Air Force and eliminate the procurement for now. After the DoD settles into its new life as a *defense* organization, we can begin buying the next model as we simultaneously sell off the preexisting aircraft it is replacing. $554 Million saved.

---

[109] http://en.wikipedia.org/wiki/General_Atomics_MQ-9_Reaper

RQ-4 Block 40

Procurement funding includes Global Hawk Block 40 integrated logistics support (to include support equipment, technical data, etc.), other support requirements, and related tasks.

A small pittance to update some of the older Reapers to be closer to the RQ-9 spec. This can stay as is ($12M), but will not be included in the final "stable" projections as it ends in 2015.

Aircraft Initial Spares

In FY 2013, the F-35, MQ-9, and C-5 RERP have large initial spare requirements in preparation for fielding. Other initial spares programs with large requirements include CV-22 and Manned Reconnaissance System. The Air Force plans to procure $56.690 of the $729.691 Initial Spares through the WCF in FY2013

Since the procurements for those aircraft have been reduced (and the C-5 wasn't mentioned at all), the spares therefor can be reduced. Cut by half and save $376 Million.

Aircraft Replacement Support Equipment

This program provides funding for the procurement of replacement organizational and intermediate level support equipment for out-of-production aircraft. These items, common (used on more than one weapon system) and peculiar (unique to one weapon system), directly support aircraft maintenance and servicing requirements.

If we reduce what needs to be supported, and factor in the reduction in wear and tear and combat losses that peacetime brings, we see a reduced need for support equipment. Cut by standard 25% and save $14 Million.

A-10 Post Production Support

FY13 funding procures an FMT for Moody AFB to replace one device that was provided to the ANG for the BRAC directed A-10C mission stand up at Ft. Wayne, IN.

It's important to keep the maintainers and pilots trained, so trainers are needed; however, this will be a one-time purchase and thus will not be included in the final projections ($5M).

B-1 Post Production Support

This effort provides funding for acquisition of essential avionics test stations, test program sets and interface test adapters to rectify unacceptable B-1B test station mission capable rates. Current B-1B ATE is becoming unsupportable and test station downtime is increasing the B-1B Line Replaceable Unit (LRU) backlog with unserviceable line replaceable units.

It's important to keep the maintainers and pilots trained, so trainers are needed; however, this will be a one-time purchase and thus will not be included in the final projections ($1M).

B-2A Post Production Support

ICS Funding requirements continue until depot activation is complete. Currently ICS continues through FY18. Without the ICS funding, Total Non-Mission Capable for Supply (TNMCS) rates will increase and Aircraft Availability Improvement Program (AAIP) goals will not be met. Additionally, lack of mission capable assets will eventually ground aircraft, prohibiting B-2 participation in Global Strike and Global Persistent Attack.

It's important to keep the maintainers and pilots trained, so trainers are needed; however, this will not be a recurring purchase and thus will not be included in the final projections ($48M).

KC-10A Post Production Support

FY13 funds will be used to procure, install, and support one KC-10 CLT.

It's important to keep the maintainers and pilots trained, so trainers are needed; however, this will be a one-time purchase and thus will not be included in the final projections ($13M).

C-17A Post Production Support

FY2013 budget funds the acquisition of required C-17 support equipment, data, material improvement projects, training equipment, obsolescence, and mission support.

It's important to keep the maintainers and pilots trained, so trainers are needed; however, this will not be a recurring purchase and thus will not be included in the final projections ($182M).

C-130 Post production Support

Procures one additional C-130 Weapon System Trainer and one Aeromedical Fuselage Trainer (AFT). The AFT is a New Start in FY13.

It's important to keep the maintainers and pilots trained, so trainers are needed; however, this will not be a recurring purchase and thus will not be included in the final projections ($32M).

KC-135 Post Production Support

Procure and support a KC-135 MTS for maintenance training courseware and infrastructure, and will fund KC-135 Pacer CRAG ICS and depot activation study & analysis. This effort is an FY13 New Start.

It's important to keep the maintainers and pilots trained, so trainers are needed; however, this will not be a recurring purchase and thus will not be included in the final projections ($13M).

F-15 Post Production Support

Provides continued support of Post production tooling storage at Granite City IL. Tooling is loaned/leased in support of manufacturing spares and support capability for future MODS or Life Extension Efforts.

It's important to keep the maintainers and pilots trained, so trainers are needed; however, this will not be a recurring purchase and thus will not be included in the final projections ($2M).

F-16 Post Production Support

This appropriation is for the continuation of prime contractor post production support, procurement of deferred peculiar ground support equipment, peculiar training equipment, mission support, interim contract support, and activities associated with F-16 production line shutdown.

It's important to keep the maintainers and pilots trained while we wait for these planes to get sold off, so trainers are needed; however, this will not be a recurring purchase and thus will not be included in the final projections ($9M).

Other Aircraft Post Production Support

FY13 funding acquires a single F-16 Block 40/50 trainer cockpit and associated Mission Training Center equipment.

It's important to keep the maintainers and pilots trained, so trainers are needed; however, this will not be a recurring purchase and thus will not be included in the final projections ($10M).

Industrial Responsiveness

FY 2013 requirements are for MPC 3000 Capital Type Rehabilitation, MPC 6000 Industrial Base Assessment, and MCP 7000 Environmental Compliance.

It's silly for the government to spend money to create environmental laws, and then spend money to follow them. Eliminate and save $21 Million.

War Consumables

> *This program provides funding for the procurement of initial/replacement War Consumables and includes commodities such as Miniature Air Launced Decoys (MALD), Fiber Optic Towed Decoys (FOTD), and Aerial Target Drone (ATD) rocket motors.*

A great way to reduce the number of consumables we need to procure is by not blowing up so many of them. This program was started in 2011, so it's obvious the Air Force could get by without it. Eliminate and save $90 Million.

Other Production Charges

> *The Miscellaneous Production Charges program provides for items which are not directly related to other procurement line items in this appropriation, cannot be reasonably allocated and charged to other procurement line items in this appropriation, can be managed as separate end items, may contain certain classified programs, and may be alternate mission equipment, not considered a modification, for out of production systems.*

This program rollup includes modifications to NATO equipment, moving aircraft around for maintenance, and other subprograms of varying importance. Cut by standard 25% and save $225 Million.

Ammo Procurement[110]

The Ammo procurement is a significant improvement over previous years; however, peacetime will require significantly reduced spending. If we aren't using our rockets and bullets, then we need not replace them. Cut by standard 25% and save $152 Million.

Missile Procurement[111]

The Ammo procurement is a significant improvement over previous years; however, peacetime will require significantly reduced spending. If we aren't using our rockets and bullets, then we need not replace them. Cut by standard 25% and save **$1.53 Billion**.

Other Procurement[112]

Vehicular Equipment

Passenger Carrying Vehicles

> *Passenger Carrying Vehicles includes the procurement of sedans, station wagons, law enforcement sedans, ambulances and buses. These vehicles are*

---

[110] http://www.saffm.hq.af.mil/shared/media/document/AFD-120207-051.pdf
[111] http://www.saffm.hq.af.mil/shared/media/document/AFD-120207-052.pdf
[112] http://www.saffm.hq.af.mil/shared/media/document/AFD-120207-054.pdf

general in nature, but they fulfill unique and distinct needs commensurate with their design.

The PCVs we procured last year should still be working, minus some basic maintenance. Eliminate and save $2 Million.

Medium Tactical Vehicles

The Family of Medium Tactical Vehicles (FMTVs) has the capability to operate in austere, adverse terrain. These important tactical assets are used by Combat Communications Units, Air Support Operations Squadrons (ASOS), Explosive Ordinance Disposal (EOD) units, and other tactical direct mission support units throughout the Air Force. The US Army uses them extensively. FMTVs are a class of M-Series Vehicles.

$21 Million to buy 130 trucks. It seems difficult to believe the Air Force lost 130 trucks in 2012. In peacetime, we'd bring home hundreds of thousands of troops, and the vehicles and such along with them. That should leave plenty of extras. Eliminate and save $21 Million.

CAP Vehicles

The Civil Air Patrol (CAP) is a Congressionally chartered non-profit corporation that serves as the Auxiliary of the Air Force. CAP uses federally provided resources to provide assistance requested by the DoD, federal, state or local government authorities and non-governmental organizations. CAP's procurement processes/standards are described in Department of Defense Grants & Agreements Regulations.

Since this proposal eliminates the CAP, they don't need vehicles anymore. Eliminate and save $1 Million.

BSA 2 Items Less Than $5 Million

This vehicle group consists of pickup trucks, trailers, semi-trailers, tractors, vans, utility trucks, maintenance and facility vehicles essential to base, and flying operations.

Since this proposal will bring many trucks, trailers, etc. back to the states, we should have plenty of extras. Eliminate all OCO spending, cut the remainder by half, and save $3.5 Million.

Security and Tactical Vehicles

This program provides funding for a variety of security and tactical vehicles essential to strategic military operations. This program currently includes: the standard diesel powered High Mobility Multi-purpose Wheeled Vehicle

(HMMWV) all configurations used by the Air Force, Guardian Angel Light Tactical Vehicle, and cargo trailers.

Since this proposal will bring many trucks and other vehicles back to the states, we should have plenty of extras. Eliminate and save $11 Million.

BSA 3 Items Less Than $5 Million

This grouping consists of various vehicles for flightline, maintenance, and facility operations used for a variety of purposes. Examples of these vehicles include the IW 40 tractor, six- and ten- passenger overthe-snow-carriers, an assortment of wreckers and refuse trucks, and water distribution trucks.

Since this proposal will bring many trucks, trailers, etc. back to the states, we should have plenty of extras. Eliminate all OCO spending, cut the remainder by half, and save $7.2 Million.

Firefighting and Crash Rescue Vehicles

Since this proposal will bring many vehicles back to the states, we should have plenty of extras. Eliminate all OCO spending, cut the remainder by half, and save $12 Million.

BSA 5 Items Less Than $5 Million

This program includes various material handling vehicles with an individual item procurement value of less than $5,000,000. These vehicles consist of lifting trucks, sequencing trucks, and other warehouse equipment critical to depot and base supply operations.

Since this proposal will bring many vehicles back to the states, we should have plenty of extras. Eliminate all OCO spending, cut the remainder by half, and save $14 Million.

Runway Snow Removal and Cleaning Equipment

This program procures snow removal vehicles and commercial sweepers used on all airfield surfaces to remove snow and help prevent foreign object damage (FOD) to aircraft engines and tires. Snow removal equipment includes front mounted brooms, multi-purpose blowers, and plows.

Since this proposal will bring many vehicles back to the states, we should have plenty of extras. Eliminate all OCO spending, cut the remainder by half, and save $800K.

BSA 6 Items Less Than $5 Million

This program procures various vehicle groups with an individual item cost of less than $5M. These vehicle groups consist of heavy wreckers, *maintenance/test vans, large capacity forklifts, extended reach deicers, and heavy construction equipment (dozers, large cranes, large dump trucks, rock crushers, motorized scrapers, well-drilling vehicles, and compactors). The assets are critical to the Air Force mission and are key to keeping many sortie generation/sortie sustainment missions supported and operational. The types of items contained within this P-1 line are critical (deployed) assets used in direct support of Air Force units engaged in contingency operations.*

Since this proposal will bring many vehicles and equipment back to the states, we should have plenty of extras. Eliminate all OCO spending, cut the remainder by half, and save $18 Million.

Electronics and Telecommunications Equipment

Comseq Equipment

This program funds procurement of Communications Security (COMSEC) equipment, ancillary encryption/decryption devices, and related equipment to enable the secure transport of information. United States Air Force (AF) and the Department of Defense (DoD) require the capability to collect, process, and disseminate an uninterrupted flow of information, while denying an adversary the ability to intercept, collect, destroy, interpret, or manipulate our information flows.

Security is important, of course; but by moving everyone back to the states, we would have much less to secure in the first place. Further, many program elements in this program group are merely upgrades to existing systems, and the existence of something new does not automatically obsolete the older versions. Cut by standard 25% and save $42 Million.

Comsec Modifications

The Communications Security (COMSEC) modification activity ensures the integration, installation, and sustainment of cryptographic equipment. This activity is a critical component in providing robust, secure global communications, enabling information superiority. It provides the warfighter with the security needed to protect the flow and exchange of operational decision-making information through the retrofit and modification of selected COMSEC equipment.

Security is important, of course; but by moving everyone back to the states, we would have much less to secure in the first place. Further, many program elements in this program group are merely upgrades to existing systems, and the existence of something new does not automatically obsolete the older versions. Cut by standard 25% and save $80K.

Intelligence Training Equipment

The Intelligence Training Equipment P-1 line procures equipment for use in initial and advanced training in the General Intelligence and Cryptologic/Signals Intelligence related career fields. The equipment supports training for intelligence officers, geospatial analysts, targeteers, operations analysts, linguists, network analysts, all communications (except communications security) and electronic intelligence analysts, and intelligence system maintainers.

Even in peacetime, the military needs to train. Keep as is ($3M).

Intelligence Communications Equipment

Intelligence communications equipment efforts procure various types of equipment to analyze and disseminate intelligence, surveillance, and reconnaissance information to warfighters and decision makers across the full range of Air Force mission areas.

In peacetime, a lot of our existing equipment will be moved stateside from overseas. Cut by standard 25% and save $82 Million.

Advanced Tech Sensors

Portal Monitors offer a method to notify appropriate personnel when nuclear material is moved outside its intended storage or maintenance area. Funding was requested to procure three sensors per year starting in FY12 and complete in FY16 for six locations (Minot AFB, Whiteman AFB, F.E.Warren AFB, Malmstrom AFB, Kirtland AFB, and Nellis AFB). This supports and is a result of the Blue Ribbon Review requirement for radiation detection checks on any missile transported out of its Weapons Storage Area.

Nuclear security is paramount. Keep as is ($877K).

Mission Planning Systems

FY13 funding will procure a variety of computers and electronic equipment to support pre-, post-, and in-flight mission planning tasks for a number of Air Force platforms. They will support legacy MPS efforts as well as newer planning systems in the final stages of development.

In peacetime, a lot of our existing equipment will be moved stateside from overseas. Cut by standard 25% and save $12 Million.

Air Traffic Control and Landing System (ATCLS)

Air Traffic Control and Landing Systems (ATCALS) procures and supports fixed-base and tactical radar, navigation aids, voice communications, and data processing/automation capabilities. ATCALS enables United States Air Force

(USAF) air traffic controllers by providing advisory, sequencing, separation, and landing guidance services to all aircraft in USAF-assigned airspace.

In peacetime, a lot of our existing equipment will be moved stateside from overseas. Cut by standard 25% and save $55 Million.

National Aerospace System

The National Airspace System (NAS) program modernizes the Department of Defense (DoD) Air Traffic Control (ATC) system in concert with the Federal Aviation Administration (FAA) modernization effort. The FAA is the overall NAS program lead and the Air Force (AF) is the DoD lead. NAS increases safety of flight, provides systems and facilities interoperable with FAA modernization, replaces aging DoD ATC systems, provides identical service to military and civilian aircraft, reduces DoD flight cancellations/delays, and reduces maintenance.

Eliminate the FAA and let airports talk to each other over the phone, the Internet, or some other easily accessible medium. A website could be built to replace the entire FAA process for probably only a few million dollars, it would be a one-time procurement, and we'd save tons in recurring costs. Eliminate NAS (though probably after a couple years) and save $31 Million.

Battle Control System – Fixed

BCS-F supports the NORAD/NORTHCOM homeland defense and air sovereignty mission for fixed Air Defense Sectors.

This proposal eliminates the Majcom echelon of command (i.e. NORTHCOM), though this program is important to tracking what's flying over America. Keep as is ($17M).

Theater Air Control System Improvement

The Theater Air Control System Improvement (TACSI) program acquires state-of-the-art equipment and capabilities essential to the survival and combat effectiveness of tactical level Battle Management Command and Control (BMC2). Collectively, they provide the flexibility, responsiveness, reliability, and maintainability necessary for effective BMC2. TACSI provides funding for the procurement of the Control and Reporting Center (CRC). CRC supports mobile ground-based command and control (C2) efforts.

This system sounds pretty important, connecting units in the battlefield to the commanders. It went through a large cut in 2013, so we can keep it as is ($23M).

Weather Observation Forecast

> The Weather Observation Forecast budget line acquires meteorological and ground based space environmental sensing equipment supporting the global missions of the Air Force (AF), Army, Special Operations Forces (SOF), combatant commands, and other government agencies.

In peacetime, our military will be in the homeland, where we can get forecasts from any number of local meteorologists. Eliminate and save $23 Million.

Strategic Command and Control

> The Strategic Command and Control (C2) program procures mission critical communications and computer systems required to ensure the United States has the capability for effective C2 of the New Triad (nuclear, conventional and missile defense). It procures hardware replacements/upgrades to maintain the only computer systems that produce the Nation's nuclear war plan and performs conventional/ contingency war planning.

In peacetime, we'll end up bringing home a lot of this equipment from overseas. Cut by 25% and save $14 Million.

Cheyenne Mountain Complex

> This program supports the NORAD Cheyenne Mountain Complex-Integrated Tactical Warning/Attack Assessment (NCMC-ITW/AA) and the US Northern Command (USNORTHCOM) Mobile Consolidated Command Center (MCCC). NCMC-ITW/AA systems provide real-time ballistic missile warning, air defense, force management, battle management and command, control and communications for existing and future North American Air Defense (NORAD) missions and US Strategic Command (USSTRATCOM) space operations and missile defense missions, including space surveillance, warning, cueing and engagement information to the theater combatant commanders.

A warning and attack assessment system of some kind is important to national security and must be maintained. Keep as is ($15M).

Tactical SIGINT Support

> Tactical Signals Intelligence supports/procures a variety of signals processing, modeling, and support equipment necessary to operate and maintain tactical cryptologic programs. FY13 funding procures equipment to support ground processing functions associated with airborne operations.

In peacetime, a lot of this equipment will be brought back from overseas, which can be used to supplant this procurement. Cut by 25% and save $50K.

General Information Technology

In peacetime, a lot of this equipment will be brought back from overseas, which can be used to supplant this procurement. Cut by 25% and save $20 Million.

Global Command and Control System

> *Procures various types and quantities of hardware and software in support of installation and unit mission requirements for Air Force personnel. These funds provide for the procurement and installation of GCCS-AF hardware and [off-the-shelf] software at warfighter Combatant Command (COCOM), MAJCOM, ANG, and AFR locations providing a full spectrum of command, control, logistics, and intelligence capability from strategic to unit level operations with total joint service connectivity.*

In peacetime, much of this hardware and software would be moved back to the states. Cut by 25% and save $40 Million.

Mobility Command and Control

> *Global Mobility Command and Control (C2) provides critical communications to manage and control national power projection force deployments, aircraft flight planning systems, airlift control elements, time sensitive logistics requirements, and Special Tactics operations.*

In peacetime, much of this hardware would be moved back to the states. Cut by 25% and save $3 Million.

Physical Security System

> *The Air Force (AF) Physical Security Systems program provides turnkey procurement, installation, integration, and acceptance testing of base defense physical security systems to protect aircraft, to include remotely pilot aircraft and infrastructure required to operate them, missiles, nuclear weapons, and other critical war fighting resources on more than 200 installations worldwide to include active AF, Air Force Reserve, and Air National Guard installations as well as numerous expeditionary, temporary, and semi-fixed locations.*

In peacetime, moving our military back to the states would mean a significantly reduced footprint. This in turn means there is less to secure. Cut by 25% and save $16 Million.

Combat Training Ranges

> *This program procures electronic telecommunication and instrumentation equipment and systems for training ranges worldwide. These systems provide real-time monitoring and control of aircrew air-to-air, air-to-ground, ground-to-air, and Electronic Warfare (EW) training along with the ability to record and play back events for aircrew debriefing and analysis. This program also*

procures weapons scoring systems and advanced threat simulator systems to satisfy EW training capability requirements. This P-1 line also procures aircraft, EW and weapons pods, and ground interfaces. This program ensures software interoperability among service ranges, the encryption of range/aircraft data links, and associated communication devices.

In peacetime, a lot of this equipment will be brought back from overseas, which can be used to supplant this procurement. Further, we can reduce the number of special operations needed against our enemies by simply not having enemies in the first place. Cut by 25% and save $14 Million.

C3 Countermeasures

U.S. military forces operate in an information age where the need for precise, instantaneous intelligence is increasing and expanding across the entire spectrum of military operations. However, this increasing technical sophistication leads to a dependency on technology that, in turn, may represent potentially crippling vulnerabilities. The Air Force (AF) addresses these vulnerabilities through Information Operations (IO). IO includes those actions taken to gain, exploit, defend, and attack information and information systems. Information Warfare (IW) consists of actions conducted to attack an adversary's information and information systems while defending one's own.

In peacetime, this equipment will be moved back to the states. This means less equipment is needed, so there is less to secure. Cut by 25% and save $3 Million.

Global Combat Support System – Air Force Family of Systems

Global Combat Support System (GCSS) is a family of information technology systems that provide integration and interoperability between combat support functions and command and control to support the operational needs of the warfighter. It directly supports Command, Control, Communication, Computers, and Information (C4I) for the warfighter and Chairman Joint Chiefs of Staff (CJCS) Joint Vision 2020. The GCSS-Air Force Family of Systems (FOS) includes standard base-level combat support applications which provide warfighters with a "one update-one time" processing environment.

In peacetime, there would be no wars to fight. By moving all our people and equipment back home, there would be fewer C4 systems to operate. Disregard the one-time update from the recurring budget and cut the remainder by half, saving around $7 Million.

Theater Battle Management C2 System

TBMCS is an integrated battle management system used to plan, execute, and assess an air campaign. It provides automated planning tools enabling consistent, coordinated battle management at entities ranging from the force level (Air Operations Centers (AOCs)) to the unit level (wings/squadrons) for operations and intelligence functions. TBMCS is a United States Air Force system with Joint interest responsible for generation and dissemination of the air tasking order and interoperates with allied units.

In peacetime, there would be no non-training air campaigns to plan. However, it does seem to increase the effectiveness thereof when the need does arise. Cut by half and save $5 Million.

Air and Space Operations Center Weapons System

The Air Operations Center (AOC) Weapon System (WS), AN/USQ-163 Falconer, the senior element of the Theater Air Control System, is the weapon system that the Commander, Air Force Forces (COMAFFOR) provides the Combined/Joint Force Air Component Commander (C/JFACC) for monitoring, planning, executing and assessing theater-wide air and space operations in support of the air battle campaign to meet the Combined/Joint Force Commander's (C/JFC) objectives.

In peacetime, there would be a reduced need for all war systems. Cut by half and save $17 Million.

Information Transportation Systems

ITS provides the core Air Force network infrastructure for over 170 fixed Air Force installations (active duty, reserve, and Air National Guard (ANG)) and Geographically Separated Units (GSU) at approved locations. ITS capabilities encompass optical cable systems and digital voice/data/video systems.

In this proposal, the number of fixed Air Force stations would be greatly reduced. Cut by half and save $26 Million.

AFNet

AFNet Systems programs and projects establish and modernize the Air Force intranet, deliver and update network management systems, and implement elements of the Air Force Network Operations (AFNetOps) transformation initiative. AFNetOps transformation includes Network Management and Network Defense, Integrated Network Operations and Security Center (I-NOSC), Regional Processing Centers (RPC), and Area Processing Centers (APC).

In this proposal, there would be a greatly reduced number of systems to network due to the reduction in number of operating locations. Cut by half and save $63 Million.

Voice Systems

Voice Switch Systems (VSS) upgrades the Multi-Function Soft Switch (MFSS) in support of the Defense Information Systems Agency (DISA) Unified Capabilities

(UC) pilot for Internet Protocol (IP)-based telephony. VSS replaces end-of-life voice switches and aging battery rectifiers for fielded switches, which if left unresolved creates a serious hazard.

In this proposal, there would be a greatly reduced number of systems to network due to the reduction in number of operating locations. Cut by half and save $8 Million.

USCENTCOM

The Air Force (AF) is the executive agent for Headquarters United States Central Command (HQ USCENTCOM) which is geographically separated from its AOR by over 7,000 miles. HQ USCENTCOM's mission is to work with its national and international partners in promoting development and cooperation among nations, responding to crises, and deterring or defeating state and transnational aggression in order to establish regional security and stability across its entire Area of Responsibility (AOR).

This proposal eliminates the Major Command echelon of command and all operations in the Middle East region. Eliminate and save $32 Million.

Space Based Infrared Systems (SBIRS) High

The Space-Based Infrared System (SBIRS) consolidates national and DOD infrared detection systems into a single overarching architecture that fulfills the nation's security needs in the areas of missile warning, missile defense, technical intelligence and battlespace awareness.

National Defense is of paramount importance and is one of the few proper roles of government. This system will be important to that end, even in peacetime. Keep as is ($47M).

Navstar GPS Space

The Navstar Global Positioning System (GPS) provides highly accurate time, three-dimensional position, and velocity information to an unlimited number of users anywhere on or above the surface of the earth, in any weather. GPS satisfies validated joint service requirements for worldwide, accurate, common grid navigation for military aircraft, ships, ground vehicles and personnel.

While the civilian use of this is not proper for a military budget, it is proper for military use and coordination. I see no reason not to let the civilians use it too since they don't increase the cost thereof. Keep as is ($2M).

Nudet Detection System Space

The United States Nuclear Detonation (NUDET) Detection System (USNDS) provides a near real-time worldwide, highly survivable capability to detect, locate, and report any nuclear detonations in the earth's atmosphere or in near space. USDNS supports NUDET detection requirements across five mission areas: Integrated Tactical Warning and Attack Assessment (ITW/AA), Nuclear Force Management (NFM), Space Control (SC), Treaty Monitoring (TM) and a classified mission.

Nuclear detonations can pose a clear and present danger to U.S. national security; keep as is ($6M).

Air Force Satellite Control Network Space

The Air Force Satellite Control Network (AFSCN) is a globally-distributed infrastructure of control centers, remote tracking stations (RTS), and communications links providing highly reliable command, control, and communications (C3) support for the nation's surveillance, navigation, communications, warning, and weather satellite operations.

The ability to communicate worldwide and surveil our enemies' military activity does directly advance national security; keep as is ($44M).

Spacelift Range System Space

The Eastern Range (ER) at Patrick Air Force Base/Cape Canaveral AFS, FL, and the Western Range (WR) at Vandenberg AFB, CA, make up the Spacelift Range System (SLRS), also known as the Launch and Test Range System (LTRS). and maintenance (O&M) costs and increased risk of launch delays.

Satellites do need to be launched and maintained; keep as is ($110M). Require civil and commercial satellite customers to fund their own operations, but allow them to use the facility.

MILSATCOM Space

Military Satellite Communications (MILSATCOM) joint-service systems collectively provide a broad range of satellite communication capabilities, including secure, jam-resistant, 24-hour worldwide communications to meet essential strategic, tactical and general-purpose operational requirements.

Satellites need to be communicated with; keep as is ($48M).

Space Mods Space

Space Mods Space enables the development of advanced Command and Control (C2) Battle Management, Intelligence Surveillance and Reconnaissance (ISR), and Command, Control, Communications, Computers, and Intelligence (C4I) systems to conduct effective predictive battle space awareness, facilitate precision attack, and compress the sensor-to-shooter kill chain.

In peacetime, there will be no need to manage or be aware of battle; and no kill chain to compress. Cut by standard 25% and save $12 Million.

Counterspace Systems

Includes systems to disrupt, deny, degrade or destroy an adversary's space systems or the information they provide (Offensive Counterspace), and active and passive measures to protect US and friendly space-related capabilities from enemy attack or interference (Defensive Counterspace).

This system can also tell our commanders when and where an attack occurs; this seems useful for defense. Keep as is ($21M).

Tactical C-E Equipment

Theater Deployable Communications Program (TDC) provides the Air Force with rapidly deployable communication infrastructure package which provides deployed users with secure and non-secure telephone service, Internet access, Local Area Network, network management, information assurance, e-mail services (NIPR/SIPRNet), and intra/interbase connectivity services similar to those established on a fixed base.

In peacetime, there will be no non-fixed bases nor deployed operations.

The Joint Tactical Radio System (JTRS) is a family of software programmable tactical radios that provide voice, data, and video communications for military users in the air, on the ground, and at sea. Common radio architecture and programmable software waveforms will provide joint interoperability between the services.

Once we buy the software, radios, and infrastructure, I don't see why it would require ongoing costs other than maintenance funding procured elsewhere.

BAO Kit will develop a Family of Systems (FoS) that provides a state-of-the-art Command, Control, Communications, Computer, Intelligence, Surveillance and Reconnaissance (C4ISR) suite for Air Force Special Operations Command's (AFSOC's) Battlefield Airmen.

The DoD shouldn't be developing its own equipment; it should buy things the private sector has already developed.

Tactical Airborne Control System Equipment encompass two types of simulators that provide scenario based training for geographically separated Joint Terminal Attack Controllers (JTACs), Combat Control Teams (CCTs), Tactical Air Control Party (TACPs), and various CAS Platforms.

Training is required even in peacetime, so we can be prepared for war if and when it comes to us. Keep this component as is.

[Battlefield Weather] Acquires meteorological and space environmental sensing equipment supporting the global missions of the AF, Army, SOF, combatant commanders, and other government agencies

Once the equipment has been procured, it should require no ongoing costs.

PATRIOT 7 is a course that trains battlefield airmen in the use of tactical intelligence, surveillance, and reconnaissance tools prior to deploying to combat.

Training is required even in peacetime, so we can be prepared for war if and when it comes to us. Keep this component as is.

Eliminate all OCO funding. PATRIOT 7 requests no 2013 funding. TACSE requestes $35M, which we can cut by our standard 25% to arrive at $26.5 Million. Compared to the total original $133 Million, we save roughly $107 Million.

Combat Survivor Evader Locator

The Combat Survivor Evader Locator (CSEL) joint program replaces antiquated PRC-90 and PRC-112 survival radios with a modern survival radio system utilizing Selective Availability Anti-Spoofing Module (SAASM) Global Positioning System (GPS), Ultra High Frequency (UHF) satellite communications, and the Integrated Broadcast Service (IBS) to quickly locate, authenticate, and communicate with isolated personnel.

This sounds like it's designed to help retrieve friendly POWs. Keep as is ($24M).

Radio Equipment

This program procures and integrates High Frequency (HF) radio equipment for 13 strategically located ground stations worldwide. The need for modern, robust, and dependable stations and radio coverage has been identified to ensure HF radio support in additional areas of interest to the United States. High Frequency Global Communications System (HFGCS) is a Command and Control/National Security System (C2/NSS), and is the only high-power HF C2 network serving the Department of Defense (DoD).

What's wrong with the old equipment other than being old? Why does this program never end? Why do we have locations across the world? Cut by half and save $3 Million.

CCTV / Audio / Visual Equipment

Imagery Acquisition and Audiovisual (AV) systems and their products are used throughout the Air Force to inform and train warfighters and to document combat operations and other events of historical significance. Combat video documentation is used for operational reporting and analysis, situational awareness, battle damage assessment, intelligence and operational analysis, casualty identification, and the historical record.

This equipment is useful, but I don't understand why it would have recurring and never ending costs. Cut by standard 25% and save $3 Million.

Base Communication Infrastructure

The Base Communications Infrastructure (BCI) program enables timely and assured delivery of data and voice communications supporting a wide range of Air Force organizations and decision makers. This program provides Air Force (AF) Major Commands (MAJCOMs), the Air Reserve Component (ARC), including the Air National Guard (ANG) and the Air Force Reserve (AFR), with effective Command and Control (C2) of information systems, and procures robust base communications infrastructure that every worker, office, and organization depends on to perform their mission.

By eliminating all overseas locations, we significantly reduce the number of bases requiring infrastructures. By eliminating the MAJCOM echelon of command, we reduce the need for a level of infrastructure. Eliminate all OCO spending, cut the remainder by half, and save $48 Million.

Comm Elect Mods

ATCALS is a combination of United States Air Force (USAF) ground facilities and equipment, both fixed and tactical, with associated avionics, personnel, and procedures that provide air traffic control worldwide to USAF/Department of Defense flying missions. The ATCALS line includes basic air navigation equipment that provides enroute and terminal navigation control and separation, approach, departure, and landing guidance.

If the military needs a way to control their aircraft, then that's fine; they do fly a lot. However, in peacetime, they will need to do so a lot less.

[Weather Observation and Forecast System] consists of meteorological and space environmental sensing equipment providing information to support the worldwide missions of the USAF, Army, Special Operations Forces (SOF), combatant commands, and other government agencies. Fixed and transportable equipment provides warfighters at in-garrison, contingency, and deployed locations with accurate, relevant, and timely terrestrial and space weather observations and forecasts.

In peacetime, there will be no such thing as "worldwide missions".

> *[Ballistic Missile Early Warning System] is a ground-based radar system whose primary mission, missile warning (MW), provides United States Strategic Command (USSTRATCOM) with credible Integrated Tactical Warning/Attack Assessment (ITW/AA) data on all Inter-Continental Ballistic Missiles (ICBMs) penetrating the coverage area.*

Necessary and proper for national defense; keep as is.

Overall, eliminate all OCO spending and cut the remainder by 25%, saving $19 Million.

Other Base Maintenance and Support Equipment

Night Vision Goggles

> *Modern warfare resulted in an increase in airborne combat under the cover of darkness. Night missions include ground operations, preparation of the aircraft for take-off and landings in complete darkness, lights-off air refueling, and visual identification of enemy targets hidden under the night sky.*

What's wrong with the night vision goggles the Air Force procured last year? Eliminate and save $24 Million.

Items Less than $5 Million (Safety)
Cut by standard 25%, save $8 Million.

Mechanized Material Handling Equipment

> *The Mechanized Material Handling Equipment line provides funding for Mechanized Material Handling Systems (MMHS) and Storage Aids Systems (SAS).*

What's wrong with the MMHS and SAS the Air Force procured last year? Also given the reduction in bases, locations, and environmental concerns, we can probably eliminate this and save $3 Million.

Base Procured Equipment

> *Organizations throughout the Air Force acquire authorized investment equipment from the General Services Administration, Defense Logistics Agency, and commercial sources when these items exceed $250,000 in cost or are unavailable through Air Force central procurement.*

Given the reduction in bases, the need for this will be commensurately reduced. Cut by 25% and save $2 Million.

Contingency Operations

> Contingency Operations, is part of the Agile Combat Support framework and provides integrated capabilities to support aircraft deployment, launch, recovery, and regeneration at air bases worldwide.

There are generally no military contingencies in peacetime. Eliminate and save $70 Million.

Productivity Capital Investments

> Funds are available to all Air Force organizations to encourage productivity enhancements for more efficient operations, focus on labor cost savings, and reductions in unit costs of operations. This program conserves critical resources, enhances unit capability, and improves combat effectiveness. Major Commands provide their own offsets from projected savings to sustain future investments for this program.

Overall, this program saves more money than it costs; keep as is ($3M).

Mobility Equipment

> This program funds procurement of Basic Expeditionary Airfield Resources (BEAR). It includes equipment to support the beddown of deployed forces (personnel, aircraft, support equipment, and munitions) at austere sites lacking infrastructure. BEAR assets are a critical enabler for the Expeditionary Air Force.

In peacetime, there should generally be no deployed forces. The equipment we have already procured should suffice if stored and maintained properly. Eliminate and save $24 Million.

Items Less than $5 Million (Base Support)

> This program provides a wide variety of base support items with worldwide application, to include but not limited to: aircraft arresting systems; electronic test stations; expandable and nonexpandable shelters; non-deployable and deployable shelters; pipe bending machines; electronic test set groups; fuels operational readiness capability equipment (FORCE); and heat treating furnaces.

Eliminate all OCO spending (which is most of it) and cut the remainder by standard 25%, saving $10 Million.

DARP RC135

> Detailed information on the DARP RC 135 program remains classified and will be provided on a need-to-know basis. For further information, please contact AF/A2RM, (703) 614-7317.

We'll just see about that. We do know that the RC-135 is a C-135 that has been modified for reconnaissance[113]. In the meantime, cut by half and save $12 Million.

DCGS – AF

> Detailed information on DCGS-AF remains classified and will be provided on a need-to-know basis. For further information, please contact, AF/A2RM, (703) 697-4723.

We'll just see about that. We do know that the DCGS is a Distributed Common Ground System[114] designed to post data, process information, and disseminate intelligence. In the meantime, cut by half and save $87 Million.

Spares and Repair Parts

> Initial Spares consist of reparable components, assemblies, subassemblies, and consumable items required as initial stock (including readiness spares package requirements) in support of newly fielded vehicles, communications electronics and telecommunications equipment, and other base maintenance and support equipment items.

In peacetime, there will be a reduced need to replace things. Eliminate all OCO spending and reduce the remainder by standard 25%, saving $6 Million.

Research, Development, Test, and Evaluation[115] [116] [117] [118]
Basic Research

Defense Research Sciences

> This program consists of extramural research activities in academia and industry along with in-house investigations performed in the Air Force Research Laboratory.

The Reliance 21 process seems to be at the very core[119] of the Military-Industrial Complex. Research and Development should be done by the R&D department of the manufacturers of the equipment and services that the DoD purchases. The Air Force should merely test and evaluate the products and services it intends to buy. Those private R&D departments should fund the programs out of the company's profits.

---

[113] http://en.wikipedia.org/wiki/Boeing_RC-135
[114] http://en.wikipedia.org/wiki/DCGS-A
[115] http://www.saffm.hq.af.mil/shared/media/document/AFD-120207-046.pdf
[116] http://www.saffm.hq.af.mil/shared/media/document/AFD-120207-047.pdf
[117] http://www.saffm.hq.af.mil/shared/media/document/AFD-120207-048.pdf
[118] http://www.saffm.hq.af.mil/shared/media/document/AFD-120208-060.pdf
[119] http://www.dtic.mil/ndia/2010SET/Kratz.pdf

The military should not directly and preemptively fund any research, period. Eliminate and save $362 Million.

University Research Initiatives

This program supports defense-related basic research in a wide range of scientific and engineering disciplines relevant to maintaining U.S. military technology superiority.

Universities should be private, and are thus no different from the R&D departments of companies. Universities and companies, however, can work together to share the research and development processes, so that students can learn while reducing costs to the companies. It's a win-win. Eliminate and save $141 Million.

High-Energy Laser Research Initiatives

This program funds basic research aimed at developing fundamental scientific knowledge to support future Department of Defense (DoD) high energy laser (HEL) systems. The HEL Joint Technology Office (JTO) sends these funds to multi-disciplinary research institutes for projects on laser and beam control technologies. In addition, funding supports educational grants to stimulate interest in HELs.

High-energy lasers show great potential both as weapons and as counter-missile defense systems. They should be researched by laser companies; eliminate and save $13 Million.

Applied Research

Materials

This program develops advanced materials, processing, and inspection technologies to reduce life cycle costs and improve performance, sustainability, availability, affordability, supportability, reliability, and survivability of current and future Air Force systems and operations.

This research should be done by companies that produce the materials in question. Eliminate and save $114 Million.

Aerospace Vehicle Technologies

This program investigates, develops, and analyzes aerospace vehicle technologies in the three primary areas of structures, controls, and aeromechanics. Advanced structures concepts are explored and developed to exploit new materials, fabrication processes, and design techniques.

This research should be done by companies that manufacture aircraft, structures, controls, and aeromechanics. Eliminate and save $121 Million.

Human Effectiveness

This program conducts applied research in the area of airmen training, airmen system interfaces, directed energy bioeffects, deployment and sustainment of airmen in extreme environments, and understanding and shaping adversarial behavior.

This research should be done by companies that make cold weather gear and related extreme environment gear. Eliminate and save $89 Million.

Aerospace Propulsion

This program develops propulsion and power technologies to achieve enabling and revolutionary aerospace technology capabilities. The program has six projects, each focusing on a technology area critical to the Air Force.

Aerospace propulsion research should be done by companies that sell aircraft engines. Eliminate and save $233 Million.

Aerospace Sensors

This program develops the technology base for Air Force aerospace sensors and electronic combat. Advances in aerospace sensors are required to increase combat effectiveness by providing anytime, anywhere surveillance, reconnaissance, precision targeting, and electronic warfare capabilities.

This research should be done by companies that sell aircraft sensors. Eliminate and save $128 Million.

Space Technology

This Program Element focuses on four major areas. First, space survivability and surveillance develops technologies to understand space weather and the geophysics environment for mitigation and exploitation of these effects to Air Force systems. Second, spacecraft payload technologies improve satellite payload operations by developing advanced component and subsystem capabilities.

The private sector has come a long way in the space sector throughout the 21st century. This research should be done by the companies that sell those things; eliminate and save $98 Million.

Conventional Munitions

This program investigates, develops, and establishes the technical feasibility and military utility of advanced guidance and ordnance technologies for conventional air-launched munitions. Program supports core technical competencies of fuze technology, energetic materials, damage mechanisms, munitions aerodynamics and guidance, navigation, and control, terminal seeker sciences, and munition systems effects.

This research should be done by companies that make munitions. Eliminate and save $77 Million.

Directed Energy Technology

This program investigates, develops, and establishes the technical feasibility and military utility of advanced guidance and ordnance technologies for conventional air-launched munitions. Program supports core technical competencies of fuze technology, energetic materials, damage mechanisms, munitions aerodynamics and guidance, navigation, and control, terminal seeker sciences, and munition systems effects.

This research should be done by weapons companies. Eliminate and save $106 Million.

Dominant Information Technology

This program develops enterprise-centric information technology for the Air Force (AF). Advances in enterprise-centric information technologies are required to increase warfighter readiness and effectiveness by providing the right information, at the right time, in the right format, anytime, anywhere in the world.

This research should be done by computer and network security companies. Eliminate and save $104 Million.

High Energy Laser Research

This program funds Department of Defense (DoD) high energy laser (HEL) applied research through the HEL Joint Technology Office (JTO). HEL weapon systems have many potential advantages including speed-of-light delivery, precision target engagement, significant magazine depth, low-cost per kill, and reduced logistics requirements.

This research should be done by weapons companies. Eliminate and save $39 Million.

Advanced Materials for Weapons Systems

This program develops and demonstrates materials technology for transition into Air Force systems. The program has five projects which develop: (1) hardened materials technologies for the protection of aircrews and sensors; (2) non-destructive inspection and evaluation technologies; (3) transition data on structural and non-structural materials for aerospace applications; (4) airbase operations technologies including deployable base infrastructure, force protection, and firefighting capabilities; and (5) advanced materials for space applications.

This research should be done by materials companies. Eliminate and save $48 Million.

Advanced Technology Department

Sustainment Science and Technology

This project develops and demonstrates sustainment technologies such as materials, corrosion, and structures for transition into Air Force systems to increase readiness and reduce life cycle costs.

This research should be done by materials companies. Eliminate and save $7 Million.

Advanced Aerospace Sensors

Divided into two broad project areas, this program develops technologies to enable the continued superiority of sensors from aerospace platforms. The first project develops and demonstrates advanced technologies for electro-optical sensors, radar sensors and electronic counter-countermeasures, and components and algorithms.

This research should be done by aircraft sensor companies. Eliminate and save $38 Million.

Aerospace Technology Development / Demonstration

This project integrates and demonstrates advanced flight vehicle technologies that improve the performance and supportability of existing and future aerospace vehicles. System level integration brings together aerospace vehicle technologies along with avionics, propulsion, and weapon systems for demonstration in a near realistic operational environment.

The companies that research and produce products should do their own demonstrations. Eliminate and save $81 Million.

Aerospace Propulsion and Power Technology

This program develops and demonstrates technologies to achieve enabling and revolutionary advances in turbine, advanced cycle, and rocket propulsion, as well as electrical power thermal management, and fuels.

This research should be done by companies that make aircraft engines. Eliminate and save $151 Million.

Electronic Combat Technology

This program develops and demonstrates technologies to support Air Force electronic combat warfighting capabilities. The program focuses on developing components, subsystems, and technologies with potential aerospace combat, special operations, and airlift electronic combat applications in three project areas.

This research should be done by companies that sell those electronics. Eliminate and save $33 Million.

Advanced Spacecraft Technology

This program develops, integrates, and demonstrates space technologies in the areas of spacecraft payloads, spacecraft protection, spacecraft vehicles, ballistic missiles, and space systems survivability. The integrated space technologies are demonstrated by component or system level tests on the ground or in flight.

This research should be done by companies that sell spacecraft, payloads, protection, missiles, and space systems. Eliminate and save $65 Million.

Maui Space Surveillance System

This program funds ground-based optical space situational awareness (SSA) technology development and demonstration at the Maui Space Surveillance System (MSSS) in Hawaii, as well as the operation and upgrade of the facility. Efforts in this program have been coordinated through the Reliance 21 process to harmonize efforts and eliminate duplication.

This isn't really research; but rather, funds a facility that is used for research. Sell the facility so someone else can do that research, eliminate, and save $29 Million.

Human Effectiveness

This program develops and demonstrates technologies to enhance human performance and effectiveness in the aerospace force. State-of-the-science advances are made in warfighter training, warfighter system interfaces, directed energy bioeffects, deployment and sustainment of warfighters in extreme environments, and understanding and shaping adversarial behavior.

The practice of researching human psychology is well established in the private sector. Research on its applications in combat should be done by companies who sell training and related equipment. Eliminate and save $22 Million.

Conventional Weapons Technology

This program develops, demonstrates, and integrates ordnance and advanced guidance technologies for air-launched conventional weapons. The program includes development of conventional ordnance technologies including warheads, fuzes, and explosives; and development of advanced guidance technologies including seekers, navigation and control, and guidance.

This research should be done by weapons companies, aircraft companies, and launch system companies. Eliminate and save $36 Million.

Advanced Weapons Technology

This program provides for the development, integration, demonstration, and detailed assessment of directed energy weapon technologies including high energy laser, high power microwave (HPM), and other unconventional weapon generation and transmission technologies, which can support a wide range of Air Force applications.

This research should be done by weapons companies. Eliminate and save $19 Million.

Manufacturing Technologies

The Manufacturing Technology (ManTech) program executes technical programs to maintain and develop an affordable and reliable industrial base and manufacturing capability that will be responsive to warfighter needs.

This research should be done by manufacturers and their vendors. Eliminate and save $37 Million.

Global Information Development and Demonstration

This program develops and demonstrates Air Force Enterprise-Centric Information technologies for the warfighter. The Global Battlespace Awareness project develops, integrates, and demonstrates advanced technologies to achieve comprehensive net-centric operations and total battlespace awareness by using and exploiting information from all sources.

This research should be done by companies that sell the equipment and services used herein. Eliminate and save $31 Million.

Advanced Component Development and Prototypes

Intelligence Advanced Development

Intelligence Advanced Development (IAD) demonstrates and validates advanced technologies required to support warfighter needs for timely all-source intelligence information. IAD research supports global awareness, consistent battlespace knowledge, precision information, and the execution of time-critical missions.

This research should be done by companies that sell the equipment. Eliminate and save $4 Million.

Physical Security Equipment

This program is a budget activity level 4 based on the concept / technology development activities ongoing within the program. The purpose of this program is to develop, demonstrate, and test Physical Security Equipment (PSE) systems, to include Force Protection.

This research should be done by companies that sell the equipment. Eliminate and save $4 Million.

Advanced EHF MILSATCOM Space

Develop and acquire Advanced Extremely High Frequency (AEHF) Military Satellite Communications (MILSATCOM) satellites, mission control segment and cryptography for survivable, anti-jam, worldwide, secure communications for the strategic and tactical warfighters.

This research should be done by companies that make the satellites and other equipment. Eliminate and save $229 Million.

Polar MILSATCOM Space

This program element acquires the Polar Military Satellite Communications (MILSATCOM) system that provides protected communications (anti-jam and low probability of intercept and detection) for users in the north polar region.

This research should be done by companies that make the satellites and other equipment. Eliminate and save $121 Million.

Space Control Technology

This program supports a range of activities including technology planning, development, demonstrations and prototyping, as well as modeling, simulations and exercises to support development of tactics and procedures in the Space Control mission area.

In peacetime, there would be no battles to manage. This research should be done by companies that sell the technology. Eliminate and save $25 Million.

Combat Identification Technology

The Combat Identification (CID) Technology program element analyzes, develops, demonstrates and evaluates promising target identification technologies to facilitate platform transition decisions prior to System

Development and Demonstration (SDD). Numerous joint needs statements, operational documents, lessons learned, and NATO requirements state the need for positive CID.

This research should be done by companies that sell the equipment. Eliminate and save $32 Million.

NATO Cooperative R&D

These funds will be used to initiate international cooperative research, and development (ICR&D) agreements with North Atlantic Treaty Organization (NATO) member states, major non-NATO allies and friendly foreign countries. Each of the selected programs and projects are required to have a concluded IA, prior to funds being released, that implements the provisions of Title 10 U.S. Code, Section 2350a.

Withdraw from NATO and evict them from our territories. This research should be done by companies that sell whatever is being researched. Eliminate all funding that goes toward international cooperative projects; save $5 Million.

International Space Cooperative R&D

These funds will be used to initiate space-related international cooperative research, and development (ICR&D) agreements with North Atlantic Treaty Organization (NATO) member states, major non-NATO allies and friendly foreign countries.

Withdraw from NATO and evict them from our territories. This research should be done by companies that sell whatever is being researched. Eliminate all funding that goes toward international cooperative projects; save $1 Million.

Space Protection Program

Growing dependence on space and demonstrated vulnerabilities have highlighted the need to actively plan for and respond to threats against national security space effects and deliver informed options to national leaders and system acquirers.

This research should be done by companies that sell the equipment and counterweapon systems in question; eliminate and save $10 Million.

Integrated Broadcast Service

The Integrated Broadcast Service (IBS) fulfills the warfighter's requirements for worldwide threat warning and situational awareness information with timely production and simultaneous dissemination of Intelligence, Surveillance, and Reconnaissance (ISR) derived combat information.

This research should be done by companies who sell the equipment. Eliminate and save $20 Million.

ICBM Demonstration and Evaluation

> This program ensures a responsive design and development engineering infrastructure to address emerging issues and technology insertion within the current Intercontinental Ballistic Missile (ICBM), future strategic systems/capability, and other common strategic mission areas, where appropriate, to develop enhanced multi-use capabilities.

This research should be done by weapons companies. Deficiencies in ICBMs, where possible, should be corrected by the companies that built them or the systems specific to the deficiency. Where not possible, other weapons companies should be contracted to correct the deficiency. Eliminate and save $71 Million.

Wideband MILSATCOM Space

> The Wideband Global SATCOM (WGS) System, previously known as Wideband Gapfiller Satellites, provides DoD users with high data rate military satellite communication services. WGS provides a new high capacity two-way Ka-band service.

This research should be done by companies that sell satellites and related equipment. Eliminate and save $12 Million.

Pollution Prevention

> Funds will be used to target R&D activities that demonstrate and prototype alternative weapon system manufacturing, remanufacturing, and maintenance materials and processes that reduce or eliminate hazardous chemicals, materials and waste streams through cost-effective programs and practices, while improving energy efficiency and reducing greenhouse gas emissions.

Anything that's important enough to involve the military is important enough not to be concerned with pollution. Eliminate and save $2 Million.

Joint Precision Approach and Landing Systems Demonstration and Evaluation

> JPALS is an Acquisition Category ID program with joint partners for requirements and acquisition including the USAF, USN/USMC, USA, and the Federal Aviation Administration (under the Next Generation (NextGen) Air Transportation System Program). JPALS development includes an incremental approach employing a family of systems (FoS) to ensure joint, allied, coalition and Federal Aviation Administration / International Civil Aviation Organization interoperability. On 16 March 2007, the Joint Requirements Oversight Council

(JROC) approved the Capability Development Document (CDD) for the JPALS FoS and Increment 1 for the Sea-Based System and designated the Navy as the JPALS lead Department of Defense (DoD) Component. On 19 January 2010, the JROC approved Increment 2 for the Land-Base System and designated the Air Force as the lead component for the Land-Based System.

Eliminate the FAA and all civil aviation regulations. Companies that sell this equipment should integrate directly with each other without the need for the military's involvement. If the military likes the demonstrations provided, they can buy all integrated technologies separately or as a package. Eliminate and save $58 Million.

Long Range Strike Bomber

[Classified] This program is reported in accordance with Title 10, United States Code, Section 119(a)(1) in the Special Access Program Annual Report to Congress. For further information, please contact the Director of Special Programs, OUSD(AT&L)/DSP.

Research on long range strike bombers should be done by the aircraft manufacturers. Eliminate and save $292 Million.

BMC2 Sensor Development

Beginning in FY12, PE 0604283F funds the development of the Three-Dimensional Expeditionary Long-Range Radar (3DELRR) which will replace the current legacy AN/TPS-75 radar.

A 3D radar is certainly an impressive idea, but this research should be done by the radar companies. Eliminate and save $114 Million.

Technology Transfer

The three-fold mission of Technology Transfer is: Integration of advanced commercial-sector technologies into Department of Defense (DoD) systems, particularly from non-traditional defense contractors; Spin-off of DoD-developed technologies to industry to make these technologies available for military acquisition; and Establishment of collaborative Research and Development (R&D) projects with the private sector for cost-sharing of new dual-use technology development.

While research should be done in the private sector, it is important to ensure those systems will integrate with the ones the DoD already has. Keep as is ($2.6M).

Hardened Target Munitions

Direct Strike Penetrator Systems project includes development of Massive Ordnance Penetrator (MOP), an advanced precision guided penetrator munition that will provide the Air Force with an improved capability using air-to-surface conventional munitions to attack HDBTs, such as bunker and tunnel facilities, with fewer weapons and number of missions necessary to defeat targets and increase overall survivability.

This research should be done by weapons companies. Eliminate and save $17 Million.

Requirements Analysis and Maturation

The Requirements Analysis and Maturation (RAM) program addresses a critical need for decision-quality information prior to initiating a new acquisition program by executing integrated material studies and analyses across the Air Force (AF) enterprise (air, space, and cyber).

It is important to tell the private sector what we want to buy, but the DoD shouldn't be ordering things for the sole purpose of keeping these companies in business. Cut by 25% and save $4 Million.

Weather Satellite Follow-On

The Defense Weather Satellite System (DWSS) program in RDT&E, AF PE 0305178F was terminated per Congressional direction in FY 2012. DoD will utilize the remaining Defense Meteorological Satellite Program (DMSP) satellites to satisfy DoD overhead weather requirements until a follow-on capability can be acquired.

This is clearly a workaround for the elimination of funding of another project. Weather satellite research should be done by companies that sell weather satellites. Eliminate and save $2 Million.

Ground Attack Weapons Fuze Development

The Hard Target Void Sensing Fuze (HTVSF) is an advanced system designed to provide fuzing and void sensing functions for a weapon to penetrate and destroy hardened targets protected by multiple layers of soil and/or reinforced concrete.

This research should be done by weapons companies. Eliminate and save $9 Million.

Technical Transition Program

The Technology Transition Program (TTP) provides funding to mature and demonstrate technologies to enable or accelerate their transition to legacy or acquisition programs of record. It addresses the gap that exists between when a technology is first demonstrated and when it can be successfully acquired as an operational capability.

Companies should fund their own demonstrations out of the profits from selling things to the military. The DoD can send them a list of concerns and requirements before the development process begins, and they can talk to each other along the way. Eliminate and save $38 Million.

NAVSTAR GPS User Equipment Space

The Global Positioning System (GPS) is a space-based radio Positioning, Navigation, and Time (PNT) distribution system. GPS User Equipment (UE) consists of standardized receivers, antennas, antenna electronics, etc., grouped together in sets to derive navigation and time information transmitted from GPS satellites. These receiver sets are used by DoD. RDT&E funds UE development, test, and analysis for new PNT receiver capabilities in Navigation Warfare (Navwar) across all military platforms using GPS services.

This research should be done by companies that make GPS User Equipment. Eliminate and save $97 Million.

Systems Development and Demonstration

Global Broadcast Service

Global Broadcast Service provides DoD with an efficient, high data rate broadcast capability from distributed information sources to dispersed warfighters who receive the broadcast directly on small, inexpensive user terminals.

In peacetime, there would be no dispersed warfighters, and this program ends in 2013. Eliminate and save $15 Million.

Nuclear Weapons Support

The Air Force is tasked with maintaining and providing technical expertise on all AF nuclear weapons and weapon systems and with developing and maintaining counter-chemical, biological, radiological, and nuclear (C-CBRN) capabilities.

This function cannot be safely privatized and falls under Necessary and Proper. Keep as is ($26M).

Specialized Undergraduate Pilot Training

Supports Air Education and Training Command's (AETC) implementation of Specialized Undergraduate Pilot Training (SUPT) and the Department of Defense initiative for joint pilot training. The Joint Primary Aircraft Training System (JPATS) is a joint USAF/USN venture to replace the Services' fleets of primary trainer aircraft (T-37 and T-34 respectively) and their associated

> *Ground Based Training Systems (GBTS) with the T-6 and its GBTS. The Air Force is the Executive Service.*

There appears to be nothing wrong with the old training planes, and they are only used to familiarize the pilots with the basics of flight. They actually train for combat on real combat aircraft. Eliminate and save $7 Million.

Electronic Warfare Development

> *This Program Element (PE) consolidates Air Force funding and management of common Electronic Warfare (EW) systems from Material Solutions Analysis through Engineering and Manufacturing Development and transition to operational capability.*

Research should be done by weapons and material companies. Eliminate and save $2 Million.

Joint Tactical Radio Systems (JTRS)

> *The JTRS Budget Item Justification is located in the Navy's FY 2013 President's Budget under Joint Tactical Radio System Program (PE 0604280N, BA 5). The JTRS development program is a joint program managed through the JTRS JPEO. The funding for the program resides in the Navy budget.*

It bothers me for some reason that the DoD's Joint Vision 2020 brochure is hosted on the Forest Service's website. There doesn't seem to be anything wrong with the radios that the military is using now, and radio research should be done by companies that sell radios. Eliminate and save $3 Million (which goes up to $30 Million in 2014).

Tactical Data Networks Enterprise

> *The Tactical Data Networks Enterprise (TDNE) contributes to the development, delivery and deployment of the next generation aerial layer network through a portfolio of legacy and advanced waveform and network management development/management efforts that advance interoperability and connectivity.*

Aerial network research should be done by companies that sell aerial network equipment. Eliminate and save $25 Million.

Physical Security Equipment

> *This program is a budget activity level 5 based on the engineering and manufacturing development activities ongoing within the program. The purpose of this program is to develop, demonstrate, and test physical security equipment (PSE) systems, to include Force Protection. This program supports*

the protection of tactical, fixed, and nuclear weapons systems, AF personnel and AF facilities.

Equipment demonstrations and testing should be done by the companies selling the equipment. The Air Force should only test the integration with their existing systems and evaluate them prior to larger purchases. In peacetime, the number of bases requiring such equipment would be reduced; cut by 25% and save $12K.

Small Diameter Bomb

Small Diameter Bomb Increment II (SDB II) is a joint interest United States Air Force (USAF) and Department of Navy (DoN) ACAT ID program, with the Air Force (AF) as the lead service. SDB II provides the warfighter the capability to attack mobile targets from stand-off, through weather.

This research should be done by weapons companies. Eliminate and save $143 Million.

Counterspace Systems

This program supports the conduct of critical planning, technology and capability insertion, and system acquisition in support of Air Force space control systems and associated command and control development to meet current and future military space control needs. Development and acquisition of counterspace systems will be conducted, capitalizing on the technology development and risk reduction efforts of PE 0603438F, Space Control Technology. This funding supports the acquisition process including concept development, risk reduction, design, and demonstration.

The development component should be done by the companies selling the equipment; the testing and integration components are justified. Cut by half and save $14 Million.

Space Situational Awareness Systems

Space Situational Awareness (SSA) is knowledge of all aspects of space related to operations. As the foundation for space control, SSA encompasses intelligence on adversary space operations; surveillance of all space objects and activities; detailed reconnaissance of specific space assets; monitoring space environmental conditions; monitoring cooperative space assets; and conducting integrated command, control, communications, processing, analysis, dissemination, and archiving activities.

This program develops sensors. This research should be done by sensor companies; eliminate and save $267 Million.

Airborne Electronic Attack

This Program Element (PE) supports the development of the critical electronic attack capabilities, from technology demonstrations through transition to operational capability, for Air Force and joint operations to include the Global Strike and Persistent Global Attack Concepts of Operations (CONOPS).

This research should be done by electronic warfare weapons companies. Eliminate and save $4 Million.

Space Based Infrared Systems (SBIRS) High

The Space-Based Infrared Systems (SBIRS) primary mission is to provide initial warning of a ballistic missile attack on the US, its deployed forces, and its allies. SBIRS will incorporate new technologies to enhance detection and improve reporting of intercontinental ballistic missile launches, submarine launched ballistic missile launches, and tactical ballistic missile launches

This approval approved SBIRS under regular Other Procurements, indicating the system is already functional. Research on improving this existing system should be done by weapons companies. Eliminate and save $449 Million.

Armament / Ordnance Development

The Armament Ordnance Development program provides for initial and continuing development of weapons/munitions (kinetic and non-kinetic) and munitions equipment for support and operational use.

Weapons should be developed by weapons companies. Materials should be developed by material companies. Eliminate and save $10 Million.

Submunitions

Project Chicken Little continues to provide vital research, development, test and evaluation (RDT&E) support to developmental smart munitions, seekers/sensors and their platforms, networked weapons, advanced weapon concepts, and innovative targeting technologies employed against a wide variety of vehicle targets, theater air defense units, and an extensive array of foreign threat systems and associated equipment.

This research should be done by weapons companies. Eliminate and save $3 Million.

Agile Combat Support

This Program Element (PE) provides capabilities to rapidly deploy, defend and sustain airfield operations, command and control activities, and force protection to ensure readiness. In addition, this PE provides tactical and strategic aeromedical evacuation systems, automated information systems, and medical treatment equipment to meet unique Air Force medical readiness and operational requirements.

In peacetime, there is no need to deploy mobile airfields. Research on how to do it better should be done by companies that sell the stuff we would buy. Eliminate and save $13 Million.

Life Support Systems

This program element provides for recapitalization, continuing research and development, and integration of aircrew flight equipment/airmen combat effectiveness equipment and subsystems to satisfy operational command requirements for improved/enhanced airmen performance capabilities.

This research should be done by companies that sell life support equipment. Eliminate and save $10 Million.

Combat Training Ranges

The Combat Training Range (CTR) Program Element (PE) provides equipment and support to Air Force units and combat training ranges for mission testing, training, and evaluation of aircrews, as well as the operational testing of weapon systems and tactics under simulated combat conditions.

Even in peacetime, people need to be trained so we're ready if war comes to us. Keep as is ($9M).

Intelligence Equipment

Intelligence Equipment (IE) Program Element (PE) performs the engineering development of software, and/or automated information operations techniques to streamline the processing, integration, exploitation, display, and dissemination of strategic and tactical intelligence information.

Software should be researched by software companies. Automation techniques should be researched by automation equipment companies. Eliminate and save $1 Million.

Joint Strike Fighter EMD

The Joint Strike Fighter (JSF) program will develop and deploy a family of highly common, affordable next generation, stealthy, multi-role strike fighter aircraft that meets the needs of the USN, USAF, USMC and allies with maximum commonality among the variants, consistent with National Disclosure Policy, to minimize life cycle costs. This is a joint program with no executive service.

If the DoD wants a new JSF right after the F-35 was approved, maybe they should send better requirements to the aircraft companies. Aircraft development should be done by aircraft manufacturers. Eliminate and save **$1.2 Billion.**

ICBM – EMD

> *Intercontinental Ballistic Missile (ICBM) Engineering and Manufacturing Development (EMD) efforts will ensure the extension of the operational life of the Minuteman III ICBM weapon system through 2030.*

Keeping our ICBMs operational is critical to national security and is thus necessary and proper. Keep as is ($135M).

Evolved Expendable Launch Vehicle

> *The Evolved Expendable Launch Vehicle (EELV) program is a space launch system that satisfies the government's National Launch Forecast (NLF) requirements. EELV is a launch service, not a weapon system, primarily funded with procurement funds. EELV is responsible for launching government manifested payloads.*

The Air Force does need a new way to launch things. Keep as is, but it shall not be included in the budget projection as its procurement seems to end in 2014. $8M saved.

Long Range Standoff Weapon

> *The Long Range Stand Off (LRSO) effort will develop a weapon system to replace the Air Force's Air Launched Cruise Missile (ALCM), operational since 1986. The LRSO weapon system will be capable of penetrating and surviving advanced Integrated Air Defense Systems (IADS) from significant stand off range to prosecute strategic targets in support of the Air Force's global attack capability and strategic deterrence core function.*

Missile development should be done by missile companies. Eliminate and save $2 Million ($353M total).

ICBM Fuze Modernization

> *The ICBM Fuze Modernization program activities will include replacement of the Mk21 fuze to meet warfighter requirements and maintain current capability; development of a new Mk12A fuze capability to integrate with W78 Life Extension Program (LEP); and provide for Air Force direction and oversight of the W78 LEP.*

Fuze development should be done by fuze companies. Eliminate and save $74 Million.

F-22 Increment 3.2B

Increment 3.2B will integrate the newest air-to-air intercept missiles (i.e., AIM-9X and AIM-120D), further improve the Electronic Protection (EP) capability over Increment 3.2A, and enhance the F-22's geolocation capability from the Increment 3.1 baseline with the addition of the Geolocation 2 candidate. Increment 3.2B will include the Enhanced Stores Management System (ESMS), as well as, an Intra-Flight Datalink (IFDL) improvement to increase IFDL bandwidth and enable cooperative functions required to realize Increment 3.2B candidates.

It seems understandable to improve existing systems, but brand-new ones? In peacetime, this can be done over a longer period; cut by 25% and save $35 Million.

KC-45 Next Generation Aerial Refueling Aircraft

Replacement of the legacy KC-135 fleet will take place in three stages, known as the KC-X (now the KC-46), KC-Y, and the KC-Z. The initial KC-46 increment will replace roughly a third of the current capability with the purchase of 179 aircraft.

Aircraft development should be done by aircraft companies; we should just buy the planes that result from that process. Maybe some of the funds need to be sent up front to fund the manufacturing; but not the development. Eliminate and save **$1.8 Billion**.

Combat Rescue Helicopter

The Combat Rescue Helicopter (CRH) program, formerly referred to as HH-60 Recapitalization, will replace the aging HH-60G. The HH-60G currently supports the Air Force's core function of Personnel Recovery. The primary mission of the HH-60G is to conduct day / night / marginal weather Combat Search and Rescue (CSAR) in order to recover downed aircrew or other isolated personnel in hostile or permissive environments.

Helicopter development should be done by helicopter companies. Eliminate and save $123 Million.

CRT-X

HC/MC-130 Recapitalization will replace and augment the aging USAF fleets of combat rescue HC-130P/N and special operations MC-130E/P aircraft which are experiencing airworthiness, maintainability and operational limitations. The HC/MC-130 Recap Capabilities Production Document (CPD) defines a common baseline configuration for the weapon system and a FY 2012 Initial Operational Capability.

Helicopter development should be done by helicopter companies. Eliminate and save $19 Million.

B-2 Defensive Management System

The B-2 Defensive Management System Modernization (DMS-M) program maintains the B-2 direct attack capability while addressing emerging 21st century threats. DMS-M is the #1 priority modification program in the B-2 program office. DMS-M will upgrade the Electronic Support Measures, antennas, and display processing units. Modernization of this system will resolve the #1 obsolescence issue in the B-2 fleet.

The Air Force shouldn't have an office for each airplane they buy. Aircraft improvement ideas should be sent to the aircraft manufacturers, who should develop the improvements. Eliminate and save $281 Million.

Nuclear Weapon Modernization

The purpose of this program element is to conduct and support Air Force and Joint DoD-DOE acquisition activities for the modernization and sustainment of nuclear weapons. B61 Life Extension Program (LEP) is a joint DoD-DOE effort encompassing feasibility, design, cost, and a down-select effort. DoD leads development and acquisition of B61 Tail Kit Assembly (TKA) as well as integration with current and future aircraft.

All nuclear weapons should be moved from the DoE to the DoD. All development activities should be done by private companies where possible. Since this might not be something we can privatize, let's leave it in and give it a standard 25% cut, saving $20 Million.

Full Combat Mission Training

Full Combat Mission Training (FCMT) supports Air Force Distributed Mission Operations (DMO) and Live-Virtual-Constructive (LVC) integration. DMO is an operational readiness initiative enabling the USAF to exercise and train at the operational and strategic levels of war while facilitating unit-level training.

In peacetime, there will be significantly reduced missions to operate and distribute. This equipment should be developed by companies that sell the equipment; eliminate and save $15 Million.

ISR for Irregular Warfare

The Air Force uses Aircrew Training Devices (ATD) to provide realistic, cost effective flight training to aircrews. Some of the training in the ATDs cannot be fully conducted in the aircraft because of safety, airspace, equipment, and security restrictions. The MC-12W Mission Training Center (MTC) Program will provide simulation for pilots and mission system operators.

Training is necessary, even in peacetime. Keep as is ($20M).

CV-22

> *CV-22 RDT&E provides development, integration, testing and enhancement of critical capability to insert, extract, and re-supply special operation forces into politically or militarily denied areas. The CV-22 Block 10 configuration added terrain following radar, additional fuel tanks, additional radios, flare/chaff dispensers, radio frequency/infrared and defensive countermeasures, weapons, situational awareness improvements, and Communications, Navigation, Surveillance/Air Traffic Management (CNS/ATM) to the V-22 Block B aircraft.*

Development of the CV-22 should be done by its manufacturers, Bell Helicopter and Boeing; but integration and testing can involve the Air Force. Cut by 25% and save $7 Million.

SLC3S-A (Senior Leader C3S)

> *The Air Force Senior Leader Command, Control, and Communications System - Airborne (SLC3S-A) provides executive airborne communications supporting worldwide command and control capabilities to US government Senior Leaders.*

The advanced communication systems in Air Force One and similar systems are necessary and proper; keep as is ($2M).

RDT&E Management Support

Threat Simulator Development

> *This PE provides funding for the elements necessary to support the Air Force Electronic Warfare (EW) Test Process, including Directed Energy (DE). This test process provides a scientific methodology to ensure the effective disciplined and efficient testing of EW and avionics systems. Each capability or facility improvement is pursued in concert with the others to avoid duplicate capabilities while at the same time producing the proper mix of test resources needed to support the AF EW Test Process and testing of EW systems which can be used in any action involving the use of electromagnetic and DE to control the electromagnetic spectrum or to attack the enemy.*

If the USAF wants a way to simulate a threat, they should order such a system from the private sector. Eliminate and save $23 Million.

Major T&E Investment

> *This PE provides planning, improvements, and modernization for test capabilities at three Air Force test organizations: 46 Test Wing (to include 46 Test Group at Holloman AFB NM, and operating locations at Wright-Patterson*

AFB OH), Arnold Engineering Development Center (AEDC), and Air Force Flight Test Center (AFFTC). The purpose is to help test organizations improve and develop their test infrastructure and capabilities to keep pace with improvements in weapon system technologies.

Testing new equipment and aircraft needs to be supported, even in peacetime; keep as is ($42M).

RAND Project Air Force

This program provides for continuing analytical research across a broad spectrum of aerospace issues and concerns. The Project AIR FORCE (PAF) research agenda is focused primarily on mid to long-term problems; in addition, PAF provides quick response assistance for senior Air Force officials on high priority, near term issues.

This is literally a brain trust to solve problems. In peacetime, there will be fewer problems. Cut by half and save $13 Million.

Initial Operational Test and Evaluation

This PE funds Congressionally mandated Initial Operational Test and Evaluation (IOT&E) to support major weapon system acquisition decisions beyond Low-Rate Initial Production (LRIP), Milestone C, full rate production, fielding, and declaration of Initial Operational Capability (IOC).

Weapons systems need to be tested and evaluated; keep as is ($16M).

Test and Evaluation Support

Test facilities, capabilities and resources operated through this program include wind tunnels, rocket and jet engine test cells, armament test ranges, hardware-in-the-loop test facilities, climatic test facilities, avionics test facilities, aircraft test beds, dry lakebed landing sites, instrumented test ranges, civilian payroll, and contractor services.

The Air Force needs places to test new stuff, but most of that testing should be done by the companies who make the stuff we buy. Cut by 25% and save $181 Million.

Rocket Systems Launch Program

Rocket Systems Launch Program (RSLP) provides responsive space and Research, Development, Test and Evaluation (RDT&E) launch vehicle support to DoD and other government agencies using commercial launch systems and excess ballistic missile assets.

The Air Force needs a way to launch things; keep as is ($16M).

Space Test Program

> *The Space Test Program (STP) conducts space test missions for the purpose of accelerating DoD space technology transformation while lowering developmental risk. The program flies an optimally selected number of DoD sponsored experiments consistent with priority, opportunity, and funding.*

Space technology needs to be tested too; but there is no funding requested after 2013.

Facility Restoration and Modernization

> *Restoration includes repair and replacement work to restore damaged facilities due to accident or failure attributable to inadequate sustainment, excessive age, or other causes.*

Facilities need to be maintained; keep as is ($43M).

Facility Sustainment

> *Provides resources for sustainment activities required for an inventory of Air Force Material Command (AFMC) T&E facilities. Facility sustainment includes regularly scheduled adjustments and inspections, preventative maintenance tasks, and emergency response and service calls for minor repairs.*

Facilities need to be maintained; keep as is ($27M).

Multi-Service Systems Engineering

> *The Multi-Service System Engineering Team (MSSET) serves as a joint acquisition effort to build the framework for future work towards achieving near-term Joint Track Management Capability (JTMC) and long-term Joint Integrated Air and Missile Defense (JIAMD) capabilities.*

This is overhead designed to make the acquisition process easier; but as demonstrated here, the true solution is simply to acquire fewer things. Eliminate and save $14 Million.

Acquisition Civilian Workforce

> *The Space and Missile Systems Center (SMC) equips US and allied forces with operational space and missile systems, launch systems, and command and control infrastructure in support of global military and national security operations.*

This is overhead designed to make the acquisition process easier; but as demonstrated here, the true solution is simply to acquire fewer things. We should never run the procurement processes of other countries. Eliminate and save $204 Million.

Acquisition and Command Support

The program funds efforts to meet the Defense Acquisition Workforce Improvement Act (DAWIA) (Public Law 101-510, Title XII), as well as Congressional and SECDEF mandates to provide acquisition and engineering process research and cost estimating, systems integration modeling and architectural analysis, information technology infrastructure development, and technical workforce.

The people doing the acquisitions should be able to figure out in their head (with the help of the Internet) whether the things they're acquiring are worth the price. This is not an expensive process. Eliminate and save $42 Million.

General Skill Training

The DoD Cyber Crime Center (DC3) is a service organization that provides on demand state-of-the-art electronic forensic services and cyber investigative and operational support to the Department of Defense (DoD). DC3 also provides leadership as a DoD center of excellence in processing an analyzing digital evidence.

There are cyber things, there are crime things, and there are military things. The three are not related. Eliminate and save $1.3 Million.

International Activities

The mission of this program is to establish, sustain, and expand mutually beneficial international partnerships through the implementation of international cooperative research, development, test, evaluation, and acquisition agreements thereby supporting the core competencies of the USAF and DoD and meeting mission requirements. These International Agreements (IAs) will significantly improve U.S. and allied conventional defense capabilities by leveraging our Allies' best defense technologies, eliminating costly duplication of research and development (R&D) efforts, accelerating the availability of defense systems, and promoting U.S. and allied interoperability or commonality.

Since the government shouldn't be doing research and development, we can remove those parts right away. The rest can be established with an E-mail or a phone call. Eliminate and save $4 Million.

Operational Systems Development

Integrated Personnel and Pay System

AF-IPPS will be a web enabled, Commercial-Off-The-Shelf (COTS) based solution aligning with the Secretary of the Air Force (SECAF) "3-1" (Active, Reserve, and Air National Guard) initiative dated 15 Oct 10 that will integrate many existing personnel and pay processes into one self-service system.

Commercial off-the-shelf personnel and pay systems can be had for much less than this procurement. The Air Force already had personnel and pay systems. There's no reason why this should have ongoing costs. Eliminate and save $92 Million.

Anti-Tamper Technology Executive Agent

The Air Force is the DoD Anti-Tamper Executive Agent (ATEA). The ATEA is responsible for implementing Anti-Tamper (AT) policy, coordinating and providing financial support for AT technology development, establishing and maintaining a data bank/library, providing proper security mechanisms, conducting effective validation and assessing AT implementations.

Computers and weapons need to be secured; keep as is ($17M).

B-52 Squadrons

Prior to FY13, all B-52 modernization programs were funded in a single BPAC, 675039 B-52 Modernization. B-52 modernization is a comprehensive program to ensure B-52 viability to perform current and future wartime missions to include datalinks, navigation, sensors, weapons, and electronic warfare (EW) and training capabilities.

There is no reason why this should be an ongoing procurement, and the program requests no funding after 2016. This should be included if necessary, but not as a part of the recurring budget. $53 Million saved.

Air Launched Cruise Missile

The AGM-86B, Air Launched Cruise Missile (ALCM), is a subsonic, air-to-surface strategic nuclear missile, operational since 1982. Armed with a W80 warhead, it is designed to evade air and ground-based defenses in order to strike targets at any location within any enemy's territory

Missiles should be developed by missile companies; eliminate and save $431K.

B-1B Squadrons

This program provides Research, Development, Test & Engineering (RDT&E) funding for the B-1B modernization program. The modernization program addresses potential aircraft obsolescent issues due to Diminishing Manufacturing Sources (DMS) and provides new and improved capabilities to the B-1B weapon system that require significant hardware and software development and testing.

There is no reason why this should be an ongoing procurement, and the program requests no funding after 2016. This should be included if necessary, but not as a part of the recurring budget. $16 Million saved.

B-2 Squadrons

> The B-2A Spirit is the world's most advanced long-range strike asset. The unique combination of range, precision, payload, and ability to operate in anti-access environments allow the B-2 to identify, locate, target, and destroy the highest value enemy targets.

There is no reason why this should be an ongoing procurement. This should be included if necessary, but not as a part of the recurring budget. $36 Million saved.

Strategic War Planning System

> The mission of USSTRATCOM is to establish and provide full-spectrum global strike, coordinated space and information operations capabilities to meet both deterrent and decisive national security objectives, and to provide operational space support, integrated missile defense, Global Command Control Communications and Computers Intelligence Surveillance and Reconnaissance (C4ISR), and specialized planning expertise to the joint warfighter.

In peacetime, there will be a significantly reduced need to strike globally, and we should not be planning war of any kind until we're actually in a war. Eliminate and save $31 Million.

Region / Sector Operations Control Center

> Battle Control System-Fixed (BCS-F) is the replacement for the fixed sites for the Region/Sector Air Operations Center (R/SAOC), also known as Region Air Operations Center-Air Defense Sector (RAOC-ADS).

This procurement doesn't request any funding after 2015, so it need not be included in the recurring budget proposal; $6 Million saved.

Warfighter Rapid Acquisition Program

> The Warfighter Rapid Acquisition Process (WRAP) provides rapid transition funding for the development and fielding of highly successful competitive experiments, demonstrations, and innovative approaches to support the Expeditionary Air Force (EAF) and other warfighters.

The military should not be funding development that should rightfully happen in the free market. Eliminate and save $15 Million.

MQ-9 Development and Fielding

> The basic MQ-9 Reaper system consists of the aircraft, sensors, a ground control station (GCS), Squadron Operations Center (SOC), communications equipment, weapon kits, support equipment, simulator and training devices, Readiness Spares Packages (RSP), technical data/training, and personnel

required to operate, maintain, and sustain the system. The system is designed to be modular and open-ended.

Development on the MQ-9 should be done by its manufacturer, General Atomics. Eliminate and save $148 Million.

Multi-Platform Electronics

Overall, this program element(PE)funds on-going sustainment, maintenance, and upgrade of Multi-Platform Electronic Attack (EA) jamming pods and associated combat test equipment as well as sustainment of various other Electronic Warfare equipment.

Electronic attack jamming pods and associated test equipment should be developed by the companies that sell them. Eliminate and save $50 Million.

A-10 Squadrons

The concept of operations for the A-10 requires an agile and survivable weapon system that provides close-air support, combat search and rescue, and special operations support.

There is no reason why this should be an ongoing procurement. This should be included if necessary, but not as a part of the recurring budget. $14 Million saved.

F-16 Squadrons

The F-16 Fighting Falcon is the world's premier multi-mission fighter. It is a fixed-wing, high performance, single-engine fighter aircraft. In its 33-year history, the F-16 has proven itself in combat in a variety of air-to-air and air-to-surface missions such as offensive and defensive counter-air, close air support, forward air control, air interdiction (day/night and all-weather) and suppression of enemy air defenses (SEAD)/destruction of enemy air defenses (DEAD).

There is no reason why this should be an ongoing procurement. This should be included if necessary, but not as a part of the recurring budget. $190 Million saved.

F-15 Programs

The F-15 is the most versatile fighter in the world today. The F-15A-D continues to provide air superiority with an undefeated and unmatched aerial combat record. The F-15E retains this air superiority capability and adds systems, such as advanced imaging and targeting systems, to meet the requirement for all-weather, deep penetration, and night/under-the-weather, air-to-surface attack. Configured with conformal fuel tanks (CFTs), the F-15E deploys worldwide with minimal tanker support and arrives combat-ready.

There is no reason why this should be an ongoing procurement. This should be included if necessary, but not as a part of the recurring budget. $193 Million saved.

Manned Destructive Suppression

> The Manned Destructive Suppression (MDS) program element funds the development, procurement, and sustainment of the Air Force's Suppression of Enemy Air Defenses (SEAD) and Destruction of Enemy Air Defenses (DEAD) capabilities.

This is a program to develop Air-to-Ground missiles, which should be done by missile companies. Eliminate and save $14 Million.

F-22 Squadrons

> The Engineering and Manufacturing Development (EMD) phase of F-22 acquisition is complete. The program is now continuing the pre-planned modernization effort through incremental development phases that enhance the F-22 Global Strike capability

Is the F-22 really so old that we already need a newer variant? R&D should be done by the manufacturer. Eliminate and save $312 Million.

Joint Strike Fighter Squadrons

> The Joint Strike Fighter (JSF) program will develop and deploy a family of highly common, affordable next generation, stealthy, multi-role strike fighter aircraft that meets the needs of the USN, USAF, USMC and allies with maximum commonality among the variants, consistent with National Disclosure Policy, to minimize life cycle costs.

Is the F-35 really so old that we already need a newer variant? R&D should be done by the manufacturer. Eliminate and save $8 Million.

Tactical AIM Missiles

> The AIM-9X Sidewinder short-range air-to-air missile is a long-term evolution of the AIM-9 series of fielded missiles. The AIM-9X missile program provides a launch and leave, air combat munition that uses passive infrared (IR) energy for acquisition and tracking of enemy aircraft and complements the Advanced Medium Range Airto-Air Missile (AMRAAM).

Missile development should be done by missile companies; eliminate and save $8 Million.

Advanced Medium Range Air-to-Air Missile

> The Air Force and Navy continue to develop improvements to the Advanced Medium Range Air-to-Air Missile (AMRAAM) to counter existing and emerging

air vehicle threats, operating at high or low altitude, and having advanced Electronic Attack (EA) capabilities. The AMRAAM Pre-Planned Product Improvement (P3I) program allows Air Force and Navy to continue a joint research and development program.

Missile development should be done by missile companies; eliminate and save $87 Million.

Joint Helmet Mounted Cueing System (JHMCS)

Develops a helmet display system capable of depicting aircraft heading data, pilot's viewing perspective, target indication tracking/cueing, and other information on the aircrew visor to enhance pilot situational awareness.

Missile accessory development should be done by missile companies; eliminate and save $87 Million.

Combat Rescue and Recovery

The HH-60G currently supports the Air Force's core function of Personnel Recovery. The primary mission of the HH-60G is to conduct day / night / marginal weather Combat Search and Rescue (CSAR) in order to recover downed aircrew or other isolated personnel in hostile or permissive environments.

In peacetime, there would be no personnel to recover. Upgrade development should be done by the manufacturer; eliminate and save $2 Million.

Pararescue – Guardian Angel Weapon System

The GA program will standardize and modernize mission essential equipment utilized in extrication, surface/underwater search and recovery, airborne infil/exfil, and ground recovery operations.

Equipment should be researched and developed by the manufacturers.

TENCAP

Air Force TENCAP is executed by the Space Innovation and Development Center (SIDC) at Schriever Air Force Base, Colorado. Established by Congress in 1977 as one of a family of service Tactical Exploitation of National Capabilities (TENCAP) programs, AF TENCAP increases warfighter awareness of Space and National capabilities, and promotes cross-domain integration of these systems into military and intelligence, surveillance and reconnaissance (ISR) operations.

This is a development program for improved satellites, which should be done by the equipment manufacturers. Eliminate and save $64 Million.

Precision Attack Systems

Advanced Targeting Pods (ATPs) provide long-range target acquisition and expanded weapon delivery envelopes for greater aircraft survivability. ATPs feature an infrared (IR) sensor, charged coupled device television (CCD-TV), laser designator, eye-safe laser, laser spot tracker, infrared marker, and real-time video data link for connectivity with ground forces.

This is a development program for improved weapon control systems, which should be done by the manufacturers. Eliminate and save $1 Million.

Compass Call

The EC-130H COMPASS CALL is the USAF's wide-area, airborne Command and Control Warfare/Information Operations (C2W/IO) weapon system. The employment of this system interdicts our adversary's use of the electronic battlespace and is a key active component in the information battlespace and prosecution of overseas contingency operations.

Weapon systems should be developed by weapons systems companies; eliminate and save $12 Million.

Aircraft Engine Component Improvement Program

The Aircraft Engine Component Improvement Program (CIP) provides the only source of critical sustaining engineering support for in-service Air Force engines to maintain flight safety (highest priority), to correct service revealed deficiencies, to improve system operational readiness (OR) and reliability & maintainability (R&M), to reduce engine Life Cycle Cost (LCC)[...]

Aircraft engines should be improved by aircraft engine companies; eliminate and save $188 Million.

Joint Air-to-Surface Standoff Missile (JASSM)

The Joint Air-to-Surface Standoff Missile (JASSM) program provides a long range, conventional air-to-surface, autonomous, precision-guided, standoff cruise missile compatible with fighter and bomber aircraft able to attack a variety of fixed or relocatable targets.

Weapons should be developed by weapons companies. Eliminate and save $8 Million.

Air and Space Operations Center Weapons System

The Air and Space Operations Center Weapon System (AOC WS) program element provides development of Command and Control (C2) capabilities across the entire spectrum of air and space operations from the strategic to the tactical level. There are three funded projects within the AOC WS program element.

C2 systems should be developed by C2 manufacturers. Eliminate and save $76 Million.

Modular Control System

> This budget activity funds development of mobile ground-based command and control (C2) capabilities of the Control and Reporting Center (CRC) program.

C2 systems should be developed by C2 manufacturers. Eliminate and save $9 Million.

Airborne Warning and Control System (AWACS)

> AWACS is the premier airborne platform providing command and control (C2)/battle management (BM) to Commander In Chief and combatant commander tasking for joint, allied, and coalition operations, humanitarian relief, and homeland defense. AWACS provides a real-time picture of friendly, neutral, and hostile air activity.

Aircraft improvements should be developed by aircraft companies; eliminate and save $65 Million.

Tactical Airborne Control System

> The Joint Terminal Control Training and Rehearsal System (JTC TRS) project, under the Tactical Airborne Control System, funds development necessary to provide a Distributed Mission Operations (DMO) capable, high-fidelity simulator for the Joint Terminal Attack Controller (JTAC), Combat Control Team (CCT) and Air Support Operations Center (ASOC).

Equipment development should be done by the equipment companies; eliminate and save $6 million.

Combat Air Intelligence System

> The mission of Combat Air Intelligence Systems (CAIS) is to process, analyze, and disseminate intelligence for air component and unit operations worldwide by providing key intelligence infrastructure and tactical production capabilities for the Air Force with true backbone type of intelligence support for air operations.

Equipment should be developed by the companies that sell it; eliminate and save $6 Million.

Tactical Air Control Party Modernization

> The TACP-M program provides equipment modernization capabilities to TACP, Air Support Operations Centers (ASOCs), and Tactical Operations Center (TOCs) personnel.

This proposal eliminates all OCO. Equipment development should be done by the companies that build the equipment; eliminate and save $16 Million.

C2ISR Tactical Data Link

As a subset of the broader Airborne Network, are used in a combat environment to exchange information such as messages, data, radar tracks, target information, platform status, imagery, and command assignments. TDLs provide interoperability, local and global connectivity, and situational awareness to the user when operating under rapidly changing operational conditions.

Equipment should be developed by the equipment companies; eliminate and save $2 Million.

C2 Constellation

The Command and Control Constellation (C2C) is the sole Air Force program for defining, developing, and assessing integrated effects of global, theater and tactical level Air Force air, space, and cyber Command and Control (C2) capabilities in support of the joint warfighter.

Equipment should be developed by the equipment companies; eliminate and save $18 Million.

DCAPES

The Deliberate and Crisis Action Planning and Execution Segments (DCAPES) Program Element (PE) includes Deliberate and Crisis Action Planning and Execution Segments (DCAPES), a system being developed as the next-generation AF interface to the Joint Operational Planning and Execution System (JOPES).

So there are actually two different things in the same procurement area with the exact same initials; that probably causes some confusion. Equipment should be developed by the equipment companies; eliminate and save $16 Million.

JOINT STARS

The Joint Surveillance Target Attack Radar System (Joint STARS) program produces the world's premier airborne ground surveillance platform, meeting joint combat capability requirements.

Equipment should be developed by the equipment companies; eliminate and save $24 Million.

> *The Air Force operates a variety of combat aircraft that carry numerous and varied stores (munitions, missiles, fuel tanks, targeting pods, range pods, electronic countermeasures pods, etc.). Stores are carried in countless different loading combinations determined by operational and training scenarios, missions, tactics, and weapon development programs.*

Evaluating procurements is an important part of responsible spending; but in peacetime, we'd need to procure much less. Cut by half and save $12 Million.

Modeling and Simulation

> *United States Air Force (USAF) Modeling & Simulation (M&S) Program Element (PE) is broken into four thrust areas: Modeling and Simulation Foundations, Accelerated Acquisition, New and Emerging Warfighting Capabilities, and Warfighter Readiness. It directly supports Air Force, Joint, Coalition composite training and rehearsal, concept development, and acquisition and testing through model and simulation development as well as the integration of these across and within Live, Virtual, and Constructive (LVC) environments.*

This sounds like a fancy way to plan future operations and training, so it can stay; keep as is ($16M).

Wargaming and Simulation Centers

> *The United States Air Force (USAF) Distributed Mission Operations Center (DMOC) is an Air Combat Command, USAF Warfare Center, 505th Command and Control Wing (505th CCW) organization. It provides joint interoperability training and testing to geographically separated Live, Virtual, and Constructive (LVC) assets--realworld weapon systems, operator-in-the-loop (OITL), and computer-driven simulations.*

Training is important in peacetime, so we're always ready for war if it comes to us. Keep as is ($6M).

Wargaming Operations (Distributed Training)

> *In September 03, the AF/CV directed the establishment of funding to increase participation in joint transformation activities including joint concept development and experimentation and joint Doctrine, Organization, Training, Material, Leadership & Education, Personnel & Facilities (DOTMLPF) recommendations.*

Training is important in peacetime, so we're always ready for war if it comes to us. Keep as is ($4M).

Mission Planning Systems

> Mission planning involves the creation of a flight plan based on threats, targets, terrain, weather, aircraft performance capability, and configuration. It is an essential task that must be completed prior to any fixed or rotary wing aircraft sortie.

In peacetime, there will be a reduced need to plan missions; cut by 25% and save $17 Million.

Information Warfare Support

> This Program Element funds research and development of strategy, assessment, and information operations (IO) capabilities required in support of Air Operation Center (AOC) command and control processes and supported combatant commanders. analysis. IWPC is a full-spectrum, offensive and defensive, planning capability.

The costs of Information "Warfare" don't seem to justify the means, especially in peacetime, given all the operational overhead associated with it. Eliminate and save $7 Million.

CYBER Command

> The US Cyber Command (USCYBERCOM) responsibilities include planning, integrating, and coordinating Computer Network Operations (CNO) capabilities; operational and tactical level planning and day-to-day employment of assigned and attached Offensive Cyber Operations (OCO) forces; integration of OCO forces with Defensive Cyber Operations (DCO) forces and planning and coordination of cyber capabilities that have trans-regional effects or that directly support national objectives; providing OCO/DCO support for assigned missions and OCO/DCO planning and integration in support of other Combatant Commanders (COCOMs) as directed.

The costs of Information "Warfare" don't seem to justify the means, especially in peacetime, given all the operational overhead associated with it. Eliminate and save $67 Million.

Space Superiority Intelligence

> Provides Electronic Support (ES) for key find, fix, track, target, engage and assess (F2T2EA) requirements supporting Space Superiority activities. Additionally funding provides for developmental intelligence collection to support new capability acquisition and development.

The Air Force doesn't need a program whose purpose is to find more stuff to buy. Eliminate and save $12 Million.

National Airborne Operations Center

The four aircraft E-4B National Airborne Operations Center (NAOC) fleet satisfies the military need for an airborne operations center with communications capabilities that permit military and civilian leadership to monitor and control military and civil national assets during all phases of nuclear and non-nuclear conflict or natural disaster

This seems important enough, and certainly necessary and proper for national defense. Keep as is ($4M).

Minimum Essential Emergency Communications Network

Will provide Nuclear Command and Control connectivity to bombers, tankers, and reconnaissance wing command posts and mobile relocation teams.

Necessary and proper; keep as is ($20M).

Information Systems Security Program

The Information Systems Security Program Element provides cradle-to-grave research, development, acquisitions, supply, sustainment, depot maintenance and demilitarization of the Air Force (AF) cryptographic and key distribution/management systems.

Necessary and proper; keep as is ($69M).

Global Combat Support System (GCSS)

Global Combat Support System-Air Force (GCSS-AF) will provide the warfighter and supporting elements with timely, accurate, and trusted Agile Combat Support (ACS) information.

Equipment should be developed by the companies that make it; eliminate and save $7 Million.

WWMCCS / Global Command and Control System

The Global Command and Control System (GCCS) is the Joint Command and Control (C2) System of Record and the designated C2 migration system for the DoD. It is an integrated Command, Control, Communications, Computer, and Intelligence (C4I) system capable of supporting all echelons of the US military command structure.

Which is all fine and dandy of course; but further development should be done in the private sector. We are, after all, still in the RDT&E procurement budgets. Eliminate and save $4 Million.

MILSATCOM Terminals

The Military Satellite Communications (MILSATCOM) Terminals program develops and fields equipment enabling users to communicate via legacy and future systems.

Equipment should be developed by equipment companies; eliminate and save $107 Million.

Airborne SIGINT Enterprise (JMIP)

This PE provides signals intelligence (SIGINT) development efforts for all USAF airborne platforms. The funds in this PE are distributed among all Airborne SIGINT Enterprise (ASE) projects based on the development priorities established by the USAF SIGINT Capabilities Working Group (SCWG) in order to build a total SIGINT capability.

Equipment should be developed by equipment companies; eliminate and save $129 Million.

Global Air Traffic Management (GATM)

Communication, Navigation, Surveillance/Air Traffic Management (CNS/ATM): This Air Force (AF) program centralizes engineering and technical expertise for CNS capability acquisitions and modifications to ensure that all AF aircraft, Unmanned Aerial Systems (UAS) and Remotely Piloted Aircraft (RPA) comply with appropriate CNS/ATM and Navigation Safety performance standards and requirements.

This may or may not be necessary and proper, but it won't be needed as much in peacetime. Cut by half and save $2 Million.

Cyber Security Initiative

The DoD Cyber Crime Center (DC3) was created as a DoD Center of Excellence to efficiently organize, equip, train, and employ scarce resources to more effectively address the proliferation of computer crimes affecting the DoD. DC3 has a digital forensics laboratory, training program, institute, and National Cyber Investigative Joint Task Force Analytical Group.

The military is not responsible for fighting crime, and if we stopped bombing and invading other countries, the DoD wouldn't be as much of a target. Eliminate DC3 and CSI, saving $2 Million.

DoD Cyber Crime Center

The military is not responsible for fighting crime, and if we stopped bombing and invading other countries, the DoD wouldn't be as much of a target. Eliminate and save $285K.

Satellite Control Network

> *The Air Force Satellite Control Network (AFSCN) mission is to command and control space systems and to distribute space system information in support of DoD, Intelligence Community (IC), and Civil operational and RDT&E missions, and other designated users.*

Equipment should be developed by equipment companies. Eliminate and save $34 Million.

Weather Service

> *This budget activity funds operational development necessary to acquire, sustain, and enhance segments of the Air Force Weather Weapon System (AFWWS). Activities also include studies and analysis to support both current program planning and execution and future program planning*

In peacetime, the weather in other countries doesn't matter. The rest of the time, we have Wunderground and thousands of weather channels. Eliminate and save $29 Million.

Air Traffic Control / Approach / Landing System (ATCALS)

> *To support the Air Force worldwide flying mission, this program element funds research, development and management of new air traffic control surveillance, positioning, and precision approach landing systems.*

Eliminate the FAA. In peacetime, the Air Force has no "worldwide flying mission". Eliminate and save $43 Million.

Aerial Targets

> *Full-scale and subscale targets assure warfighters weapon systems will perform effectively against real-world enemy fighters and cruise missiles.*

Pilots need to train, even in peacetime. However, research should be done in the private sector, and these tests should only need to be done once. Eliminate and save $50 Million.

Security and Investigative Activities

> *Air Force Office of Special Investigations (AFOSI) conducts specialized investigative activities and force protection support for Air Force (AF) commanders worldwide. This assists AF commanders in protecting their people and resources.*

While we need to reexamine seriously what is considered a crime these days, OSI plays a key role in reducing Fraud, Waste, Abuse, and other legitimately undesirable activities within the Air Force. Keep as is ($354K).

Arms Control Implementation

> *Arms Control Activities activation under the New Start Treaty drives the need to modify approximately 28 B-52s to a conventional only role by removing the Nuclear Code Enable Switch and associated equipment.*

Withdraw from the Start Treaty and allow the B-52s to continue being nuclear-capable. Eliminate and save $4 Million.

NAVSTAR GPS User Equipment Space

> *The Navstar Global Positioning System (GPS) is a space-based radio Positioning, Navigation, and Time (PNT) distribution system. GPS User Equipment (UE) consists of standardized receivers, antennas, antenna electronics, etc., grouped together in sets to derive navigation and time information transmitted from GPS satellites.*

Use equipment sets that are built by the private sector, and let them do their own development. Eliminate and save $30 Million.

NAVSTAR GPS Space

> *This Program Element (PE) funds Research and Development (R&D) for the Navstar Global Positioning System (GPS) Space and Control segments for GPS Block II satellites. It includes, but is not limited to: training simulators, Integrated Logistics Support (ILS) products, ground control segment development, sustaining engineering, space and ground segments upgrades, and R&D.*

Funding for this program ends in 2013 and need not be included in the recurring budget.

Space and Missile Test and Evaluation Center

> *R&D Space and Missile Operations (RDSMO) develops and acquires systems to: operate experimental, demonstration, and operational satellites; operate fixed and deployable satellite ground systems; perform satellite compatibility testing; act as the focal point and center of expertise for DoD experimental and demonstration space and missile operations; support space and missile R&D; and conduct/support experimental/demonstration of space and missile Developmental Test and Evaluation (DT&E) and Initial Operational Test and Evaluation (IOT&E) activities.*

This is necessary and proper to evaluate new stuff. Keep as is ($4M).

Space Warfare Center

> *Located at Schriever Air Force Base, Colorado, the Space Innovation and Development Center (SIDC) develops, evaluates, tests, and integrates space application and utility concepts, as well as new technologies, while providing*

combat effects to warfighters, such as aid in mission planning of Global Positioning System (GPS) aided/guided munitions.

This is necessary and proper to evaluate new stuff. Keep as is ($2M).

Spacelift Range System

The Eastern Range (ER) at Patrick Air Force Base (AFB)/Cape Canaveral Air Force Station, FL, and the Western Range (WR) at Vandenberg AFB, CA, make up the Spacelift Range System (SLRS), also known as the Launch and Test Range System (LTRS).

This is necessary and proper to run the satellite system; keep as is ($9M).

Dragon U-2 (JMIP)

The CIA established the Senior Year Program in 1955. The program has evolved to include the U-2 airframes, engines, sensors, cameras, recorders, data links life support systems, test facilities, and equipment. The U-2S model airframes were constructed in the late 1980s, with the last aircraft rolling off the assembly line in 1989.

The U-2 doesn't seem to do anything that we can't do with drones now, but they are still fairly new and therefore useful. In peacetime, there are no forward operationg locations; eliminate and save $24 Million.

Endurance UAV

This PE focuses USAF efforts on long endurance platforms which allow days, months, or years of endurance, as well as their associated sensors and communications suites. Efforts include, but are not limited to, airships and more standard aircraft structures.

Aircraft development should be done by aircraft companies; eliminate and save $21 Million.

Airborne Reconnaissance Systems

The Airborne Reconnaissance Systems program coordinates the development of advanced airborne reconnaissance system technologies (sensors, data links, targeting networks and products, and quick reaction capabilities) in support of multiple airborne reconnaissance platforms, both manned and unmanned.

Equipment should be developed by the companies that make the equipment. Eliminate and save $97 Million.

Manned Reconnaissance System

The RC-135 Operational Systems Development and enhancement activities project supports design studies, engineering analysis, non-recurring *engineering, and other efforts associated with the integration and modification of the RC-135 programs and their specialized mission systems - both air and ground. Extensive utilization of commercial-off the-shelf (COTS) based solutions allows rapid fielding of needed capabilities through continuous technology refresh cycles and diminishing manufacturing sources (DMS)/vanishing vendor items (VVI) logistics mitigation efforts.*

Aircraft should be developed by aircraft companies, and equipment should be developed by equipment companies. Eliminate and save $13 Million.

Distributed Common Ground Systems

The DoD Distributed Common Ground/Surface System (DCGS) Program is a cooperative effort between the Services and National Agencies to provide world-wide ground/surface systems capable of receiving, processing, exploiting, and disseminating data from airborne and national reconnaissance sensors/platforms and commercial sources.

The government should use a system that can communicate over the Internet, and just use special encryption. That is, after all, one of the major reasons why the Internet was created in the first place. Therefore no special networks are required, and the infrastructure is already provided by the private sector. Eliminate and save $64 Million.

Predator Development

The basic MQ-1 system consists of the aircraft, a control station, communications equipment, support equipment, simulator and training devices, Readiness Spares Packages (RSP), technical data/training, and personnel required to operate, maintain, and sustain the system.

Aircraft development should be done by aircraft companies; eliminate and save $9 Million.

Global Hawk Development

In FY12, P018, NATO Alliance Ground Surveillance (AGS) efforts were transferred from PE 1001018D8Z, NATO AGS, Project P018, NATO AGS, in order to transfer control of this effort from OSD to the USAF.

Withdraw from NATO. Aircraft development should be done by aircraft companies; eliminate and save $236 Million.

Network Centric Collaborative Targeting

Network Centric Collaborative Targeting (NCCT) is the Air Force program of record responsible for developing core technologies to horizontally and vertically integrate ISR sensor systems both within and across intelligence disciplines (for example SIGINT to SIGINT or GMTI to SIGINT).

This seems useful, but equipment development should be done by equipment companies. Eliminate and save $7 Million.

Common Data Link

Common Data Link (CDL) provides the DoD standard for interoperable, multi-service, multi-agency, wideband datalinks for manned/unmanned platforms performing Intelligence, Surveillance, and Reconnaissance (ISR) missions. As the CDL Executive Agent (EA), the Air Force is responsible for cross-service application of CDL RDT&E funds facilitating compliance to Congressional and DoD mandates.

Equipment should be developed by equipment companies; eliminate and save $38 Million.

NATO AGS

U.S. participation in NATO AGS was ratified by SECDEF signature of the NATO AGS Program Memorandum of Understanding (PMOU) in June 2009. The PMOU went into effect in Sept 2009.

Cabinet members do not ratify things. Withdraw from NATO. Research and development should be done in the private sector. Eliminate and save $210 Million.

Support to DCGS Enterprise

The efforts in this Program Element are those the AF is lead service for under the auspices of USD(I). The funding was previously executed within PE0305208F. Beginning with the FY13 President's Budget, the AF DCGS Program and Support to DCGS Enterprise programs are being reported separately for improved visibility.

Development should be done in the private sector. Eliminate and save $25 Million.

GPS III Space Segment

The Global Positioning System (GPS) is a space based navigation system that fills validated Joint Service requirements for worldwide, accurate, common grid three dimensional positioning/navigation for military aircraft, ships, and ground personnel.

Development should be done in the private sector. Eliminate and save $319 Million.

JSpOC Mission System

> This program will produce a net-centric collaborative environment, enhance and modernize space surveillance capabilities, create decision relevant views of the space environment, and enable efficient distribution of data across the space surveillance network.

This sounds like something that could be done with a free Wiki. Development should be done in the private sector. Eliminate and save $55 Million.

Rapid Cyber Acquisition

> Rapid Cyber Acquisition (RCA) provides combatant commanders (CCDRs) with the ability to adequately and rapidly respond to emerging cyber needs that cannot be serviced via the JUON/UON process and cannot wait for the normal DoD acquisition process to address.

Under this proposal, commanders no longer have cyber needs. Eliminate and save $4 Million.

Electronic Combat Intelligence Support

> This program expedites information and cyberspace superiority capabilities from laboratory, industry, and academia to operational platforms including the Network Attack System (NAS) via studies, rapid prototyping, technology demonstrations and other Research, Development, Testing and Evaluation (RDT&E) efforts.

Since we're eliminating the laboratories and moving the industry into the private sector, we can eliminate this and save $13 Million. The military literally has no *needs* that can't wait for the products to be released.

NUDET Detection System Space

> The United States Nuclear Detonation (NUDET) Detection System (USNDS) provides a near real-time worldwide, highly survivable capability to detect, locate, and report any nuclear detonations in the earth's atmosphere or in near space.

Necessary and proper to national security; keep as is ($65 Million).

Space Situational Awareness Operations

> Space Situational Awareness (SSA) is knowledge of all aspects of space related to operations. As the foundation for space control, SSA encompasses intelligence on adversary space operations; surveillance of all space objects and activities; detailed reconnaissance of specific space assets; monitoring space environmental conditions; monitoring cooperative space assets; and conducting integrated command, control, communications, processing, analysis, dissemination, and archiving activities.

Necessary and proper as more and more potential enemies develop space technology; keep as is ($20M).

Shared Early Warning System

> The Shared Early Warning System (SEWS) is the result of Presidential foreign policy initiatives beginning in 1996. The SEWS continues to provide Theater Combatant Commanders and foreign nation customers direct operational benefit by improving the architectural design and equipment thereby providing enhanced mission capabilities (i.e., expanding coverage, integration with active defense systems, and radar integration).

Eliminate all Presidential foreign policy initiatives. Eliminating this one saves $1.2 Million.

C-130 Airlift Squadrons

> C-130 Air Modernization Program (AMP) FY13 RDT&E funding has been deleted as a result of termination by the Department. C-130 AMP will modernize the avionics suites & cockpit configurations for 221 Combat Delivery C-130s in order to meet the International Civil Aviation Organization's (ICAO) & the FAA's mandated Communication, Navigation, Surveillance / Air Traffic Management (CNS/ATM), and Air Force Navigation and Safety mandates.

Aircraft development should be done by aircraft companies. Eliminate and save $5 Million.

C-5 Airlift Squadrons

> This program is in Budget Activity 7, Operational Systems Development because this budget activity includes development efforts to upgrade systems that have been fielded or have received approval for full rate production and anticipate production funding in the current or subsequent fiscal year.

Aircraft development should be done by aircraft companies. Eliminate and save $35 Million.

C-17 Aircraft

> The C-17 can perform the entire spectrum of airlift missions and is specifically designed to operate effectively and efficiently in both strategic and theater environments. Airlift provides essential flexibility when responding to contingencies on short notice anywhere in the world.

Aircraft development should be done by aircraft companies. Eliminate and save $99 Million.

C-130J Program

> The C-130J is a medium-sized transport aircraft capable of performing a variety of combat delivery (tactical airlift) operations across a broad range of mission environments.

Aircraft development should be done by aircraft companies. Eliminate and save $31 Million.

Large Aircraft Infrared Countermeasures (LAIRCM)

> The Large Aircraft Infrared Countermeasures (LAIRCM) system is an evolutionary acquisition program that provides significantly improved defensive systems capability for DoD aircraft to counter the infrared (IR) man-portable air-defense systems (MANPADS) missile threat.

Aircraft development should be done by aircraft companies. Eliminate and save $8 Million.

Light Mobility Aircraft

> Light Mobility Aircraft (LiMA) support contingency response forces in non-combat operations such as disaster/humanitarian response. They are also used in support of Air Force air advisors conducting Building Partnership Capacity missions that prepare partner nations to develop air mobility capabilities consistent with their military transportation needs.

Aircraft development should be done by aircraft companies. Eliminate and save $100K.

KC-10s

> The KC-10A Extender is an aerial refueling asset built on the commercial DC-10 airframe. The aircraft creates an air bridge to enable rapid global mobility and global strike missions.

Aircraft development should be done by aircraft companies. Eliminate and save $24 Million.

Operational Support Airlift

> The VC-25A Avionics Modernization Program (AMP) will enable the President of the United States to perform his duties as Commander in Chief. The VC-25A aircraft must maintain one hundred percent reliability and safe, unrestricted global access, both in civilian and military airfields.

You can't enable someone to do something they're already able to do. Aircraft development should be done by aircraft companies. Eliminate and save $7 Million.

Special Tactics / Combat Control

> *The Special Tactics (ST) System Development project focuses on modernization developments for the Battlefield Airmen Operations (BAO) Kit. The project is a program within the overarching Battlefield Airmen Modernization (BA-Mod) Program.*

Equipment development should be done by equipment companies. Eliminate and save $5 Million.

Depot Maintenance

> *This program develops, tests, and evaluates national and Air Force measurement standards (hardware) and calibration equipment in support of all Air Force programs and activities, including Precision Measurement Equipment Laboratories (PMELs) worldwide. ensure modern weapon systems meet Air Force readiness objectives.*

Equipment development should be done by equipment companies. Eliminate and save $2 Million.

Logistics Support Activities

> *The Aircraft Structural Integrity Management Information System (ASIMIS) and ASIP operate as directed by AFPD 63-10 and MIL-STD-1530C. ASIMIS responsibilities include: Receiving, storing and reporting recorder downloads from all aircraft.*

Necessary and proper; keep as is ($577K).

Logistics Information Technology

> *ECSS utilizes a Commercial-Off-The-Shelf (COTS) Enterprise Resource Planning (ERP) application to replace wholesale and retail legacy logistics Information Technology (IT) systems.*

There is no reason why this program should be a recurring procurement; eliminate and save $119 Million.

Support Systems Development

> *This program element supports an active project, Logistics Application Logistics Integration (LALI), and a project, Logistics Systems Development (LSD), that provides a budgetary accounting location for projects funded through Congressional interest.*

Development should be done in the private sector; eliminate and save $16 Million.

Other Flight Training

Program supports the Air Education and Training Command (AETC) Decision Support System (ADSS) which is an automated information system that provides AETC leadership and staff with key management information about training production status, including monitoring and assessment of training. The data and reports from ADSS provide the vital feedback mechanism essential to an effective programming and management process.

Funding for this program ends in 2015, so it need not be included in the recurring budget; $349K saved.

Other Personnel Activities

The Defense Equal Opportunity Management Institute (DEOMI) provides grants to the civilian academic community to conduct research on military and civilian equal opportunity issues using standard social science methodology and engineering analysis.

Eliminate all grants; $117K saved.

Joint Personnel Recovery Agency (JRPA)

PRMS currently in use at COCOM Rescue Coordination Centers and AF AOCs. JPRA oversaw development of PRMS during ACTD and fielding to COCOMs and Services. ACTD Transition Plan did not identify responsibility for funding further development of PRMS.

In peacetime, there would be no personnel to recover, and we're eliminating all operations in CENTCOM's area of responsibility. Eliminate and save $2 Million.

Civilian Compensation Program

This program element provides for payment of civilian compensation benefits for disability due to personal injury sustained while in the performance of duty or due to employment-related disease according to the Federal Employees Compensation Act.

Stop exposing people to employment-related diseases! Since the military is responsible for these problems, I suppose the military should pay for them. Keep as is ($1.5M).

Personnel Administration

Personnel Services Delivery (PSD), under the Personnel Administration program, funds operational developments necessary to acquire, field, and modify segments of an integrated Air Force Human Resource (HR) customer service delivery system that will effectively incorporate personnel, manpower, and pay services for the Total Force - Active Duty, Reserve, Guard, and Civilians.

Personnel need to be administered, but development should be done in the private sector. Eliminate and save $8 Million.

AF Studies and Analysis Agency

Provides for development and enhancement of modeling and simulation tools for strategic planning, operational requirements, modernization and recapitalization of systems and programs, and the Planning, Programming, Budgeting and Execution (PPBE) processes for the AF Analytic Community and Secretary of the Air Force Standard Analysis Toolkit in support of AF Senior Leadership.

Development should be done in the private sector. Eliminate and save $1.2 Million.

Facilities Operations – Administrative

The Civil Engineer's (CE) IT Transformation program's mission is to transform CE's business processes to improve operations and support AF priorities. The plan is to leverage industry best practices, optimize core business processes, and replace existing outdated IT capabilities with a set of commercial off-the-shelf (COTS) software solutions and a service provider to deploy and maintain the system.

If the CEs find a way to improve their job, they should go up through the chain of command; no third party is necessary. Eliminate and save $3 Million.

Financial Management Information Systems Development (FMISD)

Financial Management Information Systems Development (FIMSD), PE 0901538F, provides funding for the following projects; Defense Enterprise Accounting Management System, Financial Information Resource System (FIRST), and Program and Budgeting Enterprise Service (PBES).

Development should be done in the private sector; there are plenty of financial management systems out there. Eliminate and save $100 Million.

Overseas Contingency Operations

Military Personnel[120]
This proposal eliminates all OCO. **$1.4 Billion** saved.

---

[120] http://www.saffm.hq.af.mil/shared/media/document/AFD-120206-028.pdf

Operation and Maintenance[121]
This proposal eliminates all OCO. **$9.2 Billion** saved.

Reserve Operation and Maintenance[122]
This proposal eliminates all OCO. $120 Million saved.

Air National Guard Operation and Maintenance[123]
This proposal eliminates all OCO. $20 Million saved.

Base Realignment and Closure[124]
Given that this proposal moves all overseas personnel, equipment, and functions back to the United States sovereign territory, the entire BRAC budget will need to be reconsidered. For now, hold off on the Closure Package. Unfortunately the budget is not broken down in this fashion so I recommend reallocating these funds to dealing with the hundreds of thousands of incoming personnel. Keep as is for now ($2 Million).

Working Capital Fund[125]
> *In support of Air Force core functions, the AFWCF activities provide maintenance services, weapon system parts, base and medical supplies, and transportation services.*

Those needs which are necessary and proper should be taken care of within the Operation and Maintenance budget. In peacetime, with a hopeful reduction in the unnecessary shifting around of personnel and equipment, we can save a ton of money. Cut by half after the first year (as it will cost money to get all those people home), and save $63 Million.

Air Force Conclusion
Though the claimed total in the Air Force budget is $154.3 Billion, I found $187.6 Billion in total spending. All elements considered, this proposal reduces the Air Force's budget from that to $63.8 Billion for a reduction of more than half of the official budget spending and by more than two thirds of the real spending.

---

[121] http://www.saffm.hq.af.mil/shared/media/document/AFD-120206-064.pdf
[122] http://www.saffm.hq.af.mil/shared/media/document/AFD-120210-079.pdf
[123] http://www.saffm.hq.af.mil/shared/media/document/AFD-120208-060.pdf
[124] http://www.saffm.hq.af.mil/shared/media/document/AFD-120206-030.pdf
[125] http://www.saffm.hq.af.mil/shared/media/document/AFD-120207-055.pdf

Department of Defense Conclusion

This proposal reduced the Army from $224.2 Billion to $92.4 Billion, the Navy from $167 Billion to $63.4 Billion, and the Air Force from $187 Billion to $63.8 Billion; in addition to cuts across the DoD-Wide spending areas for a total reduction from $711.03 Billion to $315.27 Billion. This cut is more than half of the total requested 2013 spending.

In addition to saving $395.8 Billion, this proposal has brought peace to the American people. Your children will no longer die in faraway lands for reasons you don't fully understand. Extremists will no longer attack our buildings out of spite in a desperate last chance to get your attention and change our foreign policy.

Our military people will be home again, spending their money in the American economy instead of foreign economies. They'll be closer to their loved ones, able to eat in restaurants and pee in bathrooms again.

The Army will patrol our airports, with their owners' permission. The Marines will patrol our borders. The Navy will patrol our coasts. The Air Force will patrol the air over our cities, airports, and borders. America will be more safe and secure than ever before, while spending less than half as much.

I'm not saying this is all we can cut, but it's definitely a good start.

Department of Education (Ed)[126 127 128 129]

> *In its first three years, the Administration has combined unprecedented financial support for education with extraordinary success in pursuing and achieving fundamental reforms that will benefit students of all ages and help build a globally competitive workforce. Central to this effort has been the Race to the Top (RTT) initiative for elementary and secondary education, a competition that spurred States across the Nation to bring together teachers, school leaders, and policy makers to achieve difficult, yet fundamental improvements to our education system*

Indeed the administration has provided unprecedented funding. Let us examine the history of Ed's funding[130] and compare it to the history of SAT scores[131].

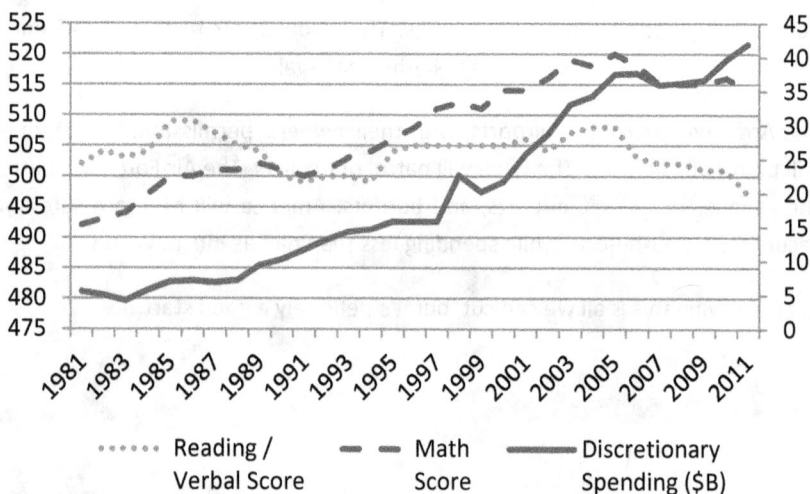

Reading / Verbal Score   Math Score   Discretionary Spending ($B)

While federal funding for education has been multiplied by more than eight times its 1981 value, math scores have only gone up a few points, and reading scores have actually gone down. Clearly, attacking the education problem from a funding perspective isn't solving the problem.

The Department of Education has ballooned far beyond the intended purpose of educating children, and only 11% of its funding actually goes to the schools.

---

[126] http://www.whitehouse.gov/sites/default/files/omb/budget/fy2013/assets/education.pdf
[127] http://www2.ed.gov/about/overview/budget/index.html
[128] http://www2.ed.gov/about/overview/budget/tables.html
[129] http://www2.ed.gov/about/overview/budget/budget13/justifications/index.html
[130] http://www2.ed.gov/about/overview/budget/history/index.html
[131] http://en.wikipedia.org/wiki/SAT#Raw_scores.2C_scaled_scores.2C_and_percentiles

The vast majority of it is bloat and unneeded programs with effectiveness that is questionable, at best.

Your tax dollars should fund only the schools in your own district; and even then, only if you wish to send your children to public school. You as a parent should have direct control over how your children are educated and what they are taught; not some committee thousands of miles away.

The Constitution provides no authority for the Congress to interfere in the education process, let alone to create a department that controls every aspect of it. Even the Department of Education's website states that "Education is primarily a state and local responsibility[132]".

Huge portions of the budget are block-granted to the states and local governments for a variety of programs, while these states and local governments could indeed just tax their own constituents.

Education starts at home. The very best education is homeschooling, followed by private schools. By every measure, the government's offering, public school, is by far the worst option there is. It's the most expensive, and it produces the dumbest students.

For all these reasons and more, we must eliminate the entire department, revert control of education back to the states where it belongs, and allow the local communities to teach their own people.

While the Department of Education doesn't appear to publish a budget in the same format as every other department, information on its hierarchy and programs can be pieced together from what information it does publish. As you read through, continue to realize that as with all other departments, removing something from the federal government doesn't mean no government can provide it. Also realize that removing something from the entire government altogether doesn't mean the people who need or want that thing won't be able to get it.

Reauthorization of the Elementary and Secondary Education Act (ESEA)[133]

> The Blueprint[134] proposes changes in the ESEA intended to help ensure that all children receive the world-class education they deserve and that America needs to compete successfully in the global economy of the 21st century. The

---

[132] http://www2.ed.gov/about/overview/fed/role.html?src=ln
[133] http://www2.ed.gov/about/overview/budget/budget13/justifications/a-eseaoverview.pdf
[134] http://www2.ed.gov/policy/elsec/leg/blueprint/blueprint.pdf

proposal does this by re-envisioning the Federal role in education to support innovative approaches to teaching and learning that make better, more productive use of existing resources. In the current fiscal environment, we can no longer afford to invest in the status quo. Instead, we must reform our schools to accelerate student achievement, close achievement gaps, and inspire our children to excel so that by 2020, America will once again have the highest proportion of college graduates in the world.

This is K-12 education. The Department of Education gets $222.4 Billion in total funding, $72 Billion in outlays, **$15.8 Billion** for ESEA; of this procurement, $15.06 Billion is reserved for grants. This leaves around $689 Million for all other federal K-12 funding; a tiny fraction of the total education budget. Now consider that the federal government is where most of the rules and regulations come from. Who are they to tell you how your children must be taught and what they can eat at school?

The Feds have demonstrated that the only way they know to improve education is to throw money at it, and clearly that hasn't been working. There is no worldwide competition for education that we need to be a part of; children should simply be educated to the level they need to function in society. For some, that will be very little; for others, that will be a lot. Maybe some should start apprenticing and otherwise training to enter a trade at a young age. These are decisions that need to be made by the parents and students, not by government bureaucrats. Eliminate and save **$15.8 Billion**.

Accelerating Achievement and Ensuring Equity[135]

The programs in the Accelerating Achievement and Ensuring Equity (formerly Education for the Disadvantaged) account provide the foundation for school improvement efforts needed to ensure that all children receive a high-quality education authorized under the Elementary and Secondary Education Act. The Administration is requesting a total of $15.6 billion in fiscal year 2013 for the programs in this account.

Ed has gone from a bad euphemism to a worse one. This is education for poor people, and it discriminates against everyone who isn't poor. All government services should be provided equally to everyone, or not at all. Whether you have money or not is irrelevant to your ability to sit in a classroom, memorize facts, and churn out rote work.

The 2013 request also includes $533.6 million for the School Turnaround Grants program to [...] require States and LEAs to use most funds to implement

---

[135] http://www2.ed.gov/about/overview/budget/budget13/justifications/b-aaee.pdf

one of four school intervention models (Turnaround, Restart, School Closure, and Transformation) in each of their schools that (1) are in the bottom 5 percent of schools in the State in terms of student achievement or (2) in the case of secondary schools, have graduation rates below 60 percent.

The U.S. has around 98,817 public primary and secondary schools[136] and 33,366 private, of which the bottom 5% is 6609 schools. Each of these schools would receive an average of $80,738.39; about enough to pay for two entry-level teachers for a year. This program is a bust.

The request would level-fund the other programs in this account, including $393.2 million for Migrant Student Education, $50.2 million for Neglected and Delinquent Children and Youth Education, and $65.2 for Homeless Children and Youth Education.

The Migrant Student Education program helps ensure that students who move from state to state aren't penalized for that move and that they are still able to meet the new state's standards.

In actuality, what we need is merely to ensure the students are learning; none of these standards should be mandatory unless they want a diploma from an accredited school. Even then, the system needs to be redesigned from scratch. K-12 is an inefficient system, especially when the states teach different things in any given grade. This program is treating a symptom.

Title 1 Grants to Local Educational Agencies

Title I Grants to Local Educational Agencies (LEAs) provide supplemental education funding, especially in high-poverty areas, for local programs that provide extra academic support to help raise the achievement of students at risk of educational failure or, in the case of schoolwide programs, to help all students in high-poverty schools meet challenging State academic standards.

The fact that taxes in your area aren't enough to fund proper schools, or that those funds aren't being well-utilized, does not justify taking money from people outside your area to make up the difference. A taxpayer in Texas should not be forced to pay for a school in California. It seems hard to believe that two thirds of all elementary schools are in high-poverty areas.

Beginning with the 2005-2006 school year, States have been required to administer their reading and mathematics assessments annually to all students in grades 3-8 and once in high school in reading and math. States also must assess annually the English proficiency of English learner (EL)

---

[136] http://nces.ed.gov/fastfacts/display.asp?id=84

students and were required to add science assessments during the 2007-2008 school year.

All this standardized testing doesn't seem to be improving the students' education. In fact, the SAT scores have been on a decline ever since 2005. Clearly something is wrong with this system.

If a school does not increase student achievement in response to corrective action, the LEA must begin planning for restructuring, which involves making a fundamental change such as closing the school and reopening it as a public charter school, replacing all or most of the school's staff, turning operation of the school over to a private management company with a demonstrated record of effectiveness, or any other major restructuring of the school's governance arrangement.

Someone in the government seems to have the right idea, but they don't take it far enough. I'll go into more detail later.

Equitable Distribution of Effective Teachers and Leaders

The Administration's ESEA reauthorization proposal also would authorize the Department to reserve up to 0.5 percent of Title I, Part A formula grant funds under a broad ESEA evaluation authority aimed at supporting the comprehensive evaluation of the implementation, outcomes, impact, and cost-effectiveness of ESEA programs, including the Title I, Part A CCRS program.

In any company, all employees receive regular performance reviews based on their actual results. Companies have operated this way for millennia, and formally for centuries. It seems odd that the government is just now getting around to it. The Feds claim that the states are the rightful place for most policy making to occur within education, and yet now the same Feds are directing that policy. The results are that students have not improved, so these changes have not been effective.

Impact Aid[137]

The Impact Aid program provides financial assistance to school districts affected by Federal activities. The presence of certain children living on Federal property across the country can place a financial burden on the local educational agencies (LEAs) that educate them. The property on which the children live is exempt from local property taxes, denying LEAs access to the primary source of revenue used by most communities to finance education.

---

[137] http://www2.ed.gov/about/overview/budget/budget13/justifications/c-impactaid.pdf

With the exception of military families, there should be no children living on federal property. All federal land, with the exception of Washington D.C. and military installations, should be released back to the states, where most of it should be sold off in a variety of lot sizes to the highest bidder. The DoD provides its own school district in areas that don't have school districts. This program is therefore obsolete; Eliminate and save **$1.2 Billion**.

Education Improvement Programs[138]

$1.6 Billion in grants and discriminatory programs riddle this program group. They have grants to supplement other grants within the same department. They have special buildings for improving the quality of education, despite most students never going near one. They try unsuccessfully to bribe schools to improve their dropout rates. This program group needs to disappear, to the tune of $4.5 Billion.

21st Century Community Learning Centers

The Department will provide technical assistance and guidance to SEAs, LEAs, and local program staff on how to form and maintain strong community-school partnerships, promote continuous quality improvement and ensure that funded programs meet the needs of individual students.

The process of human learning is no different in the 21st century than it was at any other time throughout history. In fact, most SAT scores are around the same or even lower than they were in the 20th century.

A strong community-school partnership begins with a school that grows out of the community. We should be incentivizing people and businesses to start their own schools, free from all federal shackles. If the Principal's hands are tied by No Child Left Behind, then no amount of grassroots support will set him free.

Advance Placement

The Department will use $20 million of these funds to continue the Advanced Placement Test Fee program and $7 million for continuation costs for the Advanced Placement Incentive Program.

The schools do not need $27 Million in special money to know to put smarter students in advanced classes. The teachers can just tell the principal which students are smart enough.

---

[138] http://www2.ed.gov/about/overview/budget/budget13/justifications/d-eip.pdf

Alaska Native Educational Equity

Applications from eligible entities that propose to serve schools in rural areas will undergo the same peer review process as all other applications. Historically, rural applicants have each year received a portion of the funding.

Alaska Natives aren't a special group; they have no more right to education than anyone else.

Rural Education

As called for in the authorizing legislation, the Department will continue to use half of the Rural Education Achievement program appropriation for the Small, Rural School Achievement program and half for the Rural and Low-Income School program.

Rural students aren't a special group; they have no more right to education than anyone else.

Effective Teaching and Learning for a Complete Education

The Administration requests $389 million for Assessing Achievement (State Assessments under current law) to assist States and other entities in developing and implementing assessments that are aligned with college- and career-ready standards. Formula funds would support States' implementation of the assessments currently required under Title I of the ESEA.

As we have already established, these assessments aren't getting anything done. These grants, as with the entire education system, could just be taxed676

at a more local level. Entire levels of bureaucracy could be eliminated.

Ready-to-Learn Television

Ready-to-Learn (RTL) Television is designed to facilitate student academic achievement by supporting the development and distribution of educational video programming for preschool and elementary school children and their parents, caregivers, and teachers.

Television is not a babysitter, and is no substitute for an instructor. Preapproved TV programming institutionalizes children, when they really should be engaged in the learning process. TV does not engage people; it desensitizes them.

Striving Readers

The Striving Readers program provides grants to eligible entities to support efforts to improve literacy instruction in high-need schools. In fiscal year 2010,

Congress enacted appropriations language that changed Striving Readers from an adolescent literacy program to a comprehensive literacy development and education program.

There is no actual education or reading program here; this is more grants which should rightfully be done at a lower level of government or not at all. If you want your kids to read, stick a book in their faces. Tell them they can eat one meal or watch one TV show per chapter or something along those lines. Many children can read before they ever get sent to school. Education starts at home.

Arts in Education

The Arts in Education program supports awards to VSA Arts, a national organization that sponsors programs to encourage the involvement of, and foster greater awareness of the need for, arts programs for persons with disabilities, and to the John F. Kennedy Center for the Performing Arts for its arts education programs for children and youth.

Students are put at a table and told what to paint. They are told what to draw, what songs to play and sing, and what collage to make. True art cannot be directed. Barely any students will ever even be aware of the Kennedy Center, let alone get any use of it.

College Pathways to Accelerated Learning

The College Pathways and Accelerated Learning program would support efforts to increase high school graduation rates and preparation for college matriculation and success by providing college-level and other accelerated courses and instruction in secondary schools with concentrations of students from low-income families and with low graduation rates.

Here we have more class discrimination and more grants that only serve to redistribute money while siphoning and taxing it on the way through.

Schools shouldn't be designed to prepare students to go to more schools. They should prepare students to go out into the workforce and contribute something to the world.

High School Graduation Initiative

The High School Graduation Initiative awards discretionary grants to State educational agencies and local educational agencies (LEAs) to support the implementation of effective, sustainable, and coordinated dropout prevention and re-entry programs in high schools with annual dropout rates that exceed their State average annual dropout rate

This is basically a bribe to schools to reduce their dropout rates. Students don't drop out because their school doesn't have enough funding; they drop out because they need time to support their families, or to conduct criminal activity, or just because they aren't being engaged enough by the education process. This program is treating a symptom; the underlying problems go ignored.

Other Areas

Supporting Student Success[139]

> The programs in the Supporting Student Success account assist States, local educational agencies, schools, and other organizations in developing and implementing programs and activities that increase the extent to which students are physically and emotionally safe and healthy.

More block grants; a variation on a theme. Making students physically safe is not the government's job, let alone a function of education. Making kids emotionally safe is their parents' job.

Students have always had regular access to adults: They have parents, they have teachers, and some of them have employers. At least two of these groups care about the student's success and engage with them regularly.

Emotional development is not something the government should ever be involved with. Who do you think should be teaching your children *what to feel?*

Responsible citizenship is a subjective area which should also not be institutionalized. The government should not tell people how to conduct themselves as a part of society, because the government is not responsible for creating that society.

Eliminate and save **$1.5 Billion**.

Indian Student Education[140]

> The Indian Student Education programs in this account are authorized by Title VII, Part A of the Elementary and Secondary Education Act (ESEA). These activities support a comprehensive approach to educational improvement and reform for Indian students, helping to ensure that they benefit from national education reforms and receive every opportunity to achieve to high standards.

---

[139] http://www2.ed.gov/about/overview/budget/budget13/justifications/e-sss.pdf
[140] http://www2.ed.gov/about/overview/budget/budget13/justifications/f-indianed.pdf

Native Americans have no special need for education; let them use the same schools as everyone else, if their parents decide to send them off the reservation. If they choose to remain on the reservation, they can handle the education within the tribe like they used to. Eliminate and save $131 Million.

Innovation and Instructional Teams [141]

> Programs in the Innovation and Instructional Teams account support the goal of improving student achievement in three key ways: providing incentives for States and local educational agencies (LEAs) to implement comprehensive educational reforms and to test, evaluate, and expand innovative educational strategies and practices; increasing the supply of effective teachers and principals; and providing parents with expanded options for the education of their children. The Administration requests a total of $4.3 billion for programs in this account.

States and local agencies should be incentivized directly by the parents. If the parents don't like the job they're doing, they should replace those people at their elections and local meetings.

The most effective educational strategy and practice is one-on-one instruction by a parent. The second best is a private school. If the government were allowed to run the schools, they should take their lessons from those two sources.

Hiring more teachers and principals is not the answer. The system is fundamentally broken and needs to be redesigned from scratch. I'll go into more detail on that later.

Deciding which school to send your kids to, and deciding what classes and extracurricular activities to put them in, does not constitute expanded options. Eliminate and save **$4.3 Billion**.

English Learner Education [142]

> Currently, Title III, Part A of the Elementary and Secondary Education Act (ESEA) authorizes formula grants to States to serve English Learners (ELs), the National Professional Development project, discretionary grants for Native American projects, support for the National Clearinghouse for English Language Acquisition and Language Instruction Educational Programs (NCELA), and national evaluations. The Administration is proposing reauthorizing legislation for fiscal year 2013.

---

[141] http://www2.ed.gov/about/overview/budget/budget13/justifications/g-iit.pdf
[142] http://www2.ed.gov/about/overview/budget/budget13/justifications/h-ela.pdf

The feds are seriously stealing your money and handing it over to the states to teach people English as a second language. When someone moves to a new country, they should learn that country's language on their own. Tens of thousands of people do it every year, and did so long before the government involved itself in the process.

We absolutely shouldn't be catering to multi-language areas and people. Everything the government provides should be in English only. The private sector can decide for itself what languages to support. Get out of the issue. Eliminate and save $734 Million.

Special Education[143]

> The Administration is committed to ensuring that all children, including students with disabilities, have an equal opportunity to participate in a high quality education, are expected to perform to high levels, and to the maximum extent possible, are prepared to lead productive, independent lives.

I fundamentally object to the term "Special". This is a euphemism designed to cushion the blow; to make the truth hurt less. Some people are legitimately retarded, which is to say their development has suffered from retardation, and there's nothing implicitly wrong with that, other than all students should be held to the same standard, or not at all.

Over 17% of the entire education budget is reserved for about 2% of the population. A better use for this money might be to figure out why the number of "disabled" people is increasing, and fix the problem at its root. If it turns out to be the parents' fault (i.e. smoking while pregnant, working near nuclear reactors, prescription drug use, etc.), then maybe this is a Social Services issue.

Many of these specific students are unable to learn past a certain point. The people educating them should figure out what that point is, and stop trying after that. There's no point in teaching someone something they simply cannot understand.

If there truly must be a standard for education, then that standard should be used for all students. A student who is unable to learn the same information as anyone else shouldn't be given a special exemption and awarded a diploma without having earned it. The requirements should be no different for them.

---

[143] http://www2.ed.gov/about/overview/budget/budget13/justifications/i-specialed.pdf

Of the $12.7 Billion, $12 Billion goes to state grants. The states could just tax their own people and handle everything at a more nearly local level. The remainder is funneled into a variety of programs that don't actually get used very much, and which would be better handled at the local level. Eliminate and save **$12.7 Billion**.

Rehabilitation Services and Disability Research[144]

> *People with disabilities represent a vital and integral part of our society. As a nation, our goals include independence, equal opportunity, and productivity for Americans with disabilities, many of whom require a range of services and supports in order to learn, work productively and live in the community. Numerous pieces of federal legislation establish policies to meet these requirements.*

To the contrary; people with disabilities are no more vital to our society than people without disabilities. The unfortunate truth is that not only do they not provide anything more than others, but in fact many are only capable of providing less or none at all.

It is true that many disabled people require numerous services and other support to accomplish what we generally consider to be the most basic tasks. The government, however, is not responsible for providing them. The government's responsibility should merely be to ensure their rights are protected to exactly the same extent as everyone else's, and that's it.

The government should never perform nor directly fund research of any kind.

Special programs like this discriminate against the majority. Eliminate and save **$3.5 Billion**.

American Printing House for the Blind[145]

> *The Act to Promote the Education of the Blind authorizes an annual appropriation for the American Printing House for the Blind (APH) to produce and distribute educational materials adapted for students who are legally blind and enrolled in formal educational programs below the college level.*

The World Health Organization estimates [146] that a total of 8,000,000 people are blind; about 0.1%. If we apply that same figure to the population of the United States, we can estimate that 365,714 Americans are blind. A government program specifically designed for blind people discriminates

---

[144] http://www2.ed.gov/about/overview/budget/budget13/justifications/j-rehabilitation.pdf
[145] http://www2.ed.gov/about/overview/budget/budget13/justifications/k-aphb.pdf
[146] http://www.who.int/bulletin/volumes/86/1/07-041210.pdf

against the 99.9% of us who aren't blind. As someone who can see, most of us get no benefit from this program. It does not serve the public good; the general welfare, in that the vast majority of us will never get any use of it. Let some nonprofit organization run this project and save $25 Million.

National Technical Institute for the Deaf[147]

> Congress created the National Technical Institute for the Deaf (NTID) in 1965 to promote the employment of persons who are deaf by providing technical and professional education for the Nation's youth who are deaf. The National Technical Institute for the Deaf Act was superseded by the Education of the Deaf Act of 1986 (EDA).

A study at the Gallaudet Research Institute[148] shows that there are around 640,000 deaf people in the United States. This program discriminates against the vast majority of us who will never get any use of it. Therefore it does not serve the public good; the general welfare. Eliminate and save $65 Million.

Gallaudet University[149]

> Gallaudet University, which received its Federal charter in 1864, is a private, nonprofit educational institution providing elementary and secondary education programs for students who are deaf and undergraduate, graduate, and continuing education programs for persons who are deaf and hearing. Gallaudet also conducts a wide variety of basic and applied research on deafness and provides public service programs for persons who are deaf and professionals who work with persons who are deaf.

A study at the Gallaudet Research Institute[150] shows that there are around 640,000 deaf people in the United States. This program discriminates against the vast majority of us who will never get any use of it. Therefore it does not serve the public good; the general welfare. Eliminate and save $126 Million.

Career, Technical, and Adult Education[151]

> Programs in the Career, Technical, and Adult Education account further the efforts of States and communities to improve their career and technical education programs and their adult education and literacy systems.

The states don't need any help to run their education programs; they can simply tax their own citizens more if they need more revenue. Technical

---

[147] http://www2.ed.gov/about/overview/budget/budget13/justifications/l-ntid.pdf
[148] http://research.gallaudet.edu/Demographics/deaf-US.php
[149] http://www2.ed.gov/about/overview/budget/budget13/justifications/m-gallaudet.pdf
[150] http://research.gallaudet.edu/Demographics/deaf-US.php
[151] http://www2.ed.gov/about/overview/budget/budget13/justifications/n-ctae.pdf

education – training people for specific fields of work – is not a proper government function. The feds have no authority here whatsoever. Eliminate and save **$1.7 Billion.**

Student Aid[152]

> *The Federal Government will provide in fiscal year 2012 an historic $217 billion in grants, loans, and work-study assistance to help students pay for postsecondary education. These funds help millions of Americans obtain the benefits of a higher education. The Administration is proud of this commitment to higher education. However, fiscal constraints now limit the extent to which additional Federal resources are available to help students and families cope with unrelenting increases in the costs of higher education.*

Nearly a quarter trillion dollars in student aid is historic indeed; yet we are treating a symptom here. Since the feds have made student loans guaranteed, the universities have no reason to bother with competitive tuition rates. Therefore, tuition has skyrocketed since the 90s. Rather than trying to guarantee that people can eventually pay for the costs, perhaps we should be identifying the reason why costs have gone up so sharply and address the problem at its root.

It used to be that you could pay for college on a part time job without a grant, scholarship, or loan. Some of this funding comes from elsewhere; eliminate and save **$165 Billion.**

Howard University[153]

> *Howard University was established in 1867 as a federally chartered, private, nonprofit educational institution. As a comprehensive, research-oriented, predominantly African American university, its mission is to provide a high-quality educational experience at reasonable cost.*

The federal government should never directly subsidize private companies. This university seems to discriminate against people who aren't black. Eliminate the subsidy and save $235 Million.

College Housing and Academic Facilities Loans[154]

> *Funds for this activity pay the Federal costs of administering the College Housing and Academic Facilities Loans (CHAFL), College Housing Loans (CHL), and Higher Education Facilities Loans (HEFL) programs.*

---

[152] http://www2.ed.gov/about/overview/budget/budget13/justifications/o-saoverview.pdf
[153] http://www2.ed.gov/about/overview/budget/budget13/justifications/u-howard.pdf
[154] http://www2.ed.gov/about/overview/budget/budget13/justifications/v-chafl.pdf

My copy of the Constitution says nothing about housing loans, academic loans, facilities loans, or loans of any kind. Eliminate and save $460,000.

Historically Black College and University Capital Financing[155]

> Since fiscal year 1996, the Historically Black Colleges and Universities Capital Financing Program has provided HBCUs with access to capital financing for the repair, renovation, and, in exceptional circumstances, construction or acquisition of educational facilities, instructional equipment, research instrumentation, and physical infrastructure.

This program discriminates against people who aren't black. Colleges and universities should be fully private businesses, and therefore should be responsible for their own finances. The fact that this subset happens to cater to a minority doesn't make it an exception. Eliminate and save $20.2 Million.

Institute of Education Sciences[156]

> The Administration requests $202.3 million for research, development, and dissemination, an increase of $12.5 million over the 2012 level. The requested increase would support critical investments in education research, development, dissemination, and evaluation that provide parents, teachers, and schools with evidence-based information on effective educational practice.

The Constitution doesn't say anything about improving the education process; eliminate and save $621 Million.

Salaries and Expenses[157]

If we eliminate the department, then it no longer has any salaries or expenses of any kind. Eliminate and save **$14.5 Billion**.

Yeah, that's right, 20% of the department's outlays are just *the overhead of running the department*.

Conclusion

The Department of Education is riddled with discriminatory programs, overhead, and block grants to states where states should just tax their own people. Its very existence has had a negative result on test scores. What's worse is that entire generations of children have become institutionalized and hypnotized by it into living a certain way throughout their lives. Let's put

---

[155] http://www2.ed.gov/about/overview/budget/budget13/justifications/w-hbcu.pdf
[156] http://www2.ed.gov/about/overview/budget/budget13/justifications/x-ies.pdf
[157] http://www2.ed.gov/about/overview/budget/budget13/justifications/y-seoverview.pdf

education back into the communities and homes where it belongs. Eliminate the department.

How Education Should Work

I have put together some ideas on how a truly effective education system might work. First, we need to throw out the entire system and start over. Eliminate the K-12 grade system. Eliminate ABCDF, ABCI, Advanced / Proficient / Satisfactory, and whatever other grading systems are in use.

There's no reason why the states and local communities can't run their own systems. There's no reason why education must be public to begin with. The suggestion here is merely a concept for how an effective system might run, if we actually needed such a system in the first place.

Framework

The concept of education can be broken into its component parts. We know that children generally need to be instructed in specific areas, such as mathematics, reading, and writing. There are many other areas which would be nice to include but were never core competencies, such as the sciences and the arts. We can organize the system into these components. Since these are ongoing subject areas, which begin early in life and never have to end, we can think of them as "timelines".

Each timeline can be further broken down into its component parts. Mathematics starts with counting and arithmetic, then moves into algebra and trigonometry, and ends up in number theory and fluid dynamics. The Sciences start with the basic scientific process and progresses into chemistry, biology, astronomy, computers, and quantum theory. Reading and writing begin at the alphabet and move into progressively harder concepts. The two are so inexorably intertwined that perhaps they belong in the same timeline. The arts begin at drawing and progress on through painting, music, acting, and other forms of entertainment. These component parts can be thought of as "Modules".

Each module can be further broken down into "concepts". Arithmetic consists of addition, subtraction, multiplication, and division. Biology consists of cellular, organismal, plant, and animal biology.

Physical Education has no place in school. It can be broken down into two basic areas: Health and gym. The health aspects can be taught in the biology timeline, and the gym aspect doesn't really teach anything other than how to pass gym. Gym should be at most an optional set of concepts in the health module, itself within the sciences timeline.

Progression

If we are resigned to the theory that all students should learn the same way, then all school offerings should be provided in the same way and all requirements should be the same. There should be no special cases for any individuals or groups.

School should be open year-round. If you want your children to take a summer vacation, simply don't send them to school for a few months. Take off whatever time you desire. The same modules and concepts will be there when they get back. The entire concept of semesters, hexters, and other divisions of the year is implicitly obsoleted by the timeline system.

Education should happen at the speed of the student, not the speed of the slowest kid in the room or at the speed of some committee thousands of miles away. Under this system, a student could pass a concept in a day, or in six weeks. Whenever they're ready to move on, they take a Concept Test and move onto the next concept.

We should administer tests at the end of every concept. A student must pass all concepts within a module in order to pass the module, though the order in which they do so is generally immaterial.

We should administer tests at the end of every module. A student can take any test whenever they think they're ready, and can retest as often as they like. When the student submits their test, the points they receive are added directly toward that module's timeline. Every time a student earns a certain number of points in every timeline, they get a diploma or degree. This system provides them with a real incentive to do well, and makes the impact of their grades immediately evident.

At any given point, the student knows how far along they are. They can go back and retake any test at any point. If the score is higher than the previous score, it would replace that score.

The tests would be constructed from a huge base of questions and answers, randomly generated by a computer to reduce the possibility of cheating. The only way the student could cheat would be to memorize every possible question and answer; and frankly, if they do that, they deserve to pass anyway.

The computers can analyze the answers and see which questions are correct less often, and this information can be used to improve the curriculum. If the teacher submits a list of students they taught, or the students submit a list of teachers they learn from, this information can be compared to test results to evaluate the teachers.

Environment

If we must accept that tests are the basis for evaluating a student's progression, it therefore stands to reason that those tests would be the only requirement made of the student. Homework would be solely at the discretion of the student or parents, and based on their progression through the concepts.

Schools were never intended to babysit the students. If you want your child to go to school full time, by all means they can do so. Otherwise, simply don't send them into the building. You can teach them at home. They can learn on the Internet or through books. They can study together in the cafeterias and hallways and teach each other as they learn. The school should have no opinion on the matter; it exists only to help them learn.

Students should only need to register for space planning and forecasting purposes. Even that requirement is optional, really, if you don't mind overcrowding. A student should be able to walk into any school that has space available and start interacting with any teacher. Of course, they won't be able to take a concept test until they pass the prerequisite concept tests.

Assuming the parent's permission, students would be free to come and go as they please. The only reason for them to go to a school building is to get direct instruction, especially if they're having trouble in a subject area. Classrooms should have a student to teacher ratio of no more than 10:1, and the lower the better; but there could be more than one such group per classroom for space planning purposes.

Ideally, the teacher would sit at a chair in the middle of a circular table about two to three feet deep and with a sufficient inner diameter, and the students would be seated on the far curve of that table. Behind the teacher would be a large chalkboard or whiteboard for depicting concepts visually, which could double as an overhead projector screen or have such a screen pull down in front of it.

The teacher would alternate regularly between lecture and interactive study. Ideally, these intervals would be around 30 minutes; long enough to teach, but short enough to hold the students' attention. If a student doesn't understand the concept after an interval, they can just remain seated until they do, or go find a private helper teacher. If one concept desk is empty, that teacher can go help another teacher with his student load until a student arrives.

Having the teacher only a few feet from every student would improve the teacher's ability to interact with the students. This would also improve the teacher's ability to supervise the students' conduct, although we must remember the teachers are here to teach, not to babysit.

There should be no discipline of any kind in schools; that's the parents' job. If a student is sufficiently misbehaving, just kick them out of the building for the day. They can pick up where they left off whenever they come back.

Every concept in every module in every timeline should have at least one teacher or group of teachers dedicated to it at any given time. Most teachers should have their own Concept Desk. However, not every module needs to be taught in every school. Much like today, earlier modules can be in different buildings from later modules as students graduate from one level to the next.

Students wouldn't be forced to repeat the same exercises over and over. Once you understand a concept, just take the test. Once you pass the test, walk over to another concept desk and continue learning. If a desk is full, sit at another concept desk for a little while; maybe reinforce something you need to know beforehand.

Students need not ever attend a concept desk if they are able to learn the subject without direct teacher interaction. Tests should be taken somewhere else, on demand, so the other students can focus on their learning.

The school should further offer dedicated, private study rooms for students to study on their own. The school should also offer extra teachers who aren't assigned to a concept desk, available on demand for when a student requires further or more targeted assistance. These teachers can be stationed at a "Help Desk" or used through a similar concept.

The automated nature of the testing implies that tests could be both administered and graded by kiosks placed throughout the school. Just tell it what test you want and it will generate one for you. When you're done, just slip the scantron back into the machine and receive your grade. There should be a time limit to help reduce cheating. Perhaps the machines would be located in the private study rooms and the tests would be invalidated if the student unlocks the door before submitting them.

All tests should be open-book, since people in the real world have access to books and the Internet. We should be more concerned with their ability to find and understand the information than to memorize it.

In this model, the student runs their education, not the teacher. The teacher merely teaches as has been the tradition for millennia. Parents would be free to come in and participate in the process, or simply to keep the child home full time and bring them in whenever they need to consult with a teacher. Students will be and feel more empowered, with a sense of direction and control over their own lives. These points should help reduce the dropout rate, although the definition of a dropout would become a bit fuzzier. Most of us can probably agree that education is more important than the measurement thereof.

In today's model, teachers are forced to teach down to the lowest common denominator; at the speed of the dumbest kid in the class. In this new model, the student can learn at his or her own pace, unencumbered by the progress of those around them. Allowing the students to learn in this way eliminates the need for remedial education, advance placement, study hall classes, schedules, GEDs, trade schools, charter schools, and to some extent, special education.

Certification

If we are to provide a national education system, let's do it right. Instead of providing a predetermined level of education, let's provide education to a predetermined age; say, 20. The students can continue on indefinitely, but would have to pay for it out of pocket beyond that age. As a student, you are free to make as much or as little use of the system as you and your parents desire. Your progress; your diplomas and degrees, depend solely on you.

This pay method incentivizes students to learn quickly; if you earn your secondary diploma early enough, you can get free college. No loans, no messy application process; just continue the same process you have been following. The transition from preschool to post-doctorate can be completely seamless. Of course, credits from public and private institutions would be mutually transferrable and accredited, so you can go to whatever kind of school you desire throughout the entire process.

As determined earlier, the points from each module test are applied directly to each timeline. Each concept in a module must be passed to complete the module. Each module cannot be started until the previous module in that timeline has been passed. When you get a certain number of points in all mandatory timelines, you graduate.

We can have optional timelines running in parallel with mandatory timelines to support the idea of a specialized degree or certification. A certification is awarded when an optional timeline is brought up to a certain number of points. A diploma or degree is awarded when all timelines are brought up to that number of points.

The points required would depend, of course, on the tests and what education experts determine are appropriate levels of education. Since I'm not an education expert, we'll have to use fake numbers; but the system could look like this:

Points	Award
5,000	Elementary Diploma
10,000	Secondary Diploma
12,500	Associate's Degree or Certificate
15,000	Bachelor's Degree or Certificate
17,500	Master's Degree or Certificate
20,000	Doctorate Degree or Certificate
22,250	Associate's Degree or Certificate #2

Of course, this entire system could just as easily be private; it's just a matter of getting the schools accredited. Do it right, or don't do it at all.

Department of Energy (DoE)[158]

This proposal moves the nuclear programs over to the Department of Defense, and reverts control over the energy grid back to the states where it belongs. These being the only two proper functions of the DoE, this proposal eliminates this department.

Nuclear Security Administration[159]

The NNSA has specialized programs that support the President's nuclear strategy, including those identified in the President's New Global Military Strategy released in January 2012, the New START agreement signed in 2010, the Nuclear Posture Review (NPR) report issued in 2010, and the commitments made at Prague in 2009. More specifically, the NNSA implements programs for three major national security endeavors: (1) leveraging science to maintain a safe, secure and effective arsenal of nuclear weapons and capabilities to deter any adversary and guarantee that defense to our allies; (2) accelerating and expanding our efforts here in the homeland and around the world to reduce the global threat posed by nuclear weapons, nuclear proliferation and unsecured or excess nuclear materials; and (3) providing safe and effective nuclear propulsion for the U.S. Navy.

The President should not determine the country's nuclear strategy. Withdraw from the START treaty. We should not sign defense pacts with countries that are incapable of defending us. These are all important aspects of national defense; however, nuclear weapons and materials *are* a national security concern, and therefore they belong under the Department of Defense. Transfer the NNSA over to the DoD and maintain funding levels as is ($411.3 Million).

Other Defense Activities

ODA is being transferred to the DoD in this proposal, as the DoE is being eliminated.

Health, Safety, and Security

The Office of Health, Safety and Security (HSS) demonstrates the unwavering commitment of the U.S. Department of Energy (DOE or Department) to maintain a safe and secure work environment for all Federal and contractor employees, ensure that the Department's operations preserve the health and safety of the surrounding communities, and protect national security assets entrusted to the Department.

Health, safety, and security are important aspects of working around nuclear weapons and materials, so this can stay as is ($246M).

---

[158] http://www.cfo.doe.gov/budget/13budget/index13.html
[159] http://www.cfo.doe.gov/budget/13budget/Content/Volume1.pdf

Legacy Management

The Legacy Management subprogram contains essential elements to assist the Department in achieving the strategic goal of providing a long-term solution to the environmental legacy of the Cold War and ensure that DOE fulfills its long-term commitments to protect human health and the environment and continue providing benefits to former contractor workers. By funding the long-term activities in the LM program, other DOE programs are able to concentrate on risk reduction and site closure.

It makes sense to clean up after ourselves, given the well-documented deadly nature of exposure to nuclear materials. Keep as is ($177.9M).

Defense-Related Administrative Support

Per direction provided in the FY 2004 Energy Water and Development conference report, the FY 2013 budget request reflects a proportional contribution from Other Defense Activities for Departmental Administration costs.

It makes sense to clean up after ourselves, given the well-documented deadly nature of exposure to nuclear materials. Keep as is ($119M).

Hearings and Appeals

The Office of Hearings and Appeals (OHA) provides adjudicatory and conflict prevention and resolution services for DOE's programs so that disputes may be resolved at the agency level in a fair, impartial and efficient manner.

The Constitution provides us with a court system to settle these disputes. Once we have the policies and facilities in place, there's really no need for them to be settled more than once. Eliminate and save $4.8 Million.

Departmental Administration

This is overhead needed to run the department. Moving it under the DoD allows them to use the DoD's overhead; eliminate and save $123 Million.

Inspector General

This is overhead needed to run the department. Moving it under the DoD allows them to use the DoD's overhead; eliminate and save $43 Million.

Working Capital Fund

A working capital fund exists solely to provide money to spend that they neglected to budget, or were unable to budget. The DoD has its own WCF, and most of the spending sources in the DoE are going away. Eliminate and save $273 Million.

Safeguards and Security Crosscut

> *The Safeguards and Security (S&S) program at headquarters and each DOE field site protects against theft, diversion, sabotage, espionage, unauthorized access, compromise, and other hostile acts which may cause damage to national security, program continuity, the health and safety of employees, the public or the environment.*

Necessary and proper for national security; keep as is ($1.8 Billion).

Pensions

Necessary and proper, not to mention the decent thing to do as an employer; keep as is ($1.6 Billion).

Energy Efficiency and Renewable Energy

> *The Department of Energy's (DOE) Office of Energy Efficiency and Renewable Energy (EERE) supports clean energy applied Research, Development, Demonstration and Deployment (RDD&D) for efficiency and renewable energy technologies.*

The energy sources selected for use by the country should be a pure product of supply and demand. If we eliminate regulation and allow competitive energy companies to start on their own, and people start buying energy from them instead, then those companies will expand and provide more clean energy. If people stop buying power from coal and oil, then those companies will close. Eliminate and save $2.337 Billion.

Electricity Delivery and Energy Reliability

> *The Office of Electricity Delivery and Energy Reliability (OE) leads national efforts in electric grid research and development (R&D) and electricity policy, while also serving as the Federal government's focal point in responding to energy security emergencies.*

Revert control of the energy grid back to the states. Revert to them also all property and equipment used thereby. Eliminate and save $143 Million.

Nuclear Energy

> *The Office of Nuclear Energy (NE) supports the diverse civilian nuclear energy programs of the U.S. Government, leading Federal efforts to research and develop nuclear energy technologies.*

Revert control of the energy grid back to the states. Revert to them also all property and equipment used thereby. Station a small contingent of soldiers or marines at each nuclear facility for security. Eliminate and save $770 Million.

Fossil Energy

The Office of Fossil Energy (FE) advances technologies related to the reliable, efficient, affordable, and environmentally sound use of fossil fuels which are essential to our Nation's security and economic prosperity.

Energy research should be done by energy companies. Eliminate and save $651 Million.

Naval Petroleum and Oil Shale Reserves

The NPOSR program manages a number of legal agreements that were executed as part of the 1998 sale of NPR-1 in California. These agreements direct post-sale work including environmental restoration and remediation, equity finalization, contract closeout, and records disposition.

The federal government should not involve itself in the matters internal to a state or the waters immediately next to a state, other than defense and escalated or interstate justice cases. The only proper petroleum-related programs from the federal level would be drilling out on the continental shelf, where there are no states; and that should generate revenue, not spending. However, in order to be thus allowed, the Constitution would need to be amended or a treaty would need to be signed granting the authority. Since there is no proper reason to sign a treaty over a purely internal issue, the former would be the answer. Eliminate and save $15 Million.

Strategic Petroleum Reserve

The Strategic Petroleum Reserve (SPR) protects the U.S. from future disruptions in critical petroleum supplies and meets the U.S. obligations under the International Energy Program (Energy Policy and Conservation Act, P.L. 94-163, as amended, Section 151). The mission of the SPR achieves the Secretary's Goal of Security: Protecting the Nation against interruptions in its critical petroleum supplies.

A backup fuel supply can be justified as necessary to maintaining the military, so it can stay; but as a part of the DoD and not to back up the entire country's oil supply. Cut by half and save $98 Million.

Elk Hills School Lands Fund

The Elk Hills School Lands Fund, subject to appropriation, provides a source of compensation for the California State Teachers' Retirement System as a result of a settlement with the State of California with respect to its longstanding claim to title of two sections of land within NPR-1.

Return the land back to California. Eliminate; $16 Million saved.

Northeast Home Heating Oil Reserve

> *The Northeast Home Heating Oil Reserve (NEHHOR) provides a short-term supplement to the Northeast systems' private supply of heating oil in the event of a supply interruption.*

Provides a backup heating fuel source for a very specific part of the country while others freeze to death. Heating homes is not a constitutionally authorized federal function. Eliminate; $10 Million saved.

Advanced Technology Vehicles Manufacturing Loan Program

> *Section 136 of the Energy Independence and Security Act of 2007 established the Advanced Technology Vehicles Manufacturing (ATVM) Loan Program, consisting of direct loans of up to $25 billion in total loan authority to support the development of advanced technology vehicles and associated components in the United States.*

The government is not a bank. Repeal the Energy Independence and Security Act of 2007. Eliminate; $9 Million saved.

Title 17 Innovative Tech. Loan Guarantee Program

> *The Loan Guarantee Program (LGP), as authorized under Title XVII of the Energy Policy Act of 2005, encourages early commercial use of new or significantly improved technologies in energy projects. Projects supported by DOE loan guarantees must avoid, reduce, or sequester air pollutants or anthropogenic emissions of greenhouse gases; employ new or significantly improved technologies compared to commercial technologies in service in the United States at the time the guarantee is issued; and offer a reasonable prospect of repayment of the principal and interest on the guaranteed obligation.*

The government is not a bank. Eliminate; $38 Million saved.

Energy Information Administration

> *The U.S. Energy Information Administration (EIA) is the statistical and analytical agency within the U.S. Department of Energy. EIA collects, analyzes, and disseminates independent and impartial energy information to promote sound policymaking, efficient markets, and public understanding of energy and its interaction with the economy and the environment. EIA is the Nation's premier source of energy information and, by law, its data, analyses, and forecasts are independent of approval by any other officer or employee of the U.S. Government.*

The government is not responsible for collecting statistics on, nor analyzing, information about any specific industry. The government, in fact, has constitutional no role whatsoever in the economy itself, other than to ensure states and Indian tribes are not embargoing each other. Eliminate; $116 Million saved.

Science[160]

> *The Office of Science mission is to deliver the scientific discoveries and major scientific tools that transform our understanding of nature and advance the energy, economic, and national security of the United States.*

Scientific discoveries should be made by individuals, universities, and researchers at nonprofits and companies. Scientific discoveries are rightfully made in trying to solve a problem, and the free market rewards problem-solvers by the act of customers buying the solutions to their problems. Eliminate and save $203 Million.

Power Marketing Administrations[161]

> *[Administration] exists to carry out the functions assigned by the Flood Control Act of 1944: to market the electric power and energy generated by the Federal reservoir projects to public bodies and cooperatives in the United States in a professional, innovative, customer- oriented manner, while continuing to meet the challenges of an ever-changing electric utility environment through continuous improvement.*

Repeal the Flood Control Act of 1944 and let states control their own floods. Release the reservoirs, electrical grid and its properties to the states in which they are located; let those states market their own electrical power and energy. The challenges in scaling up to the demand are best met by the free market, so hopefully the states would then sell off the assets and let the economy do its thing. Eliminate and save $333 Million.

Conclusion

In the end, the Department of Energy is responsible for two areas: Nuclear materials and the energy grid. Nuclear materials are a national security issue and belong with the Department of Defense. The energy grid is an infrastructure that provides commodities, and thus belongs in the private sector. The DoE therefore has no reason to exist. Eliminate the department.

---

[160] http://www.cfo.doe.gov/budget/13budget/Content/Volume4.pdf
[161] http://www.cfo.doe.gov/budget/13budget/Content/Volume6.pdf

Department of Health and Human Services (DHHS) [162]

The Budget for the Department of Health and Human Services (HHS) invests in health care, disease prevention, social services, and scientific research. HHS makes investments where they will have the greatest impact, build on the efforts of our partners, and lead to meaningful gains in health and opportunity for the American people.

My copy of the Constitution says nothing about healthcare, disease prevention, social services, or scientific research.

Healthcare is a commodity, which means it should be treated just like any other product or service to come out of the free market. Competition reduces prices; government regulations increase prices. The entire department needs to go away.

Unfortunately, there are many people on Medicare and Medicaid who rely on these programs; so we can't just end them all at once. Therefore, these programs are moved to the Ten Year Plan. The federal funding can be reduced while the states that choose to do so can start replacing it with their own programs. After a decade, those programs disappear.

Keep in mind that the absence of something at the federal level does not mean it cannot exist at the state level; and that this proposal merely follows the law in the Constitution to determine whether the feds can do something or not.

Food and Drug Administration (FDA)

The FY 2013 Budget requests $4.5 billion for the Food and Drug Administration (FDA), a net program level increase of $654 million, or 17 percent, over FY 2012. The FDA Budget includes investments to continue to implement the FDA Food Safety Modernization Act (FSMA); advance medical countermeasures; improve the safety of the Nation's drugs and other medical products; facilitate greater trade with China by improving the safety of imports to the United States; and further develop and implement public health strategies to prevent youth from using tobacco and help adults to quit.

Food safety is none of the government's business. It's an agreement between the supplier and the demander; the business and the customer. If your company poisons people, then people will stop buying your products and start suing you.

---

[162] http://www.hhs.gov/budget/

Much like every other industry, the government has no business in healthcare. Their involvement makes everything slower and more expensive, taxing it all on the way through, and they prevent access to medical treatments, drugs, and equipment that you could have in a *free* market.

The track record of people killed by FDA-approved drugs speaks volumes to the government's responsibility in the pharmaceutical industry. That is to say, they have no responsibility other than to ensure the drugs flow from state to state. Countless drugs are advertised every minute of every day whose "side effects may include death", yet the feds refuse to allow us to use natural medicine that cures disease simply because it can make the user feel good. Marijuana, for example, is no more habit-forming than many FDA-approved pharmaceuticals; and it has never killed a single person.

The government's facilitation of greater trade with China is one of the most destructive factors to the American manufacturing base. Chinese products are cheaper in every sense of the word, and "Made in America" doesn't mean anything to most consumers anymore. As a result, China is sitting on a cash stockpile of $3 Trillion, while we're over $16 Trillion in debt. All the while, the manufacturing jobs go with the money, and new factories just don't open anymore. This pattern must end.

There should be no such thing as a federal "health strategy". The government has no right to intervene in this private industry. Preventing children from smoking is their parents' job. What informed adults put into our own bodies is our own business and nobody else's.

Every food and drug that was ever recalled by the FDA was at some point tested and ruled as being safe by the FDA. Prescription drugs kill more people than illegal drugs. FDA-approved processed foods have been attributed to causing cancer, birth defects, obesity, and death.

The Constitution gives the federal government no power to decide for you what you're allowed to put into your body. They aren't allowed to ban or control foods or drugs by any stretch of the imagination.

Of course, the process of getting these foods and drugs approved in the first place is long, drawn out, expensive, and redundant. Companies realize that if they sell food and drugs that kill people, they'll be sued and people will stop buying their products.

The FDA has banned essential vitamins and minerals, and seeks to ban more[163]. Meanwhile, they continue to approve foods and drugs with chemicals that few have heard of and which have only existed for a term of years. As a general rule, if your great-grandmother wouldn't recognize it as food, don't eat it.

The FDA has banned perfectly natural things such as raw milk[164], but has approved Aspartame and genetically modified foods, which cause cancer[165] [166]. Meanwhile, the FDA has also suppressed[167] [168] at least two proven cures for cancer. Clearly, the FDA is not acting in the best interest of the American people.

For all these reasons and more, the Food and Drug Administration needs to go away. Eliminate it and save **$7 Billion**.

Health Resources and Services Administration (HRSA)

The FY 2013 Budget includes $8.4 billion for the Health Resources and Services Administration (HRSA), a net increase of $228 million above FY 2012. HRSA is the principal Federal agency charged with improving access to health care to those in medically underserved areas and enhancing the capacity of the health care workforce.

Access to healthcare is not a government issue. Improving that access is a function of the free market; if we let anyone open a medical office, then someone will likely do so when they realize the area has little or no competition.

The capacity of any workforce is a function of the free market. As demand increases, companies get more customers and therefore more profit. Those companies then hire people and expand their facilities to meet the additional demand so that they can make even more profit. In doing so, the demand is met and jobs are created.

Healthcare utilization by group is a poor indicator of the industry. It's true that poor people can't afford expensive things like healthcare, but this mentality is treating a symptom. To reverse this problem, we must cure the root cause: Why has healthcare become so expensive in the first place? In a nutshell, healthcare prices are increasing in price for two reasons: First, the government subsidizes the insurance companies, so the providers know they'll be paid

---

[163] http://www.healthfreedomusa.org/?p=13015
[164] http://www.fda.gov/Food/ResourcesForYou/consumers/ucm079516.htm
[165] http://www.ncbi.nlm.nih.gov/pmc/articles/PMC1964906/
[166] http://www.naturalnews.com/037249_GMO_study_cancer_tumors_organ_damage.html
[167] http://en.wikipedia.org/wiki/Royal_Rife
[168] http://en.wikipedia.org/wiki/Ernst_T._Krebs

regardless of the price. Second, government regulations add tremendous overhead to running a healthcare business; increasingly with the size of the business.

It is precisely this government intervention which is causing the problems that the government is claiming to help alleviate. The government is the very barrier that the government is proclaimed to overcome. Indeed we should reduce that barrier.

Medical, dental, and mental healthcare are commodities. You take your money to a company and trade that money for products and services, just as if you were buying a carpet cleaning, a television, or a car. Government should never involve itself in the inner workings of any industry; the commodity trades should occur organically and without this intervention.

Originally coined as recently as 1978, behavioral health is subjective and arguably is not really medicine at all, though the same principle applies. The entire alleged science of behavioral health can be reduced to practical application of common sense. Your parents and colleagues can likely teach you as much about behavioral health as any doctor, and they'll do it for free.

As for the actual mission of providing support for these practitioners to bring their skills to areas with limited access, they need merely charge the customers for the dislocation process, or move the customers closer to them.

Other than military protection and a higher level justice system, states do not require assistance from the federal government for any reason. The money that the federal government collects from the taxpayers can merely be collected by the states instead so they can run their own programs. There is no reason for a taxpayer in Texas to be forced to pay for the healthcare services of a patient in California.

Gaps in the workforce should be filled by the employers. That is to say, if your business can't keep up with the demand, hire more people. The same principle applies to addressing unmet service needs: If the customers demand a service, your business will make more profit by offering that service. Take your profit, reinvest some of it back into the company, and be done with it.

The HRSA thus has no useful services to provide, let alone any constitutional authority to exist. Eliminate and save **$14.5 Billion**.

Indian Health Service (IHS)

The FY 2013 Budget requests $5.5 billion for the Indian Health Service (IHS), an increase of $116 million over FY 2012. The FY 2013 Budget prioritizes reducing health disparities in Indian Country though purchased care with the Contract Health Services program and by providing staff for new facilities.

Grant immediate citizenship to any Native Americans who desire it. Those who choose to do so can use the healthcare system just like any other citizen. The others can handle their medical needs within the tribe as they did for centuries before we ever got involved.

Health disparities in Native Americans are no different from those of any other group; setting up special programs for specific groups is a form of discrimination in that the government provides services to some people and not to others. Eliminate and save **$5.5 Billion**.

Centers for Disease Control and Prevention (CDC)

The FY 2013 Budget request for the Centers for Disease Control and Prevention (CDC) and the Agency for Toxic Substances and Disease Registry (ATSDR) is $11.2 billion, an increase of $39 million above FY 2012.

The CDC forces parents to stick deadly viruses into their children's bodies. These often mandatory vaccines have been shown to kill people.[169] [170] [171]

The Constitution provides no authority to prevent any disease, to inspect food or any other product, to survey infections, to eradicate polio, to perform medical services of any kind, to run laboratories of any kind, nor to run the states' programs for them. Eliminate and save **$11.2 Billion**.

National Institutes of Health (NIH)

The FY 2013 Budget requests $30.9 billion for the National Institutes of Health (NIH), the same level as in FY 2012, reflecting the Administration's priority to invest in innovative biomedical and behavioral research that spurs economic growth while advancing medical science. In FY 2013.

The Constitution grants no power to do research of any kind, to be involved in the economy, to intervene in medicine, to perform science, to maintain or improve health, nor to fund anyone else to do the same. These are things the *people* should be doing, not the government.

---

[169] http://www.naturalnews.com/029911_vaccines_Bill_Gates.html
[170] http://articlesofhealth.blogspot.com/2009/08/swine-flu-vaccine-kills.html
[171] http://revlu.com/vac.htm

The NIH alone costs twice as much as the entire Department of the Interior, five Environmental Protection Agencies, or 2/3 of the Department of Energy. More than half of the NIH's budget funds grants, which this proposal eliminates entirely. Eliminate and save **$30.9 Billion**.

Substance Abuse and Mental Health Services Administration (SAMHSA)

The FY 2013 Budget requests $3.4 billion, of which $105 million is funded through the Prevention Fund, for the Substance Abuse and Mental Health Services Administration (SAMHSA), a decrease of $142 million below FY 2012. In order to maximize the effectiveness and efficiency of its resources,

The Constitution grants no power to the federal government to involve itself in mental health, to ban substances of any kind, to tell you what you're allowed to do to your own body, to offer and fund grants, to prevent societally undesired behavior which does not encroach on others, nor to direct how states and tribes can use their own funds.

As Washington and Colorado have legislated, it is the states which have the power to determine substance legality. Colorado even amended its own state Constitution to enshrine this power indefinitely. As the Tenth Amendment tells us, that power now lies with those states. The states which have not included such verbiage in their own constitutions abdicate such power by default, leaving those powers to the people thereof.

That's how the system works, and it only works if we follow it. Eliminate and save **$3.4 Billion**.

Agency for Healthcare Research and Quality (AHRQ)

AHRQ conducts and supports a broad range of health services research within research institutions, hospitals, and health care systems that informs and enhances decision-making, and improves health care services, organization, and financing. The FY 2013 Budget continues support for core health services research on delivery system cost, quality, and outcomes.

That we must repeal the Affordable Care Act goes without saying. The Constitution grants the feds no power to support research, which seems to be the AHRQ's only function. Eliminate and save $409 Million.

Centers for Medicare and Medicaid Services (CMS)

The FY 2013 Budget estimate for the Centers for Medicare & Medicaid Services (CMS) is $829.4 billion in mandatory and discretionary outlays, a net increase of $72 billion above the FY 2012 level. This request finances Medicare,

Medicaid, the Children's Health Insurance Program (CHIP), private health insurance programs and oversight, program integrity efforts, and operating costs. [...] The Budget proposes additional targeted adjustments to Medicare and Medicaid that are projected to save $358.5 billion over the next decade.

It's amusing that it costs $8.3 Trillion, not including the budgetary increases over the next decade, to save $359 Billion. The Constitution provides the feds no power to intervene in the insurance and medical industries, nor to steal from the rich and give to the poor.

Medicare Part A pays for inpatient hospital, skilled nursing facility, home health related to hospital stays, and hospice care. Part B pays for physician, outpatient, hospital, ESRD, laboratory, equipment, home health, and other medical services. Part C pays MA plans a capitated monthly payment to provide all Part A and Part B services, and Part D services depending on the patient's plan. Part D pays for prescription drugs, which as previously established, often make the patient's conditions worse and occasionally kills them.

Unfortunately there are millions of people, generally seniors, whose livelihoods absolutely depend on Medicare and Medicaid. Therefore, while strict constitutionalism demands outright elimination, we can't just cut them off all at once. Therefore these programs must be put on the Ten Year plan, so we can gradually wean them off the programs while the states who choose to do so replace them with their own systems.

It goes without saying that the system is backwards. Any system that people rely on should collect the money first, and then distribute it to its customers. As it stands, we distribute the money to the customers and then attempt to recoup the losses. Meanwhile, an increasing number, and in fact an increasing percentage, of people are being added to these programs. It must end.

As part of the Ten Year Plan, it gets an immediate 10% cut followed by an additional 10% per year for ten years. Immediate savings are **$82.94 Billion**, followed by an increase of $82.94 Billion every year for a decade, at the end of which we will have reduced the budget by what will then be over a trillion dollars. That right there is about a quarter of the budget.

Aside from Medicare and Medicaid, this agency funds Children's Health Insurance Program, state grants, Health Insurance Programs, and Centers for Medicare and Medicaid Innovations. These are clear violations of the enumerated powers and the new "No grants" policy, and can be eliminated, saving **$12.6 Billion**.

Administration for Children and Families (ACF)

The FY 2013 Budget request for the Administration for Children and Families (ACF) is $50.3 billion. ACF works in partnership with states and communities to provide critical assistance to vulnerable families while helping families and children achieve a path to success.

If the states are to be involved in a program, then the states should tax their own people and run the program themselves. Ensuring children a path to success is the responsibility of the parents, if anyone. If you can't afford to have and support children for 18 years, *don't have children*. By having a child, you accept that responsibility.

Child abuse is, of course, a serious crime in that it encroaches on the rights of the children. Although they do not yet generally possess the mental faculties to run their own lives entirely, children do have all the same basic rights as anyone else. Child abuse can generally be broken down into gross negligence, assault and battery, sexual assault, or some sort of psychological torture. Each of these is a valid encroachment upon the child and should be treated as a crime. They are not, however, valid federal issues and should be handled by friends, family, the local police, and possibly state-level social services.

Helping refugees start a new life is the responsibility of the refugee in question, not of the government at any level. Each of us is responsible to run our own life, whether we were born here or immigrated through one process or another.

Getting troubled teens "off the streets" is a vague area of responsibility, but we can infer a desired reduction in individual and gang-related crime. Of course, by legalizing drugs, many of those activities become legal for adults, but most of these people are not. Parents of troubled teens should take a more active role in their children's development. For the remainder of teen-related crime, there are local laws and therefore these crimes should be dealt with by local police. Finding or creating opportunity is the responsibility of the teen, and to a lesser extent, their parents.

Head Start

Head Start is a federal program that promotes the school readiness of children ages birth to 5 from low-income families by enhancing their cognitive, social and emotional development.

Getting your kids ready for school is *your* job. This is a simple process of teaching them how to interact with other children, and teaching some very basic reading information like the alphabet. Anyone can do this, regardless of their income level. If you plan to homeschool your children, you can skip this part altogether and teach those aspects as part of the regular curriculum that you design. Eliminate and save over **$8 Billion**.

Child Care

> *The Budget supports important improvements in the Child Care and Development Block Grant and the Child Care Entitlement to States. The Budget request for the Child Care Entitlement is an increase of $7 billion over 10 years, including an increase of $500 million in FY 2013. The request also includes a $325 million discretionary increase to the Child Care and Development Block Grant. Total child care funding for the Child Care and Development Fund is $6 billion in FY 2013.*

Childcare is an industry, and the government has no business in industries. People pay someone to supervise their child for a period of time; services are exchanged for money based on a mutual agreement of terms. This is the very basis of a free market. There is no need for any government to interfere in this perfectly natural process, let alone federal.

Any program that involves block granting money to the states is a program which the states could just tax their own people for and eliminate a layer of overhead in the process. Any program that a state administers is a program that the feds need not be involved in to any extent. Eliminate all grants.

You are not entitled to childcare. You have no right to childcare. To claim a right to one service or product is tantamount to claiming a right to all products and services. If you have a right to something, someone has to provide it to you. So tell me, what kind of car or TV should we all have? Eliminate and save **$6 Billion**.

Child Support

> *The Budget request is $3.9 billion in budget authority in FY 2013 for Child Support Enforcement and Family Support Programs. The Budget includes $2.2 billion over 10 years for an initiative to modernize the Child Support system and promote responsible fatherhood.*

Child Support is a sentence determined in local and state courts. The federal government should not be charged with enforcing state and local court decrees, and federal courts should only be used for cases of the Constitution, cases between states, and cases which have been appealed beyond the state supreme courts. The definition of "responsible" fatherhood is the responsibility of the father. Specific laws regarding it should be left at the local, or at most state, levels. Therefore, they should be enforced at those levels. The Constitution delegates the feds no power to support children or families; eliminate and save **$3.9 Billion**.

Refugee Programs

Refugees flee violence, persecution and even torture and ACF is charged with helping them to begin new lives in the United States. ACF also serves unaccompanied alien children as well as victims of trafficking and torture

People have a long history of coming to America to escape violence, persecution, and torture. The simple fact that they won't have to deal with these problems anymore is plenty to start their life anew. Running a refugee's life is the responsibility of that refugee. Their motives are irrelevant; we need simply ensure an efficient immigration process and let them go through it.

There are strong feelings on both sides of the Grandfather Clause. Since it's still part of our constitution for now, we should deal with that and let the people and their elected officials figure that out through the process. In the meantime, follow the system that is in place. If they're born here, they're citizens and should be treated like any other displaced child.

If the child is not born here, look at the parents. If the parents were deported, deport the child along with them; being a six year old with your parents in Mexico is preferable to being a six year old alone here. If the parents are dead or otherwise can't be contacted, then perhaps the child should be pushed through the immigration process. Whatever the situation, the state in which the child is located should determine what to do with it.

Once here, victims of trafficking and torture are just immigrants. Let them go through the same process as the others; we need not discriminate here. Eliminate and save $805 Million.

Foster Care

The Budget request for the Foster Care, Adoption Assistance, Guardianship Assistance, and Independent Living programs is $7.2 billion in FY 2013 budget authority. These programs, authorized by Title IV-E of the Social Security Act, support safe living environments for vulnerable children and prepare older foster youth for independence.

Adoption is a service which should be rendered by an adoption company or nonprofit. The Constitution confers no power of any kind of child management at the federal level, so those powers are reserved to the states respectively, or to the people. Repeal the Social Security Act; more on that later.

Social Services are state programs, as they should be. Providing a safe living environment for the children is the parents' responsibility. If you can't afford to raise a child, then don't have children. We have the technology and understanding of female human biology today to make these decisions very cheaply. Eliminate and save **$7.2 Billion**.

Administration on Aging (AOA)
[Now a part of the newly-formed Administration for Community Living]

> *The FY 2013 Budget requests $2.0 billion for [AOA], an increase of $7 million above FY 2012. AoA is focused on helping seniors live as independently as possible in their communities.*

Living independently is our own responsibility, and cannot possibly be achieved through dependence on government programs. Old people used to be supported by friends, family, churches, and nonprofits. At the very most, given the consent of the governed, these programs could exist at the state or local level. A more effective way to save federal funds is by simply not spending them. Eliminate and save $2 Billion.

Department Overhead

Office of the Secretary

> *The FY 2013 Budget for General Departmental Management (GDM) is $567 million, a decrease of $21 million under the FY 2012 level. This Budget supports grant programs as well as those activities associated with the Secretary's roles in administering and overseeing the organization, programs, and activities of the Department.*

If we eliminate the department, then it no longer requires a secretary, and that secretary no longer requires an office. Eliminate all grants. There is nothing left to administer or organize; eliminate and save $567 Million.

Office of the Inspector General

> *The FY 2013 Budget request for OIG is $370 million in mandatory and discretionary budget authority.*

If we eliminate the department, then there is generally nothing left to inspect. Eliminate and save $370 Million.

Office for Civil Rights

The Budget maintains its programmatic focus on improved business practices and continues to support OCR's activities as the primary defender of the public's right to nondiscriminatory access to and receipt of federally-funded health and human services. In addition, the Budget supports OCR's expanded compliance responsibilities under the Privacy and Security Rules issued pursuant to the Health Insurance Portability and Accountability Act (HIPAA).

Repeal HIPAA. If we eliminate the department, then there is nothing left to conduct in a discriminate or indiscriminate fashion. Eliminate and save $39 Million.

Medicare Hearings and Appeals

The FY 2013 Budget request for The Office of Medicare Hearings and Appeals (OMHA) is $84 million, a net increase of $12 million over FY 2012. In order to hear cases under Title XVIII of the Social Security Act and related provisions in Title XI of the Act, we request funds from the Federal Hospital Insurance and Supplementary Medical Insurance Trust Fund.

If we eliminate Medicare, then there are no more hearings or appeals to conduct. Eliminate and save $84 Million.

Public Health and Social Services Emergency Fund

To enhance the Nation's preparedness against bioterrorism and other public health threats, the FY 2013 Budget includes $1.057 billion for the Public Health and Social Services Emergency Fund (PHSSEF) in the Office of the Secretary. In addition, pandemic influenza preparedness activities will be supported using unobligated balances.

The DoD already has programs designed to protect the people in case of a biological, chemical, or nuclear attack, rendering this a duplicate function. Eliminate and save **$4.5 Billion**.

Offsetting Collections

By having no collections to offset the expenses, we incur a loss of **$1.2 Billion**.

Conclusion

All in all, eliminating the Department of Health and Human Services saves us $941 Billion, $726 Billion of which shall be recouped over the course of the Ten Year Plan. **This is a quarter of the entire federal budget.**

Department of Homeland Security (DHS)[172]

"We have continued to grow and mature as a department by strengthening our existing capabilities, building new ones where necessary, enhancing our partnerships across all levels of Government and with the private sector, and streamlining our operations and increasing efficiency." ~ Secretary Janet Napolitano

Growing a department isn't something worthy of being advertised within the first pages of your budget. Your job is to secure the homeland, not to steal our money. Of course, we already had a department to secure the homeland: The Department of Defense. The DHS is thus rendered redundant, except that it was designed to operate inside the country, even during peacetime.

Ten years after the September 11th attacks, America is stronger and more secure today, thanks to the strong support of the President; Congress; the work of the men and women of the Department of Homeland Security (DHS) and local, State and Federal partners across the homeland security enterprise.

DHS was created with the Homeland Security Act in the panic of 9-11, along with the PATRIOT act. Together, they have caused innumerable and possibly permanent losses of liberties and privacy. Now Americans graciously accept groping and irradiation in their daily travels and government access to all their Internet traffic and phone calls, despite no terrorist having ever been caught by these processes. Government surveillance of the public was well in force before all this, of course; but it has been greatly multiplied since 2002.

America could be considered stronger, in that the military has grown; and more secure, in that there are armed federal police in every department, checkpoints at every possible point of entry, as well as dotted across the country at random. In the meantime, we have expanded the list of countries which we bomb and invade, creating hundreds of millions of new enemies that we otherwise would never have had. A more accurate description would be to say "The Government is stronger and more secure", whereas the country itself is not.

The Constitution takes no stance on terrorism, in that it is actually a matter of criminal law. The Constitution does not mention any crimes other than counterfeiting, piracy, high treason, and bribery. Therefore, the creation and enforcement of all other laws falls to the states.

---

[172] http://www.dhs.gov/xlibrary/assets/mgmt/dhs-budget-in-brief-fy2013.pdf

For all these reasons and more, the Department of Homeland Security needs to go away. It does, however, include some constitutionally authorized components which can be moved elsewhere.

Departmental Management and Operations (DMO)

Provides leadership, direction, and management to DHS and is comprised of separate appropriations.

If we eliminate the department, then there is nothing to lead, direct, or manage. Eliminate and save $813 Million.

Analysis and Operations

The Analysis and Operations appropriation provides resources for the support of the Office of Intelligence and Analysis (I&A) and the Office of Operations Coordination and Planning (OPS). This appropriation includes both National Intelligence Program (NIP) and non-NIP funds for I&A and non-NIP funds for OPS.

America's intelligence needs are more than covered by the DoD, CIA, and NSA. We of course need to repeal the PATRIOT Act and eliminate the agencies which operate warrantless wiretaps and other improper search and seizure. Legalizing drugs will further reduce the need for law enforcement at all levels.

Of the four crimes mentioned in the Constitution, the DHS has been assigned to enforce zero. Therefore it has no authority to enforce law, as most of the laws it does enforce are unconstitutional in the first place. Eliminate and save $322 Million.

Office of the Inspector General

The Department of Homeland Security (DHS) Office of Inspector General (OIG) was established by the Homeland Security Act of 2002 (P.L. 107-296), an amendment to the Inspector General Act of 1978.

If we eliminate the department, then there is nothing left to inspect. Eliminate and save $144 Million.

Customs and Border Protection (CBP)

U.S. Customs and Border Protection (CBP) is responsible for securing America's borders to protect the United States against threats and prevent the illegal entry of inadmissible persons and contraband, while facilitating lawful travel, trade, and immigration. CBP performs these missions with vigilance, integrity and professionalism.

I absolutely agree with the need to secure America's borders against outside threats, and to prevent illegal entry. However, one must also consider that the proposed foreign policy would involve bringing hundreds of thousands of military personnel back from overseas.

The Posse Comitatus Act of 1878 prevents the military from being used to enforce the law of the land. It does not, however, prevent the military from being used to protect us from invasion or other unwanted entry.

If we station the Army and Marines on our borders and in our airports – not to enforce law, but to prevent such unwanted entry – this may be acceptable. The Supreme Court would likely need to pass a ruling on the subject to know for sure. Of course, we should allow landowners to secure their own law through state "Make My Day" laws. An argument could be made that border state governors should be allowed to station their own National Guard units on those borders, except where made redundant by federal faculties.

Posse Comitatus only applies to active military, and not to National Guard. Perhaps active duty military could rotate in and out of the National Guard to provide border and port protection, thus staying within the confines of the law. Of course, the ultimate purpose of Posse Comitatus is to prevent what happened in Germany in World War II, so perhaps a better solution is simply to make sure we don't have federal laws that encroach on basic human rights.

The Navy should patrol the waters off our coasts. The Coast Guard should continue to do so and patrol large inland waterways. The Air Force should fly armed patrols over major cities and along the borders and coasts. These are proper defense functions, which preexisted and thus make obsolete the need for CBP.

However, the Import Tax in this proposal must be enforced for reasons already justified. The feds could operate a small "Port of Entry" system to inspect and tax industrial and commercial goods and services which are being imported at the borders and international ports. If so, such an agency would belong in the Department of Internal Affairs, working closely with the DoD to ensure those goods aren't missed.

Another important point is the illegal immigration issue. This problem exists for two basic reasons: Drug trafficking, and jobs. Legalizing drugs would implicitly bring a sudden and direct end to all illegal drug trafficking and put the cartels out of business overnight. The jobs will be taken care of by a variety of factors including the manufacturing base newly incentivized by the import tax, an end to the minimum wage, an end to most government regulations, and a vastly more robust economy. Eliminate and save **$12 Billion**.

Immigrations and Customs Enforcement (ICE)

U.S. Immigration and Customs Enforcement (ICE) is the principal investigative arm of the U.S. Department of Homeland Security (DHS) and the second largest investigative agency in the Federal Government.

There they go again, bragging about how big their little empire is. A contingent of background checkers can be considered necessary and proper to the immigration process, but this process must be greatly streamlined. People shouldn't wait a matter of years or even decades for their citizenship to go through. The Customs aspect can be merged into the Import Tax agency. Eliminate all embargoes to check for contraband. Move to the Department of Internal Affairs and cut by half, saving **$2.8 Billion**.

Transportation Security Administration (TSA)

The Aviation and Transportation Security Act established the Transportation Security Administration (TSA) to protect the transportation system and ensure the freedom of movement for people and commerce.

"I caught a terrorist!", said no TSA agent ever. It is easy to see the irony in an agency which claims to ensure freedom, by reducing freedoms. You can't travel by air anymore without being subjected to a choice between groping and irradiation. If that's what our idea of freedom has become, then I want no part of it.

Allow the airlines and private airports to secure their own property by allowing guns on airplanes. If guns had been allowed on 9-11, then the hijackers never would have made it two steps. Eliminate and save $7.6 Billion.

US Coast Guard (USCG)

Since 1790, the Coast Guard has safeguarded our Nation's maritime interests and natural resources on our rivers, in the ports, on the high seas, and in theaters around the world. The Coast Guard saves those in peril and protects the Nation's maritime transportation system, resources, and environment.

The Coast Guard is necessary and proper to defending the nation against invaders. Move back into the DoD and cut by the DoD's standard 25%, saving **$2.5 Billion**.

US Secret Service (USSS)

The United States Secret Service carries out a unique dual mission of protection and investigation. The Service protects the President, Vice President, other visiting heads of State and Government, and National Special Security Events (NSSEs); safeguards the Nation's financial infrastructure and payment systems to preserve the integrity of the economy; investigates electronic crimes; and protects the White House and other designated buildings within the Washington, D.C. area.

We should use currency that's not only backed by gold and silver, but which is *made* out of gold and silver. We should allow states to make their own money out of the same, and we should allow people to use alternate currencies if they so desire. By fixing the value of a dollar at so much gold or silver, we reduce the counterfeiting problem in that both can be easily detected, verified, and weighed by devices which can be bought by retail stores and banks.

A small contingent of trained defenders to protect the POTUS, VPOTUS, and the White House can be justified as necessary and proper to national defense, but that's it. If someone commits an electronic crime against you, report it to the local police and they should escalate or refer away as necessary. Move into the Department of Defense, cut by 75%, and save **$1.4 Billion**.

Federal Emergency Management Agency (FEMA)

The mission of the Federal Emergency Management Agency (FEMA) is to support our citizens and first responders to ensure that, as a Nation, we work together to build, sustain, and improve our capability to prepare for, protect against, respond to, recover from, and mitigate all hazards.

It is not physically possible to *"mitigate all hazards"*. FEMA, by providing disaster relief to the entire country, incentivizes people to build in disaster-prone areas where they *know* their structures are unlikely to persist. If you build a house in Tornado Alley, expect tornadoes. If you build on the side of an active volcano, expect lava in the living room. If you build below sea level, expect flooding.

In doing so, FEMA undermines the fundamental cost-benefit analysis essential to how insurance is supposed to work. Insurance companies are businesses, and thus need profit to thrive; but never at the expense of the taxpayer.

The Constitution provides no power to manage or alleviate natural disasters, so that power is reserved to the states respectively. Eliminate and save **$14 Billion**.

US Citizenship and Immigration Services (UCIS)

United States Citizenship and Immigration Services (USCIS) processes millions of immigration benefit applications every year through a network of 235 domestic and foreign offices.

Immigration should be a simple process of learning English and passing a background check. While parts of this background check can be automated, of course, documentation in many areas of the world is lackluster or altogether nonexistent. Some degree of investigation may therefore be justified.

Special consideration should not be given to refugees nor asylum applicants. They are immigrants, just like anyone else.

The Business Transformation line item seeks to convert from a paper to an electronic filing system. This is a necessary process, but would not qualify as a recurring cost and should thus be deducted from the recurring budget. One must wonder why they didn't convert sooner. $269 Million saved.

Most of what's in UCIS isn't actually explained in the budget. Move into the Department of Defense, cut the remainder by half and save **$1.6 Billion**.

Federal Law Enforcement Training Center (FLETC)

Over the past 42 years, the Federal Law Enforcement Training Center (FLETC) has grown into the Nation's largest provider of law enforcement training. FLETC trains approximately 90 Federal law enforcement agencies, and countless State, local, and tribal departments in such critical subjects as the use of force, defensive tactics, and constitutional law.

Given that the Constitution defines only four crimes to enforce laws against, it seems the federal government shouldn't be in the business of providing law enforcement training. Let the states run their own programs; eliminate and save $258 Million.

National Protection and Programs Directorate

The National Protection and Programs Directorate (NPPD) leads the Department's mission to reduce risk to the Nation's critical physical and cyber infrastructure through partnerships that foster collaboration and interoperability.

The nation has no physical infrastructures; they belong to the states. The "cyber" infrastructure is merely basic computer and network security which should be handled internally by whatever organization has the computers and networks that need to be secured. Eliminate and save $2.5 Million.

Office of Health Affairs

The Office of Health Affairs (OHA) serves as DHS's principal authority for all medical and health issues. OHA provides medical, public health, and scientific expertise in support of the DHS mission to prepare for, respond to, and recover from all threats.

If we eliminate the department, then there are no health affairs left to officiate. Eliminate and save $166 Million.

Science and Technology Directorate

The Science and Technology Directorate's (S&Ts) mission is to improve homeland security by working with partners to provide state-of-the-art technology and solutions that help them achieve their missions. S&T partners and customers include the operating Components of the Department, as well as State, local, tribal, and territorial emergency responders and officials.

The Constitution authorizes no research of any kind. The government should merely buy the products that come out of the industrial sector, possibly telling them ahead of time what they would want to buy. The Research and Development departments of those companies would likely develop such equipment and weapons in order to procure that juicy government money. The DoD already spends billions of dollars on preventing NBC attacks, so this is also a duplicate function. Eliminate and save $831 Million.

Domestic Nuclear Detection Office

The Domestic Nuclear Detection Office (DNDO) leads the development of the global nuclear detection architecture (GNDA), carries out the implementation of the domestic portion, and serves as the coordinator and steward technical nuclear forensics efforts across the Government.

Redundant to SBIRS, Advanced Tech Sensors, Nuclear Safety Administration, DTRA / DDTA Basic Research initiative, Enhanced Sensor and Monitoring System, and Nuclear Arms Control Monitoring Sensor Network. Eliminate and save $328 Million.

Conclusion

All in all, we've reduced the spending on DHS items from $55.38 Billion to $12.13 Billion, and reduced overhead and restored liberty in the process. A good day.

Department of Housing and Urban Development (HUD) [173]

Public and Indian Housing

The role of the Office of Public and Indian Housing is to ensure safe, decent, and affordable housing; create opportunities for residents' self-sufficiency and economic independence; and assure fiscal integrity by all program participants.[174]

You do not have a right to a house, nor even to a home of your own. You *do* have a right to take your money and try to buy or rent one. You *do* have a right to improve your own skills, and go look for a job. You do have a right to look for a home in your price range and with the safety level that you desire. The banks, realtors, and landlords have a right to say no.

A resident who depends on a government program just to get by is not self-sufficient. Your fiscal integrity is your own responsibility and nobody else's.

Public and Indian Housing consists of Tenant-Based Rental Assistance (Section 8, VA housing, grants, loans, and overhead) and is projected to cost **$26.5 Billion** in 2013. The government is supposed to be neither a bank nor a landlord.

Community Planning and Development

The Office of Community Planning and Development (CPD) seeks to develop viable communities by promoting integrated approaches that provide decent housing, a suitable living environment, and expand economic opportunities for low and moderate income persons. The primary means towards this end is the development of partnerships among all levels of government and the private sector, including for-profit and non-profit organizations.[175]

Community Planning and Development consists of grants, other funding programs, and loans at a cost of **$6.7 Billion**. The same objections apply.

Housing Programs

Public housing was established to provide decent and safe rental housing for eligible low-income families, the elderly, and persons with disabilities. Public housing comes in all sizes and types, from scattered single family houses to high-rise apartments for elderly families. There are approximately 1.2 million households living in public housing units, managed by some 3,300 HAs. The U.S. Department of Housing and Urban Development (HUD) administers Federal aid to local housing agencies (HAs) that manage the housing for low-income residents at rents they can afford. HUD furnishes technical and professional assistance in planning, developing and managing these developments.

---

[173] http://portal.hud.gov/hudportal/documents/huddoc?id=CombBudget2013.pdf
[174] http://portal.hud.gov/hudportal/HUD?src=/program_offices/public_indian_housing
[175] http://portal.hud.gov/hudportal/HUD?src=/program_offices/comm_planning

Housing Programs consists of yet more Section 8 project housing, support for old and disabled people, and insurance funds at a cost of **$9.6 Billion**. The same objections apply.

Governmental National Mortgage Association

A wholly owned government corporation, the Governmental National Mortgage Association (Ginnie Mae) is actually a direct landlord at a cost of **$21 Million**, with **$500 Billion** in allowed liabilities.

By guaranteeing all banks' loans, Ginnie Mae incentivizes sellers to increase their prices and banks to increase their fees. This is why housing prices have increased so sharply over time (the housing bubble of 2008 excepted) despite having so many on the market. There is no authority in the Constitution for the federal government to be, own, or operate a landlord; eliminate.

Conclusion

There are a few additional programs designed to enforce bans on lead paints and poisons and the like. **The department's overhead alone costs nearly $2 Billion.**

The Constitution bestows no federal power to provide or guarantee housing, nor the funding thereof, nor insurance on that funding, nor security to that insurance. There is no power to coddle and babysit millions of people, nor to discriminate for or against any specific groups thereof. Eliminate the entire department, relinquish all assets to the states in which they reside, and save **$524 Billion.**

That's over half a trillion dollars annually, 12% of all federal spending, gone. At the conclusion of the Ten Year Plan, the entire federal government would cost less than this one single department.

Department of Justice (DoJ)

Led by the Attorney General, the Department of Justice (DOJ or the Department) is comprised of 43 components that have a broad array of national security, law enforcement, and criminal justice system responsibilities. DOJ prosecutes federal law offenders and represents the U.S. Government in court; its attorneys represent the rights and interests of the American people and enforce federal criminal and civil laws, including antitrust, civil rights, environmental and tax laws; its Immigration Judges ensure speedy justice for immigrants in removal proceedings; its special agents investigate organized and violent crime, illegal drugs, gun and explosives violations; its deputy marshals protect the federal judiciary, apprehend fugitives and transport persons in federal custody; and its correctional officers confine convicted federal offenders, some of whom are illegal immigrants. DOJ also provides grants and training to state, local, and tribal law enforcement partners; and brings together national security, counterterrorism, counterintelligence, and foreign intelligence surveillance operations under a single authority.

The Constitution provides no federal power for most law enforcement. It mentions a total of four crimes and therefore enforcement against those four crimes is justified. Per the tenth amendment, all other law is left to the states. Therefore the DOJ's core competency of "prosecuting federal law offenders" would be greatly reduced. There really aren't many cases of piracy.

A good point could be made, however, that the Constitution decrees all moneys shall be gold or silver, and therefore all Federal Reserve notes are counterfeit. This is a case the DOJ should definitely prosecute.

Then we have treason and bribery. Since it's illegal to bribe politicians outright, the practice often occurs in the form of campaign contributions and reciprocal policy changes and government position appointments. The DOJ should investigate and prosecute these situations as bribery. The DOJ should also investigate the voting record and orders of all past and present federal elected officials, examine those decisions for constitutionality, and prosecute, reverse, and pardon accordingly. This is at the very core of the DOJ's real mission, and these are the only four true federal crimes.

Thomas Jefferson wrote, "The most sacred of the duties of government [is] to do equal and impartial justice to all its citizens." This sacred duty to fulfill the promise of justice for all remains the guiding ideal for the men and women of the Department in carrying out their mission.

Justice is essentially reciprocity for a wrong that has been done to someone by someone else. Therefore, if something wasn't done *to someone*, it's not a *true* crime and justice is irrelevant. There are two basic rules that we need to run a free society:

1. Do all that you agree to do.
2. Do not encroach on other people or their property.

Each of us would do well to adopt these two principles as our own personal moral code. No law should be passed which does not directly advance either, which the vast majority of laws, let alone at the federal level, do not.

Jefferson also stated:

*"If a law is unjust, a man is not only right to disobey it; he is **obligated** to do so."*

And

"Rightful liberty is unobstructed action according to our will within limits drawn around us by the equal rights of others. I do not add 'within the limits of the law' because law is often but the tyrant's will, and always so when it violates the rights of the individual."

It is up to each of us as free citizens to determine which laws are just, and which are not. If a law exists to control your behavior, and not to secure the rights of the people, then you should disobey it. This mentality is at the very core of freedom.

We must fundamentally reexamine the basis of law in this country. Laws which exist only to control behavior are unjust and therefore we are obligated to disobey -- or as I would prefer, to disregard them. One should of course not go looking for laws to break merely because they are unjust, but one should also not allow an unjust law to prevent one from acting according to his own will.

Of course the Constitution does define a court system, and indeed we need one. However, there are a number of unjust laws which by their very nature require no enforcement, let alone obedience. The fewer laws we have, the less they cost to enforce. The vast majority of federal laws should either be at the state or lower levels, or should not exist at all.

State, Local, and Tribal Law Enforcement Assistance
State, local, and tribal laws should be enforced by state, local, and tribal law enforcement. Enforcing state, local, and tribal laws is not a proper federal function and is not authorized by the Constitution; eliminate and save $189 Million.

General Administration

The primary mission of the GA appropriation is to support the Attorney General and DOJ senior policy level officials in managing Department resources and developing policies for legal, law enforcement, and criminal justice activities. GA also provides administrative support services to the legal divisions and policy guidance to all Department organizations.

By reducing the scope of federal law, we reduce the need for the enforcement thereof. Cut by standard 25% to start and save $32 Million.

Justice Information Sharing Technology

The JIST account provides information technology (IT) resources so that the Department's Chief Information Officer (CIO) may effectively coordinate enterprise-wide IT investments and ensure that infrastructure enhancements are well-planned and aligned with the Department's overall IT strategy and enterprise architecture.

Much of this can be done with a wiki, which is available for free, and should be public information anyway. This cyber security nonsense has gone far enough. Cut by half and save $17 Million.

Administrative Review and Appeals

Executive Office for Immigration Review

The mission of EOIR is to adjudicate immigration cases in a careful and timely manner, including cases involving detained aliens, criminal aliens, and aliens seeking asylum as a form of relief from removal, while ensuring the standards of due process and fair treatment for all.

If we streamline the immigration process, we should be able to reduce the need for this in that there would be less to review on each case, and maybe fewer cases needing review. Further, eliminating the minimum wage and ending the war on drugs should reduce the number of illegitimate immigrants somewhat. Cut by half and save $151 Million.

Office of Pardon Attorney

The Office of the Pardon Attorney, in consultation with the Attorney General or his designee, assists the President in the exercise of his executive clemency power as authorized under Article II, Section 2, of the Constitution.

The President has unilateral power to pardon anyone for any crime, except in cases of impeachment. This is a basic tenant of the legal system and requires no attorneys to be carried out. If the Congress objects to a pardon on legal grounds such as treason, then they have the power to impeach him. Eliminate and save $3 Million.

General Legal Activities

The cuts herein show a reduction of $499 Million in spending.

Office of the Solicitor General

> *The mission of the Office of the Solicitor General is to conduct all litigation on behalf of the United States and its agencies in the Supreme Court of the United States, to approve decisions to appeal and seek further review in cases involving the United States in the lower federal courts, and to supervise the handling of litigation in the federal appellate courts.*

A significant reduction in the number of federal laws would greatly reduce the need for litigation thereby initiated. Cut by 75% and save $3 Million.

Tax Division

> *The Tax Division's mission is to enforce the nation's tax laws fully, fairly, and consistently, through both criminal and civil litigation, in order to promote voluntary compliance with the tax laws, maintain public confidence in the integrity of the tax system, and promote the sound development of the law.*

A significant reduction in the size and scope of the Internal Revenue Code (tax law) would have a subsequent and commensurate reduction in the need to enforce it. There is no such thing as voluntary compliance with any law which is enforced through the initiation of force; all tax compliance is involuntary. The Tax Reform plan in this proposal eliminates the entire federal tax code and replaces it with much simpler systems which can be enforced by a small office in the Department of Internal Affairs, which in turn can employ its own lawyers. Eliminate and save $2 Million.

Criminal Division

> *The mission of the Criminal Division is to develop, enforce, and supervise the application of all federal criminal laws (except those specifically assigned to other divisions).*

A great reduction in the number of federal criminal laws would greatly reduce the need to enforce, supervise, and apply them. Only the Congress should actually develop these laws, and even then, within a much smaller scope.

The few constitutionally justified federal laws have their own enforcement organizations. State and local laws should be managed and enforced at the state and local levels without the need for federal involvement, and state and local law enforcement should not be held responsible for the enforcement of laws outside of their jurisdiction. Cut by half and save $87 Million.

Civil Division

> The Civil Division represents the United States, its departments and agencies, Members of Congress, Cabinet officers, and other federal employees in all civil matters. Its litigation reflects the diversity of government activities involving, for example, national security issues; benefit programs; energy policies; commercial issues, such as contract disputes, banking, insurance, patents, fraud, and debt collection; all manner of accident and liability claims; and criminal violations of immigration and consumer protection laws.

This seems pretty important, so let's keep it as is for the time being ($283 Million).

Environment and Natural Resources Division

> The Environment and Natural Resources Division's mission is to enforce civil and criminal environmental laws and programs protecting the public and environment of the United States and to defend suits challenging environmental programs and activities. property by eminent domain for congressionally authorized purposes.

Civil and criminal environmental laws should not exist at the federal level, as the environment is not mentioned in the Constitution. State and local legislatures should run their own programs, if their constituents so vote, and they should have their own police enforce their own laws.

The DOJ already has the Civil and Criminal divisions for handling any cases brought against the federal government, and most or all of those 150 statutes would disappear under this plan.

Repeal the acts mentioned therein, and let the states handle their own environments. If pollution or similar property encroachments happens across state lines, then the states themselves can escalate to the federal court system, as designed. Eliminate and save $110 Million.

Office of Legal Counsel

> The mission of OLC is to assist the Attorney General in his functions as legal advisor to the President and all of the Executive Branch agencies.

A significant reduction in the number of federal laws would mean the Attorney General could perform his duties without the need for 37 people to help him do so. Eliminate and save $8 Million.

Civil Rights Division

> CRT has three significant goals: (1) to fulfill the promise of federal laws entitling all persons to basic civil rights protections as they engage in everyday conduct through the United States; (2) to deter illegal conduct through the successful judicial enforcement of these federal laws; and (3) to promote voluntary compliance and civil rights protection through a variety of educational, technical assistance, and outreach programs.

The elimination of most federal laws would greatly reduce the need for the promises thereof. Keep in mind that segregation came about through the Jim Crowe laws; not through the will of individual businesses. As a business owner, landlord, or board member, you have a right to decide who you employ and who you allow on your land. Your reasons are irrelevant. Keep in mind, of course, that if you discriminate against groups which the general public disagrees with discrimination against, then you are likely to lose a lot of business from the other groups as well.

It is impossible to legislate morality. The government, however, should not discriminate in this fashion. Eliminate and save $115 Million.

INTERPOL Washington

> The mission of INTERPOL Washington is to provide the United States' federal, state, and local law enforcement authorities a central point of communication to the international law enforcement community, and to serve as the official U.S. representative to the International Criminal Police Organization (INTERPOL).

Federal cooperation with international law enforcement organizations can be thought of as justified in the context of treaties, so let's leave this in for now and get rid of it later if it causes problems ($32M).

Antitrust Division

> The mission of the Antitrust Division is to promote economic competition through enforcing and providing guidance on antitrust laws and principles.

In theory, antitrust laws prevent corporations from becoming too large and fixing prices, and encourage competition[176]. In reality, many corporations have become too large anyway. Any company should be allowed to determine their own prices. If the prices are too low, they won't make profit. If the prices are too high, nobody will buy the product or service. Look at the prices of gasoline over the past 20 years to see how ineffective this legislation is. Competition can

---

[176] http://en.wikipedia.org/wiki/United_States_antitrust_law

be encouraged more effectively simply by eliminating all laws (at all levels of government) which prevent people from starting up their own company. Eliminate and save $165 Million.

U.S. Attorneys

The United States Attorneys serve as the Nation's principal litigators under the direction of the Attorney General. Their offices bring criminal prosecutions, pursue civil penalties, defend federal programs and guard the financial interests of the United States in court. They also provide advice and counsel to the Attorney General and senior policy leadership through the Attorney General's Advisory Committee (AGAC) and its various subcommittees.

A great reduction in the number of federal laws would greatly reduce the litigation, penalties, and prosecution required thereby. There should be no lawyers to defend federal programs; this can be done on their websites and people can petition the government for their grievances through petitions and their congressmen. If your congressmen aren't voting as you think they should, then stop reelecting them! Cut by 75% and save **$1.5 Billion**.

U.S. Trustees

USTP's mission is to promote the integrity and efficiency of the bankruptcy system for the benefit of all stakeholders –debtors, creditors, and the public.

The Constitution directly authorizes the feds to decide how bankruptcy should be handled; keep as is ($227M).

Foreign Claims Settlement Commission

The principal mission of the FCSC is to adjudicate claims of U.S. nationals against foreign governments, exercising jurisdiction conferred by the International Claims Settlement Act of 1949, as amended, and other authorizing legislation.

Article III Section 2 of the Constitution extends the Judicial power to all cases between a state or the citizens thereof and foreign States, citizens, or subjects. Therefore this program is authorized; keep as is ($2 Million).

U.S. Marshals Service

The mission of the USMS is to enforce federal laws and support virtually all elements of the federal justice system by providing for the security of federal court facilities and the safety of judges and other court personnel; apprehending fugitives; exercising custody of federal prisoners and providing for their security and transportation to detention facilities; executing federal court orders; managing and disposing of the assets seized and forfeited by federal law enforcement agencies; and assuring the safety of protected government witnesses and their families.

A great reduction in the number of federal laws would reduce the need for enforcement thereof. Cut by half and save $600 Million.

Community Relations Service

Created by the Civil Rights Act of 1964, CRS serves as the Department's "peacemaker," dedicated to assisting state and local units of government, private and public organizations, and community groups to address community conflicts and tensions arising from differences of race, color, and national origin.

If you own land or a business, you have a right to decide who to allow on your land and what they're allowed to do there. As a citizen, you have a right to decide who you are willing to interact, socialize, and conduct business with.

Some degree of discrimination is an absolute right. If you're trying to hire someone to lift heavy things, then you should be allowed not to hire someone who is wheelchair-bound. If you're looking to hire a model, then you should be allowed to discriminate on gender and appearance. Not being allowed to choose the best person for the job would undermine the purpose of the job itself.

As for discrimination based purely on personal prejudices, you should be allowed to decide who you want to work with, do business with, allow in your place of business or on your land. Doing so unfairly would probably cost you so much business from the other groups that you'd go out of business. Segregation came from the Jim Crowe Laws, not from the people. Eliminate and save $12 Million.

Assets Forfeiture Fund

The AFF's mission is to enforce federal laws and prevent and reduce crime by disrupting, damaging and dismantling criminal organizations through the use of civil and criminal forfeiture. The program attempts to remove those assets that are essential to the operation of those criminal organizations and punish the criminals involved by denying them the use of the proceeds of their crimes.

A great reduction in the number of federal laws would reduce the need for the enforcement thereof. The largest organized crime organizations in history came about as a result of prohibition, which in turn was a clear infringement upon the rights of the people. One should wonder how much organized crime today is a result of laws which shouldn't exist in the first place, such as today's prohibition on marijuana, raw milk, large sodas, and old style light bulbs.

Further, the government should never take property away from anyone without due cause: As determined in court of law, or via the very few legitimate cases of Eminent Domain. Eliminate and save **$1.4 Billion**.

Interagency Crime and Drug Enforcement

The Interagency Crime and Drug Enforcement appropriation funds the Organized Crime Drug Enforcement Task Force (OCDETF) Program. The mission of OCDETF is to reduce the supply of illegal drugs in the United States and diminish the violence associated with the drug trade by dismantling and disrupting the most significant drug trafficking organizations and the financial infrastructure that supports them.

The feds have no constitutional power to tell you what you're allowed to do to your own body. If you make a bad decision, you should live with the consequences of that decision. By legalizing all drugs, this program becomes obsolete. Eliminate and save $525 Million.

Federal Bureau of Investigation

The mission of the FBI is to protect and defend the United States against terrorist and foreign intelligence threats, to uphold and enforce the criminal laws of the United States, and to provide leadership and criminal justice services to federal, state, municipal, and international agencies and partners.

Defending the United States against terrorist and foreign threats is the responsibility of the Department of Defense. Eliminating most federal criminal laws would reduce the need for enforcement of them. The Constitution does not say that it's the federal government's job to provide leadership of any kind. Intelligence threats are more than taken care of by the NSA, CIA, and DOD. Eliminate and save **$8.2 Billion**.

Drug Enforcement Administration

DEA's mission is to enforce the controlled substances laws and regulations of the United States and bring to the criminal and civil justice system of the United States, or any other competent jurisdiction, those organizations and principal members of organizations involved in the growing, manufacture, or distribution of controlled substances appearing in or destined for illicit traffic in the United States; and to recommend and support non-enforcement programs aimed at reducing the availability of illicit controlled substances on the domestic and international markets.

The feds have no constitutional power to tell you what you're allowed to do to your own body. If you make a bad decision, you should live with the consequences of that decision. By legalizing all drugs, this program becomes obsolete. Eliminate and save $2 Billion.

Bureau of Alcohol, Tobacco, Firearms, and Explosives

ATF protects our communities from violent criminals, criminal organizations, the illegal use and trafficking of firearms, the illegal use and storage of explosives, acts of arson and bombings, acts of terrorism, and the illegal diversion of alcohol and tobacco products.

Protecting cities and states from violent criminals is the responsibility of city and state police agencies. Inanimate objects do not cause crime, and what you put into your own body is a basic human right, not a crime. The Constitution does not provide any federal power to oversee the manufacturing, distribution, possession, or use of any of these four main items. Eliminate and save **$1.2 Billion**.

Federal Prison System

The mission of the Federal Bureau of Prisons is to protect society by confining offenders in the controlled environments of prisons and community-based facilities that are safe, humane, cost-efficient, appropriately secure, and provide work and other self-improvement opportunities to assist offenders in becoming law-abiding citizens.

Eliminating most federal laws would greatly reduce the number of people who need to be incarcerated. Most laws should be at the state or local levels, and they should have their own local and state jails to put offenders into.

High Treason should be punished by death, ideally in a public manner such as hanging or firing squad. The remaining few legitimate federal crimes, which are not covered and prosecuted at a lower level, could be valid for incarceration; but the number thereof would be greatly reduced. Cut by 90% and save **$6.2 Billion**.

Office of Justice Programs

The mission of OJP is to increase public safety and improve the fair administration of justice across America through innovative leadership and programs. OJP strives to make the nation's criminal and juvenile justice systems more responsive to the needs of state, local, and tribal governments and their citizens.

Public safety is the responsibility of informed and responsible citizens, and to a lesser extent, local and state law enforcement. State, local, and tribal governments should handle their own needs internally, as each level is sovereign in their own right. Eliminate and save **$2.5 Billion**.

Community Oriented Policing Services

The mission of the COPS Office is to advance the practice of community policing as an effective strategy to improve public safety.

Policing a community is the responsibility of the community itself. Eliminate and save $290 Million.

Office on Violence Against Women

The mission of the OVW is to provide federal leadership to reduce violence against women, and to support the administration of justice for and strengthen services to all victims of domestic violence, dating violence, sexual assault, and stalking.

Women are not a special interest group; they're citizens just like any man. Any such program should be targeted to reduce violence in general and not discriminate for or against individual groups of people.

If you see someone beating up on a woman, get a few guys together and go beat up on that guy. The same principle works if someone is beating up on a particularly wimpy man, machismo aside. This should be handled at the local level; eliminate and save $413 Million.

Fees and Expenses of Witnesses

The mission of the FEW appropriation is to provide funding for all fees and expenses associated with the provision of testimony on behalf of the Federal Government. Funding is also provided to pay for private and foreign counsel.

No court fees should ever be imposed on witnesses. A great reduction in the number of federal laws should reduce the number of witnesses whose testimony is needed in the first place. Cut by half and save $135 Million.

National Security Division

The mission of the National Security Division is to carry out the Department's highest priority: to combat terrorism and other threats to national security. The Division consolidates the primary national security elements of the Department of Justice into a single Division. Community on the other, thus strengthening the effectiveness of the Federal Government's national security efforts.

The Department of Justice's highest priority *should* be to carry out justice. Combatting terrorism is generally the responsibility of the DOD or local and state law enforcement. Combatting other national security threats is generally the responsibility of the DOD or the many other intelligence agencies around the government.

Of course, the best way to combat terrorism is to identify the reasons why it has sprung up over the past century in the first place. The proposed foreign policy reform should take care of most of that. Cut by 75% and save $68 Million.

Office of the Inspector General

> *The mission of the OIG is to investigate allegations of fraud, waste, abuse, and misconduct by Department employees, contractors, and grantees, and to promote economy and efficiency in Department operations.*

A necessary bit of overhead to run the department. Cut by standard 25% and save $22 Million.

U.S. Parole Commission

> *The mission of the U.S. Parole Commission (USPC) is to promote public safety and strive for justice and fairness in the exercise of its authority to release and supervise offenders under its jurisdiction.*

A great reduction in the number of federal laws would reduce the number of incarcerations, and subsequently the number of paroles. Cut by 75% and save $10 Million.

Conclusion

All items not in the DOJ budget must not be important enough to provide an explanation for. These programs include Independent Counsel, Radiation Exposure Compensation Trust Fund, Public Safety Officers' Death Benefits, Antitrust Pre-Merger Filing Fee Collections, Diversion Control Fee, and Healthcare Fraud Reimbursements.

The items in the DOJ's budget add up to $29.53 Billion. The federal President's Budget Overview allocates $222.444 billion. I was unable to identify where the remaining $192.9 Billion is directed; any money not in the budget is money which clearly doesn't need to be spent.

All proposed changes total $2.9 Billion, for a total reduction of $219.5 Billion.

Department of Labor (DoL)[177]

> *The Department of Labor (DOL) FY 2013 request is $12.0 billion in discretionary budget authority and 17,419 full-time equivalent employees (FTE). The FY 2013 budget request fully supports the Secretary's vision of good jobs for everyone as described in detail in the Department's Strategic Plan, which outlines the Department's strategic and outcome goals for fiscal years 2011 to 2016.*

Despite requesting $12 Billion in discretionary spending, the full DOL budget requests $102 Billion, and the department has enough people to populate a small city. These are indications of something which is simply too big for our own good.

You don't have a right to a job. You have a right to spend your time developing skills, and to go out into the world looking for jobs. Employers have a right to say no. Therefore it is not the government's responsibility to provide you with one.

The Constitution provides no federal power over employment, nor the internal practices thereof, nor to oversee the economy, nor to ensure competitiveness. For all these reasons and more, this department needs to disappear. Let's look into it in more detail.

Employment and Training Administration

> *Secretary of Labor Hilda L. Solis has established a vision for the Department of Labor of —good jobs for everyone. The Employment and Training Administration's (ETA) workforce programs have a critical role to play in realizing the Secretary's vision of good jobs. ETA provides high quality employment assistance, labor market information, job training, and income support [.]*

It is physically impossible for everyone to have a good job. There are bad jobs out there which still need to be done. Nobody wants to grow up to flip burgers or clean up garbage, but someone has to do it. Governments do not provide jobs, nor is ensuring the goodness of those jobs a proper federal function.

Adult Employment and Training Activities

> *The Adult Program under Title I of the Workforce Investment Act (WIA) of 1998 provides employment and workforce development services to adults, including low-income adults, to increase their incomes through occupational and related*

---

[177] http://www.dol.gov/dol/budget

skills acquisition. The WIA Adult program prepares workers – particularly disadvantaged, low-skilled, and underemployed adults – for good jobs.

Formula grants totaling $769 Million. Taking care of poor people is not a constitutionally authorized power. As this proposal eliminates all grants, we save this amount.

Youth Employment and Training Activities

Title I of the Workforce Investment Act (WIA) of 1998 authorizes the WIA Youth program. The WIA Youth program aligns with the Secretary's goals of preparing workers for good jobs and assuring the skills and knowledge that prepare workers to succeed in a knowledge-based economy. The program targets low-income youth with barriers to employment and provides them with services that prepare them for employment and post-secondary education.

Preparing workers for the workforce is not the government's job; eliminate and save $824 Million.

Dislocated Worker Employment and Training Activities

The Dislocated Worker Assistance Program under Title I of the Workforce Investment Act (WIA) of 1998 serves to meet the complementary needs of displaced workers and employers.

The Constitution does not provide federal power for meeting the individual needs of any specific groups, nor to employ or train people. Eliminate and save $1.2 Billion.

Workforce Innovation Fund

In an increasingly competitive world economy, America's economic strength depends on the education and skills of its workers. The Federal government currently invests over $16 billion annually in employment and training programs designed to support an efficiently functioning labor market and economy.

The Constitution does not authorize the federal government to educate or manage the skills of workers, to train, nor to support a market or economy. Eliminate and save $100 Million.

Indian and Native American Programs

The Indian and Native American Program (INAP) is authorized by Section 166 of the Workforce Investment Act (WIA) of 1998.

If Native Americans desire citizenship, grandfather them in and allow to participate in the national economy. If not, let them stay in their tribes and live as they so choose. This program discriminates against people who aren't Native Americans; eliminate and save $53 Million.

Migrant and Seasonal Farmworkers

The National Farmworker Jobs Program (NFJP) provides job training and employment assistance for migrant and seasonal farmworkers (MSFW) and their dependents to counter the impact of the chronic unemployment and underemployment experienced by MSFWs.

The government is not an employment agency. The Constitution provides no federal power to train people or help them find a job. This program discriminates against people who aren't migrants and seasonal farmworkers. Eliminate and save $84 Million.

Women in Apprenticeship

Over the past few years, Congress has appropriated approximately $1,000,000 annually for the Women in Apprenticeship and Non-Traditional Occupations Act (WANTO) of 1992 (Public Law 102-530).

No funds are requested for this program, so we can probably get rid of it on that point alone. It discriminates against men, and against women who aren't in apprenticeships. Government services at all levels should be provided to everyone, or not at all. Eliminate and save nothing this year ($996K in 2012).

YouthBuild

The YouthBuild program is a workforce development program that provides significant academic and occupational skills training, and leadership development to youth ages 16-24.

All academic programs belong under the Department of Education, which this proposal eliminates, because academic programs are not authorized by the Constitution. Neither are skill training, leadership development, or education as a whole. Eliminate and save $80 Million.

Pilots Demonstrations and Research

Pilot, Demonstration, and Research (PD&R) activities are authorized under Section 171 of the Workforce Investment Act (WIA) of 1998. Under Section 171, the Employment and Training Administration (ETA) conducts pilot, demonstration, and research activities that support key areas of program and policy emphasis, inform workforce investment policies and investment decisions, and support continuous improvement of the workforce investment system.

If we eliminate the department, then there is nothing left for it to pilot, demonstrate, or research. The Constitution authorizes no research of any kind. Eliminate and save zero due to lack of funding ($7 Million in 2012).

Reintegration of Ex-Offenders

> The Reintegration of Ex-Offenders (RExO) program is carried out through authrority provided in Section 171 of the Workforce Investment Act of 1998 for both Adult Ex-Offender grants and Youthful offender grants, and Section 212 of the Second Chance Act of 2007 for adult offenders.

This program discriminates against people who haven't been convicted of a crime, which is most of us. Since the Constitution provides no authority for it, we can eliminate it and save $85 Million.

Evaluations

> As authorized under Section 172 of the Workforce Investment Act (WIA) of 1998, the Employment and Training Administration (ETA) carries out evaluations related to programs and activities authorized by Title I of WIA.

If we repeal WIA and eliminate the ETA, then there is nothing left to evaluate. Eliminate and save nothing due to funding level ($10 Million in 2012).

Workforce Data Quality Initiative

> This initiative provides competitive grants to support the development and enhancement of longitudinal data systems that integrate education and workforce data. The grants are provided under the research authority in Section 171 of the Workforce Investment Act of 1998 (Public Law 105-220).

Eliminate all federal grants. If we accept that education and employment are not proper federal functions, then the need to measure the data thereof is obsoleted. Eliminate and save $6 Million.

Job Training for Employment in High Growth Industries

> To address the Secretary's goal of preparing workers for good jobs and ensuring fair compensation, the Job Training for Employment in High Growth Industries Grants are designed to provide training for workers according to need in different sectors of the economy. The funding for this program is provided from H-1B fees.

If we accept that the Constitution provides no power to train or educate anyone, then it stands to reason that lack of power extends to people who aren't even citizens. Training foreigners to take American jobs can only hurt the American unemployment figures. **This program discriminates against Americans and costs American jobs.** Eliminate and save $125 Million.

Office of Job Corps

Job Corps is an intensive education and vocational training program that helps eligible at-risk youth, ages 16-24, with academic and career technical training to prepare them for opportunities to enter the workforce, the military or enroll in postsecondary education.

The Constitution provides no authority to educate or train, and this office discriminates against everyone who isn't between 16 and 24. Eliminate and save **$1.6 Billion**.

Community Service Employment for Older Americans

The Community Service Employment for Older Americans (CSEOA) program is the only Federally-funded program dedicated to serving unemployed low-income seniors, and is more commonly known as the Senior Community Service Employment Program (SCSEP).

This program requests no 2013 funding, so it must not be very important. The government is not an employment agency. Eliminate ($448 Million in 2012).

Federal Unemployment Benefits and Allowances

The program, collectively referred to as Trade Adjustment Assistance or TAA, provides assistance to workers who have been adversely affected by foreign trade.

The Constitution does not authorize assistance of any kind for workers for any reason, and this program discriminates against people who haven't been adversely affected by foreign trade. Eliminate and save **$1.4 Billion**.

TAA Community College and Career Training Grant Fund

The Trade Adjustment Assistance Community College and Career Training (TAACCT) program is authorized by Division B of the American Recovery and Reinvestment Act of 2009 (P.L. 111-152), and the Health Care and Education Reconciliation Act of 2010 provided the program with $500,000,000 annually in Fiscal Years 2011–2014 for competitive grants to eligible institutions of higher education.

All education programs belong under the Department of Education, which this proposal eliminates, because the Constitution provides no federal power to provide education of any kind for any reason. The government is not a community college. Eliminate and save $500 Million.

State Unemployment Insurance and Employment Service Operations

The State Unemployment Insurance and Employment Service Operations (SUIESO) account provides funding to support the Unemployment Insurance system, including State Administration, Reemployment and Eligibility Assessments, and National Activities.

The Constitution provides no authority to give money to people just because they don't have a job. Unfortunately, under recent administrations a huge number of people have become dependent on this program, many on a very long term basis. Therefore Unemployment Insurance shall be put on the Ten Year Plan. It can operate out of the Department of Internal Affairs during the decade of its demise. The remainder of this program consists of grants, certifications, and overhead which we can just outright eliminate. **$4 Billion** saved.

State Paid Leave Fund

The State Paid Leave Fund will provide funds to support States that wish to establish paid leave programs. Currently, California and New Jersey offer such programs, which they call family leave insurance. In these two states, the programs are State-run insurance programs financed by employer and/or employee contributions, and they offer up to six weeks of benefits to workers for reasons covered under the Family and Medical Leave Act who must take time off to care for a seriously ill child, spouse, or parent, or bond with a newborn or recently adopted child. Research suggests that paid leave programs can enhance job retention for many workers and help workers stay on their career paths.

If a state wishes to establish a program, then that state should fund its own program through its own state taxes. This program is brand-new in 2013. Eliminate and save $5 Million.

Program Administration

The Program Administration (PA) account finances staff for leadership, policy direction, provision of technical assistance to the system, funds management, and administration of the following programs authorized by the Workforce Investment Act (WIA): Adult, Dislocated Worker, Youth, Workforce Information, National Activities, the Indian and Native American Program, and the Migrant and Seasonal Farmworker Program.

If we eliminate the programs, then there is nothing left to administer. Eliminate and save $148 Million.

Employee Benefits Security Administration

The Employee Benefits Security Administration (EBSA) protects the integrity of pensions, health, and other employee benefits for more than 140 million people. EBSA is charged with administering and enforcing the Employee

Retirement Income Security Act (ERISA) of 1974 as amended and related federal civil and criminal laws.

Employee benefits are part of a contract between an employer and an employee. Contract law is well-established and well-enforced without the need for an administration to do so. If your employer denies you a benefit which you have paid for, sue them. If your employer simply refuses to offer a benefit which you want, then quit. Eliminate and save $183 Million.

Pension Benefit Guaranty Corporation

The Pension Benefit Guaranty Corporation (PBGC) is a wholly-owned government entity established under the Employee Retirement Income Security Act of 1974 as amended. The Corporation's mission is to guarantee the pension benefits of workers who face the loss of retirement income if plan sponsors terminate their plans or take actions that endanger the continuation of those pensions.

The government should not own corporations. If you have a contract with a sponsor and they terminate the plan, then sue them under contract law. The existence of this program is incentive for those providers to do exactly that. Eliminate and save **$7 Billion**.

Wage and Hour Division

The Wage and Hour Division (WHD) was created by the Fair Labor Standards Act (FLSA) of1938. WHD is responsible for the administration and enforcement of a wide range of laws, which collectively cover virtually all private and State and local government employment - over 135 million workers in more than 7.3 million establishments throughout the United States and its territories.

The minimum wage is a symptom of an economy which suffers from inflation and forces companies to pay employees more than they are worth. Minimum wage jobs pay so little because they can be done by literally anyone; the employee provides almost no benefit to the company whatsoever. If you don't want to work for the amount you are offered, simply refuse the job and look elsewhere. Go develop some skills. If you aren't paid what you are promised, then sue the employer under contract law. State and local government employment should be handled from within the state and local governments. Eliminate and save $238 Million.

Office of Federal Contract Compliance Programs

In 1965, President Johnson issued Executive Order 11246, which directs federal departments and agencies to include non-discrimination and affirmative action requirements in all federal contracts, including federally assisted construction contracts. Pursuant to that direction, the Secretary of Labor created the Office of Federal Contract Compliance within the Department of Labor (DOL), which was later renamed the Office of Federal Contract Compliance Programs (OFCCP). OFCCP is comprised of a national office and six regional offices distributed nationwide.

Executive Orders do not create law; however, the government absolutely shouldn't discriminate as stated. The federal government should not assist any construction projects, except the direct funding for federal projects themselves. Private employers should be allowed to decide who they hire, businesses should be allowed to decide who's allowed to do business with them, and landowners should be allowed to decide who's allowed on their land. Eliminate and save $106 Million.

Office of Labor Management Standards

The Office of Labor-Management Standards (OLMS) is responsible for administering and enforcing most provisions of the Labor-Management Reporting and Disclosure Act of 1959, as amended (LMRDA) (P.L. 86-257), 29 U.S.C. 401. The LMRDA ensures basic standards of democracy and fiscal responsibility in labor organizations representing employees in private industry. OLMS does not have jurisdiction over unions representing solely state, county, or municipal employees. OLM

If we repeal the Act, then there is nothing left to enforce. If people want to group together and elect an individual to speak for the whole, I fully support that. If they want to call it a union, so be it. If those individuals and companies choose to negotiate, so be it. The government should never be involved in this perfectly natural process. Eliminate and save $42 Million.

Office of Workers' Compensation Programs

The Office of Workers' Compensation Programs (OWCP) advances the Secretary's vision of —good jobs for everyone through the administration of four benefit programs for workers who become ill or are injured on the job. These programs ensure income support for these workers when work is impossible or unavailable due to their injury or illness.

The government is not an insurance company. Eliminate and save **$6 Billion**.

Special Benefits

The Special Benefits fund provides funding for benefits under both the Federal Employees' Compensation Act (FECA) and the Longshore and Harbor Workers' Compensation Act (Longshore). The FECA program provides workers' compensation coverage to three million Federal and Postal workers around the world for employment-related injuries and occupational diseases.

The government is not an insurance company. Eliminate and save **$3.4 Billion**.

Administrative Expenses, Energy Employees Occupational Illness Compensation Fund

This appropriation funds administrative expenses for Part B of the Energy Employees Occupational Illness Compensation Program Act (EEOICPA). All EEOICPA benefits plus administrative expenses for Part E are funded through indefinite appropriations.

If we repeal the Act, then there are no further expenses to fund. The government is not an insurance company; eliminate and save **$1.4 Billion**.

Special Benefits for Disabled Coal Miners

The Black Lung Benefits Act Part B authorizes Federal benefits to former coal mine workers who are totally disabled by occupational pneumoconiosis and their dependent survivors for claims filed on or before December 31, 1973. These monetary benefits support the Secretary's vision of good jobs for everyone and Strategic Goal 4: Secure health benefits and, for those not working, provide income security by providing income support for those who are unable to work.

The government is not an insurance company, nor is it responsible for securing your income. Giving free money to people who aren't working does not promote jobs, despite the secretary's vision. Eliminate and save $163 Million.

Black Lung Disability Trust Fund

The Black Lung Disability Trust Fund (BLDTF) was established by the Black Lung Benefits Revenue Act of 1977 to assign responsibility for Black Lung benefit payments with the coal industry. The payment of benefits provides income support and medical care for beneficiaries who are unable to perform their previous coal mine work due to occupational lung disease.

The government is not an insurance company, nor is it responsible for securing income. Eliminate and save $308 Million.

Occupational Safety and Health Administration (OSHA)

OSHA's mission, as defined in its authorizing legislation (P.L. 91-596, the Occupational Safety and Health Act of 1970), is to assure, so far as possible, safe and healthful working conditions for every working man and woman in the American workplace.

The Constitution provides no federal authority to mandate how a company is run, nor to ensure that all workplaces are pristine clean and perfectly safe. Eliminate and save $565 Million.

Mine Safety and Health Administration

The Mine Safety and Health Administration (MSHA) protects the safety and health of the nation's miners through enforcement of the Federal Mine Safety and Health Act of 1977 (Mine Act), as amended by the Mine Improvement and New Emergency Response Act of 2006 (MINER Act).

The Constitution does not authorize the government to protect the safety and health of workers against the problems caused by their jobs. If you aren't willing to live in a dangerous and unhealthy environment, then don't work in one. Eliminate and save $372 Million.

Bureau of Labor Statistics

The Bureau of Labor Statistics (BLS) produces some of the Nation's most sensitive and important economic data. The BLS is an independent national statistical agency within the Department of Labor responsible for measuring labor market activity, working conditions, and price changes in the economy. It collects, analyzes, and disseminates essential economic information to support public and private decision-making. These policies and decisions affect virtually all Americans.

There is no such thing as "sensitive economic data". Market activity, working conditions, and price changes are none of the federal government's business, and there is no constitutional power to measure them. What little authority there is can be found in the Bureau of the Census, which this proposal moves from the Department of Commerce to the Department of Internal Affairs. Eliminate and save $618 Million.

Office of Disability Employment Policy

ODEP develops policy and fosters its implementation to reduce barriers to employment for people with disabilities. This includes a continuation of the $12,000,000 investment, matched by an equal amount from the Employment and Training Administration (ETA) to build on a collaborative effort under the Disability Employment Initiative (DEI) to build disability service capacity in the Workforce Investment Act One-Stop system.

The federal government should never create entities which have a blank check to create blanket nationwide policies. All of the things which are really necessary to run the federal government are important enough to be done directly by the congress. The government is not an insurance company. Eliminate and save $39 Million.

Departmental Management

The Act to Establish the Bureau of Labor, 1884, was amended by the Act of 1913 to establish the Department of Labor (29 U.S.C. 1); this act also authorizes Departmental Management (DM) functions. The DM Salaries and Expenses (S&E) appropriation is responsible for formulating and overseeing the implementation of Departmental policy and management activities.

If we eliminate the department, then there is nothing left to manage. Eliminate and save $374 Million.

DOL IT Modernization

The FY 2013 request supports $21,852,000 for ongoing IT investments in the IT Modernization appropriation. This account includes activities for IT Infrastructure Modernization and Departmental Support Systems and is managed by the Department's Chief Information Officer.

If we eliminate the department, then there is nothing left to modernize. Eliminate and save $22 Million.

Veterans' Employment and Training Service

The Veterans' Employment and Training Service (VETS) provides veterans and transitioning service members with the resources and services to succeed in the civilian workforce by maximizing their employment opportunities, protecting their employment rights, and meeting labor market demands with qualified veterans.

Veterans have no more right to a job than anyone else. Some already leave with retirement or disability pay, and they're already covered under Veterans' Administration benefits. Eliminate and save $259 Million.

Conclusion

There are no constitutional programs within the Department of Labor. Therefore, the entire department can be eliminated to save **$102 Billion**. Unemployment Insurance remains on the Ten Year Plan at $3 Billion, and will go away in a decade under this proposal as states transition in their own programs.

Department of State (DoS)[178]

Function 150 and Other International Programs

Administration of Foreign Affairs

Diplomatic and Consular Programs

The FY 2013 enduring budget request for Diplomatic and Consular Programs (D&CP) – the State Department's principal operating appropriation – totals $7.1 billion. The request provides core funding for the people, infrastructure, and programs necessary to conduct official U.S. relations with foreign governments and international organizations, as well as to provide services to American citizens, support U.S. businesses, and reach foreign audiences through public diplomacy. The funding enables the Department to fulfill its mandates as a national security institution and engage other nations worldwide to advance American interests and values.

Many other countries are less stable than the United States. Sending people over there introduces threats like militants, insurgents, protesters, and people who just want to harm or get rid of us. The disaster in Benghazi gives testament to the DoS's inability or unwillingness to secure their embassies. What purpose do these embassies serve? How many of them are actually helping the cause of peace?

Having an installation in unstable countries increases the likelihood of an international incident, which as we've seen, tends to happen **at** the installation. Are these countries' internal affairs really any of our business?

We should reduce the number of embassies we hold in foreign countries to only those countries which are major trade partners or allies. Countries like Japan, Canada, and England. Perhaps one embassy would suffice for all of Europe.

This agency is riddled with redundant programs and programs which have not resolved the problems they set out to resolve. Cut by 75% and save **$5.3 Billion**.

Capital Investment Fund

The FY 2013 request for the Capital Investment Fund (CIF) provides $83.3 million to continue making essential investments enabling the conduct of modern business practices in Information Technology (IT) as it relates to

---

[178] http://www.state.gov/documents/organization/181061.pdf

foreign affairs. All State Department programs depend on IT, from simple e-mail to specialized systems.

A massive reduction in the scope of the DoS means a commensurate reduce in the need for investment in their IT infrastructure. Cut by half and save $42 Million.

Border Security Program

The FY 2013 request provides $2.3 billion for the Border Security Program (BSP). The BSP helps protect and assist American citizens abroad and strengthens the security of U.S. borders by preventing the entry of terrorists or others intending to engage in criminal activity in the United States.

Border security is critical to national security (though the entire Visa system needs to be rethought); leave as is.

Working Capital Fund

The Working Capital Fund does not receive direct appropriations. Revenues are generated in the Working Capital Fund (WCF) from goods and services provided to appropriated fund accounts of the Department and other federal agencies.

If you don't receive direct appropriations, then you don't need this appropriation. Eliminate and save **$1.3 Billion.**

Embassy Security, Construction, and Maintenance

The Bureau of Overseas Buildings Operations (OBO), funded through the Embassy Security, Construction, and Maintenance (ESCM) appropriation, is responsible for providing U.S. Diplomatic and Consular missions overseas with secure, safe, and functional facilities to assist them in achieving the foreign policy objectives of the United States.

A massive reduction in our global footprint means we can stop building new embassies. The government should have no foreign policy objectives. Cut by half and save $819 Million.

Conflict Stabilization Operations

The FY 2013 request provides $56.5 million for Conflict Stabilization Operations (formerly known as Civilian Stabilization Initiative). Funding for this appropriation will enable the Department to continue to build a civilian capability to prevent and respond to 21st century crises and conflicts.

Stablizing other countries' conflicts is not our problem. Eliminate and save $57 Million.

Office of Inspector General
Overhead associated with internal fraud in the department. Eliminate and save $116 Million.

Educational and Cultural Exchange Programs

The FY 2013 request for Educational and Cultural Exchange Programs (ECE) provides $587.0 million for exchanges to promote mutual understanding between the people of the United States and other countries. Exchanges communicate U.S. values and develop future leaders at home and abroad with a global perspective and individual connections worldwide.

Foreign people and our people do not need government facilitation to understand each other; the Internet allows us to talk directly to each other. Somehow I doubt the DoS is communicating accurate values. Eliminate and save $587 Million.

Representation Allowances

Representational functions convey U.S. foreign policy goals and objectives in both bilateral and multilateral fora. The Department is concentrating on representational activities that support U.S. positions on multilateral trade and economic development issues pending before the European Union (EU), the Association of Southeast Asian Nations (ASEAN), the Asia-Pacific Economic Cooperation (APEC), Central American Free Trade Agreement (CAFTA), Free Trade of the Americas (FTAA), African Growth and Opportunity Acts (AGOA) and the North American Free Trade Agreement (NAFTA).

By reducing our global footprint, we can reduce the need for these forums. We need to rethink fundamentally our stance on treaties with other countries, and the content thereof. Cut by half and save $3.7 Million.

Protection of Foreign Missions and Officials

The FY 2013 request of $28.2 million will help provide extraordinary protection of international organizations and foreign missions and officials in the United States. Of the total, $23.7 million will be used to reimburse the New York Police Department and the surrounding areas with $4.5 million for the rest of the United States.

The need for this is pretty obvious, though I don't understand why those countries can't provide their own security. Keep as is.

Emergencies in the Diplomatic and Consular Service

The FY 2013 request of $9.5 million will help meet unforeseen emergencies and other requirements in the conduct of foreign affairs. This appropriation funds emergency evacuations of American citizens and U.S. Government officials due *to civil unrest, natural disasters, or health concerns, including viral epidemics. The appropriation also pays rewards for information related to international terrorism, narcotics trafficking, and certain war crimes tribunals.*

By decriminalizing all drugs, we eliminate the need for some parts of this. Cut by 10% and save $930 Million.

Payment to the American Institute in Taiwan

The FY 2013 request of $37.2 million will fund the State Department's payment to AIT to provide economic, commercial, and agricultural services, cultural and information programs, and travel documents and services for Americans and the people of Taiwan. Of this amount, $15.3 million is to replace lost visa revenue due to Taiwan's expected entry into the Visa Waiver Program.

We are not responsible for providing any services to Taiwan. Eliminate and save $1.8 Million.

International Organizations

Contributions to International Organizations

The FY 2013 request for Contributions to International Organizations (CIO) is $1.57 billion. The requested funds will pay assessed contributions for U.S. membership in the United Nations (UN) and over 40 other international organizations. For most of these organizations, the commitment to pay assessed contributions results from treaties and conventions that the United States has signed and ratified.

By withdrawing from these organizations, especially the UN nad NATO, these fees and contributions become obsolete. Eliminate and save **$1.6 Billion**.

These memberships include the International Rubber Study Group, Seed Testing Association, and Protection of New Varieties of Plants. That should tell you something about where your tax money is going.

Contributions for International Peacekeeping Activities

The FY 2013 request of $2.1 billion for Contributions for International Peacekeeping Activities (CIPA) provides funding to pay the U.S. share of assessed expenses for UN peacekeeping missions. The funding will help support international peacekeeping operations worldwide, including critical UN missions in Darfur, the Democratic Republic of the Congo, Sudan, Haiti, Lebanon, and Liberia.

You cannot keep peace in locations where peace does not exist; there is no peace to be kept. The internal affairs of other countries are not our business. Eliminate and save **$2.1 Billion**.

International Commissions (Function 300)

International Boundary and Water Commission

> *The International Boundary and Water Commission (IBWC) is a treaty-based organization comprised of U.S. and Mexican Sections. The sections exercise respective national rights and obligations under U.S.-Mexico boundary and water treaties and related agreements and develop binational solutions to boundary and water problems arising along the 1,952-mile border.*

The kind of treaties that we should sign are the kind that do not create organizations or obligations. Treaties do not create rights. Boundary solutions should be solved through other means as addressed elsewhere in this book. America has plenty of water, and Mexico's water is not our problem. Eliminate and save $77 Million.

Related Programs

The Asia Foundation

> *The FY 2013 request provides $32.8 million for International Fisheries Commissions (IFC) to fund the U.S. share of operating expenses for ten international fisheries commissions, the International Whaling Commission, two international marine science organizations, the Arctic Council, the Antarctic Treaty, and international shark and sea turtle conservation initiatives.*

Fisheries, sharks, and sea turtles are not government issues. Eliminate and save $33 Million.

Center for Middle Eastern – Western Dialog

> *The Center for Middle Eastern-Western Dialogue was established by the Congress to further scholarship and implement programs to open channels of communication and deepen cross-cultural understanding between the United States and nations with predominantly Muslim populations.*

When you invade and bomb a country, install dictators, and tell its people how to live, they'll hate you for it. That doesn't take much understanding or communication to figure out.

The people of two countries can communicate with and understand each other better than ever thanks to the Internet; this process requires no government facilitation. We should not create agencies or treaties based on their religions. The government should not operate programs specifically to generate income. Eliminate and save $15 Million.

Eisenhower Exchange Fellowship Program

The Eisenhower Exchange Fellowship Program builds international understanding by bringing rising leaders to the United States, and sending their American counterparts abroad, on custom designed professional programs. The program's trust fund will provide an estimated $449,000 in interest earnings in FY 2013 to support these exchanges.

Here we have yet another understanding program; do you see a theme here? We don't need foreign leaders here, and they don't need our leaders over there. Eliminate and save $449K.

Israeli Arab Scholarship Program

The Israeli Arab Scholarship Program funds scholarship programs for Israeli Arabs to attend institutions of higher education in the United States. The program's trust fund will provide an estimated $374,000 in interest earnings in FY 2013 to support such activities.

We have absolutely nothing to gain by bringing foreigners into our schools. If they want to go to an American school, they can pay for it themselves. Eliminate and save $374K.

East-West Center

The Center for Cultural and Technical Interchange between East and West was established by the Congress in 1960 to promote understanding and good relations between the United States and the nations of the Asia-Pacific region. Located in Hawaii, the East-West Center has engaged more than 55,000 participants in its programs since its inception, including at the highest political levels in some nations. It can draw on extensive individual and institutional ties to work effectively on critical regional issues.

More unnecessary understanding and relations. Eliminate and save $11 Million.

National Endowment for Democracy

The National Endowment for Democracy (NED) was established by the Congress in 1983 to strengthen democratic institutions around the world. Through a worldwide grants program, NED assists those working abroad to build democratic institutions and spread democratic values.

Eliminate all federal grants. For examples of our success in sending democracy overseas, look at Iraq, Afghanistan, Vietnam, Korea, Libya, and Egypt. Eliminate and save $104 Million.

Related Agencies

Broadcasting Board of Governors

The FY 2013 request provides $711.5 million for International Broadcasting Operations. Through this appropriation, the Broadcasting Board of Governors (BBG) funds operations of its broadcasting organizations, as well as related program delivery and support activities.

The government has no business broadcasting anything, or controlling broadcasts; let alone in other countries. Eliminate and save $720 Million.

United States Institute of Peace

The United States Institute of Peace (USIP) is an independent, nonpartisan institution established and funded by the Congress. Its goals are to help prevent and resolve violent international conflicts, promote post-conflict stability and development, and increase conflict management capacity, tools, and intellectual capital worldwide.

The first step in establishing peace is to stop invading and bombing other countries. Given its record, our government is in no position to preach about how to bring about peace.

Foreign Operations and Related Programs

United States Agency for International Development (USAID)

The Quadrennial Diplomacy and Development Review (QDDR) calls for "elevating American 'civilian power' to better advance our national interests and be a better partner with the U.S. military."

Our national interests are best served by leaving other countries alone, and an increasing number of American civilians are realizing this. As much as 40% of aid to Afghanistan is said to have found its way back to donor countries through contracts and inflated costs. USAID has been accused of allowing its bidding process to be unduly influenced by political and financial interests of the then-current Presidential administration.

USAID is one of the government's ways to further its internal agenda of sending money to the dictators we like while the DoD and CIA kill the ones we don't like. By extension, we reward countries based on politics instead of furthering the cause of peace, like USAID and DoS were meant to do. USAID is known to keep a close relationship with the CIA, and CIA agents are known to operate abroad under USAID cover. [179]

USAID was convicted of influencing political "reform" in Brazil in a way that purposely benefited specific parties. A USAID contractor was arrested in Cuba in 2009 under suspicion of espionage and importing prohibited equipment to Cuban dissidents. Therefore, clearly some of our overseas Prisoners of War are through our own fault and not that of the countries in which they operate.

USAID is known to influence United Nations proceedings by directing foreign aid in illicit ways. A country's membership in the UN Security Council can cause it to receive a considerable raise in U.S. assistance. For all these reasons and more, eliminate USAID and save **$1.5 Billion** in operating costs alone.

Independent Agencies

Peace Corps

In 1961, President John F. Kennedy launched an innovative program to spearhead progress in developing countries and to promote world peace and friendship between the American people and peoples overseas. Fr

Other countries' development is their own business; not ours. The most effective way to spearhead friendship with outer peoples is to leave them alone. Stop bombing them, invading them, installing dictators, telling them how to live, and giving money to their dictators. Eliminate and save $375 Million.

Treasury Technical Assistance and Debt Restructuring

The FY 2013 request would enable OTA to maintain its current footprint of technical assistance programs globally. OTA helps finance ministries and central banks of developing countries strengthen their capacity to manage public finances and mobilize domestic resources. OTA also helps countries develop anti-money laundering regimes and fight corruption.

The Constitution provides no authority to provide global technical assistance programs, nor to run their finance ministries and central banks. We've seen the damage the Federal Reserve has done to our own country, sending tens of trillions of dollars to other countries instead of helping our own economy, endless inflation, and artificial control over interest rates. Is this the kind of "progress" we're instilling in the poor countries of Africa? It's no wonder their economies stagnate. Eliminate and save $275 Million.

---

[179] http://en.wikipedia.org/wiki/United_States_Agency_for_International_Development

International Security Assistance

International Narcotics Control and Law Enforcement

> *INCLE funded programs seek to close the gaps between law enforcement jurisdictions and strengthen law enforcement institutions that are weak or corrupt. Significant INCLE funds are focused where security situations are most dire, and where U.S. resources are used in tandem with host country government strategies in order to maximize impact.*

By decriminalizing or legalizing drugs, narcotics are no longer our problem. If it's legal to manufacture drugs within the United States, the international traffic problem will go away simply because domestic product would be cheaper to buy. Eliminate and save **$1.5 Billion**.

Nonproliferation, Antiterrorism, Demining

> *The FY 2013 Nonproliferation, Anti-Terrorism, Demining and Related Programs (NADR) request of $635.7 million will support critical security and humanitarian-related priority interventions. The request includes increases for the voluntary contribution to the International Atomic Energy Agency to demonstrate robust U.S. support for the agency, and for the Global Threat Reduction Program to strengthen biosecurity.*

The DoD and intelligence community have our nuclear defense and antiterrorism taken care of. Humanitarian intervention is not authorized by the Constitution. Eliminate and save $636 Million.

Peacekeeping Operations

> *The FY 2013 request for Peacekeeping Operations (PKO) of $249.1 million will help diminish and resolve conflict, enhance the ability of states to participate in peacekeeping and stability operations, address counterterrorism threats, and reform military establishments into professional military forces with respect for the rule of law in the aftermath of conflict.*

The all-reaching changes in foreign policy I have mentioned should go pretty far toward keeping the peace, and making new peace to be kept. Eliminate and save $249 Million.

Multilateral Economic Assistance

Our own economy is the biggest economic disaster in the world; we're in no position to help everyone else. Further, the way we have gone about conducting our economy gives testament to the damage that our "assistance" inevitably causes. Finally, our people shouldn't have to pay for it. Eliminate and save $3 Billion.

International Trade Commission

> *The International Trade Commission (ITC) is an independent, nonpartisan, Federal agency with a wide range of trade-related mandates. The ITC makes determinations with respect to unfair trade practices in import trade, as well as conducting import-injury investigations. It also conducts economic research and fact-finding investigations of trade issues, and provides technical information and advice on trade matters to the Congress and the Administration.*

The Constitution doesn't give the federal government any authority to issue trade mandates, other than to establish treaties. The feds should merely establish free trade agreements, and stay out of the issue beyond that. Eliminate and save $83 Million.

Foreign Claims Settlement Commission

> *The Foreign Claims Settlement Commission (FCSC) is a quasi-judicial, independent agency within the Department of Justice. Its principle mission is to adjudicate claims of U.S. nationals against foreign governments, under specific jurisdiction conferred by Congress, pursuant to international claims settlement agreements, or at the request of the Secretary of State.*

Departments shouldn't fund agencies within other departments; it clouds the budget and makes it difficult to see exactly where the money is going. Leave as is ($2M), but move to the DOJ.

Food for Peace Title II

> *Title II of the Food for Peace Act (P.L. 83-480, as amended, formerly the Agricultural Trade Development and Assistance Act of 1954) authorizes the provision of U.S. food assistance to meet emergency food needs around the world, and funds development-oriented programs to help address the underlying causes of food insecurity. Food for Peace Title II funding is appropriated to the U.S. Department of Agriculture and is administered by the U.S. Agency for International Development (USAID).*

There is plenty of food to feed everyone in the world. The problem is that the food is poorly distributed. The USDA pays farmers specifically *not* to farm food, and not much of the food we send ever makes it to the starving children. Nonprofits and not-for-profits have the infrastructure to feed these people purely on a donation basis, the people of one country shouldn't be forced to feed the people of any other country, and the Constitution provides no authority for it. Eliminate and save **$1.4 Billion**.

McGovern-Dole International Food for Education

> *The FY 2013 request for the McGovern-Dole International Food for Education and Child Nutrition Program Grants is $184 million. The Department of Agriculture (USDA) administers this program.*

More redistribution of food (and therefore wealth), and yet another program funded by the wrong department. By spending tax dollars on this program without the consent of the governed, it's not really a "donation" so much as "slavery", just like most of the programs in this budget. Eliminate and save $184 Million.

Overseas Contingency Operations

> *The Administration's FY 2013 International Affairs request includes $8.2 billion for Overseas Contingency Operations (OCO). This title funds the extraordinary, but temporary, costs of the Department of State and the U.S. Agency for International Development (USAID) operations in the Frontline States of Iraq, Afghanistan, and Pakistan.*

Very few of the temporary programs in the federal budget have turned out to be temporary. By overhauling our foreign policy and becoming a peaceable country for the first time in a century, we would eliminate the need for any OCO. All too often, our foreign assistance ends up in the pockets of the dictators and never helps the people of the country it is theoretically intended to help. Eliminate and save **$8.2 Billion.**

Cut the remainder of all Function 500 and Other Programs by half, with the expectation of more cuts as time progresses. Total saved: **$35.5 Billion**.

Operations[180]

Operations consists of additional overhead to run programs already mentioned under Function 150 and Other International Programs. Corresponding cuts and eliminations ensue, saving **$11.3 Billion**.

Conclusion

The Department of State has an actual 2013 budget of $92.7 Billion. This proposal authorizes $23.2 Billion, a savings of **$69.5 Billion**.

---

[180] http://www.state.gov/documents/organization/181061.pdf

Department of Transportation (DoT)

http://www.dot.gov/budget/dot-budget-and-performance

The Constitution authorizes the Congress to establish post roads[181]; that is, roads for the Post Office. That's about it. An argument could be made that the Commerce Clause authorizes roads "to keep commerce regular" between the states and Indian tribes; however, reading the Federalist Papers and writings of our forefathers, it is clear they meant "to prevent states from putting up protectionist trade barriers".

All other things transportation-related, including roads not for the post office, is left to the States per the 10th Amendment. Therefore, pretty much nothing in this department is allowed by the Constitution.

Federal Aviation Administration (FAA)[182]

Our mission is to provide the safest, most efficient aerospace system in the world.

The FAA consists of $15 Billion in spending, and it's not the government's job to provide safety or aerospace systems.

Air Traffic Organization (ATO)

This is the part of the FAA that most people are familiar with: Air Traffic Control. Apparently, controlling where planes go and at what speed requires nearly 32,000 people.

Airlines are private. Airports should be as well, though most are owned by local or state governments. Whether private or public, there is no reason why airports couldn't employ their own Air Traffic Controllers and work through mutually agreed-upon frequencies and standards, like every other part of the private sector. This is why organizations like the IEEE and ISO exist. Eliminate and save **$7.5 Billion**.

Aviation Safety (AVS)

> *AVS [promotes] aviation safety by regulating and overseeing the civil aviation industry and continued airworthiness of aircraft, as well as certification of pilots, mechanics, and other safety-related positions.*

If an airline was to use unsafe aircraft, or hire unqualified pilots and mechanics, and such employees were to cause accidents resulting in death or destruction,

---

[181] http://en.wikipedia.org/wiki/Post_road
[182] http://www.dot.gov/sites/dot.dev/files/docs/faa_%20fy_%202013_budget_estimate.pdf

those airlines wouldn't be in business for very long. Therefore they do not require government oversight to accomplish this common-sense task. Eliminate and save **$1.3 Billion.**

Commercial Space Transportation (AST)

> *AST [ensures] protection of public property and the national security and foreign policy interests of the United States during commercial space launch or reentry activities and to [encourages, facilitates, and promotes] U.S. commercial space transportation.*

Commercial transportation, in space or otherwise, requires no encouragement, facilitation, or promotion. If it makes sense to transport things and people commercially, then the private sector will meet the demand without government meddling.

Only military airstrips should be owned by the federal government; all others should be private. Since the military and state governments can handle their own security, there is no need for additional protection of any public property at this level.

National Security needs can be met through the military, Customs, and Border Patrol. Eliminate and save $17 Million.

Finance and Management (AFN)

> *AFN brings together the following four functions of the FAA: Financial Services (ABA), Acquisition and Business Services (ACQ), Information Services (AIO), and Regions and Center Operations (ARC).*

This is pure overhead for running the FAA. If we eliminate the FAA, there is no further need for any of these four functions. Eliminate and save $574 Million.

NextGen (ANG)

> *The FAA continues to make critical progress implementing the Next Generation Air Transportation System (NextGen) capabilities, which encompasses the deployment of new systems, technologies, and procedures that will help reduce delays, expand air traffic capacity, and mitigate aviation's impact on the environment, while ensuring the highest levels of safety.*

Over the past 30 years, the Space Program, public schools, and public transportation have actually gotten worse. Most other government programs have seen little to no improvement. Meanwhile, the private sector has made exponential improvements in consumer electronics, cars, and manufacturing itself. Clearly, putting the government in charge of improving things is a bad idea.

The Constitution doesn't authorize the federal government to implement any transportation system, except roads for the Post Office. By privatizing and deregulating all FAA functions, NextGen becomes obsolete. Eliminate and save $60 Million.

Human Resources (AHR)

This request provides for salaries and benefits as well as estimated non-pay AHR activities including implementing a comprehensive system of policies, procedures, and systems necessary for managing FAA's most important asset: Its people.

These 621 FTEs exists purely as overhead of running the FAA. If we eliminate the FAA, AHR becomes obsolete. Eliminate and save $99 Million.

Staff Offices

The Staff Offices include the Office of the Administrator, Chief Counsel, and seven assistant administrators who provide mission support services to the four lines of business, including legal counsel, economic trend analysis, diversity leadership, government and industry liaisons, communications, and public relations.

This is pure overhead. By eliminating the FAA, we obsolete all its offices. The fact that the FAA employs administrators of diversity and economics is a symptom of a grossly overcomplicated organization. Eliminate and save $200 Million.

Federal Highway Administration (FHWA)[183]

America is at a transportation crossroads. For too long we have put off the improvements needed to keep pace with today's transportation needs. To compete for the jobs and industries of the future, we must out-innovate and out-build the rest of the world. In support of this goal, FHWA's FY 2013 budget requests $42.6 billion to help move people and goods on roads, bridges, and tunnels throughout the U.S. as safely and effectively as possible.

The Constitution authorizes the Congress to build roads specifically for the Post Office (e.g. "Post Roads"), and that's it. Therefore, all other transportation, highways included, falls to the states per the 10th Amendment. The federal government has no authority to create or administer this organization. Eliminate in its entirety and save **$42.6 Billion**.

---

[183] http://www.dot.gov/sites/dot.dev/files/docs/fhwa_fy_2013_budget_estimate.pdf

National Highway Program

The $32.388 billion National Highway Program (NHP) will focus significant federal resources on maintaining the National Highway System (NHS) and will give States flexibility for local priorities. This request streamlines and combines several Federal-aid programs into one that is focused on preserving and improving infrastructure condition and performance on highways of national importance, includes performance management features that hold States accountable for achievement of targeted improvements, and provides flexibility to the States for making transportation investment decisions.

The National Highway System is an abomination of federal spending; a permanent solution to a temporary unemployment problem. Lo and behold, tens of billions of dollars are still being shoveled into it, and tens of percents of Americans are still out of work. While I believe Eisenhower had his heart in the right place, his highway system didn't actually solve the problem. Sell all the roads back to the states, and eliminate, saving **$32 Billion.**

Highway Safety Program

The Highway Safety Program aims to develop new and innovative ways to keep people safe on the roads. The program is designed to reduce fatalities and injuries on public roads in alignment with the Department of Transportation's (DOT) Roadway Safety Plan. This program will provide $2.2 billion for infrastructure-oriented safety improvement projects, with the flexibility to use up to 25 percent of funds for education, enforcement and emergency medical services investments if needed to address specific safety problems in the State.

This is supposed to be the land of the *free*, not the land of the *safe*. Driving safely is the responsibility of the drivers, and keeping the roads themselves safe is the responsibility of the several states. This type of safety doesn't qualify under the General Welfare clause, because it provides for *specific* welfare. That is, people are only affected by it if they use the roads.

Further, the states would handle highway safety better, in that they're closer to the roads and can oversee them more effectively. Road safety is based on simple maintenance and common sense; it does not require any special projects or progressivism. The same concepts that applied in the 1950s apply today. Eliminate and save **$2.5 Billion.**

Livable Communities Program

The Livable Communities Program establishes place-based planning, policies, and investments to help communities increase transportation choices and access to transportation services. This program will fund transportation projects that improve quality of life in both rural and urban areas, provide users with enhanced transportation choices, and improve air quality in large metropolitan areas.

The transportation choices available in a community are the responsibility of that community and of the people therein. A taxpayer in Texas shouldn't be forced to pay for a monorail in California. Eliminate and save **$4 Billion**.

Research, Technology, and Education Program

The FHWA RT&E program strives to generate new solutions, provide better decision-making information and tools, and build more effective partnerships that will allow our country to make the best investments in the nation's largest utility— our transportation system.

Automatically be suspicious of any government program that uses the term "umbrella". The federal government has no authority to conduct or finance research, technology, or education, and these concepts are most effective when they come from the private sector. People should be allowed to innovate, pitch to sell their ideas to the city or state, and be done with it. Eliminate and save $644 Million.

Federal Allocation Program

FHWA requests $1.357 billion for a Federal Allocation Program to provide funding for transportation projects on Federal and Tribal lands, to respond to natural disasters or other emergencies, to train the highway construction workforce, and to assist disadvantaged business enterprise firms compete for highway construction contracts.

The DoD budget can pay for all projects on military bases, and the Department of State can pay for all projects within the District of Columbia. All other federal lands should be given back to the states in which they are located. Indians should be allowed automatic citizenship, as they were born within the United States; however, they should be left to run their reservations on their own. The FAP is thereby obsoleted. Eliminate and save **$1.4 Billion.**

TIFIA Program

The TIFIA program provides Federal credit assistance to surface transportation projects of national or regional significance.

States should tax their own people to build their own transportation systems. The money comes from the same taxpayers anyway; they'd just be paying it to their state instead of the feds. Eliminate and save $500 Million.

> FHWA requests $700 million in FY 2013 for the Transportation Leadership
> Awards program. This competitive grant program assists State DOTs and
> tribal governments to implement bold, innovative reforms leading to
> transportation policy innovations. It also funds improvements in the
> organizational capacity of State DOTs, metropolitan planning organizations
> (MPOs) and tribal governments to support such reform.

Eliminate all federal grants. State DOTs are incentivized to innovate in that
doing so will result in better results or cheaper budgets. Individuals are
incentivized in that selling their ideas and products earns them money. Tribal
governments are none of our concern and should be left to run their own
affairs. Eliminate and save $700 Million.

Federal Motor Carrier Safety Administration (FMCSA)[184]

> FMCSA is the primary enforcement and regulatory agency responsible for truck
> and bus safety, the companies that own them, and the drivers who operate
> them. The agency proposes rules, implements enforcement programs, and
> develops systems to reduce crashes involving large trucks and buses.

Safety on trucks and busses is not a government issue in the slightest. If you sell
unsafe trucks and busses, you will go out of business. If your business uses
unsafe trucks and busses, they will cost you in maintenance and legal fees
following any damage or injuries, and you may go out of business. If you hire
unsafe drivers, they will likely cause you damage or injury that will cost you
money and possibly drive you out of business. If your company doesn't end up
dealing with any of these injuries or any damage due to your unsafe practices,
then no wrong has been done.

That government is best which governs least. The Constitution provides no
federal authority over highway safety, vehicle safety, or driver safety.
Eliminate and save $580 Million.

Motor Carrier Safety Operations and Programs

> The Operations and Programs account provides the necessary resources to
> support program and administrative activities for motor carrier safety. Under
> the Administration's surface transportation reauthorization proposal, FMCSA
> will improve safety and reduce severe and fatal commercial motor vehicles
> crashes by raising the bar to entry into the commercial motor vehicle industry,
> by requiring operators to maintain standards to remain in the industry, and by

---

[184] http://www.dot.gov/sites/dot.dev/files/docs/fmcsa_fy_2013_buget_estimate.pdf

removing high-risk carriers, vehicles, drivers and service providers from operation.

Motor carrier safety is not a government issue; it's a motor carrier issue. Driving safely is the responsibility of every driver. Hiring safe drivers is the responsibility of the employer. If you don't make good decisions in running your business, you will go *out* of business.

Law should not be passed to prevent crime; only the actual ultimate crime should be illegal. That is, it should be illegal to cause a traffic accident in which you hit another person or their property. It should *not* be illegal to drive a little faster, because you might not cause such an accident. Only the ultimate infringement upon life, body, liberty, or property should be illegal. Eliminate and save $250 Million.

Motor Carrier Safety Grants

Motor Carrier Safety Grants support States to conduct compliance reviews, identify and apprehend traffic violators, conduct roadside inspections, and support safety audits on new entrant carriers. State safety enforcement efforts and the southern and northern borders ensure that all points of entry in the U.S. are fortified with comprehensive safety measures. In addition, the Federal motor carrier Safety Administration (FMCSA) oversees

Eliminate all federal grants and federal safety laws. States will generally pass their own safety laws, and they will be responsible for enforcing the compliance thereof. While roadside inspections sometimes find compliance problems, such incompliance is generally harmless; and the inspection *always* causes delays - In every single case. Therefore, government meddling actually hurts the private sector.

Personally, I am of the opinion that licensing should not be required to drive. If you commit a crime, it doesn't matter whether you were deemed worthy to drive by the government. The same extends to CDLs. Eliminate and save $264 Million.

Driver Safety Grant Program

The Driver Safety Grant Program focuses on the operator's role in commercial vehicle safety. The grants provide resources to improve CDL programs at the State Driver Licensing Agencies and their compliance with Commercial Driver License Information System (CDLIS) standards. This program will also provide funding for training and will support systems that provide carriers with information about their drivers' violations faster.

Eliminate all federal grants. Vehicle safety is the responsibility of the driver and the vehicle owners and (somewhat) manufacturers. It should not be illegal to be unsafe; only to cause the crime that safety was meant to prevent. Eliminate and save $30 Million.

Data and Technology Grant Program

> The Data and Technology grants are essential components of the Agency's efforts to remove high risk carriers, vehicles, drivers and service providers from operating. The grants provide funding to States to improve roadside enforcement effectiveness and link carrier safety performance with State vehicle credentials (i.e., license plate registration and renewal).

Eliminate all federal grants. If we eliminate regulations on carriers, vehicles, drivers, service providers, and credentials, then there is nothing left to enforce.

Federal Railroad Administration (FRA)[185]

Established by the Department of Transportation Act of 1966, the Federal Railroad Administration's (FRA) mission is to ensure the safety of the Nation's rail operations and infrastructure and to promote, efficient, accessible, and environmentally sound rail transportation. FRA relies on the enforcement of safety regulations, administration of financial assistance programs, and research and development to accomplish this mission.

The Nation's rail operations are dwindling; people use them less and less every year. Sure, we see coal and oil being transported by rail, but when was the last time you got on a passenger car?

The Constitution does authorize the Congress "To regulate Commerce with foreign Nations, and among the several States, and with the Indian Tribes". The correct interpretation of the Commerce Clause being "to keep commerce regular" may be seen as authority to institute and maintain a rail system. However, this interpretation is on loose footing.

The federal government has been in charge of the railroad system since its inception, and it has done the opposite of thrive in that time. Old railways lie dormant and decrepit from decades of disuse. People travel by airplane, bus, or car. Perhaps some form of compromise is in order to reach a balance between the possible authority and the abysmal results thereof.

Therefore I propose that we keep the railroad system, allow the federal government to plan and build the railways, and leave everything else to the

---

[185] http://www.dot.gov/sites/dot.dev/files/docs/fra_fy_2013_budget_estimate.pdf

states. Let the states own the land, and merely build the railways on that land in cooperation therewith. This will result in a dramatic reduction in spending while ceding to the state sovereignty which was always intended.

Since we would keep the FRA, but eliminate most of the DOT, the FRA would be moved into the Department of Internal Affairs (DIA).

Safety and Operations

[FRA Requests] $196 million and 878.5 FTE to fund FRA's portfolio of rail safety and development programs. This account also funds the organizational infrastructure—staff and operations (e.g., payroll, rent, telecommunications, information technology, and contract support)—that enables the safety and development programs to accomplish their goals. In FY 2013, this account includes a proposed $80 million railroad safety user fee designed to help offset the costs of 359 safety inspectors and related railroad safety activities.

Safety and Operations will generally be a state issue under this proposal, though one must consider the safety and operations of the planning and construction efforts. Cut by 75%, move into the Department of Internal Affairs, and save $147 Million.

Research and Development

Funding requested for the Railroad Research and Development program provides science and technology support for FRA's rail safety rulemaking and enforcement efforts. In addition to improving safety, the program makes significant contributions toward DOT's state of good repair, economic competitiveness, and environmental sustainability goals.

Since Operations are left to the states, and the Constitution authorizes no R&D, eliminate and save $36 Million.

Rail Line Relocation and Improvement Program

Funds are used to redevelop the Pennsylvania Station in New York City, which involves renovating the James A. Farley Post Office building. Funding for this project was included in the Grants to the National Railroad Passenger Corporation appropriation in 1995 through 1997, and the Northeast Corridor Improvement Program in 1998. In 2000, an advance appropriation of $20 million was provided for 2001, 2002, and 2003. In 2001, Congress specified that the $20 million advance appropriation provided in 2000 for the Farley Building was to be used exclusively for fire and life safety initiatives.

Eliminate all federal grants. Since Operations are left to the states, eliminate. No funding is requested. Let Pennsylvania pay for and perform the relocations and improvements therein.

Network Development

> *Funding requested in the Network Development account will be used to develop infrastructure, stations, equipment, and capacity needed to initiate new passenger rail services, and substantially upgrade existing corridors. The FY 2013 budget request includes $1.0 billion for this account, and over 6 years, the Administration proposes to invest $34.6 billion.*

Since Operations are left to the states, we need only fund the infrastructure. Cut by 75% and save $750 Million.

System Preservation and Renewal

> *Funding requested in the System Preservation and Renewal account will ensure passenger rail assets are maintained to provide safe and reliable life-cycle service, as well as to continue operating long distance train services. The FY 2013 budget request includes $1.5 billion for this account, and over 6 years, the Administration proposes to invest $12.5 billion.*

Since Operations are left to the states, passenger rail asset maintenance, safety, and reliability are no longer federal issues. Eliminate and save **$1.5 Billion** in addition to the plans of the next six years.

Total funding for the FRA is thus reduced from $2.7 Billion to $799 Million, a savings of **$1.9 Billion**.

Federal Transit Administration (FTA)[186]

> *FTA's FY 2013 budget request continues the Administration's commitment to expand transit options for Americans and return transit systems to a state of good repair, which was first presented in the FY 2012 budget and proposed six-year reauthorization of surface transportation programs. And it restates the Administration's call for FTA to have new rail transit safety oversight authority.*

Most transit options will be abdicated back to the states, as will the maintenance thereof. All federal Rail obligations are met within what's left of the FRA. Transit system reliability, efficiency, desirability, and safety are not federal issues according to the Constitution. Therefore, the FTA is not needed.

The FTA consists almost entirely of grant programs, which merely take money from the people and give it back to the states. Therefore this money would be better taxed at the state level in the first place, while requiring less overhead on the way through and giving taxpayers more options. Eliminate and save **$10.8 Billion**.

---

[186] http://www.dot.gov/sites/dot.dev/files/docs/fta_fy_2013_budget_estimate.pdf

Maritime Administration (MARAD)[187]

> *MARAD's mission is to strengthen the U.S. maritime transportation system – including infrastructure, industry and labor - to meet the economic and security needs of the Nation. Through the management of the Maritime Security Program, the Voluntary Intermodal Sealift Agreement program, the Ready Reserve Force, and War Risk Insurance program, MARAD helps support National security and strategic mobility by assuring access to ships, crews, and port intermodal assets for Department of Defense mobilizations.*

The seaborne transportation system could be interpreted as authorized under the Commerce Clause, in that it would "keep regular" the commerce with foreign nations and among the several states. Therefore we can't just eliminate MARAD altogether.

We can, however, move as much of the operations and maintenance as possible to the states. For example, the Feds could build the ports on state coasts but let the states own and administer them. Naval ports are clearly the DoD's responsibility.

Operations and Training

> *The Operations and Training request of $146 million includes $77 million for the United States Merchant Marine Academy (USMMA), $16 million for the State Maritime Academies (SMAs), and $53 million for MARAD Operations and Programs. This request includes a total of $10 million for the Capital Improvement Program to continue the renovations and improve USMMA facilities, infrastructure, and overall student quality of life.*

The civilian component of the USMMA should not be federally funded, as it does not provide for all people equally. The military auxiliary component, however, does, as it contributes to national defense. Therefore the USMMA is somewhat authorized and can stay. Cut it by half and save $39 Million.

MARAD O&P's Environmental Sustainability can clearly go away, saving $3 Million. The remainder can stay in order to run MARAD itself. Cut the difference by the standard 25% and save a total of $15 Million.

Academy Operations can sustain a 50% cut for the same reasons, saving $34 Million.

Capital Improvement Program (CIP) is a maintenance effort, which is now the responsibility of the states. Eliminate and save $15 Million.

---

[187] http://www.dot.gov/sites/dot.dev/files/docs/marad_fy_2013_budget_estimate.pdf

Ship Disposal is an unnecessary expense. The ships can be sold as is or for parts, generating revenue instead of expenses. Further, the states and civilians own their own ships, and should thereby incur the profit and expense therefrom.

Maritime Security Program

> $184 million in new Budget authority, $10 million above FY 2012 enacted, is requested for the Maritime Security Program (MSP), which together with $2 million in unobligated balances, will fund the authorized level of $186 million ($3.1 million for each vessel in the fleet).

This is why we have a Coast Guard and a Navy. Merge into the USCG and USN, and eliminate. $184 Million saved.

Maritime Guaranteed Loan Program (Title XI)

> $3.75 million is requested for Maritime Guaranteed Loan Program (Title XI) administration to continue to increase efficiency in monitoring the loan guarantee portfolio.

The government is not a bank. Eliminate and save $4 Million.

National Highway Traffic Safety Administration (NHTSA)[188]

> Safety is the top priority – for the Department of Transportation (DOT), for the National Highway Traffic Safety Administration (NHTSA), and for the people we serve. In 2010, overall traffic fatalities reached the lowest level since 1949. This translated to a 2.9 percent decrease in fatalities from 2009 to 2010. We can attribute this decline to a combination of factors, which include high visibility enforcement, safer vehicles, safer roads, and better, more informed decisions by roadway users.

The Constitution provides no authority to provide for the safety of the highways. According to this description, all of NHTSA is a state concern. Most NHTSA funding goes to grants, meaning the states can tax their own people to run their highway safety programs more effectively. This is followed by Research and Development, which would properly be privatized. The remainder is made up of Vehicle Safety, a private industry matter, which is none of any government's business.

NHTSA includes such non-highway-related activities as "prevention of marijuana and other drug use" and "a national driver register to assist states in electronically exchanging information regarding motor vehicle driving

---

[188] http://www.dot.gov/sites/dot.dev/files/docs/nhtsa_fy_2013_budget_estimate.pdf

records".[189] There should be no federal drivers' licensing system, and no federal drivers' record system. Eliminate and save $981 Million.

Office of the Inspector General (OIG)[190]

If we eliminate the Department, we thereby eliminate the need for the detection of Fraud, Waste, and Abuse. Eliminate and save $85 Million.

Office of the Secretary of Transportation (OST)[191]

If we eliminate the Department, we thereby eliminate the need for a secretary and an office thereof. Eliminate and save $883 Million.

Pipeline and Hazardous Materials Safety Administration (PHMSA)[192]

The Pipeline and Hazardous Materials Safety Administration (PHMSA) administers nationwide safety programs designed to protect the public and the environment from the risks in the commercial transportation of hazardous materials by air, rail, vessel, highway, and pipeline.

There is no Constitutional authority for the federal government to oversee safety programs, the environment, or hazardous materials. Clearly this is a state issue. Eliminate and save $276 Million.

St. Lawrence Seaway Development Corporation (SLSDC)[193]

The SLSDC will be able to perform its core mission of serving the U.S. intermodal and international transportation system while providing a safe, reliable, efficient, and environmentally responsible deep-draft waterway, in cooperation with its Canadian counterpart, the St. Lawrence Seaway Management Corporation (SLSMC).

The government should not own corporations. States are responsible for their own waterways. Any maintenance or operations that need to be done to waterways not located in a state could be done by cooperation with the states, or by the individuals and companies who want such changes, by federal permit. Traffic can be controlled in the same ways. Vessel safety is not a government concern, until an infringement upon life, liberty, property, or body has occurred; in which case states will have their own laws handling that. Eliminate, possibly privatize, and save $33 Million.

---

[189] http://us-code.vlex.com/vid/highway-safety-research-development-19205164
[190] http://www.dot.gov/sites/dot.dev/files/docs/oig_fy_2013_budget_estimate.pdf
[191] http://www.dot.gov/sites/dot.dev/files/docs/ost_fy_2013_budget_estimate.pdf
[192] http://www.dot.gov/sites/dot.dev/files/docs/phmsa_fy_2013_budget_estimate.PDF
[193] http://www.dot.gov/sites/dot.dev/files/docs/slsdc_fy_2013_budget_estimate.pdf

Surface Transportation Board (STB)[194]

> *The Surface Transportation Board is charged with the economic oversight of the nation's freight rail system. The Board has regulatory jurisdiction over the reasonableness of rates that railroads charge shippers, mergers, line acquisitions, new rail-line construction, abandonments of existing rail lines, and the conversion of rail rights-of-way into hiking and biking trails.*

It can be argued that "regulating" the rates charged to shippers impacts interstate and international commerce, but that would be tantamount to saying the government should control all prices of everything. Therefore it merely requires that states and local governments do not charge unfair prices.

Having said that, Article I, Section 9, Clause 6 of the Constitution reads *"No Preference shall be given by any Regulation of Commerce or Revenue to the Ports of one State over those of another; nor shall Vessels bound to, or from, one State, be obliged to enter, clear, or pay Duties in another."*

Therefore the feds may only impose uniform rules across all states, even then within the parameters defined above. Clearly, this is a simple matter of passing a bill and leaving it to MARAD to administer such impositions. No regular inspection or compliance checking is necessary until someone complains. Eliminate and save $35 Million.

Conclusion

The Department of Transportation is thereby reduced in total funding from $101.4 Billion ($74.5 of which is actually budgeted within the DOT) to a paltry $1.08 Billion. **This constitutes a reduction of over $100 Billion**, over 99% reduction, and a proportional reduction in jurisdiction. What little remains can be moved into the Department of Internal Affairs.

---

[194] http://www.dot.gov/sites/dot.dev/files/docs/stb_fy_2013_budget_estimate.pdf

Department of the Interior (DoI)[195]

Our Mission: Protecting America's Great Outdoors and Powering Our Future. The U.S. Department of the Interior protects America's natural resources and heritage, honors our cultures and tribal communities, and supplies the energy to power our future.

Protection of the great outdoors falls upon a simple principle: Do not encroach on others or their property. Land that isn't yours is land that you shouldn't pollute, build upon, etc.

An argument could be made that national parks provide for the general welfare of the United States. However, these parks are very expansive, and most of their space just goes to waste. Most people stay on or near the roads and don't make use of nearly all the facilities available. Therefore I believe national parks should be state parks. Give up the land and let the states run their own parks.

Bureau of Ocean Energy Management (BOEM)[196]

In response to the Deepwater Horizon explosion and resulting oil spill in the Gulf of Mexico, the Administration has undertaken the most aggressive and comprehensive reforms to offshore oil and gas regulation and oversight in U.S. history. These reforms included significant structural changes to our offshore energy development regime, including the creation of three new entities with distinct focused missions that are designed to provide strong safety oversight and responsible management for the Nation's offshore energy resources.

BOEM is responsible for energy concerns in American waters. The presence of BOEM is necessary to oil exploration and drilling on the continental shelf, where the water is not claimed by any state. Its constitutionality could be argued under the General Welfare clause, but its strongest argument is in Article IV, Section 3:

> *The Congress shall have Power to dispose of and make all needful Rules and Regulations respecting the Territory or other Property belonging to the United States; and nothing in this Constitution shall be so construed as to Prejudice any Claims of the United States, or of any particular State.*

Because the waters on the continental shelf are not claimed by the legislatures of any state, they fall under this clause. However, the Bureau's jurisdiction would be significantly reduced: Merely allow companies to explore and exploit

---

[195] http://www.doi.gov/budget/appropriations/2013/index.cfm
[196] http://www.doi.gov/budget/appropriations/2013/upload/FY2013_BOEM_Greenbook.pdf

resources, and tax them based on what they take. For example, a 5% tax on oil drilling would be a tax of $5 per barrel when oil was at $100/bl. Due to this reduction in jurisdiction, we thusly reduce funding. However, this is offset by an increase in jurisdiction over the taxing of the resources. Let's keep it as is for now until we figure out what is needed ($160 Million).

Bureau of Safety and Environmental Enforcement (BSEE)[197]

> *The newly created [BSEE] continues to aggressively promote safety, protect the environment, and conserve resources offshore. The budget request for fiscal year (FY) 2013 supports those efforts as we institutionalize the comprehensive regulatory reforms implemented in the aftermath of the Deepwater Horizon explosion and oil spill.*

There are no other governments or agencies qualified to oversee the safety or environment of offshore waters or of territory not incorporated into a state. Therefore, the BSEE is also authorized under Article IV, Section 3 of the Constitution. It is not, however, authorized anywhere else. Further, many of its functions are unnecessary or unauthorized, such as facility inspection (other than to ensure accurate measurement), safety research, standards development, environmental compliance, etc. Move to DIA, cut by half, and save $104 Million.

Bureau of Reclamation (BR)[198]

> *Reclamation's fiscal year (FY) 2013 Budget sustains Reclamation's efforts to deliver water and generate hydropower, consistent with applicable State and Federal law, in an environmentally responsible and cost-efficient manner.*

Delivering utilities such as water and electricity are not authorized by the Constitution, and thus are rightfully state issues. There's no reason one state with demand can't buy these things from another which has a surplus. Eliminate all federal reclamation and utility laws.

> *It also supports the Administration's and Department of the Interior's (Department) priorities to tackle America's water challenge; protect and restore ecosystems; promote a new energy frontier; empower tribal nations; and establish a 21st century youth conservation workforce.*

An argument could be made that protecting ecosystems provides for the General Welfare; however, it primarily operates in the western half of the

---

[197] http://www.doi.gov/budget/appropriations/2013/upload/FY2013_BSEE_Greenbook.pdf
[198] http://www.doi.gov/budget/appropriations/2013/upload/FY2013_BOR_Greenbook.pdf

continental states, and is thus more of a *specific* welfare. Further, this task is better accomplished by the states, requiring less overhead and thus lower taxes on the way through. There's no need for a taxpayer in Alaska to pay for the restoration of the Everglades.

BR's key tasks are thus obsolete at the national level, so BR can be eliminated to save **$1.2 Billion**.

Bureau of Land Management (BLM)[199]

> *[The BLM's mission is to] manage the public lands for a variety of uses to benefit present and future generations.*

If we return most of the federal land to the states, there is significantly less land to manage. The federal government should only own and manage the Capitol area and its assorted military bases, both of which have funds allocated elsewhere. States can manage their own land. Eliminate and save $1.3 Billion.

Fish and Wildlife Service (FWS)[200]

> *The U.S. Fish and Wildlife Service (Service) is the oldest federal conservation agency, tracing its lineage back to 1871. Over its 141 year history, the Service has adapted to the Nation's changing needs to become a leader in protecting and enhancing America's biological natural resources. In the face of escalating challenges such as land-use, population growth, invasive species, water scarcity, and a range of other complex issues, all of which are amplified by accelerated climate change, the Service is meeting today's pressing conservation challenges with a strategic approach.*

The needs of a conservation effort do not change over time; merely prevent encroachments on such land. Pick up your trash; take only pictures, leave only footprints. If the states run their own land, then FWS is unnecessary in those areas. The several states can manage their own land-use, population growth, invasive species, water scarcity, and other issues. Eliminate and save $2.3 Billion.

Indian Affairs[201]

We should fundamentally rethink how we deal with Native Americans. They were here first, and the reservations are considered federal and state territory, so the Grandfather Clause of the 14th Amendment demands they are citizens of the United States.

---

[199] http://www.doi.gov/budget/appropriations/2013/upload/FY2013_BLM_Greenbook.pdf
[200] http://www.doi.gov/budget/appropriations/2013/upload/FY2013_FWS_Greenbook.pdf
[201] http://www.doi.gov/budget/appropriations/2013/upload/FY2013_IA_Greenbook.pdf

Some of them want to live on their reservations and preserve their old ways. Some of them want to try to make it in the new American society. Their vast lands didn't require any money or management before we came along, so it seems unlikely they would now.

I think we should cease all payments we make to them for staying on their reservations, so that their decisions are untarnished by what is effectively bribery. If you want to live on the reservation and follow the old ways, go for it. If you want to leave and go into a city, or wherever, go for it. Who is the government to involve itself in this process?

It is true that before we came along, their lands were vast and their numbers were thriving. Some might say this gives us the responsibility to care for them. To that I say the lands are the spoils of war.

IA has many loan programs, which can go away automatically. The government is not a bank, regardless of who you are. Settlement funds can go away per the "spoils of war" mantra. Habitat acquisitions can go away per the "Give the land back to the states" mantra.

The federal government has no more authority to provide Native Americans with land, education or healthcare than to anyone else, so those programs can go away.

The land is set aside for those who want to remain self-governed. They have a right to incorporate themselves into America as citizens. That's all they need. Eliminate IA and save $2.6 Billion.

National Indian Gaming Commission (NIGC)[202]

The National Indian Gaming Commission was created by the Indian Gaming Regulatory Act of 1988. The Indian Gaming Regulatory Act (IGRA) created a mechanism whereby NIGC operations are funded by the fees collected from tribal gaming operations. When the Commission began operations in February 1992, the Indian gaming industry generated revenue of about $3 billion per year.

The federal government has no more authority to oversee a Native American casino or other business than it does to oversee anyone else's. Let the states figure out their own laws. Eliminate and save $18 Million.

---

[202] http://www.doi.gov/budget/appropriations/2013/upload/FY2013_NIGC_Greenbook.pdf

National Park Service[203]

> *As the keeper of 397 park units, 23 national scenic and national historic trails, and 58 wild and scenic rivers, NPS is charged with preserving these lands and historic features that were designated by the Nation for their cultural and historic significance, scenic and environmental worth, and educational and recreational opportunities.*

An argument could be made that national parks contribute to the General Welfare, but how does a park in Florida help someone in Oregon? There is no clearly defined authority here.

States have programs to create and manage their own parks. Give all national park land back to the states in which they are located. Eliminate and save **$3 Billion.**

Natural Resource Damage Assessment and Restoration Program (NRDARP)[204]

> *The mission of the Natural Resource Damage Assessment and Restoration Program (Restoration Program) is to restore natural resources injured as a result of oil spills or hazardous substance releases into the environment. In partnership with other affected State, Tribal, and Federal trustee agencies, damage assessments provide the basis for determining the restoration needs that address the public's loss and use of these resources.*

There's no reason why states couldn't tax their own people to restore their own damaged lands, and there is no constitutional authority therefor. Eliminate and save $66 Million ($60M of which is a non-recurring request).

Office of Inspector General (OIG)[205]

If we eliminate the department, we thereby eliminate the need to inspect it. Eliminate and save $49 Million.

Office of Insular Affairs[206]

> *The Office of Insular Affairs (OIA) carries out the Secretary's responsibilities for U.S.-affiliated insular areas. These include the territories of Guam, American Samoa, the U.S. Virgin Islands (USVI), and the Commonwealth of the Northern Mariana Islands (CNMI), as well as the three Freely Associated States (FAS): the Federated States of Micronesia (FSM), the Republic of the Marshall Islands (RMI), and the Republic of Palau.*

---

[203] http://www.doi.gov/budget/appropriations/2013/upload/FY2013_NPS_Greenbook.pdf
[204] http://www.doi.gov/budget/appropriations/2013/upload/FY2013_NRDAR_Greenbook.pdf
[205] http://www.doi.gov/budget/appropriations/2013/upload/FY2013_OIG_Greenbook.pdf
[206] http://www.doi.gov/budget/appropriations/2013/upload/FY2013_OIA_Greenbook.pdf

An insular area is an undeveloped area which is "ignorant of or uninterested in culture, ideas, or peoples outside [their] own experience" or an area which "[lacks] contact with other people". By their very definition, they desire or require no contact with the outside world. One can easily understand why.

OIA measures the GDP of these territories and tries to identify and correct problems within them. They provide financial assistance, as if they were some third world Department of State foreign aid issue.

If these areas want the benefit of money to run their programs, then they should institute local governments to tax their own people. There's no reason why some random schmuck in Idaho should be forced to pay for the well-being of someone else in the South Pacific. Some of these programs are run by grants. Eliminate all federal grants. Eliminate and save $575 Million. What's left can be handled by nonprofits and other charities.

Office of the Secretary[207]

If we eliminate the Department, then it no longer requires a secretary, and he no longer requires an office. Eliminate and save $262 Million.

Office of the Solicitor[208]

> *The Office of the Solicitor (SOL, Office) maintains the focal mission of inspiring high ethical standards and providing quality legal counsel and advice. The Office strives to fulfill the Department of the Interior's expansive mission by performing the legal work of the Department of the Interior, managing Interior's Ethics Office and resolving Freedom of Information Act (FOIA) Appeals.*

If we eliminate the department, then it no longer has any legal or ethical obligations. Eliminate, declassify and publish all internal documents, and save $65 Million.

Office of the Special Trustee for American Indians[209]

> *In FY 2013, the Department of the Interior will maintain its emphasis on providing services to the beneficiaries of the Indian trust. The Office of the Special Trustee for American Indians (OST) will continue its role in the oversight and operations of the fiduciary trust by monitoring trust reform in accordance with the Comprehensive Trust Management Plan (CTMP) and all applicable congressional actions and regulatory requirements. Proposed funding for OST supports the Department's Indian Fiduciary Trust Responsibilities.*

---

[207] http://www.doi.gov/budget/appropriations/2013/upload/FY2013_DOI-OS_Greenbook.pdf
[208] http://www.doi.gov/budget/appropriations/2013/upload/FY2013_SOL_Greenbook.pdf
[209] http://www.doi.gov/budget/appropriations/2013/upload/FY2013_OST_Greenbook.pdf

All Native American concerns have been addressed previously in this chapter, on a higher level. Eliminate and save $588 Million.

Office of Surface Mining Reclamation and Enforcement[210]

The mission of the Office of Surface Mining Reclamation and Enforcement (OSM) is to carry out the requirements of the Surface Mining Control and Reclamation Act[211] (SMCRA or the Act) in cooperation with the States and Tribes.

SMCRA created two programs: one for regulating active coal mines, and a second for reclaiming abandoned mine lands. SMCRA also created the Office of Surface Mining, an agency within the Department of the Interior, to promulgate regulations, to fund state regulatory and reclamation efforts, and to ensure consistency among state regulatory programs.

Since we're handing all of these lands over to the states, they can manage their own active mines and reclaim their own abandoned mines. We certainly don't need entire agencies whose only purpose is to create more rules. Eliminate and save $678 Million.

U.S. Geological Survey (USGS)[212]

The Nation's largest water, Earth, and biological science and civilian mapping agency, the USGS collects, monitors, analyzes, and provides scientific understanding of natural resource conditions, issues, and problems. For more than a century, this diversity of scientific expertise has enabled the USGS to carry out large-scale, multi-disciplinary investigations and provide impartial scientific information to resource managers, planners, policymakers, and the public.

The information published by the USGS is potentially useful to all and thus qualifies as a public good under the General Welfare clause. Some programs, like WaterSMART and Youth in the Great Outdoors are simply superfluous at best and unconstitutional at worst. Cut by half and merge into the Department of Internal Affairs, under or with a dotted line to, the Office of the Census. $552 Million saved.

---

[210] http://www.doi.gov/budget/appropriations/2013/upload/FY2013_OSM_Greenbook.pdf
[211] http://en.wikipedia.org/wiki/Surface_Mining_Control_and_Reclamation_Act_of_1977
[212] http://www.doi.gov/budget/appropriations/2013/upload/FY2013_USGS_Greenbook.pdf

Wildland Fire Management[213]

The Department's Wildland Fire Management funds fire prevention, readiness, wildfire response, and rehabilitation activities performed by the land management agencies and the Bureau of Indian Affairs. The program strives to achieve both a cost-efficient and technically effective fire management program that meets resource and safety objectives, while minimizing both the cost of wildfire response and damage to resources.

Fire prevention, readiness, response, and rehabilitation can all be funded by the states themselves. States can help each other when they have resources to spare. Eliminate and save $818 Million.

Conclusion

Total funding from the Department of the Interior has been reduced from $18 Billion to $550 Million. The few constitutionally authorized sections I could find have been moved into a bureau in the Department of Internal Affairs.

There exists a difference of about **$3.3 Billion** between the master federal budget's DOI expenses and the sum of DOI's individual budgets. This money appears to go missing and thus should not be budgeted.

---

[213] http://www.doi.gov/budget/appropriations/2013/upload/FY2013_WFM_Greenbook.pdf

Department of the Treasury[214]

Mission: Maintain a strong economy and create economic and job opportunities by promoting conditions that enable economic growth and stability at home and abroad, strengthen national security by combating threats and protecting the integrity of the financial system, and manage the U.S. Government's finances and resources.

A strong economy presents itself implicitly from a free market. One prime example is that "black market" economies always thrive. Clearly, therefore, government intervention is the source of many economic problems. The free market would provide its own economic and job opportunities; the government is responsible for neither.

This meddling, combined with rampant government spending, fractional reserve banking, seemingly endless bailouts, and the media-induced consumer culture are the strongest threats to the financial system. We must break the cycle and end the pattern if we are ever to recover and thrive as a superpower once again.

Nowhere in the Constitution does it say people have a right to a job. Jobs are things, and you can't have a right to a *thing*; you can only have a right to pursue the thing.

Salaries and Expenses

Standard 25% cut; save $8 Million.

Department-Wide Systems and Capital Investments Program[215]

The Department-wide Systems and Capital Investments Program (DSCIP) is authorized to be used by or on behalf of the Treasury Department's bureaus, at the Secretary's discretion, to improve infrastructure, modernize business processes and increase efficiency through technology investments.

This is a vague and unhelpful description. They want $1.6 Million to help protect sensitive treasury data. What data could the Treasury possibly have which would need to be protected? One aspect is "Personally Identifiable Information". The new tax system I have proposed eliminates the need for the treasury to track any such information. Another is "Controlled Unclassified Information". If it doesn't need to be classified, then it doesn't need to be safeguarded. Eliminate and save $7 Million.

---

[214] http://www.treasury.gov/about/budget-performance/pages/index.aspx
[215] http://www.treasury.gov/about/budget-performance/budget-in-brief/Documents/3.%20DSCIP%20BIB%20-%20508%20Compliant%20-%20passed.pdf

Office of the Inspector General[216]

The Inspector General Act of 1978, as amended, gives the Treasury Office of Inspector General (OIG) the authority and responsibility to (1) audit and investigate the Treasury Department's programs and operations; (2) promote economy and efficiency and to detect and prevent fraud and waste in those programs and operations; and (3) keep the Secretary and Congress aware of problems and solutions.

This is overhead associated with running the department. Cut by standard 25% and save $7 Million.

Treasury IG for Tax Administration[217]

The FY 2013 President's Budget request for Treasury Inspector General for Tax Administration (TIGTA) will be used to continue to provide critical audit, investigative, and inspection and evaluation services, ensuring the integrity of tax administration on behalf of the nation's taxpayers.

Being that this proposal completely redesigns the tax system, compliance may still be an issue. Fortunately, however, the Treasury has an entire office for that, so this can go away. Eliminate and save $155 Million.

Special IG for TARP[218]

The 2013 President's Budget request for the Special Inspector General for Troubled Asset Relief Program (SIGTARP) includes funding to support and complement the Department of the Treasury's strategic goals (1) to repair and reform the financial system and support the recovery of the housing market by assessing the effectiveness of Treasury's activities and evaluating whether Troubled Asset Relief Program (TARP) recipients are satisfying their legal obligation and (5) to manage the government's finances in a fiscally responsible manner as they relate to TARP.

TARP should never have been introduced, let alone passed. The reparations and restorations needed are for damage that far outweighs TARP and indeed precedes it by a century. The housing market is none of the government's business. Eliminate and save $40 Million.

---

[216] http://www.treasury.gov/about/budget-performance/budget-in-brief/Documents/4.%20OIG%20-%20passed.pdf
[217] http://www.treasury.gov/about/budget-performance/budget-in-brief/Documents/6.%20TIGTA%20BiB%2001-31-12%20FINAL%20508%20-%20passed.pdf
[218] http://www.treasury.gov/about/budget-performance/budget-in-brief/Documents/5.%20SIGTARP%20BIB%20FINAL%20508%20-%20passed.pdf

Community Development Financial Institutions Fund[219]

The CDFI Fund expands the availability of credit, investment capital, and financial services in distressed urban and rural communities, and carries out the Community Development Banking and Financial Institutions Act of 1994, as well as certain programmatic provisions of the Community Renewal Tax Relief Act of 2000, the Housing and Economic Recovery Act of 2008, and the Small Business Jobs Act of 2010.

The government is not a bank, and credit is not a government issue. Therefore, there is no need to interfere in credit availability, investment capital, or financial services which are rightfully provided by the free market. The problems of urban and rural communities are the responsibility of their local, and possibly state, governments. Eliminate and save $221 Million.

Financial Crimes Enforcement Network[220]

The mission of FinCEN [...] is to enhance the integrity of financial systems by facilitating the detection and deterrence of financial crime. FinCEN fulfills its mission, goals and priorities by administrating the Bank Secrecy Act (BSA); furnishing analytical and financial expertise to support law enforcement investigations and prosecutions; determining merging trends in money laundering and other financial crimes; and serving as the nation's financial intelligence unit (FIU).

We absolutely need some protection against counterfeiting and large-scale fraud. Keep as is ($102 Million).

Alcohol and Tobacco Tax and Trade Bureau[221]

The Alcohol and Tobacco Tax and Trade Bureau (TTB) serves as the Nation's primary federal authority in the regulation of the alcohol and tobacco industries. TTB is responsible for the administration and enforcement of the Internal Revenue Code associated with the collection of excise taxes on alcohol, tobacco, firearms, and ammunition, and the Federal Alcohol Administration Act, which provides for the regulation of those engaged in the alcohol beverage industry and the protection of consumers of alcohol beverages.

Alcohol and tobacco are goods; they are products, just like everything else on the market. Governments should not interfere with the market in general, but

---

[219] http://www.treasury.gov/about/budget-performance/budget-in-brief/Documents/7.%20CDFI%20BIB%20-%20508%20Compliant%20-%20passed.pdf
[220] http://www.treasury.gov/about/budget-performance/budget-in-brief/Documents/8.%20FinCEN%20-%20508%20Compliant%20-%20passed.pdf
[221] http://www.treasury.gov/about/budget-performance/budget-in-brief/Documents/9.%20TTB%20-%20508%20Compliant%20-%20passed.pdf

interference in specific market segments and product lines just screams of micromanagement and bureaucratic overhead. Under this proposal, alcohol and tobacco would be subject to the same sales tax as all other products. Eliminate and save $97 Million.

Fiscal Service Operations[222]

> *The mission of the Fiscal Service is to provide guidance to improve financial management across the Federal Government and improve the efficiency of Government financial management by providing central payment services to Federal Program Agencies (FPAs), operating the Federal Government's collections and deposit systems, delivering Government-wide accounting and reporting services, managing the collection of delinquent debt owed to the Government, borrowing the money needed to operate the Federal Government and accounting for the resulting debt, and providing reimbursable support services to Federal agencies.*

Looking through these budgets, it's perfectly clear that all financial management guidance has failed. This failure is utter and complete; therefore, the entire concept of managing it in this manner is obsolete. Our elected officials either pass budgets grossly in deficit, or skip the passage of a budget altogether. Department financial decision makers ask for things which they don't need and which the people don't want. Clearly, this guidance has degenerated to the extent of pointlessness.

The government does, however, require a system to move money around, such as a collections and deposit system as mentioned here. Therefore let's keep FSO at a cut of half, saving $180 Million.

Internal Revenue Service

The new tax system implicitly obsoletes the IRS. We need only spin off a small office to enforce compliance of the few remaining taxes, and collect such revenue. The IRS itself can be eliminated, saving a total of **$11.3 Billion** and removing **96,196 FTEs.**

IRS Taxpayer "Services"

> *This budget activity funds services to assist with tax return preparation, including tax law interpretation, publication, production, and advocate services. In addition, funding for these programs continues to emphasize taxpayer education, outreach, increased volunteer support time and locations, and enhancing pre-filing taxpayer support through electronic media.*

---

[222] http://www.treasury.gov/about/budget-performance/budget-in-brief/Documents/10.%20Fiscal%20Service%20-%20508%20Compliant%20-%20passed.pdf

The new tax system I have proposed eliminates the need for tax returns. Therefore, there is nothing to prepare, and the people require no assistance with it. Eliminate and save **$2.3 Billion.**

IRS Enforcement

> The FY 2013 request provides funding to restore revenue lost from FY 2012 reductions to examination audit and collection programs; implement enacted legislation; increase compliance by addressing offshore tax evasion; make use of new information reporting to reduce the underreporting tax gap; improve treatment of complex financial situations including transfer pricing and uncertain tax positions; protect revenue by identifying fraud and preventing issuance of questionable refunds including tax-related identity theft; and strengthen return preparer compliance.

The new tax system I have proposed results in greatly reduced enforcement needs. We need simply ensure businesses submit sales tax for the first several years until the sales tax is eliminated, and ensure the compliance of the import and resource taxes. Therefore we can spin this off into a new office, under the Treasury but not under the IRS, and cut its funding. Cut by 75% and save **$4.3 Billion.**

IRS Operations Support

If we eliminate the IRS, there are no further operations to support. Eliminate and save **$4.5 Billion.**

IRS Business Systems Modernization

> This budget activity funds the planning and capital asset acquisition of information technology (IT) to continue the modernization of IT systems, including labor and related contractual costs.

If we eliminate the IRS, there are no further business systems to modernize. Eliminate and save $330 Million.

Treasury Forfeiture Fund[223]

> The mission of the Treasury Forfeiture Fund is to affirmatively influence the consistent and strategic use of asset forfeiture by law enforcement bureaus participating in the Treasury Forfeiture Fund to disrupt and dismantle criminal enterprises.

This appears to be where money comes in from seizures of crack houses, meth labs, drug lords' cars, and the like. Since most of this money comes in from

---

[223] http://www.treasury.gov/about/budget-performance/Documents/17%20-%20FY%202013%20TEOAF%20CJ.pdf

people who broke drug laws, we won't have most of this income when drugs are legalized. The budget doesn't actually break this down by law category, so let's throw out a high, wild guess: 90%. Cutting this revenue by 90% will cost us $747 Million.

Poverty Reduction and Economic Growth (MDBs)
Eliminate all international programs. This one saves **$2.1 Billion.**

Food Security
Eliminate all international programs. This one saves $164 Million.

Environmental Trust Funds
Eliminate all international programs. This one saves $364 Million.

Debt Relief
Eliminate all international programs. This one saves $250 Million.

Technical Assistance
Eliminate all international programs. This one saves $25 Million.

Additional Programs
I can't find where the Bureau of Engraving and Printing and the United States Mint fit into the hierarchy, as the department's budget is not well-organized. Therefore I shall add their budgets here. No reductions.

Bureau of Engraving and Printing: $1.9 Billion

United States Mint: $1.8 Billion

Conclusion
The Constitution authorizes the Congress to "coin money" and to "provide for the punishment of counterfeiting the securities and current coin of the United States". Other programs, such as the deposit and collections system, are "necessary and proper for carrying into execution the foregoing powers". Therefore, the treasury is authorized.

This proposal has reduced the Department of the Treasury from $16.15 Billion to $5.5 Billion, a reduction of about two-thirds, saving **$10.6 Billion.**

Social Security Administration[224]

Social Security touches the lives of nearly every American, often during times of personal hardship, transition, and uncertainty. Our 80,000 Federal and State employees serve the public through a network of 1,500 offices across the country. Each day, almost 180,000 people visit our field offices and more than 435,000 people call us for a variety of services such as filing claims and asking questions. Our fiscal year (FY) 2013 budget request is consistent with my commitment to be a good steward of our programs and provide these services to the public.

Private investments generally pay out more than Social Security, and they give you a choice in how your money is invested. The Social Security Trust Fund is insolvent at best, and broke at worst. It has been stolen from by the government, and you're still being forced to pay into it.

If you want Social Security, that's fine. Your state legislature can enact a system to provide it. That way, you could opt out by moving elsewhere.

Of course, there are millions of people who depend on it, so we can't just eliminate it altogether all at once. Therefore the entire administration goes onto the Ten Year Plan, at the conclusion of which the budget would be reduced by **$882 Billion**.

---

[224] http://www.ssa.gov/budget/

Department of Veterans' Affairs[225]

Compensation and Benefits

The number of disability compensation and pension claims received is expected to increase from 1,200,000 in 2012 to 1,250,000 in 2013. Claims receipts were 1,311,091 in 2011 and include 230,778 claims from the addition of new presumptive disabilities related to exposure to Agent Orange (ischemic heart disease, Parkinson's disease, and hairy and other B-cell leukemias). After adjusting for claims based on the new Agent Orange presumptive conditions received in 2011, there is projected to be an increase of nearly 16 percent in claims receipts between 2011 and 2013.

The increasing number of disability claims can be prevented by moving to a peacetime stance and not exposing the military to things like Agent Orange. However, this cannot be an ongoing expense. We must prevent or reduce these claims.

The VA expects 1.25 million compensation and pension claims in 2013. So if we add the two together ($57,280,483,000 + $4,239,878,000 = $61,520,361,000) and divide by that number, we get an average of $49,216.29 per claimant.

We can't just put this on the Ten Year Plan, because many of the disabled veterans will live longer than ten years, and it was the federal government that caused their disabilities in the first place. The average living Veteran is 58 years old[226]. The United States currently ranks 33rd in life expectancy[227], with an average lifespan of 78.37 years. That means we expect to pay these claims for an average of 20.37 years.

Multiplying, we find a total outstanding amount owed to our veterans of **$1.25 Trillion**. This is a legitimate expense, as it was the federal government that caused these disabilities in the first place. Pay them all a lump sum, right now, eliminate the program, and be done with it forever. Unfortunately, this results in the national debt being paid off one year later, but the long-term savings will be substantially greater. Each Veteran in the programs will get one final lump-sum check. No income taxes will be taken out. Total saved annually: **$61.5 Billion**.

---

[225] http://www.va.gov/budget/products.asp
[226] http://www.va.gov/VETDATA/docs/SurveysAndStudies/VETPOP.pdf
[227] http://en.wikipedia.org/wiki/List_of_countries_by_life_expectancy

Readjustment Benefits

Readjustment benefits consist of counseling and job training. Let Veterans with a general or better discharge, who have completed at least one full enlistment or commission, use all base facilities for free, including psychiatric therapy. Eliminate and save $12.6 Billion.

Other Benefits

Insurance

Sell off all insurance debts to private insurance companies. Eliminate and save $105 Million.

Housing

Housing is a socialism program. Put it on the Ten Year Plan.

Other

Veterans Employment and Infrastructure Enhancement Transfer Fund

This doesn't seem to exist anywhere on the Internet except in this budget. No programs without a justification can be allowed. Eliminate and save **$1 Billion.**

Trust Funds

> *Consists of gifts, bequests, and proceeds from the sale of property left in the care of VA facilities by former beneficiaries who die leaving no heirs or without having otherwise disposed of their estates.*

I don't see how this could possibly *cost* money. Eliminate and save **$1 Billion.**

General Post Fund

This doesn't seem to exist anywhere on the Internet except in this budget. No programs without a justification can be allowed. Eliminate and save $30 Million.

Proprietary Receipts

Consists mostly of income from GI Bill Receipts, and life insurance funds. Benefits should not both cost people money and also give them money; benefits should be free or privatized. Eliminate and absorb a cost of $293 Million.

Intragovernmental Transactions
Money shouldn't be shifted around within the government. This is a symptom that the money was wrongly allocated in the first place. Eliminate and absorb a cost of $713K.

Medical Research and Support
The government shouldn't do its own research of things that belong in the private sector. Allowing Veterans to use base facilities will obsolete all VA medical services. Eliminate and save $583 Million.

Medical Programs
Allowing Veterans to use base facilities will obsolete all VA medical services. Eliminate and save **$56.3 Billion.**

National Cemeteries Administration
Necessary and proper, and we owe it to them. Keep as is ($258 Million) and move to DIA or DoD.

Department Administration
Significant cuts and outright eliminations mean significant reductions in this overhead. Cut by half and save **$3.7 Billion.**

Conclusion
The biggest chunk of the VA, compensation and pension, shall be paid off in a single lump sum. A peacetime stance should pretty much eliminate any new claims, and using the facilities on military bases for free obsoletes the need for medical facilities of any kind. Not to mention the active duty folks can learn from the wisdom of the veterans who choose to do so.

The VA budget items add up to $141 Billion, but the overall federal budget allocated $190.7 Billion due to loans. The government is not a bank, so those go away as well. Total saved: **$187 Billion.**

Such massive eliminations in the department leave little to do. All that's really left is Housing Benefits, which can sit in HUD during its Ten Year Plan elimination phase, the National Cemeteries Administration, which can be moved into the Department of Internal Affairs, and Departmental Administration, which thus becomes obsolete. Thus, the department can be eliminated.

Independent Agencies & Other Expenses

Overseas Contingency Operations[228]

A combination of overseas militarism, diplomacy, and USAID. This proposal eliminates all overseas militarism and USAID, and diplomacy should be handled within the Department of State's budget. Eliminate and save **$97 Billion.**

Corps of Engineers - Civil Works[229]

Tries to restore ecosystems and harbors, which is the states' responsibility. Some inland waterways and the like, which are not within the borders of any state, are understandable and necessary for the Public Good and the General Welfare. Other programs, such as modernization and environmental concerns, are nonsense and can go away. Cut by half and move to the DIA, saving **$4 Billion.**

Environmental Protection Agency[230]

An argument could be made that this promotes the Public Good and General Welfare, but I won't make that argument here. The EPA stifles innovation, makes energy production more expensive, and is better handled at the state level. Eliminate and save **$9 Billion.**

National Aeronautics and Space Administration[231]

NASA has provided many innovations in technology, and has expanded our understanding of the universe. It has taken us to the moon, our rovers to mars, and our probes beyond our solar system. It is not certain, however, that this provides for the General Welfare of the United States.

Space technology does help provide for the common defense, in that it provides us with communications and weapons satellites; but funding for these already exists within the DoD.

The Constitution does provide for the promotion of the progress of science and the useful arts, but limits the scope thereof to what is basically the Patent and Trademark Office.

I can therefore find no authority within the Constitution for the direct funding of scientific or research programs. Therefore NASA is unconstitutional and must be eliminated, saving **$18 Billion.**

---

[228] http://www.whitehouse.gov/sites/default/files/omb/budget/fy2013/assets/overseas.pdf
[229] http://www.whitehouse.gov/sites/default/files/omb/budget/fy2013/assets/corps.pdf
[230] http://www.whitehouse.gov/sites/default/files/omb/budget/fy2013/assets/environmental.pdf
[231] http://www.whitehouse.gov/sites/default/files/omb/budget/fy2013/assets/nasa.pdf

We all love NASA, but that doesn't change the facts. It's probably for the best, as any such justification would also thus authorize hundreds of billions in scientific research in the other departments.

National Science Foundation[232]
For the same reasons as NASA, NSF is unconstitutional. Eliminate and save **$8 Billion.**

Corporation for National and Community Service[233]
The CNCS is exactly what its name implies. Community service is best handled within the community, by the people therein. Includes AmeriCorps, which serves and supports nonprofits. Claims to improve the way in which federal dollars are spent, but this book is proof of the government's rampant inability thereto. I can find no Constitutional authority for CNCS to exist. Eliminate and save $1 Billion.

Small Business Administration[234]
Provides small businesses with resources, grants, training, and loans.

Eliminate all federal grants. The government is not a charity or a bank. The training provided by SBA can be found for free on the Internet or for low prices in community colleges and by going outside and talking to people.

Eliminate and save **$25 Billion.**

---

[232] http://www.whitehouse.gov/sites/default/files/omb/budget/fy2013/assets/science.pdf
[233] http://www.whitehouse.gov/sites/default/files/omb/budget/fy2013/assets/service.pdf
[234] http://www.whitehouse.gov/sites/default/files/omb/budget/fy2013/assets/business.pdf

Department of Internal Affairs

I recommend creating a new department to house and administer all of the remaining disparate programs and agencies which are not located within another department, or which have been removed from a department by recommendation of this recovery plan, and which are still constitutionally authorized and justified at the federal level. Its organization might be thus:

Bureau of Immigrations and Customs Enforcement

Authorized under Article I, Section 8, Clause 4 of the Constitution, BICE is explained under the Department of Homeland Security under the name ICE.

Bureau of Commerce

Office of the Census

Authorized under Article I, Section 9, Clause 4 of the Constitution, the BOC is explained under the Department of Commerce as a Bureau.

Office of Weights and Measures

Authorized under Article I, Section 8, Clause 5 of the Constitution, OWM is explained under the Department of Commerce.

Office of Patents and Trademarks

Authorized under Article I, Section 8, Clause 8 of the Constitution, OPT is explained under the Department of Commerce under the name USPTO.

Office of the Geological Survey

Authorized under Article I, Section 8, Clause 1 of the Constitution, OGS is explained in the Department of the Interior under the name USGS.

Bureau of Transportation

Federal Railroad Administration (FRA)

Arguably authorized under Article I, Section 8, Clause 3 of the Constitution, the FRA is explained under the Department of Transportation.

Federal Transit Administration (FTA)

Arguably authorized under Article I, Section 8, Clause 3 of the Constitution, the FRA is explained under the Department of Transportation.

Maritime Administration (MARAD)

Arguably authorized under Article I, Section 8, Clause 3 of the Constitution, MARAD is explained under the Department of Transportation.

Bureau of the Interior

Office of Ocean Energy Management

Authorized under Article IV, Section 3 of the Constitution, the OOEM is explained under the Department of the Interior as a Bureau.

Office of Interior Safety and Environmental Enforcement

Authorized under Article IV, Section 3 of the Constitution, the OISEE is explained under the Department of the Interior as a Bureau.

Office of Veterans' Cemeteries

Authorized under the Necessary and Proper clause, and duly owed to our veterans, the OVC is explained under the Department of Veterans' Affairs.

Departmental Management

Every government organization needs a leader and a small staff to run it. Its funding can be calculated by gathering the staff and overhead funding of the organizations listed here, subtracting a percentage commensurate to the percentage therein of unauthorized projects, and summing the totals. This amount is negligible and probably doesn't need to be calculated here.

Conclusion

I will make the figures tables of this proposal available on my website[235] so you can download the spreadsheet, see how the numbers correlate, and check my math.

There are three primary budgets which circulated in the 2013 season. This proposal reverses, and indeed ends, the trend of exponential spending increases which they all exhibit. Most of the spending that remains is in defense, diplomacy, and justice. These government responsibilities generally need not increase with the population and thus remain constant after the decade of restoration.

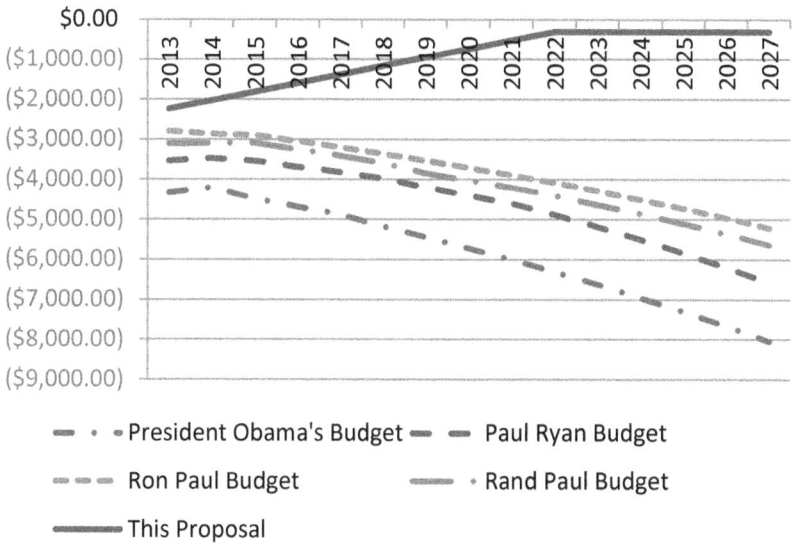

Budget Outlays

Legend:
President Obama's Budget — Paul Ryan Budget — Ron Paul Budget — Rand Paul Budget — This Proposal

Due to the complete overhaul necessitated by the Tax Plan, there is a spike in tax revenue. This doesn't mean an increase in taxes, but rather, an increase in the effective number of people being taxed. Overall, those currently paying taxes will actually pay *less*. There is a massive tax cut in the year 2020 when the National Debt is paid off, and another at the conclusion of the Ten Year Plan in 2022.

---

[235] http://www.kconnolly.net

The competing budget proposals do not provide enough information to show absolute deficit and surplus amounts, but they can be estimated through calculation. Most spending and revenue increases seem to incur a rate of around 5% annually.

Budget Deficit / Surplus ($B)

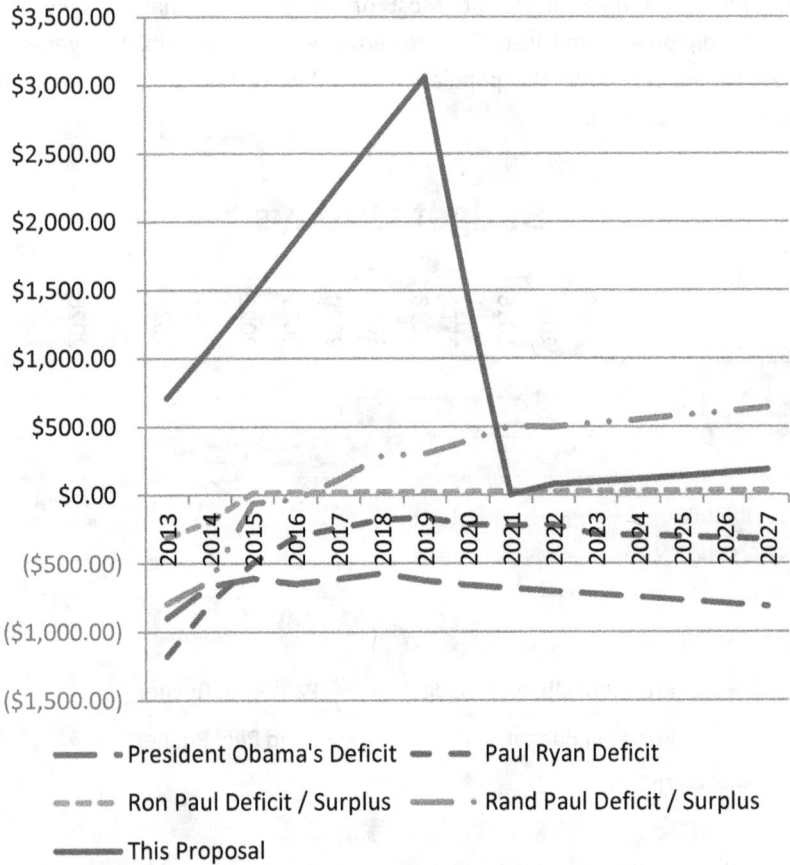

The Ten Year Plan includes the entirety of Medicare, Medicaid, Social Security, Unemployment, HUD Housing, and VA Housing. They total **$2.15 Trillion** to be eliminated over the restoration decade.

Government Size (% of GDP)

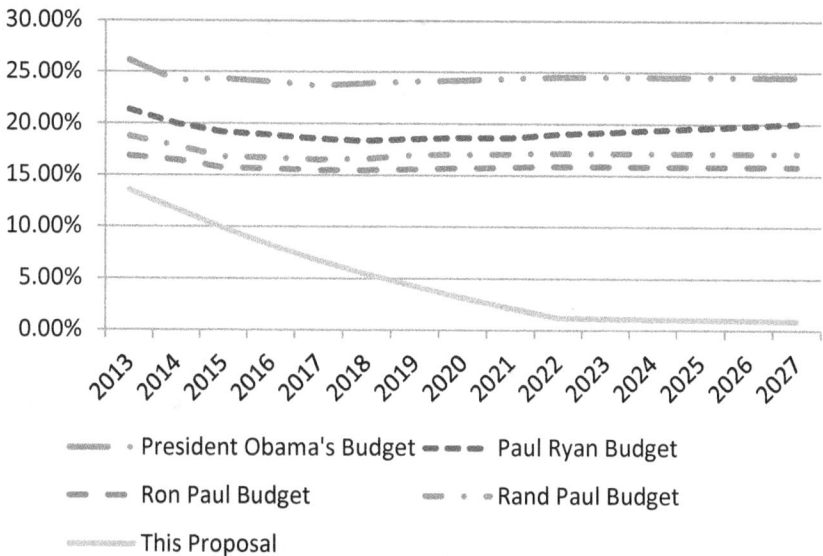

- President Obama's Budget
- Paul Ryan Budget
- Ron Paul Budget
- Rand Paul Budget
- This Proposal

Near the conclusion of the Ten Year Plan, taxes start to come down. In Year 9, we can eliminate the National Sales Tax, leaving only a 5% offshore Drilling Tax and 4.7% Import Tax. In Year 10, we can reduce those rates to 4% and 2%, respectively. The budget remains balanced, we have $5 Trillion in reserves, and stimulus packages send the extra back to the people it was stolen from in the first place.

Tax Rates

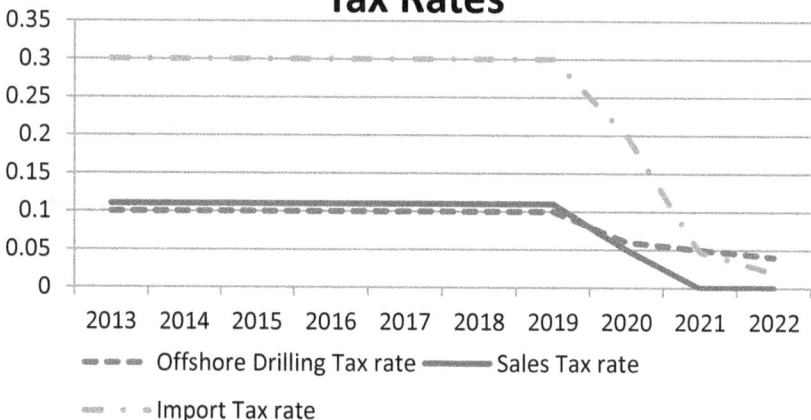

- Offshore Drilling Tax rate
- Sales Tax rate
- Import Tax rate

National Priorities shift as a result of the Ten Year Plan. Today, over half of all federal spending goes to redistribution programs. After the restoration decade, 85% is spent on defense. Diplomacy (State) and Justice remain as well, and most everything else is eliminated except a bit of overhead to run the whole thing. The new budget would allocate less than 1/11 of its current spending.

Federal Tax Revenue ($B)

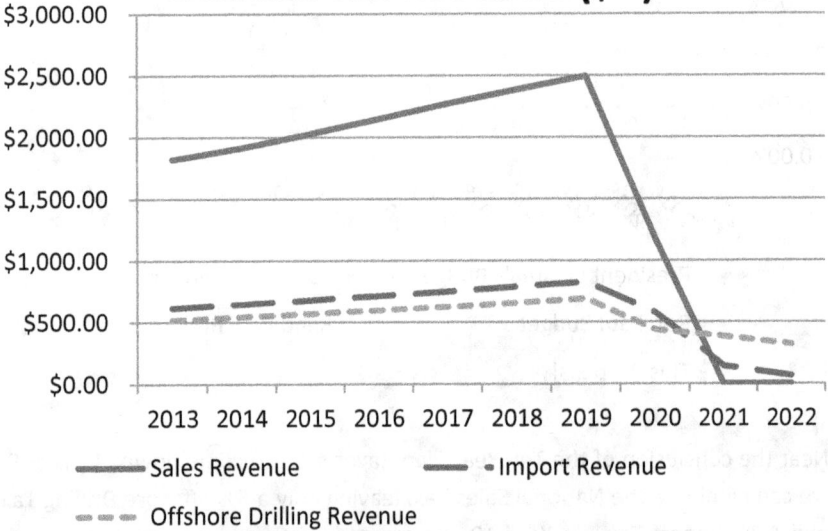

Legend: Sales Revenue · Import Revenue · Offshore Drilling Revenue

Federal Tax Revenue ($B)

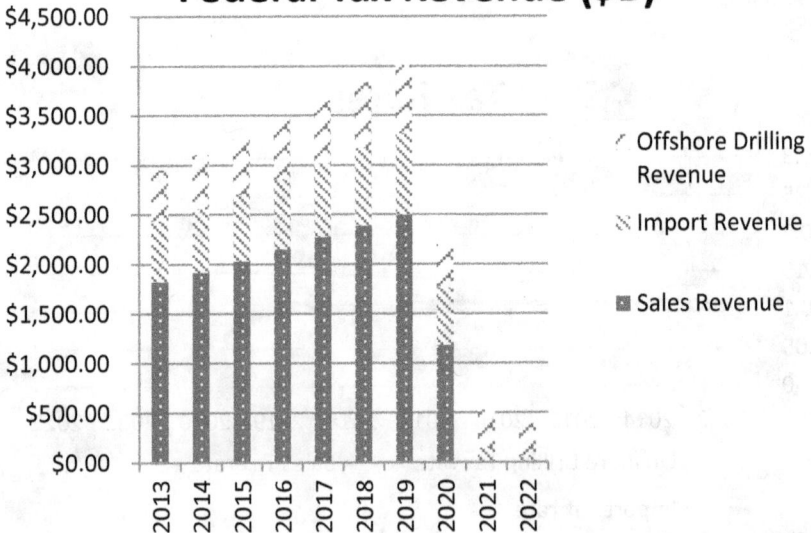

Legend: Offshore Drilling Revenue · Import Revenue · Sales Revenue

America is now completely out of debt, its numbers are green, and its taxes are low and unnoticed by most people. The government leaves you alone as long as you aren't encroaching on your neighbors, you can run your business as you see fit, you can treat your body as you see fit, and you can live your life as you see fit. America is once again whole; the embodiment of what was intended by our forebearers.

Unfortunately, this country is run by mega corporations with their lobbyists on a first-name basis with the politicians who make the laws. They'll never change the pattern until they have to. It is up to *we the people* to work within the system to affect change.

I call you to action! Involve yourself in the political process. Become a delegate to the Republican or Libertarian assemblies and conventions. Join committees, make speeches, write articles, and run for office. The Republican Party requires massive fundamental reform, and the Libertarian Party requires more mainstream publicity. Talk to your neighbors, friends, family, and total strangers. Show people my proposal – Show them *it can be done*. Spread the dream that was the United States of America.

National Income Bases

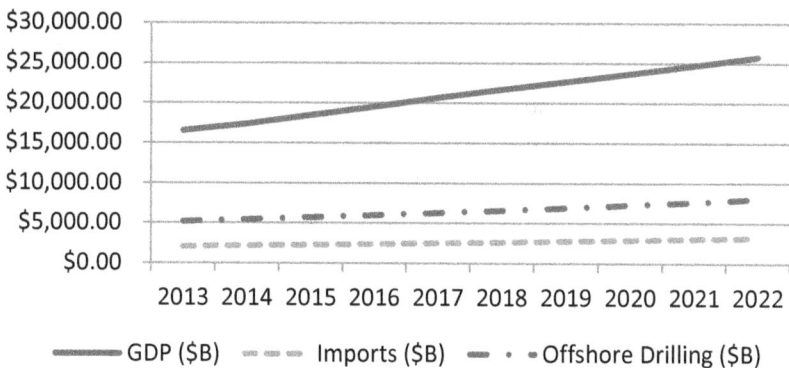

Note: National Incomes are *taxable revenue*, not federal tax revenue.

Government distribution today:

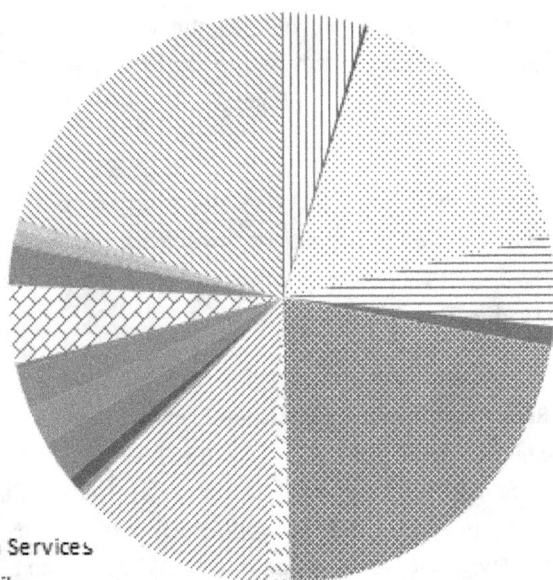

- II Agriculture
- ⫶ Defense
- = Education
- ▩ Interior
- ▩ Labor
- ▩ State
- ▩ Transportation
- ▩ Treasury
- ⟨⟩ Veterans Affairs
- ▨ Health & Human Services
- ⫶ Homeland Security
- ⫻ Housing & Urban Development
- ▩ Overseas Contingency Operations
- ▩ Corps of Engineers - Civil Works
- ▩ Environmental Protection Agency
- ▩ National Aeronautics & Space Administration
- ▩ National Science Foundation
- ▩ Small Business Administration
- ⫰ Social Security Administration
- ▩ Corporation for National and Community Service

Government distribution after initial cuts:

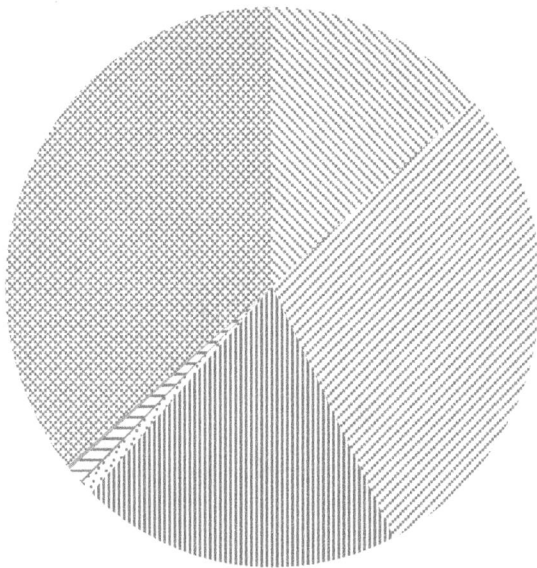

- ⟋ Defense
- ⟋ Health & Human Services
- ⦀ Housing & Urban Development
- ∴ Justice
- ▦ Labor
- ═ State
- ▩ Treasury

Final government distribution:

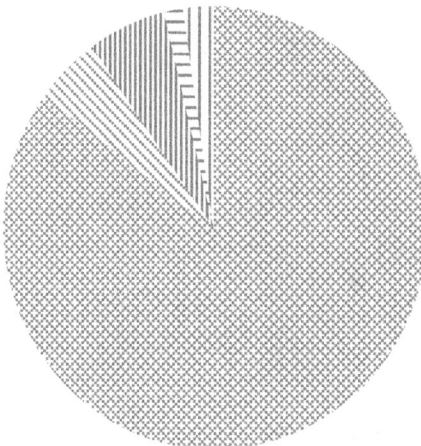

- ▨ Defense
- ⟋ Justice
- ⦀ State
- ═ Treasury
- | | Internal Affairs

Bibliography and References

Budget links can be found in footnotes within the departments.

Constitutionality and Basis in Law

1918 United States Presidential Budget
http://federal-budget.findthebest.com/l/20/1918

The Declaration of Independence
http://www.ushistory.org/declaration/document/

The Constitution of the United States
http://www.archives.gov/exhibits/charters/constitution.html

Constitutional Topic: The Preamble
http://www.usconstitution.net/consttop_pre.html

Bill of Rights
http://www.archives.gov/exhibits/charters/bill_of_rights.html

The Alleged Danger from the Powers of the Union to the State Governments[...], by James Madison
via *Yale Law School* – Lillian Goldman Law Library - Federalist Papers #45
http://avalon.law.yale.edu/18th_century/fed45.asp

Wikipedia – 9th Amendment
http://en.wikipedia.org/wiki/Ninth_Amendment_to_the_United_States_Constitution

Wikipedia – 10th Amendment
http://en.wikipedia.org/wiki/Tenth_Amendment_to_the_United_States_Constitution

General Reference

Writings, by Thomas Jefferson
http://www.amazon.com/gp/product/094045016X

Liberty Defined, by Dr. Ron Paul *(R-Texas)*
http://www.amazon.com/Liberty-Defined-Essential-Issues-Freedom/dp/145550145X

Wikileaks – 05 BAGHDAD 04237 - Saddam's message of friendship to President Bush
http://www.wikileaks.ch/cable/1990/07/90BAGHDAD4237.html

Wikipedia - Term Limits in the United States
http://en.wikipedia.org/wiki/Term_limits_in_the_United_States#Congress

Wikipedia - Old Right
http://en.wikipedia.org/wiki/Old_Right_(United_States)

Wikipedia – Keynesian Economics
http://en.wikipedia.org/wiki/Keynesian_economics

Wikipedia – Al-Qaeda
http://en.wikipedia.org/wiki/Al-Qaeda

Wikipedia – Bin Laden Issue Station
http://en.wikipedia.org/wiki/Bin_Laden_Issue_Station

Wikipedia – Operation Cyclone
http://en.wikipedia.org/wiki/Operation_Cyclone

Wikipedia – Timeline of United States military actions
http://en.wikipedia.org/wiki/Timeline_of_United_States_military_operations

Wikipedia – United States Department of Education
http://en.wikipedia.org/wiki/United_States_Department_of_Education

Wikipedia – Department of Education Organization Act
http://en.wikipedia.org/wiki/Department_of_Education_Organization_Act

Wikipedia – Interstate Commerce Clause
http://en.wikipedia.org/wiki/Commerce_Clause

Wikipedia – Copyright Clause
http://en.wikipedia.org/wiki/Copyright_Clause

Wikipedia – Sherman Antitrust Act
http://en.wikipedia.org/wiki/Sherman_Antitrust_Act

Wikipedia – Necessary and Proper Clause
http://en.wikipedia.org/wiki/Necessary_and_Proper_Clause

Wikipedia – Interstate Commerce Commission
http://en.wikipedia.org/wiki/Interstate_Commerce_Commission

Wikipedia – Spectrum Sports, Inc. v. McQuillan
http://en.wikipedia.org/wiki/Spectrum_Sports,_Inc._v._McQuillan

Wikipedia – Federalist Papers
http://en.wikipedia.org/wiki/Federalist_Papers

Wikipedia – Patient Protection and Affordable Care Act (Colloquially, "Obamacare")
http://en.wikipedia.org/wiki/Patient_Protection_and_Affordable_Care_Act

Wikipedia – Tribal Sovereignty in the United States
http://en.wikipedia.org/wiki/Tribal_sovereignty_in_the_United_States

Wikipedia – Head Start
http://en.wikipedia.org/wiki/Head_Start_Program

New York Times – US Farmers go where Workers are: Mexico
http://www.nytimes.com/2007/09/04/world/americas/04iht-export.4.7380436.html

The Organic Laws of the United States of America
http://uscode.house.gov/download/pls/organiclaws.txt

http://uscode.house.gov/uscode-cgi/fastweb.exe?getdoc+uscview+uscnst+3+4++%28organic%20law

Annual DoD budget spending, 1947-2011
http://www.data360.org/dsg.aspx?Data_Set_Group_Id=539

US Employment Overview
http://www.data360.org/report_slides.aspx?Print_Group_Id=95

The History of Education in America
http://www.chesapeake.edu/Library/EDU_101/eduhist.asp

The Difference between Socialism and Communism, and the Cognitive Dissonance Created by Lenin and Reagan
http://www.romm.org/soc_com.html

Commerce Clause Abuse, by Walter E. Williams, George Mason University
http://econfaculty.gmu.edu/wew/articles/03/abuse.html

Cherokee Nation v. the State of Georgia, 1831
http://www.mtholyoke.edu/acad/intrel/cherokee.htm

Broken Promises: Evaluating the Native American Health Care System
http://www.usccr.gov/pubs/nahealth/nabroken.pdf

America's Uncommon Sense - Science Policy and the Constitution
http://americasuncommonsense.com/blog/2010/09/01/science-policy-and-the-constitution/

CBS News - California HS Student Devises Possible Cancer Cure
http://www.cbsnews.com/8301-18563_162-57358994/calif-hs-student-devises-possible-cancer-cure/

Burzynski Clinic - Clinical Trials
http://www.burzynskiclinic.com/clinical-trials.html

Wikipedia – Dichloroacetic Acid
http://en.wikipedia.org/wiki/Dichloroacetic_acid

Wikipedia – Brownfield Land
http://en.wikipedia.org/wiki/Brownfield_land

Wikipedia – List of United States Treaties
http://en.wikipedia.org/wiki/List_of_United_States_treaties

Wikipedia – Economy of the United States
http://en.wikipedia.org/wiki/Economy_of_the_United_States

Wikipedia – United States Armed Forces
http://en.wikipedia.org/wiki/United_States_Armed_Forces

OpenCongress – H.R. 5712 – Physician Payment and Therapy Relief Act of 2010
http://www.opencongress.org/bill/111-h5712/text

Natural News – TSA Failure
http://www.naturalnews.com/033009_airports_security_breaches.html

National Review – Ten TSA Outrages
http://www.nationalreview.com/articles/274033/ten-tsa-outrages-charlie-cooke

Wolfram Alpha – USA Petroleum Production
http://www.wolframalpha.com/input/?i=USA+petroleum+production

Bloomberg – Energy & Oil Prices
http://www.bloomberg.com/energy/

National Association of Home Builders – Offsets for New Growth in Chesapeake Bay
http://www.nbnnews.com/NBN/issues/2012-01-30/Environment/index.html

ShadowStats – Alternate Unemployment Charts
http://www.shadowstats.com/alternate_data/unemployment-charts

The Economic Collapse Blog – 24 Facts about Taxes
http://theeconomiccollapseblog.com/archives/24-outrageous-facts-about-taxes-in-the-united-states-that-will-blow-your-mind

Partnership for Peace
http://www.pims.org/book/export/html/174

FAS – Security Assistance Reform: Secction 1206 Background and Issues for Congress
http://www.fas.org/sgp/crs/natsec/RS22855.pdf

Cornell Law – National Defense Sealift Fund
http://www.law.cornell.edu/uscode/text/10/2218

Government Websites

USDA - Farm Service Agency
http://www.fsa.usda.gov/FSA/

USDA - Value-Added Producer Grants
http://www.rurdev.usda.gov/rbs/coops/vadg.htm

USDA - Rural Utilities Service
http://www.rurdev.usda.gov/Utilities_LP.html

USDA – ACRE Program Backgrounder
http://www.fsa.usda.gov/Internet/FSA_File/acrebkgrd.pdf

DOC - National Institute of Science and Technology
http://www.nist.gov/public_affairs/nandyou.cfm

DOC - Economics and Statistics Administration
http://www.esa.doc.gov/about-us

DOC - National Oceanic and Atmospheric Administration
http://www.noaa.gov/about-noaa.html

Economic Development Administration
http://www.eda.gov/AboutEDA/Mission.xml

Ed - A Blueprint for Reform
http://www2.ed.gov/policy/elsec/leg/blueprint/blueprint.pdf

State of Washington – Office of Superintendent of Public Instruction – ESEA
http://www.k12.wa.us/esea/

SunShot Initiative
http://www1.eere.energy.gov/solar/sunshot/

DOE - Innovation Hubs
http://energy.gov/hubs

DOD - 2010 Nuclear Posture Review Report
http://www.defense.gov/npr/docs/2010%20nuclear%20posture%20review%20report.pdf

HUD - Community Development Block Grant Program (CDBG)
http://portal.hud.gov/hudportal/HUD?src=/program_offices/comm_planning/communitydevelop
ment/programs

Federal Register – Vol 75, No 222 – Thursday, November 18, 2010 – Rules and Regulations
http://www.gpo.gov/fdsys/pkg/FR-2010-11-18/pdf/2010-29134.pdf

Federal Register – Vol 75, No 203 – Thursday, October 21, 2010
http://www.gpo.gov/fdsys/pkg/FR-2010-10-21/html/2010-26404.htm

US Housing Act of 1937 as Amended by the Quality Housing and Work Responsibility Act of 1998
http://www.hud.gov/offices/ogc/usha1937.pdf

Public and Indian Housing – Public Housing Capital Fund
http://portal.hud.gov/hudportal/documents/huddoc?id=PH_Capital_Fund_2012.pdf

HUD - Choice Neighborhoods
http://portal.hud.gov/hudportal/HUD?src=/program_offices/public_indian_housing/programs/ph/
cn

HUD - Indian Community Development Block Grant Program
http://portal.hud.gov/hudportal/HUD?src=/program_offices/public_indian_housing/ih/grants/icdb
g

Farm Service Agency – Assets & Shared Services
http://www.fsa.usda.gov/FSA/sdlcapp?area=home&subject=assets&topic=landing

Bureau of Economic Analysis – National Income and Product Accounts Tables
http://www.bea.gov/iTable/iTable.cfm?ReqID=9&step=1

Active Duty Personnel Strengths by Regional Area and by Country
http://siadapp.dmdc.osd.mil/personnel/MILITARY/history/hst1012.pdf

DoD – Optempo and Perstempo
http://www.defense.gov/news/newsarticle.aspx?id=42131

Navy Aviation Plan 2030
http://www.navy.mil/navco/speakers/currents/Naval%20Aviation%20Plan%2027%20Feb%2008.pdf